# DENISE EBY
# ROBERT B. HORTON

# PHYSICAL
# SCIENCE

*Advances in physical science have made communication by satellite possible. This satellite uses solar cells to get energy. On the cover it is shown against a close-up of silicon crystals used in making the cells.*

# MACMILLAN

Macmillan Publishing Company
New York

Collier Macmillan Publishers
London

**Denise Eby**
Adjunct Associate Professor
  of Chemistry
Loyola College
Baltimore, Maryland

**Robert B. Horton**
Teacher of Advanced Placement
  Physics
Evanston High School
Evanston, Illinois

## PHOTO CREDITS:

**Cover:** PETER ARNOLD, INC.: © Manfred Kage

**Inset and title page:** NASA

AFTER IMAGE: © John Running, p. 437; © CLARA AICH, pp. 112L, 112R, 308, 331BL, 331BR, 516; AIP NIELS BOHR LIBRARY, William G. Meyers Collection, p. 458; © AIRSCAN® Thermogram by Daedalus Enterprises, Inc., photo courtesy National Geographic Magazine, p. 125; AMERICAN MUSEUM OF NATURAL HISTORY, pp. 154L, 154C, 154R; ANIMALS, ANIMALS: © Stouffer Productions, p. 23R; PETER ARNOLD, INC.: © Steve Allen, p. 181L, © Richard Choy, p. 447, © Bob Evans, p. 495T, © Manfred Kage, p. 534; ART RESOURCE: © Andy Sacks, p. 77, © SEF, p. 145, © Arthur Sirdofsky, p. 117; ATOZ IMAGES: © Claude Haycraft, p. 82, © Peter Pearson, p. 363; BALTIMORE GAS & ELECTRIC CO., p. 477; Courtesy A.T. & T. BELL, pp. 316, 332; Courtesy BELL LABORATORIES, p. 330; © L.V. BERGMAN & ASSOCIATES, INC., p. 192T; THE BETTMAN ARCHIVE: pp. 51, 156, 192C, 205, 459; BIOLOGICAL SYSTEMS, INC.: © Dr. David Caldwill, p. 368L; BLACK STAR: © Ricardo Ferro, p. 119, © Lee Boltin, pp. 186TR, 415BL, 415BR; BOSTON'S MUSEUM OF SCIENCE, p. 311; BROOKHAVEN NATIONAL LABORATORY, pp. 56L, 543TR, 543B; © MARY BROWN, p. 461; CAMERA HAWAII: © Werner Stoy, pp. 352L, 352C; BRUCE COLEMAN, INC.: © Robert P. Carr, p. 482L, © E.R. Degginger, pp. 328, 523CL, 523T, © Phil Degginger, p. 523B, © Larry Ditto, p. 473, © J. Fennel, p. 523CR, © Kenneth W. Fink, p. 397, © Lee Foster, p. 45R, © D.Z. Hershkowitz, p. 130L, © D. Lyons, pp. 411R, 502CR, © David Madison, pp. 131, 252L, © Alfred Pasieka, p. 522, © Michael S. Renner, p. 110C, © Ron Sherman, p. 46, © B.J. Speceley, p. 393, © Robert Weinreb, p. 489, © Jonathan T. Wright, p. 324-325; © MAR-

THA COOPER, pp. 283, 430T, CAROLINA BIOLOGICAL SUPPLY, pp. 186CT, 186CB; © DR. E.R. DEGGINGER, pp. 25L, 25R, 31, 56R, 56C, 131R, 181R, 184, 185, 186TCL, 186TL, 186B, 189C, 189B, 190T, 190LC, 190CR, 202, 208, 255, 269, 340, 381, 416L, 518BL, 518BC, 518BR; LEO DE WYS: pp. 89L, 103, © Barton Silverman, p. 101L, © Steve Vidler, p. 277R; DPI (Design Photographers, Int'l): © Wil Blanche, p. 132; Courtesy E.I. duPONT de NEMOURS & CO., pp. 476, 526; EARTH IMAGES: © Terry Domico, pp. 284, 410TL, 410BL; EKMNEPENTHE: © Tom Ballard, pp. 186, 195T; Courtesy ELECTROLUX DIAMOND JUBILEE, p. 159; © BOB EMMOTT: pp. 7, 8, 9, 19, 24, 26TL, 26B, 28, 35, 41, 47, 79, 91, 92, 94, 101R, 113, 132, 143, 157, 200-201, 215, 216, 217, 218, 230, 234, 242, 243, 246, 249, 255T, 261, 265, 266L, 269, 273, 299, 306, 307, 309, 312, 314, 317, 326, 327, 337, 355, 357, 361, 392, 397B, 402, 448, 504, 508, 510, 511, 512R, 514, 520, 530; Courtesy EROS DATA CENTER, p. 417; © SHAR FELDHEIM, p. 241R; Courtesy FORD MOTOR CO., p. 494; © DAVID R. FRAZIER, pp. 79, 226T, 430B; FUNDAMENTAL PHOTOGRAPHS, p. 463, © Richard Megna, pp. 58TR, 61, 232, 286, 288, 362, 518BR, © Kip Peticolas, p. 390, © Kip Peticolas and Richard Megna, p. 293, © Pat Peticolas, p. 29; GAMMALIASON: © Jim Pozarik, p. 296; © JOEL GORDON, pp. 111R, 256L; GRANT HEILMAN, 487, © Holt Confer, p. 332, © Barry L. Runk, pp. 179BR, 190, 195C, © Runk/Schoenberger, pp. 3, 242; © HOLIDAY FILM CORP., Courtesy of the Library Services Department, p. 153; Courtesy IBM, p. 209T; THE IMAGE BANK: © L.H. Jawitz, p. 99, © Obremski, p. 75, © Ben Rose, pp. 89-90TC, © T. Tracy, p. 401; INTERNATIONAL STOCK PHOTOGRAPHY, LTD.: © Philippe Bergeron, Nadia Magnenat-Thalman, p. 344BR, © Ken Biggs, p. 325, © Chad Ehlers, pp. 70, 78L, © Mike Freeman, p. 415T, © Judy Gurowitz, p. 2C, © B. Hospodar, p. 141, © Lonny Kalfus, p. 64B, ©
(Continued on page 596.)

Macmillan Publishing Company
866 Third Avenue
New York, New York 10022
Collier Macmillan Canada, Inc.

Printed in the United States of America

Pupil Edition: ISBN 0-02-276910-2

9  8  7  6  5  4  3  2  1

Physics   Chemistry
Strand           Strand

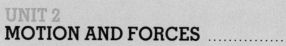

## UNIT 3

## UNIT 4
# APPLIED CHEMISTRY ..................................... 229

## CHAPTER 11   SOLUTIONS, SUSPENSIONS, AND COLLOIDS ................................................... 230

# ACTIVITIES FEATURED IN MACMILLAN PHYSICAL SCIENCE*

*In addition, there are 69 Explore activities in *Macmillan Physical Science*, including 45 Explore by Trying activities.

# ACKNOWLEDGMENTS

The authors and editors express their appreciation to these science educators,
who checked accuracy of materials and reviewed materials for teachability for this edition
of *Macmillan Physical Science.*

**Consultants:**

Dr. Richard Hermens
Department of Chemistry
Eastern Oregon State College
LaGrande, Oregon

Dr. H. Tom Hudson
Physics Department
University of Houston
Houston, Texas

Stephen Lantz
Cherry Creek High School
Englewood, Colorado

Dr. Harvey Wegner
Department of Physics
Brookhaven National Laboratory
Upton, New York

**Reviewers:**

Melody Black
Westwind School
Phoenix, Arizona

Bill Franklin
Memorial High School
Houston, Texas

Raymond Harden
Perry Junior High School
Perry, Iowa

Mary Ethel Parrott, S.N.D.
Notre Dame Academy
Covington, Kentucky

Donna Rand
Talcott Mountain Academy
    of Science and Mathematics
Avon, Connecticut

Janet Ruck
Churchville Chili
    Central School
Churchville, New York

Patricia Smith
Air Force Academy High School
U.S.A.F. Academy, Colorado

Michael Zunno
West Hempstead
    Middle School
West Hempstead, New York

# FOUNDATIONS OF PHYSICAL SCIENCE

The world you live in is very rapidly becoming more complicated. Newly invented materials that are much stronger than concrete or steel are being used to construct buildings. These materials result from advances that have been made in physical science. In this unit you will investigate the foundations of physical science. You will also study how physical science affects your world.

## UNIT

# 1

The photos show people doing very different things. But in a way, they are doing the same thing. What is it?

Each person is trying to learn why things happen the way they do. This curiosity could even be developed into an occupation. Perhaps these students could learn to use a computer to produce motion pictures. What other occupations could grow out of curiosity?

Curiosity is the beginning of all science. Scientists want to find out why things happen. As you study physical science, you will learn about some of the discoveries resulting from this curiosity. You will also investigate how these discoveries affect the way you live.

Read and Find Out:

● how the invention of the airplane led to the construction of safer bridges.

● why the ground beneath a town suddenly turned into liquid.

● about a possible source of energy in the future.

# WHAT PHYSICAL SCIENCE IS

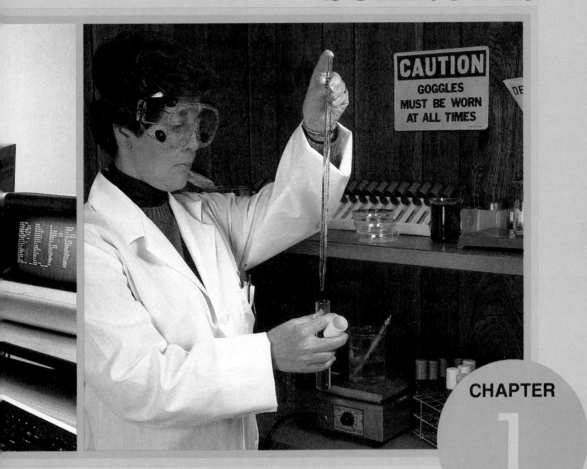

CAUTION
GOGGLES
MUST BE WORN
AT ALL TIMES

CHAPTER

1

# WORK OF SCIENTISTS

**OBJECTIVES**

**1.** Explain how science is something that everyone does.

**2.** List some of the most important activities of a scientist.

**3.** List some scientific activities you have done.

People are curious. It is natural for them to look for answers that satisfy their curiosity. When people try to answer a question about nature, they are doing *science.* **Science** *is the search for knowledge about how things behave as they do.* Science is also the knowledge that people have gained in this search.

## Doing Science

The search for knowledge involves many activities. Observing is among the most important of these activities. The opening photographs all show people observing objects in order to understand them better. An important way that scientists observe things is by measuring. Careful measurements have helped scientists answer questions about the world.

**What is an important way that scientists observe things?**

**Everyday Science** You often do science activities without realizing it. Suppose you wanted to make your school's basketball team. You might practice dribbling, passing, and shooting. You could try different types of shots. You might keep a written or mental

*Figure 1-1. Many skills used by the Egyptians are still used today.*

record of how well you shoot from different spots on the court. By keeping track of your shooting, you would be observing your performance. You might not think of yourself as a scientist while you are doing these things. But since you are searching for new knowledge about yourself, you are doing science.

**Science in the Past**   People have been doing science for centuries. Figure 1-1 shows pictures that the Egyptians painted on the walls of their tombs over 5,000 years ago. These paintings show Egyptian people using some of the knowledge that they had gained by doing science. They learned these skills by testing and observing.

**Building on Past Discoveries**   Scientists build on what other scientists in the past have reported. In the 1800s scientists like Ampère (am•PAYR) and Ohm reported on how electricity traveled through objects. In 1879 Thomas Edison, an American, discovered how to use electricity to produce light. He used the work of Ampère and Ohm to invent the light bulb. Today, scientists are still adding to the knowledge obtained by others.

## Observing and Discovering: An Example

The story of how people invented the airplane illustrates how science works. Since ancient times people have been curious about how birds fly. They wondered whether they, too, could learn to fly. Many people tried to fly by building wings that they could flap to stay in the air. Many of their attempts failed.

**The Shapes of Wings**   In the 1800s several European scientists studied the shapes of birds' wings. They wondered why birds can often glide in the air for a long time without flapping their wings. They discovered that flapping was not what kept birds in the air. The shape of the wing was the key to flying. People used this information to make gliders.

**The First Airplane**   Two Americans, Wilbur and Orville Wright, used the results of the Europeans.

# EXPLORE BY TRYING

### OBSERVING A MODEL GLIDER

**OBJECTIVE**
Observe cause and effect in a toy glider.

**MATERIALS**
light toy wood or plastic glider, thumbtacks, cellophane tape

**PROCEDURE**
**1.** Assemble a toy glider, following the maker's instructions.
**2.** Make a test flight. Observe whether the glider circles, climbs, dives, loops, or makes a long, level flight. Write down your observations.
**3.** Repeat step 2 several times. Change one part of the glider each time. For example, remove the wing, the tail pieces, or the weight in the nose. Move the wing forward or back. Replace the nose weight with thumbtacks.

**QUESTIONS**
**1.** Under what conditions did the glider make a long, straight flight? A circle to the left? To the right? A climb? A dive?
**2.** Under what conditions did the glider not fly at all?
**3.** Under what conditions did the glider make its longest flight? About how far did it fly?

*Figure 1-2.* (left) A wind tunnel helps to test how materials will react to high winds.

*Figure 1-3.* (right) After only four months, the Tacoma Narrows Bridge in Washington state collapsed in a strong wind.

They built several successful gliders. Then they designed a glider with an engine and propellers. They tested their designs carefully. Their work produced an airplane that could take off and fly under its own power. This famous flight took place at Kitty Hawk, North Carolina, on December 17, 1903.

**Using Scientists' Discoveries in New Ways** The Wright brothers learned from the work of others. Later scientists learned from the Wrights. The Wright brothers built a machine called a wind tunnel to test their designs. Improvements in the Wright brothers' wind tunnel have made it possible for people to build bigger and faster airplanes. See Figure 1-2.

● Wind tunnels have also been put to uses that the Wrights did not foresee. People who design bridges often test models of them in wind tunnels before construction begins. These tests may show what effect strong winds will have. They may help prevent disasters such as the one shown in Figure 1-3.

### OBJECTIVES AND WORDS TO REVIEW
1. Why is science something that everyone does?
2. What are some of a scientist's most important activities?
3. Name something you have done in the past month that is a scientific activity.
4. Write a complete sentence for the term below.
   science

# THE FOCUS OF PHYSICAL SCIENCE

Scientists seek knowledge of the world around them. Some scientists are most interested in studying living things, such as plants or animals. Others study nonliving things, such as metals or sound.

Each of these interests is the focus of a different area of science. Biology, or life science, is concerned with living things. The area of science concerned mostly with nonliving things is physical science. Physical science studies the materials that make up the world. It also explores the changes that occur in these materials. In this section you will look at some basic concepts of physical science. You will also read about the branches of physical science.

What does physical science study?

## Matter

All objects have certain properties. Part of the work of a scientist is to describe these properties. They make such descriptions by making measurements.

**Mass**  One of the measurements scientists make is mass. *The **mass** of an object is the amount of material it contains.* A mountain has a large mass. A grain of sand has a small mass. In general, an object with more mass feels heavier than an object with less mass.

How do you measure the mass of an object? You can use a balance as shown in Figure 1-4. A balance is an

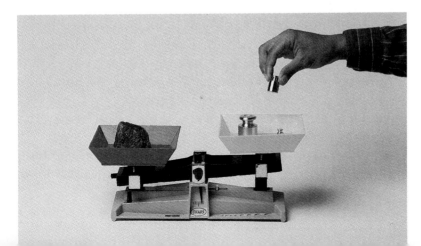

*Figure 1-4. You can find the mass of an object by balancing it with standard masses. How do you then find the object's mass?*

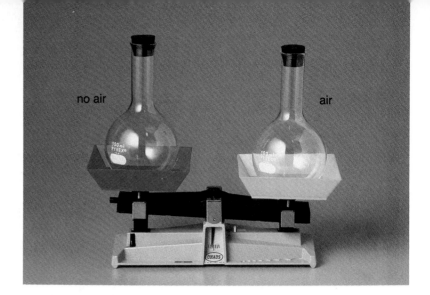

Figure 1-5. How does this photo show that air has mass?

What tool is often used to measure the volume of liquids?

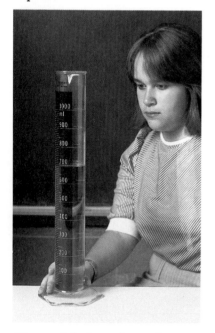

Figure 1-6. A graduated cylinder.

instrument that compares the masses of two different objects. The mass of one object is known. One object is placed on each pan of the balance. If their masses are not equal, one pan falls while the other rises. If the masses are equal, the two pans balance each other out.

Does the air you breathe have mass? Figure 1-5 shows how a balance can be used to show that air does have mass. After the air is pumped out of one container, the pans no longer balance each other. The container with air has a greater mass than the container without air.

**Volume** Scientists also measure the *volume* (VOL•yewm) of an object. **Volume** *is the amount of space an object takes up.* A basketball has a greater volume than a baseball. The basketball takes up more space.

How do you measure the volume of an object? A graduated cylinder (also called a graduate) is used most often to measure the volume of liquids. Figure 1-6 shows a graduated cylinder. This instrument is marked with graduations, or lines, to show volume. It is used just as a kitchen measuring cup is.

The two properties of mass and volume define what all objects are made of: *matter.* **Matter** *is anything that has mass and volume.* Mountains, sand, water, and air are matter. They all have mass and volume.

Figure 1-7 shows how you can prove that air is matter. Water cannot fill the space in the glass as long

Figure 1-7. *Other matter cannot occupy the same space that air does.*

as air is taking up that space. Only after the glass is tipped to let the air out can the water fill the glass.

## Phases of Matter

A cube of ice, a glass of water, and the moisture in the air are all made of the same kind of matter: water. Yet each has a different form, or phase. Most matter exists in one of three phases: *solid, liquid,* or *gas.*

You can identify the phase of matter by its shape and volume. *A* **solid** *has a definite shape and volume.* An ice cube keeps its shape and volume as long as it does not melt. *A* **liquid** *has no definite shape but has a definite volume.* As Figure 1-8 shows, 150 mL of a liq-

Figure 1-8. *The volume in each of these containers is the same.*

**TABLE 1-1.** PROPERTIES OF PHASES OF MATTER

| Phase of Matter | Has a Definite Shape? | Has a Definite Volume? |
|---|---|---|
| Solid | Yes | Yes |
| Liquid | No | Yes |
| Gas | No | No |

uid can have many shapes. But the volume is 150 mL in each case. *A **gas** has no definite shape or volume.* A gas spreads out to fill the entire space of its container. It can change both its shape and its volume. Table 1-1 summarizes the differences among the phases of matter.

## Energy

You may use the word *energy* (EN•ur•jee) in different ways. You may say you have no energy left to do anything after a long ball game. The word energy, in this case, refers to a person's ability to work or play hard. You may have heard or read news reports about energy shortages. The word energy here refers to the fuels used to run machines or cars.

There are many different kinds of energy. Heat, light, and sound are just a few examples. Since there are different kinds, the word energy is hard to define. One definition is this: ***Energy** is the ability to cause changes in matter.*

How can energy cause changes in matter? Think about what happens when you heat an ice cube. As you heat the ice, it melts. The ice changes phase and becomes liquid water. If you continue to heat the liquid water, it soon begins to boil. The liquid water changes phase and becomes water vapor, a gas. *The change in phase from liquid to gas is **evaporation***

**Figure 1-9.** *When water vapor cools, it becomes steam. What phase is steam?*

(i•vah•poh•RAY•shuhn). You cannot see water vapor. It is a colorless gas. But when water vapor cools, it changes back into a liquid. *The change in phase from gas to liquid is called* **condensation** (kahn•den•SAY•shuhn). You see droplets of water: steam. Figure 1-9 shows water collecting under the lid.

## Branches of Physical Science

Matter and energy are the main topics of physical science. Physical science is made up of branches that focus on matter and energy in different ways. The two main branches of physical science are *chemistry* and *physics.* These branches are not completely separate. In many areas, chemistry and physics overlap.

**Chemistry**   *Chemistry is the study of what substances are made of and the changes that occur in their make up.* The science of chemistry had its beginnings in the study of alchemy (AL•kuh•mee). Alchemy was the search for ways of changing cheap metals into gold. Alchemy was more a blend of science and magic than just science.

Today, the scope of chemistry has grown. Chemists, those who study chemistry, are engaged in a much wider range of activities. Some chemists work in laboratories where they study how chemicals affect the environment. Others analyze how the chemicals in foods are used by the body. Still others look for new medicines to help fight disease. The work of chemists often affects our daily lives. See Figure 1-10**A**.

**Physics**   *Physics is the study of matter and energy and how they are related.* A scientist who studies physics is a physicist (FIZ•uh•sist). A physicist searches for answers to questions such as: What is matter made of? How are energy and matter related to each other? How are the different kinds of energy related to each other?

Physicists study a very wide range of topics. Some physicists investigate the tiny particles that make up matter. Others study the motion of objects. Still other physicists explore electricity or seek new ways of

**EXPLORE** BY READING

**THE STUDY OF ALCHEMY**

**OBJECTIVE**
Learn more about alchemy.

**PROCEDURE**
Use library reference materials to learn more about alchemy, the study from which chemistry began.

**QUESTIONS**
**1.** What specific discoveries of alchemy did you find?
**2.** What mistaken beliefs of alchemy did you learn about?

*Figure 1-10A. Some chemists study how food processing methods hinder the growth of bacteria that affect the flavor or appearance of foods.*

*Figure 1-10B. Some physicists test how an object absorbs sound. They apply this information to the building of auditoriums and concert halls.*

*Figure 1-11. A slight shock turned the solid ground under these buildings into liquid mud.*

using light to communicate. The physicist in Figure 1-10**B** is investigating some of the properties of sound.

● Both chemists and physicists were needed to explain the disaster shown in Figure 1-11. A town in Sweden had stood on solid ground for many years. Suddenly, the soil turned into liquid mud, and a strange kind of landslide occurred. Buildings, roads, and railroad tracks were carried away in minutes.

Scientists discovered that an unusual kind of clay in the soil was responsible for the destruction. They learned that the clay was made up of tiny solid grains. Chemists explained that when water soaked into the ground, droplets could attach themselves to these grains. Physicists learned that the clay stayed solid until the droplets were shaken loose. The water could be shaken loose by any sudden shock, such as a slight earthquake or a train wreck. In the town shown here, the shock probably came from a machine being used by a construction crew. When this happened, the soil instantly turned into liquid mud.

**OBJECTIVES AND WORDS TO REVIEW**

1. Describe the three phases of matter.
2. Tell how energy can make changes in matter.
3. What are the two main branches of physical science?
4. Write one complete sentence for each term listed below.

| mass | solid | energy | chemistry |
| volume | liquid | evaporation | physics |
| matter | gas | condensation | |

# WHY STUDY PHYSICAL SCIENCE

Have you ever thought about what makes human activities different from those of animals? People and animals do many of the same things. Bees, ants, and birds build homes. People also build homes. Some birds migrate as the seasons change. Some people also move with the seasons.

Animals make changes in their environment by instinct. That is, they are born knowing how to do these things. They do not change their environment in new ways. People, however, are problem solvers. They learn new ways of changing their environment.

Science is one of the ways we have of solving some of our most important problems. Some scientists are trying to find ways to produce enough food for a growing world population. Others work on finding new energy sources to replace a decreasing oil supply. The solutions to these problems affect everyone. Scientists and nonscientists alike must understand both the problems and their possible solutions.

## Research

Some problems are threats. If they are not solved, life on earth could be threatened. However, other problems that scientists try to solve are simply questions. Scientists, remember, are curious.

**Basic Research**   Their curiosity leads some scientist into *basic research*. **Basic research** is a careful *study in some field of knowledge.* The purpose of basic research is to add to our knowledge of nature. For example, some physicists are curious about light. During the 1950s they investigated ways of producing powerful beams of light. Their work produced the first lasers. See Figure 1-12. These physicists did not plan to use the laser for any particular purpose. They were simply learning more about light.

**OBJECTIVES**

**1.** Describe two kinds of research.
**2.** Give two examples of how technology improves our lives.
**3.** Describe some problems of technology.

*Figure 1-12. Lasers have improved greatly since this early laser was made.*

**How have we obtained most of our knowledge about nature?**

Most of the knowledge we have gained about nature has come from basic research. Scientists have tried to apply this knowledge to serve human needs. However, scientists have sometimes found uses that were never expected.

**Applied Research** *The investigation of ways of using scientific knowledge to benefit human beings is **applied research.*** Scientists doing applied research try to find ways to put the results of basic research to work. For example, once scientists learned what a laser was, they tried to find uses that would benefit people. For example, could it be used in surgery or photography? See Figure 1-13.

**Careers in Research** At the end of each unit in this book, you will read about some of the jobs in which people use their knowledge of science. Some of these jobs involve research. Both basic and applied research need people who are interested in all branches of science. This need is expected to increase.

In all kinds of research there are jobs for *technicians* (tek•NISH•uhnz). *A **technician** is a skilled laboratory worker who carries out much of the actual work of a test.* Technicians work closely with basic and applied researchers. Some technicians' jobs require special training after high school. Others require a college education.

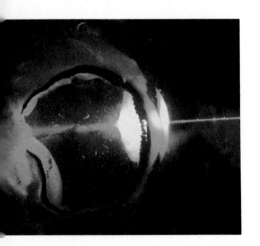

*Figure 1-13. Scientists use lasers to study the eye. They are confident their studies will help find cures for many eye problems.*

## Technology

Scientists will never run out of problems to solve. However, they have improved our lives in many ways. Basic researchers have built up a huge amount of knowledge about the world. Applied researchers have put some of this knowledge to work. You have read about the invention of the laser. Today, lasers are used in many different ways. You saw one of their uses in Figure 1-13. These and other lasers are examples of *technology.* ***Technology** is the use of scientific knowledge to serve human needs.* In other words, technology is simply the application of scientific discoveries to the real world.

**Benefits of Technology**   Technology has improved the way we live. Automobiles and jet planes have made it possible for us to reach far-off places quickly. Radio, television, and movies have made us familiar with places and events everywhere in the world.

One of the fastest-growing areas of technology is the development of computers. Just 10 or 15 years ago, only institutions such as universities and large companies had computers. Now, many homes have small computers, as you see in Figure 1-14. It will probably be as natural for your children to use a computer as it is for you to read.

**Problems of Technology**   Technology solves many problems. But it also presents a great responsibility. If technology is not used carefully, it can lead to new problems. One such problem is *pollution*. **Pollution** *is the presence of unwanted or harmful substances in the environment.* The same technology that has provided rapid transportation has created smog. Smog is a kind of air pollution that hangs over many cities.

*Figure 1-14. Home computers are now widely available.*

*Figure 1-15.* Smog over a city. What is a cause of this kind of air pollution?

See Figure 1-15. Smog results when smoke from factories and exhaust from vehicles enter the air. This pollution burns people's throats and eyes and harms their lungs. It is our responsibility to control smog and keep the air as clean as possible.

Technology also uses up *fossil fuels.* A **fossil fuel** *is a fuel that forms in the earth from the decay of dead plants and animals.* Coal, natural gas, and oil are fossil fuels. It takes nature millions of years to form them. As our technology grows, we use fossil fuels at a faster and faster pace. They are burned to run factories and automobiles and to make electricity for our homes. Many people have studied the earth's supply of fossil fuels. Some of these people believe that this supply will be nearly used up within 100 years. Then we will have to find other kinds of fuel.

List two ways that people use fossil fuels.

Sometimes the harm done by technology can be repaired by more technology. But the new technology may cause still more problems. For example, an atomic power plant produces atomic energy, but it does not use fossil fuels and it does not produce smoke. So, the use of atomic energy may solve some problems. But at the same time, an atomic power plant produces radioactive wastes. Finding a safe way to dispose of these wastes is a responsibility that must be faced if atomic energy is to be used safely.

● As the world's supplies of gas and oil are used up, scientists are searching for new sources of energy. Some scientists are studying the plan shown in Figure 1-16. These scientists are hoping to use satellites to collect solar energy. The satellites would send the energy to receiving stations on earth. There, the solar energy would be changed into electricity. This method, a product of technology, may indeed become a major source of energy in the near future.

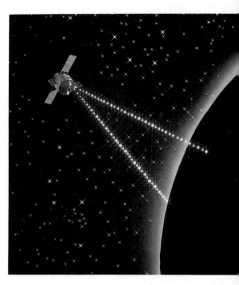

**Figure 1-16.** *Solar energy may one day become a major source of energy.*

## OBJECTIVES AND WORDS TO REVIEW
1. Describe two kinds of research.
2. Name some ways that technology has improved our lives.
3. Describe some problems of technology.
4. Write one complete sentence for each term listed below.

| | | |
|---|---|---|
| basic research | technician | pollution |
| applied research | technology | fossil fuel |

# TECHNOLOGY TRADE-OFF

## LCD's—For Better or For Worse?

If you own a wristwatch, chances are it is an LCD (liquid crystal display) type. The LCD wristwatch quickly replaced the old windup kind. It could do more, and often lasted longer, than the windup watch. One advantage of LCD's is the price. It is less expensive to get a new LCD wristwatch than to repair an old windup one. However, watchmakers found themselves without work.

Shortly after the LCD wristwatch was developed, scientists and engineers began working on other LCD devices. By 1984, the LCD television screen made it possible to fit a television in the palm of a hand. Like the LCD wristwatch, the LCD television may cause problems. For instance, tiny "hand-held" LCD televisions may cause people to watch too much television.

### Using Critical Thinking

Should society develop technology like LCD's without worrying about the effects? Might the money spent on LCD's have been better used trying to develop "more important" technology? What do you think?

# WRITING A LABORATORY REPORT

## Preparation

Imagine yourself the district attorney (D.A.) at a trial. How do you convince the jury that the accused is guilty? You try to establish a motive for the crime. You present evidence. On the basis of the evidence, the jury draws its conclusion.

Scientists use a similar procedure when they write a laboratory report. By writing a report, the scientist can support his claims later.

## Directions

A complete laboratory report has six parts.

1. The *objective* gives the purpose of the investigation. In the trial, the D.A.'s objective was to prove the defendant guilty.

2. The *materials* are anything used.

3. The *procedure* gives the steps to be followed. The procedure is important for two reasons. It shows you how to do the investigation and it shows other people how to repeat the investigation. The ability to duplicate an investigation is often a strong indication of its validity. For example, in 1976 Russian scientists reported the discovery of element 107. However, scientists of other nations could not duplicate the reaction that produced this element. So, its discovery has not been confirmed.

4. The *data* are the information obtained.

5. On the basis of the data obtained, a *conclusion* is made. The conclusion is often a statement of the truth or falsity of the objective. In the trial, the conclusion is the jury's verdict.

6. Once you have drawn your conclusion, you discuss it. The *discussion* may include answers to questions raised. It may also explain why the investigation worked or failed.

## Practice

Following the steps outlined in this skill, write a complete laboratory report for this chapter's laboratory investigation. Write your report on a separate sheet of paper.

## Application

A student was studying how fast sugar dissolves. A sugar cube was placed in two identical cups filled with water. One cup contained hot water; the other, cold. The rate of dissolving was observed. Figure 1 shows the data. On a separate sheet of paper, write out the objective, materials, procedure, data, conclusion, and discussion.

*Figure 1.*

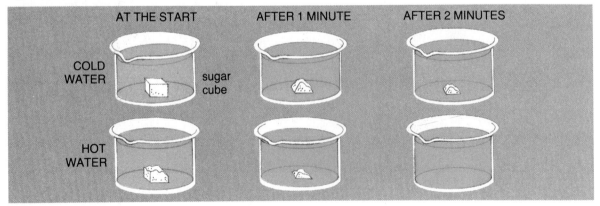

| | AT THE START | AFTER 1 MINUTE | AFTER 2 MINUTES |
| COLD WATER | sugar cube | | |
| HOT WATER | | | |

# LABORATORY ACTIVITY

## EFFECTS OF POLLUTION

### Objective
Investigate the effects of acid rain, a kind of pollution on substances, and write a laboratory report on your investigation.

### Background
Acid rain is another result of smoke in the air. Acid rain gets its name for the substances called acids that it contains. One substance in acid rain is sulfuric acid. In this activity you will study the effect of acid on marble and magnesium. The acid you will use is different from the ones in acid rain. Acid rain produces the same effects, but much more slowly.

### Materials
4 test tubes, test tube rack, goggles, apron, glass marking pencil, magnesium ribbon, marble chips, container of dilute hydrochloric acid

### Procedure
**CAUTION:** Wear goggles and an apron. If you spill acid on your clothes or skin, rinse it off at once with running water and show your teacher!

1. Number the test tubes 1, 2, 3, and 4. Stand them in a test tube rack. See Figure 1-L.
2. Place a marble chip in tubes 1 and 2.
3. Place a short strip of magnesium ribbon in tubes 3 and 4.
4. Half fill tubes 1 and 3 with water.
5. Carefully half fill tubes 2 and 4 with acid.
6. Observe for 15 minutes. Record any changes.
7. Set the tubes aside for 4 or 5 days. Then record any further changes.

### Questions
1. Compare the results in: (a) tubes 1 and 2, (b) tubes 3 and 4, and (c) tubes 2 and 4.
2. What changes occurred after several days?
3. You used acid mixed with water. Why did you test samples in acid and in water?
4. **PROBLEM SOLVING** How might acid rain affect metal and stone statues over time?
5. Write a laboratory report on this activity.

*Figure 1-L. Laboratory setup.*

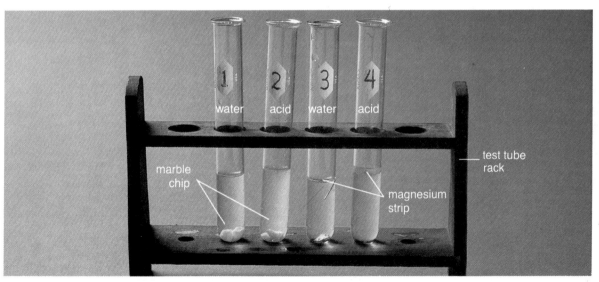

## SUMMARY

1. Science is the search for knowledge about how things behave and why they behave as they do. (1-1)

2. People do science because they are curious. Testing, observing, and measuring are scientific activities. (1-1)

3. Matter is anything that has mass and volume. Matter can occur in three phases: solid, liquid, or gas. Energy is the ability to cause changes in matter. (1-2)

4. Chemistry and physics are branches of physical science. (1-2)

5. Basic research is a careful study in some field of knowledge. Applied research is the investigation of ways of using scientific knowledge to benefit human beings. (1-3)

6. Technology is the use of applied research to serve human needs. Technology improves our lives. But if care is not used, technology can result in problems such as pollution. (1-3)

## REVIEW

Number a sheet of paper from 1 to 25 and answer these questions.

**Building Science Vocabulary**  Write the letter of the term that best matches each definition.

a. basic research    e. gas      i. physics
b. condensation      f. liquid    j. solid
c. energy           g. mass    k. technology
d. evaporation       h. matter   l. volume

1. The study of matter and energy and how they are related

2. The use of scientific knowledge to serve human needs

3. Anything that has mass and volume

4. Has a definite shape and a definite volume

5. A careful study in some field of knowledge

6. The ability to cause changes in matter

7. Has no definite shape but does have a definite volume

8. Amount of space an object takes up

9. Amount of material an object contains

10. Change in phase from liquid to gas

**Finding the Facts**  Select the letter of the answer that best completes each of the following.

11. Which of the following is a kind of energy?    (a) iron    (b) air (c) sound    (d) water

12. The beginning of scientific thinking and activity is    (a) curiosity    (b) measuring (c) discovering    (d) alchemy.

13. Which of the following is *not* a result of technology?    (a) computers (b) automobiles    (c) birds' wings (d) telephones

14. To test a model of a new jet plane, the model would probably be fastened in place in a wind tunnel by a    (a) physicist    (b) chemist (c) biologist    (d) technician.

15. Chemists are curious about    (a) matter and energy    (b) changes in matter (c) what substances are made of (d) all of the above.

16. The Wright brothers are famous for their invention of    (a) the laser    (b) the electric light bulb    (c) plastic    (d) the airplane.

17. Two different objects cannot    (a) be made of the same substance    (b) occupy the same space    (c) have the same mass (d) be studied by both a chemist and a physicist.

18. Which of these is *not* a fossil fuel? (a) oil    (b) coal    (c) wood (d) natural gas

19. Measuring things is a way of
    (**a**) observing them exactly    (**b**) changing their volume    (**c**) making them occupy space that already contains other things
    (**d**) inventing new technology.
20. A kitchen measuring cup is used to measure
    (**a**) mass    (**b**) height    (**c**) temperature
    (**d**) volume.

**Understanding Main Ideas**    Complete the following.

21. Matter is anything that has __?__ and __?__ .
22. Applied research depends on knowledge gained through __?__ research.
23. Some of the main activities of a scientist are __?__ , __?__ , and __?__ .
24. Matter with no definite shape or volume is a __?__ .
25. In a laboratory    (**a**) to measure mass, you can use a __?__ ; (**b**) to measure volume of a liquid, you can use a __?__ .

**Writing About Science**    On a separate sheet of paper, answer the following as completely as possible.

1. Many people think of science as a mysterious activity that no one but geniuses can do. Why is this idea mistaken?
2. Sometimes a solution to a problem can come from thinking about the problem in a new way. How does the development of gliders show that this statement is true?
3. Scientists often do research without any particular purpose in mind. Explain why this activity is still worthwhile.
4. Suppose modern scientists invented a technology that was able to make human

beings live forever. What problems might this technology create?
5. (laboratory question) You have observed the effect of an acid on marble. Why does acid rain take longer to wear away marble than the acid you used?

**Investigating Chapter Ideas**    Try the following project to further your study.

**A simple wind tunnel**    Hammer a nail through a wood plank. Place the plank flat on a table facing the nail up. Push the center of a long, narrow rod onto the nail's point. The rod should be free to rotate like a propeller. Tie one end of a string to the rod. Tie the other end to the hook of a spring scale that is fixed to the flat board. Arrange the setup so that moving the rod makes the pointer on the spring scale move. Put a fan in front of the other end of the rod. Tape an object to the rod. Turn on the fan. As the "wind" pushes the object, the stick moves and makes the pointer on the scale move. The reading on the scale is a measure of the object's air resistance. Build cardboard models of cars or planes. Test their air resistance. How does an object's shape affect its air resistance?

**Reading About Science**    Read some of the following books to explore topics that interest you.

Biddle, Wayne. 1979. **Coming to Terms: From Alpha to X-ray, a Lexicon for the Science Watcher.**New York: Avon.
Daintith, J., ed. 1983. **A Dictionary of Physical Sciences.** Totowa, NJ: Littlefield.
Gleasner, D.C. 1983. **Breakthrough: Women in Science.** New York: Walker.
National Geographic Society. 1983. **How Things Work.** Washington, DC: National Geographic Society.

Imagine you are playing a game. According to the rules, your partner has to identify objects from your descriptions of them. How would you start?

You learn about an object by using your senses. You see its color, size, and shape. You feel if it is hard or soft, sharp or blunt, heavy or light. You smell it or taste it. You listen to any sounds it makes. To help your partner, you use words that describe qualities learned through the senses. How would you describe a piano?

Objects, of course, are made of matter. Scientists study many different kinds of matter. They, too, begin with their senses. Then they perform tests to learn more. In this chapter you will use their methods to explore matter and how it can change.

Read and Find Out:
● how to tell if a gold object is made of pure gold.
● about the foul-smelling origin of some sweet-smelling perfumes.
● about a sports-stadium atomic model.

# BASICS OF
# PHYSICAL SCIENCE

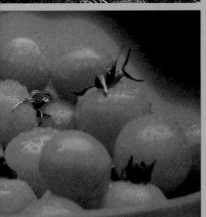

# PROPERTIES OF MATTER

**1.** Tell the difference between physical properties and chemical properties.
**2.** Give examples of a physical change and a chemical change.
**3.** Tell how to find the density of an object.

Name two important properties of an object.

*Figure 2-1. Name some physical properties of these coins.*

How would you describe an orange so that a blind-folded friend could identify it? Using your senses, you might describe its color, sweet taste, and tangy aroma. Such characteristics, or descriptions, are examples of properties of matter. In this section you will study other properties of matter. You will also study changes in properties.

## Kinds of Properties

Two important properties of any object are mass and volume. You can use your senses to describe these properties. For example, your sense of touch tells you an orange has more mass than a golf ball. Your sense of sight tells you it has a smaller volume than a bowling ball.

If you wanted to be more exact, however, you would measure the mass and volume of the orange. To make measurements, you need instruments.

**Physical Properties** The measurements or other characteristics of the orange are examples of *physical properties. A **physical property** is a property that can be observed without changing the identity of a substance.* Mass, volume, shape, and color are just a few physical properties.

You make use of the physical properties of objects many times each day. When you receive change for a dollar, how do you check to make sure it is correct? Glance quickly at Figure 2-1. Did you read the coins to see whether "penny," "dime," or "nickel" was written on them? Most people simply observe the physical properties of the coins: their color, size, and mass.

**Chemical Properties** Some properties describe the behavior of a substance when its identity is changed. Figure 2-2 shows two examples. Seltzer tablets fizz when dropped into water. They mix with water and

*Figure 2-2. Chemical properties.*

change into bubbles of gas. The candle wax burns in air. It changes into smoke and other materials. *Properties that describe the ability of a substance to be changed into new substances are* **chemical properties.**

If you have ever baked a cake, you may have used baking powder. Baking powder mixes with cake batter. Some of the substances in the baking powder change into bubbles of a gas called carbon dioxide. You observe this property of baking powder only when the powder combines with cake batter and changes into another substance. The ability to release carbon dioxide when mixed with batter is a chemical property of baking powder.

## Changing Properties

Matter is changing all around you all the time. Ice melts, toast burns, glass breaks, milk sours. Each change gives the substance new properties. Not all changes form a new substance, however.

**Physical Changes**   A change occurs when glass breaks or water freezes. But the substance does not change into another substance. The broken glass is still glass. And ice is still water. Glass breaking and water freezing are examples of *physical changes. A* **physical change** *is a change that does not produce a*

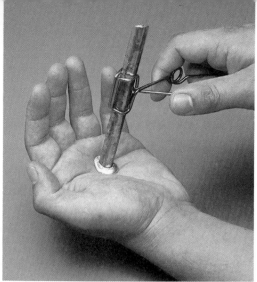

Figure 2-3. (left) The smith bends the spoon with a tap of the mallet. (right) The warmth of a human hand melts the element gallium.

new substance. Find more examples of physical changes in Figure 2-3.

**Chemical Changes**   What happens when milk is left out in the open too long? The milk curdles and has a terrible odor! What happens when bread is left in a toaster too long? The bread becomes a black, brittle substance. Milk souring and bread burning are examples of *chemical changes. A **chemical change** is any change of a substance into one or more other substances.* In chemical changes, the chemical properties as well as the physical properties of a substance change. A chemical change is also called a chemical reaction.

Chemical changes are often harder to reverse than physical changes. For example, you can easily melt ice into liquid water. Melting reverses the physical change of freezing. But you cannot easily reverse many chemical changes. You cannot "unspoil" milk or "unburn" toast.

## Density: An Important Physical Property

Both cubes in Figure 2-4 have the same volume. Each one takes up the same number of *cubic centimeters* ($cm^3$). *A **cubic centimeter** is a standard unit of volume.* The plastic cube floats in the water. The lead cube sinks to the bottom. The two cubes behave differently because of their difference in *density*

Figure 2-4. Why does the plastic cube float?

(DEN·suh·tee). **Density** *is the mass of a substance contained per unit of volume.* If the density of an object is less than the density of a liquid, the object will float in that liquid. If the object is more dense than the liquid, it will sink in the liquid.

The density of a substance is usually stated in grams per cubic centimeter. A gram (g) is a standard unit of mass. The unit "grams per cubic centimeter" ($g/cm^3$) tells the mass of 1 $cm^3$ of a substance. For example, 1 $cm^3$ of water has a mass of 1 g. The density of water is 1 $g/cm^3$. The densities of some other common substances are listed in Table 2-1.

**Using Density**   Suppose you wanted to know of what substance a spoon is made. The spoon's density could be an important clue. If you knew its density, you could check to see if the spoon was made of one of the substances in Table 2-1.

**Calculating Density**   To find the density of an object, you must first measure its mass and its volume. Then divide the mass by the volume:

$$density = \frac{mass}{volume}$$

$$D = \frac{m}{V}$$

**TABLE 2-1.** DENSITIES OF SOME COMMON SUBSTANCES

| Substance | Density ($g/cm^3$) |
| --- | --- |
| Ice | 0.90 |
| Olive oil | 0.92 |
| Water | 1.0 |
| Aluminum | 2.7 |
| Copper | 8.9 |
| Silver | 10.5 |
| Lead | 11.3 |
| Gold | 19.3 |

# EXPLORE BY TRYING

**CHEMICAL CHANGES IN THE KITCHEN**

**OBJECTIVE**
Observe some chemical changes.

**MATERIALS**
toaster or oven, 3 drinking glasses, milk, vinegar, lemon juice, bread

**PROCEDURE**
**1.** Pour just enough milk in each of three glasses to cover the bottom.
**2.** Add a small amount of vinegar to one glass. Add the same amount of lemon juice to the second glass. Leave the third glass of milk alone.
**3.** Stir the substances in each glass. Clean the stirring tool between glasses. Observe and make a note of any change in the milk.
**4.** Toast a slice of bread until it is very dark. Remove the toast and scrape off the black substance.

**QUESTIONS**
**1.** What chemical properties of milk did you observe?
**2.** What do you think was the purpose of leaving the third glass of milk alone?
**3.** What was the black substance on the burned bread?
**4.** What chemical property of bread did you observe?

*Figure 2-5. Given an object's dimensions, how do you find its volume?*

To find the spoon's density, you would first use a balance to find its mass. Then you would find its volume. Figure 2-5 shows how to find the volume of a rectangular object, such as a brick. The volume is equal to its length times its width times its height. To find the volume of an object that is not rectangular, however, you can use the method shown in Figure 2-6.

Figure 2-6 shows how to find volume by displacement of water. The water level increases slightly from **A** to **B**. This method works because water is displaced, or pushed aside, by the spoon. The change in water level is equal to the spoon's volume.

Suppose you have found that the spoon's mass is 54 g. Figure 2-6 shows that its volume is 20 cm³. Now you can find the density of the spoon:

$$D = \frac{m}{V}$$
$$D = \frac{54\,g}{20\,cm^3}$$
$$D = 2.7\ g/cm^3$$

You have found that each cubic centimeter of the metal in the spoon has a mass of 2.7 g. Table 2-1 shows that the density of aluminum metal is 2.7 g/cm³. Now you know that the spoon might be made of aluminum.

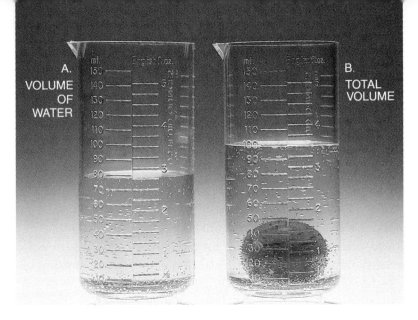

**Figure 2-6.** *To find the volume of an object by using water displacement, subtract the volume of water from the total volume.*

● There is an old story about how density was used to catch a dishonest jeweler. A king had given a jeweler enough gold to make a crown. The jeweler decided to keep some of the gold. He melted the rest of the gold together with copper, a cheaper metal. Then he used the mixture of metals to make the crown.

The crown looked like pure gold. But a wise man in the king's court suspected the trick. He knew that if the gold was mixed with another metal, the crown would not have the same density as pure gold. First, he found the mass and volume of the crown. And he found the volume of an equal mass of pure gold. Then he calculated their densities. He discovered that the crown's density was less than that of pure gold. Density proved that the crown was not pure gold!

## OBJECTIVES AND WORDS TO REVIEW

1. What is the difference between a physical property and a chemical property?
2. Use candle wax to give one example of a physical change and one example of a chemical change.
3. (a) How would you find the volume of a silver ring?
   (b) The mass of a silver ring is 21 g. Its volume is 2 cm³. Is the ring pure silver? How do you know? (Use Table 2-1 in finding an answer.)
4. Write one complete sentence for each term listed below.
   physical property    physical change    cubic centimeter
   chemical property    chemical change    density

# THE STRUCTURE OF MATTER

Suppose you owned a music shop. How would you arrange the records so that any title could be found easily? Figure 2-7 shows one possible arrangement.

To keep track of many items, people often group them. Because they study many things, scientists also group, or classify, objects. Biologists, for example, classify plants and animals. In this section you will learn how physical scientists classify matter.

## Elements

What did the ancient Greeks believe made up matter?

One of the earliest attempts to classify matter was made in Greece over 2,000 years ago. The ancient Greeks believed that all matter was made up of four *elements* (EL•uh•muhnts). *An **element** is a substance that cannot be broken down into other substances.* The elements of the Greeks were earth, fire, air, and water. All matter, the Greeks believed, was made of combinations of these elements.

Centuries later, scientists began to perform tests with matter. They found ways to break down substances in order to find out what was in them. This

*Figure 2-7. One way of arranging musical recordings.*

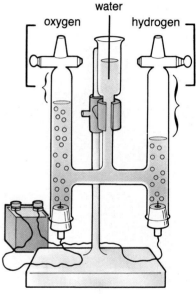

Figure 2-8. A chemical reaction may be caused by heat.

oxygen      water      hydrogen

Figure 2-9. Water is added to a tube that is safely wired to pass electricity.

breakdown of substances occurs in some chemical reactions. As a result of the tests, scientists concluded there must be more than just four elements.

Scientists use heat to break down some substances. When you burn toast, for example, you break down some of the substances that make up bread. One substance you see in burned toast is black carbon. See Figure 2-8. The carbon must have been part of the bread.

Electricity can also break down some substances. Water breaks down when electricity passes through it. It breaks down into hydrogen gas and oxygen gas. See Figure 2-9.

Bread and water can be broken down into other substances. So you know that bread and water are not elements. Carbon, hydrogen, and oxygen cannot be broken down into other substances. So, carbon, hydrogen, and oxygen are elements.

Today scientists know of 108 elements. Eighty-nine elements are found in natural substances. The others have been made in science laboratories.

## The Smallest Particles of Matter

Suppose you divided a piece of iron into two pieces. Then you continued to divide each piece into smaller and smaller pieces. Eventually you would reach a point where you could not divide the iron further and still have iron. You would have an *atom* of iron. *An*

Sulfur    S

Gold    Au

What do symbols of the
elements come from?

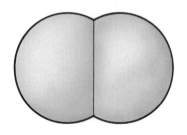

*Figure 2-10. A model of an
oxygen molecule.*

**CHART 2-1.** SOME COMMON ELEMENTS

| Name | Symbol | Name | Symbol |
|------|--------|------|--------|
| Aluminum | Al | Lead | Pb |
| Calcium | Ca | Mercury | Hg |
| Carbon | C | Nitrogen | N |
| Chlorine | Cl | Oxygen | O |
| Copper | Cu | Silver | Ag |
| Gold | Au | Sodium | Na |
| Hydrogen | H | Sulfur | S |
| Iron | Fe | Zinc | Zn |

*atom is the smallest particle of an element that has
the properties of that element.* For example, one property of iron is its ability to combine with oxygen and
form rust. An atom of iron would be the smallest piece
of iron that can combine with oxygen.

All the atoms of a particular element are alike. Each
element is made up of its own type of atom. The atoms
of one element are different from the atoms of other
elements. You will find out how atoms are alike and
different in the next section.

Chemists have given each element a *symbol. A
symbol is one or two letters that stand for an element.*
The symbols of the elements come from the English,
Latin, or Greek names for the elements. Some common
elements and their symbols are listed in Chart 2-1.

The symbol for oxygen is O. That same symbol
stands for one atom of oxygen. However, in nature,
one atom of oxygen never exists on its own. See Figure 2-10. Oxygen atoms are joined together in pairs.
To indicate a pair of oxygen atoms joined together,
use the symbol O and the number 2. The number 2 is
called a subscript. It is written to the right and
slightly below the symbol. Thus, a pair of oxygen
atoms would be indicated by $O_2$.

A pair of oxygen atoms, $O_2$, is a *molecule* (MAHL•uh•kyewl) of oxygen. *A **molecule** is the smallest particle of a substance that can exist independently.* It is the smallest particle of a substance that has all the properties of that substance. A molecule of most elements is made up of just one atom by itself. But a molecule of oxygen is a particle made of two atoms of oxygen joined together. Hydrogen, nitrogen, and chlorine molecules are also made of two atoms.

## Compounds

Every time you breathe out, you are giving off molecules of different gases. One of the gases is carbon dioxide. Figure 2-11 shows an athlete exhaling carbon dioxide. A carbon dioxide molecule is made of two different kinds of atoms. One carbon atom is joined to two oxygen atoms.

Water, too, is made of two different elements. Water is made of the elements hydrogen and oxygen. Carbon dioxide and water are *compounds* (KAHM•powndz). *A **compound** is made of two or more elements that have been chemically combined.*

When elements are chemically combined, their atoms are joined together. The atoms of elements lose their properties when they are combined. A compound, therefore, has different properties from the elements that make up the compound.

## Chemical Shorthand

Atoms are the building blocks of elements. In a similar way, elements are the building blocks of compounds. The elements in a compound have been combined chemically.

To show what elements make up a compound, scientists use *chemical formulas*. *A **chemical formula** is a shorthand way of showing the composition of substances by using symbols and subscripts.* The symbols indicate the elements in the substance. The subscripts tell how many atoms of each element are in the smallest part of the substance.

*Figure 2-11. Carbon dioxide is a gas given off when you breathe. What is its formula?*

What are the building blocks of elements?

## COMBINING AND SEPARATING SUBSTANCES

**OBJECTIVE**
Observe the properties of a mixture.

**MATERIALS**
wide pie tin, drinking glass, sugar, sand, water

**PROCEDURE**
**1.** On a sheet of paper, mix together a teaspoonful of sugar and an equal amount of sand. Observe the mixed substances carefully.
**2.** Stir the mixed substances into a tall glass of warm water. Observe what happens.
**3.** Pour the liquid slowly into a pie tin. Be careful to leave any solid substance in the glass.
**4.** Keep the pie tin in sunlight for several days until the water evaporates. Observe any substance left in the pie tin.

**QUESTIONS**
**1.** Did the sand and sugar make a compound or a mixture? How do you know?
**2.** Did the mixing of the sugar and sand cause a physical or a chemical change?
**3.** Which substance was left in the bottom of the glass?
**4.** Was there anything in the pie tin after the water evaporated? What is the substance? How do you know?

**TABLE 2-2. SOME HOUSEHOLD SUBSTANCES**

| Compound | Formula |
| --- | --- |
| Table salt | $NaCl$ |
| Baking soda | $NaHCO_3$ |
| Ammonia | $NH_3$ |
| Natural gas | $CH_4$ |
| Sugar | $C_{12}H_{22}O_{11}$ |

For example, each molecule of water is made up of two atoms of hydrogen (H) and one atom of oxygen (O). So, the formula for water is $H_2O$. Notice that if there is only one atom of an element, no number is written after its symbol.

Recall that a molecule of carbon dioxide is made up of one atom of carbon (C) and two atoms of oxygen. Can you guess the formula for carbon dioxide?

The smallest part of a given compound has the same number and kinds of atoms in it. Every water molecule has two hydrogen atoms and one oxygen atom. Every carbon dioxide molecule has one carbon atom and two oxygen atoms. Table 2-2 is a list of some common compounds and their formulas.

## Mixtures

Sometimes substances can be combined without a chemical change. If no chemical change occurs, the substances keep their own properties. *Any combination of two or more substances in which the substances keep their own properties is a **mixture**.* For example, a tossed salad is a mixture. You also make a mixture if you add sulfur and iron particles together. As Figure 2-12 shows, you can separate the parts of a mixture easily.

Mixtures are similar to compounds in that they contain more than one substance. Yet they differ from compounds in many ways. Table 2-3 sums up the differences between compounds and mixtures.

**TABLE 2-3.** PROPERTIES OF COMPOUNDS AND MIXTURES

| Compounds | Mixtures |
|---|---|
| Made up of only one kind of particle | Made up of two or more different kinds of particles |
| Formed during a chemical change | Not formed in a chemical change |
| Can be broken down only by chemical changes | Can be separated by physical changes |
| Has properties different from those of its ingredients | Has same properties as its ingredients |
| Has definite amount of each ingredient | Does not have definite amount of each ingredient |

*Figure 2-12. The parts of a mixture can always be separated by physical means.*

• Even though the substances in a mixture keep their own properties, you may not always recognize these properties. For example, perfumes are mixtures. If you separated the substances making up perfumes, you might find some of them have foul odors. Yet, when these substances are mixed together in perfumes, their odors blend to make a pleasing fragrance. If you were familiar with the odor of each substance, you could recognize it in the mixture. Perfume chemists can recognize the odors of the individual substances in a mixture.

## OBJECTIVES AND WORDS TO REVIEW

1. Name three elements and three compounds.
2. What are the meanings of the letters and numbers in the compound with the formula $HNO_3$?
3. In what way is a mixture like a compound? In what ways are mixtures and compounds different?
4. Write one complete sentence for each term listed below.

| | | | |
|---|---|---|---|
| element | symbol | compound | mixture |
| atom | molecule | chemical formula | |

# INSIDE THE ATOM

What do scientists do after they propose a model of the atom?

When you want to learn more about an object, you find out its properties. When scientists study atoms, they look at the properties of the elements. These properties give them clues about the atoms that make up the elements.

Atoms are too small to be seen. So it is difficult to tell what they are like. To help understand what atoms are like, scientists make *models* of the atom. *A **model** is a description that uses familiar ideas to explain unfamiliar ones.* A model may be three dimensional like a model boat. It may be a picture drawn on paper. Or it may simply be an idea.

Over the years, scientists have proposed many models of the atom. Once they propose it, they see if their model can explain the known properties of the elements. If the model cannot explain these properties, the scientists try a new model. In this section you will look at one particular model of an atom.

## Charged Particles

After testing many models of atoms, scientists have concluded that atoms contain a number of small particles. Some of these particles have a property called *electric charge,* or simply *charge.* Scientists do not know what charge is. But they do know that charge seems to explain how particles affect each other. ***Charge** is a model that explains how some particles attract each other and others push apart, or repel, each other.* There are two kinds of charge: positive ( + ) and negative ( − ).

Two particles with opposite charges attract each other. So, a positive charge and a negative charge attract each other. Two particles with the same charge repel, or push away, each other. See Figure 2-13.

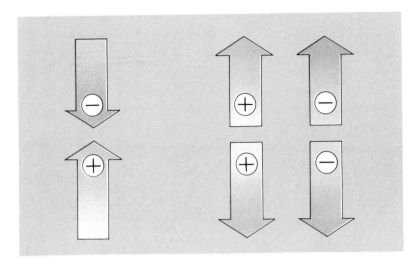

## The Particles in an Atom

You will study three kinds of particles in atoms. First, look carefully at the models of atoms of three elements in Figure 2-14. Look at the *nucleus* (NEW•kli•uhs; pl. nuclei) of each atom. *The **nucleus** is the dense central part of an atom.* Two kinds of particles are grouped together at the nucleus: *protons* and *neutrons* (NEW•tronz).

Figure 2-14. Nuclei of the atoms of three elements.

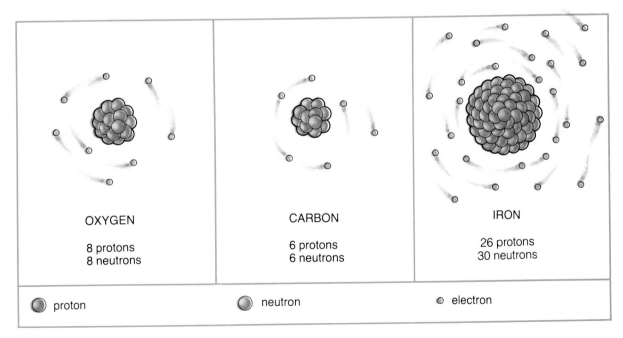

| OXYGEN | CARBON | IRON |
| --- | --- | --- |
| 8 protons | 6 protons | 26 protons |
| 8 neutrons | 6 neutrons | 30 neutrons |

⬤ proton     ⬤ neutron     ◦ electron

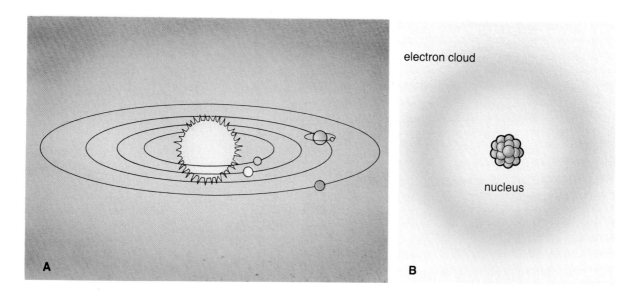

electron cloud

nucleus

A                                    B

*Figure 2-15. Comparison of the solar-system and electron-cloud models of the atom.*

**Protons** *are positively charged particles in the nucleus of an atom.* Each proton has about the same mass as a neutron. *The **neutrons** are particles in the nucleus that have no charge.* Since neutrons have no charge, they are said to be *neutral.* Because the nucleus contains positive particles, however, the nucleus has an overall positive charge.

Outside the nucleus is a third kind of particle, the electron (i•LEK•tron). **Electrons** *are negatively charged atomic particles.* Electrons have very little mass. Each one has only about 1/2000 the mass of a proton or a neutron. So most of the mass of an atom is packed into its center.

There is an attraction that holds electrons around the positively charged nucleus. The electrons are not standing still, however. They move around the nucleus, somewhat as the planets move around the sun. Planets, however, travel in definite orbits around the sun. See Figure 2-15**A**. A planet can be located at any time during its trip around the sun. But electrons do not have definite orbits. They are located somewhere in a cloud around the nucleus. See Figure 2-15**B**. Electrons are most likely to be found where the cloud is thickest.

## Numbers of Particles

Atoms can be identified by their number of protons. All atoms of any given element have the same number of protons. For example, all atoms of oxygen have 8 protons. In any atom the number of protons equals the number of electrons. That is, oxygen atoms have 8 electrons. With the same number of positive particles and negative particles, any atom has no overall charge. An atom is neutral.

The number of protons is different for atoms of different elements. Carbon, for example, has atoms with only 6 protons. And they have 6 electrons. Each of the 108 elements has atoms containing its own number of protons and electrons.

● The models shown in Figures 2-14 and 2-15 show the parts of an atom. But they do not show the sizes of these parts compared with the size of an atom.

Imagine you wanted to make a model of a carbon atom. Suppose you used marbles to represent the particles in the nucleus. To make your model, you would need a whole football stadium! First, you would place 12 marbles in the center of the playing field. These marbles represent six protons and six neutrons in the carbon nucleus. The objects that represent the electrons would have almost the entire stadium to travel in. They would travel farther from the nucleus than a football player could throw them.

From this model you can see that most of an atom is empty space. There is nothing between the nucleus and the electrons.

How can atoms be identified?

**OBJECTIVES AND WORDS TO REVIEW**
**1.** How do particles with the property of charge affect each other?
**2.** Draw a model of an atom that has 5 electrons, 5 protons, and 6 neutrons.
**3.** Describe how atoms of the same element are alike.
**4.** Write one complete sentence for each term listed below.

| | | |
|---|---|---|
| model | nucleus | neutron |
| charge | proton | electron |

# OBSERVING AND INFERRING

## Preparation

Suppose you smell an orangelike scent. You might suspect someone nearby has an orange. However, you might be wrong. The scent might be from candy or a kind of perfume. You cannot be sure unless you actually see an orange. Whenever you use your senses, you are making *observations* about the world around you. When you make a conclusion based on what you observe, you are making an *inference*. When you smell a scent you are *observing*, when you conclude the scent is from an orange, you are *inferring*.

Scientists use their senses to make observations. Based on what they observe, they make inferences. The inferences help them solve problems and predict future events.

## Directions

You can make observations and inferences about almost anything. Try improving your observing skills by looking very carefully at an object. A visual observation should be made in an orderly way. First, look at the entire object. Then, look at its parts. Observe Figure 1 carefully. Write down your observations on a separate paper.

Did you notice the (1) color of the candle, (2) blackened wick, (3) melted wax on the candle and in the holder, (4) color of the holder?

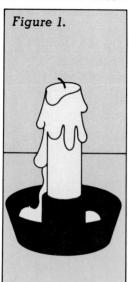

*Figure 1.*

Now try making inferences based on what you observed in Figure 1. You can base your observations about your own experience with candles. You might infer that (1) the candle was lit for a long time (based on the amount of melted wax), (2) about half the candle has melted, (3) wind blew the candle out. Inferences are based on incomplete information. Thus, they may be incorrect. The flame may have been lit for only a short time, for example.

## Practice

Look carefully at the scene in Figure 2. On a separate sheet of paper, write down (1) what you observe and (2) what you can infer from the scene. Then check your answers with your teacher.

## Application

Look at Figures 2-2 and 2-3 on pages 25 and 26. On a separate sheet of paper, write down your observations. Then write down what you can infer about the photos. Identify any changes you see as physical or chemical. Are your identifications of chemical or physical changes observations or inferences? Explain.

*Figure 2.*

# LABORATORY ACTIVITY

## CHEMICAL CHANGES IN THE LABORATORY

### Objective
Observe how iron reacts with several substances.

### Background
Chemical changes are changes in the composition of a substance. When chemical changes occur, the physical and chemical properties of the substance change.

### Materials
test tube rack, 3 test tubes, safety goggles, apron, 2 iron nails, marking pencil, medicine dropper, dilute solutions of copper sulfate, hydrochloric acid, sodium hydroxide, and iron chloride

### Procedure
**CAUTION:** Wear goggles and an apron. If you spill anything on yourself, wash the spill with water immediately and tell your teacher.

1. Label the test tubes A, B, and C as shown in Figure 2-L. Stand them in the test tube rack.
2. Half fill each of the test tubes as follows. A: dilute hydrochloric acid; B: copper sulfate; C: iron chloride.
3. *Gently* place an iron nail into test tubes A and B. Record anything that happens.
4. Your teacher will give you a small amount of sodium hydroxide solution. Put 10 drops into test tube C. Record anything that happens.

### Questions
1. In which test tubes can you infer that a chemical change took place? Explain.
2. **PROBLEM SOLVING** A clear liquid spills on a metal fender. Bubbles form. What can you infer? Explain your answer.

*Figure 2-L. Laboratory setup.*

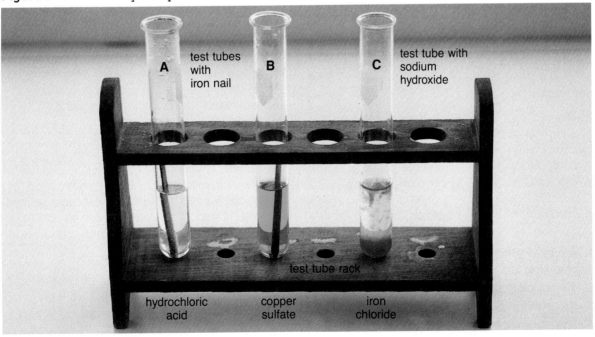

# SUMMARY

1. Every substance can be described by its physical and chemical properties. (2-1)
2. Density, a substance's mass per unit volume, is a physical property that can help identify certain substances. (2-1)
3. All matter is made up of different combinations of elements. (2-2)
4. Compounds are made up of two or more elements that have been combined in a chemical reaction. Mixtures are made up of two or more substances that have been combined physically, but not chemically. (2-2)
5. Scientists use models to study atoms. (2-3)
6. The center of an atom is its nucleus. The nucleus is made up of protons and neutrons. Electrons move around the nucleus. (2-3)

# REVIEW

Number a sheet of paper from 1 to 25 and answer these questions.

**Building Science Vocabulary**   Write the letter of the term that best matches each definition.

a. atom
b. chemical change
c. chemical
d. compound
e. electron
f. mixture
g. molecule
h. neutron
i. nucleus
j. physical change
k. physical property
l. proton

1. A property that can be observed without changing the identity of a substance
2. Two or more substances combined physically
3. An uncharged particle in the nucleus
4. The dense, central part of an atom

5. A change of a substance into one or more new substances
6. Two or more elements combined in a chemical reaction
7. A negatively charged particle traveling around the nucleus
8. The smallest particle of any substance that can exist independently
9. Particle in nucleus having positive charge
10. The smallest particle of an element that has the properties of that element

**Finding the Facts**   Select the letter of the answer that best completes each of the following.

11. All of the following are physical properties except   (a) density   (b) mass   (c) burning in air   (d) color and shape.
12. Which of the following involves a chemical change?   (a) water freezing and becoming ice   (b) baking powder making a cake rise   (c) cutting a cake   (d) using the brakes to stop a bicycle
13. The nucleus of an atom contains   (a) only neutrons   (b) only protons   (c) protons and neutrons   (d) electrons.
14. Which of the following is a unit of mass?   (a) centimeter   (b) grams per cubic centimeter   (c) cubic centimeter   (d) gram
15. The formula for water is   (a) $H_2O$   (b) $CO_2$   (c) $H_2CO_3$   (d) $HO_2$.
16. Carbon, oxygen, and hydrogen are examples of   (a) mixtures   (b) elements   (c) compounds   (d) chemical combinations.
17. When two or more elements are combined in a chemical reaction, they form   (a) a mixture   (b) an element   (c) a compound   (d) an atom.
18. If a small stone had a volume of 15 cm³ and a mass of 60 g, its density would be   (a) 75 g/cm³   (b) 0.25 cm³/g   (c) 0.25 g/cm³   (d) 4 g/cm³.

**19.** Which of the following substances cannot be broken down into other substances?
(**a**) oxygen   (**b**) water   (**c**) carbon dioxide   (**d**) air
**20.** The symbol C stands for the element
(**a**) calcium   (**b**) copper   (**c**) carbon
(**d**) chlorine.

**Understanding Main Ideas**   Complete the following.

**21.** If 10 cm³ of a substance has a mass of 50 g, the density of the substance is __?__ .
**22.** In the formula $SO_2$, the number 2 tells how many __?__ of oxygen are in a molecule of $SO_2$.
**23.** The nucleus of an atom contains __?__ and __?__ .
**24.** Ammonia, baking soda, and table salt are classified as __?__ .
**25.** A property of matter that causes some particles to attract each other and some particles to repel each other is __?__ .

**Writing About Science**   On a separate sheet of paper, answer the following as completely as possible.

**1.** Suppose you find an old bracelet in the sand at the beach. After you polish it, it looks like copper. How could you test the bracelet to find out whether it is pure copper?
**2.** A chemist works in the research laboratory for a large company. The chemist makes a new kind of plastic that seems as if it might make a good food wrap. List some of the chemical and physical properties that would make the plastic good for this use.
**3.** Sugar is a compound. Its formula is $C_{12}H_{22}O_{11}$. What kind of atoms are in a molecule of sugar? How many of each kind of atom are there?

**4.** In pioneer days, wagons had wooden wheels. In place of tires, the pioneers placed an iron band around the rim of each wheel. The iron band was heated in a fire. The pioneers would fit the band around the wheel while it was hot. When the band cooled, it contracted and fit the wheel tightly. Is this an example of a physical change or a chemical change? Explain your answer.
**5.** (laboratory question) Suppose you have two test tubes. In each test tube is an iron nail. To each test tube you add a different substance. What kinds of results would prove to you that chemical changes took place in the test tubes?

**Investigating Chapter Ideas**   Try the following project to further your study.

**Making a hydrometer**   A hydrometer measures the density of liquids. You can make one from a long test tube. Mark off a scale on a strip of paper. Glue it to the inside of the test tube. Add sand to the tube until it floats upright in the tap water with about $\frac{1}{4}$ to $\frac{1}{3}$ of its length above the water. Read the fluid level on the scale of your hydrometer when it is floating. Now dissolve a large amount of salt in the water. Does the hydrometer float higher or lower in a salt liquid? Is salt water denser than pure water? Check the relative densities of other liquids. Report your results.

**Reading About Science**   Read some of the following books to explore topics that interest you.

Challand, Helen J. 1984. **Activities in the Physical Sciences.** Chicago: Childrens.
Fritzsch, Harald. 1983. **Quarks: The Stuff of Matter.** New York: Basic.

The sun's energy makes life possible on earth. In what ways do living things use the sun's energy? The shoreline above may help you think of one important use: heat. When you stand in sunlight you absorb heat from the sun.

Recently, science has developed ways of trapping absorbed heat from the sun. Houses are being built with special panels and walls that absorb heat during the day. In some of these houses, heat is trapped in a liquid in the walls. The drums you see here store the liquid. Heat can be released from the liquid to heat houses at night. What problems can such heating solve?

Scientific tests can help answer questions like these. Testing is a way of studying problems. In this chapter you will learn how to solve a problem by testing.

Read and Find Out:
● why scientists changed their minds about how things burn.
● how a laboratory deep underground is used to study the center of the sun.
● why England changed its monetary system.

# PROBLEM SOLVING IN PHYSICAL SCIENCE

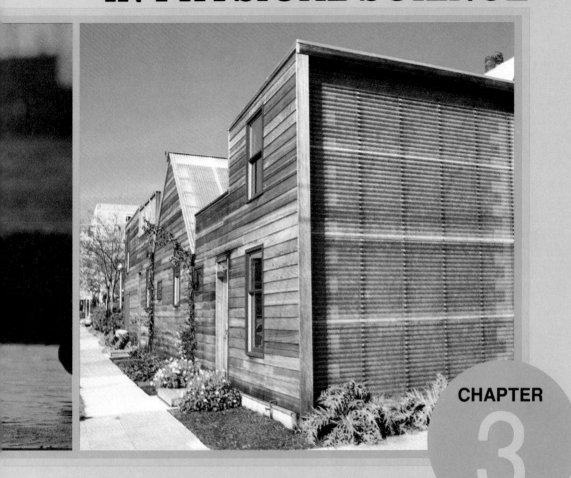

CHAPTER

3

# THINKING LIKE A SCIENTIST

During the school year, you will be doing many science activities. To work like scientists you have to think like them. In this section you will learn a process of working called the scientific method.

## Posing a Question

Suppose your class is going to do an activity on the chemistry of food. The objective of the activity is to study bread mold. Bread mold grows best in a warm, moist environment. It is easy to moisten bread and place it in a covered dish. The problem is keeping the dish warm over the weekend, when there is no heat.

The solar heating walls shown in the chapter introduction may give you an idea about how to solve this problem. Maybe the dish with moistened bread can be kept warm with solar heat. But what substance is best for storing this heat after the sun goes down? You might decide to do an *experiment* to answer this question. *An **experiment** is a scientific test designed to give information under carefully controlled conditions.*

The success of an experiment often depends on how the question it tests is stated. The more limited the question, the easier it is to set up an experiment to answer it. "What substances store heat best?" is too broad a question. Many substances could be solutions. You could not test them all.

Some students might think that water is a good substance for storing heat. Others might guess that gravel is better. Now you can ask a more limited question. "If heat can be stored, which is better for the purpose: water or gravel?"

## Forming a Hypothesis

Once the question is stated, you can form a *hypothesis* (high•POTH•uh•sis). *A **hypothesis** (pl. hy-*

*Figure 3-1. Research is an important part of scientific thinking.*

potheses) *is an educated guess about the answer to a problem or question.* A hypothesis for this question might be: "Gravel stores heat better than water." Now that you have a hypothesis, you can test it.

Before testing your hypothesis, you should find out what is already known about the question. See Figure 3-1. You might go to the library and read articles or books on materials that store heat. The information might even suggest ways to set up your experiment.

What should you do before you test a hypothesis?

## Doing the Test

Suppose you and your classmates are ready to test the hypothesis. To make your hypothesis easier to test, you could rewrite it in an "if…then" format. The hypothesis would be written "If gravel stores heat better than water, then its temperature will fall more slowly than water's." Note that the "then" part is the part that can be tested. You are now ready to perform your experiment.

To perform the gravel experiment, the class could be divided into groups. Figure 3-2 shows how the groups might begin. These students are measuring out the same mass of each of the materials to be tested. One group puts water in a beaker. A second group puts an equal mass of gravel in its beaker. A third group puts nothing in its beaker. Each group places a thermometer in its beaker. See Figure 3-3.

Each group then places its beaker in an oven set at low heat. When the temperature reaches 70 degrees Celsius (70°C), the students remove the beakers.

*Figure 3-2. (left) Beginning the experiment.*

*Figure 3-3. (right) To do an experiment properly, you must keep conditions as identical as possible.*

**TABLE 3-1.**

SAMPLE DATA TABLE

| Test Substance: | |
|---|---|
| Time (min) | Temp (°C) |
| 0 | |
| 20 | |
| 40 | |
| 60 | |
| 80 | |
| 100 | |

**Observing and Recording**   As the beakers are removed from the oven, each group reads the temperature in its beaker. Each group records this observation in a table like Table 3-1. They put this first reading in the space marked Time = 0 minutes. They continue to record temperatures every 20 minutes. When the beakers cool to room temperature, they stop recording.

The temperatures written in the table are the *data* of the experiment. **Data** *are the measurements and information that a scientist gets from an experiment.* Careful observation is needed to get the best data possible from an experiment.

**Making the Test Fair**   Why did the groups use the same mass of each substance? Using different masses might have changed the data. The data from an experiment done in this way might lead you to a false result. The data could differ, too, if the groups had used different kinds of containers. Starting the tests at different temperatures could also have given misleading results.

Mass, starting temperature, or *any condition that can be changed is a* **variable** (VAR•ee•uh•buhl). In a well-planned experiment, a variable is changed only to test the hypothesis. In this experiment, you are interested in only one variable: the materials used. The experiment can be a fair test of this variable only if you keep all the other conditions the same for each beaker.

The empty beaker is a *control* setup. *A* **control** *is an extra setup in which all the conditions are the same except for the variable being tested.* The control does not contain the variable being tested. Using a control makes sure that any changes seen in the other setups are due only to the variable being tested.

## Drawing a Conclusion

After taking your data, what do you do with them? You compare your data with that from the other groups to see which material stayed warm the longest. These results may support the class hypothesis or disprove it. Whatever the result, the class may be able to draw a *conclusion* from the experiment. *A **conclusion** is a judgment based on the data gathered in an experiment.* Your conclusion should be an answer to the question asked by the class.

**Graphing Data**   Many times, the data taken in an experiment are numbers, as Table 3-1 shows. It is often hard to draw a conclusion from a table of numbers. For this reason, scientists often graph their data. A graph is like a picture of the numbers. Such a picture often shows a pattern that you cannot see in the numbers themselves. Figure 3-4 shows how the data from the heat-storing experiment can be graphed.

*Figure 3-4. Graphs can help you see patterns that a data table may not show.*

| **TEST SUBSTANCE GRAVEL** | |
|:---:|:---:|
| Time (min) | Temp (°C) |
| 0 | 70 |
| 20 | 53 |
| 40 | 33 |
| 60 | 25 |
| 80 | 20 |
| 100 | 20 |
| 120 | 20 |

| **TEST SUBSTANCE WATER** | |
|:---:|:---:|
| Time (min) | Temp (°C) |
| 0 | 70 |
| 20 | 58 |
| 40 | 48 |
| 60 | 42 |
| 80 | 28 |
| 100 | 20 |
| 120 | 20 |

| **TEST SUBSTANCE CONTROL** | |
|:---:|:---:|
| Time (min) | Temp (°C) |
| 0 | 70 |
| 20 | 30 |
| 40 | 20 |
| 60 | 20 |
| 80 | 20 |
| 100 | 20 |
| 120 | 20 |

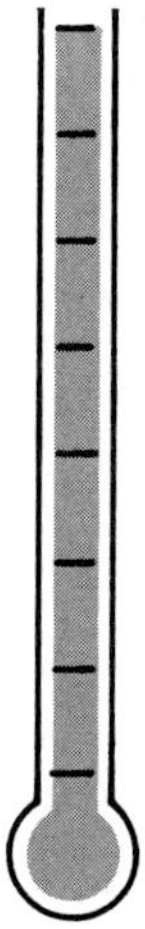

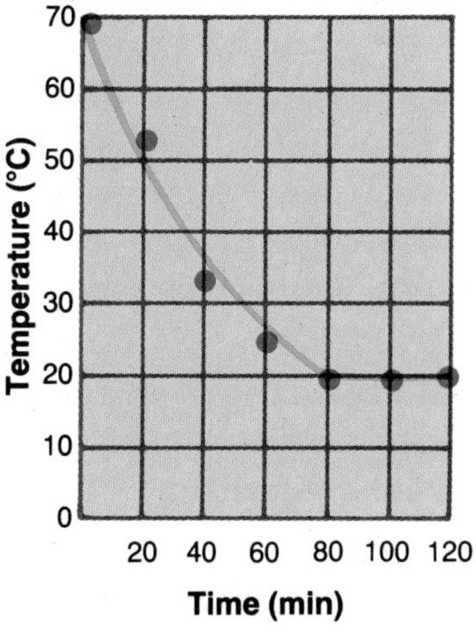

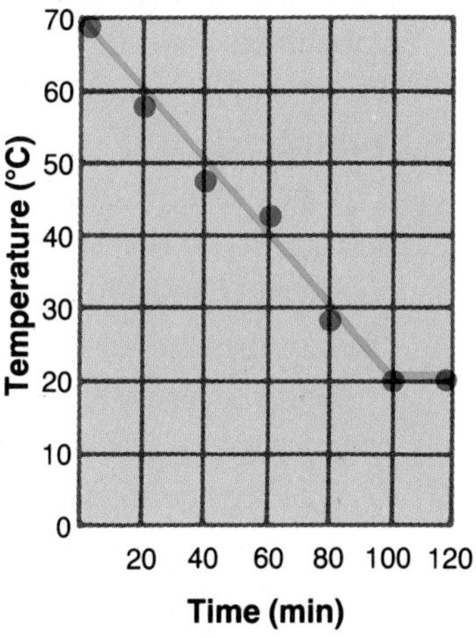

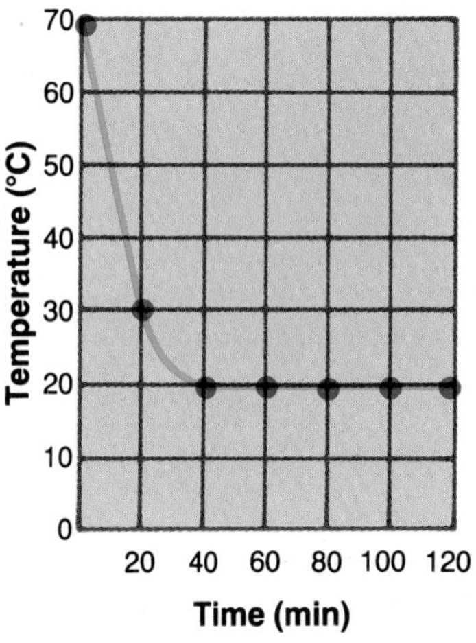

Why do scientists repeat experiments?

**Comparing and Reporting the Results**   After graphing their data, the groups compare their results. The patterns in the graphs show that the beaker with the water stayed warm longer. These results show that the original hypothesis was incorrect. The groups conclude that water seems to be a better heat-storing material than gravel.

Your class can now use its conclusion to try to find a way to keep the bread mold warm. Perhaps the class might float the dishes in a tub of hot water. Or they might want to try another method. To find the best design for a water heater, the class will have to do more tests. These tests will use the results of the first experiment.

## Laws and Theories

Scientists usually repeat experiments many times to make sure the data are accurate. If the results are the same over and over again, the conclusion may be stated as a *law*. *A **scientific law** is a statement that describes how something behaves.* A law does not explain *why* something happens. It only describes *what* happens. For example, after repeating your experiment several times you might be able to state a law. "Water stores heat better than gravel."

You may want to know why your experiment turned out the way it did. You may form a hypothesis to explain the results. Your hypothesis might be "The air spaces in gravel make gravel lose heat faster than water." You may want to experiment to test this hypothesis.

If your explanation passes many such tests, you might state a *theory*. *A **theory** is an explanation for the way something behaves.* Your theory might be "materials lose heat in air spaces."

Most scientific theories are changed or replaced many times. These changes result from new data that do not agree with the established theory.

● The phlogiston (floh•JIS•ton) theory is one example of how new data can lead scientists to change their

thinking. During the 1700s, many scientists believed that matter contained a material called phlogiston. Their theory was that phlogiston escaped from a material when burning occurred.

However, near the end of the 1700s a French scientist, Antoine Lavoisier (lah•vwah•ZYAY), showed that the theory was false. He found that when some objects burn, their ashes have more mass than the objects did before they burned. He reasoned that if part of the object escaped, the ashes should have *less* mass. He also did experiments showing that when an object burns in a closed container, some air in the container is used up. See Figure 3-5.

Lavoisier believed that phlogiston did not exist. Instead, he believed that things burn by combining with a material in the air. He named the material oxygen. More and more scientists repeated his experiments. They saw that the new theory explained burning better than phlogiston. Eventually, scientists abandoned the phlogiston theory.

## OBJECTIVES AND WORDS TO REVIEW

1. Describe some of the steps a scientist may take in solving a problem.
2. Why do scientists sometimes change theories?
3. Write one complete sentence for each term listed below.

| | | |
|---|---|---|
| experiment | variable | conclusion |
| hypothesis | control | scientific law |
| data | | theory |

# THE TOOLS OF PHYSICAL SCIENCE

**OBJECTIVES**

**1.** Name three skills that scientists need.

**2.** Identify the laboratory instruments used for measuring length, volume, mass, temperature, and time.

Scientists use many tools in experiments. During your study of physical science you will be using tools to carry out laboratory activities.

Figure 3-6 shows a physics laboratory with some specialized tools. Laboratory instruments are tools. They are the "hardware" of physical science. But scientists also use tools that you may not have considered. Scientific journals and laboratory notebooks are among the tools of the scientist. Still other tools cannot be shown in a photograph. They are the scientist's skills. Skills, the things a person does well, are among the scientist's most valuable tools.

## Skills

A scientist uses many different kinds of skills during an experiment. Some are mental skills, while others are physical skills.

**Thinking**   You have learned that an experiment is used to answer a question or solve a problem. To solve a problem, you must begin by thinking about it. The ability to think clearly is an important scientific tool.

*Figure 3-6.* 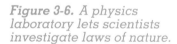 *A physics laboratory lets scientists investigate laws of nature.*

Figure 3-7. *Always know the location of safety equipment.*

Thinking clearly about a problem may include several kinds of thinking. It may include narrowing down the problem. Dividing a problem into smaller parts may make it easier to form a hypothesis that you can test. Thinking about a problem may also include comparing it with other problems with which you are familiar. Your imagination can also help you to solve a problem.

**Reading**   Scientists read books and journals to find out what is already known about the problem they want to solve. These reports and the ability to read them are valuable tools. This book is a tool for you to use in learning how to solve problems.

**Observing and Recording**   Careful observation was an important part of the heat-storing experiment. Recording the data from your observations was another important point. Observing and recording are tools of the scientist.

**Laboratory Skills**   A scientist must learn how to use laboratory instruments properly. Each instrument works best when it is used only for its intended purpose. It is also important to know and to obey safety rules in the laboratory. See Figure 3-7.

When does a laboratory instrument work best?

*Figure 3-8. Use goggles and point all test tubes away from you whenever you heat something.*

What two things should you do in an emergency in the laboratory?

## Using the Tools of Science Safely

Wearing goggles is a rule you must follow to make the science laboratory safe. In your laboratory classes you will be using tools that will develop your skills as a scientist. Tools used carelessly, however, can cause injuries. Here is a safety checklist. Read it carefully. Be sure to follow it when you are in the laboratory. For more safety information, see page 570.

1. Read all directions and cautions in your laboratory activities *before* you begin. Follow them carefully.

2. Know where safety blankets and other safety equipment such as those in Figure 3-7 are located. Learn how to use them.

3. Report any accidents to your teacher right away.

4. Wear safety goggles or glasses and a safety apron when you use chemicals, heat, glassware, and other dangerous materials.

5. Read the labels on bottles of chemicals. Never taste or touch chemicals. Never draw any substance into a glass tube with your mouth. Never inhale chemical fumes from a test tube or beaker.

6. Handle glassware carefully. Cracked or broken glass can cut you. Never touch hot glassware with your hands.

7. Be careful when you use a bunsen burner. If you have long hair, like the student in Figure 3-8, tie it back.

8. Unless you are given other instructions, if you spill acids or bases on yourself or anywhere else, wash the surface with lots of water. Tell your teacher.

9. Handle electrical equipment carefully. Do not touch metals onto electric equipment. Never use bare wire. Do not stick wires into an electric outlet.

10. Never look directly into the sun or a bright light.

Safety in the laboratory is your own responsibility. But your teacher is responsible for your safety, too. If there is an emergency, tell your teacher at once. And stay calm. Staying calm can help prevent an emergency from getting worse.

## CHART 3-1. COMMON MEASURING INSTRUMENTS

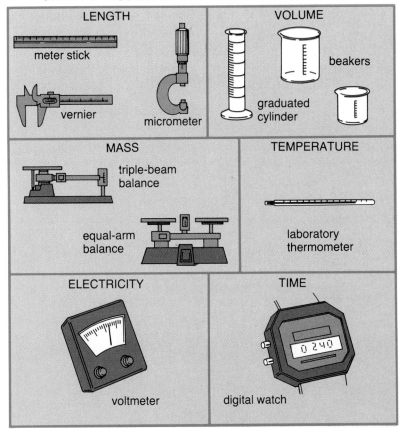

LENGTH

meter stick

vernier

micrometer

VOLUME

beakers

graduated
cylinder

MASS

triple-beam
balance

equal-arm
balance

TEMPERATURE

laboratory
thermometer

ELECTRICITY

voltmeter

TIME

0 2 40

digital watch

## Laboratory Instruments

Some of the instruments used most often by scientists are for measuring. You may recognize some of these instruments from the experiments the students did in Section 1. Chart 3-1 shows some of the more common measuring instruments. See pages 570—573 to learn how to use some of this equipment.

Not all laboratory instruments used by physicists and chemists are measuring instruments. A well-planned laboratory also contains equipment that can be used in experimental setups. In fact, some laboratory instruments are made specially for one experiment. Some other common laboratory materials are found in Chart 3-2.

## EXPLORE BY TRYING

### MAKING A LABORATORY INSTRUMENT

**OBJECTIVE**
Make a simple scientific instrument.

**MATERIALS**
coat hanger, tape, plastic sandwich bags, pennies

**PROCEDURE**
**1.** Hang a coat hanger from a hook. Tape a sandwich bag firmly to each end of the coat hanger.
**2.** Place an object whose mass you will find in one bag.
**3.** Drop pennies one at a time into the other bag. Stop when the coat hanger is level again.
**4.** Repeat steps 2 and 3 with other objects.

### QUESTIONS
**1.** What is the mass of each object in pennies?
**2.** What do the pennies represent?

## CHART 3-2. LABORATORY INSTRUMENTS

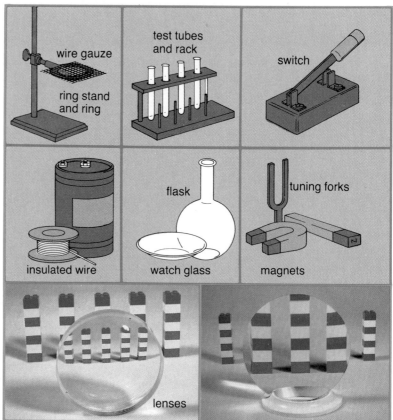

wire gauze

ring stand and ring

test tubes and rack

switch

insulated wire

flask

watch glass

tuning forks

magnets

lenses

*Figure 3-9. An instrument used to study particles created in the sun. Why is it located underground?*

● The huge tank shown in Figure 3-9 is also a scientific instrument. It contains cleaning fluid, as much as a large swimming pool would hold. Scientists use the cleaning fluid to help capture tiny particles from the sun's center. They then use special counters to tell how many particles were stopped by the fluid. To prevent all other particles from entering the tank, the tank is located far underground. The ground overhead stops these unwanted particles. Scientists study these particles from the sun to learn about its interior.

### OBJECTIVES TO REVIEW

1. Name three skills that scientists need.
2. Give examples of laboratory instruments that measure length, mass, volume, temperature, and time.

# THE METRIC SYSTEM

People have been measuring things for thousands of years. They first measured distances by counting steps. They measured the mass of an object by comparing it to the mass of a stone. They measured time by counting sunrises and sunsets.

Can you see a problem with measuring things in this way? Suppose the students who carried out the solar-heating experiment measured the mass of the test substances with stones. How would that have affected their conclusions? These primitive methods of measuring are not exact. Masses measured with different stones would have different values. The groups could not have compared their data fairly.

## Using Standard Measurements

To avoid these problems, people use exact *standards* for measuring. *A* **standard** *is a fixed quantity to which all measurements are compared.* Standards are also called *units.*

For example, the inch is a standard, or unit, for measuring length. Suppose that you measure your height and find that it is 60 inches. You are comparing your height with the inch standard. And you can use this standard to compare your height with that of someone you have never seen. By using the same standard, you will each know how tall the other is.

## Metric Standards

People have used many different systems of measurement. Most countries now use the metric system of measurement standards. The metric system makes it easier for people to understand each other. The United States is slowly changing over to the metric system. However, the English system is still used for many measurements. The inch is one of these English

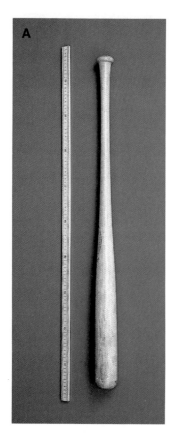

standards. Refer to page 569 to learn how to convert from English units to metric.

**Length**   The **meter** (m) *is a unit of length in the metric system.* As you have probably guessed, this unit also gives the metric system its name. You saw a meter stick in Chart 3-1. The height of a doorknob above the floor and the length of a baseball bat are each approximately one meter. See Figure 3-10.

**Volume**   The **liter** (L) *is a unit of volume in the metric system.* The volume of a grapefruit is about 0.5 L. Figure 3-11 shows several 1-L bottles.

**Mass**   The **gram** (g) *is a unit of mass in the metric system.* The mass of a paper clip is about 1 g.

*Figure 3-10. The length of objects less than one meter long is often given in centimeters. The length of the object in **B** is 10 cm.*

*Figure 3-11. One-liter bottles.*

**Temperature** *A degree Celsius* (°C) *is a unit of temperature in the metric system.* This unit is defined by the temperatures at which water freezes and boils. The freezing temperature of water is 0°C. The boiling temperature of water is 100°C. The normal temperature of your body is 37°C.

**Time** The units used to measure time are the same in the metric system as in the English system. Seconds (s) are the units used most often, but minutes and hours are also used.

## Using Metric Standards

Suppose someone asked you how far in meters it is from Los Angeles to New York. The answer is about 5,000,000 m, a very large number. It makes more sense to measure this large distance in larger units. It also makes sense to measure small things using small units. For this reason, the metric system includes many units of different sizes. Look, now, at some of these units.

**Large Units** Large units are made from the ones you already know by multiplying by 1,000. The new units are named by adding the prefix *kilo* to the name of the original unit. The prefix *kilo* means 1,000.

For example, distances between cities are often stated in units of 1,000 meters. These large units are called kilometers (km) (KIL•uh•mee•turz). The distance from Los Angeles to New York is easier to express as 5,000 km than as 5,000,000 m.

The prefix *kilo* is also used with other metric units. A kilogram (kg) is a unit of mass equal to 1,000 g. The mass of a desk telephone is approximately two kilograms.

**Small Units** Small units are made from the ones you already know by dividing by 10, 100, or 1,000. These new units are also named by adding a prefix to the name of the original unit.

The prefix *deci* means 0.1, or $\frac{1}{10}$. A decimeter (dm) is a unit of length equal to 0.1 m. The width of a business envelope is about 1 dm.

**TABLE 3-2.** METRIC PREFIXES

| Prefix | Symbol | Meaning | Common Examples |
|--------|--------|---------|-----------------|
| kilo | k | 1,000 | length: 1 km = 1,000 m<br>volume: 1 kL = 1,000 L<br>mass: 1 kg = 1,000 g |
| deci | d | 0.1 | length: 1 dm = 0.1 m |
| centi | c | 0.01 | length: 1 cm = 0.01 m |
| milli | m | 0.001 | length: 1 mm = 0.001 m<br>volume: 1 mL = 0.001 L<br>mass: 1 mg = 0.001 g |

The prefix *centi* means 0.01, or $\frac{1}{100}$. A centimeter (cm) is a unit of length equal to 0.01 m. It is about the width of a fingernail.

The prefix *milli* means 0.001, or $\frac{1}{1,000}$. A millimeter (mm) is a unit of length equal to 0.001 m. A dime is about 1 mm thick. A milliliter (mL) is a unit of volume equal to 0.001 L. A Styrofoam cup will hold about 300 mL of water. Table 3-2 shows the relationship between some of the more common metric prefixes.

One milliliter is equal to one cubic centimeter (cm³). A cubic centimeter is a cube 1 cm high, 1 cm wide, and 1 cm deep. See Figure 3-12. The volume of solids is often measured in cubic centimeters.

**SI Units** Even in the few countries that still use other measurement standards, scientists use the metric system. Scientists all over the world have agreed to use one metric unit for each kind of measurement. For example, all scientific measurements of mass are made in kilograms. All length and distance measurements are made in meters. This set of standards is called the International System, or SI. (SI is the abbreviation for the French words *Système International*.)

**Usefulness of the Metric System** More and more, measurements of common objects are being given in metric units. See Figure 3-13. You may think the metric system is hard to use. That is because you are used to

*Figure 3-12. How many cm³ = 1 L?*

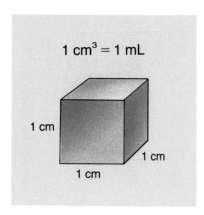

1 cm³ = 1 mL

1 cm

1 cm

1 cm

the English system. A little practice, however, will show you that the metric system is actually easier. For example, if you want to change feet into miles, you have to divide by 5280. If you want to change meters into kilometers, all you have to do is divide by 1000! So, 8594.5 m is equal to 8.5945 km. All you had to do was move the decimal point three places to the left! This ease in changing from one unit to another is what makes the metric system so useful.

Why is the metric system so useful?

● You may have already realized that our system of counting money is similar to the metric system. Our basic unit of money, the dollar, is divided by 10 to make a smaller unit, the dime. The dime is divided by 10 to make a still smaller unit, the penny. Because it is an easy system to use, many other countries use similar monetary systems.

For example, in England the pound is the basic unit of money. It is made up of 100 pence, or cents. One cent equals 0.01 pound. Until 1970, England used a monetary system that was much more complicated. Twelve pence made one shilling. Twenty shillings made one pound. Other units, such as the crown and the guinea, made the money even more confusing to people from other countries. However, the English people were used to this system. When the system was changed, they had to change their thinking over-night. You may find it hard to change your thinking from feet and inches to meters and centimeters. Imagine how hard it was to make this change in one day, as the English people had to do!

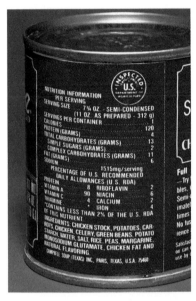

Figure 3-13. *Many labels on foods now show metric measurements.*

**OBJECTIVES AND WORDS TO REVIEW**
1. Why do people use measurement standards?
2. Name an object that has a mass of about 150 g, an object with a length of about 1 m, an object with a volume of about 500 mL.
3. The distance from Portland, Oregon to Portland, Maine is about 5,100 km. What is this distance in meters? In centimeters?
4. Write one complete sentence for each term listed below.
   standard         liter          degree Celsius
   meter            gram

# TAKING AND RECORDING ACCURATE MEASUREMENTS

## Preparation
Suppose you made a wooden model airplane. How would you make sure your friends could build an exact copy? One way would be to make and write down careful measurements of each airplane part, and share them with friends. Scientists also make careful measurements and record them.

**Figure 1.**

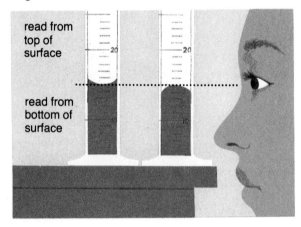

read from top of surface

read from bottom of surface

## Directions
There are two steps to keeping accurate records in science. The first step is measuring accurately.

The second is organizing data into a table.

Suppose you wanted to find the rate of evaporation of three liquids: A, B, and C. Place 10 mL of each liquid in a different graduated cylinder. Then, every 8 hr for 2 days measure the volume of each liquid. How do you make sure your data are accurate so comparisons can be made?

Measuring accurately means making a measurement that is as close to the accepted measurement as possible. One way to make sure your volume is accurate is shown in Figure 1.

Liquids do not have a flat surface in a container. The surface curves up or down. This surface is called a meniscus (mi•NIS•kuhs). To measure accurately, take the reading from the top of the curve if it curves down, or from the bottom of the curve if it curves up.

Before you take your measurements, set up a data table like Table 1. A data table consists of columns and rows. The titles of the data can be placed down or across. You usually organize the information to see changes or trends easily.

## Practice
Find out how many times three friends blink their eyes in one minute. Do three trials and record your data in a data table on a separate sheet of paper.

## Application
Measure the length, width, and height in centimeters of four objects. Then, write the measurement in a data table. How would you determine the accuracy of your measurements?

**Table 1.**

| Liquid | Volume (mL) at start | Volume (mL) after 8 hr | Volume (mL) after 16 hr | Volume (mL) after 24 hr | Volume (mL) after 32 hr | Volume (mL) after 40 hr | Volume (mL) after 48 hr |
|--------|------|------|------|------|------|------|------|
| A | 10 | 8 | 6 | 4 | 2 | 0 | 0 |
| B | 10 | 9 | 8 | 7 | 6 | 5 | 4 |
| C | 10 | 8.5 | 7.0 | 5.5 | 4.0 | 2.5 | 1.0 |

# VOLUME IN THE METRIC SYSTEM

## Objective
Measure the volume of an irregularly shaped object in metric units.

## Background
You can find the volume of a wooden block by multiplying together its length, width, and height. You cannot find the volume of an object such as a rock in the same way, however. In this experiment you will learn another way to measure volume. You will use an overflow container to catch the water the rock displaces. The volume of the water will then equal the volume of the rock.

## Materials
beaker, 50-mL graduated cylinder, string, 1-L milk carton, pencil, small rocks, plastic straw (10 cm long), scissors, metric ruler

## Procedure
1. Cut off the top of the milk carton as shown in Figure 3-L**A**. With the point of a pencil, carefully punch a hole in the side of the carton, 5 cm from the top. The hole should be just large enough for the straw to fit in.
2. Insert the straw through the hole in the carton. Two centimeters of the straw should be inside the carton. Tilt the straw down slightly.
3. Place the beaker underneath the open end of the straw. Slowly fill the carton with water until water begins to flow from the spout. Once the flow stops, discard the water in the beaker. See Figure 3-L**B**.
4. Tie a string around the rock. Place the graduate under the spout. See Figure 3-L**C**.
5. Slowly lower a rock into the carton until it is completely underwater. Catch the overflow water in the cylinder, and record its volume.

6. Repeat steps 3-5 with other rocks. Number the rocks, share them, and compare data.

## Questions
1. Why did you not find the volume of water in step 3?
2. What is the volume in mL of each rock?
3. How is it possible that several students might find different volumes for the same rock?
4. **PROBLEM SOLVING** Do larger volumes of a substance have greater densities? Offer a hypothesis and describe how to test it.

**Figure 3-L.** *Laboratory setup.*

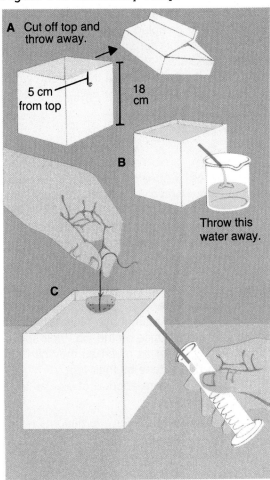

A Cut off top and throw away.

5 cm from top

18 cm

B

Throw this water away.

C

# CAREERS

CAREERS

Do you like to figure out how things work? Are you interested in science and math? Do you always try to do your homework neatly, maybe even with a typewriter? If so, the careers below might be worth looking into.

**Nuclear Physicist**  Nuclear physicists probe the inside of atoms. They use powerful machines that accelerate nuclear particles to tremendous speeds. They then aim these particles at atoms and observe what happens. Their exciting experiments have led to the discovery of new elements and subatomic particles. These experiments have also produced important sources of energy.

To become a nuclear physicist, you need advanced college training. A strong background in high school science and math is important. Experience in using computers is also helpful. When you begin your career, you might work in a university where you combine research with teaching. You might also work for an industrial firm or a government laboratory.

To find out more about this career, write:

*The American Institute of Physics*
*335 East 45th Street*
*New York, NY 10017*

**Technical Secretary**  Research scientists are often heavily involved in their projects. They have little time for keeping track of appointments, typing letters and reports, or preparing charts and graphs. Taking care of these important tasks is the job of a technical secretary.

Technical secretaries usually work for industrial and scientific firms such as oil or chemical companies. They enter the field with basic secretarial skills. They can learn these skills in high school or junior college. Once on the job, their special challenge is to learn as much as they can about the scientific work done by their firm.

To find out more about a career as a technical secretary, write:

*Professional Secretaries International*
*301 East Armour Boulevard*
*Kansas City, MO 64111*

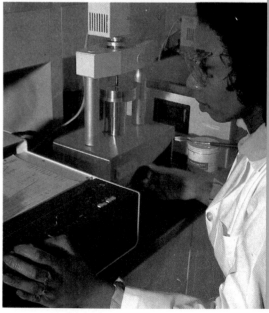

# SUMMARY

1. Scientific problem solving consists of these steps: state the problem; form a hypothesis; learn what is already known about the problem; test the hypothesis; observe and record the results; form a conclusion. (3-1)
2. A scientific law describes how things behave. A theory is an explanation of a law. (3-1)
3. The tools of a scientist include laboratory instruments, written and printed materials, and skills. (3-2)
4. Scientific laboratories use special equipment to make measurements. When using laboratory instruments, always use caution. (3-2)
5. People use standards to make it easy to compare measurements. In the metric system, the basic standards of measurement are the meter (length), gram (mass), liter (volume), degree Celsius (temperature), and the second (time). (3-3)
6. Other metric units are made from the basic units by multiplying or dividing them by 10, 100, or 1,000. Prefixes indicate the sizes of these units. (3-3)

# REVIEW

Number a sheet of paper from 1 to 25 and answer these questions.

**Building Science Vocabulary**  Write the letter of the term that best matches each definition.

**a.** control   **e.** hypothesis   **i.** meter
**b.** conclusion   **f.** kilo   **j.** milli
**c.** data   **g.** law   **k.** standard
**d.** gram   **h.** liter   **l.** theory

1. Prefix meaning 1,000
2. Prefix meaning 0.001 or $\frac{1}{1000}$
3. Part of an experiment that does not depend on the variable being observed
4. Explanation for the way something behaves
5. Unit of mass in the metric system
6. Measurements and information that a scientist obtains from an experiment
7. Educated guess about answer to problem
8. Unit of volume in the metric system
9. Statement that describes how something behaves
10. Unit of length or distance in the metric system

**Finding the Facts**  Select the letter of the answer that best completes each of the following.

11. On the Celsius thermometer the temperature of boiling water is    (**a**) 0°   (**b**) 37°   (**c**) 100°   (**d**) 212°.
12. Which prefix means 0.001 or $\frac{1}{1000}$?    (**a**) kilo   (**b**) deci   (**c**) centi   (**d**) milli
13. The monetary system of the United States is metric because its units are related to each other by the number    (**a**) 1,000   (**b**) 100   (**c**) 10   (**d**) 1.
14. Before beginning an experiment, a scientist usually    (**a**) records data   (**b**) draws a conclusion   (**c**) makes a graph of the data   (**d**) reads to learn what is known about the problem.
15. A fixed amount to which all measurements are compared is a    (**a**) standard   (**b**) control   (**c**) variable   (**d**) hypothesis.
16. A centimeter is equal to    (**a**) 0.01 m   (**b**) 0.001 m   (**c**) 100 m   (**d**) 1,000 m.
17. A balance is an instrument used to measure    (**a**) volume   (**b**) length   (**c**) mass   (**d**) time.

**18.** The set of standards used by scientists is called the **(a)** English system **(b)** SI **(c)** centimeter-gram-second system **(d)** Celsius system.

**19.** Which of the following has a mass of about 1 g? **(a)** a speck of dust **(b)** a paper clip **(c)** a telephone **(d)** a refrigerator

**20.** When should you wear safety goggles? **(a)** when using chemicals **(b)** when heating glassware **(c)** when using a bunsen burner **(d)** all of the above

## Understanding Main Ideas   Complete the following.

**21.** The purpose of an experiment is to test a __?__.

**22.** Chemists abandoned the phlogiston theory as a result of experiments that showed that substances burn by combining with __?__.

**23.** In your lab, you should always know the location of __?__.

**24.** The metric system and the English system both use the same units to measure __?__.

**25.** One important test of the value of an experiment is its ability to be __?__.

## Writing About Science   On a separate sheet of paper, answer the following as completely as possible.

**1.** Suppose you formed a hypothesis that salt water boils at a higher temperature than pure water. If you set up an experiment to measure the temperature of boiling salt water, what would you use for a control?

**2.** Explain what safety precautions you would take if your class was actually going to do the heat-holding part of the bread-mold experiment discussed in the chapter.

**3.** A certain brand of orange juice comes in containers of two different sizes. A one-liter container costs 80¢. A 750-mL container costs 55¢. Which container is a better buy, and why?

**4.** The results of experiments often prove scientists' hypotheses to be false. Yet such an experiment is not considered to be a failure. Discuss why this is so.

**5.** (laboratory question) How could you use the displacement method to find the volume of an object that floats in water?

## Investigating Chapter Ideas   Try one of the following projects to further your study.

**1. How big is a cubic meter?**   Construct a cubic meter using twelve meter sticks. Tape them together at the corners to make a cube. The space, or volume, taken up by such a cube is called a cubic meter. Then estimate the volume of your classroom in cubic meters.

**2. History and the phlogiston theory**   Antoine Lavoisier carried out experiments with oxygen that disproved the phlogiston theory. However, Joseph Priestley, who discovered oxygen, continued to believe in the phlogiston theory long after Lavoisier showed that it could not be correct. Do some research on the work of Lavoisier and Priestley. Prepare a report of your findings. Include in your report how the politics of the times had a great impact on these men.

## Reading About Science   Read some of the following books to explore topics that interest you.

Ardley, Neil. 1984. **Making Metric Measurements.** New York: Watts.

Asimov, Isaac. 1983. **The Measure of the Universe.** New York: Harper.

Grey, Vivian. 1982. **The Chemist Who Lost His Head: The Story of Antoine Laurent Lavoisier.** New York: Coward.

Gutnik, Martin. 1980. **How to Do a Science Project and Report.** New York: Watts.

# MOTION AND FORCES

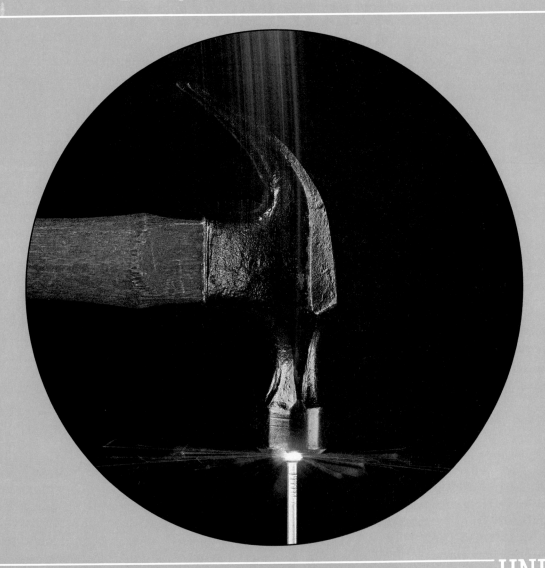

When you slam a hammer down on a nail, why does the nail move into the wood? When you release a bowstring, what provides the energy that sends the arrow skyward? Why is it easier to float in salt water than it is to float in fresh water? In this unit you will explore the world of pushes, pulls, and motion. Your investigations will lead you to answers to some of these questions.

UNIT 2

The gun fires. The 100-meter dash is on. At the start, one runner is as fast as another. But what happens near the finish line? Which runner do you think is most likely to win the dash?

Suppose you were training to run in a meet. As you train, you keep two measurements in mind. One is the length of the run. The other is time.

Would you believe that similar measurements are used to plan jet flights? Planners need to know how far a jet will travel and the time the flight will take.

Similar measurements help launch rockets and even track the movement of a storm. In fact, they are the same measurements used to describe all moving objects. In this chapter, you will learn more ways to describe moving objects.

Read and Find Out:

● how a graph can show which swimmer is faster.

● why automobile engineers perform crash tests

● what Newton's First Law tells you about seat belts.

# OBJECTS IN MOTION

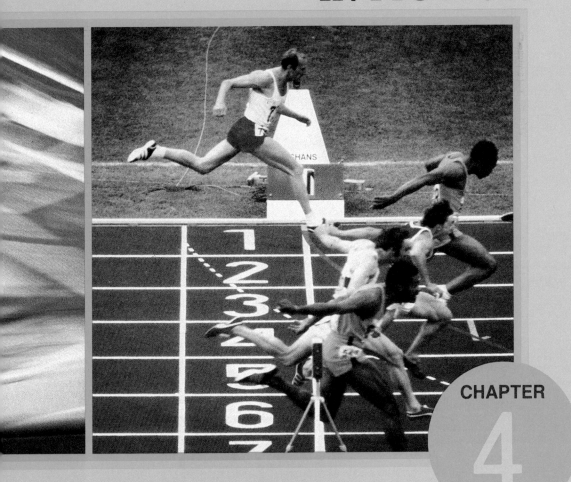

CHAPTER

4

69

# DISTANCE AND TIME

### OBJECTIVES

**1.** Calculate the speed of an object.

**2.** Contrast speed and velocity.

**3.** Compare the velocities of objects by using graphs.

*Figure 4-1. Moving objects change position relative to the background.*

*Figure 4-2. Compare the distance traveled between 1 and 2 seconds. Which runner is faster?*

Suppose you wanted to break a team record for the 100-meter dash. How fast would you have to run? To find out, you would have to know the time the record holder took to run 100 meters. You would have to run the same length in a shorter time.

From people to jets to storms, all moving objects can be described by how fast they are going. In this section you will begin to investigate moving objects. You will learn how to use length and time to calculate how fast any object is going. You will be studying objects moving in a straight line.

## A First Look at Motion

How can you tell Figure 4-1 is a photograph of a moving object? The blur indicates the bus is changing position compared with the background. **Motion** *is a change in position relative to fixed objects.*

Fixed objects, markers, can help you find how fast runners are moving in a meet. The markers in Figure 4-2 are placed one meter apart. Race officials time the runners as they pass the markers. You can use the markers to measure the *distance* the runners cover while they are timed. **Distance** *is the length between any two points in the path of an object.*

You can use distance and time to compare how fast the runners are. Runner One covers 4 meters in 1 second, 8 meters in 2 seconds, and so on. Runner Two covers 8 meters in 1 second, 16 meters in 2 seconds, and so on. These measurements show that Runner Two is moving faster.

## Distance Traveled Each Second

A simple way to tell how fast each runner is moving is to find the distance covered each second. For example, Runner One covers 12 meters in 3 seconds. Divide the distance, 12 meters, by the time, 3 seconds. By dividing, you find that Runner One covered 4 meters per second (4 m/s). This result is the runner's *speed. Speed is the distance traveled each second.*

Now find the speed of Runner Two. In 3 seconds Runner Two covered a distance of 24 meters. So:

$$\text{speed} = \frac{\text{distance traveled}}{\text{time}}$$
or,
$$s = \frac{d}{t}$$
$$s = \frac{24 \text{ meters}}{3 \text{ seconds}}$$
$$s = 8 \text{ m/s}$$

During the three seconds, each runner kept up a constant speed. That is, each ran without changing speed. During that time, Runner Two was running at twice the speed of Runner One.

## Speed and Direction

A more complete description of motion includes speed and direction. For example, the road in Figure 4-3 on page 72 stretches from south to north. So the traffic is traveling north.

*Speed in a particular direction is the* **velocity** *(vuh•LAHS•uh•tee) of a moving object.* For example, a train from New York to Chicago may be traveling at a speed of 110 km/hr. Its velocity is 110 km/hr west.

*Figure 4-3. The velocity of these cars includes their speed and their direction.*

*Figure 4-4. (right) How far has Runner Two gone after 2.5 seconds?*

## Graphing Speed

Another way to compare the speed of objects is to plot graphs. For example, suppose the runners in Figure 4-2 were timed for a total of 6 seconds. The data in Table 4-1 can be used to plot graphs of the runners. Graphs can show at a glance which runner is faster.

**TABLE 4-1.**
**DISTANCE TRAVELED BY EACH RUNNER**

| Runner One | | Runner Two | |
|---|---|---|---|
| Time s | Distance m | Time s | Distance m |
| 1 | 1 | 1 | 2 |
| 2 | 2 | 2 | 4 |
| 3 | 3 | 3 | 6 |
| 4 | 4 | 4 | 8 |
| 5 | 5 | 5 | 10 |
| 6 | 6 | 6 | 12 |

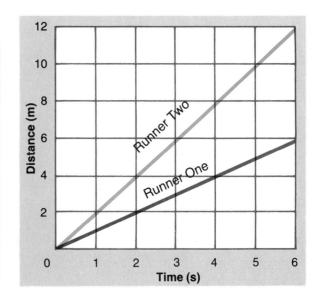

Figure 4-4 shows *distance-time graphs* for the runners. A **distance-time graph** *shows the relationship between distance and time.* Compare the graphs for the runners. The line in the graph for Runner Two is steeper than the other line. It has a greater *slope. The word* **slope** *is used to indicate the steepness of a line.*

Runner Two was the faster runner. The line for Runner Two has the greater slope. This example shows a relationship between speed and slope. The greater the speed of an object, the greater the slope of a distance-time graph.

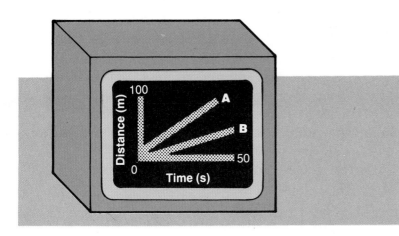

● In 1976 John Naber of the United States held the world record in the breaststroke. He swam a distance of 100 meters in 55.49 seconds. Look at the graphs in Figure 4-5. Which graph represents John Naber?

## EXPLORE BY VISITING

### COMPARING SPEEDS

**OBJECTIVE**
Compare speeds of runners with distance-time graphs.

**PROCEDURE**
**1.** Attend a track or swim meet.
**2.** Record the distance covered in a particular race. Find the time each contestant took to cover that distance.

**QUESTIONS**
**1.** Plot a distance-time graph for each contestant.
**2.** Calculate the speed of each contestant.
**3.** Which is the fastest contestant? Why?

*Figure 4-5. Why does graph B represent the slower swimmer?*

## OBJECTIVES AND WORDS TO REVIEW

**1.** A jogging path is 400 meters long. A jogger travels the entire length in 90 seconds. What is the speed of the jogger?
**2.** Can you give the velocity of the jogger in Question 1? Explain your answer.
**3.** When you are comparing distance-time graphs of two objects, how can you tell which object is moving faster?
**4.** Write one complete sentence for each term listed below.

| | | |
|---|---|---|
| motion | speed | distance-time graph |
| distance | velocity | slope |

# MOTION WITH CHANGING SPEED

**OBJECTIVES**

**1.** Calculate the average speed of an object.
**2.** Find how quickly an object is speeding up.
**3.** Find how quickly an object is slowing down.

Most moving objects are continually changing speed. Runners may pace themselves to move at a constant speed for part of a meet. But as they near the finish, they pick up speed. Planes move faster and faster along the runway just before takeoff. Cars slow down to stop at a red light. In this section you will calculate how quickly objects change speed.

## Averages

Cars, storms, and other moving objects change more than just speed. They change velocity, that is, speed and direction. A river's course may change direction many times. In some parts of its course, a river flows rapidly downhill. In other parts, the same river flows slowly over level plains.

How can you describe the motion of an object that changes speed and direction? Look at the course of the car in Figure 4-6. You can describe overall direction by comparing the car's end point with its starting point. The end point of the car is northwest of the starting point. You can describe the speed of the car by finding its *average speed. The **average speed** is the total distance traveled divided by the total time passed.*

To find the average speed of an object, you do not have to know its actual speeds. You need to know only the time the object took to travel a total distance. For example, the car in Figure 4-6 traveled 90 kilometers in 3 hours. Its average speed was:

$$\text{average speed} = \frac{\text{total distance}}{\text{time}}$$

$$= \frac{90\,\text{km}}{3\,\text{hr}}$$

$$= 30\,\text{km/hr}$$

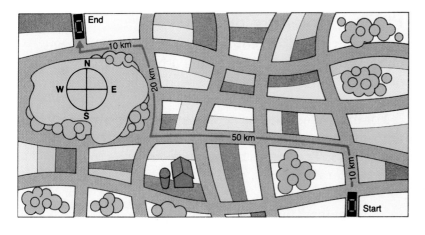

*Figure 4-6. In what general direction does the car travel on its return trip?*

Knowing the overall direction and average speed helps you describe an object with changing motion. Now look for patterns in the ways motion can change.

## Change Per Unit of Time

You can recognize a change in motion in two ways. There can be a change in speed, such as when a runner speeds up near the finish line. Or there can be a change in direction, such as when a car rounds a turn. See Figure 4-7. The car keeps the same speed as it rounds the curve. However, it changes its direction by the same amount each second.

These patterns of change are examples of *acceleration* (ak•sel•ur•AY•shuhn). **Acceleration** *is a change of velocity per unit of time.* A change in velocity can be a change in speed, a change in direction, or a change in both. Any object that is changing its speed or direction is said to be accelerating.

How do you find the distance covered in a period of time?

*Figure 4-7. Another way to change motion is to change direction.*

*Figure 4-8. Acceleration is the rate at which velocity changes.*

## Finding Acceleration

You can calculate the acceleration of an object that changes speed over a short time. First, subtract the original speed from the final speed. Then divide the difference by the time.

For example, find the acceleration of a swimmer who changes speed in the last 2 seconds of a race. See Figure 4-8. The speed increased from 1 m/s to 3 m/s. The acceleration is:

$$\text{acceleration} = \frac{\text{final speed} - \text{original speed}}{\text{time}}$$

$$= \frac{3 \, \text{m/s} - 1 \, \text{m/s}}{2 \, \text{s}}$$

$$= \frac{2 \, \text{m/s}}{2 \, \text{s}}$$

$$= 1 \, \text{m/s/s}$$

The acceleration is 1 m/s per second. However, the swimmer's speed may not have increased by exactly 1 m/s each second. It may have increased more in one second than another. The acceleration you found is actually an *average* acceleration for the 2 seconds.

## Slowing Down

Acceleration can also mean a decrease in speed. *The kind of acceleration in which speed decreases is called* **deceleration** (dee•sel•ur•AY•shuhn).

You can find the deceleration of an object the same way you find acceleration. For example, suppose a runner traveling at 4 m/s comes to a stop in 2 seconds. What is the deceleration?

$$\text{deceleration} = \frac{\textbf{final speed} - \textbf{original speed}}{\textbf{time}}$$

$$= \frac{0\,\text{m/s} - 4\,\text{m/s}}{2\,\text{s}}$$

$$= \frac{-4\,\text{m/s}}{2\,\text{s}}$$

$$= -2\,\text{m/s/s}$$

The negative sign in the answer shows that this is an example of deceleration. The runner is slowing down 2 m/s per second.

● Many safety tests made on a new car check acceleration. How quickly a car can speed up is important for helping cars to pull safely into fast lanes of traffic. Steering equipment is checked for making gentle and sudden changes of direction. Checks are made to tell how quickly a car can come to a stop to avoid a crash.

When a car crashes, its speed can change to 0 m/s in a second or less. When such a sudden drop in speed occurs, objects inside the car move forward. Crash tests are made to tell how well passengers are protected from being thrown through the windshield. See Figure 4-9.

**Figure 4-9.** *Crash tests help people make safer cars.*

## OBJECTIVES AND WORDS TO REVIEW

1. What is the average speed of a race car that travels 680 meters in 20 seconds?
2. What is the acceleration of a plane that increases its speed from 200 m/s to 250 m/s in 5 seconds?
3. Ann was swimming at a speed of 3 m/s when she started to slow down. She slowed to a stop in 2 seconds. What was her acceleration? What is this kind of acceleration called?
4. Write one complete sentence for each term listed below.
   average speed      deceleration
   acceleration

# BALANCED AND UNBALANCED FORCES

**OBJECTIVES**

**1.** List four kinds of forces.

**2.** Contrast balanced and unbalanced forces.

**3.** State Newton's First Law of Motion.

**What may indicate a change in velocity?**

Suppose you are ice skating for the first time. You push yourself away from a bench to get yourself started. A friend skates near you and gives you a pull to speed you along. Then you grab onto a handrail. You pull on the rail and come to a stop.

Pushes and pulls are needed to start and stop any object. In this section you will find how different pushes and pulls act on objects.

## Pushes and Pulls

A push or a pull can change the motion of an object. See Figure 4-10. A push or a pull is an example of a *force. A* **force** *is any cause of a change in motion.* Forces change the speed and direction of an object. In short, forces cause acceleration.

You can see two kinds of forces in Figure 4-10. When you punch a volleyball or pull a bowstring, you are applying a *muscular* (MUS•kyew•ler) *force. A* **muscular force** *comes from the expanding and contracting of muscle tissue.* When it is released, the bowstring applies an *elastic* (i•LAS•tik) *force to the arrow. An* **elastic force** *is produced by any bent or stretched object that returns to its original shape.*

*Figure 4-10. You push on a volleyball when you punch it over the net. You pull on a bowstring to fire an arrow. What is this push or pull called?*

pushing force →

← frictional force

SLIDING FRICTION

STANDING FRICTION

## A Force From Rubbing

You need to apply a muscular force to shove a crate across a floor. See Figure 4-11. At the same time, another force is also acting on the crate. That force is friction (FRIK•shuhn). **Friction** *opposes the motion of one surface past another.* Friction slows down objects and can make them stop. In this case, friction comes from the rubbing of the crate against the floor.

You can feel the effect of friction by pushing the crate along different surfaces. Push it along a waxed floor. Then push it along a carpet. It is harder to push it along the carpet because the carpet is a rougher surface. On the rougher surface, a greater friction opposes the motion.

Friction opposes motion whenever two surfaces are touching, even if they are not moving. See Figure 4-12. Friction between moving parts of machines causes parts to wear down. The amount of friction can be reduced by making surfaces smoother. Wheels and rollers also help reduce friction. See Figure 4-13.

Although friction opposes motion, it also helps objects to start moving. For example, friction between a tire and a road helps the tire grip the road. Without friction, a tire would slip and spin. A car or bicycle would not be able to move.

*Figure 4-11. (left) Frictional forces are caused by attraction between two surfaces in contact. The attraction opposes the sliding of one surface across the other.*

*Figure 4-12. (right) Standing friction is friction between two surfaces in contact, but not moving.*

*Figure 4-13. (below) Much less force is needed to overcome rolling friction than to overcome sliding friction.*

ROLLING FRICTION

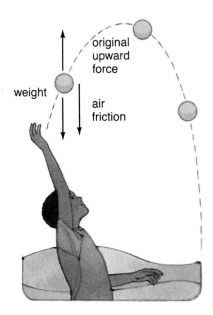

*Figure 4-14. Both gravity and friction act against the ball's motion.*

# A Pull to Earth

Friction acts on a ball that is tossed up into the air. See Figure 4-14. The ball rubs against gases in the air. The rubbing slows and stops the ball. Another force is also stopping the ball. The force, *gravity* (GRAV•uh•tee), pulls the ball to the ground.

**Gravity** *is a force of attraction between two objects.* It exists between any two objects in the universe. The closer the two objects move together, the greater the force becomes. The more mass the two objects have, the greater the force is.

There is an attraction between the earth and a ball tossed into the air. The earth's mass is so great that this attraction pulls the ball back toward the earth. It is gravity that causes all objects to fall to the ground. Gravity attracts all things to the earth's surface. It even holds the air around the earth.

# Forces on Objects at Rest

Objects do not always move when forces are applied. For example, the rower is applying a force in Figure 4-15A. So why is the boat not moving? The boat is tied to the dock. The rope is applying a force on the boat. Both the rower and the rope are applying an equal amount of force. But the forces are in opposite directions.

Equal forces applied in opposite directions are said to be balanced. When balanced forces are applied to an object at rest, the object remains still.

*Figure 4-15A. (left) The force on the boat equals the force on the rope.*

*Figure 4-15B. (right) The rower exerts a force to move the boat forward.*

What happens when the rope is untied? The boat begins to move, of course. It moves because the rowing force is no longer balanced by the pull of the rope. An unbalanced force causes an object at rest to start moving. Once the boat starts moving it picks up speed. It can even change direction. So, an unbalanced force causes acceleration.

What effect does an unbalanced force have on an object at rest?

## Forces on a Moving Object

Balanced forces can act on a moving object. See Figure 4-15. As the boat moves, for example, friction is produced by water rubbing the sides of the boat. Friction acts in a direction opposite to the rowing force. The faster the boat moves, the greater the frictional force becomes. In time, the frictional force balances the rowing force.

What happens when balanced forces act on a moving object? The boat, in this case, continues to move. But there is no more acceleration. The boat moves at a constant speed in a straight line.

Suppose the rower stops rowing. Friction then is no longer balanced by a rowing force. As an unbalanced force, the frictional force slows the boat down. If there are no currents or waves, the boat will drift to a stop.

Table 4-2 lists the conclusions you made by observing a rowboat. You can make the same conclusions by pedaling a bicycle, hitting a ball, or setting any other object in motion.

**TABLE 4-2.** FORCES ON MOVING AND UNMOVING OBJECTS

| Forces | Object | Result |
| --- | --- | --- |
| Balanced | unmoving | no motion |
| Balanced | moving | no change in speed or direction |
| Unbalanced | unmoving | object begins to move |
| Unbalanced | moving | change in speed or/and direction |

*Balanced and Unbalanced Forces* **81**

## The First Law of Motion

About 300 years ago, Sir Isaac Newton made similar observations about forces on moving objects. He put his observations together into three laws of motion. You will study the second and third law of motion in the next chapter. It is the ***First Law of Motion*** that sums up the observations from Table 4-2.

The First Law of Motion states:

1. An object at rest remains at rest unless acted upon by an unbalanced force.

2. An object in motion continues to move at a constant speed and in a straight line unless acted upon by an unbalanced force.

The first law describes a property of matter called *inertia* (in•UR•shuh). ***Inertia*** *is the tendency of any*

What is the tendency of an object at rest?

*Figure 4-17. If centripetal force acts inward, in what direction do the bikers move?*

object to oppose a change in motion. That is, an object at rest tends to remain at rest. A moving object tends to keep moving at a constant speed in a straight line. Any change in motion requires an unbalanced force.

Suppose you are in a standing bus. The bus suddenly starts up. See Figure 4-16**A**. Because of your inertia, your body tends to stay at rest. When the bus stops, your body tends to keep moving forward. See Figure 4-16**B**.

## Inertia and Circular Motion

Suppose some bikers are moving at a constant speed in a straight path. As they approach a turn, their inertia tends to keep them moving without change. It takes an unbalanced force to change their direction. The force acts inward, as shown by the direction the bikers lean in Figure 4-17. *The inward force that keeps an object moving in a circle is called* **centripetal** (sen•TRIP•uh•tuhl) *force.*

The centripetal force is provided by the high banking of the curved road and by friction between the wheels and the road.

● With the help of Newton's First Law you can help protect yourself from injury. Suppose you are in a car that comes to a sudden stop. Because of your inertia, your body tends to keep moving. You need a force to hold you back in your seat. This force is provided by a seat belt. Seat belts keep you from hitting the dashboard or windshield.

**OBJECTIVES AND WORDS TO REVIEW**
1. Give an example of each of these forces acting on an object: muscular, elastic, frictional, and gravity.
2. How can an unbalanced force change the motion of an object?
3. State Newton's First Law of Motion.
4. Write one complete sentence for each term listed below.

| force | friction | inertia |
|---|---|---|
| muscular force | gravity | centripetal force |
| elastic force | | |

## EXPLORE BY TRYING

### CIRCULAR MOTION

**OBJECTIVE**
Observe the path of an object released from a centripetal force.

**MATERIALS**
string (1 m long), beanbag

**PROCEDURE**
1. Go to a wide open area such as a gym or playground.
2. Tie the string tightly around the beanbag.
3. Swing the bag in a circle above your head.
4. Observe the motion of the bag for several seconds. Then release the string. Observe the path of the bag. Record your results. **CAUTION:** Be sure no one is near enough to be hit by the bag.
5. Repeat steps 3 and 4 several times.

**QUESTIONS**
1. Describe the acceleration of the bag as you swung it above your head.
2. What path did the bag take when it was released? Why did it take that path?

# STUDY SKILL

## INTERPRETING AND PREDICTING FROM GRAPHS

### Preparation
Look at Figure 1. You may have seen a diagram like this before. Diagrams like these are called graphs. Graphs show the relationship between two or more things. The graph in Figure 1 is a distance-time graph. The distance traveled by an object is related to the amount of time it takes to travel that distance.

Scientists use graphs to help them see relationships among data collected. They also use graphs to help them predict the results.

*Figure 1.*

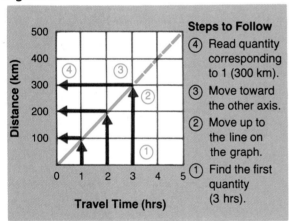

**Steps to Follow**
④ Read quantity corresponding to 1 (300 km).
③ Move toward the other axis.
② Move up to the line on the graph.
① Find the first quantity (3 hrs).

### Directions
Figure 1 is a distance-time graph of an automobile trip from Las Vegas to Los Angeles. What information does the graph give? After one hour, the auto traveled a distance of 100 km. After three hours, a distance of 300 km was traveled. Figure 1 shows how these quantities were obtained.

Graphs can be used to make predictions. Suppose you wanted to know how far the car would have traveled in 5 hours. You can predict that distance from the graph.

By looking at the graph, you notice a general direction, or trend, occurring. As time passes, the distance traveled increases. By extending the line as you see in Figure 1, you can predict that the car would have traveled 500 km.

### Practice
Look at Figure 4-4 on page 72. On a separate sheet of paper, answer the following questions.
1. How far did Runner One travel after 1 s?
2. How far did Runner Two travel after 4 s?
3. What prediction can you make for the distance Runner One would have traveled in 7 s?
4. If both runners ran at the rates shown in Figure 4-4 on page 72, which runner would have won a 6-m dash?

### Application
Figure 2 shows the motion of a falling stone. On a sheet of paper, answer the following questions.
1. How far did the stone fall after 2 seconds? After 3.5 seconds?
2. Does this graph represent accelerated motion? Explain your answer.

*Figure 2.*

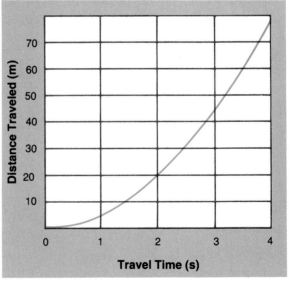

# LABORATORY ACTIVITY

## GETTING INFORMATION FROM GRAPHS

### Objective
Use a distance-time graph to describe changing speed.

### Background
You can plot a distance-time graph to show the speed of an object. A straight line shows constant speed. The steeper the line, the greater the speed. A distance-time graph can also show acceleration. For example, Table 4-L has data for a marble rolling down a ramp. A distance-time graph can show how the speed is changing.

### Materials
pencil, graph paper; optional: marble, 3 meter sticks, stop watch, marking pencil

### Procedure
1. Set up a horizontal axis on graph paper to show the time. Set up the vertical axis to show the distance. Spread out the numbers on each axis as much as possible to plot a large graph.
2. Plot each point indicated by the numbers in the table. For example, a point with a time of 1s and a distance of 3.8 cm is plotted in Figure 4-L. Draw a smooth curve through the points.

| **TABLE 4-L.** EXPERIMENTAL DATA | |
|---|---|
| Times(s) | Total Distance Traveled (cm) |
| 0.5 | 2.5 |
| 1.0 | 3.8 |
| 1.5 | 9.0 |
| 3.0 | 35.0 |
| 3.5 | 48.0 |
| 4.0 | 64.0 |

3. (optional) Place 3 meter sticks end-to-end on a floor. Roll a marble along the sticks. Mark the position of the marble on the sticks. (A partner with a watch can be a timer.) Record your data and make a graph.

*Figure 4-L.*

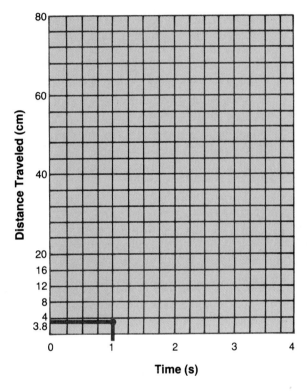

### Questions
1. In steps 1 to 2, how does the slope of the curve change (from zero to four seconds)?
2. In steps 1 to 2, how is the change in speed shown in the slope of the curve?
3. (optional) As the marble in step 3 slows down, how does the slope change?
4. **PROBLEM SOLVING** Describe the changes in the speed of a marble that rolls down a ramp and onto a level floor. How would a graph show the changing speed of the marble?

# SUMMARY

1. To describe an object's motion, find the distance it travels per unit time and its direction. (4-1)
2. The slope of the line in a distance-time graph represents the speed of a moving object. (4-1)
3. One way to describe the motion of an object with changing speed is to find the average speed. (4-2)
4. Acceleration can mean a change in speed, a change in direction, or both. (4-2)
5. Balanced forces produce no change in motion. (4-3)
6. Unbalanced forces change the motion of an object. (4-3)

# REVIEW

Number a sheet of paper from 1 to 25 and answer these questions.

**Building Science Vocabulary**   Write the letter of the term that best matches each definition.

a. acceleration
b. average speed
c. centripetal
d. deceleration
e. distance-time graph
f. force
g. frictional
h. gravity
i. inertia
j. motion
k. speed
l. velocity

1. Speed in a particular direction
2. A change of position relative to fixed objects
3. The change of velocity per unit time
4. A force that opposes motion of one surface past another
5. The distance traveled per unit time
6. A diagram showing the relationship between distance and time

7. A force of attraction between any two objects
8. Any cause of a change in motion
9. A force that keeps an object moving in a circle
10. The tendency of an object to oppose a change in motion

**Finding the Facts**   Select the letter of the answer that best completes each of the following.

11. Which of the following could be the speed of a car?   (a) 40 km   (b) 40 km/hr   (c) 1 hr   (d) 40 km/hr/s
12. The deceleration of a truck approaching a stop sign could be expressed as   (a) 7 m/s   (b) 7 m/s/s   (c) 7 m   (d) −7 m/s/s.
13. An example of acceleration is a   (a) rocket waiting in its launch pad   (b) racer going around a turn at a constant speed   (c) swimmer stroking at a constant speed in a straight lane   (d) train going due west at a constant speed.
14. The so called "bullet" train of Japan travels 510 km in 3 hrs. Its average speed is   (a) 170 m/s   (b) 170 km/s   (c) 170 km   (d) 170 km/hr.
15. The steeper the line of a distance-time graph is, the   (a) greater the speed   (b) longer the time   (c) less the distance   (d) lower the speed.
16. The force of gravity is unbalanced when   (a) a car remains at a stop sign   (b) you hold a weight   (c) you let a box fall   (d) you put a radio on a counter top.
17. A centripetal force is acting on all the following *except*   (a) cars on a dragstrip   (b) riders on a carousel   (c) cars rounding a turn   (d) a child swinging on a swing.
18. Unbalanced forces acting on a moving car can cause the car to do any of the following except   (a) speed up   (b) slow down   (c) move at a constant speed in a straight line   (d) come to a full stop.

**19.** The velocity of a jet might be **(a)** 100 km **(b)** 100 km/hr **(c)** 100 km/hr west **(d)** 100 km/hr/s.

**20.** Balanced forces are acting on all the following except a **(a)** train stopped at a station **(b)** swimmer stroking at a steady pace in a straight lane **(c)** plane landing **(d)** truck pausing at a red light.

**Understanding Main Ideas** Complete the following.

**21.** To find the speed of an object, you must know the distance traveled in a particular __?__.

**22.** In a distance-time graph of an object, the slope represents the object's __?__.

**23.** Acceleration can mean a change in speed and __?__.

**24.** Forces that act on an object without changing the object's motion are said to be __?__.

**25.** Newton's First Law of Motion describes a property of matter called __?__.

**Writing About Science** On a separate sheet of paper, answer the following as completely as possible.

**1.** For two hours of its trip from New York to Salt Lake City, a jet flew in a straight line at a constant speed. The jet covered 1,200 km in that time. Find the velocity. (Hint: For a complete answer, you may need a map.)

**2.** While riding your bicycle, you suddenly step on the brakes. Explain why you feel thrown forward slightly.

**3.** You stop pedaling your bicycle and slowly come to a stop. While you are stopping, what unbalanced force is acting on the bicycle? Explain your answer.

**4.** A car is traveling at a speed of 35 km/hr. a) Within 5 seconds, the car comes to a full stop. What is the acceleration? b) The car starts up again and within 7 seconds is traveling at 35 km/hr. What is the acceleration?

**5.** (laboratory question) Describe a distance-time graph for a runner going at a constant speed for 10 seconds and then speeding up for 10 seconds.

**Investigating Chapter Ideas** Try one of the following projects to further your study.

**1. Looking for a centripetal force** Put an old LP record on a turntable. Turn the machine on to a high speed. Set a coin down in various places on the record. Note where the coin can rotate without sliding off. Where is the centripetal force greatest?

**2. Building a bridge** A properly designed bridge must keep forces in balance under a heavy load. Build a bridge out of toothpicks. Use white wood glue and glue only the ends of toothpicks. Make the bridge about 25 cm long and no wider than one toothpick. Measure the strength of your bridge by hanging weights from it until the bridge falls.

**Reading About Science** Read some of the following books to explore topics that interest you.

Ford, Barbara. 1983. **The Elevator.** New York: Walker.

Gardner, Robert and D. Webster. 1978. **Moving Right Along.** Garden City, NY: Doubleday.

Helfman, Harry. 1975. **Creating Things That Move.** New York: Morrow.

Watson, Philip. 1983. **Super Motion.** New York: Lothrop.

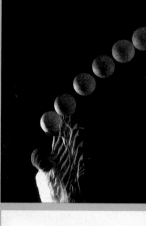

How does Newton's First Law of Motion help you understand the motion of these objects? It tells you that they stay at rest without an unbalanced force. It took an unbalanced *upward* force to move them.

What *downward* forces act on the objects? Each object rubs against air molecules. So, friction is one downward force. Gravity, too, acts downward. No matter how hard you toss a ball into the air, it returns to earth. Why, then, does the rocket not return to earth?

A rocket engine produces a great upward force as it travels. This upward force is larger than the combined downward forces due to friction and gravity. Thus, the rocket rises. If the upward force is large enough, the rocket breaks free of earth's gravity. It never falls back.

In this chapter you will study more about laws describing motion and forces.

Read and Find Out:
- how to beat a champion shot putter.
- how often you use pairs of forces.
- why balloons rise in the air.

# MORE LAWS
# OF MOTION

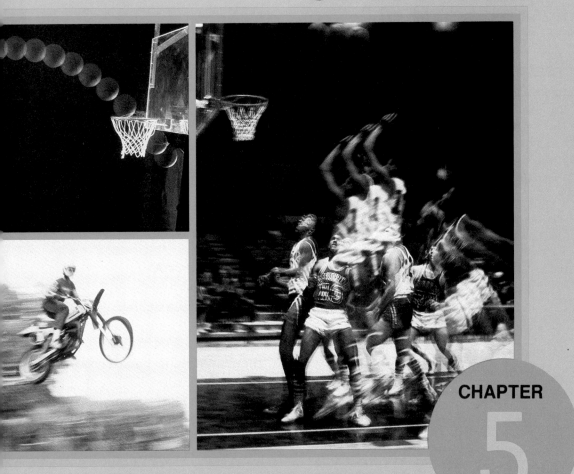

# FINDING THE AMOUNT OF FORCE

## OBJECTIVES

**1.** Relate the amount of force to a change in speed.

**2.** Use Newton's Second Law to find the amount of force applied to an object.

**3.** Contrast mass and weight.

In the last chapter, you learned that an unbalanced force can cause acceleration. That is, it can change an object's speed and direction. When a driver steps on a gas pedal, an unbalanced force makes the car go forward. What happens if the driver presses harder on the pedal?

In this section, you will see how changing the amount of force affects acceleration. You will also get a greater understanding of what you are measuring when you step onto a bathroom scale.

### Changing the Amount of Force

A bicycle can help you tell how the amount of force affects acceleration. First pedal the bicycle gently. Now pedal with a greater force. The greater force causes a greater change in the speed and direction of the bike. In general, the greater the unbalanced force, the greater the acceleration produced.

Figure 5-1 can help you study the relationship of force and acceleration more closely. At first the desk in **A** is not moving. That is, the desk is at rest. The student uses a certain force to increase the speed of the desk to 2 meters per second in 2 seconds. What is the acceleration?

*Figure 5-1. An unbalanced force can move the desk. What force must the students overcome?*

$$\text{acceleration} = \frac{\text{final speed} - \text{original speed}}{\text{time}}$$
$$= \frac{2 \text{ m/s} - 0 \text{ m/s}}{2 \text{ s}}$$
$$= 1 \text{ m/s/s}$$

In Figure 5-1**B**, two students together are producing twice the force. Starting from rest, they push the desk to a final speed of 4 meters per second in 2 seconds. What is the acceleration of the desk when the two students push together?

$$\text{acceleration} = \frac{\text{final speed} - \text{original speed}}{\text{time}}$$
$$= \frac{4 \text{ m/s} - 0 \text{ m/s}}{2 \text{ s}}$$
$$= 2 \text{ m/s/s}$$

Doubling the force doubled the acceleration. How do you think tripling the force would change the acceleration? In general, a change in the amount of unbalanced force produces the same change in acceleration.

How does a change in the amount of an unbalanced force affect the acceleration?

## Mass and Acceleration

Suppose you kick a beach ball and a football with the same amount of force. Your kick speeds up the beach ball much faster than the football. The difference in acceleration is due to the difference in mass of the objects. Mass, remember, is a measure of the amount of matter in each object. When the same unbalanced force is applied to two objects, the object with less mass has greater acceleration.

You can increase the mass of the bicycle in Figure 5-2 by adding more groceries. Suppose you try to produce the same acceleration with and without groceries. With groceries you have to pedal harder to produce the same acceleration. The greater the mass of an object, the greater the force needed to produce acceleration.

*Figure 5-2. How hard you have to pedal depends on what property of the groceries?*

## The Second Law of Motion

You have been observing how the amount of force is related to an object's acceleration. Sir Isaac Newton summed up these observations in the **Second Law of Motion.** This law states that an unbalanced force acting on an object causes acceleration. The greater the force, the greater the acceleration. And the smaller the mass, the greater the acceleration produced by a certain amount of force.

This law can be expressed in a mathematical equation:

$$\textbf{force} = \textbf{mass} \times \textbf{acceleration}$$

or simply, $$\mathbf{F} = \mathbf{m} \times \mathbf{a}$$

Until now, the amount of force was expressed by "how hard" you kicked a ball or "how many" students push a desk. Newton's equation, however, helps to define *a unit for measuring force, the **newton*** (N). One newton is the amount of force needed to give a 1 kg mass an acceleration of 1 m/s/s:

$$F = m \times a$$
$$1 \text{ newton (N)} = 1 \text{ kg} \times 1 \text{ m/s/s}$$

Define a newton in terms of the units that make it up.

## Measuring Force in Newtons

You can use a scale to find the number of newtons of force you apply to an object. See Figure 5-3. However, you can also use Newton's Second Law of Motion

*Figure 5-3. Scales have springs that stretch when a force is applied.*

to find the amount of force. For example, recall that the student in Figure 5-1**A** gave the desk an acceleration of 1 m/s/s. Suppose the mass of the desk is 50 kg. The force is

$$F = m \times a$$
$$= 50 \text{ kg} \times 1 \text{ m/s/s}$$
$$= 50 \text{ N}$$

In Figure 5-1**B**, the two students together gave the desk an acceleration of 2 m/s/s. Their combined force was:

$$F = m \times a$$
$$= 50 \text{ kg} \times 2 \text{ m/s/s}$$
$$= 100 \text{ N}$$

## Adding Forces

The two students pushing together in Figure 5-1**B** produce a combined force of 100 N to the right. This combined force is an example of a *resultant* (ri·ZUHL·tuhnt). *A **resultant** is a single force that has the combined effect of all the forces acting on an object.* In this case, the resultant has the effect of accelerating the object to the right.

What is the resultant in Figure 5-4? This person is pushing to the right on a nautilus machine with a 650-N force. The machine is pushing to the left with a 600-N force. Add the forces to find the resultant. But first, give a "+" sign to forces acting to the right. Give a "−" sign to forces acting to the left:

$$\textbf{Resultant} = \textbf{F}_1 + \textbf{F}_2$$
$$= (+650 \text{ N}) + (-600 \text{ N})$$
$$= +50 \text{ N}$$

The resultant is +50 N. The "+" sign indicates that the resultant acts to the right. So the player's feet are accelerating to the right. If the resultant were a negative number, then it would act to the left.

What would the resultant be if the player and the machine each exerted a 650-N force? The forces are balanced. When forces are balanced, the resultant is zero. The student's legs would not move.

*Figure 5-4. In which direction will the machine move?*

What is the resultant when balanced forces act on an object?

**OBJECT**

Express the weight of objects in newtons

**MATERIALS**

bathroom scale, pencil, paper

**PROCEDURE**

**1.** Use a bathroom scale to weigh yourself and objects around your home. Record the weights in pounds.
**2.** Now express each weight in newtons. The following relationship will help you: 1 pound = 4.48 newtons

**QUESTIONS**

**1.** Must you divide or multiply to change data from pounds to newtons?
**2.** Suppose a TV set weighs 25 pounds. How much is this weight in newtons?

## Weight: A Measure of Force

Newtons are used as units to measure any force, even the force of gravity. All objects on earth are pulled downward by gravity. When you step on a scale to find your *weight,* you are measuring the pull of the earth's gravity upon your body. ***Weight*** *is a measure of the pull of gravity on an object.* Since weight is a measure of force, this text expresses the weight of objects in newtons. See Figure 5-5.

An object's weight is related to its mass. Find the mass of two objects, a pen and a textbook, by putting them on a balance. Then find their weights by using a scale. The object with more mass also has a greater weight. The greater the mass of an object, the more strongly it is pulled down by gravity.

Weight and mass, however, are different measurements. No matter where an object is moved, its mass stays the same. But its weight changes from place to place. The force of gravity between two objects gets weaker as the two objects move farther apart. The farther an object is from the center of the earth, the less it weighs.

## Weight In Space

Gravity is not just a pull between objects and the earth. It exists between any two objects in the universe, depending on their masses and the distance between them. Because of the earth's great mass, objects

*Figure 5-5. Weights of some common objects.*

22 N

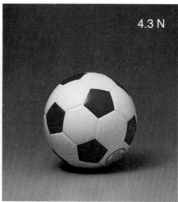

4.3 N

575 N

Figure 5-6. *The size of the arrows shows the size of the pull of gravity. The closer two objects are, the greater the gravity between them.*

within 300,000 km of the earth are pulled toward the earth. A spacecraft traveling beyond that distance, however, would be pulled toward the moon or other objects in space. See Figure 5-6.

The less mass an object has, the weaker is its pull of gravity. The moon has much less mass than the earth. So the moon has a weaker pull of gravity than earth. If you were standing on the moon you would weigh only one-sixth your weight on earth.

● The athlete in Figure 5-7 uses a muscular force to throw a metal ball or shot. In the Olympics and other major contests, a shot has a mass of about 7 kg. In high school games, shots have a mass of only about 5 kg. By Newton's Second Law, if you applied as much force as the athlete in Figure 5-7 to a shot with less mass, you could produce a greater acceleration. You would beat the champion. If you used only three-quarters the force, you could tie the champion.

Figure 5-7. *What factors affect the acceleration of the shot?*

## OBJECTIVES AND WORDS TO REVIEW

1. A student pushes a set of beams across a gym floor. She reaches an acceleration of 4 m/s/s. If she had pushed with twice as much force, what acceleration would she have reached?
2. A car has a mass of 2,300 kg. Starting from rest, it reaches a speed of 12 m/s in 4 seconds. (a) Find the acceleration. (b) Find the amount of force applied to produce that acceleration.
3. On earth a book weighs 9 N and has a mass of 0.9 kg. What are its weight and mass on the moon?
4. Write one complete sentence for each term listed below.
   newton     resultant     weight

# PAIRS OF FORCES

"What goes up must come down." You may have heard this description of gravity. Yet when you jump on a trampoline, the reverse is also true. "What comes down must go up." See Figure 5-8. How can a trampoline make you move up against gravity?

This section will help you answer this question. You will take a close look at what happens when one object applies a force on another. You will learn about a give-and-take between the two objects.

## Looking for Pairs of Forces

As you fall onto a trampoline, you apply a downward force that stretches the trampoline. The trampoline, then, applies an upward elastic force on you. It is this upward force that bounces you back up.

In short, a pair of forces is at work here. You apply a force to the trampoline. And the trampoline applies a force on you. The forces are opposite in direction. But they are equal in amount. The greater the downward

*Figure 5-8.* Forces on a trampoline occur in pairs.

force you apply on the trampoline, the greater the upward force it applies on you.

Forces always act in pairs. Each force in a pair acts on a different object. When you use a finger to push a book, the book also pushes your finger. If you push a friend while you are both on skates, you are pushed as well. Your friend accelerates in one direction and you accelerate in the opposite direction. In each case, one object (or person) applies a force to the other.

## The Third Law of Motion

Sir Isaac Newton made similar observations about pairs of forces. Newton summed up his observations in his **Third Law of Motion.** This law states that for every action there is an equal and opposite reaction. Your finger pushing a book, for example, is an action. The book pushing your finger is the reaction. The action force is equal in strength to the reaction force. But the two forces act in opposite directions.

Compare the forces of action and reaction in Figure 5-9. The balloon applies an elastic force, an action force, on the air inside. The action force pushes the air out. The air, in turn, applies a reaction force on the balloon. The reaction force pushes the balloon in the opposite direction.

A rocket is launched by a similar kind of reaction force. A rocket engine produces gases. It applies an action force that pushes the gases downward. See page 88. The gases, in turn, apply a reaction force on the rocket. They push against the rocket, causing it to lift up.

*Figure 5-9. The balloon pushes the air particles backward. The air particles push the balloon forward.*

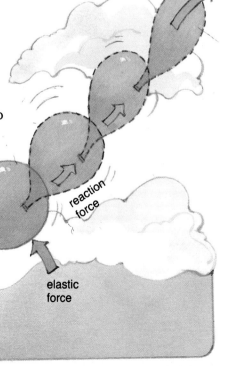

elastic force

reaction force

action force

elastic force

Relate the amount of mass and velocity to an object's momentum.

## Summing Up Newton's Laws of Motion

It takes all three Laws of Motion to describe the motion of an object. For example, the Third Law alone describes the rocket's upward force. However, you know from the First Law that a rocket will not take off if this upward force is balanced by other forces.

While the rocket is in its launch pad, gravity is acting downward on the rocket. The rocket's weight is the amount of the pull of gravity on the rocket. A rocket can take off only when the upward force is greater than its own weight.

In flight, both gravity and friction with air act downward on the rocket. The rocket can accelerate upward only if its upward force is greater than the downward forces. As the rocket rises, it gives off burned fuel. Thus, it is losing mass. Newton's Second Law relates the rocket's mass and acceleration. If the upward force stays the same, the acceleration increases as the rocket loses mass.

## Momentum

You have just seen the give-and-take that occurs when one object applies a force on another. That is, the second object, in turn, applies a force to the first. Now look carefully at Figure 5-10. Can you see another kind of give and take going on?

In **A**, the red car is moving at a certain speed. When it bumps into the blue car in **B**, it slows down. The blue car, however, now begins to move.

The red car in this example is giving *momentum* (moh•MEN•tuhm) to the blue car. **Momentum** *is defined as the mass times the velocity of an object.*

The greater the mass and velocity of an object, the more momentum the object has. The red car, for example, has a certain amount of momentum in Figure 5-10**A**. It would have more momentum if it were moving faster. It would also have more momentum if it had a larger mass.

The more momentum an object has, the more momentum it can give to another object. If the red car

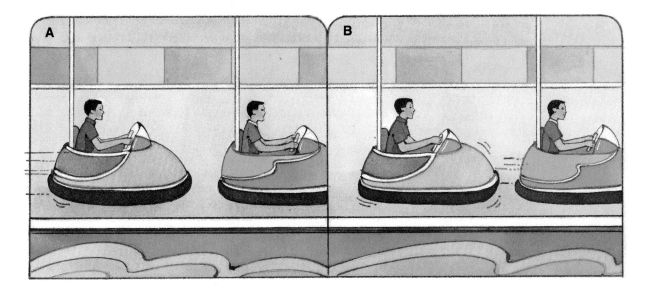

A
B

were moving faster, it would make the blue car speed up even more.

The more momentum an object has, the greater the force you need to stop it. Ask a friend to toss you a ball several times. Your friend can increase the momentum by making the ball go faster each time. You must use more force to stop the ball each time.

*Figure 5-10. Compare the speed of the red bumper car before and after it collides with the blue car.*

## Conservation of Momentum

The two bumper cars in Figure 5-10 can help you understand a law related to Newton's Laws of Motion. In **A**, the red car has all the momentum. In **B**, it has given some momentum to the blue car. Yet the total amount of momentum has not changed. The total momentum of the two bumper cars in **B** is the same as the total momentum in **A**.

Figure 5-11 illustrates the **Law of Conservation of Momentum.** This law states that the total momentum of any group of objects remains the same unless outside forces act on the group. One member of a group may lose some momentum. But the amount lost by one member is gained by another.

● Keep an eye out for examples of Newton's Third Law of Motion. You may be surprised at how many action/reaction pairs you can find. When you swim,

*Figure 5-11. Law of Conservation of Momentum.*

for instance, you apply a backward force on water. The water, in turn, applies a forward force on you.

In each example of an action/reaction pair, you can also find momentum being given from one object to another. See Figure 5-12. The ball gives momentum to the baseball player's hand as the ball hits the glove.

*Figure 5-12. State the action-reaction pair in this photo.*

**OBJECTIVES AND WORDS TO REVIEW**

1. Identify a pair of forces in each of the following situations:
   (a) You are standing on the front edge of a skateboard and carefully step onto the ground. You move forward and the board moves back.
   (b) You dive off the edge of a raft. You dive forward. The raft floats back.
2. State Newton's third law of motion. How does this law describe each force of the pairs of forces in question #1?
3. You roll a bowling ball down a lane. Describe what happens to the momentum of the ball when it hits the pins.
4. Write a complete sentence for the term below.
   momentum

# TECHNOLOGY TRADE-OFF

## The World's Fastest Bicycles

In 1984, when Tim Brummer pedaled his bicycle to a record speed of 57.91 miles per hour, he was very happy. He had set a world record for human-powered bicycling.

Cyclists have to overcome many problems to reach high speeds. One of the forces that slows cyclists down is *drag*. Drag is a force that pulls back (slows down) the bicycle and cyclist. To reduce drag, the rider and the bicycle are covered by a *fairing*. A fairing is a sleek light-weight cover over the bike and rider. A bike covered by a fairing looks like a blimp on wheels. Another problem of high speed bicycling is the danger to the rider. Falling at speeds of more than 50 miles per hour is dangerous. Finally, the rider must be in excellent physical condition to pedal so fast.

Brummer's record was broken in 1986 by a cyclist who attained a speed of 61.44 miles per hour. Today, other cyclists are trying to break this record.

### Using Critical Thinking

Will a speed record finally be set that will be impossible to surpass? Is the pursuit of a speed record that may be broken worth it? What do you think?

# FALLING, SINKING, AND FLOATING

What forces are acting on the diver in Figure 5-13? Gravity is pulling the diver down. A frictional force is opposing the diver's fall. But the force is too small to slow the diver down. When the diver hits the water, however, the diver slows down and stops before hitting bottom. How does water break a fall?

In this section you will find the answer. You will use the laws of motion to investigate objects falling in air. And you will explore forces acting on objects in water.

## Free Fall

Recall that all objects within 300,000 km of the earth are pulled to the earth by gravity. But notice what happens to the speed of an object the closer it falls to the earth's surface. See Figure 5-14. Objects speed up, or accelerate, as they fall.

The ball has a greater mass than the apple. Because of its greater mass, the ball is pulled by a greater

*Figure 5-13. (left) Air friction acts upward on the diver.*

*Figure 5-14. (right) Both objects will reach the ground at the same time.*

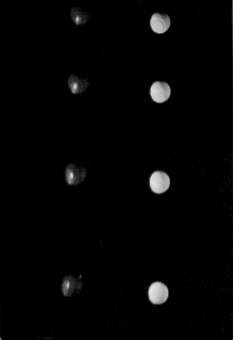

## AIR RESISTANCE

**OBJECTIVE**
Investigate the effect of air resistance on falling objects.

**MATERIALS**
two identical sheets of paper

**PROCEDURE**
**1.** Crumple one sheet of paper in a fist to make a small, tight ball.
**2.** Crumple a second loosely to make a larger, fluffier ball.
**3.** Have a friend drop both balls at the same time from a height such as a classroom window. Stand at ground level. Observe the balls fall.

**QUESTIONS**
**1.** What force is acting downward on both balls? Is the amount of this force the same for both balls?
**2.** Explain how air resistance can cause one ball to land slower than the other.

force of gravity than the apple. Yet both objects have the same acceleration. Both speed up the same amount each second and reach the ground at the same time.

A greater pull of gravity acting on a large mass produces the same acceleration as a smaller pull of gravity on a small mass. All objects near the earth's surface fall with the same acceleration due to gravity—9.8 m/s/s. That is, the speed of any falling object increases by 9.8 m/s each second.

## Falling from High Elevations

The diver in Figure 5-13 is accelerating by 9.8 m/s each second. But suppose the diver had on a parachute. Then the diver would slow down, or decelerate. A parachute provides a wide area for *air resistance* to act on a person. **Air resistance** *is a force that opposes the motion of objects in air.* Air provides an upward force along the bottom surface of a parachute.

See Figure 5-15. Air resistance is acting on these sky divers even before they open their parachutes. These divers are falling from a great height. Their speed increases 9.8 m/s each second they fall. As their speed increases, so does the air resistance acting on them. In time, the air resistance becomes great enough to balance the downward pull of gravity. From Newton's first law, you know that balanced forces produce no acceleration. When the forces are balanced, the sky divers fall at a constant speed.

Meteorites, spacecraft, and other objects too reach a constant speed as they fall to earth. *The constant speed a falling object reaches when air resistance balances gravity is called* **terminal speed.**

## Falling in Curved Paths

When you hurl a baseball, the ball first climbs. Then it falls, accelerating downward because of gravity. But it does not fall straight down. It falls in a curved path. See Figure 5-16. Can you tell why?

The curved path is the result of two forces. When you throw the ball, you apply a force on the ball. This force makes the ball move forward at a constant speed. The forward speed does not change because no other forces are acting in this direction after you throw the ball. All the time the ball moves, however, gravity keeps pulling on the ball. Gravity causes its downward speed to keep increasing. The combination of forward constant speed and downward increasing speed causes the path to curve.

The baseball is an example of a *projectile* (pruh•JEK•tuhl). *A **projectile** is any object that is thrown or shot and travels in a curved path.* Footballs, arrows, and even spacecraft can act like projectiles.

**Figure 5-15.** *Air resistance pushing against these falling divers soon stops their acceleration.*

## An Upward Force in Water

A high diver falls downward along a curved path. The diver gets a forward speed by jumping from the platform. The downward speed increases because of the pull of gravity. But the moment the diver hits water, the diver decelerates. The diver slows to a stop underwater and then comes up to the surface.

From Newton's second law, you know that such a change in motion requires an unbalanced force. Water does indeed provide such a force. *Water and other fluids apply an upward force called a **buoyant** (BOY•uhnt) force on objects immersed in them.*

Have you ever noticed how much lighter you feel when you are standing in water? Hold a heavy object

**Figure 5-16.** *After the baseball is thrown, gravity acts on the ball. So, the ball follows a curved path.*

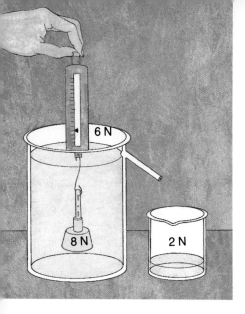

*Figure 5-17. An immersed object is acted on by a buoyant force. The weight of the water in the beaker is equal to the buoyant force acting on the object.*

like a brick underwater and it, too, feels lighter. Objects seem to lose weight in water because a buoyant force is acting on them. The amount of weight an object seems to lose is equal to the buoyant force acting on it.

Suppose, for example, that a doorknob weighs 8 N in air. When lowered into water, the same doorknob seems to weigh only 6 N. The difference in weight is 2 N. The buoyant force acting on the doorknob in water is equal to 2 N. See Figure 5-17.

Here is another way of finding the amount of the buoyant force on an object. When an object is lowered into water, remember, it displaces a certain amount of water. Figure 5-17 shows how the displaced water can be collected. The displaced water can then be weighed. The weight of the displaced water is equal to the buoyant force.

## Sinking and Floating

The amount of buoyant force acting on an object determines whether the object sinks or floats in water. When the object is underwater, it displaces a volume of water equal to its own volume.

Any object that sinks in water weighs more than an equal volume of water. The object's weight is greater than the buoyant force acting on the object.

The wooden block in Figure 5-18**A** would float if it were not held down. Held completely underwater, the block displaces its own volume of water. However, the block weighs 1 N in air. The displaced water weighs more, 2 N. When the block is released, a buoyant force of 2 N pushes the block to the surface. An object rises in water when the buoyant force acting on it is greater than its own weight.

In Figure 5-18**B** the same block is placed on the water so that it floats. Now it displaces a volume of water that is less than its own volume. The weight of displaced water is 1 N. So the buoyant force, 1 N, equals the weight of the block itself. The weight of the block balances the buoyant force. The block floats.

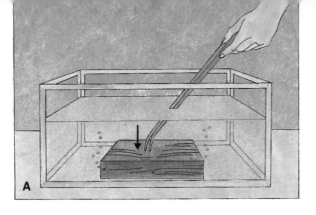
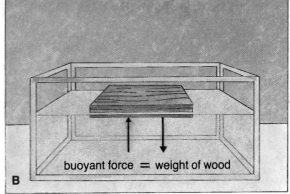

buoyant force = weight of wood

## Archimedes' Principle

Archimedes, a Greek scientist who lived over 2,000 years ago, made similar observations of sinking and floating objects. However, he observed objects in other fluids besides just water. He observed how objects behave in gases as well.

Archimedes concluded that an object placed in any fluid is acted upon by an upward force equal to the weight of the fluid displaced by the object. This statement, **Archimedes' Principle,** applies to any fluid, that is, to any liquid or gas. The principle says that an object floats when it displaces an amount of fluid equal to its own weight. If it displaces less than its own weight, it sinks.

● Balloons rise and float in air for the same reason that a wooden block rises and floats in water. See Figure 5-19. A balloon rises in air if the balloon weighs less than the air it displaces. The displaced air provides a buoyant force that pushes the balloon up. Balloons, therefore, are filled with light gases such as helium. Or they are filled with warmed air. Any volume of warmed air weighs less than an equal volume of cooler air.

*Figure 5-18. To what is the buoyant force of a floating object equal?*

*Figure 5-19. A balloon losing gas displaces less air. Thus, the balloon sinks.*

### OBJECTIVES AND WORDS TO REVIEW

**1.** What causes a sky diver to reach terminal speed?
**2.** Describe how two forces cause an arrow to fall in a curved path.
**3.** How can you measure the buoyant force acting on a rock that sinks in water?
**4.** Write one complete sentence for each term listed below.

air resistance          projectile
terminal speed          buoyant force

## RECORDING AND INTERPRETING DATA

### Preparation

Suppose the class decides to see who can throw a baseball the farthest. Each person stands on a starting line and throws the baseball. You find the distance from the starting line to the place where the ball lands. By writing down each measurement of distance, you are recording data.

You can tell who won the contest by looking at the data. The person with the longest throw is the winner. By noting the winner, you are interpreting the data.

Scientists collect and interpret data as part of their investigations. They often organize the data into a data table. They interpret the data by looking for patterns that may lead to generalizations.

| TABLE 1. | DISTANCE TRAVELED | |
|---|---|---|
| Person | Weight (N) | Distance Ball Traveled (m) |
| A | 451 | 39 |
| B | 420 | 31 |
| C | 764 | 49 |
| D | 803 | 50 |

### Directions

Table 1 shows the weight of four people and the distance each threw a baseball. Notice how the table is organized so that it is easily read. Thus, person D threw the ball the farthest—50 meters. Person B threw it the shortest—31 meters.

Now see if there is a pattern between the weight of a person and the distance the ball is thrown. Person D weighs the most, 803 N, and threw the ball the farthest. Person B weighs the least, 420 N, and threw the ball the shortest distance. By comparing weight and distance, you see a pattern emerging from the data. For this set of data, the heavier the person, the longer the throw.

| TABLE 2. | DISTANCE A BALL ROLLED |
|---|---|
| Time (s) | Distance (m) |
| 0.0 | 0.0 |
| 1.0 | 2.0 |
| 2.0 | 4.0 |
| 3.0 | 6.0 |

### Practice

Study Table 2.

1. What two types of data are recorded?
2. What general pattern do you notice?

### Application

From your reading of Chapter 5, you know that your weight on other planets differs from your weight on Earth. To find your weight on another planet, multiply your weight on Earth by the factor given in Table 3. Copy Table 3 onto a separate piece of paper. Then, calculate your weight on each planet listed and record your data.

1. On which planet(s) do you weigh more than you do on Earth? Less than on Earth?
2. On which planet(s) would you weigh nearly the same as you do on Earth?

| TABLE 3. | DATA TABLE | | |
|---|---|---|---|
| Planet | Factor | Your Weight on Earth | Your Weight on Planet |
| Venus | 0.91 | | |
| Mars | 0.36 | | |
| Jupiter | 2.3 | | |
| Saturn | 0.88 | | |
| Neptune | 1.3 | | |

# LABORATORY ACTIVITY

## FLOATING AND SINKING

### Objective
Measure the buoyant force on an object in different liquids.

### Background
When an object is placed in a liquid, a buoyant force acts upward on the object. This force acts in the opposite direction to gravity, the weight of the object. So the object seems to lose some weight in a liquid. The amount of weight an object seems to lose is equal to the buoyant force of that liquid. A great enough buoyant force can make an object float.

### Materials
spring scale, string, 3 beakers (250 mL), corn syrup, cooking oil, wood blocks, rocks, plastic wrap, paper

### Procedure
1. Copy Table 5-L onto a separate sheet of paper.
2. Fill one beaker with water, another with corn syrup, and a third with oil. (Use about 200 mL of each liquid.)

3. Wrap a block or rock tightly with cellophane. Tie a string around the object. Attach an end of the string to the hook of a small spring scale.
4. Lift the object with the scale to find its weight in air. Record its weight under "Weight in air."
5. Now hold the object in each of the three liquids. (The wrapping will keep the liquids from soaking into the object.) Record the weight in each liquid.
6. Under "Buoyant force" record the difference between the object's weight in air and in each liquid. Then indicate whether the object floats or sinks.
7. Repeat steps 1 to 7 with other objects.

### Questions
1. When an object sinks in a liquid, which is greater: the object's weight in air or the buoyant force? Explain.
2. How do the weight of an object in air and the buoyant force compare when an object floats?
3. If an object sinks in a liquid, are the forces acting on the object balanced? Explain.
4. Are the forces acting on an object balanced when an object floats in a liquid? Explain.
5. **PROBLEM SOLVING** Describe how you would test this hypothesis: "The greater the density of a liquid is, the greater is the buoyant force of the liquid."

---

**TABLE 5-L.** DATA TABLE

Name of Object _____                                                      Weight in air _____

| Weight in water _____ | Weight in oil _____ | Weight in corn syrup _____ |
|---|---|---|
| Weight in air  − _____ | Weight in air  − _____ | Weight in air  − _____ |
| | | |
| Buoyant force  = _____ in water | Buoyant force  = _____ in oil | Buoyant force  = _____ in corn syrup |
| floats _____ or sinks _____ | floats _____ or sinks _____ | floats _____ or sinks _____ |

# SUMMARY

1. The greater an unbalanced force is, the greater the acceleration produced. For any given force, the smaller an object's mass is, the greater the acceleration. (5-1)
2. Newtons are units of force. Weight depends on distance from the center of the earth. (5-1)
3. For every action there is an equal and opposite reaction. (5-2)
4. Momentum is conserved within a group of objects unless acted on by an outside force. (5-2)
5. Gravity pulls all objects close to the earth's surface with the same acceleration. Air resistance slows the speed of an object. (5-3)
6. Objects sink or float in fluids depending upon the weight of the displaced fluid. (5-3)

# REVIEW

Number a sheet of paper from 1 to 25 and answer these questions.

**Building Science Vocabulary**   Write the letter of the term that best matches each definition.

a. air resistance
b. buoyant force
c. conservation of momentum
d. first law of motion
e. momentum
f. newton
g. projectile
h. resultant
i. second law of motion
j. terminal speed
k. third law of motion
l. weight

1. Unbalanced forces causing acceleration
2. A unit for measuring force
3. A single force that has the combined effect of many forces acting on an object
4. A measure of the pull of gravity on an object
5. The mass times the velocity of an object

6. Force that opposes motion of objects in air
7. The constant speed a falling object reaches when air resistance balances gravity
8. An object that is thrown or shot and travels in a curved path
9. Actions having equal and opposite reactions
10. An upward force on objects in fluids

**Finding the Facts**   Select the letter of the answer that best completes each of the following.

11. Terminal speed may be reached by an object that    (a) falls from a great height   (b) falls a short distance    (c) stops moving   (d) is not moving.
12. A bicycle rolls into a fence. The    (a) bicycle applies a force to the fence    (b) fence applies a force to the bicycle    (c) bicycle gives momentum to the fence    (d) all of the above.
13. If you pedal with the same force all the time, you can reach the greatest acceleration with a bike that has a mass of    (a) 10 kg   (b) 15 kg    (c) 18 kg    (d) 8 kg.
14. In general, doubling the force on an object   (a) cuts the acceleration in half   (b) doubles the mass    (c) doubles the acceleration    (d) cuts the mass in half.
15. Forces acting on a diver about to dive from a platform include    (a) air resistance   (b) a buoyant force    (c) gravity   (d) friction.
16. A shopping cart hits into a stack of boxes. The cart    (a) gains momentum    (b) loses momentum    (c) conserves momentum   (d) reaches terminal speed.
17. The faster a car is traveling, the   (a) greater its mass    (b) less its mass   (c) more momentum it has    (d) less momentum it has.
18. A rock on earth weighs 60 N. The same rock on the moon would weigh    (a) 120 N   (b) 180 N    (c) 60 N    (d) 10 N.

**19.** Two people push a stalled car. When a third person helps out, the car **(a)** loses momentum **(b)** decelerates **(c)** increases mass **(d)** gains momentum.

**20.** A rail falls from a bridge. As it falls, it **(a)** decelerates **(b)** accelerates **(c)** loses momentum **(d)** loses mass.

**Understanding Main Ideas**    Complete the following.

**21.** Weight and other measurements of force are given in units called __?__.

**22.** If you increase the force to move an object, you can produce a greater __?__.

**23.** Unless a group of objects is acted upon by an outside force, the momentum of the group is __?__.

**24.** "For every action, there is an equal and opposite reaction." This statement is called __?__.

**25.** The upward force acting on an object sinking in a fluid is called __?__.

**Writing About Science**    On a separate sheet of paper, answer the following as completely as possible.

**1.** Use all three laws of motion to describe the launching of a rocket.

**2.** Suppose you have to push a crate of books across a floor. How can you use Newton's second law to complete the task?

**3.** A girl on a bicycle on a level street can produce an accelerating force of 35 N. The girl and bicycle have a mass of 70 kg. What is the girl's acceleration?

**4.** A firefighter aims a hose at a fire. When the water is suddenly turned on, the firefighter almost falls backwards. Explain why.

**5.** (laboratory question). What forces are acting on a rock that is sinking in water? Are these forces balanced?

**Investigating Chapter Ideas**    Try one of the following projects to further your study.

**1. A diving eyedropper**    Fill a bottle about ⅔ full with water. Then draw water into an eyedropper. Adjust the amount of water in the eyedropper until it just floats in the bottle without sinking. Cover the mouth of the bottle with a tightly stetched piece of balloon. Fix it firmly with a rubber band. Push the rubber cover as far as you can into the bottle without tearing it. What happens to the eyedropper? If you watch the fluid level in the eyedropper as you push on the rubber cover, you'll get a clue about what happens. Use buoyancy to explain what you observed.

**2. Galileo**    An Italian scientist named Galileo made many important discoveries about motion and the heavens. Read and write a report describing Galileo's life and his accomplishments.

**3. Finding the center of gravity**    Cut a large triangle out of cardboard. Pin the triangle by a corner to a board, allowing the triangle to pivot. Hang a weighted string from the pin. Draw a line along the string across the triangle. Repeat for the other two corners. The lines intersect at the triangle's center of gravity, the point that is evenly surrounded by the triangle's mass. How does the cardboard behave when it is pinned at its center of gravity?

**Reading About Science**    Read some of the following books to explore topics that interest you.

**Collins Young Scientist's Book of Strength.** 1977. Morristown, NJ: Silver Burdett.

Goswami, Amut with Maggie Goswami. 1983. **The Cosmic Dancers! Exploring the Physics of Science Fiction.** New York: Harper.

Schultz, Pearle and Harry Schultz. 1972. **Isaac Newton: Scientific Genius.** Champaign, IL: Garrard.

You hear and use the word "work" many times each day. People go to *work*. You do your math home*work*. You *work* on your bicycle. A sculpture is a *work* of art. In each case, the word "work" has a different meaning. In physical science, however, work has only one meaning. When you do work, you exert a force through a distance. Are the people shown in these photos doing work in the scientific sense?

The people who are walking are doing work. They are using a force to move a certain distance. You do work when you try to fix a part on your bicycle. The sculpture itself is not doing work. But the person applying the chisel certainly is. In this chapter you will find out more about work in its scientific sense.

Read and Find Out:

● how falling water can produce electric energy.

● how potential energy helps you enjoy certain sports.

● what our use of energy is doing to our world.

# WORK, ENERGY, AND POWER

# WORK AND ENERGY

**OBJECTIVES**

**1.** Calculate the work done in lifting a weight up a distance.
**2.** Describe the energy changes in a bouncing ball.
**3.** State the Law of the Conservation of Energy.

Energy is a word you have heard and used many times. You already have a good idea of what energy is. For example, you know that a rocket blasting off from Cape Canaveral has a lot of energy. You might guess that a high-speed truck has plenty of energy. A basketball player needs a lot of energy to play the entire game. You need energy to do work. That is why you must eat a good breakfast each day. Machines also need energy to do work. Whenever work is done, energy is used.

It is easy to confuse energy with other ideas you have learned, like force or momentum. To get a clear understanding of energy, you must first study the idea of work.

## Work

How can you tell when work is being done? For work to be done, a force must be applied to an object. The force must cause a change. Look at the people in Figure 6-1. Are either of them doing work? Figure 6-1**A** shows a girl trying to lift a 500-N barbell off the floor. Although she exerts a force, the barbell does not move. Since there is no change, she is not doing work. The girl in Figure 6-1**B**, however, does do

*Figure 6-1. No work is being done by the student in A because she is not lifting the barbell. The student in B is doing work while she is lifting the barbell.*

work in lifting the 100-N barbell to her knees. She does more work as she lifts the barbell to her chest and as she presses it over her head. She did work because in each case the force exerted on the barbell made it move a certain distance.

To do work you must apply a force. You must make the object move in the same direction as your force. In fact, work is defined in these terms. **Work** *is the amount of force exerted on an object times the distance the object moves in the direction of the force.*

### work = force × distance

As a boy lifts a barbell, he does work. Is he doing work if he simply carries the barbell across the room? See Figure 6-2. In the scientific sense, he is not doing work. The direction of the applied force (up) is not the same as the direction of movement (to the right).

Work does not involve time. What matters is the force exerted on the object and the distance the object moves. Once the boy presses the barbell over his head, he does no further work on the barbell. He does no work even if he holds it there for an hour.

direction of applied force

direction of movement

*Figure 6-2. Why is no work being done in the scientific sense?*

## Calculating Work

Suppose you life a heavy wooden box half a meter off the floor. The box weighs 300 newtons. How much work do you do?

The force you exert in lifting the box must overcome the force of gravity on the box. That is, you must exert a force equal to the weight of the box. The work done in lifting the box one half meter is:

$$\begin{aligned} \text{work (lifting)} &= \text{force (up)} \times \text{distance (up)} \\ &= 300 \text{ N} \times 0.5 \text{ m} \\ &= 150 \text{ joules (J)} \end{aligned}$$

The work done is 150 *joules* (JEWLZ). A *joule* (*J*) *is the amount of work done when a force of one newton is exerted over a distance of one meter.*

Now suppose you slide the box across the room, as you see in Figure 6-3. Again, you do work. This time the force you exert acts to overcome the frictional

*Figure 6-3. What force must be overcome to push the crate across the floor?*

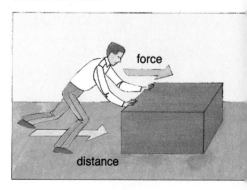

force

distance

### CALCULATING WORK

**OBJECTIVE**
Compare the work done on an object.

**MATERIALS**
string, square object, spring scale, meter stick

**PROCEDURE**
1. Tie the string around the object securely. Make a loop at the free end of the string.
2. Hook the scale through the loop.
3. Lift the object a distance of one meter. Record the force you used.
4. Now drag the object along a flat table a distance of one meter. Record the force you used. (*Do not take a reading of the force until the object is moving.*)
5. Calculate the work done in each case.

**QUESTIONS**
1. Was there a difference in the work done in each case? Why or why not?
2. When you *just* started to do step 4, you saw a much larger reading than when the object was moving. What was the cause of this extra force?

force between the box and the floor. The force of friction between a 300-newton wooden box and a wooden floor is 60 newtons. So the work done is:

$$\text{work (sliding)} = 60 \text{ N} \times 3 \text{ m}$$
$$= 180 \text{ J}$$

So more work is done by sliding the box than by lifting it. However, it may be easier to slide the box because you have to exert less force!

## Energy

Suppose you lift a super-hard ball a distance of one meter. When you release the ball, it falls. It gains speed until it hits the floor. After the ball hits the floor, it bounces back up.

The ball's motion is complex. The height and speed of the ball keep changing. These changes occur because the ball has energy. Energy is the ability to cause changes in matter. These changes are possible because you did work on the ball by lifting it. The more work you put into lifting the ball, the more energy the ball gets.

Energy comes in many forms. Some of the many forms of energy are chemical energy, mechanical energy, and light energy. See Table 6-1 for other forms of energy. All the different forms of energy can be divided into two basic kinds. These kinds are *potential* (puh•TEN•shuhl) *energy* and *kinetic* (ki•NET•ik) *energy*. **Potential energy** is *stored energy*. A ball held

**TABLE 6-1.** FORMS OF ENERGY AND THEIR SOURCES

| | Form of Energy | Source |
|---|---|---|
| Kinds of | Atomic | radioactive materials |
| Potential | Chemical | batteries |
| Energy | Gravitational | any two masses in universe |
| Kinds of | Heat | the sun |
| Kinetic | Mechanical | machines |
| Energy | Sound | vibrations |

**TABLE 6-2.** ENERGY TRANSFORMATIONS AND SOURCES

| Kind of Energy Transformation | Object(s) Producing Transformation |
|---|---|
| Chemical ⟶ electric | dry cell battery |
| Electric ⟶ chemical | battery recharger |
| Mechanical ⟶ electric | generator in power plant |
| Electric ⟶ mechanical | automobile motor |
| Mechanical ⟶ heat | moving parts in any machine |
| Heat ⟶ mechanical | steam engine |
| Heat ⟶ light | electric light bulb |
| Light ⟶ heat | laser drill |
| Light ⟶ electric | solar cell |
| Electric ⟶ light | television |
| Sound ⟶ electric | microphone |
| Electric ⟶ sound | radio |
| Nuclear ⟶ heat | nuclear reactor |

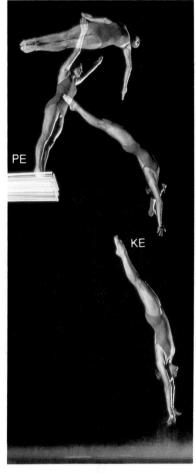

one meter above the floor has potential energy. A person on a high-dive platform has potential energy. See Figure 6-4. Potential energy comes from the work done in lifting objects.

Figure 6-4 illustrates another basic kind of energy: *kinetic energy*. **Kinetic energy** *is the energy of motion.* When the swimmer dives off the platform, she gains kinetic energy. When a ball is dropped, its speed increases and it gains kinetic energy.

*Figure 6-4. Potential energy can be changed into kinetic energy*

## The Transformation of Energy

You have seen that potential energy can change into kinetic and vice versa. This fact is true of energy in general. Whenever changes occur in matter, energy is transformed from one form into another. If a ball falls or a swimmer dives, potential energy is transformed into kinetic energy. Each time a ball bounces on the floor some of its kinetic energy is tranformed into heat and sound energy. After a few bounces, all the ball's energy is transformed into heat. When a battery is connected to a toy motor, electric energy is transformed into the kinetic energy of motion. Table 6-2 shows more examples of energy transformations.

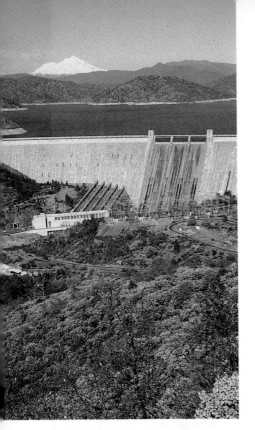

**Figure 6-5.** *The water's potential energy can be changed into electric energy. How does the water return to the lake?*

## Conservation of Energy

You observe changes all the time. Balls bounce, bicycles roll down hills, batters hit baseballs high into the air, and children swing on swings.

Energy changes from one kind into another. As the swimmer in Figure 6-4 dived, she lost potential energy. At the same time, she gained kinetic energy. The total energy of the diver is her potential energy plus her kinetic energy. The kinetic energy and the potential energy of the diver may change. However, the sum total of the kinetic and potential energies of the diver is the same. The total energy does not change. This result is an important pattern in nature called the conservation of energy. The **Law of Conservation of Energy** states that the total energy of an object, or of a group of objects, stays the same.

● Figure 6-5 shows how the potential energy of water can be changed into electric energy. There is much water in the lake, and the water is very high. So there is a lot of potential energy in the lake water. As the water flows down through the large tubes, its potential energy changes into kinetic energy. The water is moving very fast when it strikes the special paddle wheels at the bottom. The paddle wheels rotate and make electric generators turn. The generators produce electric energy.

### OBJECTIVES AND WORDS TO REVIEW

1. If your weight is 400 N, how much work would you do by climbing a flight of stairs 9 m high?
2. Describe the energy changes that take place as a ball falls to the floor, bounces, and rises back up to its starting height.
3. State the Law of Conservation of Energy.
4. Write one complete sentence for each term listed below.

   work      potential energy
   joule     kinetic energy

# THE DIFFERENT FORMS OF ENERGY

There are very many forms of energy, such as electric energy, chemical energy, and light energy. Each of these forms of energy can be thought of as either potential energy or kinetic energy. See Figure 6-6. As you study the different forms of energy, it is important to remember two things. First, whenever a change occurs in nature, energy changes from one form into another. Second, energy is always conserved. The total energy in an object, or in a group of objects, remains the same.

Energy cannot be seen or measured directly. However, the energy an object has may be determined from things that can be seen and measured. In this section you will study the ways energy can be measured.

## Measuring Energy

One way to determine the amount of energy an object has is to investigate the changes it causes. If a small marble falls from a height of 10 cm onto your finger, it produces only a small change in your finger. However, if you drop the same marble from a height of 5 meters, the change is much greater. Your finger hurts! The change depends on the potential energy of the marble. The higher an object is, the greater its potential energy.

If you replaced the marble with a heavy bowling ball, the changes in your finger would be very large indeed. The potential energy of an object depends on two things that can be measured. It depends on the weight of the object and on its height. The weight of an object, in turn, depends on the force of gravity. For this reason, the potential energy you have studied is called *gravitational potential energy* (GPE). **Gravitational potential energy** *is the potential en-*

*Figure 6-6. A battery has stored chemical energy in it. When placed in this robot, it produces electric energy. Is this energy kinetic or potential?*

Relate the height of an object to its potential energy.

## ENERGY IN AN AMUSEMENT PARK

### OBJECTIVE
Learn about the forms of energy used in rides in an amusement park.

### PROCEDURE
**1.** Choose one of the rides.
**2.** Draw a graph showing any changes in GPE and in KE as the ride progresses.

### QUESTIONS
**1.** Where does the ride depend on gravitational potential energy for its operation?
**2.** Where does kinetic energy provide the action?

*Figure 6-7. What must you know to find the kinetic energy of an object?*

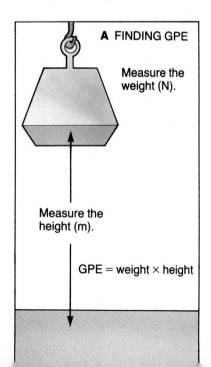

**A** FINDING GPE

Measure the weight (N).

Measure the height (m).

GPE = weight × height

ergy an object has due to its position above the earth's surface. See Figure 6-7**A**.

The formula for gravitational potential energy is:

$$\textbf{GPE} = \textbf{weight} \times \textbf{height}$$

How much potential energy does water weighing 900 N contain if it is stored in a tank 30 m above the ground? To find the answer, use the formula:

$$\text{GPE} = \text{weight} \times \text{height}$$
$$\text{GPE} = 900 \text{ N} \times 30 \text{ m}$$
$$\text{GPE} = 27{,}000 \text{ J}$$

This amount of energy would allow you to use an electric hair dryer for about half a minute. That might not seem like a lot of energy, but think about how much water you are dealing with. Nine hundred newtons is about what the amount of water in three school fish tanks would weigh. Would you like to carry three tanks of water up a ladder 30 m high?

A moving object can also cause changes. Imagine your finger is pressed against a wall close to the floor. A marble rolling across the floor hits your finger. The changes in your finger depend on the marble's speed. The greater the speed is, the greater the changes. The kinetic energy depends on the speed of the object. But what would happen to your finger if a slow-moving bowling ball banged into it? Quite a change! Study Figure 6-7**B**. Kinetic energy depends on both the mass and the speed of an object.

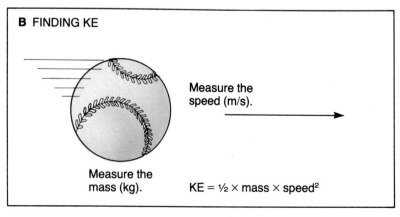

**B** FINDING KE

Measure the speed (m/s).

Measure the mass (kg).

KE = ½ × mass × speed²

You can use the following formula to calculate the kinetic energy (KE) of an object:

$$\textbf{KE} = \textbf{½} \times \textbf{mass} \times \textbf{(speed)}^2$$

Remember, (speed)² is just a shorthand way of saying speed × speed. So if the speed is 8 m/s, (speed)² would be (8 m/s) × (8 m/s) or 64 m²/s²

How much kinetic energy would a boy have traveling at a speed of 7 m/s on his bicycle? The mass of the boy and bicycle is about 70 kg.

$$
\begin{aligned}
\text{KE} &= \text{½} \times \text{mass} \times (\text{speed})^2 \\
&= \text{½} \times 70 \text{ kg} \times (7 \text{ m/s})^2 \\
&= \text{½} \times 70 \text{ kg} \times (7 \times 7) \text{ m}^2/\text{s}^2 \\
&= \text{½} \times 70 \times 49 \text{ kg} \cdot \text{m}^2/\text{s}^2 \\
&= 1{,}715 \text{ J}
\end{aligned}
$$

The kinetic energy of the boy and bicycle is 1,715 J.

## Using the Conservation of Energy

Energy is important because it is conserved. The total energy in an object, or in a group of objects, always remains the same. The total energy is the sum of the different kinds of energy an object has. As the roller coaster in Figure 6-8 starts its run, it has only gravitational potential energy. What happens to the energy of the roller coaster system during the ride? You know the total energy must stay the same. The energy just changes from one form to another.

What does the total energy of an object equal?

*Figure 6-8.* At which point is the kinetic energy of the roller coaster the greatest?

*Figure 6-9. Energy has many forms.*

On the way down the roller coaster loses potential energy and gains kinetic energy. At the lowest point during the ride, the roller coaster has the greatest speed. So it has the greatest kinetic energy. But at the same time it has the least potential energy. However, the total energy remains constant.

As the roller coaster bumps, rubs, and grinds against the rails, heat energy is produced. You may have already guessed that when the heat energy increases, the kinetic energy must decrease. If you add up the potential, heat, and kinetic energies anywhere during the ride, you always get the same answer.

● What do each of the people in Figure 6-9 have in common? They are both using gravitational potential energy to enjoy a popular sport. The person on the skateboard tries to get as high on the curve as possible. Similarly, the surfer tries to get as high on the wave as possible. In each case, the higher the person gets, the more potential energy he has. The more potential energy a person has, the more energy that can be changed into the kinetic energy of motion.

### OBJECTIVES AND WORDS TO REVIEW

1. (a) Define gravitational potential energy. (b) A stone weighing 20 N is located at the top of a cliff 300 m high. What is the stone's gravitational potential energy?
2. (a) Define kinetic energy. (b) A ball with a mass of 2 kg is moving with a speed of 7 m/s. How much kinetic energy does it have?
3. Use the conservation of energy to describe the motion of a sled traveling down an icy hill and hitting a snowbank at the bottom.
4. Write a complete sentence for the term below.
   gravitational potential energy

# FINDING THE AMOUNT OF POWER

How fast can you work? If you walk up the stairs, you do work. The work goes into your potential energy at the top of the stairs. If you run up the stairs, you do the same amount of work and your potential energy is the same. You just did the work faster when you ran up the stairs. In this section you will learn how to measure how fast you do work.

## Work Per Unit Time

Many times it is important to know how fast work is done or how fast energy changes take place. *Power is a measure of how fast work is done.* It takes more power to run up a flight of stairs than it takes to walk up. Power is measured in *watts*, abbreviated W. *One watt equals one joule per second.*

You can find the amount of power developed by using the formula:

$$\text{power} = \frac{\text{work done}}{\text{time}}$$

Suppose you had to carry a 24-newton bag of groceries from the ground floor to the fourth floor of an apartment building. See Figure 6-10. The fourth floor

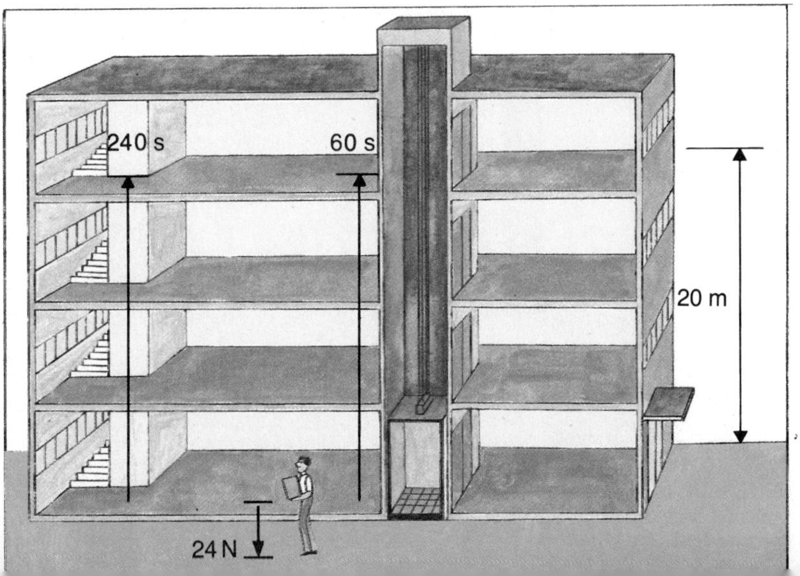

**OBJECTIVES**

**1.** Explain how power and work are related.
**2.** Find the power developed and energy changes that occur in a simple system.
**3.** Describe three different ways the sun's energy is used on the earth.

Name a unit of power.

*Figure 6-10. To calculate the power used here, you need to know the* weight *of the package, the* distance *the package moves up, and the* time *to do the job.*

is 20 meters up. How much work do you do? The work you do to carry the bag to the fourth floor is:

$$\text{work} = \text{force} \times \text{distance}$$
$$= 24 \text{ N} \times 20 \text{ m}$$
$$= 480 \text{ J}$$

Of course, you can carry the bag up yourself or you can let an elevator do the work for you. In either case the amount of work done is the same. This is because in each case the work is done against gravity. The only difference between the two methods is time. It may take you 4 minutes (240 seconds) to walk up the stairs to the fourth floor. But it may take only 1 minute (60 seconds) for the elevator to travel the same distance. What power is developed in each case?

POWER DEVELOPED BY YOU

$$\text{power} = \frac{\text{work done}}{\text{time}}$$
$$= \frac{480 \text{ J}}{240 \text{ s}}$$
$$= 2 \text{ W}$$

POWER DEVELOPED BY ELEVATOR

$$\text{power} = \frac{\text{work done}}{\text{time}}$$
$$= \frac{480 \text{ J}}{60 \text{ s}}$$
$$= 8 \text{ W}$$

## Horsepower

There is another unit that measures power. Many years ago, horses did most of the work. A good horse could lift 550 pounds of coal one foot in one second. Study Figure 6-11. Around the time of the American Revolution, steam engines replaced horses in British coal mines. If a steam engine could replace five

*Figure 6-11. A horse can lift 550 pounds a distance of one foot in one second. What is this amount called?*

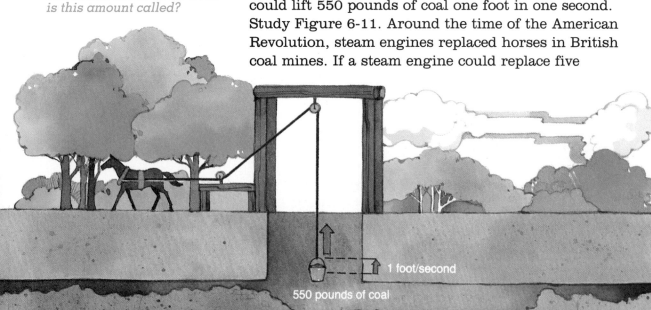

1 foot/second

550 pounds of coal

horses, the steam engine was rated at 5 *horsepower.* **Horsepower** *is a unit of power in the British system of measurement.* A five-horsepower engine could lift $5 \times 550$, or 2,750 pounds of coal up one foot in one second.

Horsepower is still used to measure how fast engines and motors can do their work. There are two units of power: watts and horsepower. They measure the same thing. They are just different units. You can change from one unit of power to the other by remembering that one horsepower equals 746 watts.

Imagine that you can run up a flight of stairs 6 meters high in 4 seconds. Your weight is 440 newtons. What is your horsepower?

Since power is the rate at which work is done, you first need to know the work you did. The work you do goes into your potential energy at the top of the stairs. The work you do is:

$$\text{work} = \text{force} \times \text{distance}$$
$$= 440 \text{ N} \times 6 \text{ m}$$
$$= 2,640 \text{ J}$$

You can now find the power:

$$\text{power} = \frac{\text{work done}}{\text{time}}$$
$$= \frac{2,640 \text{ J}}{4 \text{ s}}$$
$$= 660 \text{ W}$$

Since 746 W equals one horsepower, you can see that your power is almost one horsepower. You could not keep working at this power for very long!

## Power From The Sun

The main source of energy that powers the earth is the sun. On a clear day, about 150 joules of direct light energy hit one square meter of earth each second.

Solar energy is changed into heat energy when sunlight hits the molecules in a material. The light

**EXPLORE**
BY TRYING

### HORSEPOWER

**OBJECTIVE**
Calculate your horsepower.

**MATERIALS**
metric ruler, watch with second hand

**PROCEDURE**
**1.** Measure the total height, in meters, of a flight of stairs. Do this by measuring the height of one step and multiplying by the number of steps.
**2.** Find your weight on a bathroom scale. Multiply by 4.4 to get your weight in newtons.
**3.** Have a friend measure how long it takes you to walk up the stairs at a constant pace. **CAUTION:** Do not run.
**4.** Now change places with your friend. Measure the time it takes for your friend to walk.

**QUESTIONS**
**1.** What is your potential energy at the top of the stairs?
**2.** What is your power?
**3.** What is your horsepower?
**4.** Compare your horsepower with that of your friend.

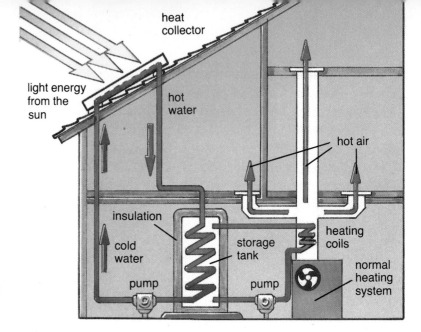

Figure 6-12. This house is kept warm during winter by energy from the sun.

heat collector

light energy from the sun

hot water

hot air

insulation

cold water

storage tank

heating coils

normal heating system

pump

pump

energy is changed into the increased kinetic energy of the molecules in the material. As Figure 6-12 shows, a solar heating system can warm a house during the winter. The sun's energy also heats the atmosphere. It causes large movements of warm air masses. The sun's energy is part of a complex system in the atmosphere that creates winds and weather.

Figure 6-13 shows how the sun's light energy can evaporate large amounts of water from the oceans. This evaporated water eventually falls back to earth as

Figure 6-13. A hydroelectric power station changes water's kinetic energy into electric energy.

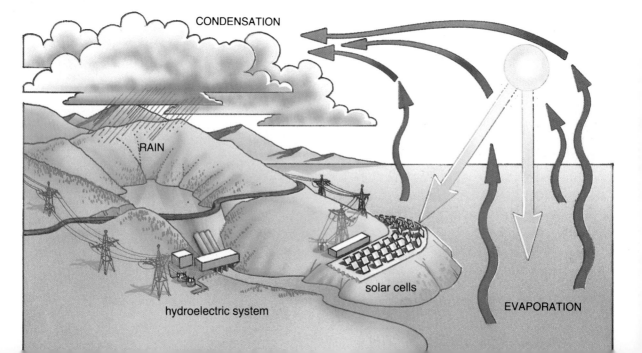

CONDENSATION

RAIN

hydroelectric system

solar cells

EVAPORATION

rain. The rain collects in lakes high above sea level. The solar energy ends up as the stored potential energy in the lake's water. As the water flows back down, electric energy can be generated in a hydro-electric power station. Sunlight can also be changed directly into electric energy with a solar cell.

The energy on the earth comes from the sun. Energy is not created or destroyed. It just changes from one kind into another. Energy is always conserved! Sometimes the sun's energy is stored for millions of years before it is released. Gasoline, natural gas, oil, and coal are called fossil fuels. Fossil fuels are plants that have been compressed for millions of years. Ancient light energy is stored in fossil fuels. The stored energy is changed into heat energy as the fuels are burned in a car engine or home furnace.

● During the last 50 years, we have been burning up our supply of fossil fuels at an alarming rate. Industries and new technologies have grown rapidly. As they grow and expand, so does the demand for energy to run them.

There is a problem with large amounts of energy we use. The energy that is used does not disappear. It ends up as useless heat energy. See Figure 6-14. Thermal pollution is a new problem on the earth. As our atmosphere, lakes, and rivers become hotter, changes in weather patterns will occur. Because of these changes, your way of life will also change.

What is the main source of the earth's energy?

Figure 6-14. *The cooling pond for this factory adds heat to the lake. The purple areas are coolest and the red areas warmest.*

**OBJECTIVES AND WORDS TO REVIEW**

1. Define power. What is your power if you lift a 98 N rock up a distance of 2 m in 2 s?
2. A microwave oven is rated at 1,500 W. How many joules of work are done in 1 second? In 10 seconds? In 1 minute?
3. List three ways the sun's energy can be used.
4. An engine is rated at 15 horsepower. What is its power in watts?
5. Write one complete sentence for each term listed below.
   power    watt    horsepower

# MAKING A HYPOTHESIS

## Preparation

Suppose you place a full glass of water on your desk and then leave the room. When you return, you notice the glass is half empty! What happened to the missing water? See Figure 1.

If you try to explain the missing water, you are making a hypothesis. A hypothesis is an educated guess about the answer to a problem or a question.

Scientists also make hypotheses. When making a hypothesis, a scientist tries to explain an observation or group of similar observations. For example, a scientist may wonder why the amount of ozone, a form of oxygen, decreases over the South Pole at times. By trying to explain why the decrease occurs, the scientist is making a hypothesis.

*Figure 1.*

## Directions

Making a hypothesis is not as easy as it seems. Time and imagination are needed. A good hypothesis has three characteristics.

*1. A hypothesis is developed from facts and observations.* In Figure 1, for example, what facts might help you form your hypothesis? Did you see the open window near the desk? Did you notice the glass was lying under a lit lamp?

*2. A hypothesis must explain known related facts.* Suppose you think the heat from the lit lamp caused the water to evaporate. Your hypothesis must explain what would happen each time water was placed under a lit lamp.

*3. A hypothesis must be testable.* In order to find out if your hypothesis is correct, you have to be able to test it. You might, perhaps, place another glass with the same amount of water under the lamp and see what happens. Notice that a hypothesis may not be correct. In the example, someone may have entered the room while you were away and drunk the water. However, the person's entrance is not an observed fact.

In many cases, it is more helpful to write a hypothesis in an "If…, then…" form. The "If…" part of the statement is the hypothesis. The "then…" part is the test with the expected result. In this example, your statement might be: "If heat evaporates water, then water placed in a glass under a lit lamp will decrease in volume."

## Practice

On a separate sheet of paper, write a hypothesis that explains each of the following observations.

**1.** An ice cube melts when placed in hot water.

**2.** A girl attaches a ball to a string. She twirls the ball and string in a circle over her head. She releases the string. The ball moves away from her in a straight line.

**3.** A man gives a cart a push and releases it. The cart slows down and stops.

## Application

You make a pendulum by tying a small washer to a string. You suspend the pendulum from a hook and start it swinging. Each time the washer reaches the highest point in its swing, you give it another slight push. The washer swings higher and higher. On a separate sheet of paper, write down a hypothesis to explain the amount of kinetic energy the washer has at the bottom of its swing.

# LABORATORY ACTIVITY

## A SYSTEM OF PENDULUMS

### Objective
Investigate how energy is transferred from one pendulum to another.

### Background
Suppose 2 pendulums are connected. One pendulum starts swinging while the other is still at rest. Energy in the system is transferred from one pendulum to the other. The total energy in the system stays the same, however.

### Materials
6 quarters, tape, string (100 cm), stop watch or watch with a second hand, metric ruler

### Procedure
1. Tape 3 quarters to make a pendulum weight. Make another weight the same way. Tie 3 lengths of string together as in Figure 6-LA. Tape the pendulum weights to strings 1 and 2 Both weights must hang down the same distance. Tape the connecting string to the underside of a table, chair, or cabinet shelf.
2. Hold one pendulum still. Pull the other one aside about 20 cm. Let both pendulums go. Observe their motion. Use a watch to measure the time it takes for kinetic energy to be transferred from the moving pendulum to the nonmoving pendulum. Repeat this step many times. Record your data. Find the average time it takes for energy to be transferred.
3. Make one pendulum shorter than the other by taping one weight 3 cm higher on the string. Start the longer pendulum swinging. Record the time it takes for the transfer of energy to the shorter pendulum. Repeat and find the average time it takes.

4. Make both pendulums the same length again, as in step 2. Slide the pendulum strings over string 3, until they are 15 cm apart. See Fig. 6-1B. Repeat step 2.
5. Repeat step 4 with the strings 8 cm apart.

*Figure 6-L. Laboratory setup.*

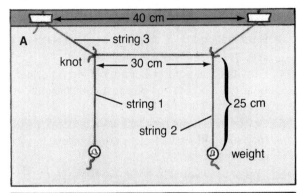

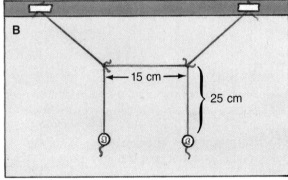

### Questions
1. At first one pendulum has all the energy. How does the second pendulum gain energy? Are any forces exerted on the second pendulum?
2. When one pendulum is shorter than the other, describe the energy transfer from one pendulum to the other.
3. As the string connecting the two pendulums gets shorter, what happens to the time needed for complete energy transfer? Why?
4. **PROBLEM SOLVING** What would happen if a third pendulum was tied between the pendulums in step 2? Offer a hypothesis and test it.

# SUMMARY

1. Energy is the ability to cause changes in matter. Energy in a system can change from one type to another, but the total energy in a system remains the same. (6-1)
2. Work is force times distance. Work and energy are both measured in joules. (6-1)
3. Potential energy is stored energy. Kinetic energy is the energy of motion. (6-2)
4. Gravitational potential energy is the potential energy an object has due to its position above the earth's surface. (6-2)
5. Power measures how fast work is done. It is measured in watts. Power equals work divided by time. (6-3)
6. The energy you use originally came from the sun. Energy is not created or destroyed. It just changes from one form into another. (6-3)

# REVIEW

Number a sheet of paper from 1 to 25 and answer these questions.

**Building Science Vocabulary**   Write the letter of the term that best matches each definition.

a. conservation of energy
b. energy
c. fossil fuel
d. gravitational potential energy
e. horsepower
f. joule
g. kinetic energy
h. potential energy
i. power
j. watt
k. weight
l. work

1. Oil or coal
2. Unit of work or energy
3. Stored energy
4. The total energy of an object or of a group of objects stays the same
5. A measure of the pull of gravity on an object
6. Energy of motion
7. Force times distance
8. One joule per second
9. Work divided by time
10. 746 watts

**Finding the Facts**   Select the letter of the answer that best completes each of the following.

11. Kinetic energy of an object depends on (a) position   (b) light   (c) speed   (d) molecules.
12. The potential energy due to gravity depends on   (a) speed   (b) molecules   (c) light   (d) height.
13. Power equals   (a) work   (b) time   (c) work × time   (d) work/time.
14. The total energy in a system   (a) stays the same   (b) can change from one kind to another   (c) is measured in joules   (d) all of the above.
15. A 100-watt light bulb   (a) changes 100 joules of electric energy into light energy in one second   (b) changes 100 joules of electric energy into light energy in one hour   (c) changes 100 watts of electric energy into light energy in one second   (d) has more power than a 150-watt bulb.
16. When a girl weighing 100 newtons runs up a flight of stairs 10 meters high in 10 seconds, (a) she does 100 joules of work   (b) her potential energy at the top is 1,000 joules   (c) she does 10 joules of work   (d) she does no work.
17. The energy in all living things can be traced to   (a) water   (b) the sun   (c) the soil   (d) animals.
18. Fossil fuels are   (a) being replaced as fast as we are using them   (b) an unlimited energy source deep inside the earth   (c) a limited energy source that will one day be gone   (d) made by nuclear reactors.

**19.** The energy produced by vibrations is
(**a**) chemical    (**b**) electric
(**c**) mechanical    (**d**) sound.

**20.** How much power does a machine develop if it does 1,000 joules of work in 10 seconds?
(**a**) 100 W    (**b**) 990 W
(**c**) 1,010 W    (**d**) 10,000 W.

**Understanding Main Ideas**   Complete the following.

**21.** A property of a system that stays the same is __?__.

**22.** The law of the conservation of energy states that __?__.

**23.** A pendulum system has 50 joules of energy. When the potential energy is 30 joules, the kinetic energy is __?__.

**24.** Force times distance is __?__.

**25.** The potential energy due to the position of an object above the earth's surface is __?__.

**Writing about Science**   On a separate piece of paper, answer the following as completely as possible.

**1.** When you rub your hands together on a cold day, is any work done in rubbing your hands?

**2.** You want to throw a baseball weighing 5 N up to a friend. Your friend is leaning out of a window on the fourth floor of a building. You must throw the ball up 16 m for your friend to catch it. If the baseball leaves your hand with a kinetic energy of 70 J, can your friend catch it?

**3.** Imagine that all the fossil fuels in the United States were used up at noon tomorrow. List all the things that would change for you for the rest of the day and night.

**4.** Calculate the total amount of energy you use each day just in lifting things. You lift yourself out of bed, you lift up objects, you climb stairs. Where does your energy come from?

**5.** (laboratory question) Describe the energy changes that take place as you move back and forth on a swing.

**Investigating Chapter Ideas**   Try the following project to further your study.

**The hydrologic cycle**   You have read how energy from the sun evaporates water from the oceans, which eventually falls to the earth as rain. This water then returns via rivers and streams to the ocean. The cycling of water from the oceans to the land and back again is called the hydrologic, or water, cycle. Read about the steps in the hydrologic cycle. Prepare a poster that diagrams the hydrologic cycle. Describe what happens in each step. Explain why the hydrologic cycle is sometimes referred to as a gigantic solar-powered engine.

**Reading About Science**   Read some of the following books to explore topics that interest you.

Asimov, Isaac. 1981. **How Did We Find Out About Solar Power?** New York: Walker.

Purcell, John. 1982. **From Hand Ax to Laser: Man's Growing Mastery of Energy.** New York: Vanguard.

Scott, Elaine. 1982. **Doodlebugging: The Treasure Hunt for Oil.** New York: Warner.

Spooner, Maggie. 1980. **Sunpower Experiments: Solar Energy Explained.** New York: Sterling.

Weitzman, David. 1982. **Windmills, Bridges and Old Machines: Discovering Our Industrial Past.** New York: Scribner's.

**S**uppose you are a crew member of a sailboat. You have to raise the sail. How would you do it? Suppose you catch a fish. Could you lift it a meter by moving your arm only a few centimeters?

You can use machines to do both jobs. A pulley at the top of the mast makes raising the sail easy. Just stand on deck and pull on a rope. A fishing pole brings the force you exert far out over the water. It also multiplies the distance over which you use the force. Just lift the handle a little to lift the fish out of the water.

Machines like pulleys and fishing poles are called simple machines. Others like steam shovels, are more complex. But complex machines are many machines working together. In this chapter you will learn how machines help make work easier.

Read and Find Out:

● how you can lift a vehicle with one hand.

● how the gears on a bicycle work.

● how to find out whether an air conditioner saves energy.

# SIMPLE MACHINES

**CHAPTER**

**7**

# FORCES AND SIMPLE MACHINES

Have you ever tried to remove the lid from a can of paint? You know that it is difficult, if not impossible, to do it using only your fingers. Yet you can easily pry off the lid with a screwdriver. The screwdriver is a kind of *simple machine. A **simple machine** is a device that helps you do work.* A machine can be used to lift a car, raise a sail, catch a fish, or open a can of paint. In this section you will investigate some kinds of simple machines. You will study how simple machines help do work. You will also learn how to find out how well a particular machine does work.

## How Machines Help Do Work

Figure 7-1 will help you analyze what happens when you use a screwdriver to open a paint can. You push *down* on the screwdriver handle. The other end goes up and lifts the lid of the can with it. This motion illustrates one way machines help make work easier. Many machines change the direction of the applied force. *An applied force is called an **effort.***

Figure 7-1 also shows you another way machines help do work. When you press down on the screwdriver handle, you use a small effort. But the force at the tip of the screwdriver, the *output force,* is great. *The **output force** is the force produced by a machine.* In this case it is enough to lift the lid off the paint can. The screwdriver, like many machines, multiplies your effort and produces a greater output force.

This example also shows the way machines do work. Machines can bring your effort to places you could not normally reach. It may be under a paint can lid or to the top of a mast.

You have learned what simple machines do. Figure 7-2 shows six basic simple machines. Look now at one of the simplest machines: a lever.

*Figure 7-1. Some machines change the direction of an applied force.*

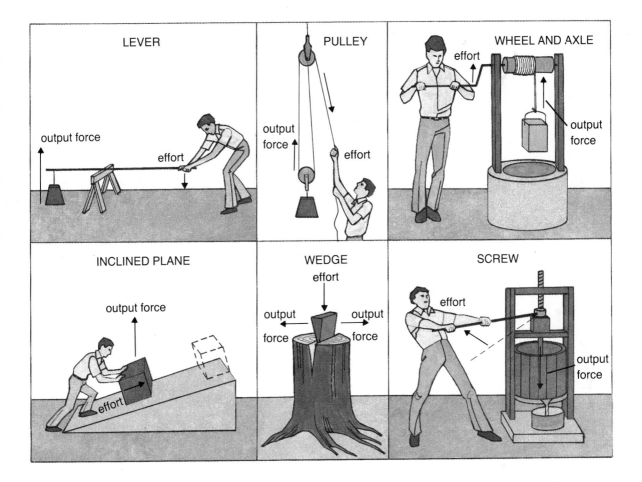

The following are labeled within the figure:

LEVER — output force, effort

PULLEY — output force, effort

WHEEL AND AXLE — effort, output force

INCLINED PLANE — output force, effort

WEDGE — effort, output force, output force

SCREW — effort, output force

## The Lever

Did you ever ride a seesaw with a friend? Your weight acting down on one end of the seesaw could balance your friend's weight on the other end. You both could sit motionless balanced in equilibrium.

A seesaw is an example of a lever. *A **lever** is a simple machine made of a rigid bar that is free to pivot. The pivot point of a lever is its **fulcrum** (FUL·kruhm).*

A lever can have the effort, output force, and fulcrum at different points along the bar. This relationship can help you identify three classes of levers. In each class the two forces are on particular sides of the fulcrum. Figure 7-3 shows the three classes of levers.

*Figure 7-2. Kinds of simple machines.*

## USING A LEVER

**OBJECTIVE**
Learn how to use a lever.

**MATERIALS**
metric ruler, pencil, eraser

**PROCEDURE**
**1.** Place the ruler on top of the pencil. The pencil should be under the 10-cm mark. Put the eraser between the 1- and 2-cm marks.
**2.** Push down on the 30-cm mark until the eraser rises. Note the effort needed.
**3.** Move the pencil to the 16-cm mark, then to the 25-cm mark. Each time repeat step 2.

**QUESTIONS**
**1.** What part of a lever is the pencil?
**2.** Where was the pencil when it was easiest to lift the eraser?
**3.** Where was the pencil when it was hardest to lift the eraser?

**First Class**   In a first-class lever, the fulcrum is between the effort and the output force. A balance and a seesaw are first-class levers. Hammers and crowbars are first-class levers that are bent at the fulcrum. First-class levers help do work by multiplying the force and changing its direction.

**Second Class**   A wheelbarrow is a second-class lever. So is a nutcracker. Second-class levers have the output force between the fulcrum and the effort. Second-class levers do not change the direction of the effort. They simply multiply the effort.

**Third Class**   A third-class lever has the effort between the fulcrum and the output force. A fishing pole and your arm are third-class levers. Look carefully at the third-class lever in Figure 7-3. With a third-class lever, the output force is less than the effort! Why would anyone want to use a third-class lever? Third-class levers multiply the distance of your effort. You only need to move your effort a short distance to make the output force move a greater distance.

E = effort
O = output force
▲ = fulcrum

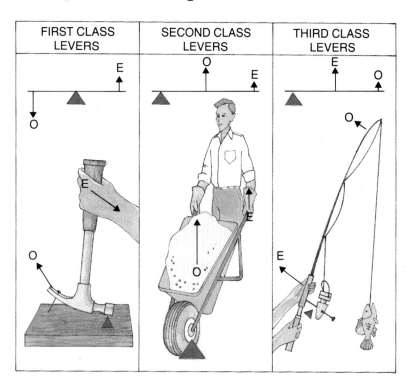

*Figure 7-3. The three classes of levers.*

## Doing Work with Levers

Most simple machines multiply effort. Suppose you wanted to lift a 500-newton boulder. You could use a lever like the one shown in Figure 7-4. How much effort must you apply to lift the boulder?

Levers are balances. They follow this rule:

**effort × effort arm = output force × output force arm**

The output force must overcome the weight of the boulder, 500 newtons. The distance between the effort and the fulcrum, the effort arm, is 200 cm. The distance from the output force to the fulcrum, the output force arm, is 20 cm. The effort is:

$$\text{effort} \times \text{effort arm} = \text{output force} \times \text{output force arm}$$
$$\text{effort} \times 200 \text{ cm} = 500 \text{ N} \times 20 \text{ cm}$$
$$\text{effort} = \frac{500 \text{ N} \times 20 \text{ cm}}{200 \text{ cm}}$$
$$\text{effort} = 50 \text{ N}$$

So instead of using 500 newtons to lift the boulder, you need apply only 50 newtons.

## Mechanical Advantage

Most machines are used because they multiply effort. When you used a screwdriver as a lever, you put in 50 newtons of effort. But you got out 500 newtons of effort. The lever multiplied your effort by ten! This value, 10, is the *mechanical* (muh•KAN•i•kuhl) *advantage* of the lever. The **mechanical advantage** (MA) *of any simple machine is the number of times the machine multiplies effort.* The MA is the output force divided by the effort. Using this formula, you can show that the MA for the lever is:

$$\textbf{MA} = \frac{\textbf{output force}}{\textbf{effort}}$$
$$\text{MA} = \frac{500 \text{ N}}{50 \text{ N}}$$
$$\text{MA} = 10$$

This is the value you expected to find.

Why are machines used?

*Figure 7-4. To just lift the boulder, the output force must equal the weight of the boulder. How large is the output force for this lever?*

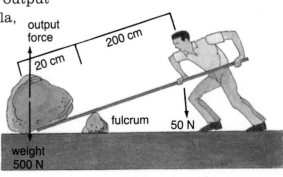

output force

20 cm

200 cm

fulcrum

50 N

weight 500 N

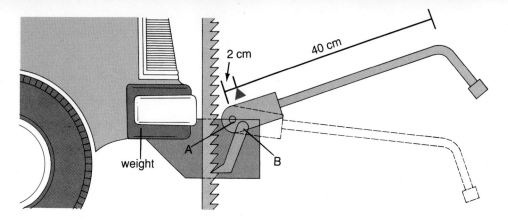

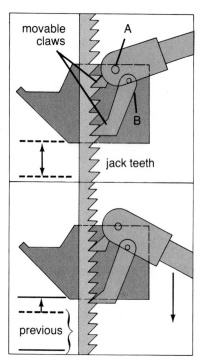

**Figure 7-5.** *Each time the jack handle moves up, the fulcrum moves up a notch.*

You can also find the MA of a lever by comparing the effort arm and the output force arm:

$$MA = \frac{\text{effort arm}}{\text{output force arm}}$$

$$MA = \frac{200 \text{ cm}}{20 \text{ cm}} = 10$$

● You can lift the front end of a car with one hand if you use a jack. Most car jacks are first-class levers. The operation of a jack is shown in Figure 7-5. The output force of the lever lifts the car at point *A*. The fulcrum of the lever is located at point *B*. As point *A* moves up, a movable claw locks in a higher tooth on the jack. Each time you push down on the handle, the car moves up a small distance and locks in place. When you lift the jack handle back up, the fulcrum locks in a new tooth.

The MA of the jack pictured is 20. The input force is increased 20 times. If you pushed down on the jack handle with a force of 360 newtons, you could lift a 7,200-newton weight.

**OBJECTIVES AND WORDS TO REVIEW**

**1.** Give two ways machines help do work.
**2.** How can a wheelbarrow and a fishing pole both be levers?
**3.** A lever can lift a load of 280 newtons with an effort of 40 newtons. What is the MA of the lever?
**4.** Write one complete sentence for each term listed below.

| simple machine | lever |
| --- | --- |
| effort | fulcrum |
| output force | mechanical advantage |

# MORE SIMPLE MACHINES

In the last section you took a close look at levers. In this section you will look at other kinds of simple machines. Some of these machines are based on a wheel. They have movable parts. But the others, as you will see, do work without having movable parts.

## Pulleys

Suppose you had to lift a television set. To help, you can use a machine that is based on a wheel, *a pulley*. *A **pulley** is a grooved wheel that turns by the action of a rope in the groove.*

There are several kinds of pulleys. Figure 7-6**A** shows a *fixed* pulley. That is, it is fixed, or attached, to one place. A fixed pulley helps make work easier by changing the direction of the effort. It is easier to pull *down* on a rope than to lift *up* the television with your bare hands. However, a fixed pulley does not multiply the effort. The effort used to lift the television is the same as the output force of the machine.

When the effort and the output force of a machine are the same, what is the MA of the machine? You can find the MA of any machine just as you did for a lever. In this case:

$$MA = \frac{\text{output force}}{\text{effort}}$$
$$= \frac{400 \text{ N}}{400 \text{ N}}$$
$$= 1$$

The MA of a fixed pulley is 1.

Figure 7-6**B** shows a *movable* pulley. A movable pulley is hooked to the object you are lifting. As you pull the rope, the object and the pulley move together. In this case, you have to pull upward. This pulley does not change the direction of the effort. But a movable

**OBJECTIVES**

**1.** Describe several machines based on wheels.

**2.** Describe how a machine with no moving parts can do work.

**3.** Describe two kinds of inclined planes.

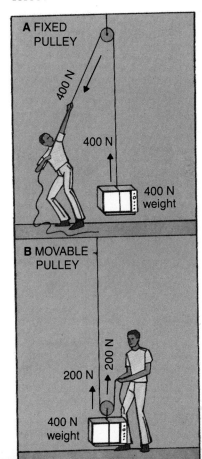

*Figure 7-6. Why does the person in B pull with less force?*

A FIXED PULLEY

400 N

400 N

400 N weight

B MOVABLE PULLEY

200 N

200 N

400 N weight

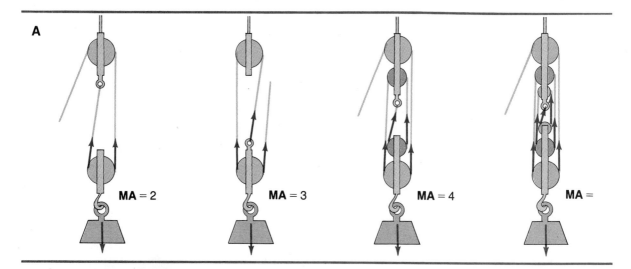

A

MA = 2        MA = 3        MA = 4        MA =

**Figure 7-7.** *Some of the most complicated machines are just combinations of simple machines.*

How can you find the MA of a pulley?

pulley does multiply effort. In this example, it takes an effort of only 200 N to lift the 400 N television with a pulley. What is the MA?

$$MA = \frac{\text{output force}}{\text{effort}}$$
$$= \frac{400 \text{ N}}{200 \text{ N}}$$
$$= 2$$

Although this pulley multiplies effort, you have to use that effort for a greater distance. To lift the television just 1 meter, you must pull a 2-meter length of rope.

## Pulley Systems

You can predict the MA of a pulley simply by counting ropes. Notice that the pulley in Figure 7-6**B** has *two* ropes that support the weight of the television. This pulley, remember, has a MA of 2—the same number as the number of supporting ropes.

You can get higher mechanical advantages by combining fixed and movable pulleys into a pulley system. See Figure 7-7**A**. As more pulleys are added, more sections of rope support the load. In each case, you can make a good prediction of the MA just by counting the supporting sections of rope.

A problem with many pulley systems, however, is friction. As you pull on a rope, the rope rubs along the grooved wheel. This rubbing can cause you to apply more effort. The more ropes in a pulley system, the more rubbing there will be. See Figure 7-7**B**. One way to reduce friction is to oil the wheel.

## Wheels and Axles

A *wheel and* axle can help your force reach places it could not reach otherwise. See Figure 7-8. *A **wheel and axle** is made of a handle or axle attached to the center of a wheel.* When you turn a wheel (or the handle of a wheel) your effort moves in a circle. The axle moves at the same rate.

Like a lever, a wheel and axle can multiply your effort. To find out how many times it can multiply your effort, compare the radius of the wheel with the radius of the axle. The radius (pl. radii) is the length between the center and edge of a circle. Look at each radius in Figure 7-8. The radius of the wheel is four times greater than the radius of the axle. The wheel and axle could multiply your effort four times.

However, friction presents a problem here. As with pulleys, there may be rubbing between the moving parts. The amount of rubbing can increase the amount of effort you need to apply.

*Figure 7-8. A wheel and axle can lift a heavy load with a small effort. The system acts like a first-class lever.*

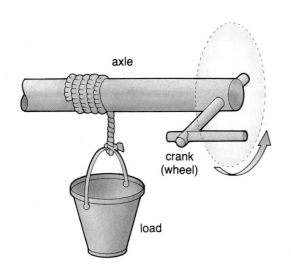

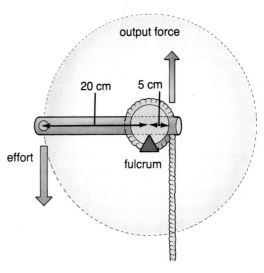

## A WHEEL-AND-BELT MACHINE

**OBJECTIVE**
See how the speed of a wheel can be changed.

**MATERIALS**
bicycle, masking tape

**PROCEDURE**
**1.** Turn the pedals until one pedal is at its highest point. If you have a multiple-speed bicycle, shift into lowest speed.
**2.** Place a piece of tape at the top of the rear tire.
**3.** Slowly revolve the pedal through a complete turn. Have a friend count the number of turns the rear tire makes.

**QUESTIONS**
**1.** Describe the motion of the rear tire compared with that of the pedal.
**2.** Explain the advantage of putting a five-speed bicycle in low speed when you begin a ride.

*Figure 7-9. Which wheel spins faster?*

## Rotating Wheels

The machine in Figure 7-9 has two wheels connected by a nonslipping belt. What can be learned about the motion of one wheel relative to the other?

**Speed and Rotation** The figure shows how far each wheel rotates in one second. The small wheel makes a half-turn while the large one makes only a quarter-turn. In two seconds, the small wheel has made one complete turn, or revolution. The large wheel has made only half a revolution. The small wheel turns twice as fast as the large wheel. So an arrangement like the one shown in Figure 7-9 can be used to change the speed of rotation of a wheel.

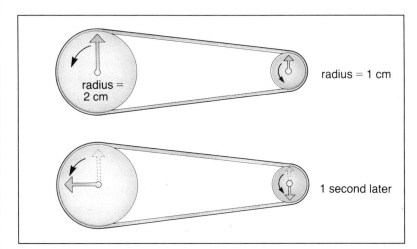

radius = 2 cm  radius = 1 cm  1 second later

**Size of Wheel and Rotation** How are the sizes of the two wheels related to their speeds of rotation? The radius of the large wheel is twice the radius of the small wheel. And the speed of the small wheel is twice that of the large one. Experiments show a connection between the radii and speeds of the wheels. The speed of the large wheel times its radius equals the speed of the small wheel times its radius.

Suppose a wheel with a radius of 4 centimeters makes one complete revolution each second. The 4-centimeter wheel is connected by a belt to a wheel having a 1-centimeter radius. How fast does the 1-centimeter wheel turn?

$$\text{speed} \times \text{radius} = \text{speed} \times \text{radius}$$
of large wheel      of small wheel

$$1 \text{ rev/s} \times 4 \text{ cm} = \text{speed of small wheel} \times 1 \text{ cm}$$

$$4 \text{ rev/s} = \text{speed of small wheel}$$

## Gears

In the National Museum of American History in Washington, D.C., there is a large clock with visible inner parts. Figure 7-10 shows two of the wheels in the clock. Each wheel has teeth cut into it. A long swinging pendulum has a hook attached to the large wheel. This wheel is connected to other similar wheels. As the pendulum swings, it makes the large wheel rotate a bit. The movement of the large wheel makes the smaller wheels rotate also. The moving wheels turn the hands of the clock.

This kind of wheel is called a *gear*. A **gear** is a *wheel with teeth cut into the rim*. A gear works by transmitting force from one gear to another where two gear teeth mesh. See Figure 7-11. The effort and the output force act on the gear shafts, each with a 1-centimeter radius. An effort of 100 newtons produces an output force of 200 newtons. The MA is 200/100, or 2.

*Figure 7-10. Gears are like a group of evenly spaced levers.*

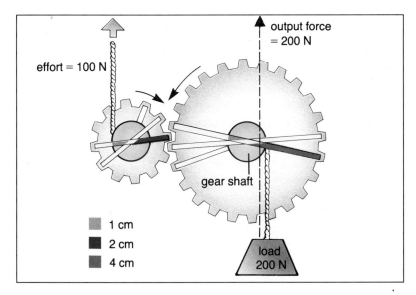

effort = 100 N

output force = 200 N

gear shaft

■ 1 cm
■ 2 cm
■ 4 cm

load 200 N

*Figure 7-11. Gears operate like spinning levers. Where gear teeth mesh, force is transferred from one gear to the other.*

## Inclined Planes

Which simple machine has no moving parts?

Up to now you have been looking at simple machines that have moving parts. Now look at a simple machine that has no moving parts. It is called an *inclined* (in•KLIGHND) *plane. An **inclined plane** is a straight, slanted surface.* A ramp is an example of an inclined plane.

How can something that has no moving parts be a machine? The movers in Figure 7-12 can help you see how. In Figure 7-12**A**, they are applying an effort to overcome gravity. Their effort is 1,200 newtons. The distance to the van is 1 meter. In **B**, they are moving the same crate up a ramp. This time they need only 600 newtons of effort.

The ramp multiplies their effort. They need an effort of only 600 newtons to get a 1,200-newton, crate to the van. At the same time, however, using a ramp has a disadvantage. You need less effort, but you have to use that effort for a longer distance. The ramp here is 3 meters long. Using the ramp, the movers must push the crate 3 meters to load it on the van. By lifting, they must move the crate only 1 meter—but they must use more effort.

*Figure 7-12. You do the same amount of work whether you lift or push the crate. In which case do you use less force?*

Figure 7-13. *A wedge can change the direction of the effort.*

## Two Kinds of Inclined Planes

Two other simple machines are actually kinds of inclined planes. See Figure 7-13. A wedge, like an inclined plane, has a slanted surface. Some wedges, in fact, have two slanted surfaces. Unlike an inclined plane, however, a wedge must be moved in order to do work. You hammer a wedge in one direction. It lifts or splits apart an object in other directions. A wedge helps your effort get under heavy objects, or inside them.

A wedge can multiply effort. With only a small effort you can tilt a safe or a heavy crate. Steep wedges are not as useful as wedges with a gentle slope. The gentler the slope of the wedge, the more it can multiply your effort.

A screw is another kind of inclined plane. See Figure 7-14. A screw is actually an inclined plane wrapped around a central bar. The steeper the inclined plane is, the farther apart the threads of a screw are.

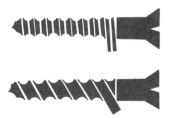

Figure 7-14. *The closer together the threads of a screw are, the less force you must exert to do work.*

*Figure 7-15. A five-speed bicycle uses different spoked wheels to make riding easier.*

● Gears multiply forces. But sometimes they are used to increase speed. Then they act like a wheel-and-belt system. A five-speed bicycle relies on such a system for its operation. See Figure 7-15.

The pedals are attached to a gear. When you push down on the pedals, you apply an effort to that gear. The effort is transmitted through the chain to a gear on the rear wheel. You can also move the chain from one gear to another. By moving the chain, you select the output force needed to move the bicycle.

The main purpose of the gear-and-chain system is to increase the rotation of the rear tire. The rotation of the pedals is slower than the rotation of the tires.

**OBJECTIVES AND WORDS TO REVIEW**

**1.** (a) You have a pulley and some rope. There is a hook on a ceiling and a hook on a heavy crate. Describe two ways of using the pulley to lift the crate from the floor.
(b) A wheel has a radius of 4 cm. It is attached to an axle that has a radius of 2 cm. How many times may the wheel and axle multiply an effort of 20 N applied to the wheel?

**2.** How can an inclined plane help do work?

**3.** How are wedges and screws kinds of inclined planes?

**4.** Write one complete sentence for each term listed below.
pulley          gear          wheel and axle          inclined plane

# EFFICIENCY OF MACHINES

The Pyramids of Egypt are outstanding examples of human effort. It is exactly that—human effort—that built these massive structures over 4,600 years ago. See Figure 7-16. Each pyramid contains thousands of blocks of stone. Some blocks weigh as much as 134,000 newtons. How could such blocks have been lifted one on top of another?

There are no written accounts of how the Pyramids were built. But pictures on the walls of tombs show that ancient Egyptians knew how to use machines. Probably, ramps made it possible for people to push blocks to the top of a pyramid. Yet, as you will see in this section, ramps often waste some of the effort that is applied to them.

## Work Output and Input

The ancient Egyptians probably used simple machines such as inclined planes. Today, people use all kinds of machines to make work easier.

All machines have some friction along their surfaces. There is friction between the rope and grooved wheel of a pulley. The moving parts of wheels and

*Figure 7-16. The Great Pyramid at Giza is one of the seven wonders of the world. About 20–30 years were needed to build the pyramids.*

axles rub each other. There is friction between the threads of a screw and the object it is being driven into. In all machines, some work is done to overcome friction.

You can use the terms *work input* and *work output* to tell how much work you are doing because of friction. **Work input** *is amount of work you put into a machine when you use it.* **Work output** *is the amount of work you obtain from a machine when you use it.*

For example, suppose you want to get a fish tank from the floor to a shelf. The tank weighs 400 newtons. The shelf is 1 meter high. You lean a 3-meter-long ramp against the shelf. With the ramp you need an effort of only 200 newtons to push the tank to the shelf. The work input is:

$$\text{work input} = \text{force} \times \text{distance}$$
$$(\text{force is } your \ effort)$$

$$= 200 \text{ N} \times 3 \text{ m}$$

$$= 600 \text{ J}$$

The work the machine did for you was the work that got the 400-newton tank to the 1-m high shelf. So the work output is:

$$\text{work output} = \text{force} \times \text{distance}$$
$$(\text{force is } weight \ of \ tank)$$

$$= 400 \text{ N} \times 1 \text{ m}$$

$$= 400 \text{ J}$$

By comparing the work input and output, you can tell how much work was done because of friction.

$$\text{work input} - \text{work output} = \text{work done}$$
$$due \ to \ friction$$

$$600 \text{ J} - 400 \text{ J} = 200 \text{ J}$$

## Efficiency

You can also compare work output and work input by finding the *efficiency* of a machine. *The* **efficiency** *of a machine is a measure of the useful work a machine can do.* It is usually expressed as a percent:

$$\text{Efficiency} = \frac{\textbf{work output}}{\textbf{100\% work input}} \times 100\%$$

The efficiency of the three-meter ramp is:

$$\text{Efficiency} = \frac{400 \text{ J}}{600 \text{ J}} \times 100\%$$
$$= \tfrac{2}{3} \times 100\%$$
$$= 66.67\%$$

If a machine had no friction at all, its efficiency would be 100%. In that case, the work output would be exactly the same as the work input. But all machines do have some friction. So their efficiencies are always less than 100%. The closer a machine's efficiency is to 100%, the less friction the machine has.

● Many newer air conditioners have numbers on their product tag. See Figure 7-17. This number is an efficiency rating. The efficiency rating tells you how good an energy saver the air conditioner is. A high rating means the machine does not have a lot of friction to overcome. So that machine produces a greater amount of useful work. A low efficiency rating means that more energy is used in overcoming friction. So more energy is needed to cool a room. Find the efficiency rating of an air conditioner in your home or in a department store. Will the air conditioner save energy or waste it?

What would be the efficiency of a frictionless machine?

**Figure 7-17.** *The efficiency rating of an air conditioner tells you how much energy a machine is saving.*

**OBJECTIVES AND WORDS TO REVIEW**

**1.** How does friction affect the amount of work you get from a machine?

**2.** In a machine, which is usually greater, the work output or the work input? Why?

**3.** A machine lifts a 1500-newton crate 4 meters. But you have to supply 7500 joules to the machine. (a) What is the work output? (b) What is the efficiency of the machine?

**4.** Write one complete sentence for each term listed below.
   work input      work output      efficiency

## USING UNITS TO CHECK YOUR ANSWERS

### Preparation

You measure time in seconds, minutes, hours, days, weeks, months, even years. Seconds, minutes, days, and so forth are units of time. A *unit* is a fixed quantity or measure that can be used as a standard.

Scientists use the following units to measure basic properties of matter: length (centimeters), mass (grams), and temperature (Celsius). They also use these units in combinations to measure more complex quantities. For example, volume and density are derived from length and mass.

$$\text{volume} = \text{length} \times \text{width} \times \text{height}$$
$$\text{cm}^3 = \text{cm} \times \text{cm} \times \text{cm}$$
$$\text{density} = \frac{\text{mass}}{\text{volume}} = \frac{\text{g}}{\text{cm}^3}$$

*Figure 1.*

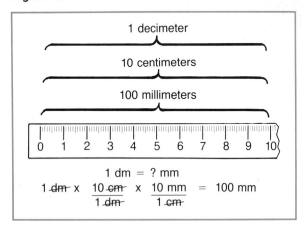

1 decimeter

10 centimeters

100 millimeters

0  1  2  3  4  5  6  7  8  9  10

$$1 \text{ dm} = ? \text{ mm}$$
$$1 \text{ dm} \times \frac{10 \text{ cm}}{1 \text{ dm}} \times \frac{10 \text{ mm}}{1 \text{ cm}} = 100 \text{ mm}$$

### Directions

The following guidelines are helpful to determine what math operations to use in solving problems.

1. Multiply to convert large units to smaller units.
2. Divide to convert small units to larger units.

3. Use conversion factors. *Conversion factors* are equalities relating one unit to another. An example of a conversion factor is 60 seconds = 1 minute.
It can be written: $\dfrac{1 \text{ min}}{60 \text{ s}}$  or  $\dfrac{60 \text{ s}}{1 \text{ min}}$

4. Set up the conversion factors so that the unwanted units are eliminated.

5. Use the size of the unit as well as the number of units to check your answer. See Figure 1.

### Practice

There are 180 days in a school year. Suppose you wanted to know how many seconds there are in a school year. Seconds are smaller units than days. So, the numerical answer in seconds must be greater than 180.

$$180 \text{ days} = ? \text{ seconds}$$

Set up the conversion factors so that all of the units except seconds are eliminated.

$$180 \text{ days} \times \frac{24 \text{ hr}}{1 \text{ day}} \times \frac{60 \text{ min}}{1 \text{ hr}} \times \frac{60 \text{ s}}{1 \text{ min}} = 15{,}552{,}000 \text{ s}$$

Notice that since the size of the unit (seconds) is smaller than the original unit (days) the quantity of the smaller unit must be greater.

Now change 7200 seconds into days.

### Application

To calculate effort when using a lever, use this rule:

$$\text{effort} = \frac{\text{output force} \times \text{output force arm}}{\text{effort arm}}$$

Suppose you are told to calculate the effort of a lever. You are given the following data: effort arm = 4 m; output force = 1,600 N; output force arm = 200 cm. Answer the following questions <u>before</u> solving the problem. Why can the values 200 cm and 4 m NOT be put into the formula <u>the way they are</u>? Why does it NOT make any difference whether you convert meters to centimeters or centimeters to meters? In what unit must effort be expressed? Calculate the effort.

# EFFICIENCY OF A SIMPLE MACHINE

## Objective
Find the efficiency of the wheel and axle.

## Background
While machines help make work easier, no machine is perfect. You always get less work out of a machine than you put in. Efficiency is a measure of how much useful work you can get from a machine.

## Materials
spool of thread, pencils, masking tape, 20 pennies, metric ruler

## Procedure
1. Stick the eraser ends of 2 pencils into the spool of thread. See Figure 7-L. Suspend the system from a table top with two loops of thread. Be sure the pencils are level. Wrap about 50 cm of thread around one pencil.

2. Wrap 6 to 8 pennies with tape and attach them to the thread hanging from the pencil. This is the load that you will lift off the floor. Attach 2 or 3 pennies to the thread hanging from the spool. These pennies will move from the spool down to the floor. You may have to experiment with the number of pennies hanging on each thread. You want the load to move up at a slow, constant speed.

3. Measure the distance the spool pennies move down and the load pennies move up.

## Questions
1. Calculate the work input by multiplying the effort (number of pennies) times the distance the pennies move down. Label your answer with units that you make up.

2. Calculate the work output by multiplying the output force (number of load pennies) by the distance the load moves. Label answer.

3. Calculate the efficiency of the wheel and axle. Use unit analysis to be sure the final answer is expressed correctly.

4. **PROBLEM SOLVING** How would the efficiency change if the load doubles? Make a hypothesis and explain how to test it.

*Figure 7-L. Laboratory setup.*

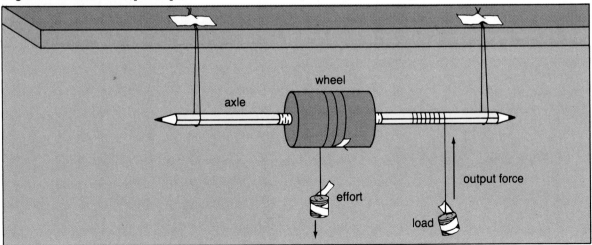

Do you enjoy fixing things? Have you ever built a model or furniture from a set of drawings? Are you always trying to improve the things you use? If you are handy with tools and machines, you might consider the careers below.

**Mechanical Engineer**   Many of our daily comforts come from the drawing boards of mechanical engineers. Mechanical engineers design, build, and test almost everything from air conditioners to electric power plants. They are also involved in consulting, teaching, and administration.

To enter the field of mechanical engineering, you need from four to five years of college training. After four years of experience, you can take exams to qualify as a professional engineer. Most mechanical engineers work in industry. However, some work for the government or for universities.

More information about this career is available from:

*The American Society of Mechanical Engineers*
*United Engineering Center*
*345 East 47th Street*
*New York, NY 10017*

**Machinist**   Machinists operate complicated machine tools that shape or form metal. They may use a lathe to cut a tiny part of a watch or a press to stamp out automobile doors. Most any industry you can think of depends on machinists for precision-made metal parts.

Machinists are employed mostly in industrial shops. They must have a wide range of experience in using different machine tools. Most train in some type of apprenticeship program for several years. A high school education is recommended. In this career, skills grow with on-the-job experience.

If you would like to know more about a career as a machinist, write:

*The National Machine Tool Builders Association*
*7901 Westpark Drive*
*McLean, VA 22102*

# SUMMARY

1. Most simple machines multiply effort or change its direction. Or they allow the effort to reach places it could not otherwise reach. (7-1)

2. The mechanical advantage (MA) of a simple machine is the number of times the machine multiplies the effort. The MA is determined by dividing the output force by the effort. (7-1)

3. Pulleys, wheels and axles, and gears are simple machines based on wheels. Friction along the movable parts increases the effort needed to do work with these machines. (7-2)

4. Screws and wedges are simple machines based on the inclined plane. (7-2)

5. All machines have some friction. The more friction there is to overcome, the more work you do. (7-3)

6. Efficiency is a measure of the usefulness of a machine. To find a machine's efficiency, compare the amount of useful work obtained with the amount of work done. (7-3)

# REVIEW

Number a sheet of paper from 1 to 25 and answer these questions.

**Building Science Vocabulary** Write the letter of the term that best matches each definition.

a. efficiency
b. effort
c. fulcrum
d. gear
e. inclined plane
f. lever

g. mechanical advantage
h. pulley
i. simple machine
j. wheel and axle
k. work input
l. work output

1. A rigid object that can rotate around a fulcrum
2. The force you apply to a machine
3. Work output divided by work input $\times$ 100%
4. A simple machine with no movable parts
5. The amount of useful work obtained by using a machine
6. Grooved wheel with a rope running through it
7. A balance point on a lever
8. Any device that makes work easier
9. A wheel with teeth
10. Output force divided by effort

**Finding the Facts** Select the letter of the answer that best completes each of the following.

11. A lever can have its fulcrum    (**a**) only at one end or the other end    (**b**) only at the middle    (**c**) almost anywhere    (**d**) only where the effort acts.

12. Compared with the work input to a simple machine, the work output    (**a**) is always the same    (**b**) is usually greater    (**c**) is never less    (**d**) is always less.

13. If the MA of a simple machine is 3, then the    (**a**) output force is 3 times the effort    (**b**) effort is 3 times the output force    (**c**) efficiency is 3%    (**d**) work output is 3 times the work input.

14. A fixed pulley is used to lift a heavy box. This machine helps do work by    (**a**) multiplying effort    (**b**) changing the direction of the effort    (**c**) both of the above    (**d**) none of the above.

15. A large pulley is connected to a small pulley by a belt. Compared with the rotation speed of the large pulley, the small pulley (**a**) rotates faster    (**b**) rotates slower (**c**) rotates at the same speed    (**d**) can rotate slower or faster, depending on the length of the belt.

16. A simple machine that is actually a kind of inclined plane is a **(a)** pulley **(b)** gear **(c)** wedge **(d)** balance.
17. An inclined plane is a machine because it **(a)** has friction along its surface **(b)** can multiply effort **(c)** tends to have an efficiency of 100% **(d)** has movable parts.
18. The work output of a simple machine is 1,500 joules. The work input to the simple machine is 2,000 joules. The efficiency of the simple machine is **(a)** 25% **(b)** 50% **(c)** 75% **(d)** 66.6%.
19. A pulley system has three sections of rope that lift the load. You might expect the MA of the system to be about **(a)** 0 **(b)** 1 **(c)** 2 **(d)** 3.
20. A first-class lever helps do work by **(a)** multiplying effort **(b)** changing the direction of the effort **(c)** both of the above **(d)** none of the above.

**Understanding Main Ideas** Complete the following.

21. The efficiency of a simple machine is always less than 100% because of __?__.
22. A screw and a wedge are both examples of __?__.
23. The MA of a fixed pulley is __?__.
24. You can find the MA of any machine by dividing the output force by the __?__.
25. A simple machine helps make work easier by __?__.

**Writing About Science** On a separate sheet of paper, answer the following as completely as possible.

1. A 50-newton block is placed 1.5 meters from the fulcrum of a lever. You apply an effort on the opposite end of the lever 2.5 meters from the fulcrum. (a) How much effort will lift the block? (b) Calculate the MA of the lever.

2. What are some of the advantages and disadvantages of using a screw?
3. You exert an effort of 350 newtons on the ropes of a pulley system. You pull the rope out 12 meters. As a result, an object weighing 1050 newtons is lifted up 1.5 meters. What is the efficiency of this system?
4. Imagine you are an engineer planning a road up to the top of a mountain. You have plenty of money. What is the best layout for the road? Why?
5. (laboratory question) Do you think a wheel-and-axle setup like the one you used in the laboratory activity could have been used in the building of the pyramids? Explain.

**Investigating Chapter Ideas** Try one of the following projects to further your study.

1. **Perpetual motion** Inventors have long sought to create perpetual motion machines. Form a committee to investigate perpetual motion machines. Describe what these machines are. Build models of some of the more famous machines. Demonstrate them to the class, explaining why they do not work.
2. **Auto efficiency** Prepare a poster that illustrates what is being done to make automobiles more energy efficient.
3. **Who's Watt?** The Scottish inventer James Watt contributed much to the development of steam engines. Write a short, one-act play describing the role Watt played in making steam engines more efficient.

**Reading About Science** Read some of the following books to explore topics that interest you.

Keen, M.L. 1973. **How It Works.** New York: Grosset and Dunlap.
Macaulay, David. 1983. **Mill.** Boston: Houghton.
Marsh, Ken. 1982. **The Way the New Technology Works.** Simon and Schuster.

# THE STRUCTURE OF MATTER

Scientists have always wondered about the composition of the planet Jupiter. The *Voyager* space probes have provided some clues, but the answer is by no means complete. However, scientists have found that not only Jupiter but all the planets and stars are made of the same elements as Earth. This unit will discuss atoms and elements, the common building blocks of matter.

**UNIT**

# 3

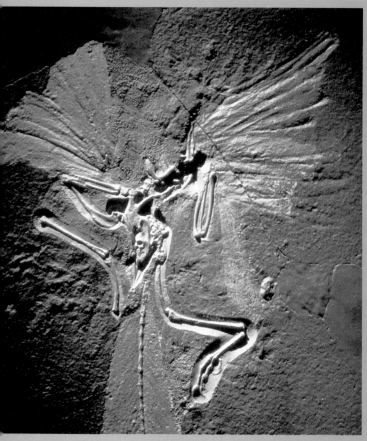

In a German mine in 1861, two workers uncovered an unfamiliar fossil. Some fossil parts resembled one animal. Other parts resembled another, completely different, animal. Yet these parts all belonged to one creature! Can you think of any modern animals with parts similar to those shown above?

Scientists wanted to know what the animal had looked like. How could they use the fossil to satisfy their curiosity? They constructed a model, using the fossil as a guide. The skeleton and the drawing are both models of the animal.

A model uses familiar ideas to explain something unfamiliar. Physical scientists use models to explain their concept of the atom. This chapter traces the development of the various models of the atom.

Read and Find Out:
● why water disappears if left for a while in the sun.
● how pictures appear on your television.
● why a neon light glows orange-red.

# THE MODEL OF THE ATOM

**CHAPTER**

**8**

# ATOMIC THEORY

Suppose you cut a strip of aluminum foil in half. You then take one of the halves and cut that in half. Now suppose you repeat this procedure over and over. Is there a smallest piece that you could make that would still have the properties of the aluminum? Of course there is! This smallest part is an atom.

What does an atom look like? As you know, no one has ever seen individual atoms. They are just too small. But scientists have observed how atoms affect each other. Based on these observations, they constructed a model of the atom. The model explained the observed facts. As new information was obtained, they changed the model to fit the new data. In this section you will study the principles on which the model of the atom is based.

## The Greeks and Atoms

The ancient Greeks were the first to record their ideas about the structure of matter. They asked themselves questions such as: Is one drop of water like any other drop? How small can a drop of water be and still be water?

**Questions and Answers** Like us, the Greeks learned with their senses. They did not do experiments, however. The Greeks questioned, observed, and thought. They concluded that matter could be broken down into particles too small to be seen. These particles were called atoms.

**The Atomists** Those who believed in atoms were called atomists. They thought that atoms came in different sizes and shapes, with much empty space between them. Very few people believed in atoms at that time. So, this first model was not accepted for over 2000 years.

*Figure 8-1. Dalton's model of the atom resulted from his study of gases.*

## Dalton and the Atomic Theory

In the early 1780's, a British school teacher named John Dalton, shown in Figure 8-1, brought back the Greek theory. He did so after making some observations about air. First, he learned that air is a mixture of different kinds of gases. He noticed that these gases do not separate on their own. They stay mixed. Second, he knew that it was possible to compress, or squeeze, gases into a smaller volume. The student in Figure 8-2 is taking advantage of this property of air. A pump can compress a large volume of air into the small volume of the basketball.

Dalton tried to explain these observations about the gases in air. He suggested that the gases were made of particles that can stay mixed. He also said that there must be large spaces between the particles. As shown in Figure 8-3, these spaces would explain why gases can be compressed.

*Figure 8-2.* What property of gases makes it possible to pump up the basketball?

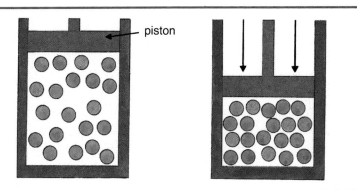

*Figure 8-3.* When the piston moves down, the gases are compressed.

**The Elements in Water**   Like the Greek atomists, Dalton thought atoms could not be broken down into smaller particles. Dalton knew from the work of others that water could be separated into two gases, oxygen and hydrogen. Nine grams of water produce 8 g of oxygen and 1 g of hydrogen. The masses of oxygen and hydrogen making up water add up to the mass of the water. These results can be obtained again and again.

What did Dalton believe about atoms?

## OBSERVING INDIRECTLY

**OBJECTIVE**
Observe particles too small to be seen directly.

**MATERIALS**
two clear glasses, bar of soap, flashlight, water

**PROCEDURE**
1. Nearly fill two glasses with water. To one glass add a piece of soap about half the size of a pea. Stir this mixture until the soap dissolves.
2. In a completely dark room direct the flashlight beam horizontally into the soapy mixture right under the surface. Repeat with the glass of plain water.
3. Observe the effects of the light beam in each glass.

**QUESTIONS**
1. What did you observe as the beam of light passed through the liquids?
2. What was the cause of the effect in the soapy mixture?
3. Why was a glass of plain water used in the experiment?

Dalton also thought that particles of different substances must be different from each other. For example, hydrogen and oxygen particles must be different, since these gases have different properties. These particles must also be different from water particles. Finally, particles of hydrogen and oxygen must retain their own mass when they join and form water.

**Dalton's Atoms**  The model of the atom accepted today began with Dalton's ideas. It has changed as new observations have been made. However, the basis of the model remains the same. Matter is made up of atoms. Atoms of an element are similar to each other. The atoms of different elements are different from each other. Atoms combine with each other and form new kinds of compounds.

● Have you ever noticed how quickly water disappears if left in the sun for a while? Dalton's model can be used to explain this disappearance of water. Water is made up of particles of hydrogen and oxygen. When left in the sun, these particles gain kinetic energy. They move about. The longer the particles are in the sun, the more kinetic energy they have. The particles move about faster. Soon, the particles are moving so fast they leave the surface of the liquid water. They enter and mix with the particles of the air. While this occurs, the amount of water goes down. Eventually, all the water has entered the air. The liquid water has disappeared.

## OBJECTIVES TO REVIEW

1. How did the way the Greeks learned about the atom differ from the way that Dalton learned about it?
2. What did the Greek atomists think the atom looked like?.
3. List three points that Dalton discovered about atoms that are still believed today.

# THE ATOM THROUGH HISTORY

The present model of the atom looks quite different from Dalton's model. In this section you will study how the model has changed.

## Thomson's Model of the Atom

A major development in the model of the atom occurred in the late 1800's. A British scientist, J. J. Thomson, was studying how electricity flowed through a glass *vacuum* tube. *A **vacuum** is a region from which all matter has been removed.* See Figure 8-4. The vacuum tube had metal strips called electrodes at each end. Certain rays had been observed in vacuum tubes when a current was passed through them. Thomson was investigating the nature of these rays. His experiments are summarized in Chart 8-1. From this work, Thomson proved that these rays were made of negative particles. These particles were later called electrons. His investigations led Thomson to develop the model of the atom shown in the chart.

## Rutherford's Discovery

Thomson and other scientists began to test his model. In 1896 it was discovered that some elements, such as uranium, give off particles with a positive charge. They have over 7,000 times more mass than electrons. Ernest Rutherford, another British scientist, called the particles alpha particles. He believed alpha particles could be used to test Thomson's model.

In the experiment illustrated in Chart 8-2, Rutherford fired alpha particles at a very thin sheet of gold foil. He coated a screen with a substance that glowed whenever an alpha particle hit it. He then used a telescope to detect the flashes of light made by the alpha particles. The results of this experiment caused Rutherford to question the Thomson model.

**OBJECTIVES**

**1.** Describe Thomson's model of the atom.

**2.** Tell how Rutherford discovered that an atom is mostly empty space and has a positive nucleus.

**3.** Compare the Bohr and wave models of the atom.

*Figure 8-4. In a vacuum cleaner, a fan pulls air through a tank, setting up a temporary vacuum inside the tank.*

**What particles did Rutherford use to test Thomson's atomic model?**

**CHART 8-1.** THOMSON'S EXPERIMENTS

| Hypothesis | Procedure | |
|---|---|---|
| If rays are made of charged particles, then an electric field will affect them. | Connected electricity source to electrodes and turned on current. | 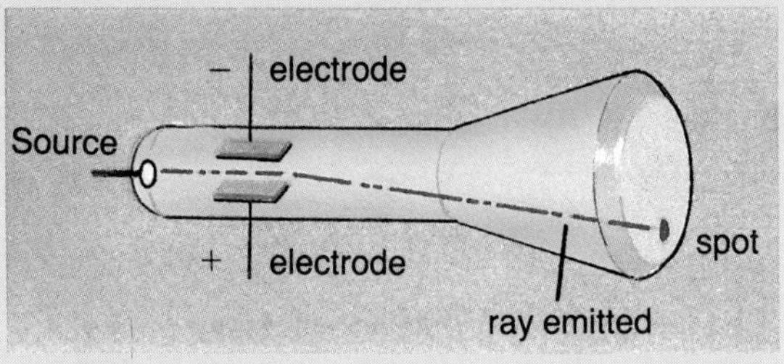 |
| If it is a charged particle, a magnet will affect its motion. | Added a magnet and did experiment over. Varied amount of current in electrodes. | 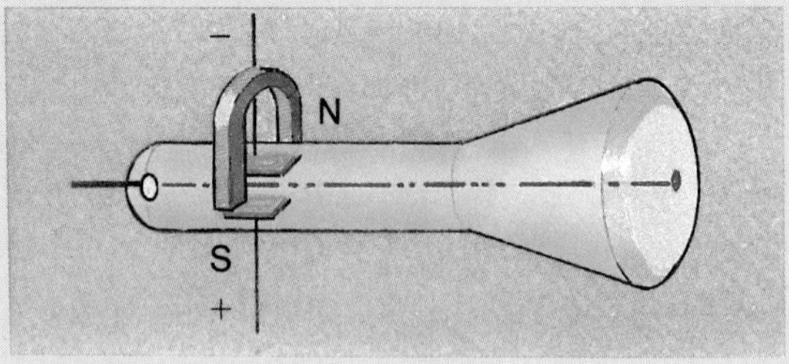 |

**CHART 8-2.** RUTHERFORD'S EXPERIMENTS

| Hypothesis | Procedure | |
|---|---|---|
| If Thomson model is right, then all of the alpha particles should pass through the foil in a straight line. | Hammered gold foil until it was less than 1 mm thick. Fired alpha particles at gold foil. Used telescope and screen to locate alpha particles. | 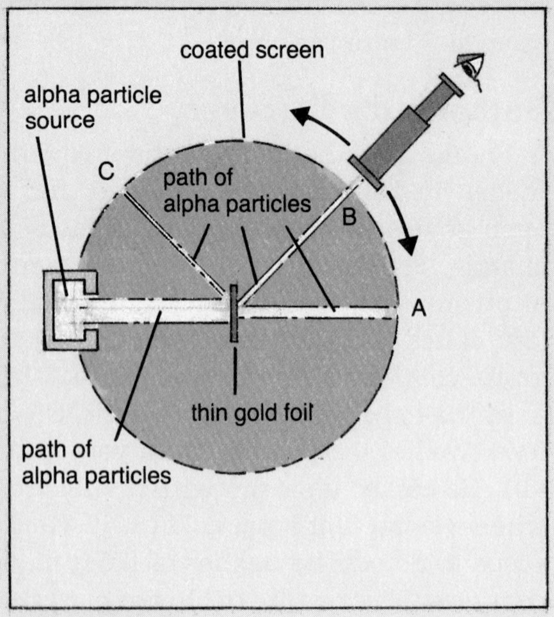 |

## Observations/Conclusions

Spot moved toward side of tube with positive electrode. This result proved that (1) rays were indeed negatively charged, (2) rays could not be light. Light not affected by electric fields. If they are not light waves, they might be particles.

No shift in spot location. This meant that fields were balanced. Using data and mathematics, Thomson could calculate the relationship of charge to mass of these cathode ray particles. Interpretation of results led him to a model of the atom.

## Thomson's Model

Atom made of negative particles equally mixed in a sphere of positive material. This model of the atom is called the plum pudding model.

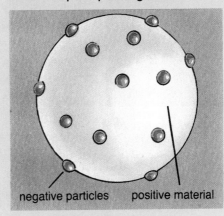

negative particles     positive material

## Observations/Conclusions

(A) Most of the alpha particles were found here. They passed straight through the foil. This result was expected.

(B) Some alpha particles were
& detected here. It was as if they
(C) had collided with a massive object and had bounced back. This bouncing back, or scattering, could not be satisfactorily explained by Thomson's model.

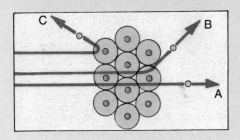

## Rutherford's Model

Most of the atom is empty space. This explained why most alpha particles passed straight through.

In the center of the atom is a nucleus containing most of the mass and all of the positive charge of the atom. Collision with nucleus reason for unusual scattering.

The region of space outside the nucleus is occupied by electrons. Hence, the atom is neutral.

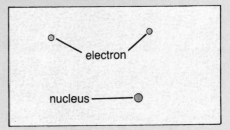

electron

nucleus

*Figure 8-5. When light passes through a prism, it breaks up into different colors.*

## The Bohr Atom

Based on the Rutherford model, scientists began to think that electrons might orbit the nucleus like planets move around the sun. But if this idea were correct, they would expect to observe two things. First, as the electrons moved about the nucleus they would give off light energy continuously. If this light energy were passed through a prism, it should produce a band of color as shown in Figure 8-5. No such band was observed. In fact, lines of color or dark lines like those in Chart 8-3 were seen! Second, as the orbiting electrons gave off light, they would lose energy. A loss of energy would mean that the electrons would spiral into the nucleus of the atom. The atom would then collapse. Thus, an atom would take up little or no space. However, you know this does not happen because matter *does* take up space.

**CHART 8-3. BOHR'S MODEL OF THE ATOM**

| Observations | |
|---|---|
| Atoms do exist and atoms are mostly empty space. Hence, electrons do not spiral into the nucleus. | 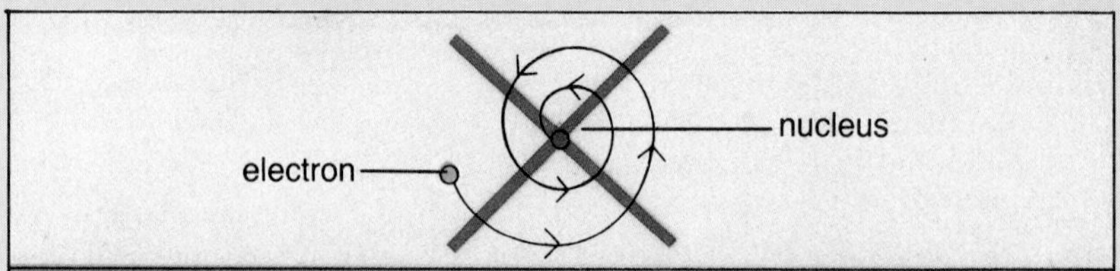 nucleus<br>electron |
| When a gas is heated, only certain colors of light are given off, or emitted, by the gas. |  hot gas tube<br>slit<br>prism<br>screen |
| When light is passed through a gas, certain colors of light are absorbed by the gas. | 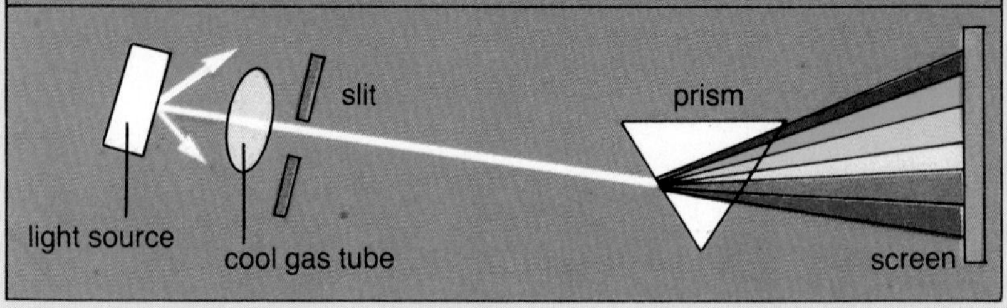 slit<br>prism<br>light source<br>cool gas tube<br>screen |

Since the current model could not explain their observations, the scientists needed a new model. Niels Bohr, a Danish scientist, came up with such a model in 1913. In the model, electrons move in certain orbits. The farther away from the nucleus, the more energy an electron has. By staying in their orbits, electrons do not lose energy continuously. They do not collapse into the nucleus. Bohr's model was just the starting point for more modern models of the atom.

## The Wave Model of the Atom

It was later shown that Bohr's model of the atom explained only the very simplest of atoms, like hydrogen. Today's atomic model is more complex than the Bohr model. It is based on mathematics and the way waves interact. The electron cloud pattern shown in Figure 8-6 is a major part of this new model. In this

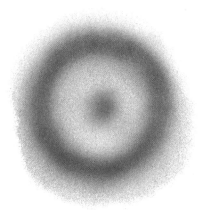

**Figure 8-6.** *According to the wave model of the atom, where do the electrons move?*

| Bohr's Model | | How Model Explains Observations |
|---|---|---|
| Electrons orbit the nucleus like planets orbit the sun. But only certain orbits are allowed. An electron moving in such an orbit will not lose energy. | 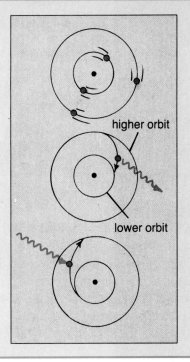 | As long as an electron stays in its orbit, it will not lose energy. Hence, the electron will not spiral into the nucleus. |
| When an electron moves from an outer orbit down to an inner orbit, it gives off energy. | higher orbit<br>lower orbit | To move to a lower orbit, an electron gives off a certain amount of energy. This energy appears as a line of a particular color. |
| When an electron moves from an inner orbit up to an outer orbit, it absorbs energy. | | To move to a higher orbit, an electron absorbs a certain amount of energy. This energy appears as a continuous band of color with dark lines. The dark lines indicate where energy has been absorbed. |

*Figure 8-7. A television picture tube uses beams of electrons to make the pictures received by the set.*

model, it is impossible to predict exactly where an electron is. Therefore, you cannot give an exact orbit for an electron. The electron cloud pattern shown in this chart represents the area where an electron is most likely to be found. The wave model forms the basis of a branch of physics called quantum mechanics.

● The experiments of Thomson and Rutherford paved the way for the invention of television. The picture tube in your television set is similar to the tubes shown in Chart 8-1. Compare the tube in Chart 8-1 with Figure 8-7. Electron guns in the picture tube fire electrons at the screen. Like Thomson's tube, a picture tube is also coated with a substance that glows when it is hit by an electron. As the electron beams move across the screen, they produce the picture sent out by the television station.

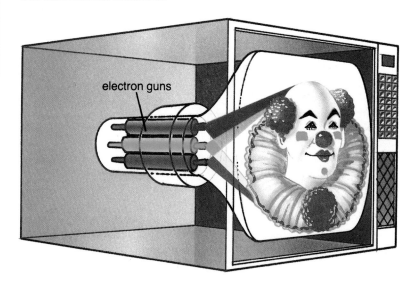

electron guns

**OBJECTIVES AND WORDS TO REVIEW**
**1.** Describe Thomson's model of the atom.
**2.** Explain how Rutherford discovered that an atom has a positive nucleus and a lot of empty space.
**3.** How does the Bohr model of the atom differ from the wave model of the atom?
**4.** Write a complete sentence for the term below.
   vacuum

# ATOMIC STRUCTURE AND ATOMIC MASS

An atom is like a peach. At the center of a peach is the pit. The pit represents the nucleus of an atom. Surrounding the peach is the fruit. The fruit represents the cloud through which electrons move.

## The Nucleus

Investigation of the nucleus began with a glass tube similar to the one used by Thomson. Again, the space inside the tube was nearly a vacuum. The small amount of gas remaining in it was hydrogen. Figure 8-8 shows what happened when an electric current made a direct hit on a hydrogen atom. The current knocked an electron away from the atom. When an electron is taken away from neutral hydrogen atoms, the remaining particles are positive.

**Protons**  These positive particles moved toward the negative end of the tube. Their mass was about 2,000 times the mass of an electron. Scientists investigating the model identified this particle as a hydrogen nucleus, or proton. Further experiments, using other gases in the tube, showed that the nuclei of all atoms contain protons. Scientists were also able to show that all atoms of the same element have the same number of protons. *The number of protons in the nucleus of each atom is called the* **atomic number** *of an element.* Elements are identified by this number.

**OBJECTIVES**

**1.** State the difference between atomic number and mass number.

**2.** Explain why the atomic mass of an element is not usually a whole number.

**3.** Describe where electrons are in atoms and what they need to change energy levels.

What particles are found in the nuclei of all atoms?

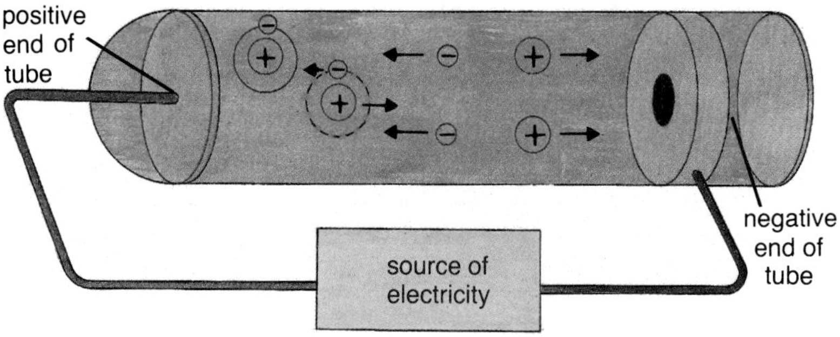

*Figure 8-8. Why do the electrons travel toward the positive end of the tube?*

positive end of tube

source of electricity

negative end of tube

**Neutrons**   Soon, a further discovery was made about the nucleus. While studying the gas neon, scientists found that not all of the atoms had the same mass. They had discovered the existence of *isotopes* (IGH•suh•tohps). *Isotopes of an element have the same number of protons in the nucleus, but have different masses.*

The discovery of isotopes presented a problem. How could two atoms of the same element have different masses and still have the same number of protons? There must be something else in the nucleus besides the proton!

In 1932 James Chadwick found another type of particle in the nucleus. This particle was called the neutron. The mass of the neutron is about the same as that of a proton, but it has no charge. It is neutral.

## Relative Mass

The discovery of neutrons explained why isotopes exist. Although all atoms of a certain element contain the same number of protons, the number of neutrons can vary. Thus, atoms of the same element can have different masses.

When you measure the mass of an object, you compare the unknown mass with a standard mass such as a gram. To find the masses of atoms, scientists begin by choosing one kind of atom to use as a standard. Then they do experiments to find how the mass of another atom compares with that of the standard atom. They find the *relative mass*. The **relative mass** of an atom is its mass expressed in terms of the mass of the standard atom. Scientists use an isotope of the element carbon as the standard atom.

The most common isotope of carbon has six neutrons and is called carbon-12. Carbon-12 is the standard atom used to find the masses of other atoms.

This isotope of carbon has been assigned a mass of 12 *atomic mass units*. The **atomic mass unit** (amu) is the standard unit for measuring the mass of an atom. It is equal to 1/12 the mass of a carbon-12 atom. Table

**TABLE 8-1.** ATOMIC PARTICLE MASSES

| Proton | 1 | amu |
|---|---|---|
| Neutron | 1 | amu |
| Electron | 0.0006 | amu |

8-1 gives the masses in amu's of particles making up atoms. If an atom of an element is twice as massive as the standard carbon-12 atom, it has a mass of 24 amu.

## Atomic Mass

In any sample of an element, there is a mixture of isotopes. For example, even the tiniest speck of carbon contains millions of atoms. As Figure 8-9 shows, most of these atoms are carbon-12. Carbon-12 has six protons and six neutrons. The 12 in carbon-12 is the *mass number. The **mass number** of an atom is the sum of its protons and neutrons.* In the same sample of carbon a few atoms are carbon-13 atoms. Still fewer are the carbon-14 atoms. See the mass number entries for the isotopes of carbon in Table 8-2.

As a result of elements being a mixture of isotopes, when scientists find the relative masses of atoms, the numbers they find are really averages. *The **atomic mass** of an element is an average of the masses of its atoms.* The atomic mass of carbon is 12.011. This decimal reflects the small amounts of heavier isotopes of carbon mixed in with carbon-12. Table 8-2 is a summary of the differences between the term atomic number, mass number, and atomic mass.

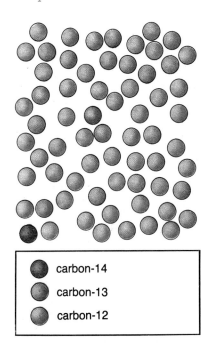

*Figure 8-9. Relative number of isotopes in a sample of carbon. Which isotope has the greatest number in the sample?*

- ● carbon-14
- ● carbon-13
- ● carbon-12

**TABLE 8-2.** TERMS USED TO DESCRIBE ATOMIC NUCLEI

| Term | Meaning | Characteristics | Examples |
|------|---------|-----------------|----------|
| Atomic number | number of protons (p) | same for all atoms of a given element | Carbon (C): atomic number = 6 (6p) |
| Mass number | number of protons plus number of neutrons (n) (p + n) | changes for different isotopes of an element | C-12 (6 p + 6 n) C-13 (6 p + 7 n) C-14 (6 p + 8 n) |
| Atomic mass | average mass of atoms of the element | usually not a whole number because many isotopes are present | atomic mass of carbon = 12.011 amu |

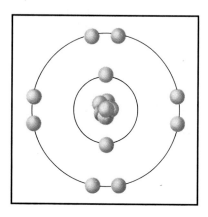

Figure 8-10. The Bohr model of neon shows complete first and second energy levels. What is the atomic number of neon?

CHART 8-4. SOME ENERGY LEVELS OF THE ATOM

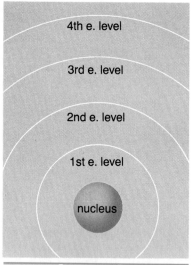

| Level | Name of Level | Max. No. Electrons in Level |
|---|---|---|
| First | K shell | 2 |
| Second | L shell | 8 |
| Third | M shell | 18 |
| Fourth | N shell | 32 |

# Electrons in Atoms

Atoms are neutral. Each atom has as many negative particles, electrons, as it has positive particles, protons. As the models of the atom have shown, electrons are thought to surround the nucleus.

**Electrons in the Bohr Model**   According to the Bohr model of the atom, electrons can orbit the nucleus only at certain distances. The more energy an electron has, the farther from the nucleus it orbits. Hence, these orbits are also called energy levels. The closer the energy level is to the nucleus, the lower the energy of the electrons. See Figure 8-10.

**Arrangement of Electrons**   Atoms range in size from having one proton and one electron to atoms with over one hundred protons and electrons. Electrons are thought to occupy energy levels in an order. The electrons tend to occupy the lowest available energy levels in an atom. *If an atom has all its electrons in the lowest possible energy levels, that atom has a* **stable electron arrangement.**

Each energy level holds a maximum number of electrons. The first level can hold up to 2 electrons. Other levels can hold more. See Chart 8-4. However, an atom with more than one energy level does not hold more than 8 electrons in its outermost level.

# Behavior of Electrons

Scientists believe that these ideas explain why chemical reactions occur. Atoms usually react with each other only when their outer energy levels are unfilled. These energy levels can become filled when atoms exchange or share electrons with each other. As a result, the atoms usually become more stable.

**Moving to Higher Energy Levels**   According to Bohr theory, as an electron gains energy, it moves from one energy level to another, higher level. See Chart 8-4. The electron will not leave its energy level, however, unless it has enough energy to reach a higher level. Otherwise, the electron will stay where it is. Thus, electrons can absorb only certain amounts of energy. Such electrons are said to be *excited*. **Excited electrons** *are electrons that have absorbed energy and have moved farther from the nucleus.*

**Moving to Lower Energy Levels**    Electrons can also lose energy. But the electrons can fall only to the lowest level that has room for them. If there is no room, they will not fall to lower energy levels. Electrons can give off only certain amounts of energy. They move to lower levels only if those levels are not filled. This idea explains why atoms do not collapse.

● You have often seen neon signs advertising a product. Such signs glow orange-red. Why does the sign give off this color?

When current goes through the gas in the sign, electrons absorb a definite amount of energy. They jump to a higher energy level for a very short time. When they return to their original level, they give off this same amount of energy as light energy. Each energy value has its own color, like the colors in a spectrum. When electrons in neon atoms drop to a lower level, the light energy they give off is orange-red. If other gases were used, they would also give off their own specific color.

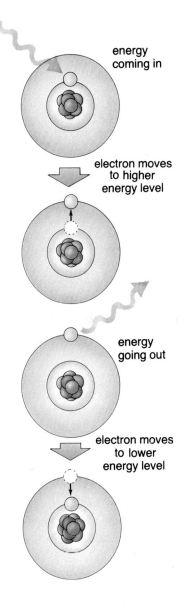

energy coming in

electron moves to higher energy level

energy going out

electron moves to lower energy level

*Figure 8-11. An electron absorbs a certain amount of energy as it moves to a higher energy level.*

### OBJECTIVES AND WORDS TO REVIEW

1. State the difference between the atomic number and the mass number of an atom.
2. Why are the atomic masses of elements not usually whole numbers?
3. What does an electron need to move farther away from the nucleus?
4. Write one complete sentence for each term listed below.

| | | |
|---|---|---|
| atomic number | atomic mass unit | stable electron |
| isotope | mass number | arrangement |
| relative mass | atomic mass | excited electron |

# MAKING MODELS BASED ON INDIRECT EVIDENCE

### Preparation

Suppose you hear sounds coming from a television set. You have not seen the television. But you can still form a mental image of what is on the screen based on what you heard. This mental image is called a model. A model is a representation of an object or an idea.

A scientist often uses models to explain something that is invisible and theoretical. In this instance, the scientific model results from data collected through indirect observations.

### Directions

Suppose you have a box in front of you whose contents are unknown. You want to find out what is inside the box, but you cannot open it. How can you determine what is inside the box?

You can determine the contents of the box by making indirect observations. For example, what will happen to the object if the box is tilted? By performing various tests and recording indirect observations, you can find out what is inside.

Table 1 lists the results of two trials performed on the box. Look at Trial 1. What conclusions can

be drawn? The unknown object is probably round since it rolls freely when the box is tilted. It is probably a solid object since it bounces hard. Based on these indirect observations, a model can be sketched. See Figure 1.

*Figure 1.*

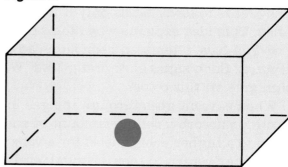

### Practice

Look at Trial 2 of Table 1. Study the results of the tests performed on the box. Then, on a separate sheet of paper, write or draw a model of the object.

### Application

After reading Chapter 8 and studying the different models of atoms, make a three-dimensional model of an electron as it moves to a higher energy level. You may wish to refer to Figure 8-11, which is a two-dimensional model.

| TABLE 1. | | |
|---|---|---|
| **Test Performed** | **Results** | |
| | **Trial 1** | **Trial 2** |
| Box is tilted. | Object rolls. | Object slides. |
| Box turned on edge and tilted. | Object still rolls. | Object rolls. |
| Box shaken up and down. | Object bounces off top and bottom very hard. | Object seems to flip inside box. |

# LABORATORY ACTIVITY

## MODELS OF ATOMS

### Objective
Investigate models of atoms using indirect evidence.

### Background
Atomic models are based on indirect evidence. Scientists observe the behavior of atoms. Then they construct a model to explain the behavior. In this experiment your group will be given a box. Inside the boxes are models of atoms. Some boxes are Thomson models, others are Rutherford models.

You may not look inside the box. By rolling marbles into the box and observing their behavior, you will decide which model you have.

### Materials
box, 10 marbles, cardboard chute, sheet of paper

### Procedure
1. Hold the chute at a 45° angle to the entrance of the box just under the fringe. See Figure 8-L.
2. Let the marble roll inside the box.
3. On a sheet of paper draw a line to represent the direction of the marble as it left the box.
4. Repeat with the other marbles, but move chute to different positions along the entrance.
5. Draw lines for each marble's path.
6. Record how many marbles remained in the box.

### Questions
1. How many marbles rolled out of the box in a straight line?
2. How many marbles, if any, rolled out at an angle?
3. How many marbles, if any, remained in the box?
4. What do the marbles represent?
5. From your data explain which model of the atom is in the box.
6. **PROBLEM SOLVING** If you decreased the angle of the chute to 15°, how would your data support your answer to #5?

*Figure 8-L.* Laboratory setup.

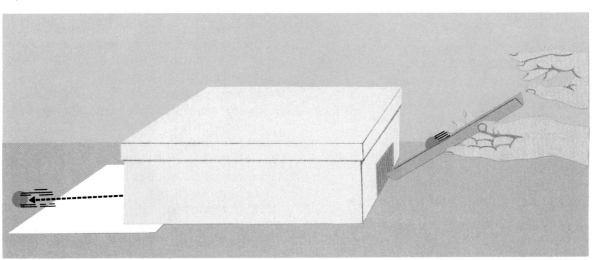

# SUMMARY

1. Dalton said that all atoms of one kind of matter are alike. Atoms combine with each other and form new kinds of substances. (8-1)

2. Thomson said the atom was made of negative particles mixed in a sphere of positive material. Rutherford suggested that the atom had a positive nucleus and electrons in a region around the nucleus. (8-2)

3. Bohr pictured the atom as having a positively charged nucleus with electrons orbiting the nucleus like planets orbiting the sun. Today the electron is pictured as being in a cloud pattern. (8-2)

4. The atomic number of an atom is the number of protons in its nucleus. The mass number is the sum of its protons and neutrons. (8-3)

5. If an atom has all its electrons in the lowest possible energy levels, the atom has a stable electron arrangement. (8-3)

# REVIEW

Number a sheet of paper from 1 to 25 and answer these questions.

**Building Science Vocabulary**   Write the letter of the term that best matches each definition.

a. atomic mass
b. atomic mass unit
c. atomic number
d. electrode
e. electron
f. excited electron
g. isotopes
h. mass number
i. neutron
j. proton
k. stable electron arrangement
l. vacuum

1. A space from which all matter has been removed
2. Metal strips at each end of a vacuum tube

3. Number of protons in nucleus of atom
4. An electron that has absorbed energy and moved farther from the nucleus
5. Positively charged particle in nucleus of atom
6. Atoms of same element with different masses
7. Equal to $\frac{1}{12}$ the mass of a carbon-12 atom
8. Sum of protons and neutrons of atom
9. The average of the masses of all the atoms of an element
10. An atom having all its electrons in the lowest energy levels

**Finding the Facts**   Select the letter of the answer that best completes each of the following.

11. According to Dalton, all atoms of hydrogen are   (a) different   (b) alike   (c) like oxygen atoms   (d) like the atoms of all other elements.

12. The first people to call the particles of matter atoms were the   (a) British   (b) Danish (c) alchemists   (d) Greeks.

13. In Thomson's model of the atom, the particles that were scattered like plums in a pudding were   (a) electrons   (b) protons (c) neutrons   (d) alpha particles.

14. The isotope of carbon that is used as a standard in finding relative atomic masses is   (a) carbon-6   (b) carbon-12 (c) carbon-13   (d) carbon-14.

15. Aluminum has an atomic number of 13 and a mass number of 27. The number of neutrons in aluminum is   (a) 40   (b) 27 (c) 14   (d) 13.

16. The atomic model in which electrons are seen as moving in a cloud pattern is the (a) wave   (b) Bohr   (c) nuclear (d) plum pudding.

17. In Bohr's model, electrons are located in (a) the nucleus   (b) energy levels (c) a positive "pudding"   (d) clouds.

**18.** The maximum number of electrons in the outermost energy level of an atom is (**a**) 2    (**b**) 4    (**c**) 6    (**d**) 8.

**19.** An atom has the same number of electrons as its    (**a**) atomic number    (**b**) atomic mass    (**c**) mass number    (**d**) isotopes.

**20.** When an electron moves from a lower orbit to a higher orbit, the electron    (**a**) gives off energy    (**b**) absorbs energy    (**c**) spirals into the nucleus    (**d**) gives off light.

**Understanding Main Ideas**    Complete the following.

**21.** Based on the results of his gold foil experiment, Rutherford proposed that most of the atom's mass is in a positively charged _?_.

**22.** Rutherford also proposed that the atom's electrons are outside the nucleus in what is mostly _?_.

**23.** The atomic mass of an element is not usually a whole number because it is an _?_ of the masses of all the isotopes of the element.

**24.** When excited electrons in a tube of neon gas fall back into lower energy levels, they give up energy in the form of _?_.

**25.** Elements usually react with each other only when the outer energy levels of their atoms are not _?_.

**Writing About Science**    On a separate sheet of paper, answer the following as completely as possible.

**1.** You have never seen radio waves travel through space from the radio station into your radio. How do you know they exist?

**2.** Suppose the results of Rutherford's gold foil experiment had turned out differently. Instead of some of the positive alpha particles being scattered when they hit the foil suppose all of them went right through. What would Rutherford have concluded about the atom?

**3.** When you open a bottle of household ammonia, the gas quickly escapes into the air. Soon you smell ammonia all over the room. How would Dalton explain this?

**4.** An isotope of element X has an atomic mass of 45. The atomic number of element X is 21. How many neutrons are in the nucleus of X?

**5.** (laboratory question) Imagine that you did an experiment to find relative masses. You use 50 buttons as a standard mass. The mass of the 50 buttons is 30 g. The mass of 50 beans turns out to be 60 g, and 50 tacks have a mass of 15 g. What are the relative masses of the beans and the tacks as compared with the standard?

**Investigating Chapter Ideas**    Try one of the following projects to further your study.

**1. Measuring atomic masses**    Scientists use a mass spectrometer to measure accurately the mass of atoms and molecules. Set up a poster to show how this device works.

**2. Images with electrons**    Electron beams are used to make TV images. They are also used to make images in powerful microscopes called electron microscopes. Sketch an electron microscope. Explain how it works.

**Reading About Science**    Read some of the following books to explore topics that interest you.

Apfel, Necia. 1981. **It's All Relative: Einstein's Theory of Relativity.** New York: Lothrop.

Ardley, Neil. 1982. **Atoms and Energy.** New York: Warwick.

Chester, Michael. 1978. **Particles: An Introduction to Particle Physics.** New York: Macmillan.

Pagels, Heinz R. 1982. **The Cosmic Code; Quantum Physics as the Language of Nature.** New York: Simon and Schuster.

Schwartz, and McGuinness. 1979. **Einstein for Beginners.** New York: Random House.

Imagine you are an engineer working on building a bridge. How can you make sure the bridge will be safe? One way is to use materials that have desirable properties. What metals might you use to make the girders or cables? Would you use gold or lead? If not, why not?

How would you decide what metals to use? There are too many metals with too many properties to remember. A table that groups metals with similar properties might be helpful. Then you could find metals with the needed properties.

Such a table exists. It is called the Periodic Table of the Elements. It does not group just metals, but all elements. You will see how this table suggests patterns in properties of the elements.

Read and Find Out:
● how a new element was produced.
● why the Statue of Liberty had to be cleaned.
● why Cleopatra may have lacked the element iodine.
● about an element that can change sunlight into electricity.

# PUTTING THE
# ELEMENTS IN ORDER

# A TABLE OF THE ELEMENTS

*Figure 9-1. Potassium reacts violently with water. It must be stored carefully to be moisture free.*

In some ways scientists are like detectives. They look for clues about the elements. From the clues they then arrange the elements until they can see patterns. From the patterns they solve riddles about properties of unknown elements. This section explains how chemists looked for patterns.

## Developing a Classification System

Many new elements were discovered during the last century. In fact, by the early 1800's chemists had noticed that some elements had similar properties. For example, sodium and potassium had similar physical properties. They are both soft, shiny metals. They have a common chemical property. They behave explosively when dropped into water. See Figure 9-1. This kind of increase in knowledge about the elements was so great that some attempt had to be made to organize them.

**Early Arrangements of Elements** Many attempts were made to group elements according to their physical and chemical properties. One chemist proposed that properties were repeated every eighth element when arranged by atomic weight. However, this pattern held true only for the first few elements. A system that was useful for all the elements was needed.

Dmitri Mendeleev (di•MEE•tree men•duh•LAY•ef), a Russian chemist, developed a table of elements that grew into the one used today. He arranged the elements according to atomic weight.

Figure 9-2 shows an early version of Mendeleev's table. He grouped elements by atomic weight so that those with similar properties were next to each other. Notice the gaps indicated by the question marks. They represent elements he predicted would be discovered one day. He studied the patterns of properties of the elements around these gaps. From his studies, he predicted the properties of these missing elements. When later chemists discovered these elements, Mendeleev's predictions were found to be largely correct.

**Modern Arrangements**   Using atomic weight to arrange the elements causes breaks in the patterns of properties. So, atomic weight is not the best way to arrange the elements. Another way to arrange the elements was needed.

In 1913 the English scientist Henry Moseley used X rays to determine the atomic number of the elements. Atomic number is the number of protons in the nucleus. When Moseley arranged the elements according to their atomic numbers, the arrangement gave truer patterns of properties than Mendeleev's. As a result, the modern Table of Elements is based on atomic number.

## The Periodic Table of Elements

The modern arrangement of the elements is called *periodic. When a property is repeated within a regular interval, that property is said to be* **periodic.** It occurs over and over, like the seasons of the year.

Study Table 9-1 on pages 182–183. It is called the Periodic Table of Elements. The table consists of rows and columns. This arrangement makes it easy to locate elements with similar properties.

## EXPLORE BY READING

**HOW THE ELEMENTS GOT THEIR NAMES**

**OBJECTIVE**
Make the names of the chemical elements more meaningful.

**PROCEDURE**
**1.** Use the Periodic Table to find elements that were named after (a) countries, (b) states, (c) scientists, (d) planets.
**2.** Make a list of the elements you found in each of the four groups. Bring your list to class.

**What did Moseley learn when he arranged elements by atomic number?**

*Figure 9-2. Mendeleev's original arrangement of the elements by atomic weight. What two elements have properties similar to the predicted element of atomic mass 68?*

### Таблица II.
Вторая нопытка Менделѣева найти естественную систему химическихъ элементовъ. Перепечатана безъ измѣненій изъ „Журнала Русскаго Химическаго Общества", т. III, стр. 31 (1871 г.).

| | Группа I. | Группа II. | Группа III. | Группа IV. | Группа V. | Группа VI. | Группа VII. | Группа VIII, переходъ къ группѣ I. |
|---|---|---|---|---|---|---|---|---|
| | H=1 | | | | | | | |
| Типическіе элементы. | Li=7 | Be=9,₄ | B=11 | C=12 | N=14 | O=16 | F=19 | |
| 1-й періодъ. Рядъ 1-й. | Na=23 | Mg=24 | Al=27,₃ | Si=28 | P=31 | S=32 | Cl=35,₅ | |
| — 2-й. | K=39 | Ca=40 | ?=44 | Ti=50? | V=51 | Cr=52 | Mn=55 | Fe=56, Co=59 Ni=59, Cu=63 |
| 2-й періодъ. — 3-й. | (Cu=63) | Zn=65 | ?=68 | ?=72 | As=75 | Se=78 | Br=80 | |
| — 4-й. | Rb=85 | Sr=87 | Yt?=88? | Zr=90 | Nb=94 | Mo=96 | - =100 | Ru=104, Rh=104 Pd=104, Ag=108 |
| 3-й періодъ. — 5-й. | (Ag=108) | Cd=112 | In=113 | Sn=118 | Sb=122 | Te=128? | J=127 | |
| — 6-й. | Cs=133 | Ba=137 | — =137 | Ce=138? | — | | | |
| 4-й періодъ. — 7-й. | — | — | — | — | | | | |
| — 8-й. | — | | — | — | Ta=182 | W=184 | — | Os=199?, Ir=198? Pt=197, Au=197 |
| 5-й | (Au=197) | Hg=200 | Tl=204 | Pb=207 | Bi=208 | — | | |

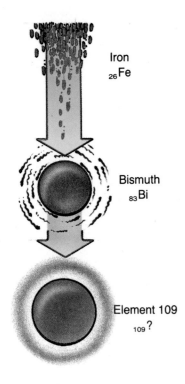

Iron
$_{26}Fe$

Bismuth
$_{83}Bi$

Element 109
$_{109}?$

*Figure 9-3. Element 109 was formed when iron nuclei were shot at bismuth. Why is the element called 109?*

**Periods**   *The **periods** are the rows across the Table.* They are referred to as first period, second period, and so on. To what period does the gas chlorine belong? If you thought the third period, you are correct.

**Groups**   Look at chlorine again. At the top of its column you see "VIIA." *The columns of the Periodic Table are called **groups**.* They are also called families. Elements in a family have similar properties. They resemble each other like members of a human family. What group, or family, does the element sodium belong to?

**Using the Table**   Mendeleev left some blank spaces in his periodic table. He listed the 63 elements known at that time, but he knew more would be discovered. By the time of his death in 1907 there were 86 elements in the table. These were discovered by using Mendeleev's table. New elements continue to be discovered.

● At 4:10 p.m. on August 29, 1983, a new element was reported. Its name is element 109. It got its name from the 109 protons in its nucleus. It was reported by scientists in the Federal Republic of Germany. Other scientists, however, must produce the element before its existence is accepted.

Element 109 was formed by shooting iron nuclei at bismuth. See Figure 9-3. Some of the iron nuclei stuck to, or fused with, the bismuth to form the new element. Element 109 broke down, or decayed, 0.0005 seconds later by releasing an alpha particle. In Chapter 8 you learned that uranium gives off particles with a positive charge. These particles, called alpha particles, are 7000 times heavier than electrons. The release of this particle told the scientists that a new element had been formed.

**OBJECTIVES AND WORDS TO REVIEW**

**1.** Give two reasons why it was necessary to organize the elements.
**2.** Why did Mendeleev leave some blank spaces in his periodic table of the elements?
**3.** Why are the elements in the modern periodic table arranged in order of atomic number rather than in order of atomic weight?
**4.** Write one complete sentence for each term listed below.
   periodic      period      group

# METALS AND THEIR PROPERTIES

Think about some of the metals with which you are familiar. What properties do they have? Many properties of metals are easily seen. However, some are not. All of these properties are important. You will now study some of the properties of metals.

## Physical Properties of Metals

Look at the metal objects in Figure 9-4. How many properties of metals can you recognize in these photos? Metals have many properties in common.

**Metals Have Luster**   Metals can be recognized by their *shininess,* or **luster.** The high luster of metals has made them valuable as material for jewelry since ancient times. All of the metals except mercury are solid at room temperatures. Notice, however, that even liquid mercury has the high luster characteristic of metals.

*Figure 9-4. The properties of metals make them useful in everyday life.*

## EXPLORE BY TRYING

### METALS CONDUCT HEAT

**OBJECTIVE**
Identify metals by their ability to conduct heat.

**MATERIALS**
plastic foam cup, hot water, silver or steel teaspoon, plastic spoon, iron nail, strip of wood, aluminum foil

**PROCEDURE**
**1.** Roll a piece of aluminum foil into a thin cylinder (about the size of a small pencil).
**2.** Stand the teaspoon, plastic spoon, wood strip, aluminum cylinder, and iron nail upright in the cup.
**3.** Add almost boiling water to the cup, leaving the tops of the objects exposed.
**CAUTION:** Do not spill the water on yourself.
**4.** Wait one minute. Carefully touch the exposed ends of the objects in the cup.
**5.** Give the best conductor a rating of 1, the worst a rating of 5. Rate all of the others.

**QUESTIONS**
**1.** Which objects were good heat conductors?
**2.** Which objects did not conduct heat?
**3.** Of what materials are the good heat conductors made?

**Metals Are Malleable and Ductile**    Look at the silverware or the aluminum foil in Figure 9-4. They exhibit another property of metals. Some metals are *malleable* (MAL•ee•uh•buhl). *A substance that can be hammered or shaped without breaking is said to be* **malleable.**

Some metals can be drawn into wires. *Substances that can be drawn into wires are* **ductile** (DUHK•tuhl). Copper and platinum are ductile materials.

**Metals are Conductors**    Metals are conductors of electricity, that is, they will allow electrons to pass through them. Copper and aluminum are both good conductors. Copper is preferred over aluminum when wiring houses for electricity. Aluminum may melt and cause electrical fires.

Metals are also good conductors of heat. Pots and pans used in cooking are made of metals such as copper or aluminum because of this property. Aluminum is used more frequently than copper because it is cheaper than copper.

## Chemical Properties of Metals

The chemical properties of all elements depend mainly on the electrons in the outer energy level. Metals have one, two, or three electrons in their outermost energy levels. These electrons play a very important role in the way metals react.

Most metals have the same general set of properties. By learning these general chemical properties, you can often predict how a metal will react.

**Metals Can Be Corroded**    Have you ever been in a junkyard like the one shown in Figure 9-5? Notice how the metal parts of the cars are rusty from being in the moist air. The metal has reacted with oxygen in the air. This reaction is a special form of *corrosion* (kuh•ROH•zhuhn). **Corrosion** *is the gradual eating away of a metal in which the metal element is changed into a metallic compound.* Whether or not a metal can be corroded is a chemical property of the metal. Iron can be corroded. Gold cannot. Corrosion affects buildings, automobiles, and other metal structures. Millions of dollars are spent each year in replacing corroded metals. What other objects have you seen corroded?

Metals can combine with oxygen. *The chemical combination of oxygen with another substance is called* **oxidation** (ahk•suh•DAY•shuhn). Oxidation results in the formation of an *oxide.* **Oxides** *are compounds of oxygen and another element.* The oxides of some metals destroy the metal. Iron oxide, rust, is an example. Other oxides, such as zinc oxide, protect the metal. See Figure 9-6.

**Metals Can React With Water**   Some metals, like sodium, react with water. In this reaction extreme heat is released. The reaction produces a gas. Because of the extreme heat, the gas sometimes catches fire. An explosion may result. Can you imagine what would happen if a metal like aluminum reacted the same way?

## Groups of Metals

The Periodic Table arranges metals into families. By studying the families, it is easier to learn about metals. Families of elements are like real families. The members have similar, but not identical, properties.

*Figure 9-5. (left) Iron combines with oxygen and forms rust.*

*Figure 9-6. (right) Steel wool can be used to polish aluminum.*

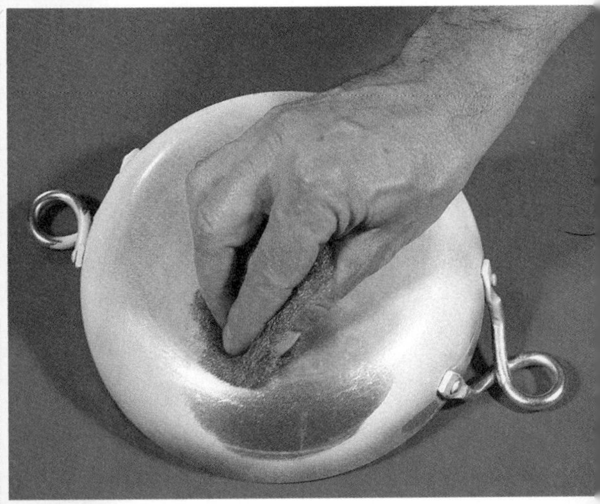

**TABLE 9-1.** THE PERIODIC TABLE OF THE ELEMENTS

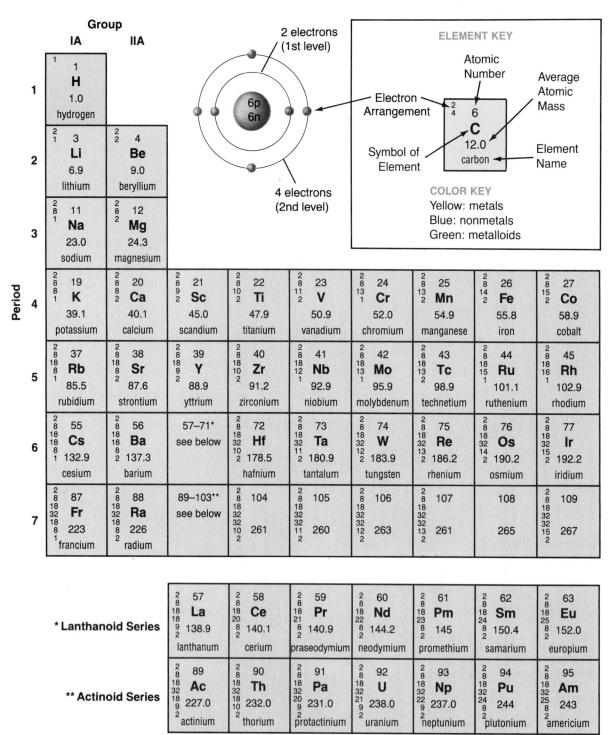

| | |
|---|---|
| **Group** | |
| IA | IIA |

**2 electrons (1st level)**

**ELEMENT KEY**

Atomic Number

Average Atomic Mass

Electron Arrangement

Symbol of Element

Element Name

**4 electrons (2nd level)**

**COLOR KEY**
Yellow: metals
Blue: nonmetals
Green: metalloids

| IIIA | IVA | VA | VIA | VIIA | VIIIA | Period |
|---|---|---|---|---|---|---|
| | | | | | 2<br>2 **He** 4.0 helium | 1 |
| 2 3 — 5 **B** 10.8 boron | 2 4 — 6 **C** 12.0 carbon | 2 5 — 7 **N** 14.0 nitrogen | 2 6 — 8 **O** 16.0 oxygen | 2 7 — 9 **F** 19.0 fluorine | 2 8 — 10 **Ne** 20.2 neon | 2 |
| 2 8 3 — 13 **Al** 27.0 aluminum | 2 8 4 — 14 **Si** 28.1 silicon | 2 8 5 — 15 **P** 31.0 phosphorus | 2 8 6 — 16 **S** 32.1 sulfur | 2 8 7 — 17 **Cl** 35.5 chlorine | 2 8 8 — 18 **Ar** 39.9 argon | 3 |
| 2 8 18 3 — 31 **Ga** 69.7 gallium | 2 8 18 4 — 32 **Ge** 72.6 germanium | 2 8 18 5 — 33 **As** 74.9 arsenic | 2 8 18 6 — 34 **Se** 79.0 selenium | 2 8 18 7 — 35 **Br** 79.9 bromine | 2 8 18 8 — 36 **Kr** 83.8 krypton | 4 |
| 2 8 18 3 — 49 **In** 114.8 indium | 2 8 18 4 — 50 **Sn** 118.7 tin | 2 8 18 5 — 51 **Sb** 121.8 antimony | 2 8 18 6 — 52 **Te** 127.6 tellurium | 2 8 18 7 — 53 **I** 126.9 iodine | 2 8 18 8 — 54 **Xe** 131.3 xenon | 5 |
| 2 8 18 32 18 3 — 81 **Ti** 204.4 thallium | 2 8 18 32 18 4 — 82 **Pb** 207.2 lead | 2 8 18 32 18 5 — 83 **Bi** 209.0 bismuth | 2 8 18 32 18 6 — 84 **Po** 209 polonium | 2 8 18 32 18 7 — 85 **At** 210 astatine | 2 8 18 32 18 8 — 86 **Rn** 222 radon | 6 |

Note — Period 4, Groups preceding (Ni, Cu, Zn):

| | | | | | | |
|---|---|---|---|---|---|---|
| 2 8 16 2 — 28 **Ni** 58.7 nickel | 2 8 18 1 — 29 **Cu** 63.5 copper | 2 8 18 2 — 30 **Zn** 65.4 zinc | | | | 4 |
| 2 8 18 18 0 — 46 **Pd** 106.4 palladium | 2 8 18 18 1 — 47 **Ag** 107.9 silver | 2 8 18 18 2 — 48 **Cd** 112.4 cadmium | | | | 5 |
| 2 8 18 32 16 2 — 78 **Pt** 195.1 platinum | 2 8 18 32 18 1 — 79 **Au** 197.0 gold | 2 8 18 32 18 2 — 80 **Hg** 200.6 mercury | | | | 6 |

| | | | | | | | |
|---|---|---|---|---|---|---|---|
| 2 8 18 25 9 2 — 64 **Gd** 157.3 gadolinium | 2 8 18 27 8 2 — 65 **Tb** 158.9 terbium | 2 8 18 28 8 2 — 66 **Dy** 162.5 dysprosium | 2 8 18 29 8 2 — 67 **Ho** 164.9 holmium | 2 8 18 30 8 2 — 68 **Er** 167.3 erbium | 2 8 18 31 8 2 — 69 **Tm** 168.9 thulium | 2 8 18 32 8 2 — 70 **Yb** 173.0 ytterbium | 2 8 18 32 9 2 — 71 **Lu** 175.0 lutetium |
| 2 8 18 32 25 9 2 — 96 **Cm** 247 curium | 2 8 18 32 27 8 2 — 97 **Bk** 247 berkelium | 2 8 18 32 28 8 2 — 98 **Cf** 251 californium | 2 8 18 32 29 8 2 — 99 **Es** 254 einsteinium | 2 8 18 32 30 8 2 — 100 **Fm** 253 fermium | 2 8 18 32 31 8 2 — 101 **Md** 256 mendelevium | 2 8 18 32 32 8 2 — 102 **No** 253 nobelium | 2 8 18 32 32 9 2 — 103 **Lr** 257 lawrencium |

Sodium

## CHART 9-1. ALKALI METALS

| Element | | Properties and Uses |
|---|---|---|
| | $^2_1$ **3** Li 6.9 lithium | Soft, silvery; reacts violently with water |
| | | Lithium compounds used to treat mental illnesses |
| | $^2_8$$_1$ **11** Na 23.0 sodium | Soft, white, silvery; reacts violently with water |
| | | Sodium compounds used to make soap |
| | $^2_8$$_8$$_1$ **19** K 39.1 potassium | Soft, silvery white; reacts violently with moisture |
| | | Potassium compounds used to make fertilizers |
| | $^2_8$$_{18}$$_8$$_1$ **37** Rb 85.5 rubidium | Soft, lustrous; reacts violently with moisture |
| | | Rubidium compounds used in space vehicle engines |
| | $^2_8$$_{18}$$_{18}$$_8$$_1$ **55** Cs 132.9 cesium | Silvery white, ductile; reacts with moisture |
| | | Cesium compounds used in photocells |
| | $^2_8$$_{18}$$_{32}$$_{18}$$_8$$_1$ **87** Fr 223 francium | Extremely rate |
| | | Francium compounds not widely used |

**Alkali Metals**   With the exception of hydrogen, all the elements in the column marked IA in the Periodic Table belong to the alkali (AL•kuh•ligh) metal family. They are softer and less dense than most metals. They can be cut with a knife. They are shiny metals, silver in color. These metals are the most chemically active metals. That is, alkali metals will react more quickly than other metals. Refer to the Periodic Table on pages 182–183 to see the relative position of these metals to

## CHART 9-2. ALKALINE EARTH METALS

| Element | Properties and Uses |
|---|---|
| 2 2 **4** **Be** **9.0** beryllium | Poisonous; among lightest of all metals<br><br>Beryllium compounds used in some types of steel; radio parts |
| 2 8 2 **12** **Mg** **24.3** magnesium | Burns with a bright white flame<br><br>Magnesium compounds used in medicine, flashbulbs, flares |
| 2 8 8 2 **20** **Ca** **40.1** calcium | Silvery, tarnishes in moist air<br><br>Calcium compounds used in metal bearings, plaster, and cement |
| 2 8 18 8 2 **38** **Sr** **87.6** strontium | Catches fire when powdered; combines with oxygen in air<br><br>Strontium compounds used in flares, fireworks |
| 2 8 18 18 8 2 **56** **Ba** **137.3** barium | Very active; combines with oxygen in air; must be kept in kerosene<br><br>Barium compounds used in paints and glassmaking |
| 2 8 18 32 18 8 2 **88** **Ra** **226.0** radium | Brilliant white<br><br>Radium compounds are used in research and treatment of cancer |

Magnesium

other elements in the Periodic Table. Some of the properties and uses of these metals are shown in Chart 9-1.

**Alkaline Earth Metals**   The metals in the column marked IIA belong to the alkaline (AL•kuh•lighn) earth metal family. These metals are harder and denser than the alkali metals. They also have higher melting and boiling points. They are chemically active. Chart 9-2 shows the alkaline earth metals and gives some properties and uses of each.

CHART 9-3. TRANSITION ELEMENTS OF PERIOD 4

| Element | 26<br>Fe<br>55.8<br>iron | 27<br>Co<br>58.9<br>cobalt | 28<br>Ni<br>58.7<br>nickel | 29<br>Cu<br>63.5<br>copper |
|---|---|---|---|---|
| |  |  | 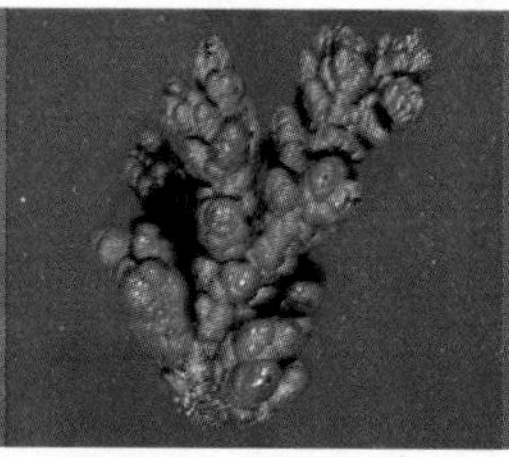 |  |
| Some Properties | strong, malleable, magnetic | hard, ductile, magnetic | malleable, ductile | good conductor |
| Uses | structural metal | machine tools, magnets | jewelry, coins, batteries | electrical wires, electrical motors |

CHART 9-4. TRANSITION ELEMENTS: SILVER AND GOLD

| Element | | Some Properties | Uses |
|---|---|---|---|
| 47<br>Ag<br>107.9<br>silver |  | ductile, malleable, good conductor of heat and electricity | electrical conductors, jewelry, dental fillings |
| 79<br>Au<br>197.0<br>gold | 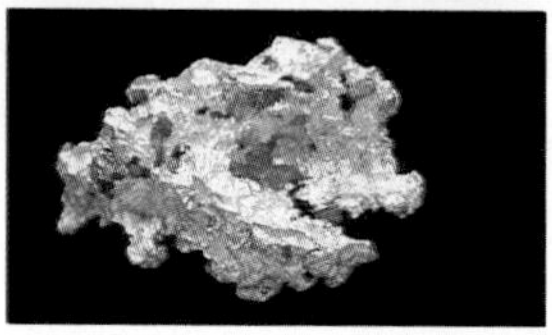 | soft, malleable, resists corrosion | jewelry, coins, dental work |

All photos Courtesy Carolina Biological Supply Company

CHART 9-5. TRANSITION ELEMENTS: CADMIUM AND MERCURY

| 48<br>Cd<br>112.4<br>cadmium |  | soft, ductile, malleable can be cut with a knife | protective layer for steels, batteries |
|---|---|---|---|
| 80<br>Hg<br>200.6<br>mercury | 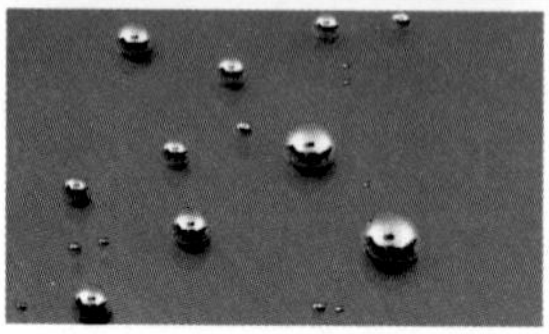 | only liquid metal at room temperature, very heavy, extremely poisonous | fluid in thermometers and barometers, mixes with other metals, paint pigments, dentistry |

TABLE 9-2. SOME COMMON ALLOYS

| Alloy | Composition | Outstanding Property | Some Uses |
|---|---|---|---|
| Solder | tin/lead | low melting point (183°C) | welding |
| Stainless steel | iron/chromium/nickel | does not rust | surgical instruments |
| Bronze | copper/tin | very hard | musical instruments |
| 14 karat gold | gold/copper | resists corrosion | coins, jewelry |

**Transition Elements**    Refer again to the Periodic Table on pages 182–183. Notice the elements that fall in the middle of the long periods. These elements are metals and are called transition elements. These special metals do not show a range in properties as you move across the Table. See Chart 9-3. They are hard, brittle, and have high melting points. Many compounds of transition elements are colorful. Charts 9-4 and 9-5 show some transition metals. For interesting facts on metals and other elements, see page 576.

## Alloys

Most metallic objects are not made of pure metals. Almost everything metallic that is familiar to you is an *alloy*. An **alloy** *is a mixture of two or more elements having properties of a metal.* Not all the elements making up an alloy are metals. For example, steel is a combination of a metal, iron, and a nonmetal, carbon.

Since the amounts of the elements in many alloys can be varied, an alloy with specific properties can be made. Usually the product is superior to the elements from which it is made. Table 9-2 lists some common alloys.

● When it was new, the Statue of Liberty in New York Harbor was a shiny copper red. Today, the statue has a dull green appearance. See Figure 9-7. Carbon dioxide in the air has attacked some of the copper. Green copper carbonate has been formed. Corrosion has occurred inside the statue, too. Oxygen has reacted with the iron supports. Rust has formed.

*Figure 9-7. The Statue of Liberty is being repaired. What might be done to metals such as these to help slow down corrosion?*

*Metals and Their Properties*    **187**

This corrosion has weakened the statue, especially the torch and the right hand. Work was done to remove the corroded metal and repair the damaged areas.

## OBJECTIVES AND WORDS TO REVIEW

1. Aluminum is a conductor of heat. How do people make use of this property?
2. You know that the alkali metal sodium reacts with water. How would you predict potassium and water would react?
3. Steel is a very common alloy. How is it superior to iron?
4. Write one complete sentence for each term listed below.

   | | | |
   |---|---|---|
   | luster | ductile | oxide |
   | malleable | corrosion | alloy |

## TECHNOLOGY TRADE-OFF

# A Future Problem For Technology

You may know that airplane engines get very hot as they operate. Indeed, aircraft engines could not function without a protective chrome plating. Do you know why? If airplane engines were made of iron or steel they would burn up. Chrome, however, forms a thin outer "skin" when it comes into contact with oxygen. This skin will not chemically combine with oxygen. The skin keeps hot airplane engines from burning. The problem is that the United States does not have chromium. Chromium is the element used in chrome plating. Today, three countries supply most of the world's chrome. They are the Soviet Union, Zimbabwe, and South Africa. A shortage of chrome would hurt air technology in the United States.

### Using Critical Thinking

Should the United States buy and store as much chromium as it can afford? Should we spend lots of money trying to create an alloy that may substitute for chromium? Can you name any other alternatives? What do you think?

# NONMETALS AND THEIR PROPERTIES

The elements in Figure 9-8 are nonmetals. Nonmetals have properties that make them very different from metals. In this section you will study the properties of some important nonmetals.

## Physical Properties of Nonmetals

Metals are easy to recognize. They have many similar properties. In contrast, nonmetals can be very different from one another. Sulfur is a yellow solid. The carbon in charcoal is a black solid. Another form of the same element carbon is diamond. Oxygen and hydrogen are both colorless gases.

Nonmetals are solids, gases, and include one liquid, bromine (Br). Solid nonmetals are brittle. A brittle substance breaks easily like a pretzel.

Nonmetals are not shiny, malleable, and ductile like metals. They are not good conductors of heat and electricity. Generally, the properties of nonmetals are just the opposite of the properties of metals.

## Chemical Properties of Nonmetals

You already know that the chemical properties of elements depend upon the electrons in the outermost energy levels of the atoms. Metals have three or fewer electrons in the outermost energy levels. Nonmetals have four to eight electrons in their outermost energy levels. Metals have a tendency to give away the few electrons in their outermost energy levels. Nonmetals have a tendency to attract electrons to their outermost energy levels. As a result of this attraction, the outermost energy levels become filled with eight electrons. This difference in the number of electrons causes the difference in properties between metals and nonmetals. The outstanding chemical property of nonmetals is that they react with metals.

*Figure 9-8. Nonmetals have properties that are different from metals and also from each other.*

## Families of Nonmetals

The nonmetals include some of the most important elements we know. Look at two important families of nonmetals.

**The Halogens**   What do table salt, fluoride toothpaste, and household bleach have in common? They all contain elements that belong to Group VIIA, a family of nonmetals called the halogens (HAL•uh•juhnz). Halogens combine readily with metals and form compounds called salts. A salt is a compound in which a metal is combined with one or more nonmetals. Ordinary table salt, for example, is formed when the halogen chlorine reacts with the metal sodium. See Chart 9-6.

**What is a salt?**

fluorine

chlorine             bromine gas

iodine

**CHART 9-6.** THE HALOGENS

| Element | Some Properties | Some Uses |
|---|---|---|
| 2 7  **9** **F** 19.0 **fluorine** | pale yellow gas; most active halogen; poisonous | etching glass; help prevent tooth decay |
| 2 8 7  **17** **Cl** 35.5 **chlorine** | green-yellow gas; very active; poisonous | purify water supplies; bleaching agent |
| 2 8 18 7  **35** **Br** 79.9 **bromine** | only liquid nonmetal; reddish brown; poisonous | photography; medicine |
| 2 8 18 18 7  **53** **I** 126.9 **iodine** | gray-black solid; least active halogen; metallic luster; poisonous | "iodize" salt (NaCl); disinfectant |
| 2 8 18 32 18 7  **85** **At** 210 **astatine** | dark-colored solid | --------- |

The halogens have different physical properties. They are gaseous (fluorine, chlorine), liquid (bromine), and solid (iodine, astatine). The halogens are the most active of the nonmetals. None of them are found in the free, or uncombined, state in nature. They are always found as part of a compound. Each halogen has seven electrons in its outermost energy level.

**The Noble Gases**   Most elements in the Periodic Table will combine chemically with other substances. The Group VIIIA elements, however, combine with other elements only under very special conditions. These elements are called *inert* (in•URT), or *inactive*. See Chart 9-7.

**REPORT ON
A NONMETAL**

**OBJECTIVE**
Learn more about an element.

**PROCEDURE**
Make a report on an element you studied in this section. Tell about its discovery, uses, properties, and most interesting aspect.

**CHART 9-7.** PROPERTIES AND USES OF NOBLE GASES

| Element | Some Properties | Some Uses |
|---|---|---|
|  2 He 4.0 helium | lighter than air, does not burn | airships, balloons, liquified and used as a coolant |
|  10 Ne 20.2 neon | does not burn | neon signs, airport lamps |
| 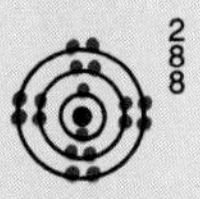 18 Ar 39.9 argon | does not burn | lightbulbs, welding |
| 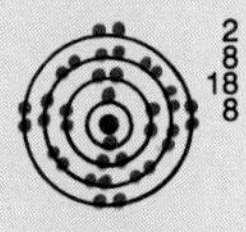 36 Kr 83.8 krypton | does not burn, can be liquified | airport lamps |
| 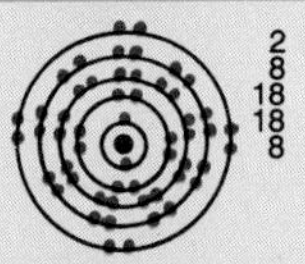 54 Xe 131.3 xenon | does not burn | photographic lamps, gas in high-intensity lightbulbs |
| 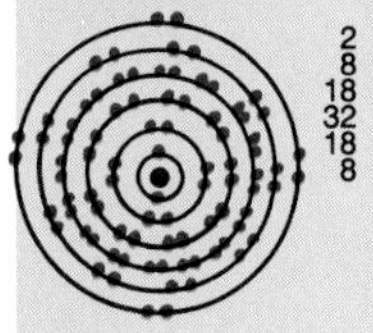 86 Rn 222 radon | heavy gas | used to treat cancer |

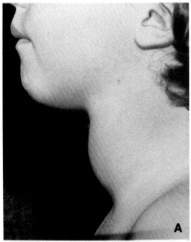

*Figure 9-9. People living in regions lacking iodine can develop goiters.*

The elements of Group VIIIA are all colorless gases. It is known that kings and other nobles did not mix with their subjects. Since the gases in Group VIIIA did not appear to react chemically with any elements, these gases were named the noble gases. Since 1962, however, research chemists have been able to prepare several compounds of krypton (Kr) and xenon (Xe). Such compounds are very difficult to produce, so reactions with noble gases are still exceptional.

The elements in Group VIIIA have eight electrons in their outermost shells. Elements with this many electrons do not usually react with other elements. Chart 9-7 gives some properties and uses of the noble gases.

● Iodine is a disinfectant. It is added to table salt in the form of sodium iodide. This "iodized salt" helps to keep your thyroid gland working properly.

People in many regions of the world do not get enough iodine from the foods they eat. This shortage of iodine can cause growths called goiters to develop in the neck. Iodized salt is used in these regions to help prevent goiters from forming.

Before the introduction of iodized salt, many people developed goiters. Even Cleopatra was thought to have had a goiter. Compare her picture shown in Figure 9-9**B** with that of the person in Figure 9-9**A**. Did Cleopatra have a goiter? What do you think?

### OBJECTIVES AND WORDS TO REVIEW

1. Give three ways metals and nonmetals differ.
2. List three properties of the halogens and two properties of the noble gases.
3. Write a complete sentence for the term below.
   inert

# METALLOIDS AND THEIR PROPERTIES

Look at the Periodic Table on pages 182–183. The metal elements are located on the left side of the table. The most active metals are the alkali metals in Group IA. When you follow the elements across a row, or period, you find that they become less and less like metals. When you come to the far right, the elements are nonmetals. The nonmetals are in the blue blocks.

In the Periodic Table there is a red stair-step line dividing the table into metals and nonmetals. Some elements on either side of the red line are in green blocks. These elements are "borderline" between metals and nonmetals. They are called *metalloids* (MET•uhl•oydz). **Metalloids** *are elements that have properties in between metals and nonmetals.* The word metalloid means "metallike." In this section you will learn about the properties of metalloids. You will also study two special metalloids.

## Physical Properties of Metalloids

The metalloids are listed in Table 9-3. All of the metalloids are solids having the appearance of metals. Most

What does the word metalloid mean?

**TABLE 9-3.** THE METALLOID ELEMENTS

| Element | Symbol | Atomic Number |
|---------|--------|---------------|
| Boron | B | 5 |
| Silicon | Si | 14 |
| Germanium | Ge | 32 |
| Arsenic | As | 33 |
| Antimony | Sb | 51 |
| Tellurium | Te | 52 |
| Polonium | Po | 84 |

## PROPERTIES OF A METALLOID COMPOUND

### OBJECTIVE
Investigate the water-softening property of borax.

### Materials
two small screw-cap jars of equal size with lids, warm water, *real* soap (not a detergent), borax (sold in the detergent section of a supermarket), metric spoon

### PROCEDURE
**1.** Half fill the two jars with very warm water.
**2.** To one of the jars add a metric teaspoonful of borax. Stir to dissolve the solid.
**3.** To each jar add equal amounts (about half a teaspoon) of real soap.
**4.** Cover each jar and shake vigorously for about 30 s.
**5.** Observe the amount of suds in each.

### QUESTIONS
**1.** Which jar contained the most suds?
**2.** If there were more suds in the water containing borax, explain this result.

of them are white or gray like metals, but are not as shiny. The metalloids are not as malleable and ductile as the metals.

Metals are good conductors of electricity. Nonmetals do not conduct electricity. Metalloids conduct electricity, but not as well as metals. This property makes metalloids very useful.

## Chemical Properties of Metalloids

Metalloids have properties that are common to metals. They also have properties that nonmetals have. Metalloids, however, do not follow patterns the way members of a group do. They are too individual in nature. In order to study the properties of the metalloids, you would have to study each element. In fact, the differences in chemical properties from element to element are what make metalloids so useful. For an illustrated description of electron arrangement in metalloids and other elements, turn to page 548.

## Two Special Metalloids

Because of their different chemical properties, the metalloids are very valuable. Boron and silicon are two important metalloids. Let us look at them.

**Boron**   Boron is the first element of Group IIIA. It has a dull luster like metals, but it is very brittle like many nonmetals. It has three electrons in its outermost energy level. It is brownish-black in color. Boron has high melting (2079°C) and boiling (2550°C) points.

Boron is a poor conductor of electricity at low temperatures. However, as the temperature of the solid is increased, boron becomes a good conductor. Boron and other elements with this property are called semiconductors. Metals, by comparison, become poor conductors as the temperature rises. This property of boron makes it useful to industry. It can be used in electrical devices that have to function at temperatures too high for metals.

Boron has other uses besides being a semiconductor. Chart 9-8 shows some ways in which boron is used.

## CHART 9-8. METALLOID ELEMENTS

| Element | Photo | Uses |
|---------|-------|------|
| 5<br>B<br>10.8<br>boron | 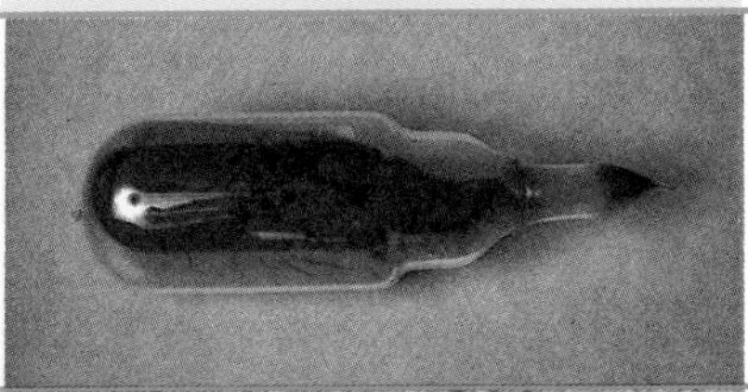 | semiconductor, fireworks, some compounds used as antiseptics, water softener, making certain types of glass |
| 14<br>Si<br>28.1<br>silicon | 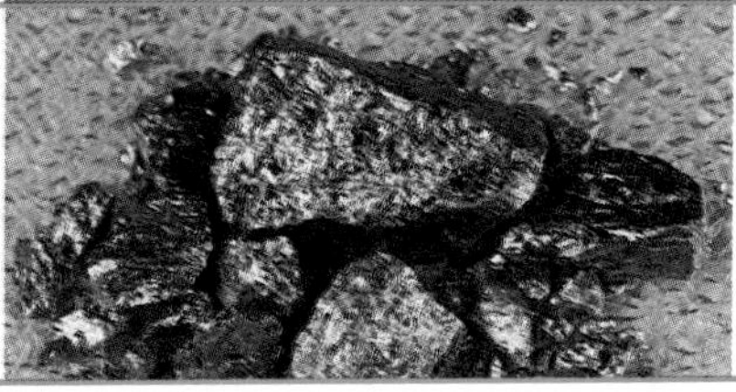 | semiconductor, transistors, solar cells, used in making glass, making steel |

**Silicon**   Silicon is the second element of Group IVA. It is a dark-gray solid, hard and brittle. It has four electrons in its outer energy level.

Almost all of the compounds of silicon contain oxygen. Silicon is the second most abundant element in the earth's crust. It is present in many rocks and minerals. Sand is made of a compound of silicon, silicon dioxide.

Silicon has many uses in industry. It, too, is a semiconductor. It is also used in making glass and in the production of cement. Chart 9-8 gives uses of silicon.

● As the aerospace industry grew, it needed a way to obtain electricity from the sun. Scientists produced extremely pure crystals of silicon. They then added tiny amounts of other substances to the pure silicon. These substances, called impurities, make silicon crystals better conductors. When the crystals are exposed to sunlight, electricity is produced. The satellite in Figure 9-10 is powered by electricity from silicon crystals.

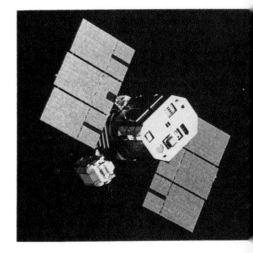

*Figure 9-10.* Solar cells provide the energy that powers this satellite.

### OBJECTIVES AND WORDS TO REVIEW
**1.** Why are metalloids important?
**2.** List three properties of boron.
**3.** Give three uses of silicon in industry.
**4.** Write a complete sentence for the term below.
   metalloid

# LEARNING HOW TO CLASSIFY

## Preparation

Do you ever do the dishes at home? After they are washed and dried, you probably put them away in some order. All the glasses may go on one shelf, all the plates on another. Forks, knives, and spoons often have separate compartments in a drawer. This sorting of things into like groups is known as classification.

By classifying objects into groups, scientists can organize information. Classifying helps them compare and contrast properties of different groups. For example, scientists classify some substances as metals or nonmetals. Once classified, these substances can be more easily studied.

## Directions

Scientists classify objects into groups or categories by first determining a common property. This may be the size, shape, color, use, or composition of the objects.

Look at the objects pictured below in Figure 1. How could you classify them? You might arrange them according to their use. A pencil, chalk, and a marker form one category: *writing tools.* A pin, a tack, and a nail form a second category: *fasteners.* They all hold things together.

Is there another way to classify these objects? Is there a property of the pencil that is common to the pin, the tack, and the nail? Yes. All have a pointed tip. You now have a third category: *pointed objects.*

## Practice

Look carefully at the list below and determine the common properties among them. Then, on a separate sheet of paper, classify the list into two groups and label each group. Answer these questions as well:

1. Why was the list classified this way?
2. Can a third category be formed?
3. What name can be given to this third category?

| | | | |
|---|---|---|---|
| Rutherford | Electron | Dalton | Neutron |
| Bohr | Proton | Thomson | |

## Application

After reading Chapter 9, you have learned much about the classification of elements. Using the Periodic Table and what you have learned, classify the following elements into categories. Label each category. Write your answers on a separate sheet of paper.

| | | | | | |
|---|---|---|---|---|---|
| F | Li | B | Cl | Si | Na |
| Br | Po | Cs | Al | He | Ni |

*Figure 1.*

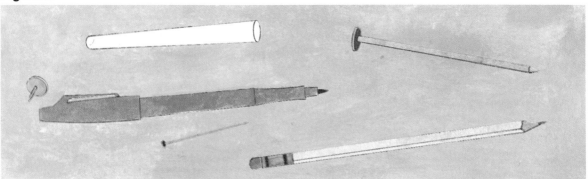

# LABORATORY ACTIVITY

## CLASSIFYING METALS AND NONMETALS

### Objective
Classify substances as metals or nonmetals.

### Background
Metals have many similar physical properties. Nonmetals are very different from one another. You can tell the difference between metals and nonmetals by comparing physical properties.

### Materials
small lump of solid sulfur, piece of charcoal, 10 cm length of uncoated copper wire, 6 cm x 6 cm piece of aluminum foil, 2 small paper dishes, hammer, wood board, bulb and lamp socket, 6-V dry cell, three 15-cm pieces coated copper wire, goggles

### Prodedure
1. Copy Table 9-L into your notebook. Record your observations in it.
2. Place the sulfur and the charcoal (carbon) in separate dishes. **CAUTION:** Wear goggles.
3. Fold the aluminum foil into a small wad. Roll the copper wire into a small coil.
4. Record the elements that have luster.
5. Place the elements on the board. Hammer each one to see if it is malleable.
6. Record which elements are ductile (by their form and appearance).
7. **CAUTION:** Never touch the bare ends of a wire. Remove 5 cm of coating from the ends of three pieces of wire. Set up a conductivity tester as shown in Figure 9-L. Test each sample for conductivity by touching it with the bare ends of the wires. If a sample is a conductor, the bulb will glow.

**Figure 9-L.** *Laboratory setup.*

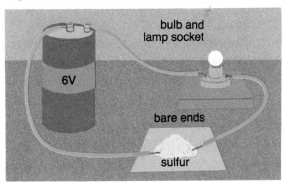

### Questions
1. Classify each sample as metal or nonmetal.
2. **PROBLEM SOLVING** A sample conducts electricity, but has no luster and is not ductile. What other kinds of tests are needed to classify the sample as metal or nonmetal?

| **TABLE 9-L.** PHYSICAL PROPERTIES OF METALS AND NONMETALS | | | | |
|---|---|---|---|---|
| **Material** | **Luster** | **Malleable** | **Ductile** | **Conductor of Electricity** |
| Sulfur | | | | |
| Carbon | | | | |
| Aluminum | | | | |
| Copper | | | | |

# SUMMARY

1. Mendeleev arranged the elements in order of their atomic weights, leaving blank spaces for elements he knew would later be discovered. (9-1)

2. In the modern Periodic Table elements are arranged in order of atomic number. The rows are called periods; the columns are called groups or families. Elements in the same group have similar properties. (9-1)

3. Metals are ductile and malleable, have luster, conduct heat and electricity, and react with nonmetals. (9-2)

4. Combinations of elements having properties of metals are alloys. (9-2)

5. Nonmetals have four or more electrons in their outermost energy levels. Halogens are the most active of the nonmetals. (9-3)

6. The noble gases are mostly inert. They do not usually react with other elements. (9-3)

7. Metalloids have properties of both metals and nonmetals. Boron and silicon are two important metalloids. (9-4)

# REVIEW

Number a sheet of paper from 1 to 25 and answer these questions.

**Building Science Vocabulary**   Write the letter of the term that best matches each definition.

| | | |
|---|---|---|
| **a.** alkali metal | **e.** halogens | **i.** noble gases |
| **b.** corrosion | **f.** luster | **j.** nonmetals |
| **c.** ductile | **g.** malleable | **k.** period |
| **d.** group | **h.** metalloid | **l.** periodic |

1. The reaction of metals with air, water, and substances in the atmosphere

2. A group of nonmetals that forms salts

3. Can be hammered into different shapes

4. Row of elements in periodic table

5. Having properties of both metals and nonmetals

6. Can be drawn into a fine wire

7. Shininess

8. Column of elements with similar properties

9. Repeated again and again

10. A group of very inert elements

**Finding the Facts**   Select the letter of the answer that best completes each of the following.

11. The periodic table classifies elements according to their     (**a**) properties   (**b**) names     (**c**) symbols     (**d**) uses.

12. To make the pattern in his periodic table work, Mendeleev had to     (**a**) leave out some of the known elements     (**b**) add extra elements     (**c**) leave some blank spaces for undiscovered elements     (**d**) change some of the atomic masses.

13. Elements in the same group always have (**a**) exactly the same properties (**b**) completely different properties     (**c**) the properties of metals     (**d**) similar properties.

14. Elements that are good conductors of heat are     (**a**) nonmetals     (**b**) inert gases (**c**) carbon and sulfur     (**d**) metals.

15. An element belonging to Group IVA found in Period 3 is     (**a**) gallium     (**b**) silicon (**c**) germanium     (**d**) phosphorus.

16. Bronze is an alloy of     (**a**) aluminum and copper     (**b**) copper and zinc     (**c**) copper and tin     (**d**) tin and lead.

17. The Statue of Liberty is coated with a green substance because its copper coating reacts with     (**a**) the iron layer under the copper     (**b**) carbon dioxide in the air     (**c**) nitrogen in the air     (**d**) water.

18. Which of the following is a nonmetal? (**a**) potassium     (**b**) copper (**c**) sulfur     (**d**) aluminum

**19.** The only liquid nonmetal is
(**a**) bromine      (**b**) mercury
(**c**) calcium      (**d**) boron.

**20.** A compound of which halogen is added to city water supplies to help prevent tooth decay?      (**a**) iodine      (**b**) astatine
(**c**) fluorine      (**d**) bromine

**Understanding Main Ideas**    Complete the following.

**21.** As you follow the elements across a row in the periodic table from left to right, the properties change from properties of metals to properties of ___?___ .

**22.** Copper is used for electrical wiring because copper is a good ___?___ .

**23.** The alkali metals have to be stored under kerosene because they react violently with ___?___ .

**24.** A metalloid element used in semiconductors is ___?___ .

**25.** Some of the elements used in making advertising lights belong to the family of ___?___ gases.

**Writing About Science**    On a separate sheet of paper, answer the following as completely as possible.

**1.** Why are metals, rather than nonmetals, used in making coins?

**2.** In what way are the seasons of the year like the periodic table?

**3.** A blank space has been left in the periodic table for an element with an atomic number of 111. How can you predict what its properties will be if it is one day discovered?

**4.** None of the noble gases were discovered until 1894. That was 25 years after Mendeleev's first periodic table. Why do you think they had not been discovered earlier?

**5.** (laboratory question) In the laboratory you observed some properties of metals and nonmetals. Why is the wiring used in electrical appliances always covered with a material having properties similar to nonmetals?

**Investigating Chapter Ideas**    Try one of the following projects to further your study.

**1. Early periodic classifications**    Mendeleev's periodic table and the modern Periodic Table are only two ways to classify elements. Methods were also proposed by Johann Wolfgang Dobereiner and John Newlands. Form a committee of four students. Each member will research one of the four methods of classification. Then, using charts or pictures, the committee can compare the four methods.

**2. Missing elements**    The importance of Mendeleev's Periodic Table was shown when he predicted the existence and properties of scandium, gallium, and germanium. Make a poster showing the names Mendeleev gave to these elements and the properties he predicted for them.

**3. Shape-memory alloys**    Special alloys can be made that have the ability to "remember" a shape. They can be bent into one shape and will return to another shape upon the proper temperature change. Called shape-memory alloys, these metals have many applications. Report on two of the most important shape-memory alloys: Nitinol and brass.

**Reading About Science**    Read some of the following books to explore topics that interest you.

Asimov, Isaac. 1974. **Building Blocks of the Universe.** New York: Abelard-Schuman.

Asimov, Isaac. 1962. **The Search for the Elements.** New York: Basic Books.

Keller, Mollie. 1982. **Marie Curie.** New York: Watts.

**W**atch what happens to the pile of orange crystals. When ignited, they sparkle like fireworks. The third photo shows what remains after burning stops. How are the substances in the first and third photos different?

The photographs show a "volcano" reaction. The mossy green volcano was made by burning the orange crystals. It is the product of a chemical change.

There are several types of chemical reactions. Familiar examples are fireworks exploding and candles burning.

How do chemical reactions take place? How can one substance change into another? These questions will be answered in this chapter.

Read and Find Out:
● what caused the explosion of the airship *Hindenberg*.
● how the Periodic Table helps people on special diets.
● how high-grade iron is separated from its ore.
● how industry obtains gasoline from petroleum.

# CHEMICAL BONDS AND REACTIONS

# BONDING AMONG NONMETALS

Most familiar substances are compounds. For example, water and sugar are compounds. If you could divide water and sugar into their smallest units, you would have molecules of these compounds. Each of these molecules contains atoms of different elements chemically combined. The world is filled with compounds because atoms combine in many ways. In this section you will see how atoms of nonmetals combine.

## Chemical Bonds

What kinds of atoms make up a molecule of water? The setup in Figure 10-1 can help you find out. Electricity is being sent through water in the middle tube. The electricity breaks down water molecules. The water molecules are broken into two elements: hydrogen and oxygen. Each element collects as a gas in one of the side tubes. At room temperature water is a liquid, while hydrogen and oxygen are gases. How can water have different properties from the elements that make it up?

*Figure 10-1. In this setup, electricity is sent through water. Water is broken down into hydrogen and oxygen, which collects in the tubes.*

Studying a model can help to answer this kind of question. Figure 10-2 shows a model of a water molecule. The molecule is made of two hydrogen atoms joined to an oxygen atom by *chemical bonds*. A **chemical bond** *is a force of attraction that holds atoms together*. Atoms of hydrogen and oxygen joined by chemical bonds into water molecules no longer have the properties of hydrogen and oxygen. They have the properties of water.

## One Kind of Bond: Covalent Bonds

The bond joining the atoms of a water molecule is only one of several kinds of chemical bonds between atoms. The bonds in a water molecule are *covalent* (koh•VAY•luhnt) *bonds. A **covalent bond** is a bond* *formed when two atoms share electrons.* For example, in a water molecule electrons are shared by both a hydrogen atom and an oxygen atom. See Figure 10-3.

**Unfilled Energy Levels**   In Figure 10-3**A** you see atoms of hydrogen and oxygen. The atoms are not yet bonded together. Look at the arrangement of electrons in the energy levels of each atom. An atom of hydrogen has only one electron in its (the first) energy level. The first level can hold up to two electrons. The level is not filled. An atom of oxygen has six electrons in its outermost level. This level can hold eight electrons. So, the outermost level of oxygen is unfilled. Recall that an atom is stable when its outermost energy level is filled. Thus, neither the hydrogen atoms nor the oxygen atom are stable. When atoms are unstable, they are readily combined with other atoms.

**Filled Energy Levels**   Now look at Figure 10-3**B**. Here, covalent bonds have formed. Each bond is represented by a boxed pair of electrons. Each hydrogen atom is attracting one electron from the oxygen atom. Thus, each hydrogen atom now has a filled outer level. So, each hydrogen atom is stable. At the same time, the oxygen atom is attracting one electron from each hy-

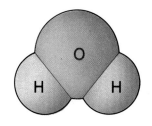

*Figure 10-2. A model of a water molecule contains two atoms of hydrogen and one atom of oxygen. What holds the atoms together?*

Relate the stability of an atom to its outermost energy level.

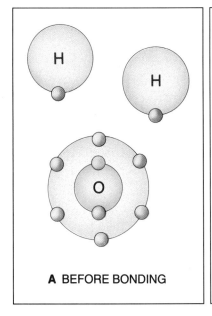

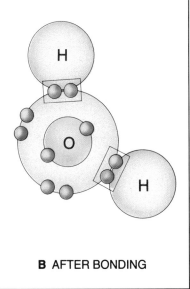

**A** BEFORE BONDING          **B** AFTER BONDING

*Figure 10-3. Each atom has a positive nucleus that attracts its own electrons. However, each nucleus can also attract electrons from nearby atoms. When this occurs, the atoms become bonded.*

**OBJECTIVE**
Construct models of molecules with covalent bonds.

**MATERIALS**
construction paper (two different colors), penny, quarter, scissors

**PROCEDURE**
1. Cut out six circles the size of a penny. These are models of H atoms.
2. Cut out four circles the size of a quarter. These are models of O atoms.
3. Use these model atoms to make models of the following molecules: hydrogen ($H_2$), oxygen ($O_2$), water ($H_2O$).

**QUESTIONS**
1. What kind of chemical bonds do your models represent?
2. To build two water molecules, how many molecules each of hydrogen and oxygen are needed?

**TABLE 10-1. COMMON COVALENT COMPOUNDS**

| Compound | Formula |
|----------|---------|
| Table sugar | $C_{12}H_{22}O_{11}$ |
| Carbon dioxide | $CO_2$ |
| Ammonia | $NH_3$ |
| Methane | $CH_4$ |

drogen atom. The oxygen atom now has a filled outer energy level. It, too, is stable. By sharing electrons, the atoms are themselves attracted to each other. They now act as a single unit: a water molecule.

The six outermost electrons of the oxygen atom and the electrons of the hydrogen atoms are called *valence* (VAY•luhns) electrons. **Valence electrons** *are the electrons that take part in a chemical bond.* These electrons are found in the outermost energy level, or "valence shell." Because they are involved in bonding, valence electrons determine the properties of an element.

**Chemical Formula for Water**   From your study of the bonds in water, you know that one oxygen atom bonds with two hydrogen atoms. Thus, the formula for water can be written. It is $H_2O$. The subscript 2 means that there are two atoms of hydrogen in the molecule. The element oxygen also has a subscript, 1, but a "1" is not written in chemical formulas.

**Covalent Compounds**   Water is a covalent compound. Its atoms are joined by convalent bonds. Table sugar and ammonia are others. In each compound, valence electrons are shared by nonmetal atoms. The sharing gives each atom a stable electron arrangement and holds the atoms together. Table 10-1 lists some common covalent compounds.

## Covalent Bonds in Elements

The atoms of many compounds are joined by covalent bonds. However, the atoms of several nonmetallic elements are also joined by covalent bonds. Hydrogen is one.

Each hydrogen atom, remember, has an unfilled valence shell. Atoms of this gas do not exist as single atoms in nature. They occur in pairs held together by covalent bonds. See Figure 10-4.

Molecules of hydrogen are examples of *diatomic* (digh•uh•TAHM•ik) *molecules.* **Diatomic molecules** *contain two of the same kind of atom joined by a covalent bond.* Table 10-2 gives diatomic molecules and their formulas.

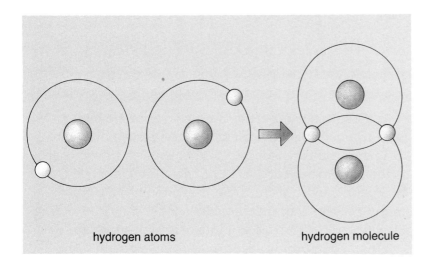

hydrogen atoms → hydrogen molecule

Figure 10-4. *Diatomic molecules are made up of two atoms.*

**TABLE 10-2.**
**SOME DIATOMIC MOLECULES**

| Name | Atom | Diatomic Molecule |
|---|---|---|
| Hydrogen | H | $H_2$ |
| Nitrogen | N | $N_2$ |
| Oxygen | O | $O_2$ |
| Fluorine | F | $F_2$ |
| Chlorine | Cl | $Cl_2$ |
| Bromine | Br | $Br_2$ |
| Iodine | I | $I_2$ |

Figure 10-5. *Explosion of the German airship* Hindenberg. *Electricity ignited a hydrogen leak.*

● Hydrogen was once used to float airships. However, hydrogen, as you know, is not stable. Its energy level is unfilled. Thus, it can combine with other substances. Often hydrogen would react so quickly that an explosion would result. The airship *Hindenberg* exploded because the hydrogen in it combined rapidly with the oxygen in the air. See Figure 10-5.

Today, helium gas is used to float airships. Helium is an inert gas. It has filled valence shell. Thus the helium atom is stable. It will not combine with other atoms and cause an explosion.

**OBJECTIVES AND WORDS TO REVIEW**

1. What is a chemical bond?
2. Draw a model of a water molecule showing how electrons are shared.
3. Draw a model showing how two atoms of hydrogen are bonded in a hydrogen molecule.
4. Write one complete sentence for each term listed below.
   chemical bond       valence electron
   covalent bond       diatomic molecule

# BONDING BETWEEN METALS AND NONMETALS

Table salt is made from two hazardous elements. Sodium metal reacts violently when placed in water. Chlorine gas is poisonous. Each element, uncombined, is too dangerous for you to handle. Yet combined in the compound sodium chloride, they are used daily by many people. Sodium chloride is table salt. How can table salt be so different from its original elements?

When compounds are formed from elements, the elements lose their properties. When they combine, atoms of the different elements are joined by a bond. As you will learn in this section, a bond between a metal and a nonmetal is different from a covalent bond. You will also learn about a bond that holds together the atoms in a metallic element.

## A Second Kind of Bond: Ionic Bonds

The bond between sodium and chlorine in table salt differs from that between hydrogen and oxygen in water. Figure 10-6 can help you see the difference.

**Electron Transfer**   Before sodium and chlorine combine, sodium has one valence electron. Chlorine has seven. Neither valence shell is filled. But if chlorine had one more electron, its valence shell would be filled.

*Figure 10-6. Formation of table salt.*

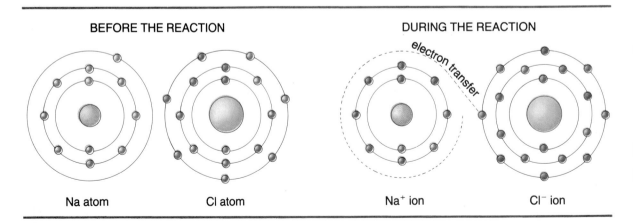

| BEFORE THE REACTION | | DURING THE REACTION | |
|---|---|---|---|
| Na atom | Cl atom | Na⁺ ion | Cl⁻ ion |

Figure 10-6 shows how the two atoms become joined. During the reaction, the sodium atom gives, or transfers, its one valence electron to the chlorine atom. Both the sodium atom and the chlorine atom now have filled shells. Both atoms are now stable. The reaction is over.

**Charged Atoms** The sodium and chlorine atoms in Figure 10-6 are no longer <u>neutral</u> atoms. A neutral atom has an equal number of electrons and protons. Both the sodium and chlorine atoms have become *ions* (IGH•uhnz). *An **ion** is an atom that has unequal numbers of electrons and protons.*

An unequal number of these charged particles gives each ion an overall charge. The sodium atom had 11 protons and 11 electrons. After it gave away an electron, the sodium ion had 11 <u>positive</u> protons but only 10 <u>negative</u> electrons. Thus, with one more proton than electrons, it has a positive charge (+1). The chlor*ine* atom had 17 protons and 17 electrons. However, after gaining an electron, it now has 17 <u>positive</u> protons and 18 <u>negative</u> electrons. By gaining an electron, it has become a chlor*ide* ion with a negative charge (−1).

Ions that are oppositely charged attract each other. An attraction holds the sodium ion and chloride ion together. This attraction between ions is a kind of chemical bond called an *ionic bond. An **ionic bond** is a bond formed by the transfer of electrons.*

## Ionic Compounds

Many compounds result from the transfer of electrons from metal atoms to nonmetal atoms. Such compounds are known as ionic compounds. Table 10-3 lists the names of some common ionic compounds.

**TABLE 10-3.** SOME COMMON IONIC COMPOUNDS

| Compound | Formula | Use |
|---|---|---|
| Sodium chloride | NaCl | table salt |
| Calcium fluoride | $CaF_2$ | lens making |
| Sodium hydroxide | NaOH | drain cleaner |
| Potassium chloride | KCl | salt substitute |

**EXPLORE** BY TRYING

### A MODEL OF SODIUM CHLORIDE

**OBJECTIVE**
Construct a model of an ionic crystal.

**MATERIALS**
gumdrops (two colors), toothpicks, table salt, hand lens

**PROCEDURE**
**1.** Use the hand lens to examine a few crystals of table salt. Observe the shape of the sodium chloride crystals.
**2.** Using gumdrops and toothpicks, make a model of a sodium chloride crystal you just saw. Figure 10-7 will also help you. Use one color gumdrop for sodium atoms, and a different color for chlorine atoms. Use toothpicks to represent the chemical bonds.

**QUESTIONS**
**1.** What shape are the salt crystals you looked at?
**2.** What kind of bonds do the toothpicks in your model represent?

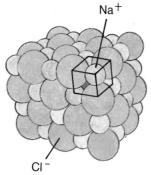

Na$^+$

Cl$^-$

*Figure 10-7. A crystal of sodium chloride. Each ion has six neighboring ions of opposite charge.*

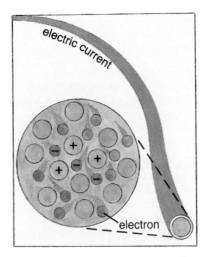

electric current

electron

*Figure 10-8. Electricity easily passes through the "sea" of electrons in a metal wire.*

**Geometric Shapes**   You can see an example of a property of many solids formed by ionic bonds. Look closely at sodium chloride with a hand lens. See Figure 10-7. Sodium chloride and many other ionic solids form *crystals* (KRIS•tuhlz). A ***crystal*** *is a solid with a geometric shape having flat surfaces at definite angles to each other.* Figure 10-7 shows a model of the arrangement of the ions in the crystal.

**Melting and Boiling**   The ions in any ionic crystal are held strongly in place by ionic bonds. A special property resulting from these strong bonds is a high *melting point.* The ***melting point*** *of a solid is the temperature at which it becomes a liquid.*

Similarly, ionic compounds have high *boiling points.* The ***boiling point*** *of a liquid is the temperature at which it begins to change rapidly into a gas.*

## A Third Kind of Bond: Metallic Bonds

You know that metals like aluminum and copper can be hammered and stretched to an extent without breaking. Why do metals have these properties? Figure 10-8 can help answer this question.

In a small piece of metal, millions of metal atoms are packed together. Each atom has a positive nucleus attracting its own electrons. The valence electrons of each atom are not held as closely as its other electrons. They are "free" to move about from atom to atom. They whiz throughout all the atoms in a kind of "electron sea." Each electron in the "sea" is equally attracted by all the nuclei of the atoms in the metal.

The atoms are held together by attracting one another's valence electrons. This attraction of electrons is a *metallic bond.* A ***metallic bond*** *is the sharing of many freely moving electrons among the atoms of a solid metal.*

Metallic bonds can help explain metal properties. Metal atoms are not held rigidly. When a metal is hammered or stretched, the atoms can change position. But they are still held together by the electron sea.

**TABLE 10-4.** COMPARISON OF CHEMICAL BONDS

| Bond | Characteristic | Examples |
|------|----------------|----------|
| Covalent | sharing of electrons | $H_2O$, $O_2$, $CH_4$, $CO_2$ |
| Metallic | movement of free electrons | Fe, Cu, Ag, Au |
| Ionic | transfer of electrons | NaCl, KCl, NaOH, $CaF_2$ |

You have learned about three kinds of chemical bonds in Sections 1 and 2. Their characteristics are summarized in Table 10-4. Remember, however, that these are only models of bonds. Such models help us understand the properties of substances.

Recent improvements in photography have offered visible support to a model explaining how atoms are joined together. See Figure 10-9. The photography involves a specialized microscope called a scanning tunneling microscope. This instrument uses electrons to illuminate different energy levels in the bonds that hold the atoms together. With this microscope, scientists can now "see" the bonds between some atoms.

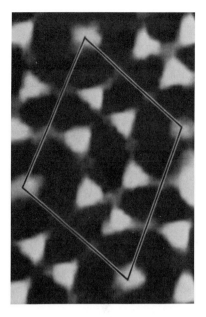

*Figure 10-9. In this photo, the triangle-shaped bright spots are the atoms in a crystal. The faint, stringlike lines connecting the atoms are the bonds.*

## Naming Chemical Compounds

You know from your study of the bonds in Table 10-4 that covalent and ionic bonds are found in compounds. Compounds, recall, are made up of elements. You can name compounds by using the names of the elements that make them up.

**Two-Element Compounds** The simplest compounds are *binary* (BIGH•nuh•ree) *compounds.* **Binary compounds** *are compounds made of two elements.* Sodium chloride, for example, is a binary compound. It is made from the elements sodium and chlorine.

Compare the name "sodium chloride" with the elements that make it up: sodium and chlorine. The first part of the compound, sodium, has the same name as the metal. The second part of the compound, chloride, has the same root as the nonmetal element: chlor-. Instead of "ine," however, the compound ends in "ide." You can write the name of other binary compounds in the same way. First, write the name of the

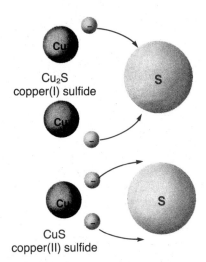

$Cu_2S$
copper(I) sulfide

CuS
copper(II) sulfide

*Figure 10-10. When copper combines with sulfur, two different compounds can be formed.*

**TABLE 10-6.** OXIDATION NUMBERS FOR VARIOUS IONS

| Ion | Formula | Oxidation Number |
|-----|---------|------------------|
| Single Ions | | |
| Hydrogen | $H^+$ | 1+ |
| Sodium | $Na^+$ | 1+ |
| Potassium | $K^+$ | 1+ |
| Copper(I) | $Cu^+$ | 1+ |
| Magnesium | $Mg^{2+}$ | 2+ |
| Calcium | $Ca^{2+}$ | 2+ |
| Copper(II) | $Cu^{2+}$ | 2+ |
| Aluminum | $Al^{3+}$ | 3+ |
| Chloride | $Cl^-$ | 1− |
| Iodide | $I^-$ | 1− |
| Oxide | $O^{2-}$ | 2− |
| Sulfide | $S^{2-}$ | 2− |
| Polyatomic Ions | | |
| Ammonium | $NH_4^+$ | 1+ |
| Hydroxide | $OH^-$ | 1− |
| Nitrate | $NO_3^-$ | 1− |
| Sulfate | $SO_4^{2-}$ | 2− |

**TABLE 10-5.** NAMING BINARY COMPOUNDS

| Elements Making Up Compound | | Formula | Name of Compound |
|------|------|---------|------------------|
| Metal | Nonmetal | | |
| Sodium | chlorine | NaCl | sodium chloride |
| Magnesium | oxygen | MgO | magnesium oxide |
| Potassium | iodine | KI | potassium iodide |
| Copper | sulfur | $Cu_2S$ | copper(I) sulfide |
| Copper | sulfur | CuS | copper(II) sulfide |

metal. Then, replace the ending of the nonmetal with "ide." Table 10-5 gives some examples.

Look carefully at the last two examples in Table 10-5. You will notice two different compounds made of the same two elements. Copper can form two different compounds when it combines with sulfur. It can produce two compounds because when forming an ionic compound, copper can lose one or two valence electrons.

To tell how many valence electrons are lost, a roman number is put in parentheses. Thus, copper(I) means that each copper atom loses one valence electron in bonding. In copper(I) sulfide, two copper atoms each donate an electron. The formula is thus $Cu_2S$. See Figure 10-10. The "2" indicates the number of copper atoms involved in bonding. In copper(II) sulfide, a single copper atom donates two electrons in forming the compound. Since only one copper atom is involved in bonding, the formula for copper(II) sulfide is CuS. (Recall a "1" is not written.)

The number of electrons involved in bonding is given a special name: *oxidation number. The **oxidation number** is the number of electrons an atom gains, loses, or shares in bonding.* Table 10-6 gives oxidation numbers for some elements. A " + " sign indicates a loss of electrons. So, $Na^+$ means that sodium loses one electron in becoming an ion. A " − " sign indicates a gain of electrons. So, $S^{2-}$ means that sulfur gains two electrons in becoming an ion. Turn to page 550 for more information.

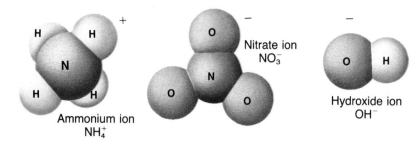

Ammonium ion
NH$_4^+$

Nitrate ion
NO$_3^-$

Hydroxide ion
OH$^-$

**Figure 10-11.** *NH$_4^+$ has lost one electron. NO$_3^-$ and OH$^-$ each have gained an electron. These polyatomic ions act as if they were one atom.*

**TABLE 10-7. TERNARY COMPOUNDS**

| Formula | Name of Compound |
|---------|------------------|
| NaOH | sodium hydroxide |
| KNO$_3$ | potassium nitrate |
| MgSO$_4$ | magnesium sulfate |
| NH$_4$Cl | ammonium chloride |
| Na$_2$SO$_4$ | sodium sulfate |
| Ca(OH)$_2$ | calcium hydroxide |

Potassium has chemical properties similar to what element?

**Many-Element Compounds** You have studied binary compounds such as sodium chloride. Figure 10-11 shows another kind of compound. Look at ammonium chloride, NH$_4$Cl. This compound has three elements in it: N, H, and Cl. *Compounds that are made of three elements are called* **ternary** *(TUR•nur•ee) compounds.* Sodium hydroxide, NaOH, is another ternary compound. Table 10-7 gives more ternary compounds.

Look at Figure 10-11 again. The group of atoms NH$_4^+$ acts as if it were one, charged ion. Such a group is called a *polyatomic* (pahl•ee•uh•TAHM•ik) *ion. A* **polyatomic ion** *is an ion made of more than one atom acting as a single unit.* The highlighted part of each compound in Table 10-7 is a polyatomic ion.

● Positive sodium ions give salt its salty taste. However, substitutes for this salt exist. Potassium lies just below sodium in the Periodic Table. It, too, has a salty taste. The labels of many salt substitutes contain potassium chloride.

## OBJECTIVES AND WORDS TO REVIEW

**1.** When sodium and chlorine bond and form sodium chloride, why are sodium ions positive (+)? Why are chloride ions negative (−)?
**2.** List two properties of ionic solids.
**3.** Name each of the following compounds. Indicate whether it is a binary or ternary compound.
  (a) H$_2$S   KCl   CaO   CuCl$_2$   Na$_2$S   CuI
     MgS   NaI   K$_2$S   AlCl$_3$   MgCl$_2$   Al$_2$O$_3$
  (b) CaSO$_4$   KOH   Ca(NO$_3$)$_2$   (NH$_4$)$_2$S   K$_2$SO$_4$   Cu$_2$SO$_4$
     Cu(OH)$_2$   CuSO$_4$   NaNO$_3$   NH$_4$NO$_3$   Mg(OH)$_2$   Al(NO$_3$)$_3$
**4.** Write one complete sentence for each term listed below.
  ion          melting point    binary compound   ternary
  ionic bond   boiling point    oxidation number    compound
  crystal      metallic bond    polyatomic ion

# CHEMICAL EQUATIONS AND REACTIONS

Have you ever spilled bleach on clothing? You know the original color becomes paler or even white. This color loss is due to a chemical change, or reaction. In this section you will study chemical reactions.

## Word Equations

A reaction scientists have studied is the formation of water. Chemists can make small amounts of it by sending an electric spark through a tube containing oxygen and hydrogen. The spark helps break the hydrogen and oxygen molecules into single atoms. Each oxygen atom reacts with two hydrogen atoms. Water results. See Figure 10-12.

Chemists sum up chemical reactions in equations (i•KWAY•zhuhnz). A simple equation using words can describe the formation of water:

hydrogen and oxygen yield water

*Figure 10-12. Every molecule of oxygen reacts with two molecules of hydrogen. Two molecules of water are produced.*

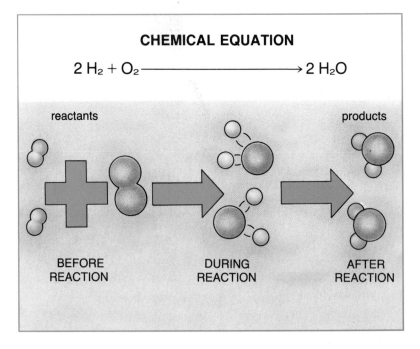

**CHEMICAL EQUATION**

$$2\,H_2 + O_2 \longrightarrow 2\,H_2O$$

reactants · products

BEFORE REACTION · DURING REACTION · AFTER REACTION

A word equation lists the reactants, or substances that react, on the left. On the right, the equation shows the product(s). But word equations do not tell how many molecules of each substance are produced.

## Chemical Equations

A more complete way to describe a chemical reaction is to use *chemical equations.* A **chemical equation** is *an arrangement of numbers and symbols that describes a chemical reaction.* Figure 10-12 shows a chemical equation that sums up the production of water.

Notice that a " + " sign replaces the word *and.* An arrow replaces the word *yield(s).* A chemical equation shows the formula for each reactant and product. The number in front of each formula tells how much of each substance reacts or is produced.

## Conservation of Mass

Chemists have described thousands of chemical reactions. In each case, substances react and yield new substances. Yet chemists have found that mass never changes in a chemical reaction. See Figure 10-13. The mass of the products is the same as the mass of the reactants. This observation that mass does not change in a reaction is the **Law of Conservation of Mass.**

A chemical reaction starts and ends with the same number of each kind of atom. Atoms are neither created nor destroyed during the reaction. So mass does not change.

## How to Balance Equations

Chemical equations should be written to show that atoms are not created or destroyed. If the equations are written correctly, they are said to be balanced. In a balanced equation, you find the same number of each kind of atom on both sides of the arrow. For example, this chemical equation for making ammonia is balanced:

$$3H_2 + N_2 \longrightarrow 2NH_3$$

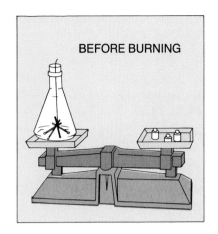

BEFORE BURNING

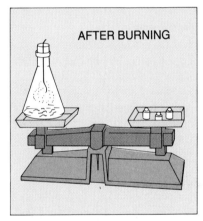

AFTER BURNING

*Figure 10-13. The mass of the substances formed after burning the matches is the same as the mass of the original substances.*

**A CHEMICAL REACTION**

**OBJECTIVE**
Observe a chemical reaction and balance its equation.

**MATERIALS**
goggles, beaker, cold water, Epsom salts, household ammonia water, spoon

**PROCEDURE**
**1.** Add about a gram of Epsom salts to 125 mL of cold water in a beaker. Stir well.
**2.** Slowly add ammonia to the solution in the beaker until you observe a change.
**CAUTION:** Do not get any ammonia on your skin or in your eyes. Do not breathe the fumes directly. Wear goggles.
**3.** Set the mixture aside for 20 to 30 minutes. Do not shake it. Observe what happens.

**QUESTIONS**
**1.** What happened when you added ammonia to the Epsom salts solution?
**2.** What happened in the beaker after 20 to 30 minutes?
**3.** Epsom salts is magnesium sulfate, $MgSO_4$. Ammonia water is ammonium hydroxide, $NH_4OH$. Your teacher will give you the formula equation. Balance it.
**4.** What type of chemical reaction is this?

How can you write a balanced equation for the reaction? Follow four rules to write a balanced equation:

1. *Write a word equation and a chemical equation.*

hydrogen and nitrogen  yield  ammonia

$$H_2 \quad + \quad N_2 \longrightarrow NH_3$$

2. *Count the number of each kind of atom on both sides of the arrow. If they are the same, the equation is balanced.*

2 H's     2 N's     1 N     3 H's

$$H_2 \quad + \quad N_2 \longrightarrow NH_3$$

In this case, there are two H atoms on the left and three on the right. There are two N atoms on the left and only one on the right. The equation is not balanced.

3. *To balance an equation, put a number in front of a formula to make the number of atoms of that substance the same on both sides of the arrow.* DO NOT CHANGE THE FORMULA OF A SUBSTANCE.
Place a 2, for example, *in front of* the $NH_3$.

2 H's   [2 N's]   $2 \times 1 =$[2 N's]   $2 \times 3 = 6$ H's

$$H_2 \quad + \quad N_2 \longrightarrow 2\,NH_3$$

Now there are two N atoms on each side.

4. *Count the other atoms to see if they are still the same on each side of the arrow.*
In step 3, there are two H atoms on the left, but $2 \times 3 = 6$ H atoms on the right. So put a 3 *in front of* the $H_2$ molecule on the left.

$3 \times 2 =$[6 H's]   2 H's   2 N's   [6 H's]

$$3\,H_2 \quad + \quad N_2 \longrightarrow 2\,NH_3$$

Now the equation is balanced.

# Chemical Reactions

Chemists have found that there are four general kinds of chemical reactions. In each kind of reaction, substances are changed in a particular way.

**Composition Reactions**   In a *composition reaction,* *two or more substances combine and form a compound.* For example, the buildup of tarnish is a composition reaction.

silver and sulfur yield silver sulfide (tarnish)
$$2\,Ag + S \longrightarrow Ag_2S$$

The formation of magnesium oxide as shown in Figure 10-14**A** is another example of a composition reaction.

*Figure 10-14A. How do the reactants change?*

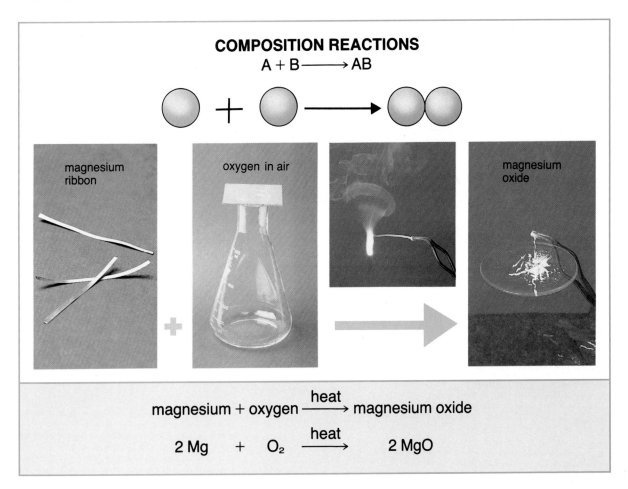

**COMPOSITION REACTIONS**

$$A + B \longrightarrow AB$$

magnesium ribbon

oxygen in air

magnesium oxide

$$\text{magnesium} + \text{oxygen} \xrightarrow{\text{heat}} \text{magnesium oxide}$$

$$2\,Mg + O_2 \xrightarrow{\text{heat}} 2\,MgO$$

**Decomposition Reactions**   *In a decomposition reaction, a compound breaks down into two or more simpler substances.* Decomposition reactions are the reverse of composition reactions. The breakdown of water is a decomposition reaction:

water breaks down into hydrogen and oxygen

$$2\ H_2O \longrightarrow 2\ H_2\ +\ O_2$$

*Figure 10-14B. How do the reactants change?*

Figure 10-14**B** shows the breakdown of mercuric oxide. This reaction produces poisonous vapors.

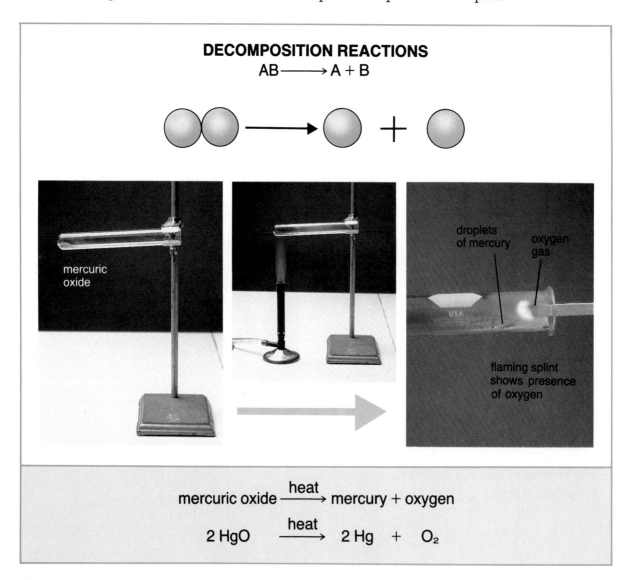

## DECOMPOSITION REACTIONS
$$AB \longrightarrow A + B$$

mercuric oxide

droplets of mercury

oxygen gas

flaming splint shows presence of oxygen

mercuric oxide $\xrightarrow{\text{heat}}$ mercury + oxygen

$$2\ HgO \xrightarrow{\text{heat}} 2\ Hg\ +\ O_2$$

**Single Replacement Reactions** *In a single replacement reaction, a free element replaces an element that is part of a compound.* For example, halogens are often involved in these reactions:

fluorine plus sodium chloride yield chlorine plus sodium fluoride

$$F_2 + 2\ NaCl \longrightarrow Cl_2 + 2\ NaF$$

Another example of a single replacement reaction is shown in Figure 10-14C.

*Figure 10-14C. How do the reactants change?*

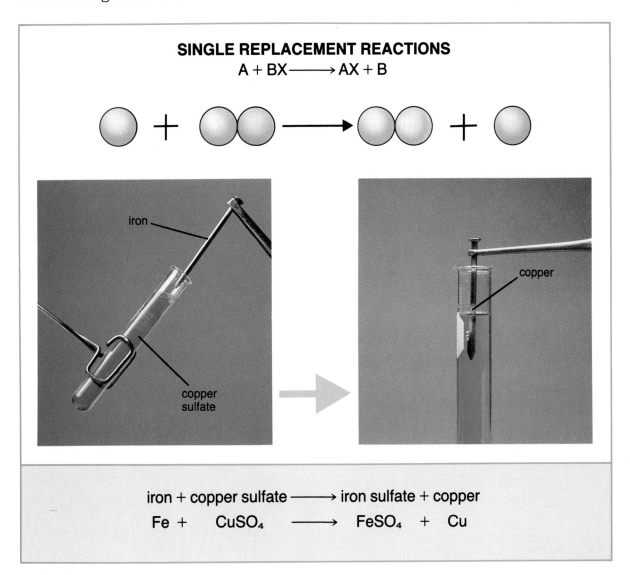

**SINGLE REPLACEMENT REACTIONS**
$$A + BX \longrightarrow AX + B$$

iron

copper sulfate

copper

iron + copper sulfate ⟶ iron sulfate + copper

$$Fe + CuSO_4 \longrightarrow FeSO_4 + Cu$$

**Double Replacement Reactions**   In a *double replacement reaction,* parts of two compounds replace each other. In this kind of reaction, two compounds seem to "switch partners." The yellow pigment in paint, cadmium yellow (cadmium sulfide), is a product of a double replacement reaction:

| cadmium chloride | plus | hydrogen sulfide | yield | cadmium sulfide | plus | hydrogen chloride |
|---|---|---|---|---|---|---|
| $CdCl_2$ | $+$ | $H_2S$ | $\longrightarrow$ | $CdS$ | $+$ | $2\ HCl$ |

*Figure 10-14D.* *How do the reactants change?*

Figure 10-14D illustrates another example of a double replacement reaction.

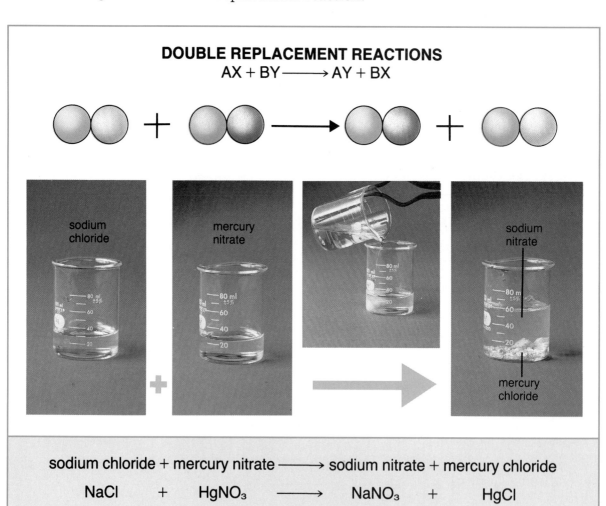

## DOUBLE REPLACEMENT REACTIONS
### AX + BY ⟶ AY + BX

sodium chloride

mercury nitrate

sodium nitrate

mercury chloride

| sodium chloride | + | mercury nitrate | ⟶ | sodium nitrate | + | mercury chloride |
|---|---|---|---|---|---|---|
| NaCl | + | HgNO₃ | ⟶ | NaNO₃ | + | HgCl |

● Iron is one of our most useful metals. Most of it is used to make steel. Before it can be used, iron must first be separated from iron ore.

Most of the iron ore in the United States is a compound of iron and oxygen called iron oxide ($Fe_2O_3$). The iron oxide is loaded into a blast furnace like the one you see in Figure 10-15. Inside the furnace besides other chemicals there is carbon.

The carbon combines with the oxygen from the iron oxide. This reaction is represented by the equation

| carbon | plus | iron oxide | yield | iron | plus | carbon monoxide |
|---|---|---|---|---|---|---|
| 3C | + | $Fe_2O_3$ | $\longrightarrow$ | 2 Fe | + | 3 CO |

After the oxygen is removed from the oxide, pure iron is left.

*Figure 10-15. A blast furnace operates at a temperature of several thousand degrees. It removes oxygen and sandy impurities from iron ore.*

## OBJECTIVES AND WORDS TO REVIEW

**1.** Balance these equations:
 a. $KCl + F_2 \longrightarrow KF + Cl_2$
 b. $Na + H_2O \longrightarrow NaOH + H_2$
 c. $Fe_2O_3 + CO \longrightarrow Fe + CO_2$
 d. $MnO_2 + HCl \longrightarrow MnCl_2 + Cl_2 + H_2O$
 e. $BaCl_2 + Na_2SO_4 \longrightarrow NaCl + BaSO_4$
 f. $KOH + H_2SO_4 \longrightarrow K_2SO_4 + H_2O$

**2.** Balance each equation if necessary. Tell which kind of reaction each represents.
 a. $Ba + Cl_2 \longrightarrow BaCl_2$
 b. $KClO_3 \longrightarrow KCl + O_2$
 c. $NaBr + Ag_2SO_4 \longrightarrow Na_2SO_4 + AgBr$
 d. $CaBr_2 + F_2 \longrightarrow CaF_2 + Br_2$
 e. $H_2O + N_2O_3 \longrightarrow HNO_2$
 f. $Fe + H_2O \longrightarrow Fe_3O_4 + H_2$
 g. $CuCl_2 + H_2S \longrightarrow CuS + HCl$
 h. $PbO_2 \longrightarrow PbO + O_2$
 i. $Br_2 + KI \longrightarrow KBr + I_2$
 j. $Na_2O + H_2O \longrightarrow NaOH$
 k. $Ag_2O \longrightarrow Ag + O_2$

**3.** Write one complete sentence for each term listed below.
 chemical equation          single replacement reaction
 composition reaction        double replacement reaction
 decomposition reaction

# SPEED AND ENERGY OF REACTIONS

List three factors that can speed up a reaction.

*Figure 10-16. Fireworks are examples of reactions that must be heated.*

Some chemical reactions occur slowly. Others happen very quickly. All chemical reactions involve energy changes. In this section you will study factors that affect the rate of a chemical reaction. You will also find out how reactions release and absorb energy.

## The Speed of a Reaction

When fireworks explode, a chemical reaction takes place as Figure 10-16 illustrates. Chemists can control factors that can make reactions speed up or slow down. A model can help you understand how the speed of a reaction can be changed.

In a reaction model, the particles of the reacting substances collide with each other. Collisions allow energy to be transferred from particle to particle. This energy is used in breaking and forming bonds. If collisions take place more often, the reaction will occur faster. Factors that increase the numbers of collisions will speed up the reaction.

**Numbers of Particles** Compare how many particles collide in each part of Figure 10-17. More particles collide in **B** than in **A**. The particle *concentration* (kahn•sen•TRAY•shuhn) is higher in Figure 10-17**B**. *Concentration is the number of particles present in a given volume of space.* In general, the higher the concentration is, the more collisions that occur. The more collisions that occur, the faster the reaction rate.

**A**

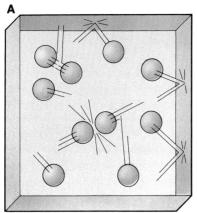

**B**

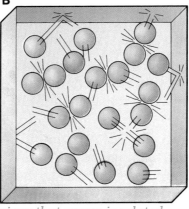

*Figure 10-17. The number of collisions that occurs is related to the number of molecules.*

**Temperature** Hard boiling an egg is a chemical reaction. It might take ten minutes to hard cook an egg with hot, but not boiling, water. It might take only three minutes to hard cook the egg with boiling water.

Most reactions go faster when the temperature is raised. As the temperature increases, the particles of substances move about more rapidly. Particles that move faster collide more often.

**Catalysts** Some chemical reactions take place very slowly. For example, the exhaust gases from an automobile engine contain poisonous carbon monoxide (mon•OK•sighd) (CO) and unburned gasoline. These substances will react and change into carbon dioxide ($CO_2$) and water. But the reaction is normally very slow. In some cases, a catalytic (kat•uh•LIT•ik) converter helps the reaction along. It contains small beads of a substance that causes the change to be very

A.

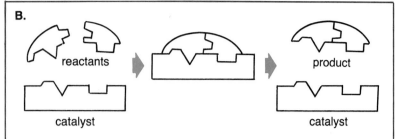

B.

reactants → product

catalyst          catalyst

*Figure 10-18. **A.** A catalytic converter changes carbon monoxide and unburned gasoline into carbon dioxide and water. **B.** Some catalysts provide a site on which chemical reactions take place. However, the catalyst itself is not changed.*

rapid. See Figure 10-18**A.** The beads are a *catalyst* (KAT•uh•list). *A substance that speeds up a chemical reaction is called a **catalyst.*** A catalyst itself is not changed during a reaction. It can be used over and over. See Figure 10-18**B.**

Scientists are trying to understand how catalysts speed up a reaction. It is believed that catalysts make it easier for collisions to occur.

Some catalysts play an important role in food processing. The production of margarine involves the use of a catalyst. Margarine is made by adding hydrogen to liquid oils, such as soybean oil. The hydrogen and the oil react and yield solid margarine. This chemical change takes place in the presence of a catalyst, finely divided nickel.

## Reactions That Give Up Heat

Have you ever warmed your hands at a fire? The burning wood supplies the heat you need to warm yourself. Burning is an example of an *exothermic* (ek•soh•THER•mik) *reaction. A reaction that releases heat is **exothermic.*** The word "exothermic" comes from "exo," which means "out" and "therm," which means "heat." The heat and light produced in a fireworks display result from an exothermic reaction.

When wood burns, it combines with oxygen in the process of oxidation. Oxidation can be slow, as in rusting, or rapid, as in burning. *Rapid oxidation with the release of heat and light is **combustion*** (kuhm•BUS•chuhn). Thus, burning, an exothermic reaction, is classified as combustion. Many exothermic reactions are classified as combustion reactions.

*Figure 10-19. You burn wood to keep warm because this reaction releases heat. Is burning exothermic or endothermic?*

## Reactions that Absorb Heat

The decomposition of mercuric oxide that you studied in Section 3 is an example of another type of reaction:

$$2\ HgO \xrightarrow{\text{heat}} 2\ Hg + O_2$$

This reaction is *endothermic* (en•doh•THUR•mik). *Any reaction that absorbs heat as it progresses is* **endothermic.**

Many chemical reactions absorb heat. Baking powder contains chemical compounds that react in dough and make it rise. But the chemical reaction does not take place until you put the dough into a hot oven. Then the dough absorbs heat, and tiny bubbles of carbon dioxide gas form. The gas causes the dough to rise. This is an endothermic reaction.

● In the early 1900's gasoline for the few cars on the road could be obtained by distilling petroleum. Today the enormous demand for gasoline requires other methods. The petroleum industry uses a process called catalytic cracking. A catalyst is used to "crack," or break up, large petroleum molecules into smaller gasoline molecules.

## OBJECTIVES AND WORDS TO REVIEW

1. Why does raising the temperature usually make chemical reactions go faster?
2. Give two examples of chemical reactions in which a catalyst is used.
3. For each of the following reactions tell whether it is exothermic or endothermic:
   (a) decomposition of mercuric oxide
   (b) burning fuels
   (c) baking powder reacting in dough
4. Write one complete sentence for each term listed below.
   concentration  combustion
   catalyst  endothermic reaction
   exothermic reaction

## EXPLORE BY TRYING

### A SELTZER TABLET REACTION

**OBJECTIVE**
Observe a temperature change in a reaction.

**MATERIALS**
thin plastic cup, water, two seltzer tablets

**PROCEDURE**
1. Add water to the cup to a depth of about 3 cm. Feel the bottom of the cup.
2. Break two seltzer tablets. Add them to the cup.
3. Touch the bottom of the cup. Note any temperature changes for 5 minutes.

**QUESTIONS**
1. Why did you feel the cup in step 1?
2. How did the temperature change after seltzer tablets were added to the water?
3. What type of reaction is this? Explain your answer.

# IDENTIFYING CONTROL AND VARIABLE FACTORS

## Preparation

You may have participated in a taste test. A company gives you two identical cups labeled A and B. The drinks to be tested look alike. You are asked to taste the same amount of each drink, and to say which drink tastes better. The use of two identical cups with the same amount of similar-looking drink makes the taste test valid. The test uses control and variable factors.

The control factors are all the factors that are the same except the variable being tested. In the taste test, the control factors are the identical cups, amounts, and appearance of the two drinks. The variable is the part of the experiment that is different. The taste-test variable is the drink.

Scientists design experiments in much the same way. They take great care to make sure only one factor in the experiment, the variable factor, is changed. Scientists always also include control factors. Control factors provide a basis for comparison.

## Directions

It is important to be able to recognize the factors that are control or variable in an experiment.

Suppose you want to test whether dissolving salt in water lowers its temperature. You measure the same amount of water in similar beakers as in Figure 1. You make sure that to begin with, the water in each beaker is at the same temperature. The only difference between the beakers of water is that you add salt to one of them. You stir the water in each beaker (until all the salt has dissolved). Now you take the temperature of the water in both beakers. The salt is the only variable factor. All the other factors in the experiment are the control factors.

## Practice

Read the experiments below. Then on a separate sheet of paper, identify the control and variable factors for each experiment.

1. Ten grams of sugar dissolves more quickly in a liter bottle of pure, hot tap water than it does in a liter bottle of pure, cold tap water.

2. Five small tomatoes in the vegetable bin of a refrigerator get moldy faster in a plastic bag than five similar tomatoes in a paper bag.

## Application

Design an experiment to see if water causes the exposed metal parts of bicycles to rust faster than when they are dry. On a separate sheet of paper, list all the control factors, as well as the variable factor.

*Figure 1.*

# THE EFFECT OF A CATALYST

### Objective
Observe how a catalyst controls the rate of a chemical reaction.

### Background
Hydrogen peroxide ($H_2O_2$) changes chemically into water and oxygen. This change occurs very slowly when hydrogen peroxide is stored in a dark bottle. However, a catalyst can be used to change the speed of a reaction.

   If this reaction is speeded up, more oxygen will be made. In this experiment you can test for the presence of oxygen by using a wood splint. Oxygen gas supports burning. A glowing split put into a tube of oxygen bursts into flame.

### Materials
4 test tubes, test tube rack, marking pencil, metric teaspoon, 3% hydrogen peroxide, sodium chloride (NaCl), sodium bicarbonate (baking soda, $NaHCO_3$), manganese dioxide ($MnO_2$), graduated cylinder, splint, matches, goggles, apron

### Procedure
1. Label four test tubes *A, B, C,* and *D.* Stand them in the test tube rack or beaker.
2. Add nothing to test tube *A.*
3. Add half a teaspoon NaCl to tube *B.* Add half a teaspoon $MnO_2$ to tube *C.* Add half a teaspoon $NaHCO_3$ to tube *D.* See Figure 10-L. **CAUTION:** Wear goggles and apron.
4. Now add 5 mL of $H_2O_2$ to each test tube. Immediately observe any reactions that occur.
5. If you see gas bubbles in any of the tubes, test the gas with a glowing splint. To do this, light a splint with a match. Quickly blow out the flame. The splint should be glowing but not on fire. Insert the splint part way into the test tube. **CAUTION:** If a flame appears, blow it out. Keep long hair tied back.

6. Test the other tubes the same way.
7. Record all your observations.
8. After 15 minutes look at each tube again.

### Questions
1. What is the purpose of test tube *A*?
2. In which tube(s) did you see a reaction? What happened to the glowing splint?
3. Was the solid used up in the tube(s) that showed a reaction? Explain why or why not.
4. Why did nothing happen in the other tube(s)?
5. **PROBLEM SOLVING** Suggest several ways to speed up this reaction. **CAUTION:** Do not test them yourself.

***Figure 10-L.*** *Laboratory setup.*

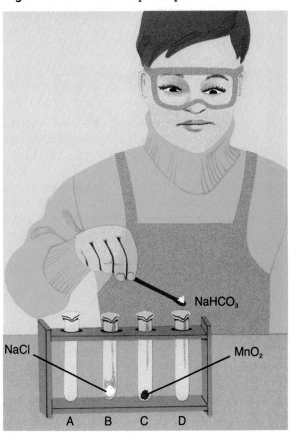

NaHCO₃

NaCl

MnO₂

A   B   C   D

Have you ever made a piece of pottery? Would you like to know how glass is shaped? Do you like to watch construction crews working with concrete? If you have some of these interests, you might look over the careers below.

**Ceramic Engineer** Ceramic engineers develop new ceramic materials or applications for ceramics. Their work may involve porcelain, china, heat-resistant coatings, brick, tile, abrasives, or glass products. Among the unique products they have developed are teacups that can fall nine stories without breaking and glass pipes that can hammer nails. Ceramic engineers also manufacture computer parts and other electronic components.

Like other engineering careers, ceramic engineering requires at least four years of college. Additional college training is important for research engineers. The largest employers of ceramic engineers are the stone, clay, and glass industries.

To find out more about this career, write:

*The National Institute of Ceramic Engineers*
*757 Brooksedge*
*Brooksedge Plaza Drive*
*Westerville, OH 43081-2821*

**Cement Mason** Concrete has been known and used since the days of the Roman Empire. Yet it is still one of the most important structural materials used by builders. Workers who have the special skills needed to form and finish concrete are called cement masons. They work on buildings, bridges, highways, and many other construction projects.

Cement masons usually learn their trade through at least two years of apprenticeship. The training includes both on-the-job experience and classroom education. To qualify for the apprenticeship program, it helps to have a high school education or vocational training.

More information about this career can be obtained from:

*Associated General Contractors of America*
*1957 E Street, NW*
*Washington, DC 20006*

# SUMMARY

1. Covalent bonds result from a sharing of valence electrons between atoms. (10-1)

2. In many nonmetallic compounds and several nonmetallic elements, atoms are held together by covalent bonds. (10-1)

3. Atoms of metals and nonmetals become ions when they bond together. An attraction between oppositely charged ions is an ionic bond. (10-2)

4. Atoms of a metal are bonded together by sharing freely moving valence electrons. (10-2)

5. Chemical equations list the reactants and products of a reaction. Equations are balanced to show that atoms are not created or destroyed in a reaction. (10-3)

6. There are four general types of chemical reactions: composition, decomposition, single replacement, and double replacement. (10-3)

7. Concentration, temperature, and use of catalysts are factors that affect the speed of a reaction. (10-4)

8. Chemical reactions may release energy (exothermic) or absorb energy (endothermic). (10-4)

# REVIEW

Number a sheet of paper from 1 to 25 and answer these questions.

**Building Science Vocabulary**   Write the letter of the term that best matches each definition.

a. boiling point
b. catalyst
c. chemical equation
d. covalent bond
e. crystal
f. endothermic
g. exothermic
h. ion
i. ionic bond
j. melting point
k. metallic bond
l. valence electrons

1. A reaction that gives off heat
2. Electrons that form bonds with other atoms
3. Temperature at which solid changes to liquid
4. Bond formed when two atoms share electrons
5. A bond in which freely moving electrons are shared among atoms
6. Temperature at which liquid changes to gas
7. The force of attraction between ions having opposite changes
8. An expression that uses formulas to represent what is happening during a chemical reaction
9. A substance that speeds up a reaction without changing itself
10. An atom having an unequal number of protons and electrons

**Finding the Facts**   Select the letter of the answer that best completes each of the following.

11. A reaction in which a compound is formed by two or more elements is    (a) single replacement    (b) double replacement    (c) composition    (d) decomposition.

12. Two atoms of hydrogen can acquire a stable electron pattern by    (a) transferring an electron from one atom to the other    (b) sharing electrons between atoms    (c) giving one electron away    (d) obtaining an electron from helium.

13. Zinc chloride is formed when zinc reacts with copper chloride. This is an example of a    (a) single replacement reaction    (b) composition reaction    (c) decomposition reaction    (d) double replacement reaction.

14. Which type of bond occurs in a crystal of KCl?    (a) covalent    (b) ionic    (c) metallic    (d) none of the above

15. Which of the following substances exists as crystals at room temperature?    (a) sodium chloride    (b) natural gas    (c) oxygen    (d) hydrogen peroxide

16. An ion that tastes salty is a (**a**) chloride ion (**b**) hydrogen ion (**c**) potassium ion (**d**) oxide ion.

17. Most chemical reactions go faster at higher temperatures because (**a**) a catalyst is present (**b**) there are more collisions among molecules (**c**) there are more molecules present (**d**) most chemical reactions are exothermic.

18. A chemical reaction that requires the use of a catalyst is (**a**) burning natural gas (**b**) baking powder causing dough to rise (**c**) burning hydrogen in oxygen (**d**) cracking petroleum to produce gasoline.

19. When a sodium atom transfers an electron to a chlorine atom, chlorine becomes (**a**) a negative ion (**b**) a positive ion (**c**) a different element (**d**) neutral.

20. An example of an exothermic reaction is (**a**) a cold pack (**b**) the freezing of water (**c**) the burning of natural gas in a furnace (**d**) baking powder reacting with dough.

**Understanding Main Ideas** Complete the following:

21. In the compound $CO_2$, the number 2 below the letter O stands for the number of oxygen atoms in each __?__.

22. Examine this equation: $2 Hg + O_2 \longrightarrow HgO$ The number that must be placed in front of HgO to balance the equation is __?__.

23. In the reaction $2 NaCl + F_2$, the products are $Cl_2$ and __?__.

24. Metals are good conductors because their valence electrons are moving __?__.

25. A chemical reaction goes faster in the presence of a catalyst because scientists believe the catalyst causes the reaction to require less __?__.

**Writing About Science** On a separate sheet of paper, answer the following as completely as possible.

1. Potassium (K) is in Group IA of the Periodic Table. Bromine (Br) is in Group VIIA. What kind of bond holds potassium and bromine together in potassium bromide (KBr)?

2. Suppose you hear someone say that one of the guests was a catalyst at a party. What do you think the person meant by this?

3. Suppose you drop two seltzer tablets into a glass of water. The seltzer reacts in the water and fizzes. After a few minutes the glass feels cold. Explain why the glass became cold.

4. Balance this equation:

$$Ca + HCl \longrightarrow CaCl_2 + H_2$$

5. (laboratory question) Suppose you have two test tubes. To each tube you add a pinch of a different chemical compound. Then you add 5 mL of hydrogen peroxide to each tube. What observation would tell you which of the two compounds is a catalyst for the decomposition change of hydrogen peroxide $(H_2O_2)$?

**Investigating Chapter Ideas** Try the following project to further your study.

**Slow oxidation** Float iron filings on a cork in a tray of water. Place a glass tumbler over the filings and cork. Explain what changes you see over a period of days.

**Reading About Science** Read some of the following books to explore topics that interest you.

Cherrier, François. 1978. **Fascinating Experiments in Chemistry.** New York: Sterling.
Gleasner, Diana C. 1983. **Dynamite.** New York: Walker

# APPLIED CHEMISTRY

A huge rig removes oil from chambers far below the ocean's surface. This precious fluid is a major source of energy. However, chemical research has discovered other uses for oil. For example, the fabric of some kinds of clothing is made from compounds contained in oil. In this unit you will study how the knowledge of chemistry is applied to the world around you to make it a more comfortable place to live.

UNIT

4

A

B

The first beaker seems to contain just plain water. However, it also contains something else. This something is broken up and spread evenly throughout the liquid. It is a solid that has been dissolved in the liquid.

Look what happens when a small crystal of the solid, used as a seed, is dropped into the beaker. The dissolved solid comes out of the liquid. The solid collects on the seed crystal, making it grow larger.

Seeding is one way to remove a dissolved solid from a liquid. The geyser pool illustrates another way. The hot water evaporates, leaving the solid behind. In this chapter you will study dissolved substances.

Read and Find Out:

● why coins are mixtures of valuable and cheap metals.

● how table salt is taken from ocean water.

● how some dissolved substances help keep traffic moving.

● how to make a mixture that you can use in salads.

# SOLUTIONS, SUSPENSIONS, AND COLLOIDS

# SOLUTIONS ARE MIXTURES

Suppose you wanted to make iced tea from an instant tea mix. All you have to do is add water to the instant tea and stir. What happens to the tea particles and the water as you stir?

The tea particles are *soluble* (SAHL•yuh•buhl) in water. **Soluble** *means "can be dissolved."* The particles become dissolved in water. As they are dissolved, they spread evenly throughout the water. The result is a mixture that looks the same throughout the pitcher. Not all mixtures look the same throughout. You have made a special kind of mixture called a *solution* (suh•LEW•shuhn).

*A **solution** is a mixture of one substance dissolved in another so that the properties are the same throughout.* All parts of a solution have the same properties, such as color, odor, and taste.

Salt water is a solution. So are many soft drinks. These examples are all liquid solutions. In this section you will learn about other kinds of solutions as well.

*Figure 11-1. Particles of the solid break away in water. These particles fit into the spaces between the water molecules.*

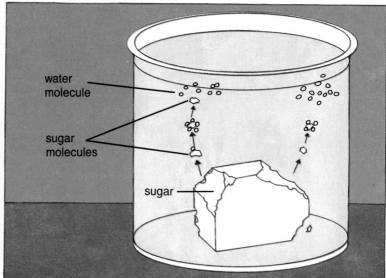

water molecule

sugar molecules

sugar

## Parts of a Solution

All mixtures are made of at least two parts added together. Solutions, as special kinds of mixtures, have two special kinds of parts. One part dissolves the other. When you add sugar to water, for example, water dissolves the sugar. See Figure 11-1.

Even if you do not stir the sugar and water, in time the water tastes sweet. Water molecules are in motion. Gradually they surround molecules of sugar. The surrounded sugar molecules are spread throughout the water. Without stirring, you have made a sugar solution.

The water in this solution is a *solvent* (SAHL•vent). *A **solvent** is the part of a solution that dissolves a substance.* Water is not the only solvent. Other liquids can also be solvents. For example, turpentine is a good paint solvent. Acetone "removes" nail polish. *Alcohol is the solvent in solutions called **tinctures*** (TING•churz), such as tincture of iodine.

The other part of a solution is the *solute* (SAHL•yewt). *The **solute** is the substance that becomes dissolved,* such as the sugar or the tea particles.

## Separating the Parts

Compounds and mixtures both have at least two parts added together. The parts of a compound lose their properties. They form a new substance during a chemical change. The parts of a mixture, however, do not lose their properties. In the sugar solution, you still have molecules of sugar and water. They did not change chemically.

The parts of a solution are so well mixed that even a filter cannot separate them. See Figure 11-2 on page 234. However, a simple physical change can help separate the two parts of a solution. Boiling, for example, is a physical change. If a sugar solution is boiled, the water evaporates. The evaporated water is still water, only it has changed from liquid to gas. After all the water has boiled away, particles of sugar will remain behind.

*Figure 11-2.* The parts of a solution go right through a filter. Is a sand and water mixture a solution?

## Kinds of Solutions

In the sugar solution, the solute (sugar) is a solid. The solvent (water) is a liquid. The instant iced tea is also a solid-in-liquid solution. You are probably familiar with other solutions that fit this description.

However, there are many other kinds of solutions. Liquids are dissolved in other liquids. Liquids are dissolved in gases. Gases are dissolved in gases, and so on. Table 11-1 shows examples of these and other solutions.

How are alloys made?

Most "metal" objects around you are actually solid solutions called alloys. Alloys are solutions of one or more metals and other solids. Alloys are made by heating, melting, and mixing the parts together. The solution, then, cools and hardens. The parts remain dissolved in each other in the solid phase.

● Most "metal" jewelry is made of alloys. Pure gold, considered 24 carat gold, is too soft for most jewelry. Fourteen carat gold—an alloy of gold, copper, and silver—is more durable. Pure silver is also too soft for jewelry and silverware. Sterling silver, an alloy of silver and copper, is much more useful.

Coins are also made of alloys. A nickel coin is only 25% nickel metal. The rest is copper. Pennies used to be made of pure copper. Pennies today are an alloy of copper and the metal zinc. Quarters and dimes, once silver, are today alloys of copper and nickel. Alloys are used to make coins mainly because they are less expensive than pure metals. If pure metals were used, coins would be worth more than their face value.

### TABLE 11-1. TYPES OF SOLUTIONS

| Kind of Solution | Solute | Solvent | Solution |
|---|---|---|---|
| Gas in liquid | carbon dioxide | water | club soda |
| Liquid in liquid | alcohol | water | rubbing alcohol |
| Solid in gas | sulfur vapor | air | sulfur vapor in air |
| Liquid in gas | water | air | humid air |
| Gas in gas | oxygen | nitrogen | air |

### OBJECTIVES AND WORDS TO REVIEW

1. What are the two parts of a solution?
2. How is a solution different from a compound?
3. List five kinds of solutions and give an example of each. List the solute and solvent of each.
4. Write one complete sentence for each term listed below.
   soluble    solvent    solute    solution    tincture

# MAKING SOLUTIONS

**OBJECTIVES**

**1.** List three ways to increase the rate at which a solute is dissolved.

**2.** Contrast dilute and concentrated solutions.

**3.** Contrast unsaturated and supersaturated solutions.

Have you ever used tea bags to make iced tea? If so, you know that the first step is to boil the water. Why do you need hot water to make iced tea? Boiling helps water dissolve tea particles. In this section, you will learn more about the process of dissolving and how you can speed up the process.

## The Rate of Dissolving

You have seen how water dissolves sugar. Water molecules surround the sugar molecules. The amount of sugar that the water dissolves per second is called the rate of dissolving. Heating is a way of increasing the rate of dissolving. That is, heating can increase the amount of solute that a solvent dissolves per second.

List three ways to increase the rate at which a substance dissolves.

Heating speeds up the motion of molecules in the beaker. The faster the molecules move, the faster the solvent molecules surround and spread out the solute molecules. So the faster the molecules are moving, the more solute is dissolved each second.

A second way to increase the rate of dissolving is stirring. Like heating, stirring also speeds up the molecules in the beaker and helps them mix together.

Grinding is a third way to increase the rate of dissolving. For example, grinding or crushing a sugar cube breaks it into small particles. The smaller the particles, the faster the solvent can surround them. See Figure 11-3.

*Figure 11-3. A pharmacist prepares powders with a mortar and pestle.*

## Making a Concentrated Solution

Stir a teaspoonful of sugar into a saucepan of water. With such a small amount of sugar, the solution tastes only slightly sweet. It is a *dilute* (digh•LEWT) solution. *A **dilute** solution has only a small amount of solute compared with the amount of solvent.*

Now add two more teaspoonfuls of sugar to the solution. Stir until all of it is dissolved. Has the solution changed? Of course, it is sweeter. The solution is more *concentrated* (KAHN•sen•tray•tid). *A **concentrated** solution has a relatively large amount of solute compared with the amount of solvent.*

## Reaching a Limit

Make the sugar solution more concentrated by adding sugar. Keep stirring, but do not heat it. Is there a limit to the amount of sugar that can be dissolved?

*A solution is said to be **unsaturated** (un•SACH•uh•ray•tid) as long as more solute can be dissolved.* As you keep adding sugar and stirring, however, eventually your solution becomes *saturated*. *In a **saturated** solution at any one temperature, no more solute can be dissolved.*

Suppose six teaspoonfuls is all the sugar that you can dissolve in the pan of water without heating. You have found the *solubility* (SAHL•yew•bil•uh•tee) of the sugar at room temperature. *The **solubility** is the amount of solute that can be dissolved in a given amount of solvent at any one temperature.* It is the amount of solute that makes a solution saturated.

## Solubility and Temperature

Is there a way to make more solute dissolve in a saturated solution? Heat the solution. As the temperature increases, more sugar can be dissolved. So, increasing the temperature of a solution can increase the solubility of many solutes. See Figure 11-4.

Suppose you made a saturated sugar solution at a high temperature. Then you let it cool. The sugar stays dissolved as long as the solution is not disturbed. The undisturbed, cooled solution is *supersaturated*. *A **supersaturated** solution contains more solute than it normally has at a given temperature.*

Drop an extra sugar crystal into the solution. Or shake it. Any such disturbance can make the extra solute come out of the solution. The solution shown in

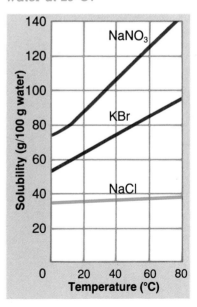

*Figure 11-4. Table salt (NaCl), potassium bromide (KBr), and sodium nitrate (NaNO$_3$) are used by photographers. How many grams of each substance could you dissolve in 100 g of water at 20°C?*

## SUPERSATURATING A SOLUTION

**OBJECTIVE**
Make rock candy.

**MATERIALS**
0.25 L water, saucepan, sugar, tumbler, pot holders

**PROCEDURE**
**1.** Boil the water in a saucepan. Turn off the heat.
**CAUTION:** Use potholders.
**2.** Slowly stir sugar into the water until no more dissolves.
**3.** Cool the solution 5 minutes. Pour the clear liquid into the tumbler. Let the liquid stand undisturbed for 3 hours. Record your observations.
**4.** Drop a sugar crystal into the liquid. Record what you see.

**QUESTIONS**
**1.** Describe how the tumbler looked after 3 hours.
**2.** What happened when you dropped the sugar crystal into the solution? Explain.

beaker **B** in the chapter opener was supersaturated. A tap was all it took to make the solute settle to the bottom of the beaker.

● Ocean water contains a large number of dissolved compounds, including table salt. Table salt can be taken from ocean water by simple evaporation. See Figure 11-5. Ocean water collects in shallow basins along a shore. The sun's energy evaporates water from the basins. Less and less salt can stay dissolved in the remaining water. In time, salt comes out of the ocean water and settles to the bottom of the basins. The salt can then be collected and purified for use.

*Figure 11-5. Some extraction plants use solar energy to obtain salt from sea water.*

### OBJECTIVES AND WORDS TO REVIEW

**1.** You want to dissolve a bouillon cube in water to make a cup of broth. List three things you can do to make the cube dissolve quickly.
**2.** How can you make a dilute solution of salt more concentrated?
**3.** How can you make supersaturated solution from a glass of water and a bag of sugar?
**4.** Write one complete sentence for each term listed below.

| | | |
|---|---|---|
| solubility | concentrated | saturated |
| dilute | unsaturated | supersaturated |

# THE "UNIVERSAL SOLVENT": WATER

In most of the solutions discussed so far, water has been the solvent. Water is sometimes called "the universal solvent," that is, a solvent that dissolves everything. However, there are many substances that water cannot dissolve.

For example, water cannot dissolve oil. Water and oil remain separate even when they are stirred. Oil is *insoluble* (in•SAHL•yew•buhl) in water. **Insoluble** *means "cannot be dissolved."*

Yet, thousands of substances are soluble in water. In this section you will learn why water is such a good solvent. You will also find out how water can be purified of solutes that may be harmful.

## Water Molecules

The structure of a molecule of water can help you understand how water can dissolve so many substances. A water molecule, remember, is made of one atom of oxygen bonded with two atoms of hydrogen. The atoms are bonded by sharing some electrons.

The sharing, however, is like an unequal tug of war. See Figure 11-6. The oxygen atoms attract the electrons more strongly than the hydrogen atoms. The shared electrons are attracted closer to oxygen than to hydrogen. As you see in Figure 11-6, the oxygen "end" of the water molecule is more negative than the hydrogen "end." Likewise, the hydrogen end is more positive than the oxygen end. The oxygen end is said to have a partial negative charge. The hydrogen end of the molecule is said to have a partial positive charge.

*Molecules that have ends with partial negative and partial positive charges are called* **polar** *(POH•lur)* **molecules.** Water is a polar molecule.

**OBJECTIVES**

**1.** Show how water dissolves sugar and salt.

**2.** Tell why water cannot dissolve oils.

**3.** List some ways to purify water.

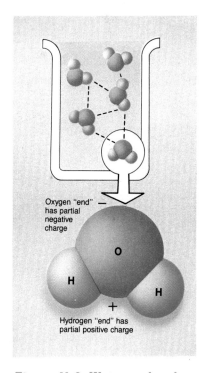

Oxygen "end" has partial negative charge

O

H        H

+

Hydrogen "end" has partial positive charge

*Figure 11-6. Water molecules in the glass exert attractive forces (dotted lines) on each other. What happens to these forces when the water is heated?*

**A SOLUTION CALLED
OCEAN WATER**

**OBJECTIVE**
Report on the substances
dissolved in ocean water.

**PROCEDURE**
**1.** In the science section of
the library, look for books
about the oceans.
**2.** Make a list of substances
that are dissolved in ocean
water. Also list materials that
settle or collect at the ocean
floor.
**3.** Find out how people obtain
and use the materials listed
above.

**QUESTION**
Set up a poster to report your
findings. Divide the poster
into sections. In each section,
list a material that we get from
ocean water. Explain how the
material is taken from the
water and how the material is
used.

*Figure 11-7. A table salt
crystal dissolving in water.*

## The Dissolving Action of Polar Molecules

Water molecules attract each other, as you see in Figure 11-6. The slightly negative "end" of one molecule attracts the slightly positive "end" of another. Water molecules can also attract particles of other substances. It is this attraction that makes water such a good solvent.

**Other Polar Molecules**   Many of the substances that water dissolves also are made of polar molecules. For example, alcohol is a polar molecule. Water dissolves alcohol. The partially charged ends of water molecules attract the partially charged ends of the alcohol molecules.

**Ions**   Many of the substances that water dissolves are made of ions, charged atoms, or groups of atoms. Table salt (sodium chloride) is made of sodium ions and chloride ions. See Figure 11-7. When table salt is mixed with water, the slightly charged ends of the water molecules attract the ions of the salt. As a result, a salt solution consists of sodium ions and chloride ions spread evenly among the water molecules.

**Nonpolar Molecules**   Grease, oils, and many other substances are not made of polar molecules. Water cannot dissolve these substances. To dissolve these substances, other nonpolar solvents are used. "Like dissolves like" is a useful saying to remember when choosing a solvent.

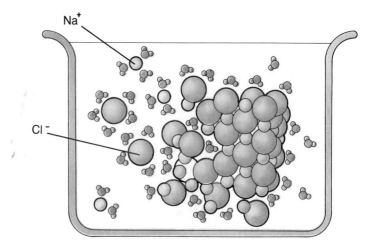

## Impurities in Water

Water is such a good solvent that it dissolves many substances in nature, including air and minerals. Streams and lakes dissolve some of the minerals from soil and rocks at the bottom. The water supply in some areas contains dissolved ions of many metals.

The water supply in some areas is called *hard water.* **Hard water** *contains dissolved metal ions that keep the water from lathering when soap is added.* When hard water evaporates, these ions are left behind in a scaly residue called a "water spot."

Chemicals can be added to soften water, that is, to remove the ions. Ion exchange units can be installed on faucets to remove the ions. See Figure 11-8.

## Pollutants

**Pollutants** (pah•LEWT•nts) *are impurities in air and water that may be harmful to life.* Water in some areas may contain such pollutants as chemical wastes and sewage. Fertilizers added to soil become dissolved in ground water and may drain into lakes and streams. Waste gases from cars and factories rise into the atmosphere and may be dissolved in rainwater.

Pollutants can be harmful to animals and plants. Dissolved fertilizers, for example, can encourage the growth of water plants at the surface of a lake. These plants use up dissolved oxygen and other substances needed by other living things in the lake. Fish and other forms of life in the lake may die.

## Purifying Water

When chemists purify water in a laboratory, they do it by *distillation* (dis•tuh•LAY•shuhn). **Distillation** *is a process that evaporates a liquid by heating and changes the gas back to a liquid by cooling.* See Figure 11-9 on page 242. Impurities are left behind when water is evaporated. Because of the heat energy, however, distillation is an expensive process for large amounts of water.

What effect does water have on table salt when the two substances are mixed?

Figure 11-8. Ions that form a scaly crust can be removed by attaching an ion exchange unit to a faucet.

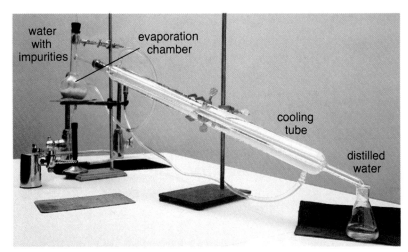

*Figure 11-9.* The water evaporated at the left is changed back into a liquid when it passes through the cooling tube. Where are impurities left behind?

water with impurities

evaporation chamber

cooling tube

distilled water

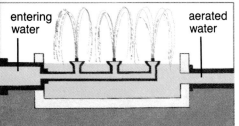

entering water

aerated water

*Figure 11-10.* In many water treatment plants, water is sprayed into the air. The oxygen in the air removes the foul odor and taste the water may have.

Large water supplies are often purified in a number of steps. See Figure 11-10. In one step, water is filtered to remove undissolved particles. In a step called **aeration** (ayr•AY•shuhn), *water is sprayed into the air.* Aeration improves the taste of water. Some chemicals may be added to remove certain minerals and to kill harmful organisms.

● Pure water boils at 100°C and freezes at 0°C. However, water containing dissolved minerals such as salt must be heated above 100° before it will boil. Water with dissolved materials will not freeze until the temperature drops below 0°. Materials such as antifreeze and rock salt are dissolved into water to keep it from freezing until the temperature drops well below 0°. Antifreeze, a solution containing alcohol, is used to keep water from freezing in a car's radiator. Rock salt, sodium chloride, keeps water from freezing on sidewalks and streets.

### OBJECTIVES AND WORDS TO REVIEW

1. Draw a diagram showing how water molecules dissolve sodium chloride.
2. Why is oil insoluble in water?
3. In the distillation setup in Figure 11-9, what is needed to make water evaporate? In what part of the setup are impurities left?
4. Write a complete sentence for each term listed below.

| | | |
|---|---|---|
| insoluble | hard water | distillation |
| polar molecule | pollutant | aeration |

# SUSPENSIONS AND COLLOIDS

In this section you will learn about more kinds of mixtures. You will find out how each one is different from a solution. For example, look at the mixture at the left in Figure 11-11A. How is it different from the solution, the mixture at the right?

## Suspension

Solutions are clear. The dissolved particles are so small that you cannot see them. The particles do not settle shortly after they have been dissolved.

The mixture at the left in Figure 11-11A, soil and water, is cloudy. You can see the soil particles. They are not dissolved. They are simply hanging, or suspended, in the water in **A**. In **B**, many of the particles have settled.

soil and water          tea and water

soil and water          tea and water

*Figure 11-11.* (A) *Both mixtures have just been stirred.* (B) *Ten minutes later. Compare the two mixtures. Tea shows no change; soil has settled to bottom.*

*The "Universal Solvent": Water* **243**

A mixture of soil and water is an example of a *suspension* (suh•SPEN•shuhn). *A **suspension** is a mixture made of parts that separate upon standing.* The particles mixed into a suspension are larger than molecules or ions. Products marked "Shake well before using" are often suspensions. Find more kinds of suspensions in Table 11-2.

Solid particles separate from a suspension by settling to the bottom. Fine particles, however, often remain suspended a long time. You can separate them by using a strainer or filter. When you pour a solution through a filter, the solute particles go through. But when you pour a suspension through a filter, the particles get trapped.

How can you separate the parts of a suspension?

## Liquid-in-Liquid Suspensions

Oil and water, remember, stay mixed only moments after shaking. For the short time that they are mixed together, however, they make up a kind of suspension called an *emulsion* (ee•MUL•shuhn). *An **emulsion** is a suspension of two liquids that usually do not mix together.*

Add a few drops of liquid soap to the oil and water. Shake again. The soap helps break up the oil into droplets. The droplets now stay mixed for a longer time. Using soap, you have made the parts of the emulsion stay mixed. *Any substance that keeps the parts of an emulsion mixed together is called an **emulsifier** (ee•MUL•si•figh•ur).*

**TABLE 11-2.** SUSPENSIONS

| Kind of Suspension | Particles (or Droplets) of | Mixed in | Suspension |
|---|---|---|---|
| Solid in gas | dust | air | dusty air |
| Liquid in gas | water | air | steam inside a covered pot |
| Gas in liquid | air | cream | whipped cream |

*Figure 11-12.* The tiny droplets making up fog scatter the light from a beam passing through it.

## Colloids

A headlight can help you learn about a special kind of mixture. See Figure 11-12. Fog is a mixture of fine water droplets in air. The droplets *do not* settle out. So fog is not a suspension. Rather, it is an example of a mixture called a *colloid* (KAHL•oyd).

A **colloid** *contains undissolved particles or droplets that stay mixed in another substance.* Fog is a liquid-in-gas colloid. An emulsion in which liquid droplets stay *permanently* mixed in another liquid is another kind of colloid. Find more kinds in Table 11-3. The particles or droplets mixed in each kind of colloid are too small to be seen. They go through filter paper.

**TABLE 11-3.** COLLOIDS

| Kind of Colloid | Particles (or Droplets) of | Mixed in | Colloid |
|---|---|---|---|
| Gas in solid | air | soap | floating soap |
| Liquid in liquid | butterfat | water | homogenized milk |
| Solid in liquid | gum | water | liquid glue |
| Solid in gas | ash and soot | air | smoke |

## IDENTIFYING MIXTURES

### OBJECTIVE
Identify a solution, suspension, and a colloid by using light.

### MATERIALS
3 clear glasses, 3 egg whites, cornstarch, water, flashlight, instant coffee, metric teaspoon

### PROCEDURE
**1.** Fill two glasses with water. Stir a teaspoon of cornstarch into one glass. Stir 5 grains of the coffee into the second.
**2.** Pour three egg whites into a third glass.
**3.** In a darkened room, beam a flashlight into each glass.
**4.** Observe each glass for the path of light. Note any other features of the mixtures.

### QUESTION
Identify each mixture as a solution, suspension, or colloid. Support your answers.

*Figure 11-13.* The path of a beam of light is seen only as it passes through a colloid, not through a solution.

*Figure 11-14.* *Brownian motion occurs when molecules of the suspending medium collide with the particles of the colloid.*

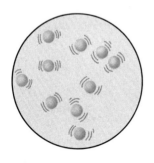

Colloids are much like solutions. Both mixtures contain small particles that stay mixed and go through filter paper. But a beam of light can help you see how a colloid differs from a solution. See Figure 11-13.

The particles in a colloid are larger than molecules. They are large enough to scatter light. So you can see the path of light through a colloid. This scattering of light by colloids is known as the Tyndall effect.

Dissolved particles in a solution, on the other hand, are the size of molecules. They are too small to scatter light. Because light is not scattered, you cannot see a path as a light beam goes through a solution.

Colloids can help demonstrate an important property that all molecules have. Molecules are constantly moving. If you looked at a colloid under a microscope, you would see rapidly moving pinpoints of light. See Figure 11-14. This zigzag movement was first seen by the biologist Robert Brown. It is called *Brownian motion.* **Brownian motion** *is the random movement of colloid particles suspended in a fluid.*

Brownian motion is like the motion of food on the surface of a fishtank. As fish below the surface nibble at the food, they push it in many directions. The food moves first one way, then another. This zigzag movement is like that of a colloid showing Brownian motion.

● Oil and vinegar do not stay mixed. Moments after you stop shaking them, they separate into two layers. However, add an egg yolk to the oil and vinegar. Shake again. The egg yolk acts like an emulsifier. It breaks the oil into droplets that stay mixed permanently with the vinegar. You have made a colloid out of two liquids. The colloid is mayonnaise.

## OBJECTIVES AND WORDS TO REVIEW

1. How is a suspension different from a solution?
2. How could you separate coffee grains from coffee?
3. Tell one way a colloid is like a solution and one way a colloid is like a suspension.
4. Write one complete sentence for each term listed below.

| suspension | emulsifier | Brownian motion |
|---|---|---|
| emulsion | colloid | |

## TECHNOLOGY TRADE-OFF

### Is Jello "Alive?"

You may know that living nerve cells produce very small amounts of electricity. When doctors are not sure if a person is alive, they sometimes use an electroencephalograph (i·LEK·troh·en·SEF·uh·luh·graf) machine (EEG). The EEG measures and records the voltages, or electrical impulses, produced by nerve cells in the brain.

There is probably no question in your mind about whether a bowl of Jello is alive or dead. Jello is a colloid. Doctor Adrian Upton, however, decided to test the EEG machine. He attached it to a bowl of Jello. Surprisingly, the EEG "reported" that the Jello *was alive*. The normal activity in the room, such as the body heat and sweat of the doctors and nurses, had been "sensed" by the machine. Dr. Upton's experiment raises some very basic questions about modern technology.

### Using Critical Thinking

How much should doctors rely on technology? What kind of safeguards should society demand when it comes to "sophisticated" technology? What do you think?

# COMPARING AND CONTRASTING

## Preparation

Are you an educated consumer? You are when you learn about a product before you buy it. Suppose you want to buy a stereo. How do you go about it? You read all the available information on the various models. Then, you find properties that each stereo has in common. That is, you compare the models. However, you also consider the options available. Each model has its own options. They make each model different. When you consider differences between the stereos, you are contrasting.

Comparing and contrasting are important tools for scientists also. For example, to learn more about impurities in water, a scientist may compare and contrast many water samples.

| TABLE 1. | |
|---|---|
| **Similarities (comparing)** | **Differences (contrasting)** |
| Both round or oval shape | Grapefruit large and yellow; orange small and orange |
| Both citrus fruits | Grapefruit: bitter taste; orange: sweet taste |

## Directions

You can compare and contrast common objects, such as a grapefruit and an orange. By noting the similarities between the two objects, you are comparing them. By noting their differences, you

are contrasting them. Table 1 shows some results of these two processes.

## Practice

Scientists compare and contrast in their writings. Read the following paragraphs. Then, on a separate sheet of paper, copy out Table 2. Fill in the missing information on the basis of the paragraphs.

A solution and a suspension are two kinds of mixtures. A solution is a mixture of one substance dissolved in another so that the properties are the same throughout. Sugar dissolved in water is an example of a solution. It appears clear and the particles do not settle out once dissolved.

On the other hand, a suspension is a mixture made of parts that separate upon standing. Soil mixed in water is a suspension. It appears cloudy because the particles are hanging suspended in the water. They do not dissolve.

## Application

After reading Chapter 11, make up a table like Table 2 for solutions and colloids. Then, write a short paragraph comparing and contrasting solutions with colloids.

| TABLE 2. | | |
|---|---|---|
| | **Solutions** | **Suspensions** |
| Appearance | | |
| How particles found in mixture | | |
| Example | | |

# LABORATORY ACTIVITY

## TEMPERATURE AND SOLUBILITY

### Objective
Investigate the effect of temperature on the solubility of potassium nitrate ($KNO_3$) in water.

### Background
You will measure how much $KNO_3$ dissolves in 10 mL of water at a particular temperature. You will compare results with students working at other temperatures.

### Materials
balance, standard masses, Pyrex 50 mL beaker, ringstand and ring support, wire gauze, filter paper, bunsen burner, stirring rod, thermometer, $KNO_3$, water, graph paper, goggles, apron

### Procedure
1. Place standard masses totaling 20 g on one pan of a balance.
2. Place a filter paper circle on the other pan. Gradually add $KNO_3$ to the filter paper until the pans are balanced. The combined mass of the paper and $KNO_3$ is now 20 g. Remove the masses and bring the $KNO_3$ to your work space.
3. Set up the materials shown in Figure 11-L to heat 10 mL of water to the temperature your teacher assigns you.
4. **CAUTION:** Do not stir the water with a thermometer. When the water reaches the temperature, turn off the burner. With a stirring rod, gradually stir in $KNO_3$ from your supply until no more can be dissolved. **CAUTION:** Do not touch hot glassware. Wear goggles and an apron.
5. Find the mass of the filter paper and remaining $KNO_3$. Subtract this mass from the original mass of 20 g. The difference is the amount of $KNO_3$ that is dissolved in the solution.

### Questions
1. Share your data with other students. Record how much $KNO_3$ dissolves at 20°, 30°, 40°, 50°, and 60°C. Make a graph of the data of masses on the vertical axis and temperatures on the horizontal axis. Based on the graph, how does the solubility of $KNO_3$ change with temperature.
2. **PROBLEM SOLVING** Compare and contrast your graph with the three graphs in Figure 11-4 on page 237. Which graph in Figure 11-4 is most like yours? Which is least like yours? Which of all the compounds is most soluble at 60°C?

*Figure 11-L.* *Laboratory setup.*

# SUMMARY

1. A solution contains particles the size of molecules evenly distributed throughout another substance. (11-1)
2. The parts of a solution can be separated by physical changes. (11-1)
3. Grinding, stirring, and heating increase the rate of dissolving by helping mix molecules of solute and solvent. (11-2)
4. An increase in temperature increases the solubility of a solute. (11-2)
5. The polar molecules of water enable it to dissolve other polar molecules as well as ions. (11-3)
6. Water in lakes, streams, and oceans contain dissolved minerals and sometimes harmful pollutants. (11-3)
7. The particles of a suspension settle and are large enough to be seen. (11-4)
8. The particles of a colloid do not settle. They scatter a beam of light passing through the colloid. (11-4)

# REVIEW

Number a sheet of paper from 1 to 25 and answer these questions.

**Building Science Vocabulary**  Write the letter of the term that best matches each definition.

a. aeration      e. distillation   i. solute
b. colloid       f. hard water    j. solvent
c. concentrated  g. pollutant     k. suspension
d. dilute        h. saturated     l. tincture

1. A mixture in which particles settle out on standing
2. A process in which water is sprayed into air

3. A solution that contains a large amount of solute compared with the amount of solvent
4. A solution having alcohol as the solvent
5. A solution that contains very little solute
6. Water containing large amounts of certain metal ions
7. A solution in which no more solute can be dissolved
8. An impurity in air or water that can be harmful
9. The process that evaporates a liquid by heating and changes the gas back to a liquid by cooling
10. A substance that dissolves another substance

**Finding the Facts**  Select the letter of the answer that best completes each of the following.

11. Which of the following is not a solution?
    (a) air   (b) tea   (c) soil and water
    (d) sugar and water
12. Oil does not dissolve in water because
    (a) water is made of nonpolar molecules
    (b) oil is made of nonpolar molecules
    (c) water is made of ions   (d) oil is made of polar molecules.
13. Which of the following is a property of colloids?   (a) The particles settle out.
    (b) The particles are large enough for you to see.   (c) The particles scatter light.
    (d) The parts can be separated with a filter.
14. Oil and water will stay mixed together if you
    (a) shake them   (b) stir them   (c) mix them with soap   (d) strain them.
15. Fog is an example of a   (a) solution
    (b) solute   (c) alloy   (d) colloid.
16. An alloy is a kind of   (a) solution
    (b) suspension   (c) solute   (d) colloid.
17. Which of the following is an example of a colloid?   (a) metal coins   (b) oil
    (c) mayonnaise   (d) tea.
18. Which of the following is usually not a way to increase the rate of dissolving?   (a) heating
    (b) grinding   (c) cooling   (d) stirring.

**19.** Homogenized milk is best described as a    **(a)** colloid    **(b)** solvent    **(c)** solution    **(d)** solute.

**20.** Distilling water includes evaporating the water and    **(a)** adding chemicals    **(b)** spraying it into air    **(c)** changing it back to liquid    **(d)** filtering it.

**Understanding the Main Ideas**    Complete the following.

**21.** The two parts of a solution are the __?__ and the __?__.

**22.** A way of increasing the rate of dissolving a solute are __?__, __?__, and __?__.

**23.** Water molecules, with partially charged ends, are called __?__.

**24.** Suspensions and solutions differ because, upon standing, particles mixed in a suspension gradually __?__.

**25.** When you aim a light through a solution and a colloid, you can see the path of the beam through the __?__.

**Writing About Science**    On a separate sheet of paper, answer the following as completely as possible.

**1.** When you start to set up an aquarium you spread a layer of gravel on the bottom. Then you add water. The water mixes with particles from the gravel. In time the particles settle. But how could you separate the particles more quickly?

**2.** When you open a bottle of soda, you see bubbles of gas. Where did the bubbles come from?

**3.** Ocean water contains valuable dissolved substances. What would be one possible way to separate these substances from the ocean water?

**4.** How could filter paper help you to identify a suspension from a solution or a colloid?

**5.** (laboratory question) Suppose you dissolve sodium chloride in water to find its solubility. How does its solubility change as you heat the water? Suppose you graph your data. The vertical axis represents solubility. The horizontal axis represents temperature. What would the line made by your data look like?

**Investigating Chapter Ideas**    Try one of the following projects to further your study.

**1. Water Treatment**    Read about how sewer water is purified. Prepare a poster that shows a diagram of the steps followed in treating sewage. Be sure to mention primary, secondary, and tertiary treatment. Include a written description of each step and sketches of some of the important equipment used at sewage treatment plants.

**2. Wetting Agents**    Using tweezers, carefully place a paper clip on the surface of water in a small bowl. If done properly, the paper clip will float. It floats owing to *surface tension.* Now add a few drops of soap solution to the bowl. Soap is an example of a *wetting agent.* Read about surface tension and wetting agents. Then describe what happened to the paper clip when you added the soap solution. Explain what happened in terms of what you read.

**Reading About Science**    Read some of the following books to explore topics that interest you.

Dickinson, E. 1982. **Colloids in Food.** New York: Elsevier.

Gay, Kathlyn. 1983. **Acid Rain.** New York: Watts.

Watson, Philip. 1983. **Liquid Magic.** New York: Lothrop.

Acids are a group of compounds sharing certain properties. One property is shown in the photos. In the first photo, a board is being removed from a vat of acid. The acid has eaten into, or etched, lines into the board. Does this photo display a physical or a chemical change?

The second photo shows a closeup of an electric device. Here, too, acid was used in its manufacture. In this case, the acid removed a protective coating on the surface of the material.

Reacting with materials is a property that some acids have. This chapter will present more properties of acids. It will also present properties of another group of compounds: bases.

Read and Find Out:
● why an acid that can burn your skin does not burn your stomach wall.
● how a substance that destroys some fibers strengthens others.
● why you must leave a swimming pool during a lightning storm.

# ACIDS, BASES, AND SALTS

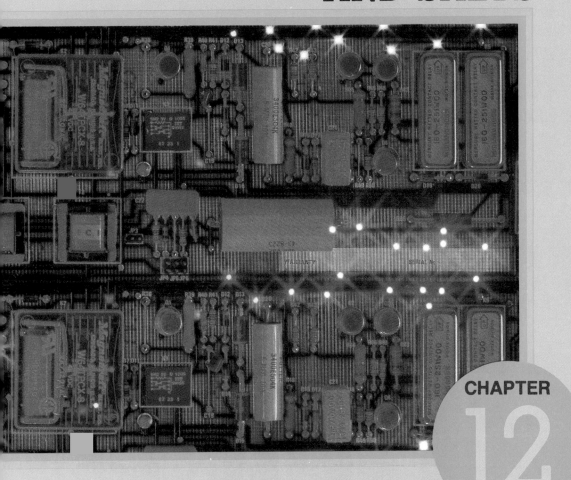

# ACIDS AND THEIR PROPERTIES

**OBJECTIVES**

**1.** List three properties of acids.

**2.** Describe a safe way to test for the presence of an acid.

**3.** List three acids and give a use for each.

Acids are a group of compounds that share some special properties. One such property is sour taste. Lemon juice, buttermilk, and vinegar taste sour because they contain acids. In this section you will learn about other properties of acids. These properties will then lead you to a definition of acids.

## Properties of Acids

The word *acid* refers to a wide variety of compounds with different properties and uses. Yet, different as they are, these compounds share several properties when they are dissolved in water.

Sour taste is one common property of acids dissolved in water. However, it is not safe to taste a solution for the presence of an acid. Some acids are corrosive. They can wear away metal, as well as burn skin.

However, there are safer properties that can help you test for acids. In particular, acids have some special chemical properties when they are dissolved in water.

**Effect on Indicators**   A safe way to test for acids is to use an *indicator* (IN•duh•kay•tur). *An* **indicator** *is a substance that changes color in the presence of a test substance.*

For example, litmus is an indicator for acids and bases. Litmus comes in the form of red and blue paper strips. Figure 12-1 shows the effect of acids on litmus paper. Acids cause blue litmus paper to turn red. Suppose you dip litmus paper into an unknown solution. If you see a change from blue to red, you know the solution contains an acid.

**Reaction with Metals**   Have you ever noticed a scaly crust on the top of a car battery? This crust is a result of another property of acids. Acids react with many metals. In a car battery, metal atoms react with

*Figure 12-1.* Litmus paper is made by soaking paper in a litmus solution and allowing it to dry. What color is litmus in the presence of acid?

an acid and form the crust as a product. A second product is hydrogen gas. See Figure 12-2.

You may have seen the result of a similar reaction in buildings and statues made of stone. Stone often contains compounds of metals. The metallic compounds in the stone react with small amounts of acid

*Figure 12-2.* Crust on a car battery.

*Figure 12-3. Acids dissolved in the air can corrode metals and stone.*

in the air. See Figure 12-3. Substances from factory and car exhaust dissolve in rain water, forming acids. When this rain water soaks into stone, acids can react with metallic compounds and gradually wear the stone away.

## Chemists' Definition of an Acid

List three common industrial acids.

Sulfuric acid ($H_2SO_4$), nitric acid ($HNO_3$), and hydrochloric acid (HCl) are common industrial acids. Look carefully at the formula of each acid. Can you see something the acids have in common?

If you noticed that these formulas contained hydrogen, you are right. All acids contain hydrogen. However, many compounds that contain hydrogen are not acids. For example, water contains hydrogen. But water is not an acid. How is an acid different from water?

A special model of water can help you see the difference. See Figure 12-4**A**. Remember that water is made of molecules with the formula $H_2O$. Some of these molecules split into ions, $H^+$ and $OH^-$. The hydrogen ions are attracted to unsplit water molecules. The result is the formation of *hydronium* (high•DROH•nee•uhm) *ions.* See Figure 12-4**B**. *A **hydronium ion** is an ion group made of a water molecule and a hydrogen ion. It has a positive charge. Its formula is $H_3O^+$.*

Now look carefully at Figure 12-4**C**. Acids split into ions in water. Hydrogen ions from the acid combine with water molecules. The result is still more hydronium ions.

The model in Figure 12-4 can help you understand how chemists define acids. ***Acids** are substances that, when added to water, increase the concentration of hydronium ions.*

This definition can help you understand how compounds are classified as acids. For example, table sugar ($C_{12}H_{22}O_{11}$) contains hydrogen. But it does not increase the hydronium concentration of water. So table sugar is not an acid.

## Strong Acids and Weak Acids

Some foods such as pickles, tomatoes, and citrus fruits contain acids. Yet how can you eat these foods when certain acids can burn the skin? The acids in foods are not as strong, or as acidic (a•SI•dik), as some others.

The properties of acids depend on the concentration of hydronium ions. Strong acids have greater concentrations of hydronium ions than weak acids do. With higher concentrations, strong acids react vigorously with metals. They can also cause severe skin burns. Sulfuric acid and hydrochloric acid are examples of strong acids.

Strong acids are dangerous. But diluting them with water can make them safer to handle. That is, an amount of acid can be carefully added to a volume of water. The resulting solution has a lower concentration of hydronium ions than the original acid. It reacts less vigorously than the original.

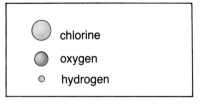

chlorine

oxygen

hydrogen

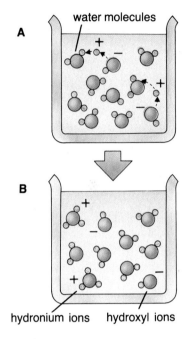

water molecules

**A**

**B**

hydronium ions     hydroxyl ions

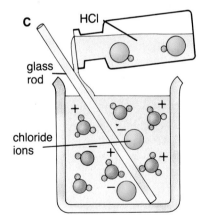

**C**       HCl

glass rod

chloride ions

*Figure 12-4. What effect does adding an acid have on the number of hydronium ions?*

## DISSOLVING MINERALS IN BONES

**OBJECTIVE**
Show how an acid reacts with the minerals in a bone.

**MATERIALS**
two chicken bones, vinegar, jar, plastic wrap

**PROCEDURE**
1. Clean and wash two chicken bones. Let them dry overnight.
2. Place the bones in separate jars. Add enough vinegar to cover the bone in one jar. Put the same amount of water in the other jar.
3. Cover the jars with plastic wrap. Let both jars stand four days.
4. Remove both bones and rinse them off.
5. Compare the stiffness of the two bones.

**QUESTIONS**
1. What difference did you observe between the two bones?
2. What caused this change?
3. What was the purpose of soaking one bone in water?

Table 12-1 shows some common weak acids found around the house. Weak acids do not produce as high a concentration of hydronium ions in water as strong acids do. However, they are still acids. So, they are still hazardous and must be handled with care.

## Using Industrial Acids

Three strong acids have very important uses in science laboratories and in industry. They are sulfuric acid, nitric acid, and hydrochloric acid. These acids must always be handled with care. If handled carelessly, they can burn your skin and clothes. See Appendix 1 on page 549 for safety in handling acids.

**Sulfuric Acid**   Concentrated sulfuric acid is a thick, oily liquid that has a strong attraction for water. This attraction is so strong that the acid absorbs water vapor from the air. If you leave a beaker of concentrated sulfuric acid in the open for a few hours, the acid will increase in volume. The acid will have absorbed the water vapor and trapped it among its molecules. Industry makes good use of this property. Sulfuric acid is used in the *dehydration* (dee•high•DRAY•shuhn) of air and other gases. **Dehydration** *is the removal of water from a material.*

**Nitric Acid**   Nitric acid is also a liquid. Nitric acid has many uses. It is useful in etching metals. It is used to make explosives such as TNT and nitroglycerin (nigh•truh•GLIS•er•in). Compounds obtained

**TABLE 12-1. COMMON HOUSEHOLD ACIDS**

| Name | Formula | Found in |
|------|---------|----------|
| Acetic acid | $HC_2H_3O_2$ | vinegar |
| Citric acid | $H_3C_6H_5O_7$ | citrus fruits |
| Carbonic acid | $H_2CO_3$ | soda water |
| Boric acid | $H_3BO_3$ | eyewash |
| Hypochlorous acid | $HOCl$ | bleaches |
| Phosphoric acid | $H_3PO_4$ | dental cement |

from nitric acid are also used making fertilizers. It supplies the element nitrogen, which is needed by growing plants. See Figure 12-5.

**Hydrochloric Acid**   Hydrochloric acid is a solution of a gas (hydrogen chloride) in water. Hydrochloric acid is used to clean metals before they are painted or plated with other metals. This cleaning process is called pickling. Hydrochloric acid removes tarnish and impurities from the surfaces of most metals. However, hydrochloric acid is not used as a tarnish remover in the home for two reasons. First, it is too dangerous. Second, it corrodes many metals. It cleans a metal object by removing some of the metal. If you cleaned the same utensil over and over again with the acid, it would be eaten away.

● Your stomach produces hydrochloric acid. Hydrochloric acid helps digest certain foods. Your stomach muscles contract and mix the food with the acid and other chemicals.

As you know, hydrochloric acid is a strong acid. It can burn the skin. Why, then, does the acid not burn the wall of your stomach? Your stomach wall is coated with a secretion called mucus. Mucus prevents the hydrochloric acid from eating into your stomach wall. However, if too much acid or too little mucus is produced, the acid can eat into your stomach wall. The wound produced is an ulcer.

*Figure 12-5. Farmers add fertilizers to soil to replace those minerals that are missing.*

What acid does your stomach contain?

## OBJECTIVES AND WORDS TO REVIEW

1. List three properties that acids have in common.
2. Describe a safe way to find out whether an unknown solution is an acid.
3. Name three acids and give a use for each.
4. Write one complete sentence for each word listed below.
   indicator      hydronium ion      acid      dehydration

# BASES AND THEIR PROPERTIES

**OBJECTIVES**

**1.** List four properties of bases.

**2.** List three bases and give a use for each.

Like acids, bases are a group of compounds that share some special properties. Also like acids, bases display properties when they are dissolved in water. In this section you will learn about these properties. Then you will find out exactly how bases are defined.

## Properties of Bases

Have you ever felt household ammonia, a common base? It feels slippery. Water solutions of most bases share this property. However, many bases can be harmful to skin. So never test a solution for the presence of a base by touching it.

**Bitter Taste**   Have you ever had to take milk of magnesia? Many people would say that it has a bland, or even bitter, taste. Bitter taste is one common property of bases. Of course, you should *never* taste a solution to see if it contains a base. Most bases are poisonous.

**Effect on Animal Substances**   Strong bases react with animal substances. They dissolve hair, wool, and fingernails. See Figure 12-6. This property makes them useful for cleaning clogged drains. Many drain

*Figure 12-6. Compare the effect of a strong base on wool, an animal product, and on cotton. Where does cotton come from?*

Figure 12-7. *What color is litmus in the presence of a base?*

cleaners contain the base sodium hydroxide, or lye. Lye dissolves grease from dirty dishes. It also dissolves hair. However, this property makes strong bases dangerous. Read the warning label on any can of drain cleaner.

**Effect on Fats and Oils**   Bases can dissolve fats and oils. This property explains why household ammonia water is used to clean greasy materials. The ammonia water dissolves the grease and allows it to be washed away.

**Effect on Indicators**   Indicators can be used to identify bases as well as acids. Litmus is red in the presence of an acid. But in the presence of bases, red litmus turns blue. See Figure 12-7.

*Phenolphthalein* (fee•nohl•THAY•leen) *is another indicator.* In acid solutions phenolphthalein is colorless. But it is deep pink in a base solution. See Figure 12-8.

Figure 12-8. *Phenolphthalein in the presence of a base.*

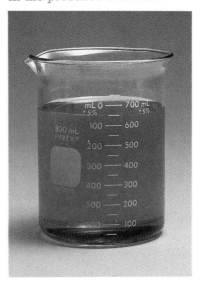

## Chemists' Definition of a Base

Sodium hydroxide (NaOH), ammonium hydroxide ($NH_4OH$), and potassium hydroxide (KOH) are common bases. Look carefully at their names and formulas. As you can see, the chemical name of each base ends with the word *hydroxide* (high•DRAHK•sighd). Hydroxide indicates that the formula of each base

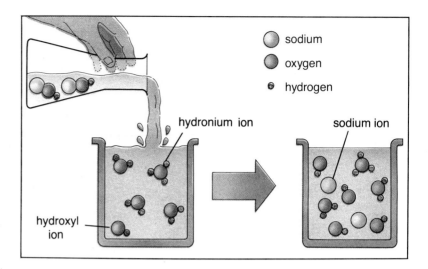

*Figure 12-9. When bases are added to water, they increase the concentration of hydroxyl ions.*

ends in OH. For example, sodium hydroxide has the formula Na*OH*.

The OH in the formula of a base represents the *hydroxyl* (high•DRAHK•sil) *ion. The **hydroxyl ion** is an ion group made of an oxygen atom joined to a hydrogen ion.* The hydroxyl ion has a negative charge. Its formula is $OH^-$.

All bases produce the hydroxyl ion. But so does water. Recall that in a special model of water, a few water molecules split and form two ions: $H_3O^+$ and $OH^-$. So how is a base different from water?

Figure 12-9 will help you see the difference. Pure water has an equal number of $H_3O^+$ ions and $OH^-$ ions. But when you add a base to water, the base splits into ions. The base increases the number of $OH^-$ ions of any sample of water.

The model in Figure 12-9 will help you understand how chemists define bases. ***Bases** are compounds that increase the concentration of hydroxyl ions in water.* The properties of bases depend on the number of hydroxyl ions they produce in water. The more hydroxyl ions a base produces, the stronger it is. Strong bases react vigorously with human and animal substances.

As you can see, bases have properties that are almost the opposite of acids. Table 12-2 summarizes properties of acids and bases.

On what factor do the properties of bases depend?

**TABLE 12-2. ACIDS AND BASES**

| Properties of Acids | Properties of Bases |
|---|---|
| affect indicators | affect indicators |
| conduct electricity | conduct electricity |
| taste sour | taste bitter |
| neutralize bases | neutralize acids |
| react with metals and form hydrogen | react with human and animal substances |
| | feel slippery |
| | dissolve fats and oils |

## Using Bases

The most extensive use of bases in industry is in reactions with acids. You will explore this use of bases in the next section. However, many bases are used in the home. You already know that lye (sodium hydroxide) is used in drain cleaners. Ammonium hydroxide, or ammonia water, is used to clean floors, bathtubs, and windows. Aluminum hydroxide is an ingredient in many deodorants.

● Bases are also used in industry. Strong bases often destroy animal fibers such as wool. However, they do not usually have the same effect on plant fibers, such as cotton. In fact, cotton cloth is often treated with concentrated sodium hydroxide to make it shiny. Chino pants show the effects of this treatment, which is called mercerizing (MUR•suh•righ•zing)

### OBJECTIVES AND WORDS TO REVIEW
1. List four properties that bases have in common.
2. Name three bases and give a use for each.
3. Write one complete sentence for each term listed below.
   phenolphthalein      hydroxyl ion      base

## EXPLORE BY TRYING

### TESTING FOR ACIDS AND BASES

**OBJECTIVE**
Identify bases.

**MATERIALS**
household liquids, medicine dropper, red litmus paper

**PROCEDURE**
1. Put 5 red litmus strips on a flat dish.
2. Place two drops of a liquid on a strip of litmus paper. Use a different liquid for each strip. Wash the dropper thoroughly in water before using the next liquid. You might try liquids such as fruit juices, milk of magnesia, soda, tea, milk.
3. Record what happens to the litmus paper.

**QUESTIONS**
1. Which liquids tested are basic? How can you tell?
2. Which liquids tested are acidic? How can you tell?

# ACIDS, BASES, AND SALTS IN SOLUTION

So far in this chapter, you have learned to tell acids and bases by their properties. In this section, you will learn how chemists measure the strength of acids and bases. You will investigate what happens when acids and bases react with each other.

## Measuring Ions in Acid and Base Solutions

The strength of an acid depends on the number of hydronium ions it produces in solution. The strength of a base depends on the number of hydroxyl ions it produces in solution. Chemists express the strength of acids and bases by using a scale of numbers, the *pH* scale. *The **pH** of a solution is a measure of the concentration of hydronium ions.* The pH scale in Figure 12-10 shows the pH of several common substances.

Find water on the pH scale. Its pH is 7. Remember that water has both $H_3O^+$ ions and $OH^-$ ions. Pure water has an equal concentration of both ions. Water or any solution with an equal concentration of $H_3O^+$ ions

*Figure 12-10. The pH scale is a way of measuring the strength of an acid or a base. Your stomach contains hydrochloric acid. What is its approximate pH?*

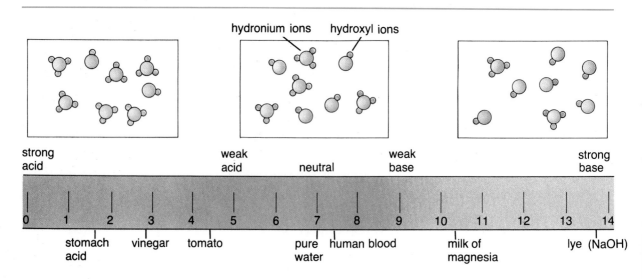

and OH⁻ ions is said to be *neutral*. *A **neutral solution** has the properties of neither an acid nor a base.* A pH of 7 indicates that a solution is neutral.

Solutions that have a pH less than 7 are acidic. A pH less than 7 indicates a greater concentration of $H_3O^+$ ions than $OH^-$ ions. The stronger an acid is, the lower its pH.

On the other hand, solutions that contain bases have a pH greater than 7. A pH greater than 7 indicates a greater concentration of $OH^-$ ions than $H_3O^+$ ions. The stronger a base is, the more $OH^-$ ions it produces and the greater its pH.

## Indicators and pH

You can use indicators to help estimate the pH of a solution. The pH scale has a large range of numbers. Each indicator is limited to just a certain range of pH values. Litmus, for example, is sensitive to pH values from 4.5 to 8.

Red cabbage juice can also be used as an indicator. It is sensitive over a wider range of pH values than litmus. Figure 12-11 shows the colors that red cabbage juice has in different types of solutions.

An indicator often used in the laboratory is pH paper. This paper is sensitive over a very wide range of

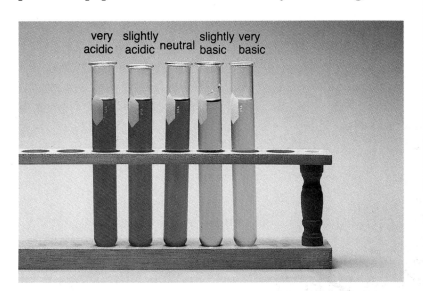

very slightly     slightly very
acidic acidic neutral basic basic

*Figure 12-11. The color of an indicator depends on the pH of a solution.*

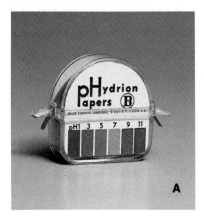

*Figure 12-12. Hydrangeas have pink flowers in basic soil; blue in acidic soil. What kind of chemicals do these flowers contain?*

**A**

**B**

pH values. See Figure 12-12**A.** Indicators are also found in nature. For example, the hydrangeas (high•DRAYN•juhz) shown in Figure 12-12**B** contain an indicator. Thus, the flowers will be blue or pink depending on the pH of the soil.

For very accurate measurements of pH, a pH meter is sometimes used. This device uses electricity to measure the concentration of hydronium ions.

## Reactions Between Acids and Bases

You know that your stomach contains hydrochloric acid. Many of the foods you eat contain acids. Such foods can increase the concentration of acid in the stomach. You have probably heard commercials for products that relieve "excess stomach acid." Most of these products contain a base. Milk of magnesia tablets are one example of this kind of product. They contain magnesium hydroxide, $Mg(OH)_2$. If you swallow one of these tablets, the following reaction occurs in your stomach:

hydrochloric acid   plus   magnesium hydroxide   yield   magnesium chloride   plus water

$$2 \ HCl + Mg(OH)_2 \longrightarrow MgCl_2 + 2 \ H_2O$$

Look at this equation carefully. Two products result.

**Water is Formed** The acid in your stomach has formed hydronium ions. Upon reaching your stomach, the magnesium hydroxide splits into magnesium ions

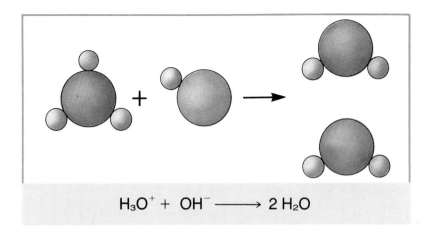

$$H_3O^+ + OH^- \longrightarrow 2\,H_2O$$

*Figure 12-13. Water is one of the products of a reaction between an acid and a base.*

and hydroxyl ions. The hydronium ions from the acid combine with the hydroxyl ions from the base. Water is formed. See Figure 12-13.

**A Salt is Formed**   The reaction that occurs in your stomach produces magnesium chloride, $MgCl_2$. Magnesium chloride belongs to a class of compounds called *salts*. A **salt** *is a compound formed from the positive ions of a base and the negative ions of an acid.* Table 12-3 lists some salts formed when an acid reacts with a base.

**Acids and Bases Cancel Each Other's Effects**
When an acid reacts with a base, a chemical change takes place. This chemical change is known as *neutralization* (new•truh•luh•ZAY•shuhn). **Neutraliza-**

| **TABLE 12-3.** PRODUCTS OF NEUTRALIZATION REACTIONS | Acids | |
|---|---|---|
| | **Hydrochloric** | **Sulfuric** |
| **Sodium hydroxide** NaOH | sodium chloride NaCl | sodium sulfate $Na_2SO_4$ |
| **Ammonium hydroxide** $NH_4OH$ | ammonium chloride $NH_4Cl$ | ammonium sulfate $(NH_4)_2SO_4$ |
| **Magnesium hydroxide** $Mg(OH)_2$ | magnesium chloride $MgCl_2$ | magnesium sulfate $MgSO_4$ |

B a s e s

*tion is a chemical reaction in which hydronium ions combine with hydroxyl ions and form water.* In a neutralization reaction, the properties of the acid and the base are lost. The acid and the base are said to neutralize (NEW•truh•lighz) each other. See Figure 12-14. Neutralization reactions always result in the formation of water and a salt.

List the two products of any neutralization reaction.

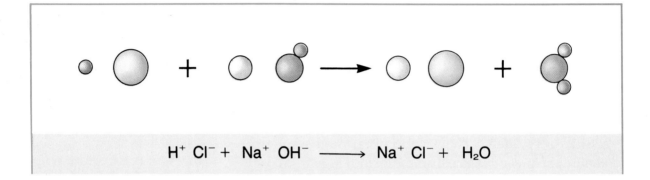

$$H^+ \ Cl^- + \ Na^+ \ OH^- \longrightarrow \ Na^+ \ Cl^- + \ H_2O$$

*Figure 12-14. In a neutralization reaction the acid and base break up into ions and then recombine. Why is this reaction a double replacement reaction?*

## Some Properties of Salts

Salt is not just the name of ordinary table salt (NaCl). It is the name of an entire class of compounds. As a group of compounds, salts have certain properties in common.

**Ionic Bonds**   Most salts contain positive metal ions and negative nonmetal ions. The ions are held together by ionic bonds. Recall from Chapter 10 that an ionic bond is a strong attraction between positive and negative ions. This attraction causes ions to become packed in special patterns. Such packing gives each salt a particular crystal pattern.

**Solubility in Water**   What happens to the magnesium chloride that forms in your stomach in an acid-base reaction? This salt remains dissolved in the water in the stomach. Eventually the salt is either used by the body or eliminated as waste. However, not all salts behave in this way. When some acids and bases react, salts are formed that are only slightly soluble in water. Most of these salts leave the solution and settle to the bottom of the container. Such salts

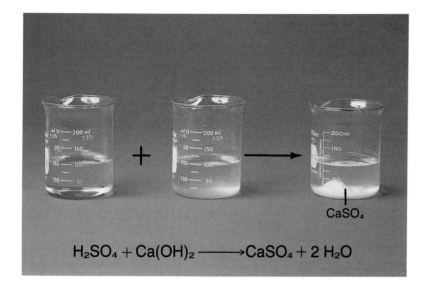

$$H_2SO_4 + Ca(OH)_2 \longrightarrow CaSO_4 + 2\,H_2O$$

CaSO₄

Figure 12-15. *Some acid-base reactions form salts that settle to the bottom. What name is given to this type of solid?*

are called *precipitates* (pri•SIP•uh•titz). *A **precipitate** is an insoluble solid that separates out of a solution.* Figure 12-15 shows what happens when sulfuric acid is mixed with calcium hydroxide Ca(OH)₂, which is also called limewater.

## Uses of Some Salts

Hundreds of salts exist. They have many different uses. For example, magnesium sulfate is commonly called Epsom salts. If you have ever had a sprain, you may have used Epsom salts as a soak to reduce the swelling. Magnesium sulfate is also used on the heads of matches. Potassium chloride is used as a substitute for table salt in low-sodium diets. Ammonium nitrate is an ingredient in some rocket fuels and fertilizers.

When sulfuric acid neutralizes aluminum hydroxide, Al(OH)₃, the salt aluminum sulfate, Al₂(SO₄)₃, is made:

$$3\,H_2SO_4 + 2\,Al(OH)_3 \longrightarrow Al_2(SO_4)_3 + 6\,H_2O$$

This salt is often added to paper. It prevents paper from soaking up too much ink in the printing process. However, its use has had an unexpected side effect. See Figure 12-16. Aluminum sulfate reacts slowly with water vapor and produces sulfuric acid.

Figure 12-16. *Paper that has been destroyed slowly by acid.*

# SCIENCE EXPLORERS

## Dr. Isabella Karle

Suppose you had a crystal and wanted to know what molecules were in it. How might you find out without destroying the crystal? You might ask Dr. Isabella Karle for help.

To investigate a crystal, Dr. Karle directs beams of X rays at it. After passing through the crystal, the X rays produce a pattern of light- and dark-colored bands. Each kind of molecule makes a characteristic pattern. The pattern is recorded on a photographic plate. The chemical composition of the crystal is determined from that pattern formed on the plate. Dr. Karle has written about her techniques in many scientific journals. Her articles are among the most widely read by chemists all over the world. She received the Chemical Pioneer award from the American Institute of Chemists in 1984.

Although the acid has a low concentration, it can still weaken the paper. As a result, the pages of many older books are cracking and crumbling.

Chemists are trying to find ways to slow down or stop this crumbling of paper. They are trying to treat the paper with other chemicals. These chemicals will react with the acid and neutralize it. Some libraries have begun spraying the pages of important old books with these neutralizing chemicals. By spraying, the people running the libraries hope to protect the books so future generations will be able to use them.

## Solutions that Conduct Electricity

Look carefully at the setup in each part of Figure 12-17. The wires in the setup provide a pathway for electricity. Usually electricity cannot travel through a pathway that has unconnected wires. But in this case, the unconnected ends of wire are put into different liquids. Charged particles, ions, in each liquid can help carry the electricity from one end of wire to the other.

The liquid in **A** is water. Water does contain $H_3O^+$ ions and $OH^-$ ions. However, the concentration of these ions is too low to carry enough electricity to cause the bulb to light up. Adding acids, bases, and salts to water, however, increases the concentration of ions. So in **B** and **C** the solutions do carry enough electricity to light the bulb.

Acids, bases, and salts are examples of compounds called *electrolytes* (e•LEK•truh•lightz). ***Electrolytes** are substances that conduct electricity in water solutions.* They conduct electricity because they break into ions in water. Electrolytes that supply many ions to a solution are said to be strong electrolytes. Weak electrolytes supply fewer ions to a solution.

● Your body fluids contain electrolytes. Blood needs a balance of acids and bases. Other body fluids need salts. Salts containing sodium and potassium ions are especially important. Because of electrolytes, your body is a conductor of electricity. Dry skin helps to insulate your body. Wet skin, however, makes your body a good

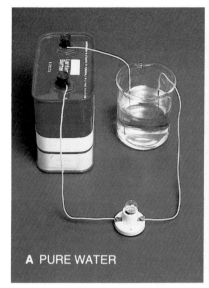

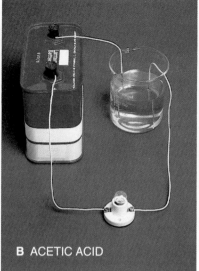

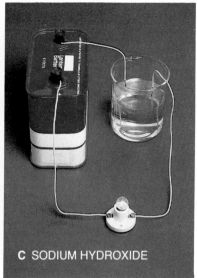

**A** PURE WATER

**B** ACETIC ACID

**C** SODIUM HYDROXIDE

conductor. That is why you must get out of a swimming pool during a lightning storm. If a lightning bolt hit the water, its electricity would pass right through your body. The electric shock could burn or even kill you.

*Figure 12-17. Electrolytes can carry electricity through them. The brighter the bulb, the stronger the electrolyte is. Which of the above is the weakest electrolyte?*

**Distinguish between strong and weak electrolytes.**

## OBJECTIVES AND WORDS TO REVIEW

**1.** What two products are always formed when an acid reacts with a base?
**2.** What are three properties of salts?
**3.** Name three salts and give a use for each.
**4.** Write one complete sentence for each word listed below.

| | |
|---|---|
| pH | neutralization |
| neutral solution | precipitate |
| salt | electrolyte |

# STUDY SKILL

## READING A SCIENTIFIC DIAGRAM

### Preparation

Have you ever tried to set a digital watch? You know that you could randomly press buttons. Or you could look at the instruction sheet provided by the manufacturer. See Figure 1. It diagrams the steps of the procedure.

In science, diagrams are often used to explain how an investigation is set up. For example, see Figure 12-L on page 273.

### Directions

Reading a diagram can be a complicated task. Follow these steps when reading a diagram.

*Step 1* Look at the entire diagram. If a diagram has a caption, read it carefully.

*Step 2* Identify each part in the diagram. Parts may be labeled with letters or symbols.

*Step 3* Look for any dimensions. This kind of measurement is often given between two arrows: ←20 cm→. The arrow heads indicated where the measurement begins and ends.

*Step 4* Try to understand how the various parts are related or interact. How are the parts connected?

### Practice

Figure 2 shows how to make a paper helicopter. Using the materials provided and the diagram in Figure 2, construct a working helicopter.

### Application

After reading Chapter 12, turn to Figure 12-10 on page 264. How many hydronium ions do you see in the diagram of a strong base? How many hydroxyl ions are there in the diagram of a strong acid? The concentration of which ion increases as the pH reading increases?

*Figure 1.*

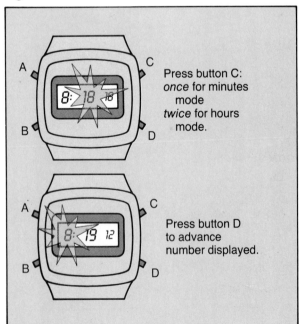

*Figure 2.*

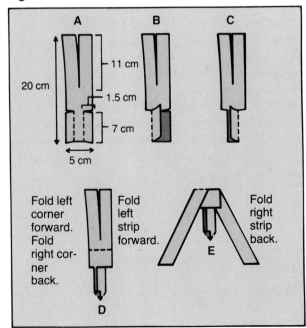

## ELECTROLYTES

### Objective
Observe electric properties of solutions.

### Background
Electricity will pass through solutions of electrolytes such as acids, bases, and salts. The ions that are produced when the electrolyte dissolves in water are charged particles. These ions can carry the electricity from a dry cell (battery) through a light bulb and make it glow. The more ions there are in the solution the brighter the bulb will glow.

### Materials
solutions of hyrochloric acid (HCl), sodium hydroxide (NaOH), sodium chloride (NaCl), 6-V dry cell, light bulb and socket, coated copper wire, scissors, graduated cylinder, 250 mL beaker, goggles, pencil, water, glass microscope slide, apron

### Procedure
1. Remove about 5 cm of the wire coating from the ends of two pieces of wire as shown in Figure 12-L. **CAUTION:** Wear goggles and an apron.
2. Prepare the setup shown in Figure 12-L.
3. Add 50 mL of water to the beaker. Does the light bulb glow? Record your observations.
4. Lift the pencil to remove the wires from the beaker. **CAUTION:** Never touch bare wires while a circuit is connected to a battery. Add 3 mL of hydrochloric acid to the water by pouring the acid slowly down the glass slide tilted into the water. **CAUTION:** If you spill acids or other solutions on yourself, rinse with cold water and tell your teacher.
5. Insert the wires into the beaker again. Record your observations.

*Figure 12-L. Laboratory setup.*

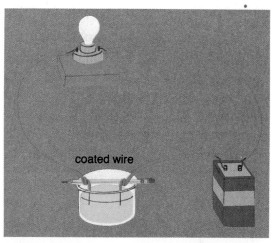

coated wire

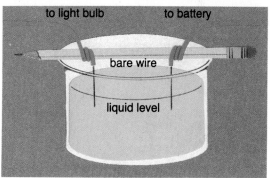

to light bulb      to battery

bare wire

liquid level

6. Add another 6 mL of hydrochloric acid to the beaker. Repeat step 5.
7. Remove the wires and empty the beaker carefully. Clean and dry it.
8. Repeat steps 3-7 with sodium hydroxide.
9. Repeat steps 3-7 with sodium chloride solution. Record all observations.

### Questions
1. Why does the bulb not glow in pure water?
2. How can you tell which of the solutions are electrolytes? Explain.
3. **PROBLEM SOLVING:** Based on your results, explain why you must not be in water outdoors (salt or fresh) during a storm.

# SUMMARY

1. Acids have properties that include having a sour taste, reacting with metals, and causing color changes in indicators. Acids increase the concentration of hydronium ions in water. (12-1)

2. Bases have properties that include having a bitter taste, dissolving animal substances, feeling slippery, dissolving fats and oils, and causing color changes in indicators. Bases increase the concentration of hydroxyl ions in water. (12-2)

3. The pH of a solution is a measure of its hydronium ion concentration. (12-3)

4. Acids and bases react with each other and form a salt and water. Acids, bases, and salts are electrolytes. (12-3)

# REVIEW

Number a sheet of paper from 1 to 25 and answer these questions.

**Building Science Vocabulary**   Write the letter of the word that best matches each definition.

| | | |
|---|---|---|
| **a.** dehydration | **e.** hydronium ion | **i.** pH |
| **b.** electrolyte | **f.** neutralization | **j.** salt |
| **c.** precipitate | **g.** phenolphthalein | **k.** acid |
| **d.** hydroxyl ion | **h.** litmus | **l.** base |

1. A positive ion made up of a water molecule and a hydrogen ion

2. An indicator that turns pink in the presence of a base

3. A compound made up of the positive ion from a base and the negative ion from an acid

4. A compound that increases the concentration of hydronium ions when it is dissolved in water

5. A substance that conducts electricity in water solutions

6. The reaction between an acid and a base

7. The removal of water

8. A compound that increases the concentration of hydroxyl ions when it is dissolved in water

9. A measure of the concentration of hydronium ions in a solution

10. An insoluble solid that separates out of a solution

**Finding the Facts**   Select the letter of the answer that best completes each of the following.

11. Which formula represents an acid?   **(a)** $H_2O$   **(b)** HCl   **(c)** NaOH   **(d)** $CH_4$

12. Which of the following substances is a poor conductor of electricity?   **(a)** an acid solution   **(b)** salt water   **(c)** a base solution   **(d)** pure water

13. The removal of water is called **(a)** precipitation   **(b)** neutralization   **(c)** dehydration   **(d)** corrosion.

14. Vinegar and lemon juice taste sour because they contain   **(a)** salts   **(b)** bases   **(c)** lye   **(d)** acids.

15. Which substance turns litmus paper blue? **(a)** sulfuric acid   **(b)** sodium chloride   **(c)** calcium hydroxide   **(d)** vinegar

16. The pH of pure water is   **(a)** 0   **(b)** 7   **(c)** 10   **(d)** 14.

17. Base solutions contain   **(a)** hydronium ions   **(b)** hydroxyl ions   **(c)** hydrogen ions   **(d)** salts.

18. Phenolphthalein is   **(a)** an indicator **(b)** a salt   **(c)** a base   **(d)** an acid.

19. Neutralization reactions produce   **(a)** an acid and a base   **(b)** water and an indicator   **(c)** water and a salt **(d)** hydronium ions and hydroxyl ions.

20. A solution that has a pH of 3 is   **(a)** neutral **(b)** an acid   **(c)** a base   **(d)** not able to conduct electricity.

**Understanding Main Ideas**  Complete the following.

**21.** When an acid, such as sulfuric acid, reacts with a metal, such as zinc, the gas formed is __?__.

**22.** The acid in your stomach is __?__.

**23.** An acid that is useful for its dehydrating ability is __?__.

**24.** Substances that conduct electricity are called __?__.

**25.** The correct way to mix an acid with water is to __?__.

**Writing About Science**  On a separate sheet of paper, answer the following as completely as possible.

**1.** Some drain cleaners contain lye, a strong base. Lye is able to dissolve hair and grease that may clog pipes. A strong acid would also dissolve these substances. Why are acids not used in drain cleaners?

**2.** Why is salt water, a solution of sodium chloride, a good conductor of electricity?

**3.** Sugar's formula is $C_{12}H_{22}O_{11}$. Explain why sugar is not an acid even though it contains hydrogen.

**4.** If wood is dipped into concentrated sulfuric acid, it turns black. What conclusions can you draw about the elements making up wood?

**5.** (laboratory question) Suppose you placed the conduction apparatus into a liquid and the bulb glowed. Explain this observation.

**Investigating Chapter Ideas**  Try one of the following projects to further your study.

**1. How are they made?**  Two important industrial acids are sulfuric acid and nitric acid. Choose one of these acids and report on how it is made industrially. Include diagrams of the process in your report.

**2. Other ways of classifying acid**  In this chapter, you learned how to define acids and bases. These definitions are part of the Arrhenius concept of acids and bases. However, there are other ways to classify acids and bases. One way is the Bronsted-Lowry acid-base scheme. Another is the Lewis acid-base scheme. Write a report on these acid-base classifications. Compare them with the Arrhenius acid-base concept.

**3. Common antacids**  Milk of magnesia contains the base magnesium hydroxide. What do some other common antacids use as a base? Find a reference that discusses commercial antacids. Write a report that lists some of the various ingredients used in antacid preparations. Try to write chemical equations for the neutralization reactions between the bases in the antacids and HCl, the acid in the stomach. Can you suggest why people on low-sodium diets should be careful about antacids tablet they use? What other problems can occur with improper use of antacids?

**4. Crystal systems**  The crystals of salts and other substances can be classified into six or seven basic systems. Do some research on crystal systems. Use toothpicks and glue to make models that represent the angles and axes found in each crystal system. Cite examples of substances that crystallize in each of the various crystal forms.

**Reading About Science**  Read some of the following books to explore topics that interest you.

Jensen, William B. 1980. **The Lewis Acid-Base Concepts: an Overview.** New York: Wiley.

Luoma, Jon. 1984. **Troubled Skies, Troubled Waters: the Story of Acid Rain.** New York: Viking.

Tanabe, Kozo. 1971. **Solids, Acids, and Bases: Their Catalytic Properties.** New York: Academic Press.

Can you name an element contained in both the disk and the yarn? Here are some clues. It is an element found in over three million compounds. Its atomic number is 6. Its atomic mass is 12. And it is an element found in compounds in all living things.

If you named the element carbon, you are correct. Carbon compounds are found in many fuels, fabrics, and foods, as well as in all the tissues of living things. How can the same element make up so many different kinds of compounds? Think about what you have already learned about atomic structure. In this chapter you will use models to show how carbon atoms form bonds with other atoms. You will learn about the properties and uses of carbon and its many compounds.

Read and Find Out:
● how a form of carbon used in rocket engines can also be used in making tennis rackets.
● about some organic compounds that are used in cosmetics.
● how "muscles" can run a car.

# THE CHEMISTRY OF CARBON

# CARBON AND ITS COMPOUNDS

So far in your study of chemistry you have studied metals and nonmetals. You have learned about solutions of acids and bases. But, since chemistry is the study of matter, you must have wondered about the matter in the common objects around you. What makes up the food you eat, the clothes you wear, and the gasoline that powers cars? In this section you will study the element carbon, which is the backbone of these compounds. You will learn about the very simplest carbon compounds and the models chemists use to study them.

## The Element Carbon

In Figure 13-1, you can see two forms of the element carbon: graphite and diamond. Graphite is a very soft form of carbon. It is so soft you can scratch it with a fingernail. It also feels very slippery. Because it is slippery, graphite is useful as a lubricant.

Diamond, on the other hand, is a hard form of carbon. In fact, it is one of the hardest substances known. It can scratch glass, steel, and granite, a hard rock. Its hardness makes diamond a useful cutting tool.

*Figure 13-1. What do graphite (A) and diamonds (B) have in common?*

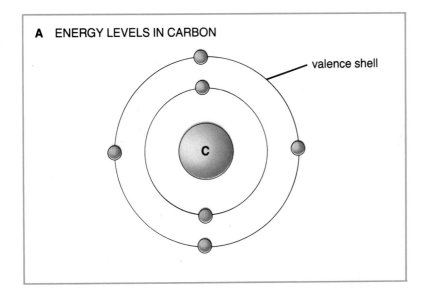

**A  ENERGY LEVELS IN CARBON**

valence shell

C

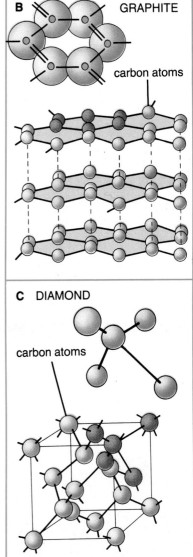

**B**  GRAPHITE

carbon atoms

**C  DIAMOND**

carbon atoms

Both graphite and diamond are pure carbon. They are made entirely of carbon atoms. How can these two substances made of the same kind of atom have such different properties? One explanation is the kinds of bonds between carbon atoms.

An atom of carbon has four electrons in its valence shell. This energy level can hold eight electrons. A carbon atom fills this energy level by sharing its four valence electrons with other atoms and forming covalent bonds. See Figure 13-2**A.**

In a piece of pure carbon, carbon atoms form covalent bonds with each other. Look at models of carbon atoms in graphite and diamond in Figures 13-2**B, C.**

In the model of graphite, carbon atoms are arranged in layers. Within each layer, each atom is joined to three other atoms by covalent bonds. But there are no covalent bonds joining atoms of different layers. The layers are free to slide over each other. This sliding of layers explains how graphite can be slippery and soft.

In the model of diamond, however, the atoms are joined in a rigid network. Within this network, the atoms are not free to slide. They are held tightly in place. This rigid network explains why diamonds are so hard.

*Figure 13-2. In graphite, each carbon atom shares electrons with three other carbon atoms. In diamond, each carbon atom shares electrons with four other carbon atoms.*

What kind of bonds holds the atoms together in pure carbon?

**CHART 13-1.** SOME IMPORTANT FACTS ABOUT CO₂ AND CO

| Compound | Formula | Shape of Molecule | Some Uses | Some Dangers |
|---|---|---|---|---|
| Carbon dioxide | $CO_2$ | | ingredient in fire extinguishers

provides the "fizz" in soda pop | too much $CO_2$ in an unventilated room can cause a headache

cause of "greenhouse effect" |
| Carbon monoxide | $CO$ | | removes oxygen from iron ore

ingredient in some types of fuels | interferes with ability of red blood cells to carry oxygen

substance in smog |

## Carbon Compounds

In pure carbon, carbon atoms share electrons with each other. However, carbon atoms can also share electrons with atoms of other elements in a variety of ways. Thus, carbon forms many compounds.

**Compounds with Oxygen**  Carbon atoms form covalent bonds with atoms of oxygen. Under different conditions, two different compounds can be produced: carbon dioxide ($CO_2$) and carbon monoxide ($CO$).

carbon dioxide:  $C + O_2 \longrightarrow CO_2$
carbon monoxide:  $2\,C + O_2 \longrightarrow 2\,CO$

Chart 13-1 gives more information about these compounds. The compounds can be produced by the burning of many fuels. Respiration, a reaction that occurs in all living cells, also produces carbon dioxide.

**Organic Compounds**  Figure 13-3 shows one of the great number of compounds of carbon and hydrogen. Many of these compounds are produced by living things. *A branch of chemistry,* **organic chemistry,** *studies the compounds of carbon.* Such compounds are

*Figure 13-3. Paraffin, used to make candles and wax paper, is a carbon compound that comes from petroleum.*

called organic compounds. Note that simple carbon compounds like CO and $CO_2$ are not considered organic.

Over 100 years ago chemists found ways of producing organic compounds in laboratories. Today over three million organic compounds have been made in chemistry laboratories. New organic compounds are being made, or synthesized (SIN•thuh•sighzd), daily.

## Models of Carbon Compounds

How can so many compounds be made of just a few kinds of atoms? Scientists construct models of organic compounds to provide an explanation. For example, Figure 13-4 shows a model of a molecule of one organic compound, methane gas. The carbon atom shares its outermost electrons with four hydrogen atoms. Each line stands for a pair of shared electrons. This model is called a *structural formula*. A **structural formula** shows the number and arrangement of atoms in a molecule.

Figure 13-4 shows other structural formulas of organic compounds. In many organic compounds, mole-

What does a line in a model of an organic compound represent?

*Figure 13-4. Models of molecules of organic compounds. How many bonds does each carbon atom form?*

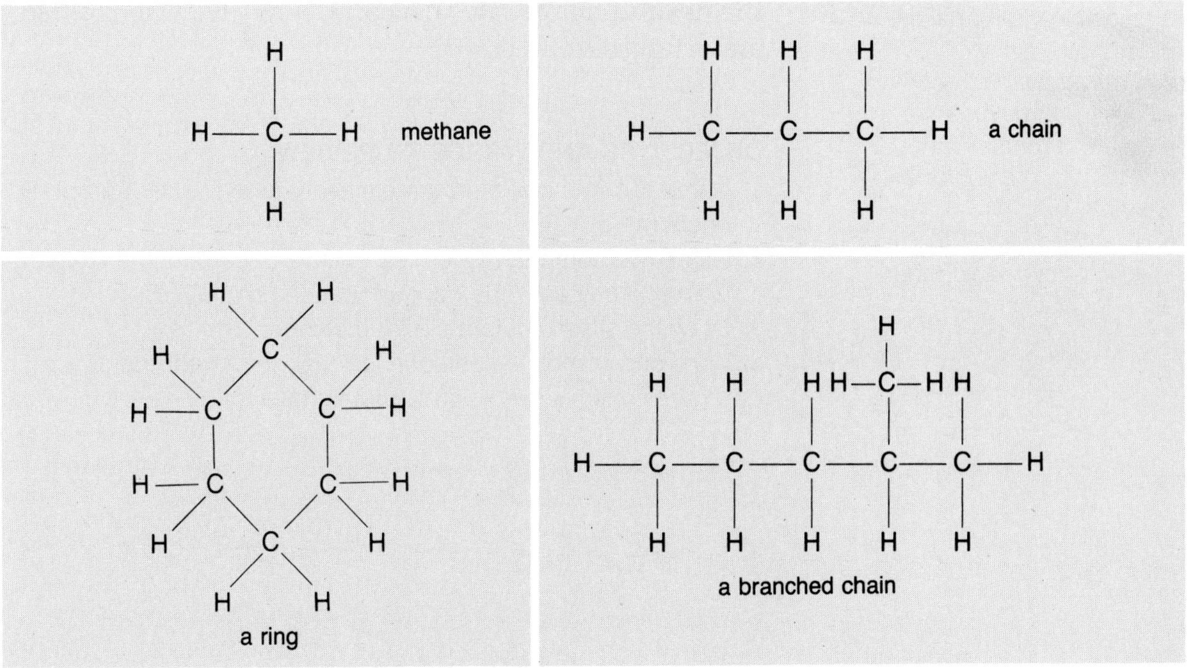

methane

a chain

a ring

a branched chain

## DIAMONDS

**OBJECTIVE**
Learn about the origin, properties, and uses of diamonds.

**PROCEDURE**
**1.** Go to a jewelry store. Interview the jeweler by asking the following questions. Write down the answers and bring them to class for discussion.

**QUESTIONS**
**1.** How are diamonds formed in the earth? How are they made artificially?
**2.** From what countries do most diamonds come?
**3.** Is it possible to tell the difference between a real diamond and an artificial diamond? How?
**4.** What does each of the following terms mean to a jeweler: hardness, facet?
**5.** Why are diamonds so valuable?
**6.** Diamonds are often used in jewelry. Give two other uses for diamonds.

cules contain carbon atoms joined together in chains or rings. The chains may have only two carbon atoms or many hundreds of carbon atoms. Some molecules are made of branches of carbon atoms.

Notice that the structural formulas in Figure 13-4 contain atoms of just two elements. These formulas can give you some idea of the enormous number of possible arrangements with just these two kinds of atoms. Now you can understand how carbon atoms form millions of organic compounds when other kinds of atoms are also involved. You will learn about different groups of organic compounds in the next section.

● Tennis rackets, golf clubs, fishing poles, and many other objects are being made of a material that was first used in rocket engines. The material is largely carbon.

The material comes from a yarn made of organic compounds. The yarn is burned at very high temperatures in an airless oven. After burning, very little is left of the yarn. All that remains is fibers of almost pure carbon. These fibers are lightweight and strong. They are added to plastic, which is then molded into the desired shape. The carbon fibers give this molded material great strength.

### OBJECTIVES AND WORDS TO REVIEW

**1.** Name two forms of the pure element carbon. Give a property of each.
**2.** Name two compounds formed entirely of carbon and oxygen. Give one use and one danger of each compound.
**3.** Draw the structural formula for methane.
**4.** Write one complete sentence for each term listed below.
    organic chemistry      structural formula

# GROUPS OF ORGANIC COMPOUNDS

There are many kinds of organic compounds. In this section you will learn about gasoline, waxes, alcohols, and acids like vinegar, just to name a few.

## Hydrocarbons

Hydrocarbons (high•droh•KAHR•buhnz) are very important organic compounds. *A **hydrocarbon** is an organic compound that contains only hydrogen atoms and carbon atoms.* There are thousands of hydrocarbons. They range from tiny molecules of gases used as fuels in gas stoves to dense solids. How can so many different compounds be made of just two kinds of atoms?

The properties of each compound depend on the structure of its molecules. A change in the structure changes one molecule into another. Reactions that change the arrangement or number of atoms in molecules change one organic compound into another organic compound.

## The Bonds in Hydrocarbons

Hydrocarbons are divided into two groups based on how their carbon atoms share electrons.

**Saturated Hydrocarbons** Look carefully at the model of propane in Figure 13-5. Count the bonds around each carbon atom. These are single bonds. A single bond is the sharing of one electron pair between atoms. By sharing a pair of electrons each with four other atoms, the carbon atom fills its outermost energy level. The molecule represented in Figure 13-5 is a *saturated* (SACH•uh•rayt•uhd) *hydrocarbon.* In a **saturated hydrocarbon,** *each carbon atom is joined by single bonds to four other atoms.* The gases methane and ethane (found in natural gas) and octane (found in gasoline) are saturated hydrocarbons.

**OBJECTIVES**
**1.** Draw models of molecules with double and triple bonds.
**2.** Describe two groups of organic compounds that contain oxygen.
**3.** Show how two different compounds can have the same chemical formula.

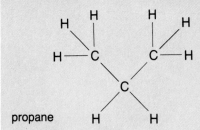

propane

*Figure 13-5. Propane is the gas burned to heat the air that fills balloons. What kind of organic compound is propane?*

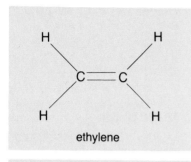

ethylene

H—C≡C—H

acetylene

*Figure 13-6. How many bonds does each carbon form?*

**Unsaturated Hydrocarbons**  Figure 13-6 shows two models of *unsaturated hydrocarbons. An* **unsaturated hydrocarbon** *contains carbon atoms that are bonded to only two or three other atoms.* Double or triple bonds are unsaturated bonds. In a double bond, two carbon atoms share two pairs of electrons. How many pairs of electrons are shared in a triple bond?

You are familiar with the term unsaturated as it is used in nutrition. Unsaturated refers to the type of carbon bonds found in some foods. Research has shown that foods, especially fats, with unsaturated carbon bonds may be very useful. They are less likely to cause disease of the heart and blood vessels than foods with saturated fats are.

## Aromatic Hydrocarbons

Many unsaturated hydrocarbons share a common property. They have a strong odor or aroma. These compounds are called *aromatic* (ar•uh•MAT•ik) *hydrocarbons.* **Aromatic hydrocarbons** *have molecules built from a ring of six carbon atoms joined by single and double bonds.*

Benzene is a well-known aromatic hydrocarbon. Figure 13-7 shows a model of the benzene molecule. Benzene is a solvent for fats, oils, and rubber. It is the basis of many important reactions that form synthetic materials.

*Figure 13-7. The shape of a benzene molecule resembles a honeycomb. What is the molecular formula of benzene?*

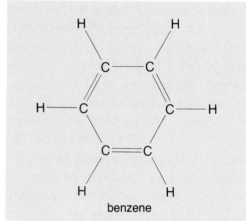

benzene

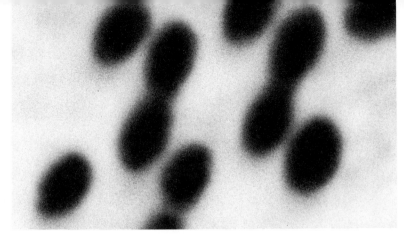

*Figure 13-8. X rays can be used to reveal the structure of molecules.*

You are also looking at an aromatic hydrocarbon in Figure 13-8. Scientists estimate the structure of a molecule by the ways it reacts with other substances. But now they can use X rays to find the position of atoms in a molecule. The black spots in Figure 13-8 are shadows of carbon atoms. The structural formula of the compound had been determined years earlier. But you can see how closely the X-ray picture supports the structural formula.

## Other Organic Compounds

The hydrocarbons are only one group of organic compounds. Many other organic compounds contain other elements besides just hydrogen and carbon. Some of these compounds are *substituted hydrocarbons*. A **substituted hydrocarbon** *is a compound made by replacing some of the hydrogen atoms of a hydrocarbon with other atoms.* Halogens are used to replace the hydrogen in many hydrocarbons. The substituted hydrocarbons that result have many uses. Table 13-1 lists just a few substituted hydrocarbons.

**TABLE 13-1.** SUBSTITUTED HYDROCARBONS

| Name | Formula | Based on | Some Uses |
|------|---------|----------|-----------|
| Iodoform | $CHI_3$ | methane: $CH_4$ | antiseptic |
| Chloroform | $CHCl_3$ | methane: $CH_4$ | general anesthetic |
| Methyl chloride | $CH_3Cl$ | methane: $CH_4$ | refrigerant |

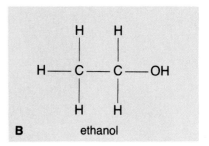

A      ethane             B      ethanol

*Figure 13-9. Ethanol is derived from ethane.*

Three other groups of organic compounds follow. They contain oxygen as well as hydrogen and carbon.

**Alcohols** Have you ever used rubbing alcohol? Rubbing alcohol is a water solution of ethanol or iso-propanol (IGH•soh•proh•puh•nawl). These compounds belong to a group of organic compounds called *alcohols*. **Alcohols** *are organic compounds that contain a hydroxyl group of atoms (—OH).*

Alcohols have a hydroxyl group. Yet they are not bases. Alcohols do not form hydroxyl ions in water. However, alcohols can be derived from hydrocarbons. For example, look at Figure 13-9. Ethane, in **A**, is a hydrocarbon. Ethanol, in **B**, has only one difference in its structure. It has an —OH group in place of one of the hydrogen atoms in the ethane molecule. All alcohols contain this —OH group.

The name of all alcohols ends in "ol." Each alcohol is named after the hydrocarbon that has a similar structure. Ethanol, for example, has a structure similar to ethane. Methanol, an alcohol used in car deicers, has a structure similar to methane. See Figure 13-9**C**.

**Organic Acids** Many foods have a sour taste. This taste is due to the presence of acids. Lemons, for example, contain citric acid. Vinegar contains acetic (uh•SEE•tik) acid. Citric acid and acetic acid are *organic acids*. **Organic acids** *are organic compounds that contain a —COOH group of atoms.* The —COOH group is circled in Figure 13-10. This group produces hydronium ions in water. Most organic acids are weak acids. They produce fewer hydronium ions in water than strong acids do.

*Figure 13-10. Organic acids have a—COOH group.*

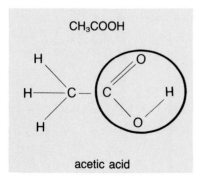

CH₃COOH

acetic acid

**TABLE 13-2.** COMPARISON OF TWO ISOMERS OF PENTANE ($C_5H_{12}$)

| Isomer | Structural Formula | Boiling Point (°C) | Melting Point (°C) | Density (g/cm³) |
|--------|-------------------|--------------------|--------------------|-----------------|
| Normal pentane | | 36.1 | −130 | 0.626 |
| Isopentane | | 27.8 | −159.9 | 0.620 |

**Esters**   Have you ever noticed the pleasing fruitlike aroma of some substances? The aroma of many of these substances is caused by an *ester*. An **ester** *is an organic compound formed by the reaction of an organic acid with an alcohol.* For example, acetic acid reacts with ethanol and forms ethyl acetate (an ester) and water.

acetic acid plus ethanol yields ethyl acetate plus water
$$CH_3COOH + C_2H_5OH \longrightarrow CH_3COOC_2H_5 + H_2O$$

Ethyl acetate is the solvent in some fingernail polish removers.

The production of esters shows an interesting sign of a chemical change: a change of scent. Some of the organic acids esters are made from have foul odors.

## Isomers

Now that you have learned about some organic compounds, perhaps you can solve a puzzle. How can two compounds have the same chemical formula and yet have different properties? Table 13-2 shows the structural formulas of pentane and isopentane. If you look at the structural formula of each compound, you can tell they are different. Each compound has a different

**How are isomers alike? How are they different?**

*Figure 13-11. The properties of petrolatum make it useful as an ingredient in cosmetics. Its more familiar forms are mineral oil and petroleum jelly.*

arrangement of atoms. They are examples of *isomers* (IGH•soh•murz). *Compounds are called* **isomers** *when they share the same chemical formula, but have different structural formulas.* There are many sets of organic compounds that are isomers. Each member of the set has the same number and kind of atoms. Yet each compound has a different structure. Each also has different properties. Refer again to Table 13-2.

● Cosmetic chemists perform many tests to be sure that a cosmetic ingredient is safe. Petrolatum, a mixture of hydrocarbons, is one of these safe ingredients. See Figure 13-11. Petrolatum is odorless, tasteless, soft, smooth, greasy, and harmless to the skin. It is used in some forms of eye makeup and in lipstick. Petrolatum is also used as a skin softener.

**OBJECTIVES AND WORDS TO REVIEW**

1. Draw a structural formula for the following unsaturated hydrocarbons:
   a. ethylene ($C_2H_4$)  b. acetylene ($C_2H_2$)
2. Name two groups of organic compounds that contain oxygen. Give an example and properties of each group.
3. Hexane and isohexane are isomers. Below is the structural formula for isohexane.

$$
\begin{array}{cccccccc}
 & & & & H & & & \\
 & & & & | & & & \\
 & & & H-&C&-H & & \\
 & & H & H & | & H & H \\
 & & | & | & | & | & | \\
H-&C-&C-&C-&C-&C&-H \\
 & | & | & | & | & | \\
 & H & H & H & H & H
\end{array}
$$

   What is the chemical formula for isohexane? What is the chemical formula for hexane? Draw its structural formula.
4. Write one complete sentence for each term listed below.
   hydrocarbon                    alcohol
   saturated hydrocarbon          organic acid
   unsaturated hydrocarbon        ester
   aromatic hydrocarbon           isomers
   substituted hydrocarbon

# USING ORGANIC COMPOUNDS

You use organic compounds every day. They make up the foods you eat, the clothes you wear, even the fuels that warm your home. In this section you will get a closer look at some of these important kinds of organic compounds.

## Compounds That Give Energy

Your body needs energy to do just about anything. Organic compounds are the source of this energy. They act as fuels in your body much as gasoline does in a car. What are some of these energy-containing compounds?

**Carbohydrates** Think of the taste of a sun-ripened peach. The sweetness of this and other fruits is due to sugars. Sugars belong to a group of compounds called *carbohydrates* (kahr•boh•HIGH•drayts).

*Carbohydrates* are organic compounds that contain carbon, hydrogen, and oxygen, with two atoms of hydrogen for every atom of oxygen. The sugar glucose has the formula $C_6H_{12}O_6$. Notice there are twice as many hydrogen atoms (12) as oxygen atoms (6). See Figure 13-12.

**OBJECTIVES**
**1.** List three kinds of organic compounds that are used as foods.
**2.** Describe how enzymes help change food molecules.
**3.** Explain how hydrocarbons are separated from petroleum.

*Figure 13-12. Glucose is produced by green leaves in sunlight.*

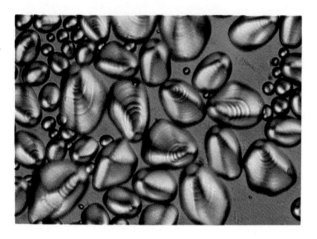

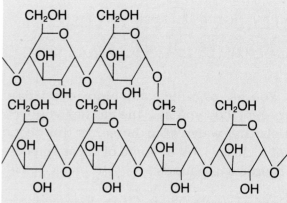

*Figure 13-13. A short section of a starch molecule.*

How are starches related to glucose molecules?

Glucose has an isomer, fructose. Fructose is a sugar found in many fruits. Glucose and fructose will combine and form sucrose, $C_{12}H_{22}O_{11}$, a more complex sugar.

Starches are another carbohydrate with which you are familiar. Starch molecules are made of long chains of glucose molecules hooked together. See Figure 13-13. Starches are the main form of stored food in plants.

**Fats** Fats are also a group of compounds found in living things. Like carbohydrates, fats are made from carbon, hydrogen, and oxygen. Fat molecules are large and complex. They store about twice the energy of carbohydrates. Unused fats are stored by the body and add to body weight.

Fats are formed when an alcohol reacts with organic acids called fatty acids. The alcohol from which fats are made is glycerol (GLIS•ur•awl).

## Compounds That Build and Repair

All living cells perform activities such as growing and reproducing. These activities require *proteins* (PROH•tee•inz). **Proteins** are organic compounds used in building and repairing cells. All proteins contain carbon, hydrogen, oxygen, and nitrogen. A few proteins also contain sulfur or phosphorus.

Proteins are made of smaller molecules bonded together in long chains. These smaller molecules are called amino (AM•i•noh) acids. There are about 20 common amino acids. Most proteins are made of these common amino acids. You see the formula for the amino acid glycine (GLIGH•seen) in Figure 13-14.

Meat, seafood, dairy products, and beans are major sources of proteins. However, in certain countries where such foods are hard to obtain, people use soybeans as a substitute.

## Making Carbon Compounds Useful to the Body

Your breakfast may have contained carbohydrates, fats, and proteins. What do you think happens to these substances after you have eaten them?

Once you take in food, your body begins a breakdown process. It breaks down the food molecules into smaller molecules. Sugars and starches are broken down into glucose molecules. Fats are split up into glycerol and fatty acids. Proteins are broken down into amino acids.

In each case the same process occurs: *digestion. The breaking down of proteins, fats, and carbohydrates into smaller molecules is called* **digestion.** Once these large molecules are split into smaller ones, they can enter the blood stream.

Digestion is a chemical reaction. Digestion requires water. Water helps split the food into smaller molecules. However, with just water, digestion occurs slowly. But your body contains other substances that speed up digestion. These substances are *enzymes* (EN•zighmz). **Enzymes** *are catalysts that help speed up chemical reactions in living things.* You have an enzyme in your saliva that changes starches into sugars. If you chew an unsalted cracker about a minute without swallowing it, the cracker will begin to taste sweet.

Besides the mouth, many other organs in your body play an important part in digestion. In each digestive organ, certain foods are digested. And in each organ,

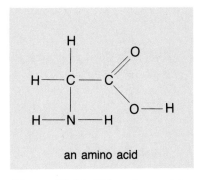

an amino acid

*Figure 13-14. All amino acids contain nitrogen. How can you tell this molecule is an acid?*

What are the products of digestion?

**CHART 13-2.** DIGESTION AND WHERE IT OCCURS

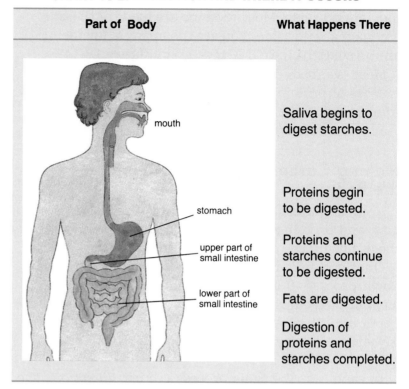

| Part of Body | What Happens There |
|---|---|
| mouth | Saliva begins to digest starches. |
| stomach | Proteins begin to be digested. |
| upper part of small intestine | Proteins and starches continue to be digested. |
| lower part of small intestine | Fats are digested. |
| | Digestion of proteins and starches completed. |

certain enzymes help speed up the process. Your body's transport system carries the smaller molecules to your cells. Your cells use them for repair, growth, and energy. Chart 13-2 outlines digestion.

## Petroleum—A Source of Useful Compounds

What do a can of paint, a nylon rope, and a box of detergent have in common? Each substance was obtained from *petroleum* (puh•TROH•lee•uhm) products. **Petroleum** *is a liquid mixture of hydrocarbons obtained from below the earth's surface.* Figure 13-15 shows many common products that come from petroleum.

How did petroleum form? Plants and animals that lived millions of years ago died. Their bodies sank to the bottom of seas and oceans, where they were buried.

As time went by, their remains decayed. Chemical reactions broke down the bodies into the hydrocarbons in petroleum.

In order to use the hydrocarbons in petroleum, they must be separated. They are separated by distillation in a tower such as in Figure 13-16 on page 294. Petroleum is heated at the bottom until it evaporates. The evaporated petroleum then rises. As it rises, it cools gradually. Each hydrocarbon in the petroleum con-

*Figure 13-15. Many household products are made from petroleum.*

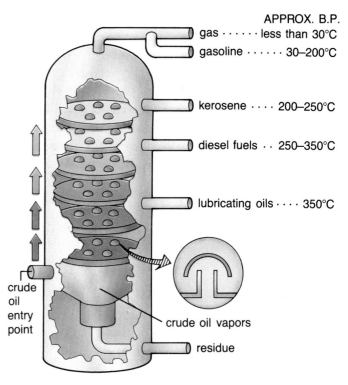

APPROX. B.P.

gas · · · · · · less than 30°C

gasoline · · · · · · 30–200°C

kerosene · · · · 200–250°C

diesel fuels · · 250–350°C

lubricating oils · · · · 350°C

crude oil entry point

crude oil vapors

residue

*Figure 13-16. At each temperature range shown, a rising hydrocarbon condenses. What is the purpose of the pipes on the side of the tower in the photograph?*

denses back to a liquid at certain temperatures along the way up the tower. As each hydrocarbon condenses it is collected and removed. Oils are collected near the bottom of the tower. Gasoline, however, condenses at a lower temperature than oils. So it will rise higher in the tower before it turns back into a liquid.

## Soaps and Detergents

*Soaps* and detergents are organic compounds very familiar to you. **Soaps are metallic salts of fatty acids.** They are made by boiling fats and lye. Lye is a solution of the base, sodium hydroxide.

$$\text{fat} + \text{lye} \longrightarrow \text{glycerin} + \text{soaps}$$

Soaps act as emulsifiers when placed in contact with water and oil or greasy dirt. The metallic end of a soap molecule dissolves in water. The hydrocarbon end dissolves in oil. The oil is surrounded by the soap molecules. This process allows water to work away the oil or greasy dirt. Figure 13-17 shows how this action works.

Detergents, like soaps, are substances that remove dirt. However, soaps do not suds well in hard water because they react with the metal ions in hard water. Detergents have different chemical compositions from soaps. Unlike soaps, detergents suds well in hard water because they do not react with the metal ions.

How are detergents different from soaps?

## Polymers

Modern synthetic fabrics are often made of organic compounds called *polymers* (PAHL•i•murz). **Polymers are organic compounds that have molecules made of long chains of smaller molecules.** The molecules of some polymers are made of thousands of smaller molecules linked together.

*Figure 13-17. A model of the grease-dissolving action of soap. What elements are contained in the soap molecule?*

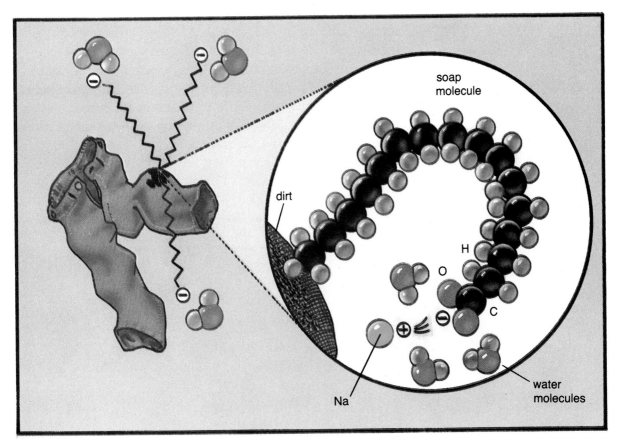

## OCTANE NUMBER

**OBJECTIVE**
Learn why automobile gasoline is given an octane number.

**PROCEDURE**
You see an octane number, or octane rating, posted on the gasoline tanks at the service station. Using reference books in the library find out what "octane number" means.

**QUESTIONS**
**1.** What causes "knocking" in an automobile engine?
**2.** What type of hydrocarbon in gasoline prevents knocking?
**3.** What does octane rating, or number, tell you?

Many polymers are made from only one repeating unit, or monomer. Starches, for example, are made of repeating glucose units. The glucose units are the monomers. Proteins are polymers made of amino-acid units linked together. Polyesters and rubber may have thousands of monomers. Nylon and most *plastics* are also examples of polymers. *A **plastic** is a material that can be molded while soft, and then hardened by heat, cooling, or exposing to air.* Most people think of a plastic as a synthetic material. Some natural plastics, like asphalt and shellac, do exist.

Most synthetic plastics are polymers. Look at Figure 13-18. The shoes ball players wear have cleats made from a synthetic plastic. It is called polyethylene (pahl•ee•ETH•uh•leen). Polyethylene is a polymer made up of about forty thousand monomers of ethylene. The prefix "poly," meaning "many," is part of the names of synthetic plastics to indicate the many monomers that make them up.

Polypropylene (pahl•ee•PROH•puh•leen) and poly-urethane (pahl•ee•YEWR•uh•thayn) are two other common polymers. Polypropylene is molded into auto parts and cooking utensils. Polyurethane is an ingredient in foam insulation. However, it is also used to add strength to airplane metals.

Wood and cotton contain a natural polymer called cellulose (SEL•yew•lohs). Cellulose is a polymer made up of many molecules of glucose. Like starch, cellulose is a carbohydrate. But unlike starch, it is woody

*Figure 13-18. One of the many uses of polyethylene plastic is to make these shoes. What property do you think this materal must have?*

and tough. If cellulose is treated with acetic acid, a plastic called cellulose acetate is made. See Figure 13-19. Cellophane is made by chemically treating cellulose. If the treated cellulose is forced through tiny holes, it forms threads. Acetate, a silky fabric, is made by twisting these threads together.

● Can you imagine a car propelled by "muscles" made of polymers? Some scientists can. They know that the structures of some proteins resemble coiled springs. Slight chemical changes can cause these proteins to coil and uncoil. These scientists believe that a similar coiled spring made of polymers can be used as a muscle. By placing these muscles in an electrolyte solution that keeps changing, they can make the muscles contract and relax like living muscle. This contracting and relaxing would provide a moving force that would propel a car.

## OBJECTIVES AND WORDS TO REVIEW

1. List three types of organic compounds that are used as foods.
2. Describe the role of enzymes in digestion.
3. Describe the process petroleum undergoes in the production of useful compounds.
4. Write one complete sentence for each term listed below.

| | | |
|---|---|---|
| carbohydrate | enzyme | polymer |
| protein | petroleum | plastic |
| digestion | | |

# LEARNING TO USE RATIOS

## Preparation

Ratios may look strange, but they are used in down-to-earth ways. Have you ever made orange juice from frozen concentrate? By itself, the concentrate is too sweet. When you mix it with water in a $1:3$ ratio, you get good-tasting orange juice.

Ratios can be written as fractions. The ratio of concentrate to water is $\frac{1}{3}$. An equation of two such ratios is a proportion. For example: $\frac{3}{5}=\frac{6}{10}$. If any one number of a proportion is missing, you can find its value by solving the equation.

Scientists also use ratios. For example, a chemist must know the ratio of hydrogen to oxygen to tell whether a compound is water ($H_2O$) or hydrogen peroxide ($H_2O_2$).

## Directions

To solve a proportion, follow these steps:

1. Make sure the units in each ratio of a proportion are the same. When you mix the concentrate, the units you use are *cans*. You add 1 *can* of concentrate to 3 *cans* of water. If you mixed 1 *can* of concentrate with 3 *teaspoons* of water, the juice would not taste right.
2. Represent the unknown by an "x".
3. Multiply the first term by the fourth. (See Figure 1.)
4. Multiply the second term by the third.
5. Set the two products equal to each other.
6. Solve the equation algebraically.

For example, an official United States flag may be any size. But the ratio of length to width must be $19:10$, or $\frac{19}{10}$. You want to make a flag 2 meters wide. What must its length be?

$$\frac{\text{length of flag}}{\text{width of flag}} = \frac{19}{10}$$
$$\frac{x}{2} = \frac{19}{10}$$
$$10 \times = 19 \times 2$$
$$10 \times = 38$$
$$\times = 3.8 \text{ meters}$$

## Practice

Use proportions to solve these problems.

1. The ratio of sulfur to oxygen in a compound is $1:2$. How many grams of oxygen are needed to make the compound with 3 grams of sulfur?
2. In an architect's blueprint, 2 cm represents 1 meter. What will be the actual dimensions of a room shown in the blueprint as 6.6 cm by 8 cm?

## Application

In Chapter 13 you learned that carbohydrates contain carbon, hydrogen, and oxygen atoms. In most carbohydrates the ratio of carbon atoms to hydrogen atoms is $1:2$. The ratio of hydrogen atoms to oxygen atoms is $2:1$. Thus, the chemical formula of glucose (6 carbon atoms) is $C_6H_{12}O_6$. A pentose is any carbohydrate with 5 carbon atoms. Use proportions to find its formula. A triose is any carbohydrate with 3 carbon atoms. What is its formula?

**Figure 1.**

$$\frac{\text{1ST TERM}}{\text{2ND TERM}} = \frac{\text{3RD TERM}}{\text{4TH TERM}}$$

1ST TERM $\times$ 4TH TERM = 2ND TERM $\times$ 3RD TERM

# ORGANIC COMPOUNDS IN A PET FOOD

## Objective
Learn what organic compounds are in cat food.

## Background
A dog or cat food label tells you the percentage of carbohydrates, fats, and proteins in the food.

You can test for the presence of fat in a food by rubbing some of it on a piece of brown wrapping paper. If fat is present it will leave a grease spot that does not dry. You can see light through the spot. See Figure 13-L.

To test for starch, add a few drops of iodine to the food. If starch is present it will turn blue-black.

To test for proteins, add copper ions and sodium hydroxide to the food. If proteins are present, they will turn a violet color.

## Materials
cat food, 0.05 M copper sulfate, 6 M sodium hydroxide, iodine solution, test tubes, 3 droppers, brown wrapping paper, goggles, apron, marking pencil, label from food can, corks

## Procedure
1. Your teacher has already dissolved out any fat that may be in the pet food with a dry cleaning solvent. The solvent has been evaporated.

Feel some of the greasy substance left in the dish. Rub it on a small square of brown paper. Mark the paper *fat.*

2. Rub a bit of water on a second square of paper. Mark this square *water.* Allow both papers to dry until the end of the experiment.

3. Add an amount of cat food about the size of a cherry and 10 drops of water to two test tubes. Mark one test tube *starch,* and the other *protein.* **CAUTION:** Wear goggles, and an apron.

4. To the tube marked *starch,* add a few drops of iodine solution. Cap and shake the mixture. Note any changes.

5. To the tube marked *protein,* add 10 drops of copper sulfate solution and 5 drops of sodium hydroxide solution. Cap and shake the mixture. Note any changes.

6. Examine the squares of paper. If the water has dried, hold the squares up to the light. Can you see light through either spot?

## Questions
1. What observations revealed that the cat food contains fat, starch, and protein?
2. Why did you test water on brown paper?
3. Using the food label, find the ratio of fats to proteins and of carbohydrates to proteins.
4. **PROBLEM SOLVING** Does egg white contain protein? Make a hypothesis and test it.
5. **PROBLEM SOLVING** Does bread contain carbohyrates? Proteins? Fats? Make hypotheses and test them.

*Figure 13-L. Laboratory setup.*

TEST FOR FATS

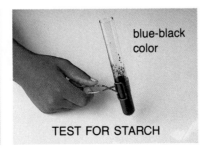

TEST FOR STARCH

TEST FOR PROTEINS

Do you like doing experiments with chemicals? Are you curious about how permanents, hair dyes, and other beauty aids work? Would you like to help people feel and look better? If so, the careers below may appeal to you.

**Pharmacist** Doctors often prescribe medications for us when we get sick. Pharmacists have the job of preparing and dispensing these medications. Although most medications are now ready made, pharmacists still may have to compound a medicine from its separate chemicals. This process requires accuracy, cleanliness, and a thorough knowledge of the chemicals to be used.

To become a pharmacist you must enroll in a special five-year college program. Upon graduation, you may work in a drugstore, pharmacy, or hospital. As you work, your challenge will be to keep up with new developments in drug research.

You can find out more about a career in pharmacy by writing:

*American Association of Colleges of Pharmacy*
*Office of Student Affairs*
*4720 Montgomery Lane, Suite 602*
*Bethesda, MD 20814*

**Beauty Operator** Beauty operators use a variety of skills to improve the personal appearance of their clients. They may apply skin treatments, color and condition hair, or manicure nails. However, they must be aware of the effects on the skin of chemicals in cosmetic products. Beauty operators also must be able to use tools such as scissors, dryers, and curling irons.

Beauty operators can learn their trade in vocational school or private beauty colleges. High school courses in chemistry are desirable. However, some beauty operators enter trade school after the eighth grade. After graduating, they usually start work in an established shop.

To find out more about this career, write:

*National Cosmetology Association*
*3510 Olive Street*
*St. Louis, MO 63103*

# SUMMARY

1. All organic compounds contain carbon. Carbon atoms have four electrons in their valence shell. They share electrons with other atoms by forming covalent bonds. (13-1)

2. A great variety of organic compounds exist because the same atoms can be arranged in many ways. (13-1)

3. Hydrocarbons contain only hydrogen and carbon. Some hydrocarbons are unsaturated. Such hydrocarbons have double or triple covalent bonds. (13-2)

4. Alcohols contain an—OH group. Organic acids have a—COOH group (13-2)

5. Carbohydrates and fats are organic compounds that supply living things with energy. Proteins are organic compounds that help build and repair body tissues. (13-3)

6. Petroleum is a thick mixture of many hydrocarbons. Distillation separates petroleum into its parts. (13-3)

# REVIEW

Number a sheet of paper from 1 to 25 and answer these questions.

**Building Science Vocabulary**    Write the letter of the term that best matches each definition.

a. alcohols
b. carbohydrates
c. fats
d. enzymes
e. isomers
f. organic acids
g. petroleum
h. plastics
i. polymers
j. proteins
k. saturated
l. unsaturated

1. Compounds that have the same chemical formula but a different structural formula

2. Hydrocarbons in which carbon atoms are bonded to four other atoms

3. A group of organic compounds that contain an —OH group

4. Hydrocarbons in which carbon atoms are bonded to two or three other atoms

5. Organic compounds that have two hydrogen atoms for every oxygen atom

6. Organic compounds used for cell repair

7. Catalysts that speed up chemical processes in living things

8. Liquid mixture of many hydrocarbons obtained from below the earth's surface

9. Large molecules made of long chains of smaller molecules

10. A group of organic compounds containing the —COOH group

**Finding the Facts**    Select the letter of the answer that best completes each of the following.

11. Diamond and graphite are two forms of pure    (a) carbohydrate    (b) carbon    (c) hydrocarbon    (d) organic compound.

12. Hydrocarbons contain only    (a) carbon    (b) carbon and oxygen    (c) carbon and hydrogen    (d) carbon and nitrogen.

13. Saturated hydrocarbons contain    (a) only single bonds    (b) single and double bonds    (c) double and triple bonds    (d) single, double, or triple bonds.

14. Benzene is a type of    (a) saturated hydrocarbon    (b) alcohol    (c) aromatic hydrocarbon    (d) alcohol.

15. An organic compound that contains a —COOH group is    (a) an alcohol    (b) a carbohydrate    (c) a protein    (d) an organic acid.

16. A compound that supplies energy to your body is    (a) an enzyme    (b) a carbohydrate    (c) water    (d) an aromatic hydrocarbon.

17. Fats are made from    (a) benzene    (b) ethane    (c) glycerol    (d) enzymes

18. Meats and seafood are major sources of (**a**) proteins (**b**) fats (**c**) carbohydrates (**d**) hydrocarbons.
19. Which is not a polymer? (**a**) proteins (**b**) rubber (**c**) nylon (**d**) ethane
20. Cellophane is made from (**a**) resin (**b**) fructose (**c**) cellulose (**d**) polyethylene.

## Understanding Main Ideas    Complete the following.

21. Carbon atoms share electrons with other atoms by forming __?__.
22. A molecule having the formula $C_3H_7OH$ would be classified as a type of __?__.
23. The breakdown of long molecules of food into shorter molecules is called __?__.
24. The separation of petroleum into its hydrocarbon compounds is __?__.
25. Long chains built up by linking small molecules are called __?__.

## Writing About Science    On a separate sheet of paper, answer the following as completely as possible.

1. The "lead" in a lead pencil is really a mixture of graphite and hard clay. Why is pure graphite not used?
2. Oleomargarine is made from plant oils containing hydrocarbon chains. On the package of some margarines you see the word "polyunsaturated." What do you think that means?
3. Vinegar is a mixture of two liquids, acetic acid and water. How could you separate these two liquids?
4. In some undeveloped countries of the world protein foods are scarce. Children are fed mostly carbohydrate foods. Their bodies look undeveloped and wasted away. Explain why this is so.
5. (laboratory question) Suppose you want to test a cooked cereal, such as cream of wheat, to see if it contains starch and protein. What chemical tests would you perform? What observations would tell you if the cereal contains these compounds?

## Investigating Chapter Ideas    Try one of the following projects to further your study.

1. **Isomers**   Use gumdrops and toothpicks to make three-dimensional models of organic isomers. See how many ways you can attach the carbon atoms in a 4-carbon compound. Which of these arrangements may represent isomers? Which arrangements appear to be just a rotation of some other arrangement?
2. **Heat and an enzyme**   Beef liver contains the enzyme catalase. Catalase breaks down hydrogen peroxide. Place a small piece of raw beef liver in a glass. Add several mL of fresh 3% hydrogen peroxide solution. **CAUTION:** Wear goggles. What evidence is there of a chemical reaction? Repeat the procedure with a piece of cooked liver. What effect does heat have on the activity of catalase in liver?

## Reading About Science    Read some of the following books to explore topics that interest you.

Asimov, Isaac. 1974. **Inside the Atom.** Rev. Ed. New York: Abelard-Schuman.
Cross, Wilbur. 1983. **Coal.** Chicago: Children's.
Cross, Wilbur. 1983. **Petroleum.** New York: Children's.
Kraft, Betsy H. 1982. **Oil and Natural Gas.** Rev. Ed. New York: Watts.
Milne, Lorus and Margery Milne. 1983. **Nature's Great Carbon Cycle.** New York: Atheneum.

# ELECTRICITY AND MAGNETISM

Falling water rushes past wheels, making them spin. The spinning wheels produce the electricity that provides light and power to cities. What is electricity? Would you believe that a magnet can also produce electricity? In this unit you will learn about electricity and magnetism. You will also investigate the relationship between electricity and magnetism and how it is put to use.

**UNIT 5**

Lightning is very dangerous. Yet people are fascinated by this sudden burst of electricity. Why is electricity so fascinating? One reason may be the effects it produces. These effects can be harmful or helpful. You know its harmful effects. What are some useful effects?

Electricity is a form of energy. Energy, remember, causes changes in matter. How does electricity affect matter? A simple activity can help answer this question. Tear some tissue paper into very tiny bits. Stroke your hair three times with a rubber or plastic comb. Bring the comb near the tissue. What happens?

Objects that display this effect are said to be charged. Those that do not are uncharged or neutral. In this chapter you will study how objects can be charged and how they affect each other.

Read and Find Out:

● how a machine makes giant sparks.

● why you can use many appliances at the same time.

● why you must be careful when using an electric heater.

# BASICS
# OF ELECTRICITY

# STATIC ELECTRICITY

**OBJECTIVES**

**1.** State what property of matter causes the electric force.

**2.** Explain how an object can become charged.

**3.** Explain how an instrument can be used to detect charge.

Try rubbing an inflated balloon with a piece of wool. Then bring the wool near the balloon. What happens? As Figure 14-1**A** shows, the balloon moves toward the wool. Now rub two balloons with the wool and hang them as shown in **B**. This time they move apart. Why do two objects attract each other one time and repel each other another time? This section will investigate the answer to that question.

## Electric Forces

What caused the balloons to move? Recall that any object is made of atoms. Atoms, in turn, are made of particles that have charge. Charge is a property that causes some particles to attract each other and others to repel each other. There are two kinds of charge: positive (+) and negative (−). Protons have a positive charge. Electrons have a negative charge. Charged particles exert forces on each other. As you know, forces can cause motion. The balloons moved because a force was exerted on them.

The force resulting from the charge on particles is called the *electric force*. The **electric force** is a force *that attracts or repels charged objects.*

Look again at Figure 14-1. Why did the balloons move the way they did? A model of electron transfer can help you understand. When you rubbed the bal-

*Figure 14-1A. Opposite charges attract.*

loon in **A** with wool, electrons in the wool were transferred to the balloon. The balloon gained electrons and obtained a negative charge. At the same time, the wool lost electrons. Since it now had more protons than electrons, the wool acquired a positive charge. When objects have opposite charges, they attract each other. Thus, the balloon was attracted to the wool.

In Figure 14-1**B**, each balloon gained electrons when it was rubbed with the wool. So, both balloons became negatively charged. Objects with the same charge repel each other. Thus, the balloons moved apart.

## Electric Fields

When the balloons in Figure 14-1 were brought together, they attracted or repelled each other. However, they had to be near each other before movement occurred. Why was there no attraction or repulsion when the balloons were far apart? These effects occur because charged objects have *electric fields* around them. An **electric field** *is the region around a charged object where electric forces on other charged objects can be observed.* The electric field is strongest near the object. It is weakest far away from the object. If you are far enough from an object, its electric field will be too weak to be noticed.

Rubbing contact between two objects can cause them to become charged. You can think of the charge on an object as *static electricity.* **Static electricity** *is a charge that is not moving.* "Static" means "not moving." Static electricity can cause charged objects to move, but the charges themselves do not move.

How do charged objects affect each other?

How can two objects become charged?

*Figure 14-1B. Like charges repel.*

## A Path for Electricity

Have you ever felt a shock when you touched a metal doorknob after walking across a rug? Figure 14-2 can help explain this effect. As you walk, electrons from atoms of the rug are rubbed off onto your shoes. The extra electrons give your shoes a negative charge. The electrons on your shoes spread throughout your body. So your entire body becomes negatively charged. This charge builds up in your body. As you reach for the doorknob, your body repels the electrons in the doorknob. As a result, the doorknob becomes positively charged. Opposite charges attract each other. So electrons in your body jump through the air to the doorknob. The spark you see is caused by this sudden flow of electrons.

The electric spark you see indicates that an amount of energy is being transferred from your body to the doorknob. This transfer occurs because flowing electrons, like all moving objects, have kinetic energy while they move. The slight shock you feel is due to this transfer of energy.

## Conductors and Insulators

You know you sometimes see sparks when you touch a metal doorknob. But you do not see sparks when you touch a doorknob covered with rubber. Metals and rubber have different electric properties. Metals such as copper, silver, and aluminum have *free electrons*. **Free electrons** *are electrons in a metal that are not tightly held by the atoms.* Because of their free electrons, metals such as copper, silver, and aluminum are good *conductors*. A **conductor** *is a material that allows electricity to flow through it easily.* When a negatively charged object is brought near one end of a conductor, free electrons in that end are repelled. They move toward the other end of the conductor. Refer again to Figure 14-2.

Rubber, glass, and wood are poor conductors of electricity. Their electrons are more closely bound to their nuclei. Such materials are called *insulators*

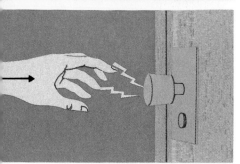

*Figure 14-2. As you walk across a floor, charges build up in your body. When you reach for the door, electrons jump from you to the doorknob.*

Figure 14-3. *The insulator material prevents the other end from attracting the paper.*

(IN•suh•lay•turz). *An **insulator** is a material that hinders the flow of electricity through it.* Figure 14-3 shows a rod made of an insulator. It has been charged by rubbing at one end only. Note that the rod attracts the paper at that end only. The insulator material prevents free electrons from traveling to the other end of the rod. So that end cannot attract the paper.

## Measuring Static Electricity

An **electroscope** (i•LEK•truh•skohp) *is a device used to study static electricity.* Figure 14-4 shows how to make a simple electroscope. An electroscope is most useful for detecting charge.

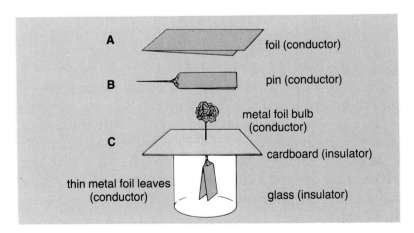

A — foil (conductor)

B — pin (conductor)

metal foil bulb (conductor)

C — cardboard (insulator)

thin metal foil leaves (conductor)

glass (insulator)

Figure 14-4. *A simple electroscope.* (**A**) *Fold foil (20 × 1 cm) in half.* (**B**) *Pinch foil around pin. Push pin through cardboard. Put crushed foil ball on top of pin.* (**C**) *Completed electroscope.*

*Static Electricity* **309**

**Detecting Charge** What happens if you place a charged object near the top of a neutral electroscope? A positively charged object attracts free electrons in the metal leaves to the top of the electroscope. Since the leaves lose electrons, both obtain a positive charge. Like charges repel, so the leaves spread apart. The spreading shows that there is charge. See Figure 14-5.

If you use a negative object, free electrons move in the opposite direction. Again, the leaves have like charges and spread apart. So an electroscope shows *whether* an object has charge. It cannot show *what kind* of charge an object has.

**Giving Charge** If you actually touch the top of an electroscope with a positive object, what happens? Free electrons are again attracted to the top. Now, however, they can leave the device. The object touching the bulb provides a path for the electrons to move along. They flow into the positively charged object.

If you then remove the charged object, electrons cannot return to the leaves. The leaves keep their positive charge. They stay spread apart.

**Removing Charge** Now suppose you touch the bulb with your finger. Living things, including people, are conductors. Free electrons in your finger flow toward the positively charged leaves. As a result, the leaves become neutral and hang straight down.

**Grounding Charge** After touching a charged electroscope, why do you not become charged yourself? You do not become charged because your feet are touching the earth. Or they are in contact with something touching the earth. The earth is so large it can give up or accept huge numbers of free electrons. Your body gave a path for the electrons to move between the earth and the electroscope.

Charge can be removed from an object by connecting it to the earth through a conductor. *The removal of static electricity by conduction to the earth is called* **grounding**. When you touch a metal doorknob, you are grounding yourself. You are removing electrons from your body.

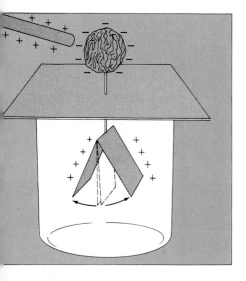

*Figure 14-5. The position of the leaves of an electroscope indicates if the device is charged. Which position indicates the electroscope is neutral?*

● Figure 14-6 shows a machine that produces large amounts of static electricity. Part **A** shows a rubber belt, similar to a giant rubber band, inside the machine. A motor drives the belt around a set of wheels. Electrons jump from a metal comb at the bottom onto the rubber belt. The belt carries these electrons to the top. There, they collect on the large metal sphere. When too many electrons have collected on the sphere, a large spark results. See Figure 14-6**B**.

*Figure 14-6.* A Van de Graaff machine produces large amounts of static electricity.

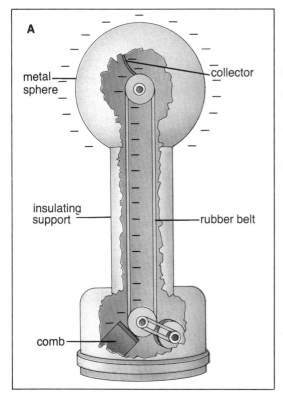

## OBJECTIVES AND WORDS TO REVIEW

1. What property of matter causes the electric force?
2. How can rubbing two objects together make one object positive and the other object negative?
3. Explain how you can use an electroscope to detect charge.
4. Write one complete sentence for each term listed below.

electric force     free electrons     electroscope
electric field      conductor          grounding
static electricity  insulator

# ELECTRONS IN MOTION

**OBJECTIVES**

**1.** Explain how a dry cell keeps electrons flowing.

**2.** Name three basic parts of a circuit.

**3.** Describe how the two types of electric circuits differ.

You flick on a switch. Lights go on. A stereo begins to play. A computer begins to print out information. Many appliances run on electricity, but not static electricity. Computers and other electric devices work by using moving electrons. In this section you will learn what happens to electrons as they flow through objects.

## Giving Energy to Electrons

Energy is needed to keep electrons moving through electric devices. This energy is provided by a source. Sources that you may be familiar with are dry cells and batteries. Both use a chemical reaction to produce a flow of electrons.

The model shown in Figure 14-7 can help you understand how a dry cell provides energy to electrons. The top of a dry cell has two connection points, or terminals. One terminal is the top of a carbon rod inside the dry cell. The other terminal connects to a zinc can enclosing the dry cell.

A dry cell contains a mixture of chemicals. When a wire, which is a conductor and has free electrons, connects the terminals, a chemical reaction occurs. The

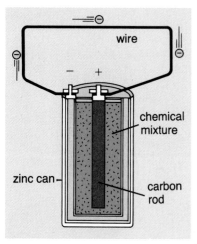

*Figure 14-7. Electrons in a dry cell move from the negative terminal to the positive terminal.*

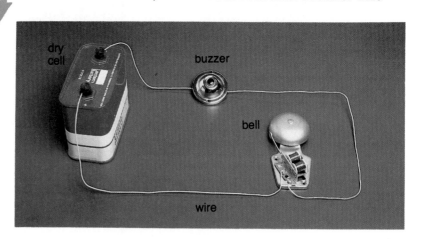

*Figure 14-8. A simple circuit.*

reaction removes electrons from the carbon rod. As a result, the carbon rod becomes positive. At the same time, extra electrons build up in the zinc.

The electrons in the zinc repel each other and repel the free electrons in the wire. Thus, a flow of electrons is started along the wire. They flow from the negative zinc terminal to the positive carbon terminal. There they move onto the carbon rod. Then the electrons are removed by the mixture of chemicals and the flow starts all over again.

## Parts of a Circuit

In Figure 14-7, the electrons flow from the source, through the wire, and back to the source. The setup you see in this figure is an *electric circuit. An **electric circuit** is a path along which electrons can flow.* Electrons flow only when the circuit is complete, or closed. Any break in the circuit will cause electrons to stop flowing. In such a case the circuit is said to be open.

Figure 14-8 shows a circuit consisting of a dry cell, a bell, and a button. This figure illustrates the parts of a simple circuit. The dry cell is the source that supplies energy to the flowing electrons. Electrons transfer this energy to the bell. The bell is an example of a *load. A **load** is a device that uses energy.*

The circuit in Figure 14-8 is open. You know this because the bell does not ring. However, if you press the button, the bell rings. The buzzer is a kind of *switch. A **switch** is a device that opens or closes a circuit.* When you press the button, you close the circuit. Electrons flow through the circuit and the bell rings.

Circuits usually have at least these three parts. However, most circuits are much more complicated.

## Kinds of Circuits

How many ways can you connect two light bulbs to a dry cell? Figure 14-9 on page 314 shows two ways. Now suppose you remove one light bulb from each circuit. Removing a bulb is like opening a switch. What

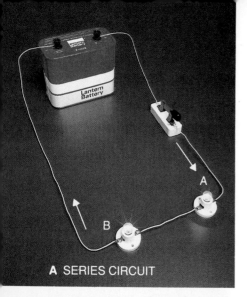

**A** SERIES CIRCUIT

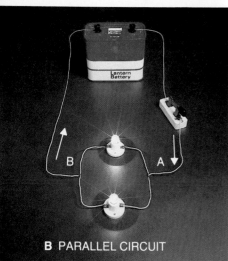

**B** PARALLEL CIRCUIT

*Figure 14-9. In what kind of circuit must an electron flow through both lamps?*

happens to the other light bulb? Follow the path that electrons must take to get from point *A* to point *B*.

**Series Circuits**   In Figure 14-9**A**, an electron has only one way to get from point *A* to point *B*. It must travel through both light bulbs. Since electrons cannot reach point *B*, the circuit is open. The other bulb will not light.

This circuit is an example of a *series circuit*. A **series circuit** *is one in which electrons have only one path along which they can move.* When one load in a series circuit goes out, the circuit is opened. That is why many holiday lights go out if even one bulb breaks.

**Parallel Circuits**   In Figure 14-9**B**, an electron has two ways to get from point *A* to point *B*. It need not travel through both light bulbs. If you remove one bulb, the electrons can still reach point *B*. The circuit is closed. The other bulb stays lit.

This circuit is a *parallel circuit*. A **parallel circuit** *is one in which electrons have more than one path along which they can move.* Each path is known as a branch. If a load in a parallel branch goes out, there is still a path electrons can follow to get to point *B*.

● When you turn off an appliance, you are opening a circuit. Most circuits in your home are parallel circuits. Each wall outlet plugs into a separate branch of a main circuit. When you turn off an appliance in one branch, electrons can still flow through the other branches. So appliances plugged into those other branches will still work. If your home were wired only in series, every appliance would go out as soon as you turned off one.

## OBJECTIVES AND WORDS TO REVIEW

**1.** How does a dry cell keep electrons flowing in a wire?
**2.** What are three basic parts of an electric circuit?
**3.** Distinguish between series and parallel circuits.
**4.** Write one complete sentence for each term listed below.
   electric circuit      switch            parallel circuit
   load                  series circuit

# MEASUREMENTS IN A CIRCUIT

Figure 14-10 can help explain what happens to an electron as it moves through a circuit. Suppose you place a penny on the raised cover of a book. Gravity exerts a force on the penny. The penny slides from point *B* down to point *A*. As the penny slides down, it loses potential energy.

When you lift the penny back to the top of the book, you do work against the force of gravity. The penny gains potential energy equal to the amount of work you do in lifting it. So the penny once again slides down the cover. As long as you lift the penny, the cycle continues.

The penny circuit is much like an electric circuit. In this model, the penny represents an electron. The book cover represents a wire. In the model, you provide energy to the penny. In a similar way, a source provides energy to an electron. The penny circuit can help you understand some of the measurements you can make on an actual electric circuit. Look now at three of the most important measurements.

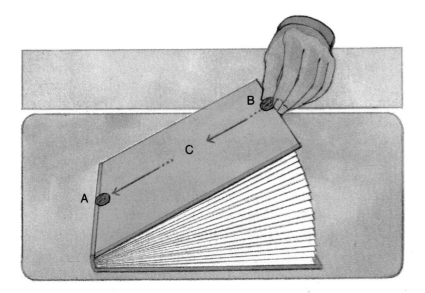

*Figure 14-10. Potential energy lost during the trip from B to A is regained during the trip from A to B.*

## Potential Difference

A penny has more potential energy at the top of the book than at the bottom. So, too, an electron has more electric potential energy before it goes through a load than after. In going through a load, an electron does work. As a result, it loses some of its energy. You can measure the amount of energy lost by finding the *potential difference*. The **potential difference** between *two points is the work needed to move a charge from one point to another.*

**Volts** *are the units used to measure potential difference.* For this reason, potential difference is sometimes called voltage (VOHL•tij). The higher the voltage, the more energy electrons have. A nine-volt source will give an electron nine times as much energy as a one-volt source.

Figure 14-11**A** shows an instrument that measures potential difference. It is called a *voltmeter* (VOHLT•mee•tur). *A* **voltmeter** *measures the amount of work done as electrons move between two points.* To use a voltmeter, place it in parallel with the load whose potential difference you are measuring.

## Current

In a penny circuit you could count the number of pennies that slide past a point each minute. For example, you might find that 30 pennies slid past point *C* in one minute. You have found the *current* in the penny circuit.

You can also find the current in an electric circuit. **Current** *is the number of electrons that flow past a point in a circuit each second.* Current is a flow of electrons. The greater the current is, the greater the number of electrons flowing.

Figure 14-11**B** shows an *ammeter* (AM•mee•tur). *An* **ammeter** *is an instrument that measures current.* An ammeter measures the number of electrons that go through it each second. *Current is measured in units called* **amperes** (AM•payrz). To use an ammeter, put it in series with the load you are measuring.

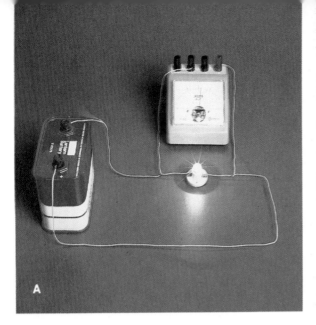
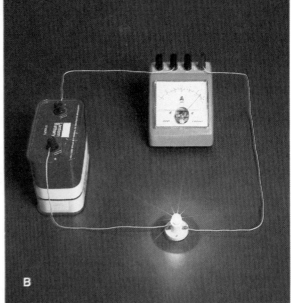

Figure 14-11. Voltmeters (A) and ammeters (B) are used to make measurements in a circuit. What does each measure?

## Resistance

Electric energy flows in a closed circuit. As electrons flow through a wire in a circuit, they lose potential energy. Some of this energy is changed into heat energy. Electric energy changes to heat because of the *resistance* of the material in the circuit. **Resistance is the ability of a material to resist, or oppose, the flow of electrons through it. Resistance is measured in units called ohms.** All substances have resistance. Even copper, a good conductor, resists the flow of electrons slightly. We say it has a low resistance. The resistance of a wire depends on certain conditions.

**Kinds of Atoms**   In the penny circuit, what would happen if you changed the sliding surface? If you used wax paper instead of the book cover, more pennies would slide down each minute. If you used sandpaper, fewer pennies would slide down each minute. The sliding surface provides the resistance in the penny circuit. A sandpaper surface has more resistance than a wax-paper surface. Likewise, the resistance in a wire depends on the kind of atoms that make it up. The atoms of some substances have tightly bound electrons. Such substances do not allow electrons to flow through them easily. Their resistance is very high. Silicon atoms in glass behave this way. That is why glass is a good insulator.

What units are used to measure resistance?

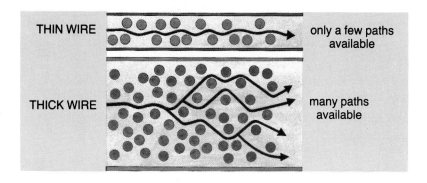

THIN WIRE — only a few paths available

THICK WIRE — many paths available

**Thickness of a Wire**   Look at Figure 14-12. Think of a wire as if it were a tube. If a wire is thick, electrons have more room to travel through the wire. The thinner the wire, the less room there is for electrons to travel. So the thinner a wire, the greater its resistance.

*Figure 14-12. Which wire has the higher resistance?*

**Length of a Wire**   Electric resistance also depends on the length of a wire. As the length of a wire increases, its resistance increases.

## Ohm's Law

Potential difference, current, and resistance in a circuit are related to each other. This relationship is known as Ohm's Law. **Ohm's Law** states that the current is equal to the potential difference divided by the resistance. If potential difference is represented by the letter V, current by I, and resistance by R, you can write:

What is Ohm's Law?

$$I = \frac{V}{R}$$

Suppose a wire has a resistance of 10 ohms. What is the current in the wire when the potential difference is 100 volts? Using Ohm's Law, you obtain:

$$I = \frac{V}{R}$$
$$I = \frac{100 \text{ volts}}{10 \text{ ohms}}$$
$$I = 10 \text{ amperes}$$

A current of ten amperes or more can cause the wire to get hot. The electric energy changes into heat energy.

● In some homes, portable electric heaters are used to help warm a room. A heater changes electric potential energy into heat energy. Suppose an electric heater has a resistance of 5 ohms. What is the current in the heater if you plug it into a 110-volt wall outlet? To find the current, use Ohm's Law:

$$I \text{ (amperes)} = \frac{V \text{ (volts)}}{R \text{ (ohms)}}$$

$$I = \frac{110 \text{ volts}}{5 \text{ ohms}}$$

$$I = 22 \text{ amperes}$$

In most homes, 22 amperes is about the maximum current any room circuit can handle. The circuit wires in the walls become hot when they carry a high current. Currents greater than 25 amperes could start a fire inside the wall. So when an electric heater is used in a room, nothing else should be plugged into the room circuit. For a look at how electricians work with electric circuits, see page 558.

## OBJECTIVES AND WORDS TO REVIEW

1. What happens to the potential energy of an electron as it goes through a wire?
2. Give three conditions that control the resistance of a wire.
3. In your own words, state Ohm's Law.
4. The current through a lamp is 2 amperes when the potential difference is 120 volts. What is the resistance of the lamp?
5. Write one complete sentence for each term listed below.

| potential difference | ammeter |
| volt | ampere |
| voltmeter | resistance |
| current | ohm |

## EXPLORE BY READING

### IMPORTANT NAMES IN ELECTRICITY

**OBJECTIVE**
Learn about three scientists connected with electricity.

**PROCEDURE**
1. Go to your library and read about the work of the following scientists: Georg S. Ohm, André Marie Ampère, and Alessandro Volta. On a separate piece of paper, answer the following questions.

**QUESTIONS**
1. What unit of electricity is named after each of these scientists?
2. Which scientist's work was ignored for a long time?
3. Who invented the electric battery?
4. Who discovered that an electric current could decompose water?
5. Which scientist found out that an electric current flowing through a coiled wire acts like a magnet?

# SEQUENCING BY USING FLOW CHARTS

## Preparation
Every day you do things in a certain order. For example, you may have a schedule that tells the order of your classes. English may be first, followed by science, math, and so on. When you go to your classes in a certain order, you follow a sequence. A sequence is a series of things or events arranged in a specific order.

For scientists knowing the sequence of a set of events can be very important. Sequencing helps scientists better understand a process under study or predict what may happen next.

To help them outline a particular sequence, many scientists make a *flow chart,* a detailed description of the operations and decisions needed to solve a problem. A flow chart breaks a process down into its most basic steps.

## Directions
To understand flow charts, think about when you make a telephone call. What steps do you take?

Figure 1 shows the sequence of steps taken for the above activity in the form of a flow chart. Each step is written in a special kind of box. A ○ begins and ends a chart. A ◇ shows that a question is being asked. A □ indicates something you do. A ▱ represents a result. Whenever you ask a question, you must provide two paths. One path shows what to do if the answer is yes. The other path is for a "no."

## Practice
Use flow charts to describe how to find the mass of an object, using a dual-beam balance. You have standard masses of 1, 5, 10, and 25 g. Write your chart on a separate piece of paper.

## Application
Look at Figure 14-L of the laboratory activity. Use a flow chart to show the path an electron might take in going through the circuit.

*Figure 1*

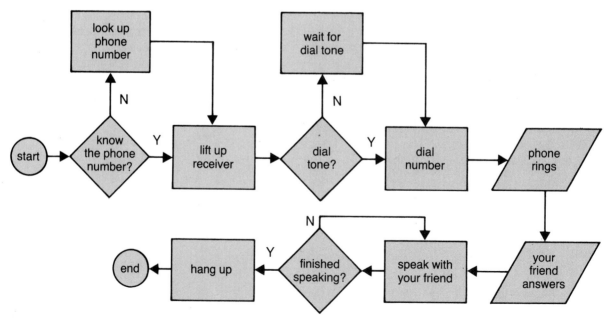

# A COMPLEX CIRCUIT

## Objective
Make measurements on a complex circuit.

## Background
Complex circuits are a combination of series and parallel circuits. Different amounts of current travel throught the parts of a complex circuit. You will use miniature lamps to investigate current in a complex circuit. The brighter a light bulb glows, the more current going through the bulb.

## Materials
four miniature lamps, wire 1.5-volt dry cell, four lamp sockets, switch

## Procedure
1. Set up your electric circuit as shown in Figure 14-L. **CAUTION:** Let your teacher look at your circuit before you close the switch and do the investigation.
2. Close the switch. Leave it closed for the rest of the investigation. Compare the relative brightness of each lamp.

3. Unscrew each lamp one at a time, beginning with lamp A. In each case, record what happens to the other lamps. Note any changes in brightness. Then tighten the lamp until it glows again and unscrew the next lamp.

## Questions
1. Compare the brightness of each lamp before you loosened lamp A.
2. Use your sequencing skills to describe the path and amount of current going through the other lamps when A is unscrewed.
3. Compare what happened when lamp B was unscrewed with your answer to question 2.
4. What happened to the other lamps when you unscrewed lamp C.?
5. Compare what happens when lamp D was unscrewed with your answer to question 4.
6. Are lamps A and B connected in series or parallel? Why?
7. Are lamps C and D connected in series or parallel? Why?
8. **PROBLEM SOLVING** Describe how the circuit might be rearranged so that if any lamp is unscrewed the other three remain lighted. (**CAUTION:** Do not actually try this.)

*Figure 14-L. Laboratory setup.*

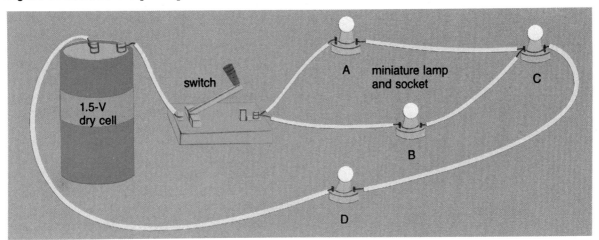

# SUMMARY

1. Charge is a property that causes some particles to attract each other and others to repel each other. Opposite charges attract. Like charges repel. (14-1)

2. Static electricity is electricity that is not moving. Rubbing can build up static electricity. (14-1)

3. An electric circuit is a path along which electrons flow. (14-2)

4. Circuits can be series, parallel, or a combination of both. (14-2)

5. In going through a circuit, electrons must work against the resistance of conductors. The potential difference is the work needed to move an electron from one point in an electric circuit to another point. (14-3)

6. Current is a flow of electrons. Ohm's Law states that the current is equal to the potential difference divided by the resistance. (14-3)

# REVIEW

Number a sheet of paper from 1 to 25 and answer these questions.

**Building Science Vocabulary**    Write the letter of the term that best matches each definition.

a. ammeter      e. electroscope    i. series circuit
b. charge        f. grounding       j. source
c. conductor    g. ohm             k. volt
d. current       h. parallel circuit  l. voltmeter

1. A property that causes some particles to attract each other and others to repel each other

2. A substance with many free electrons

3. A device that uses conducting foil to detect charge

4. The removal of static electricity by conduction to the earth

5. A device that gives energy to electrons

6. A circuit that gives electrons more than one path along which to move

7. A unit used to measure potential difference

8. An instrument used to measure current

9. A flow of electrons

10. A unit used to measure resistance

**Finding the Facts**    Select the letter of the answer that best completes each of the following.

11. What kind of charge do electrons have?
(**a**) positive     (**b**) negative     (**c**) no charge
(**d**) sometimes positive, sometimes negative.

12. Electrons may be moved from one substance to another by     (**a**) using an insulator
(**b**) heating     (**c**) rubbing     (**d**) all of the above.

13. An electroscope has been given a negative charge. If you ground it by touching its top, the leaves will     (**a**) spread farther apart
(**b**) fall back together     (**c**) show no change
(**d**) shoot out sparks.

14. Charges that can move between atoms are
(**a**) free electrons     (**b**) free protons
(**c**) free neutrons     (**d**) all of the above.

15. Copper is a better conductor than glass. This is because     (**a**) copper has more atoms
(**b**) glass has more free electrons
(**c**) copper has more free electrons
(**d**) the electrons in copper are bound tightly to their atoms.

16. As two charges move closer to each other, the electric force between them
(**a**) increases     (**b**) decreases     (**c**) stays the same     (**d**) increases, then decreases.

17. Current is measured in     (**a**) volts
(**b**) ohms     (**c**) voltage     (**d**) amperes.

18. A device that opens or closes a circuit is a
(**a**) load     (**b**) source     (**c**) switch
(**d**) battery.

**19.** If you connected two equal lengths of the same wire together, the **(a)** current would increase **(b)** potential difference would increase **(c)** resistance would decrease **(d)** resistance would increase.

**20.** A 9-volt battery is connected to a piece of wire that has a resistance of 36 ohms. The current in the wire in amperes is **(a)** ⅑ **(b)** ¼ **(c)** 4 **(d)** 27.

### Understanding Main Ideas    Complete the following.

**21.** Opposite charges __?__.

**22.** As an electron moves through a wire, its potential energy __?__.

**23.** Electricity that is not moving is __?__.

**24.** A path along which electrons flow is a __?__.

**25.** The work needed to move a charge from one point to another is the __?__.

### Writing About Science    On a separate sheet of paper, answer the following as completely as possible.

**1.** Why do clothes dried in a dryer often have "static cling"? Why does fabric softener prevent this from happening?

**2.** A person working near a car battery must be careful not to touch both terminals at the same time. Why is it dangerous to ignore this warning?

**3.** Describe a way of using light bulbs and switches to show the pattern "ON-OFF-ON-OFF". You may use a circuit diagram in your answer if you wish.

**4.** Why are people in a modern steel-frame building not hurt when it is hit by lightning?

**5.** (laboratory question) Draw a circuit showing a dry cell and three lamps. Arrange the circuit so that if one lamp is unscrewed the other two lamps will still light up. Indicate which lamp is to be unscrewed.

### Investigating Chapter Ideas    Try one of the following projects to further your study.

**1. Light bulbs**    Obtain a fairly large glass jar. Cut out a cardboard circle slightly larger than the mouth of the jar. Punch two No. 16 nails about 5 cm apart into the cardboard circle. Connect a short piece of thin picture wire between the nails. Place the cardboard circle on the mouth of the jar so the nails and wire filament are suspended inside the jar. Next, use insulated wire to connect the positive terminal of one 1.5-V dry cell to the negative terminal of another. Then hook one of the nails to one of the remaining terminals of the batteries. Finally, attach an insulated wire to the last battery terminal and cautiously touch it to the other nail. **CAUTION:** Hold the wire with a towel to make sure you do not get burned. What happens to the thin wire filament between the nails? Explain why.

**2. Electroplating**    The shiny chrome you see on cars is a coating deposited by a technique called electroplating. Report on how electroplating works. Explain some of its uses.

### Reading About Science    Read some of the following books to explore topics that interest you.

Bender, Alfred. 1977. **Science Projects with Electrons and Computers.** New York: Arco.

Irwin, Keith G. 1966. **The Romance of Physics.** New York: Scribner's.

Leon, George de Lucenay. 1983. **The Electricity Story: 2500 Years of Experiments and Discoveries.** New York: Arco.

Math, Irwin. 1981. **Wires and Watts: Understanding and Using Electricity.** New York: Scribner's.

What is a source of electricity in a simple circuit? You know that a battery is one such source. Your home, however, is a much more complex circuit. What is the source of electricity in your home circuit? Electric energy that powers your home comes from a generator, often located near a dam. Electricity produced by the generator may travel large distances before it reaches your town.

All the buildings in your town are part of an enormous circuit. What kind of circuit is it? When you turn off a light, do the lights in your neighbor's home also go off? Of course not! The buildings in your town are all wired in parallel.

You know how a battery provides electricity. This chapter will show you how a generator provides electricity.

Read and Find Out:
● how scientists "see" magnetic fields.
● how an electromagnet can make sounds.
● why you should not use a penny to fix a broken fuse.
● how computers operate with numbers.

# MAGNETISM AND ELECTRICITY

# MAGNETIC FIELDS

## OBJECTIVES

**1.** State two rules of magnets.
**2.** Show that there is a region of force around a magnet.
**3.** Describe a model showing why some materials are magnetic.

You live in a world of electric appliances. Would you believe that the electricity for the appliances is produced by a magnet? You will see how magnets are used to produce electricity in the next section. But first find out more about magnets in this section.

## Rules of Magnets

Magnets attract paper clips, iron nails, and many other metal objects. But do magnets attract each other? Suppose you brought two iron magnets close to each other as you see in Figure 15-1**A**. What would you feel? You would feel the magnets repelling each other. If you then turned one magnet around, as in **B**, the magnets would attract.

All magnets have two ends, or poles. One pole is called north (N). The other pole is called south (S). Figure 15-1 illustrates two important rules of magnets. *Like poles repel. Opposite poles attract.* Where have you seen this kind of relationship before? A similar set of rules holds for charged objects. Like charges repel and opposite charges attract.

## Magnetic Fields

The closer you bring two magnets together, the stronger the force between them becomes. Move them apart and the force gets weaker. If you move them apart still farther, you will eventually feel no force. The force changes strength as you move within each magnet's *magnetic field. A **magnetic field** is the space around a magnet in which its force affects objects.* A good picture of a magnetic field can be made by sprinkling small iron filings around a magnet. See Figure 15-2.

Notice that near a magnet's poles iron filings are crowded close together. The magnetic field here is

*Figure 15-1. Interaction of magnetic forces. To which force is the magnetic force similar?*

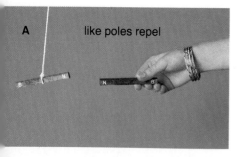

A  like poles repel

B  opposite poles attract

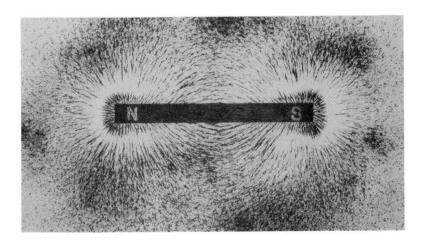

*Figure 15-2. Iron filings are attracted to both poles, depending on how far they are from the magnet.*

very strong. Farther away from the poles, the filings are more scattered. The force gets weaker farther from the magnet.

In Figure 15-2 the iron filings make a pattern of curved lines. These curved lines are called magnetic lines of force. Lines of force define the magnetic field of an object.

What defines an object's magnetic field?

## Earth's Magnetic Field

The earth exerts magnetic forces on magnets and compasses. Our planet acts as if it has a giant magnet buried deep within it. You cannot photograph the earth's magnetic field. However, a model of our planet's magnetic field can be drawn as in Figure 15-3.

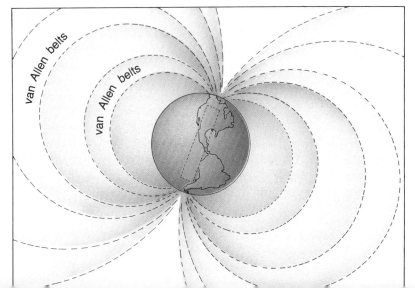

*Figure 15-3. A model of the earth's magnetic field.*

*Figure 15-4. Sometimes particles trapped by the earth's magnetic field penetrate the atmosphere near the poles. The particles collide with oxygen and nitrogen atoms. The atoms then emit light.*

**Give one explanation of the earth's magnetism.**

Many scientists have tried to explain the cause of the earth's magnetic field. One explanation suggests that moving particles in the planet's core cause the earth's magnetism.

The earth's magnetic field exerts forces on charged particles moving in space near the earth. These particles include particles from outer space called cosmic rays. They also include charged particles emitted by the sun at high speeds. When these particles reach the earth, they are trapped in zones called the van Allen belts. Refer to Figure 15-3 again.

Sometimes these trapped particles escape the van Allen belts. As a result, colored bands of light dance high in the atmosphere near the earth's north and south poles. See Figure 15-4.

## Magnetic Materials

You can make a magnet out of an iron nail. Simply stroke the nail with the magnet many times in the same direction. After a number of strokes, the nail acts like a magnet. The iron nail attracts metal paper clips.

Now try stroking an aluminum nail with a magnet. Then bring the nail near the paper clips. The nail does not attract the clips. You cannot make a magnet out of aluminum using this method. Actually, only a few materials can be made into magnets by stroking. Iron, cobalt, and nickel are among these materials. Such materials are said to be magnetic. Magnetic materials can be attracted to a magnet or made into one.

**What property identifies magnetic materials?**

## Magnetic Domains

Why are some materials magnetic and others not? Some scientists have proposed a model to explain these observations. Magnetism, they suggest, is a property of electrons in motion. The most important motion is the spinning of the electrons. The spinning of an electron can set up a magnetic field around the electron.

In most atoms, most electrons spin in pairs in opposite directions. See Figure 15-5**A**. Each spinning electron has its magnetic field canceled out by the field of its partner.

In an atom of iron, however, there are four unpaired electrons. See Figure 15-5**B**. The magnetic fields of these electrons are not canceled out. Their fields add up to make a tiny magnet.

Since iron atoms act like magnets, they exert forces on each other. These forces set up small regions in a piece of iron called *magnetic domains* (doh•MAYNZ). *A **magnetic domain** is a region where atomic magnetic*

**A** ELECTRONS SPINNING IN OPPOSITE DIRECTIONS

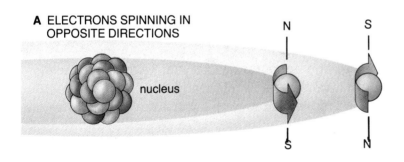

**B** ELECTRONS SPINNING IN SAME DIRECTION

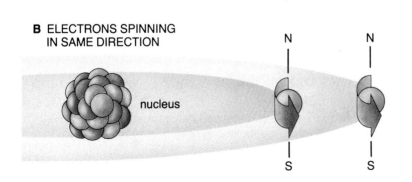

*Figure 15-5. Which picture is a model of a magnetic material?*

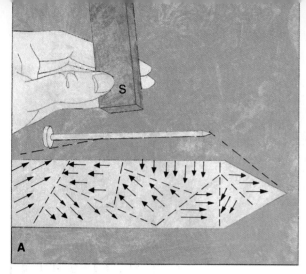
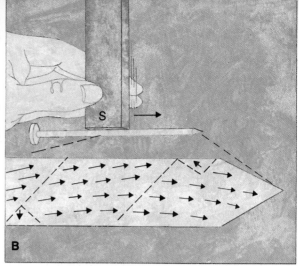

**Figure 15-6.** *Magnetizing a magnetic material.*

**Figure 15-7.** *When scientists sprinkle iron oxide particles onto a crystal of iron, the magnetic domains become visible.*

*fields line up in the same direction.* As Figure 15-6**A** shows, a piece of iron can have many domains.

The model of magnetic domains explains how a piece of iron becomes a magnet. If a strong magnet is near an iron nail, the magnet attracts the poles of the atomic magnets in the nail. The tiny magnetic fields line up in the direction of the magnet. The magnet causes the domains pointing in its direction to grow. See Figure 15-6**B**. The other domains become smaller. One large domain results. Most of the tiny magnetic fields in the nail now point in the same direction. The nail has become a magnet.

● Magnetic domains are normally invisible. However, scientists have developed a way of making these domains visible. See Figure 15-7. They sprinkle a single crystal of iron with particles of iron oxide. In this way, physicists can photograph magnetic domains. They can then study how external magnetic fields affect them.

**OBJECTIVES AND WORDS TO REVIEW**

1. State two rules of magnets.
2. How are the van Allen belts and the northern lights related?
3. How do domains explain how a piece of iron becomes a magnet?
4. Write one complete sentence for each term listed below.
   magnetic field      magnetic domain

# USING MAGNETISM AND ELECTRICITY

Would you believe that you can make a magnet out of a coil of wire? Just connect the ends to a battery. When current goes through a wire, the wire acts like a magnet. It attracts iron the same way a bar magnet does. See Figure 15-8. *A coil of wire that acts like a magnet when electric current goes through it is called an **electromagnet*** (i•lek•troh•MAG•nit).

In this section you will study how electricity and magnetism are related. You will also learn about devices that use both electricity and magnetism.

## Electromagnets

A current in a coil of wire creates a magnetic field just like that of a bar magnet. One end of the coil becomes a north pole. The other end becomes a south pole. The end that becomes the north pole depends on the direction of electron flow. If you change the direction of the current, you reverse the poles.

The electromagnet shown in Figure 15-8 can lift only a few paper clips. However, you can make it stronger. See Figure 15-9. You can put an iron core inside the coil of wire. With a core inserted, the coil can often pick up twice as many clips. Second, you can put more turns of wire in the coil. The greater the number of turns you make, the stronger the magnet

**OBJECTIVES**
**1.** Explain how a coil of wire and a bar magnet can produce motion.
**2.** Name two devices that use electromagnets.
**3.** Explain the difference between a motor and a generator.

*Figure 15-9. Compare this figure with Figure 15-8. Give three ways to make an electromagnet stronger.*

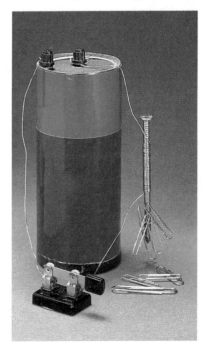

*Figure 15-8. What happens when you open the switch?*

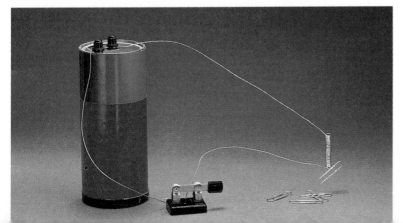

becomes. Third, you can increase the number of batteries you use. That is, you can use more current. You can also combine all these methods to produce a very strong magnet.

## Electromagnets at Work

Electromagnets have two "handy" properties. First, they can be turned on and off by flicking a switch in a circuit. Second, they can change electric energy into the mechanical energy of motion. These properties make electromagnets very useful in a number of devices.

*Figure 15-10. A telegraph key.*

For example, telegraphs use electromagnets. See Figure 15-10. When you press a telegraph key, current flows through the circuit. The electromagnet is turned on. It attracts an iron bar. The iron bar hits a sounder board and makes a click. Release the key and the current and the electromagnet go off. The bar springs back. A code has been developed based on varying the time between clicks. This code, Morse code, has made it possible to communicate as far around the world as electric wires can reach.

Electromagnets are used in many other devices as well. A doorbell uses an electromagnet to make a hammer clang the bell. Huge machines use electromagnets to lift up large pieces of scrap metal. See Figure 15-11.

*Figure 15-11. Electromagnets can be used to move scrap metal.*

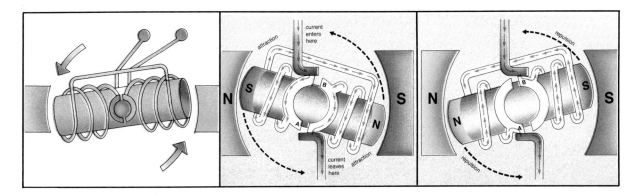

Figure 15-12. *A motor spins by the constant changing of the poles of the armature. What causes the change in the poles?*

## The Electric Motor

A very important device that uses an electromagnet is a motor. A motor has an electromagnet that is free to rotate. *The rotating electromagnet is called an* **armature** (AHR•muh•chur). The armature is allowed to rotate because it is placed in the field of a strong magnet.

Figure 15-12 shows a model of how a motor works. When current flows through the coil, the ends of the coil become magnetic poles. The poles of the armature are repelled by the poles of the large magnet. Then the armature begins to rotate. It spins quickly to the opposite poles of the magnet. Just before the armature reaches the opposite poles, the current changes direction, or reverses. When the current reverses direction, the poles of the armature switch. So, once again the poles of the armature and the large magnet repel each other. The armature continues to rotate. The poles of the armature reverse each time it spins halfway through the field of the large magnet. As long as the current keeps reversing, the armature keeps rotating.

Figure 15-12 shows how the current reverses just at the right time to keep the motor running. Current reverses because of a split-ring *commutator* (KOM•yew•tay•tur). *A* **commutator** *is a split ring where wires from the circuit touch the armature.* When the armature reaches the large magnet's poles,

What action makes the poles of an armature switch?

## MAKING AN ELECTROMAGNET

**OBJECTIVE**
Build a simple electromagnet.

**MATERIALS**
insulated wire, 4 nails, rubber band, 9-V battery, staples

**PROCEDURE**
**1.** Wrap the rubber band around the four nails to make a core.
**2.** Wrap 10 loops of wire around the core. Bring the core near some staples and connect the wire ends to the battery. Note the effect on the staples.
**3.** Carefully wrap 10 more loops of wire on top of the first loops. Connect the ends to the battery. Note what happens.
**4.** Repeat step 3 until you have 4 layers of wire.
**5.** Carefully pull the nails out of the wire. Bring each nail near the staples. Note what happens.

**QUESTIONS**
**1.** How does the strength of your electromagnet depend on the number of loops of wire?
**2.** If you increased the current in the wire, what would happen to the strength of the electromagnet?
**3.** What did you observe when you did step 5? Now bang the nails on a hard surface. Do they still attract the staples? Why or why not?

each wire slides onto a different part of the commutator. At this point the current through the armature reverses direction and the motion continues.

The spinning motion of the armature in a motor can be used to move things. A long rod or shaft attached to a motor can turn pulleys, fan blades, or wheels. Electric motors are used to run golf carts, elevators, record turntables, and many other useful machines.

## Electromagnetic Induction

Suppose you held a coil of wire next to a strong magnet. Now suppose you move the coil back and forth across the magnetic field. If you connect the ends of the coil to a meter, the meter needle moves when the coil moves.

The coil connected to the meter makes a complete circuit. When you move the coil across the magnetic field, electrons flow through the circuit. That is, a current is produced. When you reverse the direction of the moving coil, the current reverses direction. See Figure 15-13.

*Producing a current by moving a coil of wire across a magnetic field is called* **electromagnetic induction.** (in•DUHK•shuhn). *The current that is produced is called an* **induced current.** Electromagnetic induction is the key to another important device, the generator.

## The Generator

A motor changes electric energy into mechanical energy of motion. It uses an electric current to magnetize an armature, causing it to spin. In these respects, a motor is the opposite of a *generator. A* **generator** *is a device that uses the energy of motion to produce electricity.* See Figure 15-14.

Basically, a generator is a coil of wire moving within a very strong magnetic field. A large generator has a coil with thousands of loops of wire mounted on a shaft. The shaft is placed within a strong magnetic field. Falling water, steam, or wind sets the shaft in spinning motion within the field. As

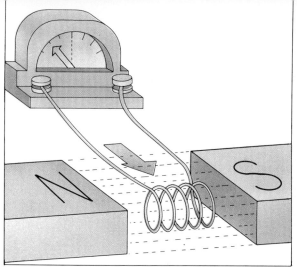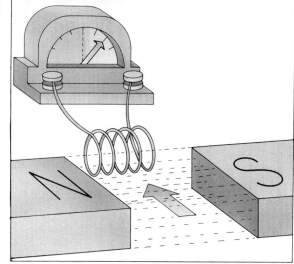

it spins, an electric current flows through the coil and lead wires.

The current here keeps changing direction. You have seen that a current reverses when you move a coil back and forth across a magnetic field. Instead of moving back and forth, the coil in a generator spins around within a magnetic field. With each half-spin of the coil, the current reverses once. With each complete spin, the current reverses twice. In most generators the coils spin thousands of times each second. So current reverses twice as many times each second.

*Figure 15-13. Moving a coil of wire through a magnetic field produces a current in it.*

*Figure 15-14. Most of the electricity you use is produced by large generators like this one.*

## Two Kinds of Current

A dry cell and a generator are both sources of electric current. Each source, however, produces a different kind of current. A dry cell supplies *direct current*. **Direct current** *is current that flows in one direction only.* Electrons flow from the negative terminal to the positive terminal of the dry cell.

A generator, on the other hand, produces current that reverses its direction after each half-turn of the shaft. This kind of current is *alternating current*. **Alternating current** *is current that reverses its direction of flow.* Most generators supply alternating current to cities and factories. In the United States, these generators usually provide current that changes direction 60 times a second.

● The speaker in a radio, television, or stereo uses an electromagnet. So does the speaker in the earpiece of a telephone receiver. See the telephone speaker in Figure 15-15. In these devices, the current flowing through the electromagnet gets alternately stronger and weaker. A strong current makes the electromagnet attract a thin metal disk. A weak current causes the electromagnet to release the disk. The current changes strength many times per second. So the disk is attracted and released many times per second. The back and forth motion of the disk produces the sounds that you hear from the speaker.

List two kinds of current.

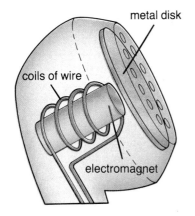

*Figure 15-15. In a telephone speaker, a metal disk vibrates many times a second. What makes the metal disk vibrate?*

labels: metal disk, coils of wire, electromagnet

### OBJECTIVES AND WORDS TO REVIEW

1. How does an electromagnet produce motion?
2. Name two electric devices that use electromagnets.
3. What is the difference between how a motor works and how a generator works?
4. Write one complete sentence for each term listed below.

| | |
|---|---|
| electromagnet | induced current |
| armature | generator |
| commutator | direct current |
| electromagnetic induction | alternating current |

# ELECTRICITY AT HOME

Power lines carry electric energy from a generator to your home. This energy then runs the appliances you use. How does electric energy get from the power plant to your home? And what measures can you take to make sure this energy is used safely? This section will answer these questions.

## Electric Power

Power is the rate at which work is done. But you can also think of power in another way. Doing work requires energy. So, you can think of power as the amount of energy used each second as work is done.

The new "definition" of power is very useful in your understanding of electric energy. You know that when current goes through a load, electric energy is used. This energy may be used to light a lamp or toast bread. Or it may be used to run a hair dryer. The amount of energy that a load uses each second is electric power. Figure 15-16 shows the power rating of an electric appliance.

How much power does a light bulb use in an hour? Suppose a light bulb has a rating of 100 watts. Recall that a watt is a unit of power. A 100-watt bulb uses 100 joules of electric energy each second. In one minute (60 seconds) the bulb uses 6,000 joules of energy. So, in one hour a 100-watt light bulb uses 6,000 joules/min × 60 min or 360,000 joules of energy.

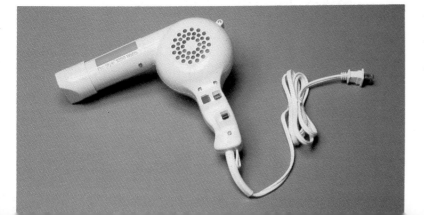

*Figure 15-16. A 200-W appliance uses 200 J of energy each second. How much energy does a hair dryer use in 5 minutes?*

What does electricity cost? Suppose for every kilowatt (1000 watts) used for 1 hour, the electric company charges 11 cents. A kilowatt-hour is the unit of electric energy that electric companies use. At 11 cents per kilowatt-hour, how much does it cost to run a 500-watt refrigerator for a day? Five hundred watts is 0.5 kilowatt. The total energy used is:

$$\text{total energy used} = 0.5 \text{ kilowatts} \times 24 \text{ hours}$$
$$= 12 \text{ kilowatt-hours}$$

The cost of the electric energy used is 11 cents per kilowatt-hour. So, the total cost per day is

$$\text{total cost} = 11 \text{ cents per kilowatt-hour}$$
$$\times 12 \text{ kilowatt-hours}$$
$$= \$1.32$$

## Transmitting Electric Power

Power lines span thousands of kilometers, carrying electric energy from generators to cities. Some of the electric energy traveling in the lines is changed into heat due to the wire's resistance. This heat is wasted.

*Figure 15-17. Transformers help bring electric energy from a generator to your home. What do transformers do?*

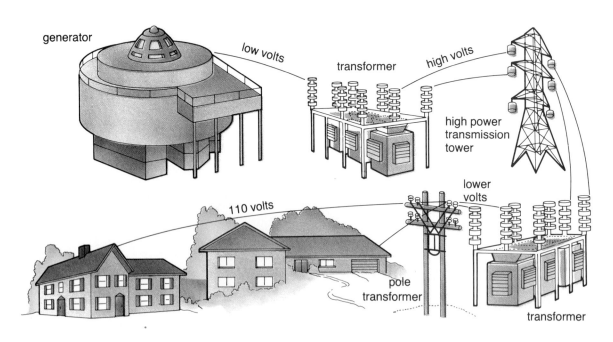

One way to prevent such waste is to send low currents through power lines. In order to transmit useful amounts of electric power using low currents, thousands of volts are required. However, most generators produce electricity at a low voltage. How can the voltage be increased?

Electric energy coming from a generator is usually conducted to a *transformer*. *A **transformer** is a device that changes voltage.* A transformer near a generating station increases voltage. At the same time, the current is lowered. The high-voltage electricity is then sent through power lines to your community. See Figure 15-17.

High voltages, however, are dangerous. As a safety precaution, high-voltage power lines are held high above the ground on steel wires. Before the electricity reaches your home, it first reaches a power distribution station. Here the electricity flows through another kind of transformer. This transformer lowers the voltage to safer levels.

From the power station the electricity is sent to your home. Before entering your home, the electricity passes through one more transformer. This transformer lowers the voltage to 110 volts. This level is safe for household circuits.

## Safety at Home

The electricity that enters your home is safe, but you must know how to use it safely. Electric outlets are branches of a main parallel circuit in your home. And each time you turn on an appliance, current flows through a branch. The more appliances you plug into a branch, the more current that goes through that branch. Greater currents result in more heat produced in the wires.

Household wires are covered with insulation. The insulation protects wall materials from heat in the wires. If you put too many appliances into the same branch, too much current will go through the wire. The excess current in the wire can cause the wire to

## EXPLORE BY TRYING

### CIRCUITS IN YOUR HOME

**OBJECTIVE**
Determine which fuse or circuit breaker controls each outlet in your home.

**PROCEDURE**
1. Draw a floor plan of your home. Indicate the location of each outlet.
2. Find your fuse box or circuit breaker panel. Number each fuse or circuit breaker if it is not already numbered.
3. Leaving all the other fuses or circuit breakers on, have your parent or other adult turn one off.
4. Go through each room to find those outlets or devices that no longer work. Do this by plugging a small lamp into an unused outlet or turning on an appliance already plugged into an outlet.
5. On your floor plan, write the number of the fuse or circuit breaker next to each outlet protected by it.
6. Repeat steps 3 through 5 until all the fuses or circuit breakers have been checked.

**QUESTIONS**
1. Which fuse or circuit breaker protects an entire room?

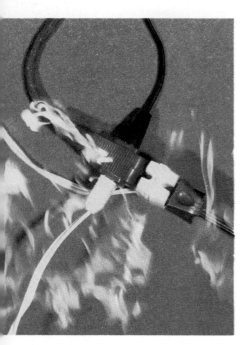

**Figure 15-18.** *Too many appliances plugged into a wall outlet caused this fire. How can you reduce the risk of fire?*

melt. As a result, the insulating material can catch on fire. See Figure 15-18.

To protect against fire, household circuits have safety devices. One such device is a *fuse*. A **fuse** *is a safety device in a circuit that melts before the wires in the circuit become too hot.* When a fuse melts, the circuit is opened. The current stops flowing in time to prevent a fire from breaking out.

In many homes, wires can carry 20 amperes of current without melting. If your household wires can carry 20 amperes, be sure never to use a fuse that is marked greater than 20 amps. Such a fuse conducts more than 20 amperes without melting. Then the fuse would not melt in time to prevent the wires in the wall from overheating and starting a fire.

Another safety device found in many homes is a *circuit breaker*. A **circuit breaker** *is a safety device that switches off when too much current goes through it.* When too much current flows, a breaker switch jumps up. As a result, current stops flowing. Once the cause of the high current is corrected, the breaker switch can be reset.

● People sometimes use a metal coin to fix a burned-out fuse. While this action may close the circuit and allow current to flow again, it is very dangerous. Most coins conduct more current than household wires can. So if a coin is placed into a fuse box, large currents may flow through the coin without causing it to melt. These large currents can cause the wires in the wall to overheat and start a fire.

**OBJECTIVES AND WORDS TO REVIEW**

1. A microwave oven uses 0.72 kilowatt-hour of energy when it is used for half an hour. How much power in watts is this?
2. How does a power substation reduce voltage so that it can be used safely in your home?
3. Name two electric devices that help protect the circuits in your house.
4. Write one complete sentence for each term listed below.
   transformer     fuse     circuit breaker

# THE WORLD OF ELECTRONICS

Almost every month new and exciting electric devices are invented. These devices are just a part of the expanding field of *electronics* (i•lek•TRON•iks). *Electronics is the study of the motion of electrons for use in devices in home and industry.* In this section you will study some of these devices that have had such an impact on your life.

## Electronic Devices

Engineers use basic laws of electricity to design and build electronic devices. These devices are built of electronic parts, or components.

**Cathode Ray Tubes** An important part of a television set is a *cathode ray tube (CRT). A **CRT** is an electronic component that produces a stream of electrons.* In a TV set, a CRT is used to make an image. See Figure 15-19. Electrons pass through a small slit in a positively charged plate. They form an electron beam. Electrons in the beam travel to a screen. The screen is coated with a substance that glows when it is hit by an electron. By changing the number of electrons hitting the screen each second, you vary the brightness of the light.

**Rectifiers** Most electronic components need direct current to work. The current in your home is alternating current. A *rectifier* allows electronic parts to use alternating current. *A **rectifier** changes alternating current into direct current.* You use a rectifier to charge a calculator.

**Amplifiers** The small current that flows through a phonograph cartridge cannot operate a speaker. The speaker needs an *amplifier. An **amplifier** converts a small input current into a large output current.* An amplifier increases current, making the speaker work.

What produces the image on a television?

*Figure 15-19. If the top charging plate of a CRT is positive, the electron beam moves up. How could you make the beam move down?*

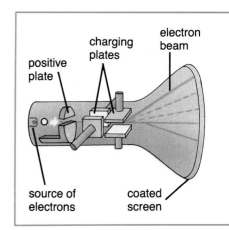

# EXPLORE
## BY VISITING

### COMPARING COMPUTERS

**OBJECTIVE**
Discover the advantages of different types of computers.

**PROCEDURE**
Visit the computer division of your local department store and speak with a salesperson.

**QUESTIONS**
**1.** What advantage does each type of computer have?

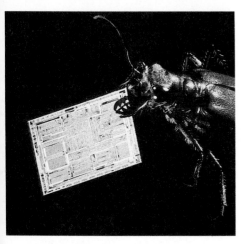

*Figure 15-20. Integrated circuits have hundreds of electronic parts on a small chip.*

**Semiconductors**  *Semiconductors are materials that have a resistance between that of an insulator and a conductor.* Many semiconductors are crystals. Some crystals, like silicon, are good insulators in pure form. However, adding another kind of atom to the crystal can add or remove electrons from the crystal. The crystal becomes a better conductor.

There are two types of semiconductors: n-type and p-type. The n-type (negative type) semiconductor has many free electrons in the crystal. The p-type (positive type) semiconductor has empty spaces, holes, in the crystal. Because holes can be filled by free electrons, p-type crystals act like positive charges.

**Transistors**  You can use n- and p-type semiconductors to make *transistors* (tran•ZIS•turz). *A **transistor** is a small device that controls current flow.* Because transistors control current flow, they are sometimes used in building amplifiers.

## Integrated Circuits and Computers

Figure 15-20 shows one of the great breakthroughs in electronics. Advances in technology have made it possible to fit electronic parts in small spaces. These electronic parts can be made directly on a small slice of silicon crystal, called a "chip." Many of these chips are small enough to be carried away by a large ant.

Silicon chips are the basis for *integrated* (IN•tuh•gray•tuhd) *circuits.* **Integrated circuits** *combine hundreds of electric components on a single chip.* Integrated circuits are used in televisions, radios, and computers. Today you can buy a small calculator to do what once needed a large computer. See the photo essay on computers on pages 344–345.

● Digital computers use thousands of electronic components to do simple arithmetic. The computer is useful because it can do a tremendous number of calculations in a very short time.

Computers operate with a special kind of number system called a binary number system. See Figure 15-21. The binary system has only two numbers: 0

and 1. You can express any number as a combination of 0's and 1's. For example, the number 4 is written as 100 in the binary system.

In a computer, transistor switches are used to represent binary numbers. A switch is "on" when there is a current flowing through it. If the switch is "on," the binary number is "1." If the switch is "off," the binary number is "0." Four transistor switches in the series "on, off, off, on" would represent the number "9." Computers use thousands of switches in integrated circuits to operate with numbers.

### OBJECTIVES AND WORDS TO REVIEW

1. How can you change alternating current into direct?
2. Name three devices in your home that use integrated circuits.
3. Give four uses of computers.
4. Write one complete sentence for each term listed below.

| | | | |
|---|---|---|---|
| electronics | rectifier | semiconductor | integrated circuit |
| CRT | amplifier | transistor | |

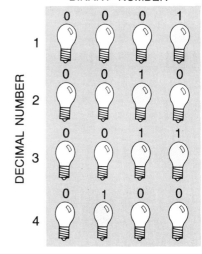

*Figure 15-21. A model of the binary system. How would the number "5" appear?*

## Universal Product Codes

Have you been to one of those supermarket checkout counters with electronic scanning devices? Do you know how they work? Scanning devices "see" the Universal Product Codes (UPC) that appear on every product in supermarkets. The Universal Product Codes are the series of coded black lines that appear on every package. Computers attached to the scanners use the codes to identify products, find prices, and add up bills. Computers then send all this information to the cash register, which prints out the names and prices of every item. Supermarket computers (and scanners) help clerks. The computer can do a clerk's work in a fraction of his or her time. However, some people feel that this technology costs jobs. Fewer clerks are needed. There are other problems as well.

### Using Critical Thinking

Besides costing jobs, will checkout counter devices make it more difficult for small businesses that cannot afford them to compete? What do you think?

# THE FAST-PACED WORLD OF COMPUTERS

Computers are devices that process data rapidly. The speed with which computers process data has made them important industrial tools. In fact, more than a million computers are in use in the United States and Canada today. A few of the many uses of computers are represented below.

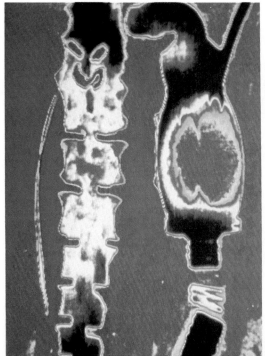

**Weather Forecasting** Weather satellites collect data on conditions such as pressure. This information is then run through computers. The computers produce images showing hour-by-hour changes in high and low pressure areas. Scientists then use this information to predict the weather.

**Medicine** (above) Computers help doctors see inside the body. Thus, they can diagnose disorders without surgery.
**Architecture** (right) Computers can be programmed to rotate images of objects. Thus, architects can study an object from many angles without having to draw them all.

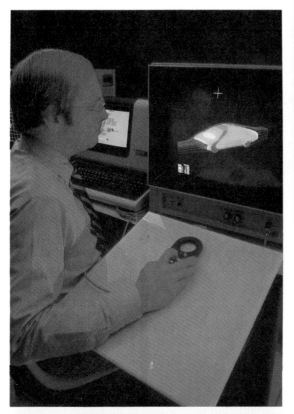

**Air Traffic Control** (above) Computers are being used to store and process data on arrivals and departures from airports. This helps air traffic controllers make sure that aircraft reach their destinations safely.

**Automobile Design** (left) Automobile makers use computers to test car designs. Engineers study how air flows around different computerized car models. These tests help them decide which designs are most fuel efficient.

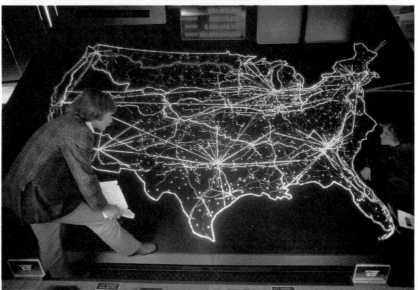

**Communication** The fast and dependable transfer of data is vital to business and industry. Computerized communication systems can relay information between cities on opposite coasts within seconds.

# STUDY SKILL

## USING SCIENTIFIC INSTRUMENTS

### Preparation
Can you read a fever thermometer? To use a thermometer properly, you must perform certain steps.

Scientists must also be careful when using scientific instruments. Many scientific instruments are very delicate. And some instruments can be hazardous if handled improperly.

### Directions
To use scientific instruments, follow these steps.

1. *Orienting*   Place the instrument in its proper position in the laboratory set up. If a diagram is provided, compare it with your set up. Look for any warnings or special instructions. Check all electric connections carefully. Some instruments will not work or can be damaged if they are incorrectly attached. Call your teacher if you are not sure.

2. *Zeroing*   Zeroing an instrument puts it in perfect balance. Thus, any readings are caused by the quantity itself, not the measuring instrument. Figure 1 shows how to zero a voltmeter. **CAUTION:** Be careful when you turn any knobs or tighten any strings on an instrument. A broken knob or a twanging string can harm you.

3. *Reading*   When you read an instrument, examine the scale carefully. What are the smallest divisions? Figure 2 shows how to read a voltmeter.

4. *Caring*   After you have finished using an instrument, you must clean it, set all dials back to zero, and store it.

**Figure 2.**

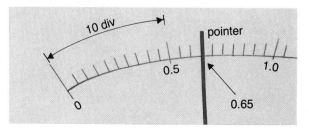

### Practice
A meter stick is a familiar scientific instrument. On a separate sheet of paper, answer the following.

1. What is the proper way of measuring length with a meter stick?

2. There is no zeroing knob on a meter stick. What might you do to make sure that the readings you take are accurate?

### Application
Refer to Figures 1 and 2. On a separate sheet of paper, answer the following.

1. What clues to the proper use of this instrument are given in the figure?

2. What are the smallest scale divisions?

3. How might you care for such an instrument?

**Figure 1.**

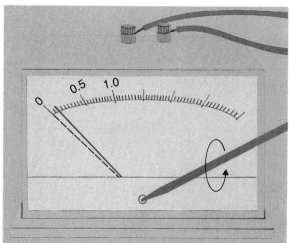

# ELECTROMAGNETIC INDUCTION

### Objective
Study the current made by a coil moving in a magnetic field.

### Background
A coil moving in a magnetic field creates a current. You will detect this current with a sensitive "current meter." Your current meter will be a compass with a coil of wire wrapped around it. When a current is in the coil, the compass needle moves.

### Materials
compass, 4 meters of insulated wire, bar magnet

### Procedure
1. Cut off 1 m of your wire. Wrap 20 loops of wire around your compass as shown in Figure 15-L. Turn the compass so that the needle lines up with the wire. Place it on the table so it cannot move.
2. Starting in the middle of the remaining wire, wind 10 loops of wire around your fingers. Make sure the hole in the coil is big enough for the magnet to go through.
3. Connect the coil to your current meter by twisting the bare wires together. The coil should be 1 m away from your current meter.

Slowly move the north pole of the magnet *into* the coil. Note how the current meter moves.
4. Add 10 more loops of wire to your coil in the same direction as before. Repeat step 3. Note the motion of your current meter.
5. Keep adding 10 loops of wire to your coil until you have a total of 50. Repeat step 3 each time.
6. Slowly move the south pole *into* the coil. Observe the current meter.
7. Repeat steps 3 and 4. This time begin with the bar magnet in the coil and slowly move it *out of* the coil. Look at the meter.
8. Move the bar magnet faster into the coil. Observe what happens to the meter.

### Questions
1. How do your results from step 4 compare with those from step 3?
2. How does the number of loops of wire affect the current produced?
3. How do your results from step 3 compare with those of step 6?
4. What does changing the pole of the magnet do to the direction of the current? Hint: Your current meter shows the direction of the current by which way the compass needle moves.
5. How does the current produced by the coil depend on the speed of the bar magnet?
6. **PROBLEM SOLVING** What would happen if you made a coil of wire with 10 loops in one direction and 10 more loops in the opposite direction? Try it.

**Figure 15-L.** *Laboratory setup.*

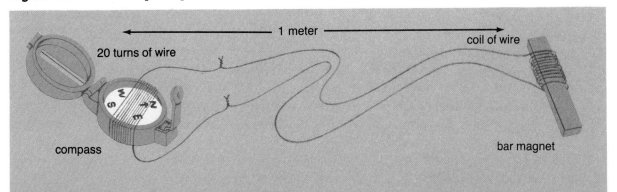

Have you ever written your own computer programs? Do you wish you could spend more time using a computer at school or at home? Do you like to work with electric equipment? If so, you might want to consider the careers below.

**Computer Programmer**   Without a computer programmer to tell it what to do, a computer would be nothing more than an idle pile of electronic parts. Computer programmers use symbols, codes, and languages to write sets of instructions—programs—that make computers carry out tasks.

Some programmers work for firms that specialize in developing and selling computer programs. Others work for large banks, corporations, or agencies that hire their own programmers. To train for a career in programming, you need four years of college. You are also likely to receive further training from the company that employs you.

You can find out more about a career as a computer programmer by writing:

*Institute for Certification of Computer
   Professionals
35 E. Wacker Drive, Suite 2828
Chicago, IL 60601*

**Electronics Technician**   The growing use of tape recorders, computers, and other electronic equipment has produced a need for people who can repair these machines when they break down. Repair is just one of the duties of an electronics technician. Electronics technicians install, care for, and repair electronic components and systems.

Many industries, from aviation to publishing, employ electronic technicians. Most train for about four years in a formal apprenticeship program. These programs combine on-the-job experience with specialized courses such as mathematics, blueprint reading, and electronics. Apprenticeship programs usually require that applicants be high school graduates. High school courses in physics and electronics are helpful.

To find out about this career, write:

*National Joint Apprenticeship and Training
   Committee for the Electrical Industry
1730 Rhode Island Avenue, NW
Washington, DC 20036*

# SUMMARY

1. Like poles of magnets repel. Opposite poles attract. Magnetism in some materials is caused by spinning electrons. (15-1)

2. Only iron and a few other materials can be made into magnets. They are magnetized by causing the domains that point in a certain direction to grow. (15-1)

3. A current through a coil of wire creates a magnetic field. The field of an electromagnet reverses when the current reverses direction. Alternating current and direct current are two types of current. (15-2)

4. A motor changes electric energy into mechanical energy. A generator changes mechanical energy into electric energy. (15-2)

5. A transformer can increase or decrease the voltage in a circuit. (15-3)

6. A fuse and a circuit breaker are two devices that protect household circuits. (15-3)

7. Most electronic devices run on direct current. Rectifiers change alternating current into direct current. (15-4)

8. Integrated circuits combine many electric components in a very small space. (15-4)

# REVIEW

Number a sheet of paper from 1 to 25 and answer these questions.

**Building Science Vocabulary**   Write the letter of the term that best matches each definition.

a. alternating current
b. armature
c. circuit breaker
d. commutator
e. direct current
f. electromagnetic induction
g. generator
h. magnetic domain
i. magnetic field
j. rectifier
k. transformer
l. transistor

1. A small region in a piece of iron where atomic magnetic fields line up in the same direction

2. A device used to change voltage

3. The rotating coil in an electric motor

4. A device that converts mechanical energy into electric energy

5. A device that changes alternating current into direct current

6. The production of current in a wire that is moving across a magnetic field

7. A device that reverses the direction of current in a motor

8. Current that reverses its direction of flow

9. A device that controls the flow of current

10. The space surrounding a magnet that can be affected by it.

**Finding the Facts**   Select the letter of the answer that best completes each of the following.

11. A magnet will attract a wire if     (**a**) the wire has a small mass     (**b**) the wire exerts an electric force     (**c**) the wire is long     (**d**) the wire has current flowing through it.

12. The iron atom acts as a magnet because (**a**) it has an equal number of protons and electrons     (**b**) the electrons have a spinning motion     (**c**) the electrons have negative charge     (**d**) the neutrons have no charge.

13. A steel sewing needle can be made into a magnet by     (**a**) stroking it with a magnet in one direction only     (**b**) soaking it in mercury     (**c**) banging it on a table (**d**) placing it near a compass.

14. A piece of copper cannot be made into a magnet because     (**a**) copper cannot be charged     (**b**) the copper atoms have no charge     (**c**) electrons spinning in opposite directions in copper cancel each other (**d**) the domains are already aligned.

**15.** To increase the strength of an electromagnet, (**a**) increase the current in the coil (**b**) add an iron center to the coil (**c**) increase the number of loops of wire in the coil (**d**) any of the above.

**16.** If a magnet is brought near a magnet suspended on a string, the (**a**) N poles attract each other (**b**) N poles attract the S poles (**c**) S poles attract each other (**d**) N poles repel the S poles.

**17.** In sending electric energy over long distances, the main cause of energy loss is (**a**) the use of transformers (**b**) the size of the wires (**c**) the high current (**d**) the use of direct current.

**18.** A material that has a resistance between that of an insulator and a conductor is (**a**) a commutator (**b**) an amplifier (**c**) a semiconductor (**d**) an armature.

**19.** A device that turns electric energy into sound energy is (**a**) a speaker (**b**) a transformer (**c**) a CRT (**d**) generator.

**20.** A hair dryer has a rating of 1000 watts. If it is used for ¼ hour, the total energy in kilowatt-hours used by this machine is (**a**) 250 (**b**) 500 (**c**) 1000 (**d**) 4000.

**Understanding Main Ideas** Complete the following.

**21.** Current flowing in only one direction is __?__.

**22.** A magnet whose magnetism is caused by a current in a wire is a(n) __?__.

**23.** A device that changes electric energy into mechanical energy is a __?__.

**24.** Charged particles trapped in the earth's magnetic field produce a glow in the sky called the __?__.

**25.** A safety device that switches off when too much current goes through it is a __?__.

**Writing About Science** On a separate sheet of paper, answer the following as completely as possible.

**1.** Describe two ways in which knowledge of electromagnets made it possible for people to communicate over long distances.

**2.** Permanent magnets can be "de-magnetized" by banging on them with a hammer or by heating them over a flame. Why?

**3.** Why is a compass not part of the equipment carried by astronauts on space voyages?

**4.** A television contains a CRT. If you bring a magnet near a color television, the image on the screen becomes distorted and the color may be destroyed. Why does this distortion occur?

**5.** (laboratory question) The electromagnet in a telephone is much stronger than the simple electromagnet you made in the lab. How are the two different?

**Investigating Chapter Ideas** Try one of the following projects to further your study.

**1. Silicon chips** Find out how integrated circuits are placed onto thin silicon wafers.

**2. P and n silicon** Report on how silicon is laced, or *doped,* with impurities to create p- and n-type silicon. Explain how layers of p- and n-silicon are used to make transistors.

**Reading About Science** Read some of the following books to explore topics that interest you.

Arley, Neil. 1984. **Exploring Magnetism.** New York: Watts.

Jespersen, James. 1981. **Mercury's Web: The Story of Telecommunications.** New York: Atheneum.

# WAVES

How do you see light? Why do you see color? Would you believe there are kinds of light that you cannot see, but that can be seen by other animals? In this unit you will investigate light as you study waves. Light is a kind of wave. So, too, is sound a kind of wave, as your reading of this unit will illustrate. In this unit you will learn about some of the properties and uses of each of these kinds of waves.

## UNIT

351

An alarm sounds in a small coastal town. The alarm signals the approach of a tidal wave, or tsunami (tsew•NAH•mee). What effects will the wave have on the town?

How can a wave destroy a town? Think about what happens when you shake one end of a rope. As you shake the rope, you send waves through it. The waves carry your energy from one end of the rope to the other. Similarly, a tsunami begins with an earthquake on the ocean floor. The earthquake shakes the water. The shaking sets up a wave in the water. The wave carries the energy of the earthquake to the town.

Waves are energy carriers. The ability of waves to carry energy explains how a wave can have enough energy to destroy a town. In this chapter you will explore the properties of waves. You will see how different kinds of waves travel.

Read and Find Out:
● how you can see an invisible wave.
● what Lake Michigan has in common with your bathtub.

# WAVE MOTION

# THE MOTION OF WAVES

## OBJECTIVES

**1.** Define waves.
**2.** Contrast the movement of energy and matter in a wave.
**3.** Describe two kinds of wave motion.

*A **wave** is a disturbance that travels through matter or space.* As a wave travels, energy is carried from one place to another. Later in this unit you will learn about energy from the sun that travels through space as waves. But you will start your study of waves by learning about the motion of waves through matter. In this section you will take a close look at two kinds of wave motion.

## Waves Through Matter

Suppose you are on a raft. A motorboat speeds by. What happens to your raft? The boat sets up waves in the water that travel outward. The waves soon reach you and make your raft bob up and down. Like the tsunami you just read about, these "little" waves are also energy carriers. They carry the energy of the motorboat to your raft.

Water waves are easy to study because you can see them. See Figure 16-1. And you can also see their effects. However, many invisible waves are traveling around you all the time. Waves can travel through solids, liquids, and gases. Although you cannot see the waves, you can study them by observing their effects.

For example, wave a large book up and down. Moments later you can see a curtain across the room flutter. Your energy of motion set up waves through the air. The waves carried your energy to the curtains, causing them to move.

A stereo and foil can also demonstrate waves moving through air. Turn on a stereo and hold a sheet of aluminum foil about one meter in front of the speaker. As the music plays, you can feel the aluminum foil rattle. Waves from the speaker travel through air to the foil.

*Figure 16-1. Suppose you time how long it takes the ripples to cross the pond. And you measure the distance they travel. What do you know about the ripples?*

All sounds travel as waves. Sound waves can travel through all three phases of matter. Rest your ear on top of a wooden desk and tap on the far end of the desk with a pencil. You hear the tapping because the sound travels through the desk. If you have ever swum underwater, you know that sounds also travel through liquids.

Through what phases of matter can sound waves travel?

## The Medium of a Wave

The **medium** (pl. media) of a wave is the material through which the wave travels. Water is the medium of waves set up by a boat. Water, air, and wood are just three media through which sound waves can travel. Waves can also travel through the earth. When large sections of rock suddenly slip, they create a disturbance. This disturbance sends waves through the earth medium. An earthquake occurs.

Figure 16-2 shows how a medium can be affected as a wave travels through it. The medium here is the rope. The student's energy sets waves moving to the right through the rope. But notice the rope. As the wave passes forward, the rope bobs up and down. It does not travel forward with the wave. When a wave travels through a medium, the medium itself is not carried along. Only the energy travels forward.

Waves travel at different speeds through different media. For example, dip a finger up and down in a bowl of water. Dip a finger of your other hand in a bowl of syrup. You can see waves travel across each substance. They travel faster through water.

*Figure 16-2. The piece of rope moves up and down, not forward. In what medium is the wave traveling?*

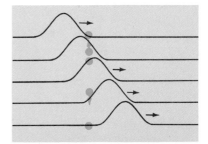

## Transverse Waves

All waves carry energy from place to place. But the way a wave carries energy depends on the kind of wave motion. There are two kinds of wave motion through matter. Figure 16-3 shows a model of one kind of wave motion.

In this model waves move by one part of the medium pushing, pulling, or twisting on the next part. The medium for this model is soda straws and tape. You generate waves by twisting the first straw up and down several times. As the first straw moves up, it twists the tape. The twisting motion transfers energy to the next straw, causing it to move. The twisting and moving continue over the entire length of the straw-tape medium. The waves move to the left, carrying energy along with it.

Notice that the parts of the straw-tape medium move up and down, while the waves move to the left. The straw-tape model illustrates the motion of *transverse* (tranz•VURS) *waves*. *A **transverse wave** is one that moves at right angles to the moving particles of the medium.* Rope waves, and water waves, and soda-straw waves are examples of transverse waves.

Give three examples of transverse waves.

## Longitudinal Waves

Figure 16-4 shows a model of a second kind of wave motion. This model uses a spring as the wave medium. You set up the wave motion by vibrating one end of the spring. That is, you move that end back

*Figure 16-3. Waves travel through a medium made up of soda straws connected by tape.*

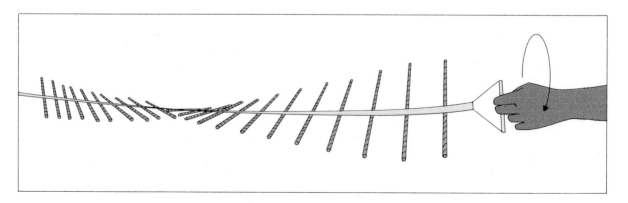

and forth, over and over. Your motion makes the vibrations of the coils travel from one end of the coil to the other.

The areas where the coils are squeezed together are called *compressions*. *A* **compression** *is a region where particles of a medium are close together.* Outside each compression, the coils of the spring are spread apart. *These regions, where the particles of a medium are spread apart, are called* **rarefactions** (rayr•uh•FAK•shunz).

This kind of wave motion is a series of compressions and rarefactions, one following the other. As the coils of the spring vibrate, they move back and forth in the same line of motion as the wave. They do not move up and down as in a transverse wave. *The kind of wave that moves along the same direction as the moving particles of the medium is called a* **longitudinal** (lawn•juh•TEW•di•nuhl) **wave.** Again, the coils of the spring do not move forward. They move back and forth. It is the energy, not the matter, that is carried

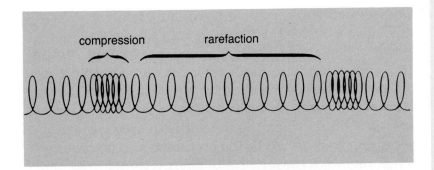

compression   rarefaction

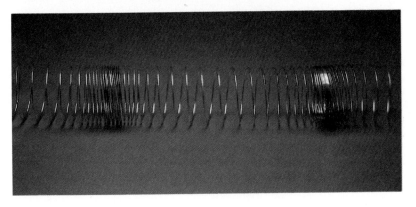

**ROPE WAVES**

**OBJECTIVE**
Study properties of rope waves.

**MATERIALS**
jump rope

**PROCEDURE**
1. Tie one end of the rope to a chair. Hold the other end in your hand. Make a wave by snapping your wrist with a quick, vertical motion.
2. Send a wave through the rope. Observe what happens when it hits the chair.
3. Send a wave toward the chair. When the wave hits the chair, send out another wave. Watch the two waves when they meet.

**QUESTIONS**
1. What happened to the wave in step 2?
2. Describe the wave in step 2 that returned to you.
3. When two waves meet, do they bounce off each other or pass through each other?

*Figure 16-4. The spring moves back and forth while the wave moves forward.*

## CHART 16-1. TRANSVERSE AND LONGITUDINAL WAVES

| Type of Wave | Direction of Wave | Direction of Motion of Medium | Waves |
|---|---|---|---|
| Transverse | → | ↕ | 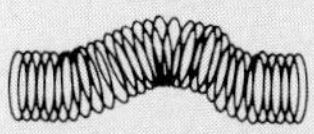 |
| Longitudinal | → | ↔ | 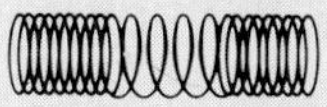 |

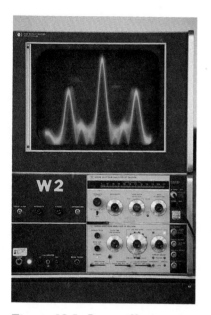

*Figure 16-5. An oscilloscope lets you "see" sound waves.*

along with the wave. Chart 16-1 shows how you can use a spring to produce both longitudinal and transverse waves.

● You know that although you can hear sound, a longitudinal wave, you cannot see it. However, scientists have a device that "sees" sound waves. This device is called an oscilloscope (uh•SIL•uh•skohp). Figure 16-5 shows how a sound wave looks on an oscilloscope.

The "picture" of the sound wave is caused by the energy of the wave. As the sound wave moves, it carries energy with it. When the wave hits the receiver, the energy is transferred to the oscilloscope. The oscilloscope registers the amount of energy transferred and converts it into a picture.

### OBJECTIVES AND WORDS TO REVIEW

**1.** What is a wave?

**2.** Are both matter and energy carried forward by a wave? Give an example to support your answer.

**3.** Distinguish between transverse and longitudinal waves.

**4.** Write one complete sentence for each term listed below.

| | | |
|---|---|---|
| wave | transverse wave | rarefaction |
| medium | compression | longitudinal wave |

# LOOKING AT WAVES

Sending waves through ropes and springs allows you to see the waves. In this section you will observe interesting properties of waves, including some measurements.

## Measurements on Waves

All waves have certain points that you can identify. Figure 16-6 shows these points in a transverse wave.

**Wavelength** By snapping a rope with your hand many times, you send a series of transverse waves through the rope. Notice that each wave has a high point and a low point. *The high point of a wave is its* **crest**. *The low point of a wave is its* **trough** (TRAWF).

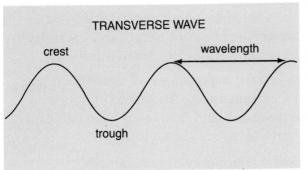
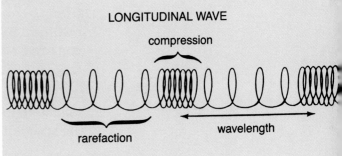

Each wave is made up of one crest and one trough. Each wave has a certain *wavelength*. *A* **wavelength** *is the distance from one crest to the next crest.* The wavelength changes if you snap the rope faster. The faster you snap the rope, the shorter the wavelength becomes.

You can make the same kind of measurements on a longitudinal wave. Figure 16-6 shows that a longitudinal wave is made of one compression and one rarefaction just as a transverse wave is made of a crest and trough. The wavelength of a longitudinal wave is the distance between two compressions.

*Figure 16-6. Parts of a transverse wave and a longitudinal wave.*

What is the wavelength of a longitudinal wave?

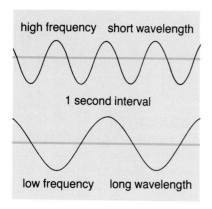

high frequency    short wavelength

1 second interval

low frequency    long wavelength

*Figure 16-7. A wave with a short wavelength has a high frequency.*

**Frequency**    The faster you vibrate a rope or spring, the more waves you make each second. *The number of waves produced each second is the* **frequency** (FREE•kwuhn•see). The frequency of a wave can be thought of as the number of vibrations per second. You can measure the frequency of a rope wave by counting how many times the rope moves up and down each second. In a spring wave, you can find the frequency by counting how many times a coil vibrates back and forth each second.

Frequency is measured in a unit called the *hertz* (HURTZ). *One* **hertz,** abbreviated Hz, *is one wave per second.*

Frequency and wavelength are related. As the frequency of a wave increases, its wavelength decreases. See Figure 16-7.

**Amplitude**    You can make big waves and small waves in a rope. The size of a wave is measured by its *amplitude* (AM•pluh•tewd). **Amplitude** *is the distance from the crest of a wave to the normal position of the medium.* By measuring the rope height in Figure 16-8, you are finding the amplitude of a transverse wave.

**Speed**    Once a wave is produced, it moves through the medium at a certain speed. The speed of a wave is related to its wavelength and frequency. You can find the speed of a wave by using the equation:

**speed = frequency × wavelength**

Suppose you generate rope waves with a frequency of 2 Hz. You find the wavelength of the rope waves to be 3 cm. What is the speed of the waves as they travel along the rope?

speed = frequency × wavelength
speed = 2 Hz × 3 cm
speed =  6 cm/s

The crest of this wave moves forward at the rate of 6 cm/s. This formula works for both transverse and longitudinal waves.

*Figure 16-8. The height of a wave is its amplitude.*

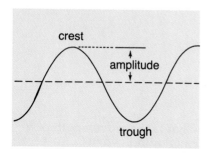

crest

amplitude

trough

## Comparing Transverse and Longitudinal Waves

In the last section you saw a picture of a longitudinal wave. The picture looked similar to that of a rope wave, a transverse wave. This similarity is not accidental. The two kinds of waves are described in similar ways. Look at Figure 16-9. In **A** you see a longitudinal wave in a spring. Notice that in compressions, more coils are located in a small area. So, compressions are regions where the "density" of the coils is high. Rarefactions, on the other hand, have a low "density" of coils.

Figure 16-9**B** shows a graph of the "density" of the coils during wave motion. Notice that the graph looks like a transverse wave. The highest points on the graph show regions of highest density. These are regions of compression. From the graph you know they are crests. The lowest points are regions of lowest density. These are regions of rarefaction. They correspond to troughs.

## Energy of Waves

Whenever you snap a rope, the energy you use can affect the waves you produce. When you snap the rope gently, you make waves like those in Figure 16-10**A**. When you snap the rope harder, you use more energy. You produce a wave more like the one in Figure 16-10**B**. Notice, the waves are bigger. The energy in a wave is related to the amplitude of the wave. Larger amplitude waves have more energy than smaller ones.

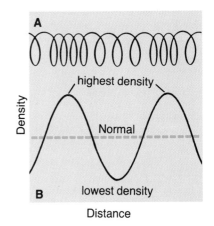

*Figure 16-9. Regions of high and low density in a longitudinal wave.*

*Figure 16-10. What does the height of a transverse wave measure?*

*Figure 16-11. A light above the ripple tank shines through the water. An image of the waves appears on the floor.*

*Figure 16-12. Waves coming from the left are reflected upward.*

*Figure 16-13. Waves bend as the medium they travel through changes a property (depth).*

## Properties of Waves

By observing water waves in a device called a ripple tank, you can learn about some properties of all kinds of waves. See Figure 16-11.

**Reflection**   Figure 16-12 shows what happens when a wave hits a surface. The waves bounce off the surface and change their direction. All waves show this property of *reflection* (ri•FLEK•shuhn). **Reflection** is *the bouncing of a wave off a surface.*

**Refraction**   When a wave travels from one medium into another medium, it may bend or change direction. The water waves in Figure 16-13 change direction as they move from deep water into shallow water. The bending of waves is called *refraction* (ri•FRAK•shuhn). **Refraction** is *the change in direction of a wave as it moves into a different medium.* Notice that the wavelength of the water waves also changes in the shallow water. The troughs get closer together.

**Interference**   When two waves meet, they can add or subtract. If two wave crests meet at one place, the result is one big wave. Figure 16-14 shows *interference* (in•tur•FEER•uhns) regions where two water waves meet. They add and form large waves. **Interference** is *the interaction of two or more waves when they meet.* When a wave crest meets a wave trough, the amplitudes subtract, resulting in little or no wave at all.

**Diffraction**   When waves pass through a small opening they continue moving in a straight line. However, they also bend a little at the sides of the opening. Figure 16-15 shows this property of all waves: *diffraction* (di•FRAK•shuhn). **Diffraction** is *the bending of waves around the edges of an object.*

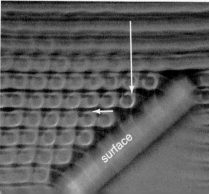

surface

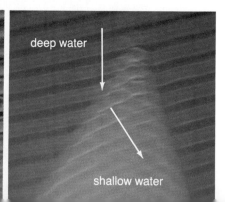

deep water

shallow water

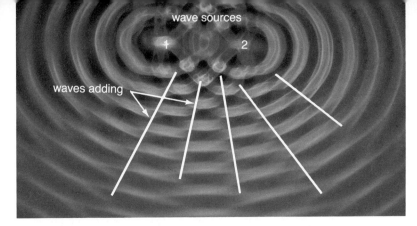
wave sources

waves adding

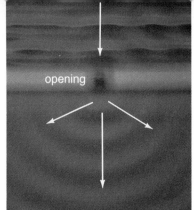
opening

● Think of times you took a bath when you were young. Did you ever move back and forth in the tub? Did you ever notice that if you moved back and forth in step with the motion of the water, the wave you made got higher and higher? Did the wave ever get so high that it spilled over the edge of the tub and onto the floor?

This "bathtub" effect is also found in nature. See Figure 16-16. Called a seiche (SAYSH), this phenomenon has at times occurred on Lake Michigan. The winds that blow across the lake create the waves. As the wind continues to blow, new waves are formed. These new waves are in step with the previous ones. After the wind stops, the wave continues to travel across the lake from one side to the other. A seiche can cause the water level at the shore to rise and fall by several meters. If the amplitude becomes great enough, the wave overflows the shore. This effect is just like the water going over the top of the bathtub.

*Figure 16-14. Interference of water waves.*

*Figure 16-15. Diffraction of water waves.*

*Figure 16-16. Winds blowing over Lake Michigan can cause a seiche.*

## OBJECTIVES AND WORDS TO REVIEW

1. Draw a picture of both a longitudinal wave and a transverse wave. On each, label a wavelength and the amplitude.
2. The speed of a wave is 12 cm/s. The wavelength is 2 cm. What is the frequency of the wave?
3. Wave X has an amplitude of 30 cm. Wave Y has an amplitude of 10 cm. Which wave has more energy? How can you tell?
4. Write one complete sentence for each term listed below.

   | | |
   |---|---|
   | crest | frequency |
   | trough | hertz |
   | wavelength | amplitude |

*Looking at Waves* **363**

# IDENTIFYING SOURCES OF ERROR

## Preparation

How many times have you missed catching a fly ball? And how often have you thought about why you missed it? You might have said: "The ball got lost in the sun's glare," or "I only took my eye off the ball for a second," or "Someone called my name and I was distracted." Well, believe it or not, you are acting like a scientist when you ask yourself a question like this. You are considering sources of error.

Scientists consider sources of error whenever they do a laboratory activity. Identifying sources of error helps scientists decide how valid the results of their investigation are. It also helps them think about ways of improving the investigation to obtain better results.

## Directions

Identifying sources of error may be very difficult. So many possibilities exist. However, here are some questions you can ask yourself. A "no" answer to any of them is a strong indication of a source of error.

1. Determine if an error could have been caused by the equipment itself. For example, are the divisions on the meter stick readable, or have they been worn away through use?
2. Is the equipment I am using accurate? Is it sensitive enough? For example, you cannot use an egg-timer to clock a 100-meter dash.
3. Are the measuring instruments properly zeroed?
4. Have I followed the procedure correctly? Did I omit any steps?
5. Have I taken my readings correctly? Did I look directly at any scales?

6. How accurate are the readings I took?
7. Have I used the correct data in the formulas?

## Practice

On a separate sheet of paper, write down possible sources of error for each of the cases cited below.

1. You do an activity meant to show that if equal amounts of heat are added to different masses of water, the smallest mass heats up fastest. Your results indicate that the middle mass of water heated fastest.

*Figure 1.*

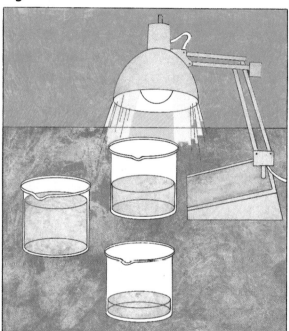

2. You perform a chemical experiment that is supposed to show that the total mass of the reactants equals the total mass of the products. Your results do not show this equality.

## Application

Read the laboratory activity for this chapter. Then, on a separate sheet of paper, identify any possible sources of error for this activity.

# LABORATORY ACTIVITY

## THE SPEED OF A WAVE

### Objective
Study how wave speed depends on the medium.

### Background
The setup in Figure 16-L allows you to watch transverse waves travel across a straw-tape medium. With it, you can study the effects of tension, a pulling force, on the waves.

### Materials
20 soda straws, 40 paper clips, 50-g masses, cord, tape (4 meters), mass hanger, stick (or pencil), stop (or digital) watch

### Procedure
1. Construct the straw-tape medium in Figure 16-L. Tapes 1 and 2 are each 2m long. Make sure to space the straws exactly 6 cm apart at right angles to the tape.

2. Attach one end of the tape to a ring stand. Attach the other to a stick tied to a cord. See Figure 16-L. Run the cord over the mass hanger and hang a 50-g mass on the cord.

3. Send a wave into the straw-tape medium by moving the first straw up and down. With a stop watch, measure the time it takes for the wave to travel to the end of the tape. You can find the speed by dividing the distance traveled (2 meters) by the time it took (in seconds) to move this distance. Record your answer.

4. Increase the tension in the medium by adding 100 grams to the mass hanger. Find the wave speed. Keep adding masses until 500 grams are hanging. Find and record each time you add a mass.

5. Attach clips to the ends of the first 10 straws. You now have two different media joined together. Send a wave into the medium. Observe what happens. Think of other combinations. Try them.

### Questions
1. In what direction do the straws move? Which way does the wave move?

2. How does the wave speed depend on the tension in the medium?

3. **PROBLEM SOLVING** In step 5, what happens to the speed as the wave travels along the tape?

**Figure 16-L.** *Laboratory setup.*

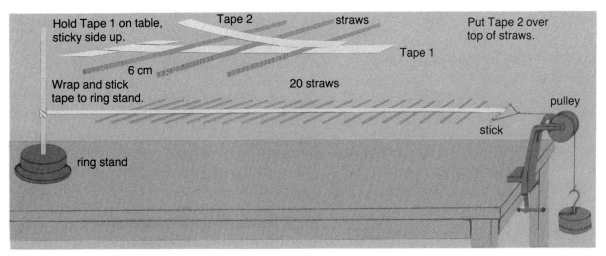

# SUMMARY

1. Waves carry energy. A wave is a disturbance that moves through a medium without carrying the medium along with it. The energy of a wave depends on its amplitude. (16-1)

2. In a transverse wave, the medium vibrates up and down as the wave moves horizontally. In a longitudinal wave, the medium moves back and forth as the wave moves horizontally. (16-1)

3. All waves have a wavelength, a frequency, and an amplitude. (16-2)

4. The speed of a wave is equal to the product of the frequency and the wavelength. (16-2)

# REVIEW

Number a sheet of paper from 1 to 25 and answer these questions.

**Building Science Vocabulary**   Write the letter of the term that best matches each definition.

| | | |
|---|---|---|
| **a.** amplitude | **e.** hertz | **i.** trough |
| **b.** compression | **f.** medium | **j.** vibration |
| **c.** crest | **g.** rarefaction | **k.** wave |
| **d.** frequency | **h.** speed | **l.** wavelength |

1. A disturbance moving through matter
2. A low point on a wave
3. A material that carries a wave
4. The number of waves each second
5. The height of a wave
6. Region where particles are close together
7. The distance between two crests
8. A unit used to measure frequency
9. Frequency times wavelength
10. A high point on a wave

**Finding the Facts**   Select the letter of the answer that best completes each of the following.

11. As a transverse wave in a rope moves from left to right, in what direction does a point on the rope move?   (**a**) left to right (**b**) right to left   (**c**) it does not move (**d**) up and down

12. The energy of a wave is measured by its (**a**) wavelength   (**b**) frequency (**c**) amplitude   (**d**) direction.

13. The low point on a wave is its   (**a**) trough (**b**) crest   (**c**) wavelength   (**d**) frequency.

14. A series of compressions and rarefactions is a (**a**) water wave   (**b**) longitudinal wave (**c**) transverse wave   (**d**) longitudinal or transverse wave.

15. The speed of a wave depends on its (**a**) amplitude   (**b**) medium   (**c**) neither of the above   (**d**) both of the above.

16. A water wave has a frequency of 2 Hz and a wavelength of 7 cm. The speed of the wave is (**a**) 14 cm/s   (**b**) 9 cm/s   (**c**) 5 cm/s (**d**) 3.5 cm/s.

17. Which of the following statements does not apply to *all* waves?   (**a**) They transfer energy.   (**b**) They are a series of disturbances.   (**c**) They travel in a direction parallel to the direction of motion of the medium.   (**d**) They are caused by something vibrating.

18. As the wavelength of a wave increases, its frequency will   (**a**) increase (**b**) decrease   (**c**) remain the same (**d**) decrease, then increase.

19. Sound waves can travel through   (**a**) solids only   (**b**) liquids only   (**c**) gases only (**d**) all of the above.

20. If you double the frequency of some water waves   (**a**) the speed doubles   (**b**) the wavelength doubles   (**c**) the speed is one half   (**d**) the wavelength is one half the original.

**Understanding Main Ideas**   Complete the following.

21. Waves carry __?__ from place to place.
22. A region of a wave where particles are far apart is a region of __?__.
23. The speed of a wave is different in different __?__.
24. As the amplitude of a wave increases, its energy __?__.
25. Frequency is measured in a unit called a __?__.

**Writing About Science**   On a separate sheet of paper, answer the following as completely as possible.

1. Two students each attach one end of a long string to the bottoms of two plastic cups. They stand far apart, each holding a cup and pulling the string tight. Explain how one girl, talking into her cup, can communicate with her friend.
2. The shape and size of ocean beaches change from year to year. Explain.
3. How do transverse waves differ from longitudinal waves?
4. Sometimes you feel a room shake when a heavy truck or train passes. Describe how this shaking can happen.
5. (laboratory question) Suppose you have two ropes: one thin and light, the other thick and heavy. You tie them together and attach the thick rope to a chair. Holding the thin rope, you make a wave. In which rope will the wave move faster? Explain your answer.

**Investigating Chapter Ideas**   Try one of the following projects to further your study.

1. **A simple telephone**   A simple model of a telephone is a string stretched between two plastic cups. Obtain the appropriate materials and see if you can get such a "telephone" to work. Try varying the tension, thickness, and length of the string. Try different cups to see how the thickness and size of cup affect the transmission of sound. Try all of the above tests using tin cans and various types of wire. Report on your observations.
2. **Tides**   Report on the causes of ocean tides. How can tides act in step to produce large changes in the water level at the shore in certain areas?
3. **Gravity waves**   Einstein believed that waves of gravity are continually rippling through space. Report on what gravity waves are. How might they be produced? How are scientists trying to detect them?

**Reading About Science**   Read some of the following books to explore topics that interest you.

Communications Research Machines, Inc. 1973. **Concepts in Physics.** Del Mar, CA: CRM Books.

Kentzer, Michael. 1980. **Waves.** Morristown, NJ: Silver Burdett.

Taffel, Alexander. 1981. **Physics: Its Methods and Meanings.** Boston: Allyn and Bacon.

Young, Frank. 1984. **Radio and Radar.** New York: Watts.

Cobb, Vicki. 1981. **How to Really Fool Yourself.** New York: Lippincott.

Think about the sounds a train makes. From its sounds you can tell when it is approaching you. But how do these sounds reach your ears? That is, through what medium can sound travel?

The sound you hear from a train whistle has traveled through the air—a gas. The vibrations you feel as the train nears the station are sounds moving through the tracks or the ground—a solid.

So, sound waves can travel through a solid or gas. However, they can also travel through a liquid. A diver can attract his buddy's attention by tapping on his air tank. And a scientist can "call" a dolphin by making a noise underwater. This chapter will investigate sound waves.

Read and Find Out:

● how people use sounds they cannot even hear.

● how sounds from a jet can shake dishes.

● how electricity is used to imitate musical sounds.

# THE WORLD OF SOUND

# SOUND AND HEARING

What sounds can you hear right this moment? Whenever you hear a sound, sound waves from some object are reaching your ears. How does an object produce waves? How do sound waves travel? This section will answer these questions.

## Sources of Sound

All sounds are produced by objects that are vibrating. When you pluck a guitar string, for example, you make it vibrate. As it vibrates, the string sends out sound waves. A stereo speaker produces sound waves when a paper cone in the speaker vibrates. When you talk, vocal cords in your voice box vibrate.

## How Sound Waves Travel

Sound waves reach your ear by traveling through a medium. Often the medium is air, a mixture of gases. But sound waves can also travel through solids and liquids. Sound waves are longitudinal waves that can go through all phases of matter.

In Chapter 16, you saw how to send longitudinal waves through a spring. You vibrate the end of the spring in the direction of the waves. The waves, a series of compressions and rarefactions, travel from that end of the spring to the other.

Figure 17-1 shows how a vibrating guitar string sends sound waves through any kind of matter. All

*Figure 17-1. How a vibrating string creates sound waves.*

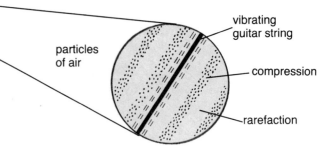

particles of air

vibrating guitar string

compression

rarefaction

matter is made of molecules. When the string vibrates to the right, molecules crowd together into a compression. Each molecule collides with a molecule to its right. As a result, the compression moves to the right.

As the string vibrates to the left, it leaves a space. Molecules spread out in the space, forming a rarefaction. As the string keeps vibrating, a train of compressions and rarefactions moves away from the string.

## How You Hear

Sound waves transfer the energy of a vibrating object to your ear. Actually, it is the molecules of the medium that transfer the energy by colliding with each other. The transfer of energy continues when the sound waves reach your ear.

Figure 17-2 shows the three sections of your ear. Sound waves enter the outer ear. They travel through

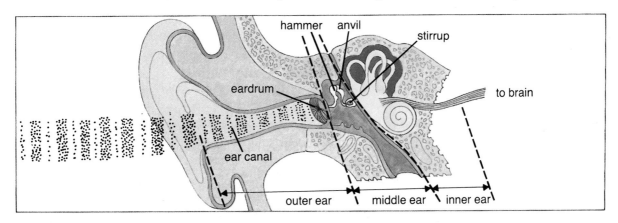

the air in the ear canal. The sound waves hit a thin membrane, the eardrum, at the end of the canal. The eardrum vibrates. It sends, or transmits, the sound waves to three small bones in the middle ear.

The bones vibrate. One of them, the stirrup, vibrates against the oval window, a thin membrane over the inner ear. The oval window vibrates and sends the sound waves into a liquid-filled chamber of the inner ear. The sound waves are converted to coded signals that are sent by nerves to the brain. The brain interprets the signals as sounds.

*Figure 17-2. The ear is divided into three parts: the outer, the middle, and the inner ear. Through what medium does sound travel in each part?*

What is the thin membrane at the end of the ear canal?

**OBJECTIVE**
Study sound wave motion.

**MATERIALS**
marbles, 2 thick books, soft sponge, watch, towel

**PROCEDURE**
1. Put two books side by side on a smooth counter. Leave a narrow space between them. Fill the space with a row of marbles about 1 cm apart.
2. Stop up one end of the space with a sponge.
3. Poke the first marble at the open end of the row. Time how long it takes for all the marbles to move.
4. Repeat step 3 on a soft towel.

**QUESTIONS**
1. How is this setup a model of sound wave motion?
2. Do the colliding marbles move faster on the counter or on the towel? Explain.
3. Relate your answer to question 2 to the speed of sound in different media.

## Pitch and Frequency

Sounds have many differences. You can hear one difference by stroking your hand along a piano keyboard from left to right. How do the sounds differ from key to key? They get higher. If you play the keys from right to left, the sounds get lower (or deeper). *The highness or lowness of a sound is called* **pitch.** You hear differences in pitch when singers reach for high notes, or when a record slows down.

With a baseball card and a bicycle, you can investigate how pitches change. Attach the card to the back of the bicycle so that the card hits the spokes when you turn the wheel with your hand. As you turn the wheel, the card vibrates and makes a sound. The faster you turn the wheel, the faster the card vibrates—and the higher the pitch becomes.

Pitch depends on the frequency of sound waves. When the card, or any object, vibrates faster, it produces more waves per second. See Figure 17-3. These waves have higher frequencies. The higher the frequency, the higher the pitch.

The frequencies of sound waves are measured in hertz. People, in general, can hear sound waves with frequencies of about 20 Hz to 20,000 Hz. Most people cannot hear **infrasonic** (in•fruh•SAHN•ik) **waves,** *sound waves with frequencies below 20 Hz.* Nor can most people hear **ultrasonic** (uhl•truh•SAHN•ik) **waves,** *sound waves with frequencies above 20,000 Hz.* Many animals can hear frequencies that people cannot hear. Dolphins and bats can hear frequencies higher than 100,000 Hz.

*Figure 17-3. As a string vibrates faster, the sound's frequency increases.*

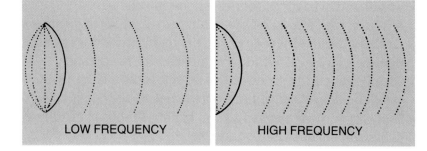

LOW FREQUENCY HIGH FREQUENCY

## Volume and Amplitude

Another way you can hear how sounds differ is to hit one piano key harder and harder. The more energy you use to make a sound, the louder the sound becomes. *The loudness, or* **volume,** *of a sound* depends on the amplitude of sound waves. When you use more energy to make a sound, you produce sound waves with greater amplitude. The greater the amplitude, the louder the sound.

*The volume of a sound is measured in units called* **decibels** (DES•i•buhlz), *or dB.* Table 17-1 shows the decibel rating of common sounds. Sounds above 90 dB can cause temporary hearing loss. People who work near loud noises must wear protective devices over their ears. See Figure 17-4.

*Figure 17-4. Ear protectors muffle loud sounds so they will not harm the ear.*

What must people working near loud noises wear?

**TABLE 17-1.** VOLUME OF FAMILIAR SOUNDS

| Source of Sound | Loudness in Decibels |
|---|---|
| Large rocket engine | 200 |
| Jet engine | 160 |
| Lower limit of pain | 120 |
| Nearby rock band | 115 |
| Subway | 100 |
| Vacuum cleaner | 85 |
| Busy street | 75 |
| Normal talking | 65 |
| Whisper | 40 |
| Rustling of leaves | 15 |

## The Speed of Sound

Sound waves have different frequencies and amplitudes. But the speed of sound waves in any medium at a certain temperature does not change. Table 17-2 shows the speed of sound waves in different media. In each medium, the speed depends on how close the mol-

**TABLE 17-2.** SPEED OF SOUND IN MATERIALS

| Material | Speed of Sound (m/s) |
|----------|----------------------|
| Aluminum | 5,100 |
| Copper | 3,560 |
| Water | 1,460 |
| Air | 340 |
| Vacuum | 0 |

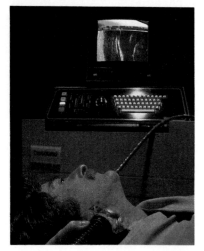

*Figure 17-5. Ultrasonic waves are used in medical diagnosis.*

ecules are to each other and on how easily they can collide with each other. Sound waves travel through some solids faster than through air.

The speed, frequency, and wavelength of a sound wave are all related. This relationship, as you learned in Chapter 16, can be summed up as:

$$speed = frequency \times wavelength$$

The speed of sound in air at 20°C is 340 m/s. The highest frequency you can hear is about 20,000 Hz. What wavelength would this sound wave have?

$$speed = frequency \times wavelength$$
$$340 \text{ m/s} = 20,000 \text{ Hz} \times wavelength$$
$$\frac{340 \text{ m/s}}{20,000 \text{ Hz}} = wavelength$$
$$0.017 \text{ m} = wavelength$$
$$1.7 \text{ cm} = wavelength$$

● Even though people cannot hear ultrasonic waves, they can use them. These waves are produced by devices that have rapidly vibrating parts. Such devices focus the waves into a narrow beam. This sound beam can shake loose dirt from watches and other objects. Sound beams are also used to test metals and plastics. In medicine, doctors use ultrasonic waves to help detect malfunctioning organs. See Figure 17-5.

**OBJECTIVES AND WORDS TO REVIEW**

**1.** How do sound waves travel through air?

**2.** Describe the path of a sound wave through your ear.

**3.** Explain the difference between pitch and volume.

**4.** The lowest frequency you can hear is about 20 Hz. To what wavelength does this correspond?

**5.** Write one complete sentence for each term listed below.

| | |
|---|---|
| pitch | volume |
| infrasonic wave | decibel |
| ultrasonic wave | |

# BEHAVIOR OF SOUND WAVES

You can observe some interesting properties of sound waves simply by listening. Sound waves can bounce off objects. They sometimes become louder or quieter. Sometimes they seem to change pitch. In this section you will investigate these properties.

## Reflections and Echoes

Suppose you are standing in your schoolyard and you clap your hands once. You hear the sound of the clap. But in a moment, you hear the sound a second time. Why do you hear the sound twice? See Figure 17-6.

You heard the first clap almost instantly as sound waves traveled from your hands to your ears. However, sound waves travel in all directions from a source. Some of the waves you produced by clapping reached the wall of the school. They bounced off the wall and returned to your ear. So you heard a second sound.

Figure 17-6 illustrates a property of all waves, reflection. Recall from Chapter 16 that reflection is the bouncing of a wave off a surface. The second sound of a clap in the example is an *echo*. **Echoes are sounds produced by reflected sound waves.**

*Figure 17-6. The production of an echo.*

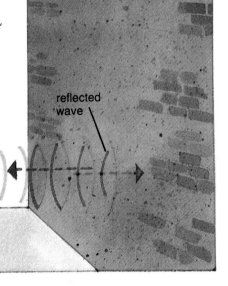

reflected wave

**A**
CONSTRUCTIVE INTERFERENCE

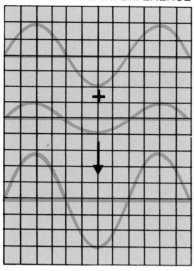

**B**
DESTRUCTIVE INTERFERENCE

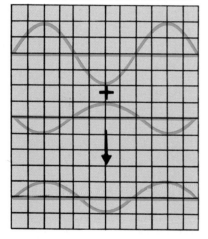

*Figure 17-7. When two sound waves meet, you may hear a louder sound or a softer one. Under what conditions will you hear a louder sound?*

You can listen for an echo in a hallway, a stadium, or wherever there is a hard reflecting surface. But if you are too close to the surface, the reflected waves may reach you almost as soon as the original waves. If so, you will not detect an echo. To hear an echo, the reflected waves must reach you at least 0.1 second after the first waves. How far must you stand from a wall to hear an echo of a clap? Look again at Figure 17-6. The speed of sound in air is about 340 m/s. To tell how far the student is from the wall, use this formula:

$$\text{distance} = \text{speed} \times \text{time}$$
$$= 340 \text{ m/s} \times 0.1 \text{ s}$$
$$= 34 \text{ m}$$

The distance 34 m is the round-trip distance of the wave to the wall and back. The student must be at least 17 m from the wall to hear the echo of the clap.

## Interference

Suppose you have two tuning forks. When you strike each tuning fork separately, you hear the same sound. Each tuning fork vibrates at the same frequency and produces sound waves with the same frequency. If you cover one ear and stand between the two vibrating tuning forks, you can hear no sound at all! By moving your head slightly, you can find regions in which the sounds produced are loud. You can also find regions of soft sounds. Can you tell why?

You might find an answer if you could "see" the sound waves from each fork. To see the waves, you can use an oscilloscope. This device shows sound-wave patterns on a screen. The pattern, however, is displayed as a transverse wave.

An oscilloscope would show the wave patterns you see in Figure 17-7. The patterns show the interference of the waves from the two forks. You may remember that interference is the interaction of two or more waves when they meet. In **A**, the waves interfere *constructively*. The crest of one wave meets the crest of the other. They combine into a crest with a greater amplitude. As a result, you hear a louder sound. In **B**, the waves interfere *destructively*. The crest of one wave meets the trough of the other. They produce a wave with a lower amplitude. As a result, you hear a softer sound.

## Beats

Suppose you have two tuning forks that have different pitches. One produces sound waves with a slightly higher frequency than the other. Strike the two forks. You may hear **beats,** *a series of loud and soft sounds.* Again, an oscilloscope can show that the beats result from the interference of the waves. When the two waves meet, the crests combine at some points and produce loud sounds. At other points, they nearly cancel each other out and produce soft sounds.

## The Doppler Effect

Have you ever heard a car blow its horn as it passed you? If you listened to the horn carefully, you may have heard a change in pitch. When a car approaches you, the horn has a higher pitch than when it moves away. Figure 17-8 can help you understand the change in pitch.

**E**XPLORE
BY TRYING

**THE DOPPLER EFFECT IN WATER**

**OBJECTIVE**
Observe the Doppler effect.

**MATERIALS**
large flat dish or baking tray

**PROCEDURE**
1. Fill a large flat dish with 5 cm of water.
2. Dip your finger in and out of the water at a steady rate. Observe the waves you make.
3. Now slowly move your hand toward one side of the dish as you dip your finger. Observe the waves behind your finger and ahead of it.

**QUESTIONS**
1. What properties of the waves changed as you moved your finger?
2. In step 3, how were the waves ahead of your finger different from waves behind your finger?

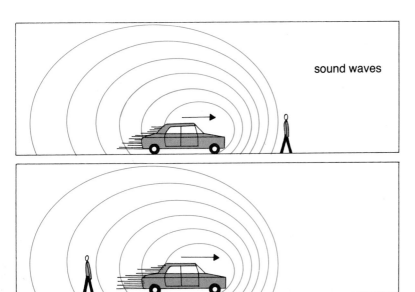

sound waves

*Figure 17-8. The Doppler effect.*

As the car approaches you, its sound waves crowd together. The wavelength decreases. And the frequency increases, producing a higher pitch. As the car moves away, the waves spread apart. The wavelength increases and the frequency decreases. The pitch gets lower.

*The change in the frequency of waves from a moving source is called the* **Doppler** (DAHP•lur) *effect.* You can listen for this effect when trains, trucks, and other vehicles pass you. Patrol cars have devices that can detect changes in frequency. They use these devices to identify speeding cars.

## Speeds Faster than Sound

You can hear the Doppler effect as jets pass. However, some jets move so fast you do not hear them until they have passed. They travel at **supersonic speeds,** *speeds greater than the speed of sound.* See Figure 17-9.

*Figure 17-9. Sound wave patterns made by a jet flying at different speeds.*

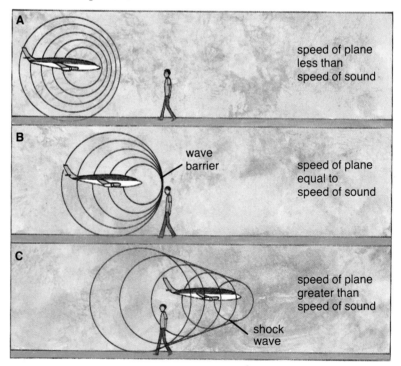

## Dr. France Córdova

Some people find out what their goals in life are in unusual ways. Dr. France Córdova became interested in astronomy while watching a television special on the origins of the universe. Wishing to find out if astronomy was truly for her, she took a part-time job in an astronomy laboratory. She ended up getting her degree in astrophysics (as•troh•FIZ•iks).

Dr. Córdova now specializes in studying objects in the sky that emit X rays. She was one of the first scientists to hypothesize that "white dwarfs" (collapsed stars) *should* emit X rays. She proved her hypothesis by taking pictures from X-ray satellites of hundreds of white dwarfs. By using mathematics, she later described *why* white dwarfs emit X rays.

In **A**, the jet is traveling at a speed slower than sound. The sound waves from the jet are traveling faster than the jet. They reach you before the jet passes overhead. In **B**, the jet has speeded up so that it is traveling as fast as the sound waves. The waves do not move ahead of the jet. Instead they pile up in front of the jet. Molecules of air in front of the jet are closely crowded together.

In **C**, the jet is traveling faster than sound. It breaks through the piled up waves in front. The sound waves now trail behind the jet and combine into a *shock wave*. A ***shock wave*** *is a moving region of crowded molecules produced when the source is traveling faster than sound.* When the shock wave reaches the ground, the jet has already passed overhead.

● Shock waves travel at the speed of sound. They reach the ground after the jet that produces them has passed overhead. When it reaches the ground, this region of crowded air molecules produces a thunderlike sound called a sonic boom. A sonic boom transfers a great deal of energy to the ground. It can cause dishes and windows to vibrate. If windows vibrate too much, they may shatter.

At what speed do shock waves from a jet travel?

## OBJECTIVES AND WORDS TO REVIEW

**1.** What property of waves results in echoes? Under what conditions may you hear an echo?

**2.** Under what conditions may you hear a beat?

**3.** How does the sound of a car's horn change as the car passes you? What causes the change?

**4.** Write one complete sentence for each term listed below.

echo    Doppler effect    shock wave
beat    supersonic speed

# MUSIC: PATTERNS OF VIBRATIONS

**OBJECTIVES**

**1.** Describe how musical instruments produce sounds.
**2.** List three features of a string that determine pitch.
**3.** Explain why the same note sounds different played on different instruments.

reed

CLARINET

sound waves

*Figure 17-10. Holes in a clarinet control changes in pitch.*

When you pluck a guitar string, it vibrates. You hear a sound. If you learn how to play a guitar, you can pluck all the strings to make them vibrate at different rates. When you produce a regular pattern of vibrations on the strings, you hear music. In this section you will learn how musical instruments produce different sounds.

## The Sounds of an Orchestra

Music, like all sounds, is produced by something that is vibrating. Musical instruments produce sound waves from vibrations of different kinds of matter.

For example, when you hit a bar on a xylophone, the bar vibrates and produces sound waves. When you hit piano keys, hammers hit strings inside the piano. The strings vibrate and produce sound waves. You make violin strings vibrate by plucking or bowing them.

Clarinets and oboes have a reed, a small piece of cane, in the mouthpiece. See Figure 17-10. By blowing into the mouthpiece, you make the reed vibrate. The vibrating reed sends sound waves throughout a column of air inside the instrument. Sound waves travel out of openings at the end and along the sides of the instrument.

Trumpets and trombones also produce sounds from a vibrating column of air. But these instruments have no reed. The musician's lips send vibrations through the column.

## Making Musical Sounds Louder

Suppose you take a string from a guitar. Tie one end to a doorknob. Hold the other end tightly. Now pluck the string. The string vibrates and produces sound waves. But the sound you hear is much softer than when the string is attached to a guitar. You would also hear a softer sound if you made a reed vibrate outside of a clarinet.

A vibrating string produces very little sound because of the small area of air it can compress. So, the strings of pianos and guitars are connected to sounding boards. The strings make the boards vibrate in the air, producing louder sounds.

The reed of a clarinet vibrates at many frequencies. However, the air column for a certain note will only produce a loud sound for one frequency. Most wind instruments produce sounds by *resonance* (REZ•uh•nuhns). **Resonance** *is a large-amplitude vibration produced at a certain frequency.*

## Notes and Strings

Have you ever looked inside a piano? See Figure 17-11. When any string vibrates in a piano, it produces a note, or musical sound. Each string produces a note with a definite pitch. When a long string at the left vibrates, you hear a note with a low pitch. When any of the short strings at the right vibrate, you hear a note with a high pitch.

Pitch, remember, depends on frequency. Each string in a piano vibrates at a certain rate and produces sound waves at that rate. The string that produces middle C vibrates 262 times per second. It produces sound waves with a frequency of 262 Hz. Shorter strings vibrate faster than longer ones. Therefore, the shorter strings on a piano produce sound waves that have greater frequencies and higher pitches than those produced by the longer strings.

Length is only one feature of a string that determines pitch. Thickness and tension (TEN•shuhn), or tightness, are two others. See Figure 17-12. Thinner strings vibrate faster than thicker ones. The thinner strings of a guitar produce higher notes than the thicker strings. And by increasing the tension of a string, you make the string vibrate faster. As a result, it produces higher notes.

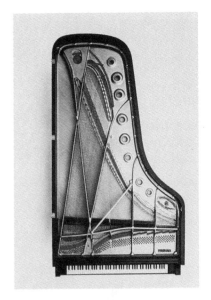

*Figure 17-11. What produces the vibrations of a piano string that result in a musical note?*

What does the pitch of a sound wave depend on?

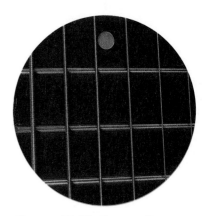

*Figure 17-12. As a guitar string is tightened, what happens to the pitch of the sound produced?*

## Notes on Instruments Without Strings

Clarinets and trombones have no strings. How do
they produce notes with different pitches? To play
each instrument, you vary the length of the vibrating
air column inside. For example, a clarinet with all the
holes closed produces a low pitch. When you open
some of the holes, waves travel a shorter distance inside. Therefore, the pitch becomes higher. When you
pull in the slide of a trombone, you shorten the length
of the air column. As you do so, the pitch gets higher.

## Fundamentals and Overtones

Can you recognize an instrument from its sound?
Suppose you were hearing a band warm up. Each instrument plays a middle C at about the same volume.
You can hear a difference between a middle C from a
piano and the same note from a guitar. *The difference
between sounds of the same pitch and volume is the*
**quality** *of the sounds.*

The quality of a sound depends on the vibrations
that produce the sound. For example, Figure 17-13
shows that a string can vibrate in different ways. A
string vibrates as a whole. But it can also vibrate in
parts. *Vibrating as a whole, the string produces sound
waves with the lowest frequency, the* **fundamental
frequency.** *Vibrating in parts, the string produces*
**overtones,** *sound waves with frequencies higher than
the fundamental frequency.*

Each overtone has a frequency that is a multiple of
the fundamental frequency. Because each overtone has
a higher frequency, it also has a higher pitch than the
fundamental frequency.

*Figure 17-13. The whole
string vibrates as well as
parts of it. Which of the
vibrations shown produces
the highest pitch?*

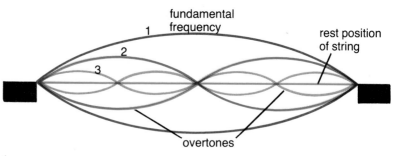

The same note played on different instruments has the same fundamental frequency. But each instrument produces that note with a different number and strength of overtones. The combination of number and strength of overtones gives a note from any instrument its own sound—its quality.

## Standing Waves

A time-lapse photo of a plucked guitar string might show one of the vibrations in Figure 17-13. Each vibration is a *standing wave.* A **standing wave** *is a wave that results from the meeting of two waves with the same frequency and amplitude traveling in opposite directions.*

To understand standing waves, tie a rope to a tree. Set up equal rope waves at a constant rate. Outgoing waves travel to the tree, are reflected, and return. When the outgoing and reflected waves meet, they interfere. If the frequency of the rope waves is a multiple of the rope's fundamental frequency, the two waves will interfere at the same points. At some points the waves will interfere constructively, forming crests and troughs. At other points the waves will interfere destructively, forming points of no motion, nodes. A pattern like Figure 17-14 results.

● One of the latest musical instruments is an electric synthesizer (SIN•thuh•sigh•zur). See Figure 17-15. An electric current in this instrument makes the speaker vibrate, producing sounds similar to many musical instruments. Synthesizers can produce notes with complex overtones that give the notes a quality unlike that of any other instrument.

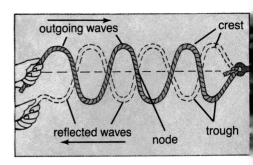

*Figure 17-14. The outgoing and the reflected waves forming a standing wave both have the same frequency and amplitude.*

What conditions give a note its quality?

*Figure 17-15. An electric synthesizer uses electricity to produce musical sounds.*

### OBJECTIVES AND WORDS TO REVIEW

**1.** What produces vibrations in a piano, a clarinet, and a trombone?
**2.** What three characteristics of guitar strings determine pitch?
**3.** What is the quality of a sound? What gives a musical note its special quality?
**4.** Write one complete sentence for each term listed below.
resonance    fundamental frequency    standing wave
quality    overtone

## DETERMINING CAUSE AND EFFECT

### Preparation

Finding out why something happens is a part of daily life. For example, you may wonder why your party was not a success. Finding the reason can help make your next party better.

*Figure 1.*

Answering the question "Why?" is also important in science. After observing an event, scientists try to find out why it happened. The connection between an event and why it happened is called cause and effect. An effect is what occurs. A cause is the reason it occurs.

### Directions

You can begin looking for cause and effect by observing the order in which events occur. For example, did people leave your party right after your friends from another school arrived? Does the order of events always show cause and effect? If you had bad luck after a black cat crossed your path, that does not prove the cat caused the bad luck.

You can also look for the cause of an effect by comparing the effect to similar events for which you know the causes. Compare your unsuccessful party with your successful ones. How were they alike? How were they different? Their differences might give you a clue to the cause.

### Practice

Look for possible cause and effect relationships in Figure 1. Determine whether any event in one drawing may have led to an event in another drawing. Does any drawing represent both a cause and an effect? Explain. Does any drawing represent an event that seems to have no cause or effect relationship with the others? Explain.

### Application

In 1761, Benjamin Franklin invented a musical instrument called the glass harmonica. The instrument consisted of rotating glass discs. A musician plays it by lightly touching the discs as they turn. The discs have to be kept wet. Franklin designed the instrument so that the discs are always partially immersed in water.

Find out about the glass harmonica. Fill a stemmed glass about a third full of water. Wet the rim of the glass and lightly rub your fingers on it. Do not touch any part of the glass except the rim and the stem. Now fill a second glass with water about halfway to the top. Rub the wetted rim the same way. Are different sounds produced by each glass? If so, after reading Section 17-3 discuss possible causes for the effects you hear.

# LABORATORY ACTIVITY

## INVESTIGATING STRING INSTRUMENTS

### Objective
Investigate how strings produce sounds.

### Background
When a stretched string is plucked, it vibrates back and forth. The vibration of the string sends sound waves into the air. The pitch of the sound waves is related to the string's frequency. The vibration of the string depends on the kind of string and its length. It also depends on the tension, how tightly the string is stretched.

### Materials
wood board about 50 cm long, 2 nails, 2 screw eyes, 100 cm of nylon fishing line or steel wire

### Procedure
1. Build a sound board, using Figure 17-L. Tighten a string with its screw eye. **CAUTION:** If you tighten the string too much, it may snap. Pluck the string and listen to the pitch. Watch the string as it vibrates.

2. Tighten the string further by giving the screw eye a one-quarter turn. Pluck the string and listen to the pitch. Tighten the string once more and repeat.

3. Press down in the middle of the stretched string with your fingernail. Pluck the right half of the string. Listen to the pitch of the half-string. Compare the pitch of the half-string with that of the whole string. Repeat several times, pressing down at other points along the string.

4. Try to tune both strings to the same pitch. Pluck both strings. Listen for beats.

### Questions
1. How does the pitch of the sound waves depend on the tension in the string?

2. How does the pitch of the sound waves depend on the length of the string? In step 3, was the tension in the string the same no matter where you pressed the string?

3. **PROBLEM SOLVING** Imagine that you have 2 strings with the same length and tension, but one string is thicker. How would the pitch of the thicker string compare with the pitch of the thinner string? Try it.

4. Did you hear beats in step 4? If so, does anything happen to the beats as both strings approach the same pitch?

**Figure 17-L.** *Laboratory setup.*

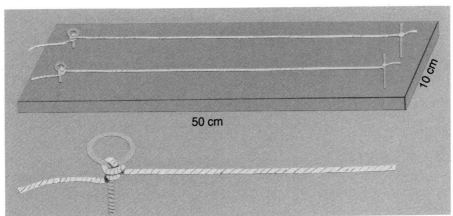

50 cm

10 cm

# SUMMARY

1. Sound is made by a vibrating object. (17-1)
2. Pitch is the highness or lowness of a sound wave. Volume refers to the loudness of a sound. (17-1)
3. Echoes are reflected sound waves. Beats are a series of loud and soft sounds. (17-2)
4. The Doppler effect is a change in the frequency of waves from a moving source. (17-2)
5. The pitch of a stringed instrument depends on the strings' length, thickness, and tension. The pitch of a reed or horn instrument depends on the length of the air column. (17-3)
6. Two different musical notes of the same pitch can sound different because they have different overtones. (17-3)

# REVIEW

Number a sheet of paper from 1 to 25 and answer these questions.

**Building Science Vocabulary**   Write the letter of the term that best matches each definition.

| | | |
|---|---|---|
| a. beat | e. infrasonic | i. quality |
| b. decibel | f. interference | j. supersonic |
| c. Doppler effect | g. overtone | k. ultrasonic |
| d. echo | h. pitch | l. volume |

1. One of a series of loud and soft sounds
2. A sound wave with a frequency greater than 20,000 Hz
3. The highness or lowness of a sound
4. A unit that measures the volume of a sound
5. A higher frequency produced when a part of a string vibrates

6. Speeds that are greater than the speed of sound
7. The reflection of a sound wave
8. The loudness of a sound wave
9. The change in frequency of waves from a moving source
10. A characteristic determined by the overtones in a music note

**Finding the Facts**   Select the letter of the answer that best completes each of the following.

11. You cannot see sound waves because (**a**) you cannot see air particles    (**b**) they travel too fast    (**c**) the wavelength is too long    (**d**) the frequency is too high.
12. The human ear cannot hear frequencies that are    (**a**) equal to 15,000 Hz    (**b**) greater than 20 Hz    (**c**) greater than 20,000 Hz    (**d**) less than 20,000 Hz.
13. Sound waves are created by    (**a**) short wavelengths    (**b**) vibrations    (**c**) the medium    (**d**) the speed of sound.
14. An object vibrates at 512 Hz. Which frequency would a second object have to vibrate at to produce a beat?    (**a**) 288 Hz    (**b**) 400 Hz    (**c**) 509 Hz    (**d**) 730 Hz
15. The stirrup is a part of the    (**a**) ear canal    (**b**) outer ear    (**c**) middle ear    (**d**) inner ear.
16. In which material is the speed of sound the greatest?    (**a**) water    (**b**) air    (**c**) copper    (**d**) aluminum
17. A region of crowded air molecules formed when a jet moves faster than the speed of sound in air is    (**a**) an overtone    (**b**) a shock wave    (**c**) an echo    (**d**) a beat.
18. Decibels measure    (**a**) pitch    (**b**) resonance    (**c**) quality    (**d**) volume.
19. An increase in the amplitude of sound waves at certain frequencies in a piano is due to    (**a**) pitch    (**b**) quality    (**c**) resonance    (**d**) volume.

**20.** Bats use the reflections of ultrasonic waves (130,000 Hz) to guide their flight in darkness. In a dark room with carpeted floors, walls, and ceilings **(a)** there would be no echoes **(b)** bats could not "see" **(c)** bats would crash **(d)** all of the above.

## Understanding Main Ideas   Complete the following.

**21.** Temporary loss of hearing can result from sounds greater than about __?__ .

**22.** The same notes from a guitar and a banjo sound different because __?__ .

**23.** When two sound waves with slightly different frequencies combine, they produce a __?__ .

**24.** The speed of sound is 340 m/s. The wavelength of middle C (256 Hz) is __?__ .

**25.** The lowest frequency of a note is the __?__ .

## Writing About Science   On a separate sheet of paper, answer the following as completely as possible.

**1.** There is a band at the head of a long parade. Why are marchers at the end of the parade probably out of step with the marchers at the head of the parade?

**2.** Explain why all swings attached to the same frame may move even though only one of them is being pushed.

**3.** Pilots in high-flying airplanes must use oxygen masks because there is very little air at high altitudes. The pilots press the microphones against their throats to talk. Why?

**4.** Would you hear noises from your bicycle if you were riding at the speed of sound? Explain your answer.

**5.** (laboratory question) A piano string has a fixed length and produces one particular pitch. How can you produce *many* pitches by plucking just one guitar string?

## Investigating Chapter Ideas   Try one of the following projects to further your study.

**1. Phonograph needles**   Investigate how a record reproduces sound by doing the following. Roll a piece of notebook paper into a cone. Make the narrow end as pointed as possible. Stick a straight pin firmly through the pointed end of the paper cone at a 90° angle. Put an old record (one you do not need any more) on a turntable. Turn on the record player, leaving the needle up. Touch the straight pin in the paper cone lightly to the surface of the spinning record and listen. Report and explain your findings to the class. (You may need to research information about records and record players.)

**2. Noise pollution**   Residents in areas exposed to high levels of noise may become agitated. Keep a record for a week of common sounds in your neighborhood. Use Table 17-1 or other reference to estimate their decibel level. Do you think your neighborhood is polluted with too much noise? If so, what could be done to ease the problem?

**3. How far is the lightning?**   To find how many miles away a lightning strike is, you count the seconds between the flash and the thunder and divide by five. Show mathematically why this method works. Assume that the speed of sound is 344 m/s.

## Reading About Science   Read some of the following books to explore topics that interest you.

Aldous, Donald. 1984. **Sound Systems.** New York: Watts.

Heuer, Kenneth. 1981. **Thunder, Singing Sands, and Other Wonders.** New York: Dodd.

Kettelkamp, Larry. 1982. **The Magic of Sound.** Rev. Ed. New York: Morrow.

Knight, David C. 1980. **Silent Sound: The World of Ultrasonics.** New York: Morrow.

plate 1
(yellow)

plate 2
(cyan)

plate 3
(magenta)

**W**hat image comes to mind when you think of a sailboat? Perhaps you imagine a long, streamlined craft with many sails. Or maybe you think of a small boat with a single sail. Whatever your mental image, it is made of many parts. The combination of these parts produces the final image.

The photo of the sailboat at the far right is also an image. It is called a four-color print. A four-color print is made from four images, each of a different color. When the four single-color images are combined, the photo shown at the far right results.

The color photo above is possible because of the properties of light. Color is related to the wavelength of light. In this chapter you will study this and other properties of light.

Read and Find Out:
● how a fiber helps you communicate.
● how lenses help correct vision problems.
● how fine details of distant objects can be obtained.

# LIGHT

plate 4
(black)

final
print

# LOOKING AT LIGHT

Stand in a room just after sunset. Do not turn on any lights. What happens to the objects around you as the room gets darker? Everything slowly seems to disappear. Without light you cannot see anything.

What is light? How does light enable you to see? Light is a form of energy. In this section you will investigate the basic properties of this form of energy.

## Two Basic Properties of Light

Have you ever put your hands in front of a movie projector and made shadow figures? Shadows illustrate a basic property of light. Light travels in straight lines. Your hand, put between a projector and a screen, blocks the light and produces a shadow. If light traveled in curves, it would curve around your hand and you would see no shadow.

*What property of light do shadows illustrate?*

Figure 18-1 shows another basic property of light. When light hits a surface, it is reflected. Reflected light follows a simple law. The angle of the incoming light—the angle of incidence—is the same as the angle of reflected light—the angle of reflection. This law of reflection applies to all waves.

*Figure 18-1. Light from the candle hits the mirror and is reflected. How are the incoming and reflected angles related?*

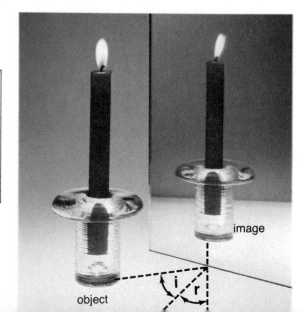

**i** = angle of incidence

**r** = angle of reflection

image

object

Reflected light enables you to see objects. All objects reflect light from the sun and from lamps. You see the objects when the reflected light reaches your eyes. You can see this page because the paper reflects light from a lamp to your eyes.

## Paths of Reflected Light

The same law of reflection applies to all surfaces. Yet different surfaces reflect light differently. See Figure 18-2. Rough surfaces scatter light in many directions. Smooth surfaces reflect light in one direction. If a surface is smooth *and shiny,* like a mirror, reflection enables you to see your image in the surface.

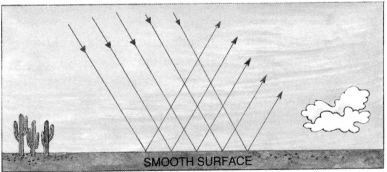

In Figure 18-2 and in other figures in this chapter, *rays* are drawn to show the direction of light. *A **ray** is a straight line that starts at one point and keeps going in one direction.* The starting point of a light ray is a source of light. The source may be a lamp, or it may be the sun.

### MEASURING SHADOWS

**OBJECTIVE**
Study the effect of distance on shadows.

**MATERIALS**
tape, sheet of white paper, flashlight, pencil, metric ruler

**PROCEDURE**
**1.** Tape the paper to a wall. Place a flashlight at the far end of a darkened room. Hold a pencil about 30 cm from the paper. Point the flashlight at the paper so that the pencil's shadow falls on the paper. Observe the shadow.
**2.** Move the flashlight 1 m closer to the paper. Keep the pencil 30 cm from the paper and observe its shadow.
**3.** Repeat step 2 two more times. At each new flashlight position, note the appearance of the shadow.

**QUESTION**
**1.** What happens to an object's shadow as the flashlight gets closer to the object?

*Figure 18-2. Most light hitting a smooth surface is reflected in the same direction. Light hitting a rough surface is reflected in many directions.*

## Light Can Be Refracted

A twig appears bent when part of it is underwater. See Figure 18-3. This effect illustrates a third basic property of light, refraction. Recall that refraction is a change in direction of a wave as it enters a different medium. When applied to light, refraction is the bending of light as it enters a substance. Light is bent, for example, when it goes from air into water.

Refraction results from a change in speed of light. See Table 18-1. Light travels in air at a speed of $3.00 \times 10^8$ m/s. However, notice that light travels faster in air than in water and the other materials. So light slows down when it passes from air to water. When it slows down, it is refracted.

Notice the *index of refraction* of each material in Table 18-1. *The **index of refraction** is a measure of the amount of refraction as light passes into a substance.* Find the index for any two materials. The greater the difference between them, the more a light ray is bent as it goes from one material to the other.

## Interference Patterns

One evening, squint at a distant streetlight. If your eyes are almost closed, your eyelashes form tiny openings in front of your eyes. Light coming through the openings produces a pattern of light and dark bands, as in Figure 18-4. This pattern illustrates the property of interference. Light traveling through one opening interferes with light from the other openings. Turn to page 560 for an illustrated description of interference.

## Light Can Be Diffracted

You learned in Chapter 16 that water waves diffract, or bend around the edges of an object. Light also diffracts. Diffraction occurs when light goes through a narrow slit. As the light passes through the slit, it bends slightly around the slit's edges.

You can do a simple activity to see what diffraction looks like. Press your index and middle fingers together, making a very thin slit between them. Hold the

**What causes refraction?**

*Figure 18-3. As light enters another substance, it bends. What is this bending called?*

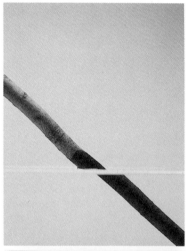

**TABLE 18-1.** INDEX OF REFRACTION AND SPEED OF LIGHT OF SOME MATERIALS

| Material | Index of Refraction | Speed of Light in meters/second |
|---|---|---|
| Air | 1.00 | $3.00 \times 10^8$ |
| Water | 1.33 | $2.26 \times 10^8$ |
| Methanol | 1.33 | $2.26 \times 10^8$ |
| Acetic acid | 1.37 | $2.19 \times 10^8$ |
| Salt crystals | 1.54 | $1.95 \times 10^8$ |
| Calcite | 1.66 | $1.81 \times 10^8$ |
| Diamond | 2.42 | $1.24 \times 10^8$ |

fingers about 8 cm in front of your eyes. Look through the slit at a distant light such as a neon sign or a fluorescent light. The pattern you see will resemble the one in Figure 18-4. This pattern is a diffraction pattern.

## Light Can Be Polarized

Interference is a property of waves, as you saw when you studied sound waves. Because light causes interference patterns, light, too, must travel by wave motion. But does light travel as transverse or longitudinal waves?

One property suggests that light travels as transverse waves. Light behaves like the transverse rope waves in Figure 18-5. At first, the waves are vibrating in many directions. But as the waves pass through the

*Figure 18-4. When light interferes, it acts like a wave.*

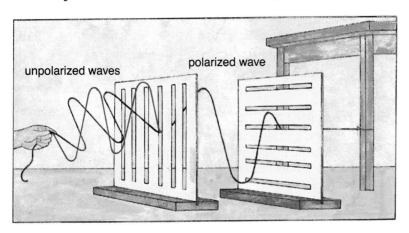

unpolarized waves

polarized wave

*Figure 18-5. A model of polarized light.*

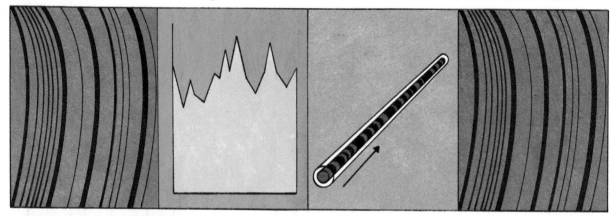

Sound waves from human voice . . .  are changed into electric signals . . .  translated into computer code and sent through fiber to destination . . .  where code is then changed back into human voice.

*Figure 18-6. Optical fibers can carry over a thousand telephone messages at the same time.*

How can light be polarized?

screens, many directions of vibration are blocked. The waves become *polarized* (POH•lur•ighzd). **Polarized waves** *are waves that vibrate along a single plane.*

Light can be polarized by letting it pass through special filters. Such filters block all vibrations except those in a single plane. This property is used in polarized sunglasses. By blocking out all but one place of vibration, these sunglasses cut down glare.

● Light can travel through thin fibers of glass or plastic without escaping the sides. Light inside these fibers is reflected so that it stays in the fiber until it reaches the fiber's other end.

Such optical fibers are being used today to carry telephone messages. See Figure 18-6. Sound waves are first converted to electric signals. The signals are coded into a series of light pulses. These pulses move through the fibers at great speeds and are converted back to sound.

### OBJECTIVES AND WORDS TO REVIEW
1. List five basic properties of light.
2. How is the bending of light related to the speed of light?
3. Which wave model better explains light: shaking a rope up and down or vibrating a spring back and forth? Explain.
4. Write one complete sentence for each term listed below.
   ray    index of refraction    polarized waves

# FORMING IMAGES

Light seems to play tricks with your eyes. Look into a spoon. You see a tiny image of yourself. Look at an object through a hand lens. As you back away from the object, the image gets larger and even turns upside down.

Mirrors produce images by reflecting light. Lenses produce images by refracting light. *The production of images by the reflection and refraction of light is called* **optics.** This section introduces basics of optics.

## Mirrors and Images

Look carefully at your image in a flat mirror. Not only is your image about your real size, it also seems to be behind the mirror. If you stand one meter in front of the mirror, your image seems to be one meter behind it.

Figure 18-7 shows how a flat mirror produces such an image. Follow the solid rays from the object to the mirror. The mirror reflects the rays to your eyes. But your eyes see light as if the light were coming in a straight line from behind the mirror. The dotted rays in the figure extend the reflected rays to points behind the mirror where the image seems to be.

**OBJECTIVES**

**1.** Describe two kinds of images made by mirrors.
**2.** Explain how a convex lens can form tiny and enlarged images.
**3.** Relate vision to muscle action.

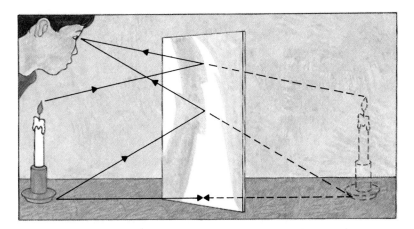

*Figure 18-7. Rays from the candle hit the mirror and are reflected. What is the size of the image formed?*

## IMAGES WITHOUT LENSES

**OBJECTIVE**
Produce an image without using a lens.

**MATERIALS**
aluminum foil, small candle, dish, matches, pencil, 2 index cards

**PROCEDURE**
**1.** Wrap the foil around the bottom of the candle, forming a base for the candle to stand in. Place the candle on the dish. Light the candle.
**2.** Use a pencil to punch a small hole in one of the cards. This is your "lens." The other card is the screen.
**3.** Place the screen about 20 cm away from the candle.
**4.** Place the "lens" halfway between the candle and the screen. Record what you see.
**5.** Vary the distances between the candle, "lens," and screen. Make notes of any combinations you try.

**QUESTIONS**
**1.** What combinations produced an image?
**2.** Were the images produced real or virtual?
**3.** How did the size of the image compare with the size of the object?

The image you see in a flat mirror is a *virtual image*. A **virtual image** *is an image that only seems to be where it is.* But a mirror that curves inward, such as the inside of a shiny bowl, can produce a *real image*. A **real image** *is produced when light actually passes through the point where the image appears.* A real image can be projected onto a screen.

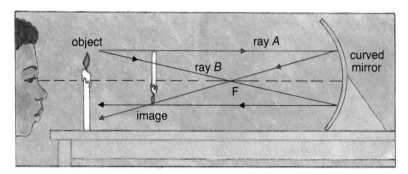

*Figure 18-8. The student sees the image due to reflection of light.*

The rays in Figure 18-8 show how a curved mirror produces a real image. First look for ray A. Ray A is traveling parallel to the *optic axis*. The **optic axis** *is a line drawn through the center of a mirror.* All rays striking a mirror parallel to the optic axis are reflected through the same point, the **focus** (FOH·kuhs). Find where the reflected ray A passes through the focus (F). *The distance between the focus and the mirror is the* **focal length.**

Ray B goes through the focus before it reaches the mirror. Then the reflected ray B travels parallel to the optic axis. The real image forms where the reflected ray A and reflected ray B meet. Notice the image is upside down, small, and in front of the mirror.

## Convex Lenses

A lens is a clear piece of glass or plastic with one or more curved sides. An image is produced when light from an object is refracted on its way through a lens. The kind of image you see depends on the shape of the lens and the position of the object.

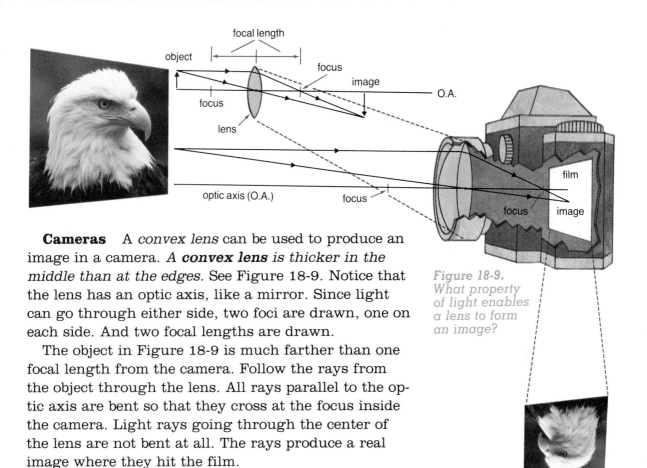

focus

Figure 18-9.
*What property
of light enables
a lens to form
an image?*

**Cameras**   A *convex lens* can be used to produce an image in a camera. ***A convex lens** is thicker in the middle than at the edges.* See Figure 18-9. Notice that the lens has an optic axis, like a mirror. Since light can go through either side, two foci are drawn, one on each side. And two focal lengths are drawn.

The object in Figure 18-9 is much farther than one focal length from the camera. Follow the rays from the object through the lens. All rays parallel to the optic axis are bent so that they cross at the focus inside the camera. Light rays going through the center of the lens are not bent at all. The rays produce a real image where they hit the film.

The real image on the film is, of course, smaller than the object. The image size depends on the focal length of the lens. The focal length, in turn, depends on how curved the lens is. The longer the focal length of a lens is, the larger the image size. Figure 18-10 shows three photos of the same view. Each was taken with a lens having a longer focal length.

**Magnifying Lenses**   A hand lens and the lenses in a microscope are all examples of convex lenses. A con-

On what property of a lens does image size depend?

Figure 18-10. Image size is related to focal length.

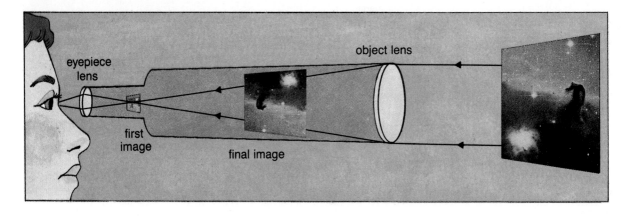

**Figure 18-11.** *The eyepiece lens of a telescope magnifies the first image.*

vex lens can produce a virtual image. If the object is less than one focal length from the lens, an enlarged image appears. The image seems farther away than the object actually is. Turn to page 562 for an illustrated description of image formation with a convex lens.

**Refracting Telescopes** Some telescopes use convex lenses to gather light from distant objects. See Figure 18-11. The object lens produces a real, inverted, small image. The eyepiece lens magnifies the real image so you see an enlarged, virtual image.

## Concave Lenses

Convex lenses converge parallel light rays. They bring parallel light rays together at a focus. But *concave lenses* diverge, or spread out, light. *A concave lens is thinner in the center than at the edges.* See Figure 18-12. Concave lenses produce virtual images. As you look at an object through a concave lens, the image seems to be behind the lens. It appears to be closer to the lens than the object is, between the lens and its focus.

What kind of image does a concave lens make?

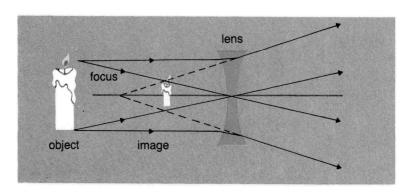

**Figure 18-12.** *A concave lens spreads light rays out.*

# The Eye and Vision

Like a camera, the lens in your eye is a convex lens. See Figure 18-13. Your ability to see clearly depends on the activity of eye muscles. Eye muscles change the shape of the lens, and thus affect the focal length. The change in focal length allows clear images of objects from different distances to appear on the *retina*. *The **retina** is a layer of light-sensitive cells in the rear of the eye.* The image formed on the retina is changed into nerve impulses that travel to the brain.

● When the muscles surrounding the lens do not function properly, poor vision results. A person may become nearsighted or farsighted. Chart 18-1 shows how different lenses can correct these problems.

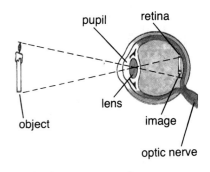

*Figure 18-13. A real image is formed on the retina. Notice the image is inverted. The brain translates the image into a right-side-up image.*

### CHART 18-1. DEFECTS OF THE EYE

| Defect | What Causes It | How It Is Corrected |
|---|---|---|
| Nearsightedness | lens focuses images in front of retina | concave lens placed between object and eye |
| Farsightedness | lens focuses images behind retina | convex lens placed between object and eye |

## OBJECTIVES AND WORDS TO REVIEW

1. What two kinds of images can be made by mirrors?
2. Explain how a convex lens can make tiny and enlarged images.
3. How does the eye see objects?
4. Write one complete sentence for each term listed below.

| | | |
|---|---|---|
| optics | optic axis | convex lens |
| virtual image | focus | concave lens |
| real image | focal length | retina |

# 18-3

# THE WORLD OF COLOR

**OBJECTIVES**

1. Describe how different colors can come from light.
2. Explain how a yellow pencil appears yellow.
3. Describe how your eye sees color.

One of the most pleasing properties of light is color. You see red shirts, yellow pencils, and green grass. In this section you will learn about color and how you detect it.

## White Light and Color

Figure 18-14 shows a simple demonstration using light. Light from the sun, white light, passes through a *prism* (PRIZ•uhm). *A* ***prism*** *is a clear piece of glass or plastic shaped like a wedge.*

sun
prism
prism


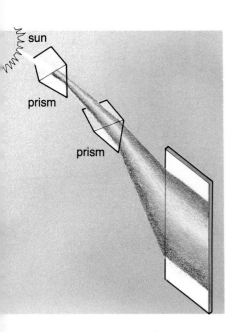

*Figure 18-14. White light entering a prism leaves it as a band of colors.*

Notice that white light enters the prism and colored light comes out. Does a prism change white light into different colors or is white light a mixture of colors? When light from the first prism enters the second, the colors spread out more. These results show that white light is a mixture of many colors.

Colors of light are similar to musical notes. Musical notes have different wavelengths. Colors, too, are different wavelengths of visible light. The longest wavelengths of visible light are red. The shortest visible wavelengths are violet. See Chart 18-2.

**CHART 18-2. PROPERTIES OF COLORS OF VISIBLE LIGHT**

| Color | | Wave Properties |
|---|---|---|
| Red | R | |
| Orange | O | |
| Yellow | Y | |
| Green | G | |
| Blue | B | |
| Violet | V | |

long wavelength
low frequency
bent least by a prism
short wavelength
high frequency
bent most by a prism

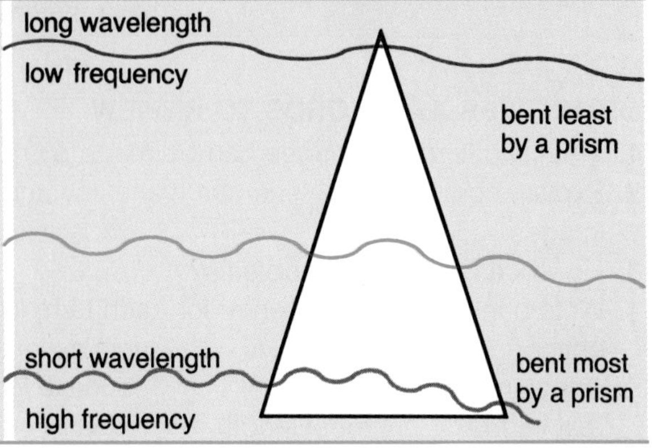

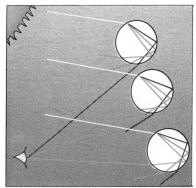

Figure 18-15. A rainbow forms when raindrops spread out sunlight into a spectrum. Each raindrop refracts a different wavelength of light toward your eye. The color of the spectrum that you see depends on the angle between you and the raindrop. The colors from all the raindrops produce the rainbow.

How does a prism separate light into colors? Recall that light waves are refracted as they enter another medium. When white light enters a prism, it is refracted. The amount of refraction depends on the wavelength of the light. Shorter wavelengths bend more than longer wavelengths. So blue light bends more than red light. As a result, each color leaves a prism at an angle slightly different from the other colors. This is why you see colored light leaving the prism. You see the same colors in a prism as you do in a rainbow. See Figure 18-15.

The colors from the prism in Figure 18-14 and from a rainbow are examples of a *spectrum* (SPEK•truhm). A **spectrum** *(pl. spectra) is a band of colors produced when wavelengths of white light are separated.*

## The Colors of Matter

Why is a leaf green or a sweater red? The color of an object depends on what happens as light hits the object. See Figure 18-16.

**Opaque Materials** Different materials absorb some colors and reflect others. The colors you see are the colors reflected by the object. For example, a green leaf absorbs all colors except green. It reflects green, so green is the color you see. A black material absorbs all colors and reflects none. That is why you do not see any colors. A white material absorbs very little light and reflects all colors. As you have seen, all the colors blending together produce white light.

Figure 18-16. A leaf is green because it reflects green wavelengths.

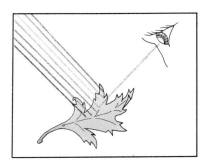

Figure 18-17. Why does the tomato appear black in green light?

Figure 18-18. Red, green and blue light blend into white light. What color do you get when you add blue light and green light?

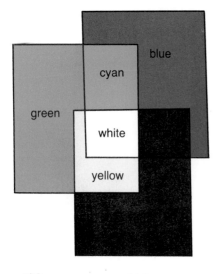

*Materials that absorb light without transmitting it are said to be* **opaque** (oh•PAYK) **materials.** You cannot see through an opaque object.

**Transparent Materials** Some materials, like glass or water, are *transparent* (trans•PAR•uhnt). *Materials that you can see through are said to be* **transparent materials.** Sometimes a transparent material transmits only certain colors of light. Such materials are called *filters. A* **filter** *is a material that transmits certain colors of light and absorbs others.* Refer to Figure 18-17.

Suppose you shine a flashlight on a tomato. You see its red color. Now place a red filter in front of the flashlight. The red filter allows red light to go through and absorb all other colors. Red light now hits the tomato and it is still red. See Figure 18-17.

Now replace the red filter with a green one. This time, green light is passed through and all other colors are absorbed. Since the red tomato reflects only red light, it appears black. See Figure 18-17 again.

## Adding Colors

As Figure 18-18 shows, you can use filters to produce colored light. Notice that only three colors of light are needed. These colors are called the *primary colors. The* **primary colors** *are red, green, and blue.* Adding the proper amounts of these three colors produces any color including white. For example, red and green light add together and produce yellow light. Blue and red add and make magenta (muh•JEN•tuh).

The color picture on a television screen is produced by adding the primary colors together. A screen contains groups of red, blue, and green dots. A group of these three dots makes a color by producing different amounts of red, green, and blue. The light from these colored dots then blends together in your eye and produces the color picture.

## How the Eye Sees Color

When light enters your eye, it hits light-sensitive cells in the retina. Some of them, the cones, react to color. Each cone responds to a particular primary color. When light from a yellow object hits your cones, only those cones sensitive to yellow react. These are the red and green cones. So the object appears yellow. Other colors are detected in the same way. Cones perform the same job for your eyes that the dots do for the television screen.

Stare at the lower right-hand star of the flag in Figure 18-19 without moving your eyes for one minute. Then quickly look at the black dot in the white rectangle. What image appears? From your study of color so far, can you think of an explanation?

Where light from the cyan stripes hit your retina, the cones sensitive to cyan reacted. (Recall that cyan results from adding blue and green light). The cones sensitive to red rested. No light from the black stripes and stars hit your retina. So all the cones in those areas rested. And where the field was yellow, only the cones sensitive to yellow (red and green) reacted. The blue cones rested. By staring at the flag, all the cones that reacted became "tired." Then, when you looked at the white paper, only the rested cones were stimulated. So instead of cyan, black, and yellow, you saw red, white, and blue.

An image such as the flag you saw often results from eye fatigue. The eye gets tired of seeing a certain color. As a result it sees every color except that one. It is as if the color has been subtracted from the white

What kind of cells in the eye are sensitive to color?

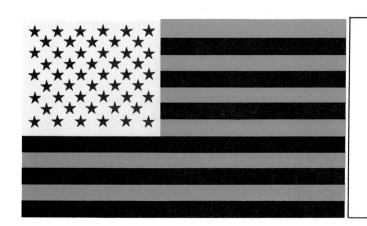

*Figure 18-19.* When you stare too long at a color, the cones sensitive to that color get tired. As a result, you see the color's opposite. What is the opposite of yellow?

light. Subtracting colors explains the effect caused by staring at the flag. But it can also explain what happens when you mix paint pigments together.

## Subtracting Colors

Making or blending paints is different from the way your eye blends colored light. Paints are made from three *primary pigments,* which are different from the primary colors. *The* **primary pigments** *are magenta, yellow, and cyan.* Each pigment absorbs some colors and reflects others. You see the colors that are reflected. By mixing the primary pigments, you pick the colors that are absorbed and those that are reflected.

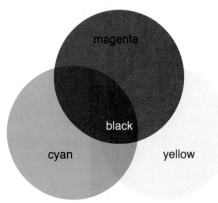

*Figure 18-20. The primary pigments subtract colors. What happens when all three primary pigments are mixed?*

Figure 18-20 shows how the primary pigments absorb and reflect light. When white light hits cyan pigment, blue light and some green are reflected. Red, orange, and yellow light are absorbed. Yellow pigment reflects red and some green, but absorbs blue. When cyan and yellow pigments are mixed, all colors are absorbed except green. As a result, the pigment is green.

● Color is not just a pleasing property of matter. Color also has valuable uses. One use is shown in Figure 18-21. When *Voyager 2* flew past Saturn in 1981, it sent back many signals. These signals were converted into color pictures. However, some of these sig-

*Figure 18-21. False-color photographs bring out details not seen in true-color photos.*

nals were fed into a specially programmed computer. The computer then produced a false-color image of Saturn as shown in the insert. Scientists use the false-color image to study the cloud bands in Saturn's atmosphere. These bands are not as noticeable in the true-color images of Saturn.

**OBJECTIVES AND WORDS TO REVIEW**

1. White light passes through a prism. Why is a spectrum produced?
2. White light hits a yellow pencil. What colors are reflected? What colors are absorbed?
3. How does the eye see color? What three colors does the eye detect?
4. Write one complete sentence for each term listed below.

| | |
|---|---|
| prism | filter |
| spectrum | primary colors |
| opaque material | primary pigments |
| transparent material | |

# WRITING NUMBERS IN SCIENTIFIC NOTATION

## Preparation
How well do you work with numbers? For example, there are 365.25 days in a year. In one day there are 24 hours. So, in one year there are 365.25 x 24 = 8766 hours. These numbers are relatively easy to read and write. But what would you do if you had to use very large or very small numbers?

Scientists often have to deal with very large or very small numbers. For example, the speed of light is 300,000,000 meters per second. The mass of an electron is 0.000,000,000,000,000,000,000, 000,000,000,910,953.4 kilogram. Suppose you had to multiply these numbers together! These numbers are inconvenient to write and hard to use. Fortunately, scientists have a way to ease the amount of work. They use scientific notation.

## Directions
A number written in scientific notation has the form

$$P \times 10^Q$$

P will always be a number between 1 and 10. The exponent Q is a positive or negative integer.

## Figure 1.

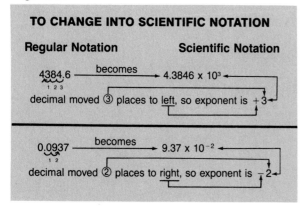

**TO CHANGE INTO SCIENTIFIC NOTATION**

**Regular Notation**          **Scientific Notation**

4384.6 — becomes → 4.3846 x 10³
1 2 3
decimal moved ③ places to left, so exponent is +3

0.0937 — becomes → 9.37 x 10⁻²
1 2
decimal moved ② places to right, so exponent is −2

To write a number in scientific notation, follow these steps. Refer to Figure 1 as you read.

*Step 1*    Find P by moving the decimal point in the original number to the left or to the right until only one nonzero digit is to the left of the decimal point. In the first example in Figure 1, P is 4.3846.

*Step 2*    Find Q by counting the number of places the decimal point has been moved. If the decimal point has been moved to the left, Q is positive. The plus sign is not written. If it has been moved to the right, then Q is negative. The minus sign is always written. In the first example in Figure 1, Q is 3. In scientific notation 4384.6 is written $4.3846 \times 10^3$.

*Step 3*    To add or subtract numbers in scientific notation, the exponents must be the same. To see how to change exponents, see Figure 1.

*Step 4*    To multiply numbers in scientific notation, multiply the Q values and add the exponents: $(4.00 \times 10^2) \times (2.00 \times 10^3) = 8.00 \times 10^5$. If your answer is not in scientific notation, follow steps 1 and 2 to put the number back into scientific notation.

*Step 5*    To divide numbers in scientific notation, divide the P values, then subtract the divisor's exponent from the dividend's exponent:

$$\frac{8.20 \times 10^5}{2.00 \times 10^3} = 4.10 \times 10^2$$

If your answer is not in scientific notation, follow steps 1 and 2 to put the number back into scientific notation.

## Practice
On a separate sheet of paper, write each answer below in scientific notation.

**1.** The speed of light. **2.** The mass of an electron. **3.** Your weight. **4.** Your mail or zip code.

## Application
The index of refraction of a substance is found by dividing the speed of light in air by the speed of light in the substance. Using Table 18-1 on page 393, show by dividing that the index of refraction of each substance is as given by the table.

# LABORATORY ACTIVITY

## THE SIZE OF AN IMAGE

### Objective
Investigate magnification with a lens.

### Background
In an object is 2 cm high and its image is 4 cm high, the image is magnified. Its magnification is 2. Find the magnification by using the formula:

Magnification = Image size/Object size

### Materials
tracing paper, flashlight, black felt marker, convex lens with a focal length of 10 cm, mound of soft clay, meter stick, tape

### Procedure
1. Cut out a circle of the paper to fit the front of the flashlight. Draw a black arrow 2 cm high in the middle of the circle. The arrow is the object for the experiment. The object size is 2 cm. Fit the paper onto the front of the flashlight.

2. Place the lens into a mound of clay as shown in Figure 18-L. Make an image screen by taping a clean white piece of paper to a book.

3. Turn on the flashlight. The arrow should point to about 2 o'clock. Arrange the object, image screen, and lens as shown in Figure 18-L. Place the object about 1 m from the lens. Move the image screen until a sharp image forms.

4. Measure the height of the image (image size). Compute the magnification.

5. Change the object distance (distance from the flashlight to the lens). Adjust the image screen until a sharp image is formed. Repeat step 4.

6. Repeat step 5 for 3 different object distances. Make a table showing object distance and the resulting magnification.

### Questions
1. Describe the images you saw. Are they upside down? Are they reversed right for left?

2. As the object gets closer to the lens, what happens to the magnification?

3. **PROBLEM SOLVING** Find the magnification in steps 4-6 in scientific notation. Does this notation change your answers? Explain.

*Figure 18-L. Laboratory setup.*

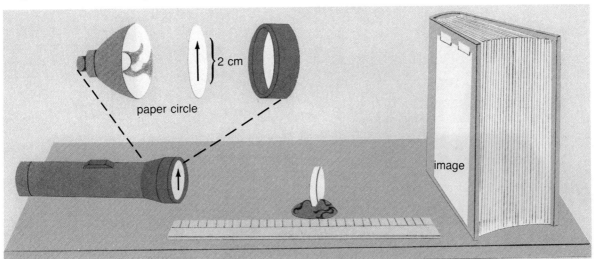

paper circle

2 cm

image

# SUMMARY

1. Light travels in straight lines at a speed of $3.00 \times 10^8$ m/s. Light can be reflected and refracted. It can also be interfered with and polarized. (18-1)

2. The index of refraction is a measure of the amount of bending light will undergo. (18-1)

3. Optics is the study of how images are made by mirrors and lenses. Scientists use rays to show how images are made. (18-2)

4. Only two light rays are needed to find the location of an image. One ray leaves the object parallel to the optic axis and hits the lens. The other ray passes through the center of the lens. (18-2)

5. When white light goes through a prism, it produces a spectrum of colors. Different colors of light have different wavelengths. (18-3)

6. The primary colors your eyes use are red, green, and blue. The primary pigment colors used to mix paints are cyan, yellow, and magenta. (18-3)

# REVIEW

Number a sheet of paper from 1 to 25 and answer these questions.

**Building Science Vocabulary**   Write the letter of the term that best matches each definition.

a. concave
b. convex
c. filter
d. focus
e. primary colors
f. primary pigments
g. prism
h. real image
i. refraction
j. retina
k. spectrum
l. virtual image

1. An image that is upright
2. All rays parallel to the optic axis of a lens or mirror pass through this point
3. A lens that is thick in the middle and thin at the edges
4. A wedge-shaped piece of clear glass or plastic
5. An upside-down image
6. A band of colors produced when wavelengths of white light are separated
7. The part of the eye where an image is made
8. Red, green, and blue
9. The bending of a light ray as it enters a substance
10. A material that allows only one wavelength of light to pass through it

**Finding the Facts**   Select the letter of the answer that best completes each of the following.

11. The primary pigment colors are (a) magenta, green, and yellow (b) green, red, and blue (c) cyan, yellow, and magenta (d) yellow, cyan, and green.

12. When cyan pigment and yellow pigment are mixed, you see (a) green (b) magenta (c) blue (d) black.

13. A light ray traveling parallel to the optic axis of a curved mirror will (a) pass through the mirror (b) reflect off the mirror and pass through the focus (c) reflect off the mirror and travel parallel to the optic axis (d) make an image at the focus.

14. Your eye can make sharp images of far objects and near objects because (a) the retina changes its distance to the eye lens (b) the light-sensitive cells in the retina change their positions (c) only three colors are used by the cones (d) the eye lens can change its focal length.

**15.** Shadows are made because     (**a**) all colors are waves     (**b**) light travels in straight lines     (**c**) light rays bend around opaque objects     (**d**) light passing through the atmosphere is polarized.

**16.** Polarized light waves     (**a**) contain all the colors in the spectrum     (**b**) reflect off filters     (**c**) vibrate in only one direction     (**d**) vibrate in all directions.

**17.** Light will travel fastest through     (**a**) diamond     (**b**) methane     (**c**) calcite     (**d**) acetic acid.

**18.** On which property of light is the usefulness of an optical fiber based?     (**a**) interference     (**b**) total internal reflection     (**c**) polarization     (**d**) straight-line motion

**19.** The spectrum of colors made when white light goes through a prism is due to     (**a**) different wavelengths being bent different amounts in the prism     (**b**) all the wavelengths in the white light being polarized     (**c**) only the primary colors being bent     (**d**) all the wavelengths in the white light being interfered with.

**20.** A red shirt is red because     (**a**) one of the primary colors is red     (**b**) red is the only color that is not polarized     (**c**) red is the only color that is not abosrbed     (**d**) all the colors except red are reflected.

**Understanding Main Ideas**    Complete the following.

**21.** When light strikes a material, it can be reflected, transmitted, or __?__.

**22.** When you look at a car through a green filter, everything looks green because __?__.

**23.** The speed of light is __?__.

**24.** An instrument that magnifies extremely small objects is a __?__.

**25.** The image size in a camera depends on the __?__.

**Writing About Science**    On a separate sheet of paper, answer the following as completely as possible.

**1.** You want to invent a material that is completely invisible. What must happen to all light hitting this material? Would this material cast a shadow?

**2.** Why does the shadow of an object get bigger when it is moved closer to a light source?

**3.** Light reflecting off snow is polarized. If you rotate a pair of sunglasses in front of your eyes, the reflected light fades. Why?

**4.** A spotlight shines on a dancer in a brilliant green shirt. If a magenta filter is put in front of the spotlight, what color will the shirt appear?

**5.** (laboratory question) An 0.25-cm object in a slide is enlarged to 12.5 cm by a slide projector. What is the magnification?

**Investigating Chapter Ideas**    Try one of the following projects to further your study.

**1. Color photography**    Write a report about color photography. Explain how color film is exposed and developed to make color photographs.

**2. Newton's rings**    Fill a shallow pan with soapy water. Set up a flashlight about a meter away from the pan at a low angle. Use a bubble wand to place a large bubble on the water in the pan. Turn on the flashlight and look at the bubble. The moving bands of color you see are called Newton's rings. Find out what causes them. Report your results.

**Reading About Science**    Read some of the following books to explore topics that interest you.

Simon, Hilda. 1981. **The Magic of Color.** New York: Lothrop.

Watson, Philip. 1983. **Light Fantastic.** New York: Lothrop.

The sun is setting and it is getting dark. Small animals are stirring. Suddenly a rattlesnake lunges and captures a rodent.

How does a rattler find its prey in the dark? It has a deep pit in its head below the eyes. This pit has a sensitive nerve that detects heat. The rattlesnake knows where its prey is because it senses the animal's heat.

Many animals see things that people cannot. The flower to the upper left is how you see it. The one to the lower left shows how a bee sees the same flower. Which image is more useful for locating nectar?

People, rattlesnakes, and bees see because of visible light. But rattlesnakes and bees are also sensitive to light that is invisible to people. This chapter will discuss other kinds of light.

Read and Find Out:
● how invisible light waves help the farming industry.
● how scientists can identify elements in stars.
● why a beam of light can melt metals.

# ELECTROMAGNETIC WAVES

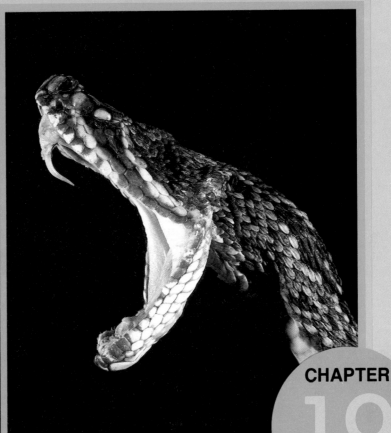

# ELECTROMAGNETIC WAVES: PROPERTIES

## OBJECTIVES

**1.** Compare sound and water waves with electromagnetic waves.

**2.** Compare and contrast electromagnetic waves.

**3.** Describe the properties of four wavelengths of electromagnetic waves.

Every day you use energy that travels by wave motion. Your eyes detect waves of visible light. However, your eyes cannot detect most waves of energy. For example, radio waves are used to broadcast radio and television programs. Radio waves are whizzing past you this moment. The only way to detect them is to turn on a radio or television set. In this section you will study properties of these invisible waves.

## The Electromagnetic Spectrum

The sun and other stars are constantly producing energy in the form of waves. For example, they produce waves of visible light. They also produce waves of invisible energy: radio waves, X rays, gamma rays, and more. These invisible waves travel through space at the same speed as light, $3.00 \times 10^8$ m/s.

All waves that can travel through space are known as *elecromagnetic* (i•lek•troh•mag•NET•ik) *waves.* **Electromagnetic waves** *are transverse waves that can travel through a vacuum.* Water waves and sound waves are not electromagnetic. They need a medium, some form of matter, in which to travel. Sound waves cannot travel through space. See Figure 19-1. However, electromagnetic waves can travel where there is no matter, that is, through a vacuum.

Electromagnetic waves can also be produced on earth. And they can also travel through many kinds of matter. Through space and matter, *electromagnetic waves travel as tiny packets or bundles of energy called* **photons** (FOH•tahnz). Photons travel through matter at different speeds from those at which they travel through space.

Figure 19-2 arranges electromagnetic waves in order of their wavelengths (and frequencies). This arrangement is known as the electromagnetic spectrum.

*Figure 19-1. How did the astronauts communicate with each other on the moon?*

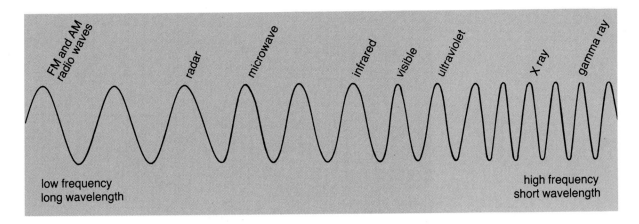

low frequency
long wavelength

high frequency
short wavelength

*Figure 19-2. The electromagnetic spectrum.*

The waves with the longest wavelength (at the left) have the lowest frequencies. Waves with the shortest wavelengths (at the right) have the highest frequencies. The colors of visible light make up only a small portion of the spectrum. They are medium wavelengths. All the other wavelengths are invisible. Now look at each of the main divisions of invisible wavelengths.

## Radio Waves

*Radio waves* have the longest wavelengths of the electromagnetic spectrum. On the sun and on earth, radio waves are produced by charged particles. For example, the motion of electrons in the antenna of a broadcasting station generates radio waves. Some are transmitted directly to radio and television receivers nearby. Others are transmitted to the ionosphere (igh•AHN•uh•sfeer), a layer of charged particles in the atmosphere. They are reflected back to earth, far from their source. See Figure 19-3.

Your radio or television receives these waves through its antenna. Energy from these waves is transferred to electrons in the antenna and produces a current. The current from the antenna is amplified and sent to the loudspeaker or picture tube.

**AM and FM**  Programs are carried on radio waves by two methods: AM and FM. AM radio waves carry information as a pattern of changes in their amplitude.

*Figure 19-3. Television and radio waves are sent to relay stations or satellites before reaching your home.*

ionosphere

relay satellite

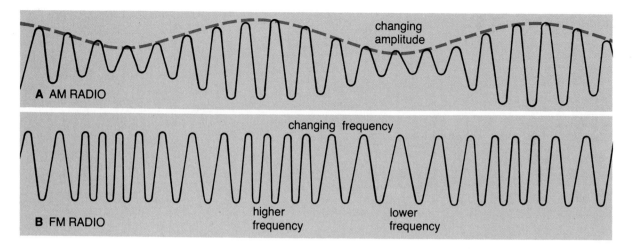

A  AM RADIO

changing
amplitude

changing  frequency

B  FM RADIO

higher
frequency

lower
frequency

*Figure 19-4. (top) Music may be transmitted by changing the amplitude.*

*Figure 19-5. (bottom) Music may also be transmitted by changing the frequency.*

See Figure 19-4. FM waves, as shown in Figure 19-5, carry information as a pattern of changes in their frequency. Television stations use high-frequency waves just as FM radio stations do. In general, television stations broadcast sound (audio) by AM waves. For the picture (video), they use FM radio waves. Many radio stations also use FM waves. FM signals do not have as much static noise as AM signals.

**Radar**   Some bats send out sound waves to find objects. They know an object's location by its echo. Echoes can also be made by using waves. The method is called radar, or RAdio Detecting And Ranging. Higher-frequency radio waves are ideal for radar because they reflect off most objects. They can even penetrate dense fog or rain.

A radar system measures the time of a round trip of a reflected radio wave. From these data the distance to the object is calculated. Radar systems can also measure the speed of an object. Many law enforcement agencies use radar to monitor vehicles on highways.

**Microwaves**   Microwaves are the highest-frequency radio waves. Microwaves are used for communication over short distances.

Because they are absorbed by most foods, microwaves are often used in cooking. And since energy is absorbed directly by the food, it cooks faster than more conventional methods take.

## Infrared Rays

When you stand in sunlight, it is the sun's *infrared* (IN•fruh•red) *rays* that warm you. **Infrared rays** *are electromagnetic waves with wavelengths between those of visible light and radio waves.*

All objects give off infrared rays, the amount depending on their temperature. Hot objects emit more infrared radiation than cool objects do. Thermometers, special photographic film, and electronic sensors can be used to detect infrared rays. Figure 19-6 shows a picture of a person taken with infrared rays.

## Ultraviolet Rays

**Ultraviolet rays** *are electromagnetic waves with wavelengths just shorter than those of visible light.* They make up the invisible part of the spectrum right next to violet light.

Ultraviolet rays can cause chemical changes. For example, ultraviolet rays produce vitamin D in your skin. Your body needs vitamin D to make healthy bones and teeth. They also make your skin produce a substance that gives you a tan. Ultraviolet rays can also kill germs. For this reason, many hospitals use ultraviolet rays to sterilize surgical equipment.

Ultraviolet rays can be detected by electronic devices and by *fluorescent* (floor•ES•uhnt) *materials.* **Fluorescent materials** *absorb ultraviolet rays and change some of the energy into visible light.* Fluorescent materials can sometimes produce interesting visual effects. See Figure 19-7.

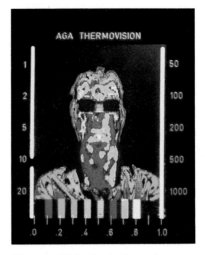

*Figure 19-6. An infrared photo shows that some parts of the body are warmer than others. Which part of the body shown is coolest?*

*Figure 19-7. The same mineral can look different when seen in daylight and under ultraviolet light.*

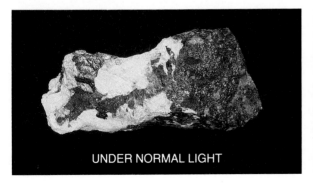

UNDER NORMAL LIGHT

UNDER ULTRAVIOLET LIGHT

## X Rays

*X rays* are electromagnetic waves with wavelengths just shorter than those of ultraviolet rays. They have higher frequencies than all the other waves you have been reading about. They have great penetrating power. As Figure 19-8 shows, most X rays pass right through an object. However, denser or thicker parts of an object tend to absorb X rays. Some substances, such as lead, are so dense that they absorb almost all the X rays that hit them. Special photographic films can detect and record X rays. The denser parts of an object show up as darker regions on the film. Refer again to Figure 19-8.

## Gamma Rays

*Gamma rays* have the shortest wavelengths of all electromagnetic waves. Gamma rays are emitted from the nuclei of some atoms such as cobalt. They also come from outer space. Gamma rays are even more penetrating than X rays. They can penetrate up to about 60 cm of concrete before being stopped. Gamma rays are used in medicine to destroy cancer cells.

*Figure 19-8. X rays help dentists locate cavities.*

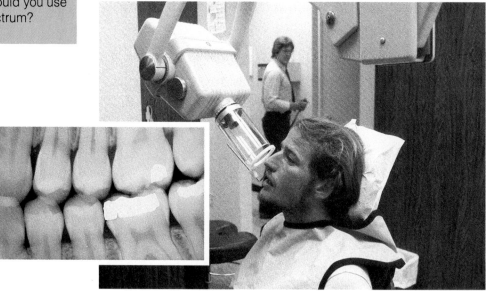

*Figure 19-9. Infrared waves can be used to determine the health of farm crops. Where is the city in this photograph?*

● Figure 19-9 is a photograph made by combining several satellite pictures. Each picture was made using a different color, or wavelength. The infrared wavelengths are used to detect the health and growth patterns of farm crops. A healthy crop radiates most of its electromagnetic energy at a slightly different infrared wavelength from that of a diseased crop. The planning and harvest of large farm crops are improved by the use of these satellite photographs.

**Why are infrared waves used to detect the health of crops?**

## OBJECTIVES AND WORDS TO REVIEW

1. How do electromagnetic waves differ from sound or water waves?
2. How are all electromagnetic waves alike? How do they differ?
3. Name four divisions of the electromagnetic spectrum and list properties of each division.
4. Write one complete sentence for each term listed below.

| | | |
|---|---|---|
| electromagnetic wave | infrared ray | X ray |
| photon | ultraviolet ray | gamma ray |
| radio wave | fluorescent material | |

# SIGNATURES OF MATTER

## OBJECTIVES

**1.** Relate an object's temperature to electromagnetic waves.
**2.** Compare and contrast two kinds of spectra.
**3.** Explain how spectra can identify matter.

What do electromagnetic waves emitted by an object depend on?

With just a little ink, you can make a set of fingerprints. Fingerprints can be used to identify people because no two people have the same set. In this section you will learn about a different kind of fingerprint. You will see how electromagnetic waves can provide a way of identifying substances.

## Electromagnetic Waves and Temperature

You have probably seen the glowing embers in a charcoal grill. But have you ever paid attention to these bricks of burnt wood? As a piece of charcoal heats up, it first glows a faint red, then a bright red, then yellow. However, long before you saw the ember's red glow, it was emitting infrared rays. You can feel the infrared rays as they are absorbed by your skin.

All objects—even a book and a snowball—give off electromagnetic waves. See Table 19-1. The waves emitted by an object depend on the object's temperature. At higher temperatures, electric charges on the surface of an object move about more rapidly. As they move more rapidly, the object emits waves with shorter wavelengths (and higher frequencies).

If a book emits electromagnetic waves, why do you not see them? Remember, only a small portion of the electromagnetic spectrum is visible. At room temperatures, materials give off mostly infrared rays. Your eyes are not sensitive to these wavelengths.

**TABLE 19-1.** TEMPERATURE AND THE ELECTROMAGNETIC SPECTRUM

| Object | Temperature of Object | Region of Electromagnetic Spectrum |
|---|---|---|
| Snowball | 0°C | infrared |
| Book | 20°C | infrared |
| Glowing hot metal | 5000°C | visible |

## Wavelengths From Atoms

At very high temperatures, gases begin to glow. Under certain conditions, solids and liquids at high temperatures vaporize and also begin to glow. The glow is light coming from the atoms of the elements that make up these materials. As the atoms are heated to high temperatures, they absorb energy. They give off the energy in the form of light. When this light is passed through a prism, patterns of lines show up instead of the usual spectrum of white light.

**Emission Spectra** An object as a whole gives off a range of wavelengths. However, a single atom in that object gives off only a few exact wavelengths. Each kind of atom gives off its own pattern of wavelengths. For example, the pattern of wavelengths given off by helium atoms differs from the pattern of all other atoms. Because patterns differ, you can identify atoms by the wavelengths they give off. Figure 19-10 shows the wavelength patterns for hydrogen and helium atoms. *The wavelength pattern given off by single atoms is called an* **emission spectrum.**

*Figure 19-10. The emission spectrum of hydrogen (top) and of helium (bottom). How do the two spectra differ?*

**A** EMISSION SPECTRUM OF HYDROGEN

low frequency                                                          high frequency

**B** EMISSION SPECTRUM OF HELIUM

low frequency                                                          high frequency

**The Hydrogen Atom** How does an atom produce an emission spectrum? In 1913 Niels Bohr presented a simple model. See Figure 19-11 on page 420.

The Bohr model shows the atom giving off photons. Each photon is a packet or bundle of energy with a

**HOW INDUSTRY
USES SPECTRA**

**OBJECTIVE**
Learn about some industrial uses of spectra.

**PROCEDURE**
Go to an optics laboratory or chemical plant and obtain the answers to the following questions.

**QUESTIONS**
**1.** What is a spectroscope? How does it work?
**2.** How is an emission spectrum or an absorption spectrum obtained?
**3.** How are these two kinds of spectra related?
**4.** What are some of the uses of spectra in industry?

particular wavelength. An atom gives off photons when an electron jumps from a higher energy level to a lower energy level. An orbiting electron can make only a few particular jumps between levels. It may jump, for example, from level 3 to level 2, or from level 3 to level 1. With each jump an electron makes, it gives off a photon with a particular wavelength. Each line in the spectrum in Figure 19-10 comes from photons given off when electrons make a particular jump.

**Absorption Spectra**   Atoms do not just give off electromagnetic energy. They also absorb it. As they absorb energy, electrons make jumps to higher orbits. See Figure 19-12. For example, an electron that absorbs energy may jump from level 1 to level 2, or level 2 to level 3. For each jump an electron makes, it absorbs a photon with a particular wavelength. Photons with wavelengths that are not absorbed pass right through the atom.

*The radiation pattern absorbed by single atoms is called an* **absorption spectrum.** Figure 19-12 is an absorption spectrum of hydrogen. The dark lines show the wavelengths that have been absorbed. Compare this spectrum with the emission spectrum of hydrogen in Figure 19-10.

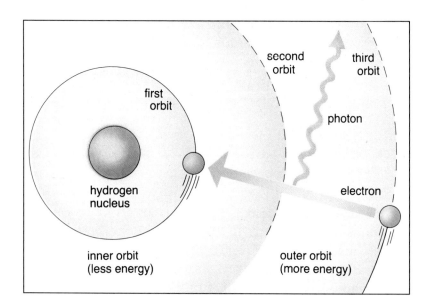

*Figure 19-11. When an electron drops from orbit 3 to orbit 1, it emits a photon.*

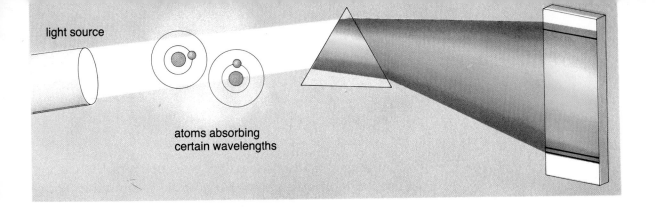

light source

atoms absorbing
certain wavelengths

## Waves or Particles?

You have learned that electromagnetic waves travel as photons. Photons, then, have properties of waves, such as interference. Yet if a photon hits an electron, it can bounce off like one marble bouncing off another marble. This bouncing is a property of particles!

Electrons, on the other hand, are particles. They can collide with other particles, just like one marble hitting another. However, electrons passing through a thin crystal produce an interference pattern. However, interference is a property of waves! Scientists need both wave and particle properties to explain how photons and electrons behave.

Scientists use absorption spectra to identify elements in stars. The spectrum of a star is actually a combination of spectra made by all the elements in the star. Scientists compare a star's spectrum with the spectra of elements on earth. By matching spectra they can identify elements in stars that are very far away. Figure 19-13**A** shows a spectrum of the metal sodium. Figure 19-13**B** shows a spectrum of a star. Does this star contain the metal sodium?

*Figure 19-12. How is this spectrum similar to an emission spectrum?*

*Figure 19-13. Spectra of stars can be compared with spectra of elements on earth. **A** shows the spectrum of sodium. Does the star in **B** contain sodium?*

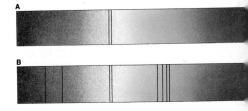

A

B

### OBJECTIVES AND WORDS TO REVIEW

1. When an object is heated to higher temperatures, how do wavelengths of emitted energy change?
2. How is an emission spectrum similar to an absorption spectrum? How are the two spectra different?
3. How can you use spectra to identify an element?
4. Write one complete sentence for each term listed below.
   emission spectrum   absorption spectrum

# ELECTROMAGNETIC WAVES: USES

**OBJECTIVES**

**1.** Name two kinds of electromagnetic waves used in medicine, and two kinds used in space studies.

**2.** Give two ways laser light differs from sunlight.

You may already be familiar with some of the uses of electromagnetic waves. Microwave ovens cook food. Ultraviolet rays kill germs. Infrared "heat lamps" help soothe aching muscles. But electromagnetic waves have other uses with which you may not be so familiar. This section will present some of these other uses.

## Imaging in Medicine

Doctors are always looking for new, more accurate ways of diagnosing medical problems. For example, they use X rays to find the location of a broken bone. However, X rays cannot show tissues. And they can be dangerous if used improperly. Scientists have found other wavelengths that can be used to study the human body.

**Gamma Cameras** A gamma camera forms an image of a patient's body by detecting gamma rays. The patient to be imaged is placed in the camera, as shown in Figure 19-14**A**. The patient is injected with a fluid

*Figure 19-14. Medical science is finding new ways to diagnose and treat disease by using electromagnetic waves.*

**A**

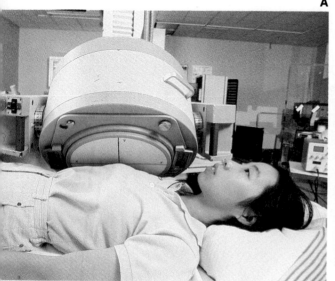

**B**

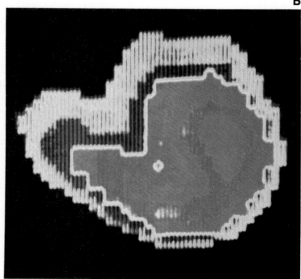

that emits gamma rays. The camera revolves around the patient in one plane, detecting the gamma rays. The image obtained resembles a slice taken from the body. See Figure 19-14B.

**MR Imaging**   Another way to see into the body is by using magnetic resonance imaging, abbreviated MRI. MRI uses radio waves and magnetic fields to obtain images. The patient is placed within a coil that makes a magnetic field. A beam of radio waves is transmitted into the patient. The waves cause hydrogen nuclei in the person's body to line up opposite to the direction of the magnetic field of the coil. When the radio waves are turned off, the nuclei return to their original alignment. As they return, the nuclei emit radio waves, which are detected by the machine. These waves form the image. See Figure 19-14C.

MRI has advantages over using gamma cameras. MRI does not use gamma rays. And it does not require the patient to be injected with a fluid. However, MRI also has some drawbacks. For example, images made with a gamma camera are clearer than images made using MRI. (Compare parts **B** and **C**.) However, scientists are confident that this and other problems will be solved.

List two advantages of MRI over gamma cameras.

C

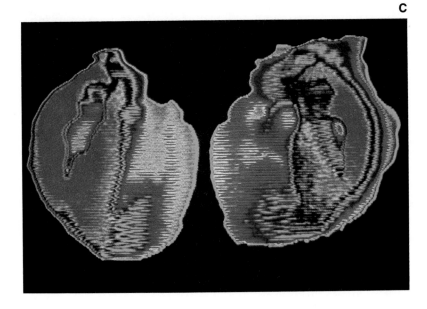

## Space Studies

Before space flight, astronomers could only study the universe with ground-based telescopes. These instruments were sensitive only to visible and radio wavelengths. Now, rockets carry telescopes outside earth's atmosphere. These instruments have taken photos of the sky in all wavelengths, from radio waves through gamma rays. Figure 19-15 displays an ultraviolet photograph of the sun. Photographs like these have helped astronomers learn about the composition of the sun's atmosphere.

Astronomers also study the sky in the infrared region of the electromagnetic spectrum. The infrared photos in Figure 19-16 show jets of gas being emitted by a quasar (KWAY•zahr). Quasars appear to be galaxies moving away from the earth at nearly the speed of light. By studying the infrared photographs, astronomers measured the speed of these jets of gas.

SIZE OF EARTH

*Figure 19-15. This ultraviolet photo of the sun gives scientists information not available in other kinds of photographs.*

## Lasers: A Special Source of Light

You have read about electronic instruments that amplify sounds. Scientists have built *a device that amplifies light, a **laser.*** A laser concentrates a great deal of

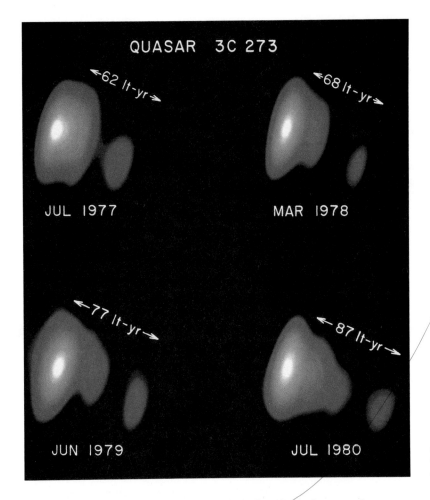

QUASAR 3C 273

←62 lt-yr→

JUL 1977

←68 lt-yr→

MAR 1978

←77 lt-yr→

JUN 1979

← 87 lt-yr→

JUL 1980

*Figure 19-16. What do the different positions of the jets of gas indicate?*

energy into a narrow beam of light that does not spread. A laser produces a pencil-thin beam of light that travels in one direction. This property makes laser light quite different from light from a lightbulb or from the sun. Ordinary light spreads out in many directions as it travels.

Laser light also differs from other light because of its wavelengths. Light from a glowing object is made of a range of wavelengths. For example, the light from the sun is yellow. But you know that it also shines in the ultraviolet, infrared, X ray, and so forth. Light from a laser, on the other hand, contains a very narrow range of wavelengths. So a laser may emit light only in the infrared or visible or ultraviolet.

**How does laser light differ from other kinds of light?**

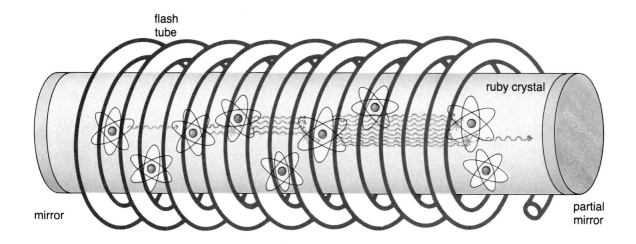

flash tube

ruby crystal

mirror

partial mirror

*Figure 19-17. Diagram of a laser. What causes the normal atoms to become excited?*

Figure 19-17 shows one of the earliest kinds of lasers. It contains a solid rod made of ruby crystal. Each end of the rod has a mirror. However, one of the mirrors is a partial mirror. That is, not all of the light that hits it will be reflected. Very strong light will pass through it. Coiled around the rod is a tube called a flash tube. Atoms in the ruby will absorb the energy provided by the flash tube. It is this absorption of energy that is important to the operation of the laser.

To understand how a laser works, think about the electrons in orbit around an atom. Refer again to Figure 19-17. When an atom absorbs energy, an electron moves to a higher energy level. Very quickly the electron returns to its original energy level. As it drops down, it releases a photon of light. This photon then interacts with an electron from another excited atom, causing it to jump to a lower level. Another photon is emitted, with the same wavelength as the first.

**When an atom absorbs energy, what happens to its electrons?**

The process is repeated over and over. As more photons are released, the light builds up, or amplifies. The released photons travel back and forth along the rod. They reflect off a mirror at each end. However, the light in the rod soon becomes strong enough to pass through the thinner mirror at one end. An intense beam of laser light is then emitted.

● The unusual properties of laser light make lasers very valuable. Laser light does not spread out like normal light does. So laser light can be focused to a pinpoint. The focusing also concentrates the energy of the light into a point. Very high temperatures are produced. Industry uses this property of laser light to melt extremely hard materials. See Figure 19-18.

Lasers are also used in medicine. The high temperatures produced allow surgeons to repair ruptured blood vessels in the eye.

## OBJECTIVES AND WORDS TO REVIEW

1. Name two kinds of electromagnetic waves used in medicine. Name two kinds used in space studies.
2. What is a laser? How does laser light differ from sunlight?
3. Write a complete sentence for the term below.
   laser

**Figure 19-18.** *The energy in a laser beam can melt the hardest metals.*

# X Rays Vs Terrorism

If you have ever traveled by air, you probably have put your luggage through X-ray machines. These machines can detect metal guns hidden in the luggage. The X-ray machine was a very useful protection against terrorism. Then, plastic guns made their appearance. Plastic cannot be detected by "ordinary" X-ray devices. Their X rays pass right through plastic as if it were not there.

However, a company has developed a device called the "Model Z" X-ray machine. The machine produces a thin beam of X rays that scan luggage. Together with a computer, the machine creates an image of the plastic weapons on the screen. A guard operating the new machine can see *everything* in a passenger's bags.

### Using Critical Thinking

Suppose a passenger refused to allow his/her baggage to be X-rayed. Does the passenger have any basis for objection? Does an airline company have a right to say that a passenger cannot fly unless the luggage is X-rayed? What do you think?

# EXPANDING YOUR SCIENTIFIC VOCABULARY

## Preparation
What does the word *intramural* mean? One way to find out is to break the word up into parts. The word *intramural* is made up of the prefix *intra* (within), the root *mura* (wall), and the adjective suffix *al* (action). So, intramural sports are sports that take place within the (school) walls.

As scientific knowledge increases, new terms are constantly appearing. However, you can still learn the meaning of these words by breaking them apart into prefixes, roots, and suffixes.

## Directions
To learn the meaning of an unfamiliar science term, follow these steps.

*Step 1* Divide the word into prefix, root, and suffix.

*Step 2* Write down the meaning of each part.

*Step 3* Combine or rearrange the meanings to form the meaning of the entire word.

For example, Figure 1 shows how these steps are applied. When you divide the word

*photograph,* you find it means "light writing." A photograph does use light to produce an image.

*Figure 1.*

| | |
|---|---|
| STEP 1 | PHOTO GRAPH |
| STEP 2 | LIGHT ⌄ WRITING |
| STEP 3 | LIGHT WRITING |

## Practice
Table 1 gives some common prefixes, roots, and suffixes used in physical science. On a separate sheet of paper, break each of the terms below, using Figure 1 as a guide. Then, using Table 1, write the meaning of the term.

ultraviolet    saline    geothermal
electroscope    infrared    diatomic

## Application
The following terms are found in the laboratory activity for this chapter. On a separate sheet of paper, break up each of the terms, using Table 1 and a dictionary. Then write down the meaning.

solution    hydrochloric    hydroxide
chloride    electrolyte

**TABLE 1.** PREFIXES, ROOTS, AND SUFFIXES COMMONLY USED IN PHYSICAL SCIENCE

| | | | | | |
|---|---|---|---|---|---|
| **al** | action; characteristic of | **hydro** | water | **poly** | many |
| **ate** | object of an action | **ic, ical** | relating to, belonging to | **sal** | salt |
| **bi, di** | two | | | **sci** | know |
| **carbo** | carbon | **ine** | like | **scope** | instrument for observing |
| **electro** | electric | **infra** | below, beneath | **son** | sound |
| **endo** | inner | **logy** | study of | **super** | above |
| **exo** | outer | **mer** | a part | **techno** | art, skill |
| **geo** | earth | **photo** | light | **thermo** | heat |
| **graph** | writing | **physi** | nature | **ultra** | beyond |

# LABORATORY ACTIVITY

## OBSERVING ELECTROMAGNETIC WAVES

### Objective
Investigate the electromagnetic radiation given off by a lamp.

### Background
You can use a thermometer to detect some of the regions of the electromagnetic spectrum. When some electromagnetic waves strike a thermometer, they transfer energy to the thermometer. As a result, the thermometer shows a rise in temperature. However, not all of these electromagnetic waves affect the thermometer equally.

### Materials
prism, lamp and convex lens, cardboard shoe box, black paint, sensitive thermometer, scissors

**Figure 19-L.** *Laboratory setup.*

### Procedure
1. Arrange the materials as shown in Figure 19-L. Adjust the prism until the entire spectrum is on the back of the cardboard box. Paint the thermometer bulb to make it absorb all the radiation that hits it.
2. Place the thermometer bulb at various parts of the spectrum. Be sure to place the thermometer at points beyond each side of the visible spectrum. Allow a few minutes for the thermometer to register the temperature.
3. Make a table showing the increase in temperature for each part of the spectrum.

### Questions
1. Where is the "hottest" part of the spectrum?
2. Did you detect infrared or ultraviolet waves? How do you know?
3. **PROBLEM SOLVING** Repeat the experiment with a bottle of water in front of the prism (outside the box). Does water absorb infrared waves? How can you check if the bottle itself absorbs infrared waves? Try other liquids besides water.

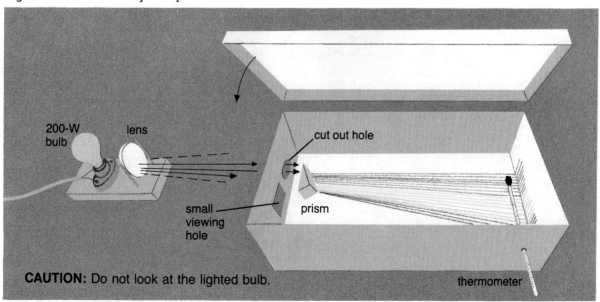

200-W bulb
lens
cut out hole
small viewing hole
prism
thermometer

**CAUTION:** Do not look at the lighted bulb.

Have you ever opened a pocket radio to see what was inside? Have you wondered how televisions produce images? Do you enjoy listening to music? If you have these interests, you might look into the careers below.

**Recording Engineer** Recording engineers reproduce sounds for television, films, and records. Their challenge is to record a full range of pitches of an orchestra, voices, and other sounds. The volume levels of the recording must be as loud and as quiet as the actual sounds.

To become a recording engineer, you need special two-to-four-year college programs. Your training will grow as you work in an actual recording studio. In this career practice makes perfect.

For more information on this career, write:

*The National Association of Broadcast Employees and Technicians*
*7101 Wisconsin Avenue, Suite 800*
*Bethesda, MD 20814*

**Television Technician** Television technicians repair faulty and broken electronic video products. Mostly they fix televisions, but some technicians also work on tape recorders and videodisc players.

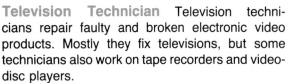

Television technicians usually work in repair shops or in homes. Some, however, work in industrial plants where home entertainment and other electronic products are made.

To become a television technician, you must train for from two to four years. This training usually is done in a vocational school or a junior college. Training includes taking science courses and on-the-job experience. Some technicians start out as assistants or apprentices. Others take special courses offered by employers and trade organizations.

To find out more information about a career as a television technician, write:

*International Brotherhood of Electrical Workers*
*1125 15th Street, NW*
*Washington, DC 20005*

# SUMMARY

1. Electromagnetic waves are transverse waves that travel through a vacuum at $3.00 \times 10^8$ meters per second. (19-1)
2. The electromagnetic spectrum consists of radio waves, infrared rays, visible light, ultraviolet rays, x rays, gamma rays. (19-1)
3. An emission spectrum is the radiation pattern given off by single atoms. An absorption spectrum is the radiation pattern absorbed by single atoms. (19-2)
4. The Bohr model of the atom describes how electrons can jump from one orbit to another. As they jump, electrons emit photons. (19-2)
5. Electromagnetic waves are used in many fields, from medicine to astronomy. (19-3)
6. Lasers are devices that amplify light. They cause photons released by an excited atom to trigger a similar release in other excited atoms. (19-3)

# REVIEW

Number a sheet of paper from 1 to 25 and answer these questions.

**Building Science Vocabulary**     Write the letter of the term that best matches each definition.

a. absorption spectrum
b. emission spectrum
c. fluorescent material
d. gamma
e. infrared
f. laser
g. microwave
h. photon
i. radar
j. radio
k. ultraviolet
l. x ray

1. Electromagnetic radiation that can be used for cooking
2. Invisible wavelengths lying next to the red region of visible spectrum
3. A packet or bundle of electromagnetic waves
4. Absorbs ultraviolet rays and then changes some of the energy into visible light
5. Radio detecting and ranging
6. Electromagnetic waves having the shortest wavelengths
7. Electromagnetic wavelengths responsible for sun tans
8. A device that amplifies light
9. Long electromagnetic waves that carry music
10. A pattern of electromagnetic waves given off by single atoms

**Finding the Facts**     Select the letter of the answer that best completes each of the following.

11. Of the following, the wave with the shortest wavelength is     (a) microwave     (b) x ray     (c) infrared     (d) visible light.
12. All electromagnetic waves     (a) travel with different speeds     (b) have the same frequency but different wavelengths     (c) can travel through a vacuum     (d) have the same wavelengths.
13. Radar is used     (a) to kill germs     (b) to take "pictures" of the interior of your teeth     (c) to warm food     (d) to find the distance to an object.
14. Electromagnetic waves are     (a) produced by vibrating charges     (b) produced by electrons in atoms changing their orbits     (c) produced by high-speed electrons orbiting the nucleus     (d) all of the above.
15. The electromagnetic wave with the longest wavelength is     (a) radio     (b) x ray     (c) gamma     (d) infrared.
16. Which electromagnetic wave produces vitamin D in your skin?     (a) ultraviolet     (b) infrared     (c) visible light     (d) radio
17. Which kind of radio wave carries information by changing the frequency of the electromagnetic wave?     (a) radar     (b) microwave     (c) FM     (d) AM

18. When an electron jumps to a higher energy level, it **(a)** loses energy **(b)** emits energy **(c)** spirals into the nucleus **(d)** absorbs energy.

19. A device that uses radio waves to form an image is a **(a)** gamma camera **(b)** MRI camera **(c)** quasar **(d)** x-ray machine.

20. A device that provides the energy that runs a laser is a **(a)** flash tube **(b)** ruby crystal **(c)** gamma camera **(d)** none of the above.

**Understanding Main Ideas** Complete the following.

21. Transverse waves that can travel through a vacuum are known as __?__.

22. A radio wave that carries information by changes in its amplitude is __?__.

23. The wavelengths emitted by an object depend on its __?__.

24. The radiation pattern absorbed by single atoms is called __?__.

25. Galaxies that appear to be moving away from the earth at nearly the speed of light are __?__.

**Writing About Science** On a separate sheet of paper, answer the following as completely as possible.

1. Describe how an astronomer can use electromagnetic waves to find the distance to the planet Venus.

2. You have learned that laser light can be focused to produce great heat. How might this property of laser light be used in medicine?

3. Diseased tissues are warmer than healthy tissues. How could hospitals use electromagnetic waves to detect diseased tissues?

4. How can electromagnetic radiation explain why a mosquito can locate you even when it is completely dark?

5. (laboratory question) Suppose you were a doctor looking at a photo like the one in Figure 19-6. Which part of the person's body is warmer? Why? (Use what you learned in the laboratory activity.)

**Investigating Chapter Ideas** Try one of the following projects to further your study.

1. **A shoebox spectroscope** Cut a 2-cm opening at one end of a shoebox. Tape a small square of diffraction grating plastic over the opening. At the other end of the shoebox, cut a *narrow* slit about 2 cm high. The slit should be parallel to the grating pattern. Point the box at a bright lamp and look through the diffraction grating end. Be sure the lid is on. Move the box back and forth until a spectrum appears to the side of the slit at the other end. If a spectrum is not visible, retape the grating turned 90° from its original position. Use your spectroscope to examine light from street-lamps, fluorescent lights, and moonlight. **CAUTION:** Do not look at the sun with this device. Sketch the spectra you see and discuss them in class. Explain why the spectra appear the way they do.

2. **Holograms** Laser beams can be used to make three-dimensional images called holograms. Construct a display showing how holograms are produced.

**Reading About Science** Read some of the following books to explore topics that interest you.

Burroughs, William. 1982. **Lasers.** New York: Warwick.

Maurer, Allen. 1982. **Lasers: Light Wave of the Future.** New York: Arco.

Pringle, Laurence. 1983. **Radiation: Waves and Particles/Benefits and Risks.** Hillside, NJ: Enslow.

White, Jack R. 1984. **The Invisible World of the Infrared.** New York: Dodd.

# ENERGY

Imagine a colony in outer space orbiting a quarter of a million miles from the earth! Imagine energy obtained from ores that have been mined on the moon or from particles coming directly from the sun! In this unit you will study some of the many forms of energy that people rely on. You will also investigate some of the alternatives that scientists hope will provide energy in the future.

If you rub your hands together, they get hotter. Their temperature rises. What causes this effect?

The *Space Shuttles* are covered with protective tiles. Look at the photos that show the shuttle after landing. Why are the tiles needed?

Your hands and the shuttle are both doing the same thing. They are moving. Motion and temperature are related. The more rapid the motion is, the higher the temperature. Thus, as you rub your hands faster, the temperature rises. And the shuttle is moving fast enough to make even its tiles burn. Imagine what would happen to the ship if the tiles were not there! In this chapter you will find out more about motion and temperature.

Read and Find Out:

● what factor affects home heating systems.

● how a change of state cools air in a refrigerator.

● how a jet plane moves.

# HEAT

# HEAT: A TRANSFER OF ENERGY

**OBJECTIVES**

**1.** Relate temperature to kinetic energy.
**2.** Define heat and temperature.
**3.** List three kinds of energy transfer.

What does the word *heat* mean to you? Does it mean the same thing as *temperature?* A simple example may help you to see a difference between these two. If you roast a hot dog on a metal rod, you hold one end of the rod and put the other end over a fire. In a few minutes, the end you are holding gets hot. This example can serve as a model for what scientists call *heat.*

## Temperature and Heat

Why does the end of a metal rod get hot? To find out, look at a model showing the molecules that make up the rod. See Figure 20-1**A**. The molecules in a solid rod or in any form of matter are moving. All molecules have a certain amount of kinetic energy, the energy of motion. ***Temperature** is a measure of the average kinetic energy of the molecules in a material.*

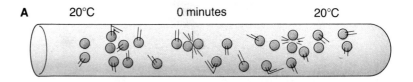

A    20°C      0 minutes      20°C

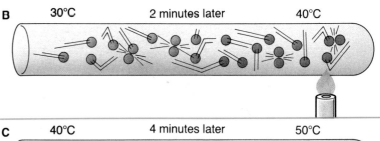

B    30°C      2 minutes later      40°C

C    40°C      4 minutes later      50°C

*Figure 20-1. The movement of molecules transfers energy from the flame through the rod. How does the temperature of each end of the rod change in time?*

**Figure 20-2.** *Heated air rises, transferring energy upward. As you look through the rising air, the background seems to shimmer.*

The flame is a source of kinetic energy. The tip of the rod held over the flame absorbs kinetic energy. The molecules in the tip move faster and faster. The temperature of the tip increases. See Figure 20-1**B**.

The faster molecules begin to collide with slower molecules to the left. When they collide, the faster molecules transfer kinetic energy to the slower molecules, making them speed up. As the slower molecules speed up they, in turn, collide with their neighbors.

The collisions continue along the rod toward the end you are holding. The temperature at that end is much lower than the temperature of the tip in the flame. But as kinetic energy is transferred to the end you are holding, the molecules speed up. See Figure 20-1**C**. And the temperature increases.

Why does a handle of a metal rod heat up if the opposite end is held over a flame?

So the end you hold gets hotter because of a transfer of energy. *Transfer* is the basis for understanding what is meant by *heat*. **Heat** *is the energy transferred between materials (or parts of a material) that have different temperatures.* See Figure 20-2.

## Three Kinds of Transfer

The collisions in a solid rod are only one model of energy transfer. Energy can be transferred through various forms of matter in three different ways.

**OBJECTIVE**
Watch convection in action.

**MATERIALS**
glass pot, water, range or hot plate, sourball candy

**PROCEDURE**
**CAUTION:** Do this activity under an adult's supervision.
**1.** Half fill the glass pot with water. Place it over the range or hot plate. The source of heat should be under one side of the pot.
**2.** Gently drop the candy at the corner of the pot directly over the source of heat. Turn the flame on. Observe what happens.

**QUESTIONS**
**1.** What happened to the candy after you placed it in the water?
**2.** What is this effect called?

**Conduction** The kind of energy transfer that took place in the solid rod is *conduction*. **Conduction** *is the transfer of energy from molecule to molecule by collisions.* Can you see how conduction is taking place in Figure 20-3**A**?

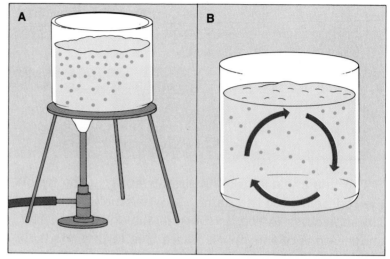

*Figure 20-3. Conduction (**A**) and convection (**B**). Which kind of energy transfer involves a current?*

Molecules of gases absorb kinetic energy from the flame. These molecules speed up and collide with molecules of the beaker. Molecules of the beaker, in turn, collide with water molecules along the bottom of the beaker. The collisions transfer kinetic energy from one substance to the next.

**Convection** Most of the water in the beaker is heated by a second kind of energy transfer, *convection* (kuhn•VEK•shuhn). **Convection** *is the transfer of energy by the flow of a liquid or gas.* In Figure 20-3**B** convection starts where water is heated by the flame at the bottom of the beaker. As the molecules are heated, they move faster and spread apart, or expand. When the molecules expand, the density of the water decreases. The warm water, less dense than cooler water around it, rises.

The rising water carries energy to the top. A constant flow is set up as cooler, denser water sinks to the bottom and is heated. *The flow within a fluid due to changes in density is a* **convection current.**

**Radiation**   A fireplace provides another kind of energy transfer, *radiation.* **Radiation** *is the transfer of energy by electromagnetic waves.* Electromagnetic waves, you may recall, can travel through space as well as through air and other kinds of matter. When sunlight warms you, the sun's energy is reaching you by radiation through 15 million kilometers of space. The warmth you feel when you stand in front of an electric heater is also due to radiation.

By which kind of energy transfer does sunlight reach earth?

## Household Heating Systems

Various kinds of energy transfer are used to heat homes and buildings. Many heating systems, as in Figure 20-4**A,** use steam to warm rooms. A furnace heats water to boiling. The steam moves through baseboard pipes. Energy from the steam is transferred throughout the air in a room by convection and radiation. As energy is transferred from the steam, the steam cools and condenses into liquid water. The liquid water returns to the boiler. It is heated to boiling again and the cycle is repeated.

Some systems use hot air to heat rooms. See Figure 20-4**B.** A furnace heats the air. A blower directs the

*Figure 20-4. In* **A** *and* **B,** *heat is transferred by conduction from the pipes to the air touching the pipes. How is heat transferred throughout the room?*

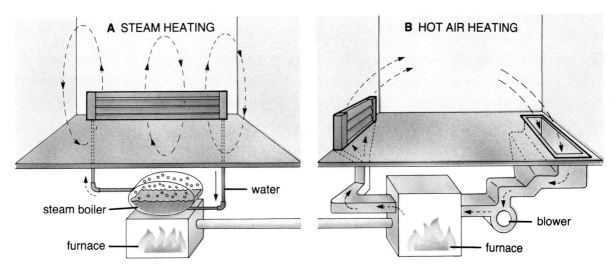

**A** STEAM HEATING

water

steam boiler

furnace

**B** HOT AIR HEATING

blower

furnace

*Figure 20-5. Insulating material is used to fill in spaces in walls. These materials oppose the flow of energy through the walls. What effect do they have in the summer? In the winter?*

hot air through pipes called ducts to each room. The air cools off when energy is transferred out of it to the rooms. Ducts lead the cool air back to the furnace. The air is reheated and the cycle is repeated.

● The effectiveness of your home's heating system depends on the use of insulating materials. Insulating materials such as those in Figure 20-5 help retain heat. That is, they help prevent the transfer of energy to the outdoors. Poorly insulated homes waste energy by having to burn too much fuel to replace the energy that is lost to the outdoors.

### OBJECTIVES AND WORDS TO REVIEW

**1.** How is kinetic energy related to temperature?
**2.** How does heat differ from temperature?
**3.** Name three kinds of energy transfer.
**4.** Write one complete sentence for each term listed below.

| | | |
|---|---|---|
| temperature | conduction | convection current |
| heat | convection | radiation |

# MEASURING HEAT

Do you think it is possible to measure something that you cannot even see? For example, if you leave a cup of cold water in sunlight, the water absorbs, or gains, heat. Of course, you cannot see heat being transferred into the water. But is there a way to find out just how much heat the water absorbs?

You cannot measure heat directly. But you can measure changes in temperature. In this section you will measure changes in temperature to find out how much heat is transferred into or out of a substance.

## Specific Heat

It takes different amounts of heat to change the temperatures of equal masses of different substances. See Figure 20-6. Substances that warm up slowly absorb large amounts of heat for each degree the temperature rises. When a substance cools off, it releases heat. Substances that cool slowly lose large amounts of heat for each degree the temperature drops.

**OBJECTIVES**

**1.** Calculate the heat lost or gained by an object.
**2.** State a law relating heat loss and heat gain.
**3.** Relate a change in temperature to a change of phase.

*Figure 20-6. Although these materials are heated at the same rate, their temperatures increase at different rates. Which material has the greatest rate of temperature increase?*

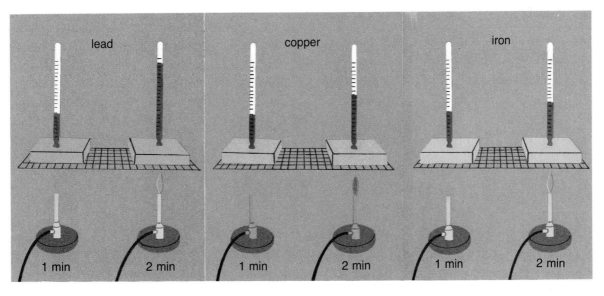

## TABLE 20-1. SPECIFIC HEAT

| Material | Specific Heat (J/g · C°) |
|----------|--------------------------|
| Water | 4.18 |
| Iron | 0.45 |
| Copper | 0.39 |
| Silver | 0.24 |
| Lead | 0.13 |

Each material has its own *specific heat*. **Specific heat** *is the amount of heat needed to change the temperature of 1 g of a substance 1 C°.* Water has the highest specific heat of all the substances on Table 20-1. Water warms up and cools off slowest of all these substances.

Note that the unit for specific heat is a combination of three units. The specific heat of water, for example, is 4.18 J/g · C°. That is, when one gram of water rises in temperature by 1 C°, it has absorbed 4.18 joules of heat. When one gram of water goes down in temperature by 1 C°, it gives off 4.18 joules.

## Calculating Heat Gain and Heat Loss

By using specific heat, you can find the amount of heat a substance absorbs when it is being warmed. First, you have to make three simple measurements. Measure the mass and temperature of the substance before you heat it. And measure the temperature again when you have finished heating it. Then use this formula:

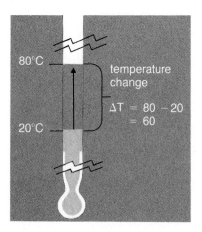

*Figure 20-7. The change in temperature (ΔT) is found by subtracting the lower temperature from the higher temperature.*

$$\text{Heat} = \text{mass} \times \begin{array}{c}\text{temperature} \\ \text{change}\end{array} \times \begin{array}{c}\text{specific} \\ \text{heat}\end{array}$$
$$= \text{m} \times \Delta\text{T} \times c_P$$

In this equation, $c_P$ represents the specific heat and ΔT means "the change in temperature." For example, a sheet of aluminum foil has a mass of 20 g. At first, it is at room temperature, about 20°C. You leave it in a heated oven until its temperature is 80°C. (So the temperature went up by 60 C°. See Figure 20-7.) How much heat did the aluminum foil absorb? The specific heat of aluminum is 0.92 J/g · C°. So:

$$\text{Heat Gain} = \text{m} \times \Delta\text{T} \times c_P$$
$$= 20 \text{ g} \times 60 \text{ C°} \times 0.92 \text{ J/g} \cdot \text{C°}$$
$$= 1{,}104 \text{ J}$$

You can use the same formula to find how much heat a substance loses when it cools off. Suppose you take the aluminum foil in the previous example away from the heated oven. The temperature drops from 80°C to 30°C, or 50 C°. How much heat did the foil lose?

$$\text{Heat Loss} = m \times \Delta T \times c_P$$
$$= 20 \text{ g} \times 50C° \times 0.92 \text{ J/g} \cdot C°$$
$$= 920 \text{ J}$$

What is the formula used to calculate heat loss or gain?

## A Law of Conservation

You have seen that when you heat an object, it gains energy. When the object cools off, it loses energy. Figure 20-8 shows that the heat loss and heat gain between two or more substances are related.

The setup in **A** shows two insulated cups of water connected by an insulated metal bar. CUP 1 has 100 g of water at 80°C. CUP 2 has 100 g of water at 60°C. What has happened to the temperature of each cup after an hour passes, as you see in **B**?

The temperature of CUP 1 dropped by 10 C° to 70°C. The temperature of CUP 2 rose by 10 C° to 70°C. Can you tell why the temperatures changed? CUP 1 was originally at a higher temperature than CUP 2. Energy

*Figure 20-8. Heat gain in one part of a system is equal to heat loss in another part of the system. How is energy transferred in this system?*

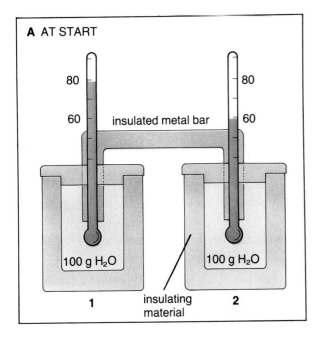

A AT START

insulated metal bar

100 g H₂O

100 g H₂O

insulating material

1

2

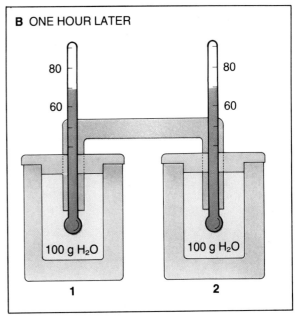

B ONE HOUR LATER

100 g H₂O

100 g H₂O

1

2

**OBJECTIVE**
Compare temperature scales currently in use.

**PROCEDURE**
In the library read about the Fahrenheit, Celsius, and Kelvin temperature scales. Answer the questions below.

**QUESTIONS**
**1.** How did each temperature scale get its name?
**2.** What is the boiling point of water in each scale at one atmosphere?
**3.** What is the freezing point of water in each scale?
**4.** How do you convert from Celsius to Kelvin degrees?
**5.** How do you convert from Fahrenheit to Celsius degrees?

was transferred from CUP 1 to CUP 2 by way of the metal bar. CUP 1 lost heat. CUP 2, on the other hand, gained heat. When both cups reached the same temperature, energy was no longer transferred.

Now find the heat lost by CUP 1 and the heat gained by CUP 2. And compare the two amounts.

CUP 1

$$\Delta T = 10 \text{ C}°$$
$$\text{Heat Loss} = \quad m \quad \times \quad \Delta T \quad \times c_P$$
$$= 100 \text{ g} \times 10 \text{ C}° \times 4.18 \text{ J/g} \cdot \text{C}°$$
$$= 4,180 \text{ J}$$

CUP 2

$$\Delta T = 10 \text{ C}°$$
$$\text{Heat Gain} = \quad m \quad \times \quad \Delta T \quad \times c_P$$
$$= 100 \text{ g} \times 10 \text{ C}° \times 4.18 \text{ J/g} \cdot \text{C}°$$
$$= 4,180 \text{ J}$$

The amounts are equal. The heat lost by one material in the insulated system is equal to the heat gained by the other materials in the system. These results agree with the ***Law of Conservation of Energy.*** The total energy of an object or a group of objects stays the same.

## Change of Phase

When an ice cube melts or water boils, a change of phase takes place. What makes a material change its phase? A change of phase, as Figure 20-9 shows, involves heat transfer—either heat gain or heat loss.

**Heat Gain**   When an ice cube absorbs heat, its molecules vibrate faster and faster. The temperature rises. When the ice cube reaches 0°C, it keeps on absorbing heat. But its temperature stops rising. Why does the temperature stop rising even though the cube is gaining heat?

The answer is that the ice cube is melting. The absorbed heat enables the molecules of the ice to break away from their crystal structure. The temperature does not rise again until all the ice is melted. *The heat needed to change one gram of a material from a solid*

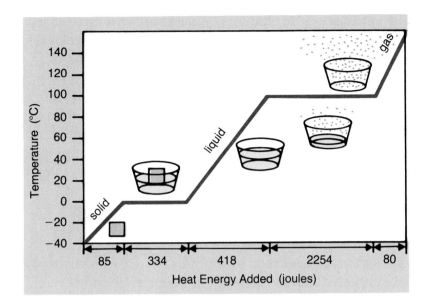

**Figure 20-9.** *From left to right the graph shows how a gram of ice changes phase when it is heated. What does the graph show if you read it from right to left?*

*into a liquid is the* **heat of fusion.** As Table 20-2 shows, it takes 205 joules to melt 1 gram of copper at its melting point.

After all the ice has melted, the temperature of the liquid water rises once again. However, at 100°C another change of phase occurs and the temperature stops rising. The liquid is evaporating. The absorbed heat enables the molecules to break the bonds that held them together in the liquid phase. *The heat needed to change 1 gram of a liquid into a gas is called the* **heat of vaporization** (vay•pur•i•ZAY•shuhn). See Table 20-2.

When does the temperature of heated water stop rising?

**TABLE 20-2.** HEATS OF FUSION AND VAPORIZATION

| Material | Heat of Fusion (J/g) | Heat of Vaporization (J/g) |
|---|---|---|
| Water | 334 | 2254 |
| Aluminum | 393 | 10,544 |
| Iron | 33 | 6694 |
| Copper | 205 | 4812 |
| Silver | 108.8 | 2364 |
| Mercury | 11.8 | 295.4 |
| Lead | 22.9 | 866 |

**Figure 20-10.** *Why does liquid Freon evaporate as it circulates around the freezer?*

**Heat Loss**   The changes of phase are reversed when a substance cools down. When a gas cools off, it releases energy and condenses back to a liquid. Each gram of gas releases an amount of heat equal to the heat of vaporization. If the liquid continues releasing heat, it changes back into a solid. Each gram of the liquid releases an amount of heat equal to its heat of fusion. Turn to page 564 for an illustrated description of how molecular motion can be used to explain phase changes.

● A change of phase is used to cool the inside of a refrigerator. As Figure 20-10 shows, liquid Freon—$CCl_2F_2$—is stored in a tank. A pump pushes the liquid Freon through pipes into the freezer. Here it changes into a gas. As the Freon evaporates, each gram absorbs 167 joules of energy, the heat of vaporization for Freon. The Freon takes this energy from the air inside the freezer. So the air in the freezer gets cold. After the Freon evaporates, it flows away from the freezer to the pump. The Freon is changed back into a liquid as it flows through narrow coils. Then the cycle starts over.

Another kind of cooling system is an air conditioner. An air conditioner cools the inside of a room in a manner similar to that of a refrigerator. Turn to page 565 for an illustrated description of cooling with an air conditioner.

**OBJECTIVES AND WORDS TO REVIEW**

1. Suppose 20 grams of silver are heated from 20 °C to 120 °C. How much heat does the silver absorb?
2. State a law relating heat loss to heat gain.
3. Why does the temperature of a material remain constant during a change of phase?
4. Write one complete sentence for each term listed below.
   specific heat      heat of vaporization      heat of fusion

# HEAT CAUSES EXPANSION

Why do you think there are separations in the road-way of a bridge? See Figure 20-11. These separations have been placed there to avoid a problem that heat can cause. Heat affects materials in different ways, as you will see in this section.

## Expansion in Solids

High-tension wires sag in the summer. The summer heat makes the wires expand. Most matter expands in response to heat. This response explains why spaces are left in bridge roadways. If no space is left for the roadway to expand into, the surface will buckle.

Scientists have developed a model to explain why solids expand when heated. The molecules in a solid vibrate about fixed positions. As energy is added to a solid, its temperature increases. That is, the molecules' kinetic energy—and speed—increase. The molecules vibrate faster and move farther away from their fixed positions. As the molecules separate, the solid expands.

**OBJECTIVES**

**1.** Explain how heat affects matter.
**2.** Explain how changes in pressure, volume, and temperature affect a gas.
**3.** Name the four cycles that operate a gas engine.

**Explain why solids expand when heated.**

*Figure 20-11. Cracks are left in sidewalks for the same reason as separations in a bridge. Heat makes concrete expand.*

*Figure 20-12. The strip bends because the metals expand at different rates when heated.*

Different materials expand at different rates. This property is shown by a bimetallic strip. The bimetallic strip is made of two metals fused together. Each metal expands at a different rate. See Figure 20-12.

## Expansion in Liquids

Like the molecules of a solid, the molecules of a liquid also move apart when they are heated. The mercury thermometer is a common everyday example. As heat is transferred to the bulb, the mercury molecules speed up and move apart. The liquid expands. You interpret this expansion as a rise in temperature.

## Expansion in Gases

A tightly sealed can containing water may explode if heated too long. See Figure 20-13. At 100°C the water changes into steam. As the temperature of the steam rises, molecules move about faster. They hit the sides of the can harder, exerting a greater force on the sides. The faster the molecules move, the greater the force they exert. If the force becomes great enough, it makes the can split apart at the seams. The can explodes.

As the gas molecules hit the sides of the can with increasing force, the *pressure* is said to build up. **Pressure** *is the force exerted on each unit of area of a*

*Figure 20-13. What happens to water molecules in the can the longer they are heated?*

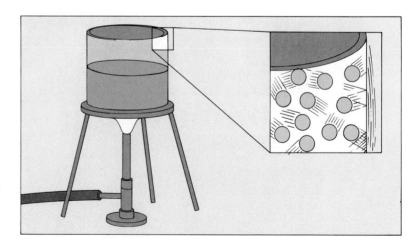

*surface. Pressure is measured in a unit called the* **pascal** *(pas•KAL). One pascal (Pa) is equal to one new-ton of force pushing on one square meter of area.*

## The Gas Laws

You have read about the volume, temperature, and pressure of a gas. How are these quantities related?

**Pressure and Temperature**   When you ride a bicy-cle, friction between the road and the tire heats up the air inside the tire. How does this rise in temperature affect the air pressure? As the temperature of the air increases, the molecules move about more rapidly. The molecules hit the inner wall of the tire more often and harder. The pressure increases. So, as the temperature of a gas increases, its pressure increases.

**Pressure and Volume**   What effect does changing the volume of a gas have on its pressure? If you have ever used a bicycle pump, you know that the gas pres-sure increases as you push the pump handle down. See Figure 20-14. Suppose all the gas molecules stay trapped inside the tire pump, and the temperature stays the same. As you push down on the handle, you decrease the volume. Molecules of air hit the sides of the pump more often. More hits each second result in greater pressure.

The relationship between the pressure and the volume of a gas is called **Boyle's Law.**  This law states

### EFFECT OF HEAT ON A GAS

**OBJECTIVE**
Study how heat affects a gas.

**MATERIALS**
2 identical balloons, pan of hot water, pan of ice water

**PROCEDURE**
**1.** Blow up the balloons so that both are the same size. Tie the mouth of each balloon so that no air escapes.
**2.** Put one balloon aside, away from either pan of water.
**3.** Put the second balloon into the hot water for 5 minutes.
**4.** Remove the balloon from the water. Compare its size with the size of the first.
**5.** Place the second balloon in the ice water for 5 minutes. Repeat Step 4.

**QUESTIONS**
**1.** Why did you put the first balloon aside?
**2.** What happened when you put the balloon in hot water?
**3.** What happened when you put the balloon in ice water?
**4.** How does heat affect a gas?

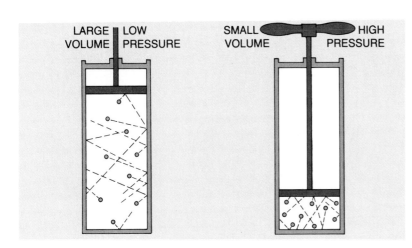

LARGE VOLUME | LOW PRESSURE       SMALL VOLUME | HIGH PRESSURE

*Figure 20-14. The smaller the volume, the more often the gas particles hit the walls of the container.*

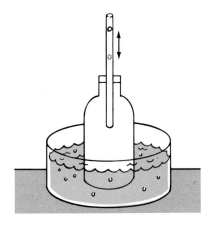

*Figure 20-15. The greater the water temperature, the higher the drop rises in the tube. What happens to the drop when the water cools?*

*Figure 20-16. Note how the piston moves from stroke to stroke.*

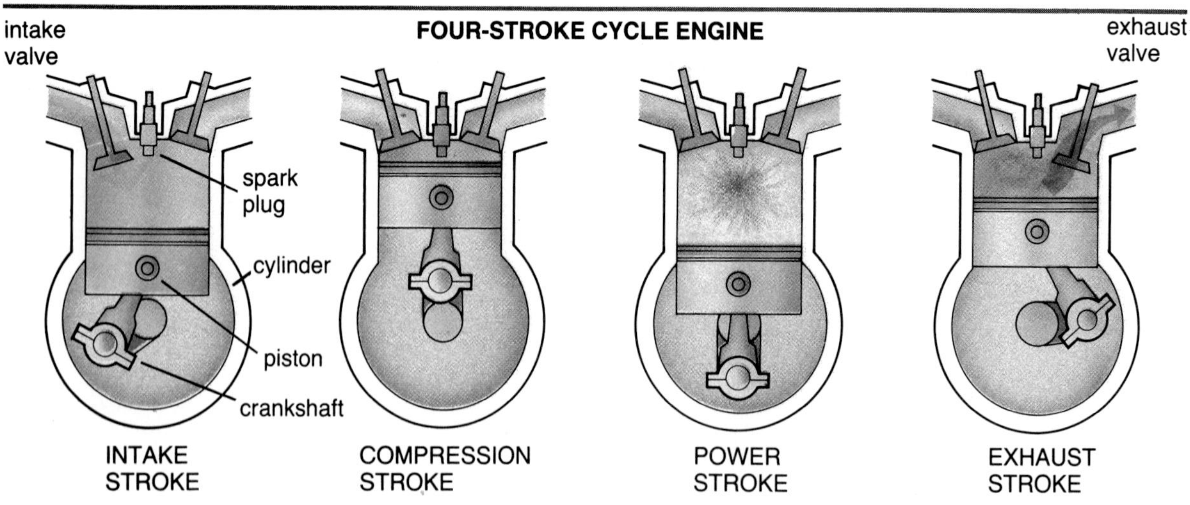

that at a constant temperature, a decrease in the volume of a gas causes an increase in its pressure.

**Temperature and Volume**   What happens to the volume of a gas when its temperature increases? Study Figure 20-15. A gas is trapped inside a bottle that has a straw attached to its top. A drop of water in the straw confines the gas inside the bottle. It also lets the gas expand without changing the pressure.

If you place the bottle in hot water, the temperature of the gas increases. As the temperature rises, the water drop inside the straw rises. This action occurs because the volume of the gas has increased. **Charles' Law** states that at a constant pressure, an increase in temperature causes an increase in the volume of a gas. For a closer look at the gas laws, see page 566.

## Heat Engines

Would you believe that hot gases can run a machine? This is the principle behind *heat engines*. A **heat engine** *uses energy from a burning fuel to make something move.* A gasoline engine is an example of a heat engine. Burning occurs inside the engine. So, a gasoline engine is called an internal combustion engine.

Figure 20-16 illustrates how a gasoline engine works. Most gasoline engines burn fuel inside tubes

**FOUR-STROKE CYCLE ENGINE**

intake valve

exhaust valve

spark plug

cylinder

piston

crankshaft

INTAKE STROKE

COMPRESSION STROKE

POWER STROKE

EXHAUST STROKE

called cylinders. A cylinder has two valves: an intake valve and an exhaust valve. A cylinder also has a movable part called a piston. The piston is connected by a rod to the crankshaft. The crankshaft rotates each time the piston moves up and down. The crankshaft is connected to gears, which move the car.

Most gasoline engines have a four-stroke cycle. A stroke is one up or down movement of a piston. During the first—or intake—stroke, the piston moves down. The intake valve of the cylinder opens and its exhaust valve closes. A partial vacuum is created in the cylinder. The partial vacuum draws in gasoline vapor that has been mixed with air. At the second stroke—the compression stroke—the intake valve closes and the piston moves up. The upward movement of the piston compresses the air-fuel mixture.

During the third—or power—stroke, a spark plug ignites the mixture. The high temperature makes the gas molecules expand. The expanding gas drives the piston down. In the fourth stroke—the exhaust stroke—the exhaust valve opens. The burned fuel leaves the cylinder. Then the cycle repeats itself.

● What propels a jet plane forward? See Figure 20-17. The principle behind the motion of a jet plane is similar to that behind the motion of an automobile. Air enters the jet engine and passes through a number of blades. The spinning of these blades compresses the air, making its temperature rise. The hot air enters the combustion chamber. Fuel is injected into the chamber and is ignited by the hot air. The rapid expansion of the burned gases drives the gases out of the rear of the engine. In reaction to this backward force, the jet moves forward.

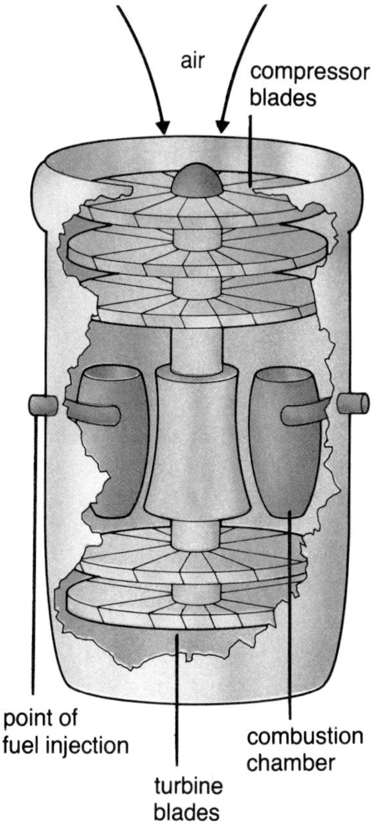

*Figure 20-17. What is the purpose of the spinning blades?*

## OBJECTIVES AND WORDS TO REVIEW

**1.** How does heat affect most materials?
**2.** Which two factors are related by Charles' Law? by Boyle's Law?
**3.** Describe the four-stroke cycle in a gasoline engine.
**4.** Write one complete sentence for each term listed below.
  pressure  pascal  heat engine

# CALIBRATING A SCIENTIFIC INSTRUMENT

### Preparation

Suppose you buy some liquid plant food. The directions specify one drop of plant food for 300 mL water. All you have is a 500-mL soda-pop bottle, an unmarked 200-mL beaker, a meter stick, and tape. How can you prepare the food solution exactly? To measure out 300 mL exactly would be very difficult. However, the task becomes much easier if you *calibrate* (KAL•i•brayt) the soda bottle. That is, if you mark the bottle with equal subdivisions.

Scientists always calibrate their scientific instruments. The process helps them make sure readings are accurate.

### Directions

To calibrate an instrument, you can follow three basic steps. First, choose any two fixed quantities to use. As Figure 1 shows, the two fixed quantities for the plant problem are the levels of water after one and two beakers of water were added.

*Figure 1.*

Second, indicate these two fixed points on a scale. In this case, the points are indicated by a piece of tape at the water level.

Third, divide the scale between the two fixed points into equal divisions. As Figure 1 shows, in this case the distance between the two fixed points was measured. Then a line was marked off halfway between these two points. Then another line was marked off halfway between these two points on each side of the midline.

### Practice

Professor X has invented a machine that can measure the entire range of human hearing. Outline on a separate sheet of paper a way of calibrating the instrument. What might you use as fixed points on the scale?

### Application

A thermometer is a laboratory instrument that is calibrated. The fixed points on a Celsius thermometer are the freezing point and boiling point of water. On a separate sheet of paper describe how you would make a thermometer from the following: a narrow, unmarked tube, colored alcohol; and a glass-marking pencil. Indicate what you will use as fixed points.

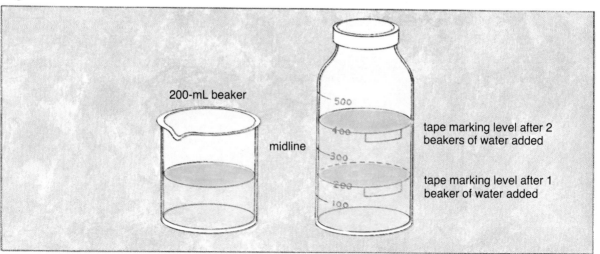

200-mL beaker

midline

500

400

300

200

100

tape marking level after 2 beakers of water added

tape marking level after 1 beaker of water added

# LABORATORY ACTIVITY

## CHANGES IN PHASE

### Objective
Observe how heat affects the phase of water.

### Background
Water can exist as a solid, a liquid, or a gas. When water absorbs or loses heat, it changes phase.

### Materials
beaker (100 mL), crushed ice, thermometer, ring stand, heat source, graph paper, wire screen

### Procedure
1. Fill a 100-mL beaker with 50-mL of ice.
2. Insert the thermometer about three-quarters into the ice. Record the temperature in a copy of Table 20-L. This is the temperature at time t = 0 minutes.

| TABLE 20-L. DATA TABLE | |
|---|---|
| Time (min) | Temperature (°C) |
| 0.0 | |
| 0.5 | |
| 1.0 | |
| 1.5 | |
| 2.0 | |

3. Place the beaker on the ring stand and heat as shown in Figure 20-L. **CAUTION:** Do not touch hot glassware.
4. Record the temperature of the ice water every half minute. Note the exact time when the last of the ice melts. Continue to heat the water and record its temperature.

5. Note the exact time when the water begins to boil. Continue to heat and record the temperature of the water until 25 mL of water remains. At that point turn off the heat.
6. On a sheet of graph paper, make a graph of temperature (y axis) versus time (x axis).

*Figure 20-L. Laboratory setup.*

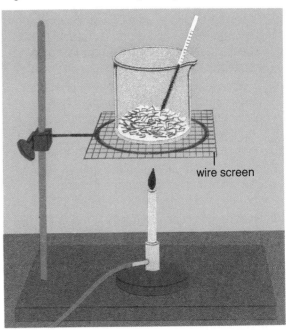

wire screen

### Questions
1. Which parts of the graph show changes of phase? What happens to the temperature during a change of phase? (Use your data.)
2. Discuss what the other parts of your graph (those not mentioned in question #1) indicate.
3. Discuss some sources of error that might affect the parts of your graph.
4. **PROBLEM SOLVING** For safety reasons you boiled away only half the water. To find the time it would have taken to boil away all the water, just double your recorded time. How does this reading differ from the time it took to melt all the ice? Explain the difference.

# SUMMARY

1. Temperature is a measure of the average kinetic energy of the molecules of a material. Heat is the energy transferred between materials of different temperatures. (20-1)

2. Heat can be transferred by conduction, convection, or radiation. (20-1)

3. Specific heat is the energy needed to change the temperature of 1 gram of material by 1 C°. Specific heat helps indicate how fast material heats up or cools off. (20-2).

4. When a material absorbs (gains) heat, the temperature rises or the material changes its phase.In any insulated system, the energy transferred out of one material equals the energy transferred into another. (20-2)

5. Heat makes most materials expand. Boyle's Law and Charles' Law relate the pressure, volume, and temperature of a gas. (20-3)

6. Heat engines use energy from a burning fuel to make something move. (20-3)

# REVIEW

Number a sheet of paper from 1 to 25 and answer these questions.

**Building Science Vocabulary** Write the letter of the term that best matches each definition.

a. Boyle's Law
b. Charles's Law
c. conduction
d. convection
e. heat engine
f. heat of fusion
g. heat of vaporization
h. pascal
i. pressure
j. radiation
k. specific heat
l. temperature

1. The heat needed to change 1 gram of a material from a solid to a liquid

2. The heat transferred by electromagnetic waves

3. One newton per square meter

4. As gas pressure goes up, volume goes down

5. A machine that uses heat from a burning fuel to make something move

6. Heat transfer due to collision of particles

7. Average kinetic energy of molecules

8. The heat needed to change 1 gram of a material from a liquid into a gas

9. Force exerted per unit area of surface

10. The heat needed to change the temperature of 1 gram of a material by 1 C°

**Finding the Facts** Select the letter of the answer that best completes each of the following.

11. During which stroke of a four-stroke cycle in a gasoline engine is the fuel-air mixture ignited? (**a**) intake (**b**) compression (**c**) power (**d**) exhaust

12. As the kinetic energy of the molecules of a gas increases, the temperature of the gas (**a**) goes down (**b**) goes up (**c**) stays the same (**d**) is divided in half.

13. The specific heat of water in $J/g \cdot C°$ is (**a**) 0.13 (**b**) 4.18 (**c**) 0.92 (**d**) 0.23.

14. When a piece of ice at a temperature of 0 °C absorbs energy, the temperature (**a**) goes down (**b**) goes up (**c**) goes down, then goes up (**d**) stays the same.

15. Equal masses of copper and lead each absorb 1,000 joules of heat. Compared with the lead, the temperature rise in the copper will be (**a**) the same (**b**) greater (**c**) less (**d**) three times as much.

16. If the temperature of a gas remains the same and the volume of the gas increases, (**a**) the pressure decreases (**b**) the energy transfer increases (**c**) the speed of the molecules increases (**d**) the pressure increases.

17. The specific heat of copper is $0.39 \ J/g \cdot C°$. How many joules of heat does 100 grams of

copper absorb when its temperature goes up by 10 C°? **(a)** 39 **(b)** 1,000 **(c)** 390 **(d)** 3,900

18. The energy transferred between materials that have different temperatures is **(a)** pressure **(b)** heat **(c)** expansion **(d)** Boyle's Law.

19. An up or down motion of a piston in a gasoline engine is **(a)** a compression **(b)** a pascal **(c)** an exhaust **(d)** a stroke.

20. Water at 20°C is put in a refrigerator. The mass of the water is 200 g. It cools to 10°C. How many joules are released? **(a)** 838 **(b)** 4.19 **(c)** 8,380 **(d)** 2,000

**Understanding Main Ideas**   Complete the following.

21. Heat flows from a region of higher temperature to a region of __?__.

22. A gas exerts a force on the walls of its container by __?__.

23. The heat of vaporization of water is __?__.

24. The transfer of energy by the movement of a liquid or a gas is called __?__.

25. When a material changes from the liquid phase to the solid phase, heat is __?__ .

**Writing About Science**   On a separate sheet of paper, answer the following as completely as possible.

1. Explain how the handle of a cold spoon becomes hot a few moments after it is placed in a cup of hot water.

2. An air conditioner works by absorbing energy from the air in the room. Explain why the temperature of the air in the room goes down.

3. Suppose you will be riding your bicycle for a long time on a hot day. Should you inflate the bicycle tires fully? Why or why not?

4. Hot water is often run over the lid of a jar that cannot be unscrewed. Why is this done?

5. (laboratory question) **a.** When you place an ice cube into a glass of water, what happens to the temperature of the water? What happens to the ice cube? **b.** How does a melting iceberg affect its surroundings?

**Investigating Chapter Ideas**   Try one of the following projects to further your study.

1. **Rotary engines**   Instead of gasoline engines with pistons and cylinders, some cars are powered by rotary engines. Find out how rotary engines work. Set up a model showing their operation.

2. **Making a barometer**   Find a glass jar with a mouth about 8–10 cm in diameter. Stretch part of a rubber balloon over the mouth of the jar (like the head of a drum). Seal it tightly with a rubber band. Lay a straw on the top of the jar with one end positioned in the middle of the rubber cover. Glue this end to the rubber cover. Set the jar on a wood base. Attach a scale so that the free end of the straw points to the scale. As the barometric pressure varies daily, the straw will move. Calibrate your barometer by calling the weather service periodically to find the actual barometric pressure. Mark this on the scale where the straw is pointing. Explain how your barometer works.

**Reading About Science.**   Read some of the following books to explore topics that interest you.

Gewirtz, Herman. 1974. **Essentials of Physics.** Woodbury, NY: Barron's.

Kavaler, Lucy. 1981. **A Matter of Degree: Heat, Life and Death.** New York: Harper.

Rahn, Joan C. **Keeping Warm, Keeping Cool.** New York: Atheneum.

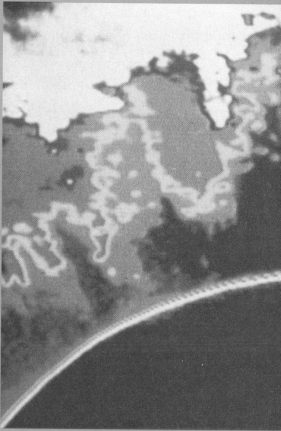

**F**ossil fuels provide most of the electricity in the United States. What is the source of the energy contained in fossil fuels? It is the same source that supplies most of the world's energy: the sun.

The apparently peaceful sun is actually a fiery furnace of intensely hot gases. These gases swirl in enormous convection currents. Huge amounts of energy are transferred from the core to the solar surface. There it escapes into outer space. How does this energy reach earth?

What is the source of the sun's energy?

It has no fossil fuels. Special reactions deep within it supply the sun's energy. These reactions do not involve the electrons of atoms. They involve their nuclei. As you will see in this chapter, nuclear reactions can also be carried out on earth.

Read and Find Out:
● how the astronauts kept their food fresh.
● how an isotope led to the discovery of a radioactive particle.
● how scientists are hoping to find a new source of energy.

# NUCLEAR ENERGY

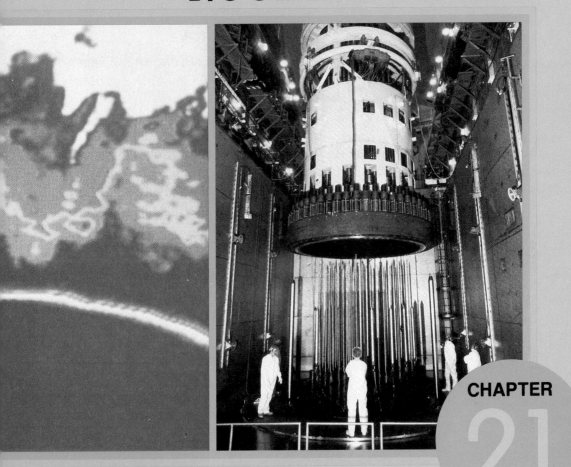

# AN INTRODUCTION TO RADIOACTIVITY

Have you ever looked for something and, almost by accident, found something else? One of the greatest discoveries in science was made almost by accident. In 1896 a French scientist, Henri Becquerel (ahn•REE bek•REL), wanted to see if a uranium compound gave off X-rays. However, he discovered that it gave off something that had not been known before. In this section you will find out what that mysterious "something" is.

## Becquerel and the Curies

Becquerel knew that certain materials glow when they are exposed to sunlight. That is, they give off visible light. You may have seen watch dials made of these materials. Do these materials also give off invisible X-rays?

To answer this question, Becquerel left a sample of uranium salt in sunlight. The sample was on top of photographic film wrapped in lightproof paper. If it gave off X-rays, the rays would go through the wrap and produce an image of the sample on the film. When Becquerel developed the film, he saw the image. So he believed that the salt gave off X-rays when exposed to sunlight.

*Figure 21-1. What caused this image of a uranium salt to show up on Becquerel's photographic plate?*

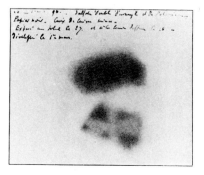

Becquerel left another uranium salt sample on wrapped film in his desk drawer for future use. After waiting for sunlight after several cloudy days, he decided to develop the film anyway. He saw an image of the sample. See Figure 21-1. Even without sunlight, the sample had given off "something" that went through the wrapping and produced an image.

In time, that "something" was named *radiation.* After testing many uranium compounds, Becquerel concluded that the element uranium was the source of the radiation. Uranium was said to be *radioactive.*

Marie Curie, a Polish scientist working in France, wanted to learn more about Becquerel's mysterious radiation. She suspected that a uranium ore called pitchblende contained other elements that give off radiation. Marie Curie and her husband Pierre began a search for these elements. See Figure 21-2.

In 1898 the Curies discovered a new element in pitchblende. They named it *polonium* in honor of her native country. Polonium gives off radiation as uranium does. Later that year the Curies separated still another radiation-emitting element from the ore. They named it *radium*, which means "shining element." Both radium and polonium give off more radiation than uranium.

*Figure 21-2. Which uranium ore did the Curies investigate?*

## Radiation from Nuclei

Becquerel and the Curies were not quite sure what they were observing. But their curiosity and hard work led to our present knowledge of *radioactivity* (ray•dee•oh•ak•TIV•uh•tee). **Radioactivity** *is the breaking down of atomic nuclei by releasing particles or electromagnetic radiation.*

Radioactive nuclei give off radiation in the form of streams of particles or energy. An electric field can

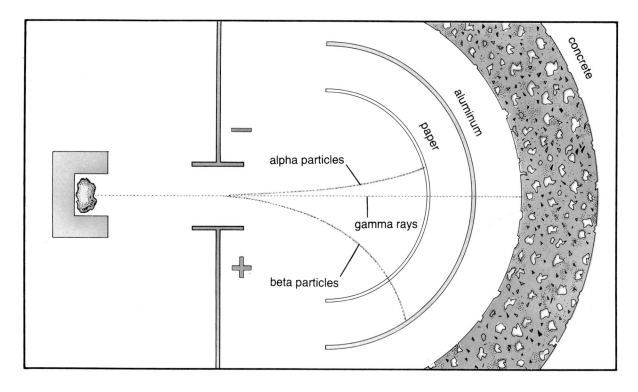

*Figure 21-3. An electric field separates radiation into three forms. Which form is deflected to the negative plate? To the positive plate?*

What is the symbol for an alpha particle?

help identify three forms of radiation. See Figure 21-3. These forms are *alpha* (AL•fuh) *particles,* *beta* (BAY•tuh) *particles,* and *gamma rays.*

**Alpha Particles** *An **alpha particle** is a positively charged particle consisting of two protons and two neutrons.* Its makeup and mass are the same as the nucleus of a helium atom. So the symbol for an alpha particle is often written as $_2^4\text{He}$.

One beam in Figure 21-3 is a stream of alpha particles. At a speed of 15,000 km/s, it is the slowest of the three forms of radiation. Also, it has the least ability to penetrate matter. It can be stopped by paper.

**Beta Particles** *A **beta particle** is an electron.* A beta particle is produced when a neutron in the nucleus breaks up into a proton and an electron. The proton remains inside the nucleus, increasing its atomic number by one. But the electron is given off.

The stream of beta particles in Figure 21-3 is strongly deflected by the positive plate. This strong deflection results from the low mass and negative charge of a beta particle. The mass and charge are shown in its symbol, $_{-1}^{0}e$. Beta particles move at about half the speed of light. They can penetrate about 3 centimeters of wood, but are stopped by a centimeter of aluminum.

**Gamma Rays**   *Gamma rays* *are electromagnetic waves with extremely short wavelengths,* as you may recall from Chapter 19. They are not particles of matter, so they have no mass. They have no charge, so they are not deflected by an electric field. Gamma rays travel at the speed of light. They are the most penetrating of the three forms of radiation. It takes a thick block of lead or concrete to stop them. All three forms of radiation are reviewed in Table 21-1.

*Figure 21-4. The badge you see is a dosimeter. A film inside detects radioactivity.*

## Detecting Radioactivity

Becquerel found that radioactive elements expose photographic film. Film is still used to detect radioactivity in elements. See Figure 21-4. However, there are other ways of detecting radioactivity.

**Electroscopes**   Radioactive materials remove electrons from molecules in the air. The molecules of air become ionized. They acquire a positive charge. If a negatively charged electroscope is brought near a radioactive substance, air molecules (that is, ions) attract electrons from the leaves. (See page 310.) The leaves lose their charge and move closer together.

**TABLE 21-1.**  PROPERTIES OF NUCLEAR RADIATION

| Kind of Radiation | Symbol | Charge | Atomic Mass | Approximate Speed (km/s) | Stopped By |
|---|---|---|---|---|---|
| Alpha | $_{2}^{4}He$ | positive (+) | 4 | 15,000 | sheet of paper |
| Beta | $_{-1}^{0}e$ | negative (−) | 0 | 150,000 | 1 cm of aluminum |
| Gamma | $\gamma$ | none | 0 | 300,000 (speed of light) | 60 cm of concrete, 30 cm of lead |

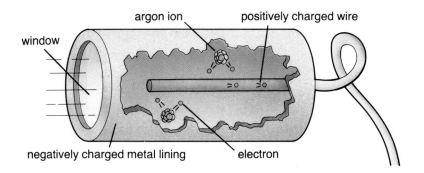

**Figure 21-5.** *Freed by radiation, electrons from the argon are attracted to a positively charged wire and set up a brief current.*

argon ion   positively charged wire

window

negatively charged metal lining   electron

**Geiger Counters**   *A **Geiger counter** is an instrument that detects radioactivity by an electric current.* See Figure 21-5. Inside a Geiger counter is a tube filled with argon gas. Whenever radiation enters a window in the tube, it removes electrons from atoms of the gas. The gas atoms are, thus, ionized. The electrons move to a wire in the tube and set up a current. The current produces a flashing light and a sound.

**Cloud Chambers**   *A **cloud chamber** is a container in which radioactive particles are detected by leaving a trail.* The chamber contains evaporated alcohol. Ice surrounding the chamber makes the alcohol condense into liquid droplets. See Figure 21-6. If a radioactive substance is put inside the chamber, the droplets condense around particles of radiation. The condensing alcohol droplets form a trail that shows up along the chamber lining.

**Bubble Chambers**   Figure 21-7 shows a trail produced in a more complex kind of cloud chamber, a bubble chamber. These chambers usually contain liquefied hydrogen. The passage of radioactive particles through the liquid makes it boil. The track you see is a trail of bubbles from the boiling liquid.

● The food the astronauts ate on the moon and in orbit was preserved by radiation. Radiation from a radioactive substance kills bacteria that spoil food. The radiation dose required to kill these bacteria is low. This level of radiation does not seem to have any effect on the taste of the food. Nor does it make the food radioactive.

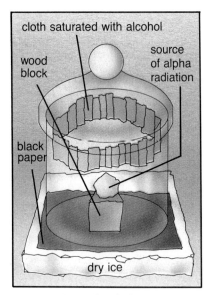

cloth saturated with alcohol

source of alpha radiation

wood block

black paper

dry ice

**Figure 21-6.** *As radioactive particles move in a cloud chamber, droplets collect around them and make their trails visible.*

## OBJECTIVES AND WORDS TO REVIEW

1. How did Becquerel and the Curies contribute to our present knowledge of radioactivity?
2. Name two kinds of radiation in the form of particles. How are they different from gamma rays?
3. List two radioactivity detection devices and explain how they work.
4. Write one complete sentence for each term listed below.

   | | | |
   |---|---|---|
   | radioactivity | beta particle | Geiger counter |
   | alpha particle | gamma ray | cloud chamber |

*Figure 21-7.* A bubble chamber contains a liquefied gas at a low temperature. How is the liquid used to show trails of radiation?

## TECHNOLOGY TRADE-OFF

### Gamma Rays and Unspoiled Food

You probably, at times, have found rotten food in your refrigerator. About 30% of the world's food spoils before it is ever eaten. Do you know why? Food spoils because germs such as bacteria and mold growing on it decompose it. Tests show that gamma rays can destroy germs in foods. Thus, foods that are treated with gamma rays ("irradiated") are less likely to spoil for longer periods of time than nonirradiated foods. Several food companies hope to use gamma rays to keep food from spoiling. However, there are people who do not want to irradiate foods. They feel that irradiated foods may be dangerous. These people fear that gamma rays may change some natural chemicals in foods into cancer-causing substances. Other people who own homes near gamma-ray treatment centers are also concerned. They say that radioactive materials produced at the centers may affect their health.

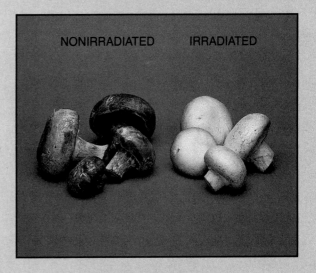

NONIRRADIATED    IRRADIATED

### Using Critical Thinking

How can society decide whether or not to irradiate foods? What do you think?

# 21-2

# RADIOACTIVE DECAY AND HALF-LIFE

**OBJECTIVES**

1. Give an example of radioactive decay.
2. Write an equation for a nuclear reaction.
3. Find the amount of substance left after a given number of half-lives.

The work of the Curies was just the beginning of the search for radioactive elements. In time, all the elements in the periodic table beyond bismuth (atomic number 83) were found to be radioactive. See Table 21-2. However, radioactivity has been detected in a great many other elements as well. In this section you will find out more about radioactive elements. You will learn what happens to an element that gives off radiation.

## Radioactive Isotopes

Most elements, you may recall, have a number of isotopes. Isotopes are atoms of an element that have different mass numbers. For example, two isotopes of Uranium are uranium-235 ($^{235}_{92}U$) and uranium-238 ($^{238}_{92}U$). See Figure 21-8. Both have the same atomic number (number of protons). But they have different numbers of neutrons. So they have different masses.

These two isotopes of uranium are radioactive. In fact, all isotopes of all elements with atomic numbers above 83 are radioactive. Elements with atomic numbers 93 to 109 are synthetic (sin•THET•ik). Synthetic elements are produced in laboratories. All isotopes of synthetic elements are radioactive.

(atomic mass) 235 = 92 p + 143 n

U

(atomic number) 92 = 92 p

(atomic mass) 238 = 92 p + 146 n

U

(atomic number) 92 = 92 p

*Figure 21-8. Isotopes of an element differ only in the number of neutrons in the nucleus. How many neutrons are there in U-234?*

**TABLE 21-2.** RADIOACTIVE ELEMENTS

| Element | Symbol | Atomic Number | Atomic Mass | Element | Symbol | Atomic Number | Atomic Mass |
|---------|--------|---------------|-------------|---------|--------|---------------|-------------|
| Technetium | Tc | 43 | 99 | Curium | Cm | 96 | 247 |
| Promethium | Pm | 61 | 145 | Berkelium | Bk | 97 | 247 |
| Polonium | Po | 84 | 209 | Californium | Cf | 98 | 251 |
| Astatine | At | 85 | 210 | Einsteinium | Es | 99 | 254 |
| Radon | Rn | 86 | 222 | Fermium | Fm | 100 | 253 |
| Francium | Fr | 87 | 223 | Mendelevium | Md | 101 | 256 |
| Radium | Ra | 88 | 226 | Nobelium | No | 102 | 253 |
| Actinium | Ac | 89 | 227 | Lawrencium | Lr | 103 | 257 |
| Thorium | Th | 90 | 232 | Element 104 | | 104 | 261 |
| Protactinium | Pa | 91 | 231 | Element 105 | | 105 | 260 |
| Uranium | U | 92 | 238 | Element 106 | | 106 | 263 |
| Neptunium | Np | 93 | 237 | Element 107 | | 107 | 261 |
| Plutonium | Pu | 94 | 244 | Element 108 | | 108 | 265 |
| Americium | Am | 95 | 243 | Element 109 | | 109 | 267 |

However, many elements with atomic numbers below 84 also have radioactive isotopes. For example, two common isotopes of carbon are carbon-12 ($^{12}_{6}C$) and carbon-14 ($^{14}_{6}C$). Carbon-12 is not radioactive. But carbon-14 is. In any sample of carbon, some radioactivity can be detected from the carbon-14 isotopes in the sample.

Name a radioactive isotope of carbon.

Other light elements also have some radioactive isotopes. See Table 21-3. Why are some isotopes of the elements radioactive, while others are not? Many fac-

**TABLE 21-3.** NONRADIOACTIVE AND RADIOACTIVE ISOTOPES

| Element | Nonradioactive Isotope | Radioactive Isotope |
|---------|------------------------|---------------------|
| Hydrogen | $^{1}_{1}H$ | $^{3}_{1}H$ |
| Helium | $^{4}_{2}He$ | $^{6}_{2}He$ |
| Oxygen | $^{16}_{8}O$ | $^{14}_{8}O$ |
| Potassium | $^{39}_{19}K$ | $^{40}_{19}K$ |

## Dr. Carlo Rubbia

"Make no mistake about it, physics is fun," says Carlo Rubbia. Dr. Rubbia had achieved the outstanding feat of creating matter from energy. He created the subatomic (particles smaller than atoms) "W" and "Z" particles.

To produce W and Z particles, Rubbia designed a device that hurls protons into antiprotons. Antiprotons are very rare. They are identical to protons except that they have a negative charge. When a single proton and antiproton collide, 1.8 billion electron volts of electricity are produced. Rubbia predicted that W and Z particles would be created from so much energy. He was right. Dr. Rubbia (b. 1934) was awarded the Nobel Prize in physics in 1984.

tors are probably involved. But since isotopes differ only in their number of neutrons, the neutron number may be one important factor.

Scientists have compared the number of neutrons to the number of protons in each isotope. See Figure 21-9. When the number of protons and neutrons in an isotope are the same or close, the isotope often is not radioactive. It is said to be *stable.* For example, carbon-12, with 6 protons and 6 neutrons, is stable. Isotopes with a much greater number of neutrons than protons tend to be radioactive. Radioactive isotopes are said to be *unstable.* All isotopes of elements heavier than bismuth have many more neutrons than protons, and these are all unstable.

The relationship of neutron number to radioactivity is not completely understood. It is still being explored, particularly as new isotopes are still being discovered.

*Figure 21-9. Each vertical set of dots represents the stable isotopes of an element.*

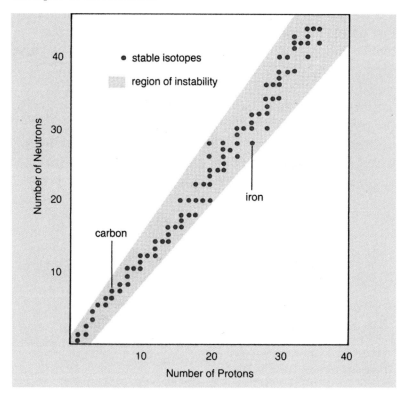

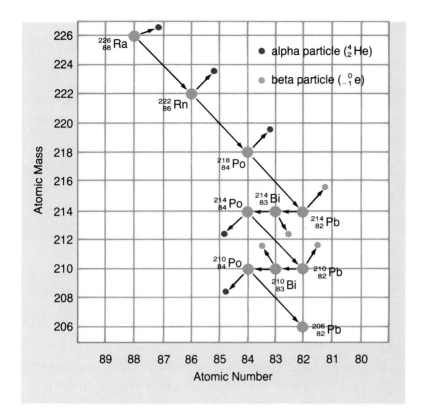

Figure 21-10. Radioactive decay of radium-226. The decay stops when stable lead-206 is formed.

## Radioactive Decay

What happens to an unstable isotope? Does it change in any way when its nucleus gives off radiation? Figure 21-10 shows what happens to an isotope of radium, radium-226, when it gives off an alpha particle. The nucleus loses two protons and two neutrons. It becomes an isotope of another element, radon. The radon isotope then gives off an alpha particle and changes into an isotope of polonium. Each newly formed isotope continues to give off radiation. The radiation stops when a stable isotope of lead is formed, lead-206 ($^{206}_{82}$Pb).

The process shown here is called *radioactive decay*. **Radioactive decay** is the changing of one element into another element by the release of radiation. All radioactive isotopes undergo decay. The decay continues until a stable isotope is formed.

When does radioactive decay stop?

**OBJECTIVE**
Make a working model of radioactive decay.

**MATERIALS**
two kinds of dried beans, jar, periodic table

**PROCEDURE**
1. The jar represents an "empty" nucleus. Fill it with 20 beans of one kind (protons) and 32 beans of another (neutrons).
2. The jar now represents an unstable nucleus of atom X. Make this nucleus give off an alpha particle (that is, remove 2 of each kind of bean).
3. Make the nucleus emit 2 more alpha particles and form a stable nucleus of atom Y.

**QUESTIONS**
1. Give the mass number and atomic number of atom X.
2. Give the mass number and atomic number of atom Y.

## Decay: A Nuclear Reaction

Radioactive decay is a nuclear reaction. It is a change that takes place only in the nucleus of an atom. The electrons surrounding the nucleus are not involved, as they are in chemical reactions. However, nuclear reactions can be expressed as equations, much as chemical reactions are. Here is an example.

When uranium-238 decays, it changes into thorium, a simpler element. The decay equation is:

$$^{238}_{92}\text{U} \longrightarrow ^{234}_{90}\text{Th} + ^{4}_{2}\text{He} + \text{gamma rays}$$

Note how the equation is written. The atomic mass of the element is written to the upper left of the element's symbol. The atomic number of the element is written to the lower left. Nuclear equations are often written this way. This notation makes it easier to balance them. For more information on balancing nuclear equations, see page 568.

If you add up the atomic masses of thorium-234 and helium-4 they add up to the atomic mass of uranium-238. Similarly, if you add up the atomic numbers of thorium and helium, they add up to 92, the atomic number of uranium-238. If a nuclear equation is written correctly, these two sums will always be true. You can also use this property to determine the products of radioactive decay. In the above equation you know that the atomic number of the product must be 90. Only thorium has this atomic number.

## Half-Life of Radioactive Elements

A form of a radioactive isotope of technetium ($^{99}_{43}\text{Tc}$) is used in hospitals. It is given to patients and is followed with a Geiger counter as it travels through the patients' bloodstream. Suppose you held a Geiger counter near a sample of the isotope. You would get a certain reading. As time went by, the reading would go down. In six hours, you would get half the original reading. Can you tell why?

The isotope is decaying. Each radioactive isotope decays at a constant rate. Every six hours, for example,

**TABLE 21-4.** HALF-LIVES OF SOME RADIOACTIVE ELEMENTS

| Element | Half-Life |
|---|---|
| Carbon-14 | $5.730 \times 10^3$ years |
| Cobalt-60 | 5.26 years |
| Iodine-131 | 8.07 days |
| Polonium-212 | $3 \times 10^{-7}$ seconds |
| Polonium-218 | 3.05 minutes |
| Radium-226 | $1.600 \times 10^3$ years |
| Uranium-235 | $7.10 \times 10^8$ years |
| Uranium-238 | $4.5 \times 10^9$ years |

half an amount of technetium-99 decays. Six hours is the *half-life* of this isotope. *A **half-life** is the time it takes for half an amount of a radioactive material to decay.* As Table 21-4 shows, some isotopes have very long or very short half-lives.

**A Half-Life Problem** Suppose 2 grams of radium-226 are stored away. The half-life of radium-226 is about 1,600 years. How much radium-226 will be left after 1,600 years (1 half-life) go by? After 3,200 years (2 half-lives) go by? See Figure 21-11.

*Figure 21-11. How many half-lives of radium-226 are shown here?*

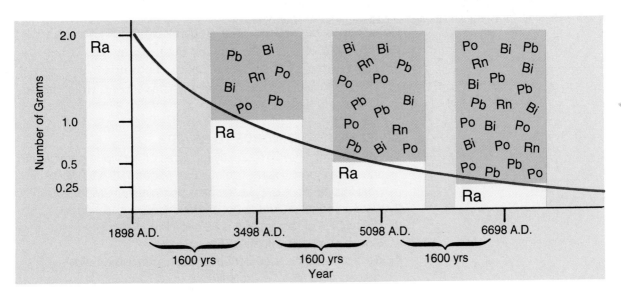

To find the answers, just reduce the mass of radium by one half for every half-life that passes:

$$\text{after 1 half-life: } \tfrac{1}{2} \times 2 \text{ g} = 1 \text{ g}$$
$$\text{after 2 half-lives: } \tfrac{1}{2} \times 1 \text{ g} = \tfrac{1}{2} \text{ g}$$
$$\text{after 3 half-lives: } \tfrac{1}{2} \times \tfrac{1}{2}\text{g} = \tfrac{1}{4} \text{ g}$$

**Half-Life Dating**   The half-life of a radioactive element can be used to tell the ages of rocks and fossils. For example, all living things have a constant level of carbon-14. When they die, the level drops because of decay. Carbon-14 has a half-life of 5,700 years. Suppose a fossil skeleton is found. Careful measurement shows the fossil has only half as much carbon-14 as a living thing. In this case, the age of the fossil is estimated to be about 5700 years.

**What isotope is used to date fossils?**

● For years scientists have known that decaying radioactive isotopes may emit alpha particles, beta particles, or gamma rays. Now, studies of the decay of aluminum-22 have shown that other forms of radioactivity may exist. Aluminum-22 has 13 protons and 9 neutrons in its nucleus. This odd-odd combination of protons and neutrons makes aluminum-22 very unstable. In 1/70,000 of a second the nucleus decays into magnesium-22. This isotope then decays into neon-20.

The decay seems to indicate that two protons are ejected from the nucleus as a single particle. This particle would be helium-2, a helium nucleus that has no neutrons. Helium-2 has never been observed. If scientists find that this decay produces helium-2, a new product of radioactive decay will have been discovered.

**OBJECTIVES AND WORDS TO REVIEW**

1. When thorium-226 (Th) decays, it gives off an alpha particle and another element. Using Table 9-1 on pages 182–183, find out what this element is. Give its mass and atomic number.
2. Write an equation for the decay described in question 1.
3. The half-life of radium-222 is 38 seconds. How much of a 6-gram sample is left after 76 seconds?
4. Write one complete sentence for each term listed below.
   radioactive decay        half-life

# HARNESSING THE NUCLEUS

A large mound of coal will supply the energy needs of the average house for about three months. A small pellet of uranium about the size of a jelly bean could also run the house for about three months. How can so small an amount of uranium produce so much energy? In this section you will learn the answer to that question.

**OBJECTIVES**

**1.** Explain what is meant by a chain reaction.

**2.** List the parts of a nuclear reactor.

**3.** Describe how nuclear reactors generate electricity.

## Nuclear Fission

You have seen that natural and synthetic radioactive elements are unstable. Their nuclei decay, emitting radiation, until they change into stable elements. Decay happens continuously. It is a *spontaneous* nuclear reaction. It occurs naturally, on its own. However, some nuclear reactions can be induced.

If you have played marbles, you have set up a model of induced radioactive decay. If you shoot one marble into a pack of marbles, you can split the pack apart. You have to aim the shooter marble carefully, however.

A similar situation can occur with radioactive nuclei. For example, uranium-235 can be made to split apart. The "shooter" in this case is a neutron. When a slow-moving neutron is shot into a uranium-235 atom, it enters the nucleus. The nucleus becomes unstable and immediately splits apart into two smaller nuclei. Also, three neutrons are emitted as products of the reaction. One nuclear equation for this induced decay reaction is:

*Figure 21-12. A uranium-235 nucleus may split apart when it is hit by a slow-moving particle. What is the name of this particle?*

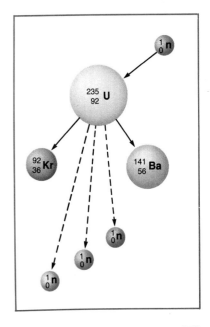

$$^{235}_{92}\text{U} + ^{1}_{0}\text{n} \longrightarrow ^{141}_{56}\text{Ba} + ^{92}_{36}\text{Kr} + 3\,^{1}_{0}\text{n} + \text{energy}$$

The symbol $^{1}_{0}\text{n}$ represents a neutron.

The nuclear reaction represented by this equation is an example of *nuclear fission* (FISH•uhn). **Nuclear fission** *is the splitting of a nucleus with a large mass into two nuclei with smaller masses.*

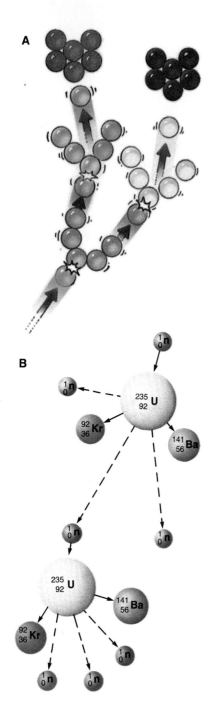

## A Case of Missing Mass

The first successful nuclear fission test took place in 1939. A huge amount of energy was released. Scientists were curious about where so much energy came from. Later they calculated the total mass of the barium, krypton, and the neutrons. This mass was less than the mass of the uranium-235 plus the initial neutron. What happened to the missing mass?

Albert Einstein had provided the answer to the question of missing mass years before the first fission test. In the early 1900s he predicted that in some reactions mass could be changed into energy. This prediction was later proven to be true. His famous equation $E = mc^2$ is now used to calculate the energy produced in nuclear reactions.

## Chain Reactions

What happens after a nucleus splits? Once again, marbles can be used as a model. When the shooter in Figure 21-13**A** hits the first pack of marbles, the pack splits. However, some of the marbles from the pack now become shooters for the other packs. This process continues until there are no more unsplit packs.

The fission of uranium-235 nuclei follows a pattern similar to that of the marbles. See Figure 21-13**B**. In splitting apart, the U-235 nucleus emits three neutrons. These neutrons then enter three other uranium-235 nuclei. They, in turn, split. Now there are nine neutrons. These nine then enter nine other uranium-235 nuclei, and the process continues.

The process described above is a *chain reaction*. A **chain reaction** is one in which some of the products of the reaction cause the reaction to keep going.

## Nuclear Fusion

Up to now you have been exploring how a nucleus with a large mass can made to split into nuclei with smaller masses. An opposite kind of nuclear reaction seems to be going on inside the sun and other stars. Stars release energy during a reaction in which nuclei

*Figure 21-13.* In a chain reaction, particles set in motion by a collision can cause additional collisions.

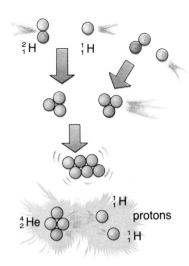

Figure 21-14. *In the sun, hydrogen nuclei are fusing into helium nuclei and releasing energy.* What other products result from this fusion?

with small masses fuse, or join together. By fusing, they become a single nucleus with greater mass. In a series of steps, four hydrogen-1 nuclei fuse and become one helium-4 nucleus. See Figure 21-14.

The nuclear reaction going on in the sun and other stars is *nuclear fusion*. **Nuclear fusion** *is the joining of several nuclei with smaller masses into one nucleus with a larger mass.* During the reaction, a certain amount of mass is lost. This missing mass is changed into huge amounts of energy.

The energy released by this reaction produces a tremendous temperature in the sun's core. Such temperatures are necessary to keep nuclear fusion going. Enough nuclear fuel is present in the core, in the form of hydrogen and other elements, to keep fusion going for billions of years.

At the high temperatures of the sun, matter does not consist of atoms. Instead, electrons are separated from atoms, resulting in ions, charged atoms. Thus, matter on the sun is neither solid, liquid, nor gas. It is in a fourth phase, the *plasma* phase. **Plasma** *is a gaslike phase consisting of free electrons and ions.*

In what phase does matter exist on the sun?

## Nuclear Reactors

You read earlier that a pellet of uranium could produce as much energy as a large mound of coal. Uranium and other radioactive materials are used as fuels in *nuclear reactors*. A **nuclear reactor** *is a device that produces energy from radioactive fuels through controlled chain reactions.*

**CORE**
contains nuclear fuel

**MODERATOR**
slows neutrons down

**CONTROL RODS**
control rate of chain reaction

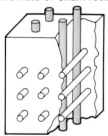

**SAFETY SYSTEM**
protects workers from radioactivity

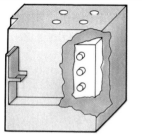

*Figure 21-15. A nuclear reactor has four main parts.*

Figure 21-15 shows the main parts of a fission reactor. These parts include the core, the moderator, the control rods, and the safety system.

**Core**   The core contains the nuclear fuel. This fuel is often a mixture of many isotopes. The core is the central part of the reactor, and is the place where the fission actually occurs.

**Moderator**   The neutrons emitted during the fission of uranium-235 travel too fast to be captured easily by other uranium-235 nuclei. A moderator slows down these neutrons to a speed that makes it easier for uranium-235 nuclei to capture them.

**Control Rods**   Once a chain reaction begins, it continues until there is no more nuclear fuel. In a reactor, a fast chain reaction would not be efficient. The fuel would be used up too soon and there would be no way of controlling the reaction. Control rods help control the rate of a chain reaction by absorbing neutrons. The farther a control rod is pushed into a reactor, the more neutrons are absorbed. The chain reaction slows down. Control rods are usually made of cadmium or boron steel.

**Safety System**   The safety system of a reactor is the set of devices designed to prevent serious reactor accidents. The safety system has many components. It includes rods that can be dropped into the reactor that will stop the chain reaction at once. The system also includes a coolant that circulates through the reactor. It removes the heat from the core. Both these parts of the system help to prevent a meltdown—a melting of the nuclear fuel. The safety system also contains shielding to prevent the escape of radioactivity to the outside.

Two nuclear accidents show the need for shielding. The 1979 Three Mile Island accident produced a meltdown. However, the reactor's safety system had thick concrete shielding. Very little radiation escaped into the air. The 1986 Chernobyl accident also caused a meltdown. However, this reactor did not have thick concrete shielding. Very high levels of radiation escaped.

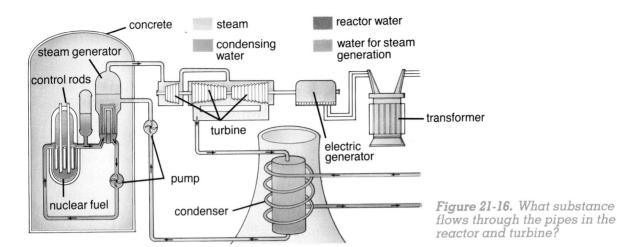

concrete — steam — reactor water

steam generator — condensing water — water for steam generation

control rods

transformer

turbine

electric generator

pump

nuclear fuel — condenser

*Figure 21-16. What substance flows through the pipes in the reactor and turbine?*

## Electricity From Nuclear Energy

The huge amount of energy released in a chain reaction can be used to generate electric energy. Figure 21-16 shows a nuclear power plant, where this energy conversion occurs. Using a fuel like uranium-235, the energy produced by the chain reaction changes water into steam. The steam turns a **turbine,** *a rotating wheel with blades.* The rotating turbine spins the generator to which it is connected. The generator, as you know, then changes this mechanical energy into electric energy. After the steam runs the turbine, it is condensed and returned to the reactor.

Nuclear power plants of this kind are in use all over the United States. They produce energy by fission. The only real way that nuclear power plants differ from fossil-fuel power plants is in the kind of fuel.

## Effects of Radioactivity

You saw that radioactive particles can expose a photographic plate. They also ionize the air they travel through. Radioactive particles also produce another important effect. They can kill cancer cells and harmful bacteria. But if powerful enough, they can also cause illness or even death. Gamma rays are especially harmful. They can penetrate the body and damage its cells. That is why people working with radioactive materials wear protective clothing. See Figure 21-17.

*Figure 21-17. Protective clothing is worn to prevent radioactive contamination.*

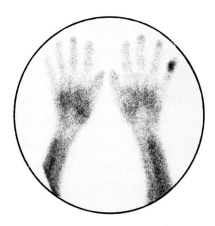

*Figure 21-18. A radioactive isotope located a tumor in this hand.*

*Figure 21-19. Water is used to block radiation from stored radioactive wastes.*

## Uses of Radioactivity

Radioactivity can be dangerous to a person's health. Yet when used wisely, it can be beneficial. The nucleus of cobalt-60 is unstable. As it decays, the cobalt-60 nucleus emits radiation. The radiation it produces can destroy cancer cells. However, this radiation can also kill healthy cells. So the radiation must be carefully aimed at the cancer tissue.

Radioactivity can also help detect tumors. A solution containing a small amount of radioactive material is used. This solution, called a tracer, is injected into a patient. The radioactive tracer collects in the tumor. As a result, the location of the tumor can be found. See Figure 21-18.

## Pluses and Minuses of Nuclear Energy

The use of nuclear power plants saves oil and natural gas, which are becoming scarce. A fission reactor uses much less fuel than coal or oil power plants. One gram of uranium a day can generate a million watts of electric power a year. This saves the consumer money. The use of nuclear fuel also reduces air pollution. No polluting soot, ashes, or waste gases are given off by fission reactors.

Fission reactors, however, produce radioactive elements and waste materials. These materials can destroy body cells. Overexposure can cause cancer. Workers in these plants must be protected by special clothing.

One of the greatest problems facing nuclear power plants is the disposal of nuclear waste. Such materials have long half-lives. Some nuclear power plants store waste in a pool of water at the plant. See Figure 21-19.

As you have seen in this section, nuclear energy can have beneficial effects. However, there can also be disastrous effects. Nuclear weapons are a case in point. Nations of the world have long known of the great power locked within the atom. Some governments encourage research in nuclear weapons for national defense. However, many people are concerned about the effects of nuclear attack. Recently, some scientists have predicted that such an attack could cause a "nuclear winter." In a nuclear winter, dust thrown into the air from a nuclear explosion would plunge large parts of the earth into a long period of darkness. Below-freezing temperatures would result throughout the year. Violent windstorms, toxic smog, and radioactive fallout would be widespread. Such a nuclear winter would affect most or all life on earth.

This prediction places an even greater responsibility on the governments of the world. It is the responsibility of everyone to prevent this prediction from becoming a fact.

● In an effort to find other ways to use nuclear energy, scientists are trying to build fusion reactors. One such device, called a tokamak (TAH•kah•mahk), is being investigated. This reactor would not need uranium-235. It could use hydrogen obtained from sea water. This reactor would also be very efficient. Much less heat would be wasted. Also, the radioactive products from this reactor have short half-lives. So they would not have to be stored very long.

Although tokamaks hold great promise, there are still problems that scientists have to solve. The temperatures required for fusion exceed 100 million degrees. At present, tokamaks cannot produce these high temperatures. However, if scientists find a way to achieve such temperatures, tokamaks may become practical.

## OBJECTIVES AND WORDS TO REVIEW

1. Explain why the nuclear fission of uranium-235 is called a chain reaction.
2. List the parts of a nuclear reactor. State the purpose of each part.
3. How does a nuclear reactor produce electricity?
4. Write one complete sentence for each term listed below.

| | |
|---|---|
| nuclear fission | plasma |
| chain reaction | nuclear reaction |
| nuclear fusion | turbine |

## EXPLORE BY VISITING

### RADIOACTIVITY AND HEALTH

**OBJECTIVE**
Learn about effects of radioactivity on living things.

**PROCEDURE**
Go to a radiology department of a hospital. Find the answers to the questions below.

**QUESTIONS**
1. What are radionuclides?
2. What effect do radionuclides have on living things?
3. What precautions must be taken by people using radionuclides? Why?
4. What is a gamma camera?
5. How are tracers used in medicine?

# FINDING THE PROBABILITY OF AN EVENT

## Preparation

You often hear the word "probability." Radio reports may speak of a 70% probability of snow tomorrow. Or you might say there is a small probability that you will live to be 100 years old.

Scientists also speak in terms of probability. They may talk about the probability of Mt. St. Helens erupting again. Or they might consider the probability of finding a particular isotope of oxygen in a sample of oxygen gas. The probability of an event is an estimate of the number of times that event will occur after many observations are made.

## Directions

To find the probability of an event, use the formula:

$$\text{Probability} = \frac{\text{Chance an Event Can Occur}}{\text{Total Number Possible Events}}$$

For example, suppose you have a jar containing 15 blue marbles and 45 green marbles. Without looking at the jar, you pull out a marble. What is the probability of pulling out a blue marble? There are 15 blue marbles, so there are 15 chances that

you could pull one out. The total number of possible pulls of a marble is 60 (15 blue + 45 green). So the probability of pulling a blue marble is $\frac{15}{60} = 0.25$. (Probability is usually expressed as a decimal.)

In a similar way, the probability of pulling out a green marble is $\frac{45}{60} = 0.75$. See Figure 1. The sum of the probabilities of all possible cases is 1.0. A probability of one means certainty. In the case of the marbles, for example, the sum of the probabilities is 0.25 + 0.75 = 1.0. This means that when you put your hand into the jar, you will pull out either a blue marble or a green marble.

## Practice

On a separate sheet of paper, find the probability of each event described.

1. Getting a head when you flip a coin.
2. Pulling out a jack from a regular deck of 52 playing cards (no jokers).
3. Pulling out a red marble from a jar containing 16 red, 8 white, and 24 blue marbles. Pulling out a white marble. Pulling out a blue marble. What is the sum of the probabilities?

## Application

Read the Laboratory Activity. On a separate sheet of paper, find the chance that a "radioactive" lima bean will decay. (Hint: This case is like getting a head or a tail when tossing a coin.)

*Figure 21-L. Laboratory setup.*

$$\text{Prob. of Picking a Green Marble} = \frac{\text{Chance of Picking a Green Marble}}{\text{Total Number of Marbles}}$$

$$\text{Probability} = \frac{45}{60}$$

$$= \frac{3}{4}$$

$$= 0.75$$

# HALF-LIFE

## Objective
Use models to show what happens during radioactive decay.

## Background
The half-life of a radioactive element is the time it takes for one half of the atoms to decay. Decay is a matter of chance. In a small amount of radioactive element there are millions of atoms. So the chance that exactly half of them will decay in one half-life is very great.

In this experiment you will use lima beans as models of radioactive atoms. The chance of half of them decaying during the first half-life is good. However, after several half-lives the number of "radioactive" beans becomes smaller.

## Materials
glass or beaker, 200 lima beans with an ink spot on one side, graph paper

## Procedure
1. Put 200 lima beans in a glass or beaker. Shake them well and toss them on the table.
2. The beans that land painted side up have "decayed." Remove them. Count the number of beans that are still "radioactive." Record this number in a data table set up like Table 21-L.
3. Return the radioactive beans to the glass. Shake and toss them again. This is the second half-life. Repeat step 2.
4. Repeat steps 2 and 3 one more time.

5. Pool your data with the data obtained by other teams. Obtain an average number for atoms remaining radioactive after each half-life. Record these numbers in your data table.
6. Use the average data to make a graph of radioactive decay. Plot "atoms remaining radioactive" along the y axis. Plot "half-life (0,1,2,3)" along the x axis. Draw a smooth curve as close as possible to the points you have plotted.

## Questions
1. Contrast your graph with the one in Figure 21-11 on page 469. Explain any differences.
2. Find the probability for each bean to decay. Use the formula on page 478.
3. **PROBLEM SOLVING** Suppose you began this activity with 1,000 beans. How many half-lives would pass until only 125 beans remain "radioactive"? Would you ever reach a time when no beans remain radioactive? Explain. Do you think a radioactive sample could ever become completely decayed? Explain.

| TABLE 21-L. DATA FOR THE HALF-LIFE EXPERIMENT | | |
|---|---|---|
| Half-Life | Atoms Remaining Radioactive | Atoms Remaining Radioactive (class average) |
| 0 | 200 | 200 |
| 1 | | |
| 2 | | |
| 3 | | |

# SUMMARY

1. Three forms of radiation from radioactive elements have been identified: alpha particles, beta particles, and gamma rays. (21-1)
2. Radioactivity can be detected by photographic film, electroscopes, Geiger counters, cloud chambers, and bubble chambers. (21-1)
3. Radioactive isotopes of one element decay by giving off radiation until they change finally into stable isotopes of another element. (21-2)
4. The half-life of a radioactive element is the time it takes for half of the starting amount to decay. The age of fossils can be found by measuring the amount of carbon-14 in them. (21-2)
5. The nuclear fission of uranium-235 is a chain reaction that produces huge amounts of energy. (21-3)
6. Nuclear reactors produce isotopes and energy by nuclear fission. The energy, in the form of heat, is used to produce steam to run electric generators. (21-3).

# REVIEW

Number a sheet of paper from 1 to 25 and answer these questions.

**Building Science Vocabulary**   Write the letter of the term that best matches each definition.

a. alpha particle
b. beta particle
c. cloud chamber
d. gamma ray
e. Geiger counter
f. half-life
g. isotope
h. nuclear fission
i. nuclear fusion
j. radioactive decay
k. radioactivity
l. turbine

1. Nuclear radiation in the form of electro-magnetic waves with a very short wavelength
2. An instrument that detects radioactivity by way of an electric current
3. The time it takes for one half of the starting amount of a radioactive element to decay
4. The release of streams of particles or energy from the nuclei of atoms of certain elements
5. A positive particle consisting of two protons and two neutrons
6. The splitting of a nucleus with a large mass into two nuclei with smaller masses
7. A rotating wheel with blades
8. The joining of several nuclei with smaller masses into one nucleus with a large mass
9. The change of one element into another by the release of radiation from atoms of the element
10. A container in which radioactive particles are detected by the trails they leave behind

**Finding the Facts**   Select the letter of the answer that best completes each of the following.

11. Becquerel detected radioactivity by using   (a) a Geiger counter
   (b) photographic film   (c) an electroscope
   (d) a nuclear reactor.
12. In a nuclear reactor, nuclei of uranium-235 are split by slow-moving   (a) neutrons
   (b) protons   (c) electrons   (d) beta particles.
13. At the high temperatures of the sun's core, matter exists as   (a) solid   (b) liquid
   (c) gas   (d) plasma.
14. A radioisotope used to treat cancer is
   (a) uranium-235   (b) hydrogen-1
   (c) cobalt-60   (d) carbon-14.
15. Beta particles are   (a) electromagnetic waves   (b) positively charged
   (c) negatively charged   (d) neutral.

**16.** Gamma rays can be stopped by     (**a**) thick concrete     (**b**) 1 cm of aluminum     (**c**) paper     (**d**) cardboard.

**17.** The age of a fossil is determined by measuring the amount of     (**a**) uranium-235     (**b**) uranium-238     (**c**) carbon-12     (**d**) carbon 14.

**18.** The chain reaction in a nuclear reactor is regulated by a control rod made of     (**a**) uranium-238     (**b**) cadmium or boron     (**c**) concrete     (**d**) carbon-14.

**19.** The sun produces energy by     (**a**) nuclear breakdown     (**b**) nuclear fusion     (**c**) radioactive decay     (**d**) nuclear fission.

**20.** Unstable nuclei often have     (**a**) an equal number of protons and neutrons     (**b**) no neutrons     (**c**) more neutrons than protons     (**d**) no protons.

### Finding the Facts     Complete the following.

**21.** Three forms of radiation that have been identified from radioactive elements are __?__.

**22.** Of the two common isotopes of carbon, carbon-12 and carbon-14, only carbon-14 is __?__

**23.** Two devices which detect radiation by using radiation's effect of knocking electrons off gas molecules are electroscopes and __?__.

**24.** In the nuclear fusion reaction going on in the sun hydrogen nuclei fuse and form a nucleus of __?__.

**25.** Radioactive isotopes continue to decay until they become __?__.

### Writing About Science     On a separate sheet of paper, answer the following as completely as possible.

**1.** Describe the parts of a nuclear reactor. Be sure to include the function of each part.

**2.** Suppose you bought a wrapped, unexposed sheet of photographic film. How could you use it to detect radioactivity in rocks or other objects?

**3.** Explain how nuclear fission is different from nuclear fusion. If they are different, why are they both nuclear reactions?

**4.** How are nuclear reactors used to produce electricity?

**5.** (laboratory question) In the laboratory activity for this chapter, you graphed the number of undecayed atoms left after each half-life. Describe how your graph may differ from the curved line in Figure 21-11. Explain why they differ.

### Investigating Chapter Ideas     Try one of the following projects to further your study.

**1.** **A model nuclear power plant**     Make a model of a nuclear fission power plant. Use your imagination in selecting materials for the parts of your model reactor. You might use cardboard for the building walls and a can for the reactor core. You might use straws for the control and fuel rods. Prepare a report describing the function of the parts shown in your model

**2.** **Where do elements come from?**     Elements are thought to be formed in stars. Read and report on the nuclear processes in stars that form both the lighter and heavier elements.

### Reading About Science     Read some of the following books to explore topics that interest you.

Kiefer, Irene. 1982. **Nuclear Energy at the Crossroads.** New York: Atheneum.

Lampton, Christopher. 1982. **Fusion: The Eternal Flame.** New York: Watts.

Weiss, Ann. 1981. **The Nuclear Question.** New York: Harcourt.

The world is running out of oil? Impossible! That might have been a common reaction 30 years ago. But in the world of the 1980s this statement is unfortunately true. Our use of fossil fuels is depleting the world's supply. Thus, people are looking for energy alternatives.

What alternatives are available? What is the source of their energy? Three possibilities are shown here. The photos show machines that use different forms of energy to produce electricity.

The spinning blades of a windmill are connected to a generator. Water heated within the earth is sent through turbines. Energy from the sun creates an electric current in the solar cells it strikes.

In this chapter you will investigate these and other sources of energy.

Read and Find Out:
● how mirrors are being used to generate electricity.
● how tides can produce electric energy.
● about a plant that feeds on sewage.

# ENERGY FOR THE FUTURE

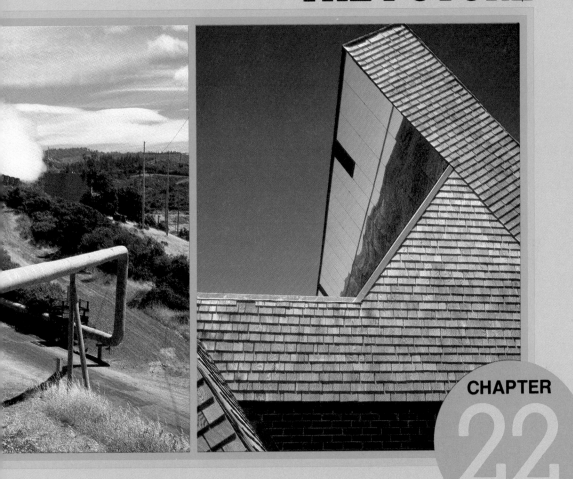

# SUN AND WIND POWER

The energy appetite of our modern societies continues to grow. Transportation, communication, and other advances in technology create a huge demand for energy. Satisfying this demand requires vast amounts of fossil fuels. Fossil fuels—coal, natural gas, oil—were formed from the remains of life forms that died long ago. These energy supplies are now running low.

It is our responsibility to assure that future generations have fuel. Scientists are seeking alternatives to replace our dwindling energy supply. In this section you will learn how the sun is being used as an alternative energy source. Finding new energy sources is not enough. It is important to conserve energy now. Failure to do so will result in a lack of fuel for future generations. Enacting conservation laws is a first step. However, it takes all nations working together to find appropriate solutions.

*Figure 22-1. Why are solar collectors placed on a roof facing the sun?*

## Solar Heating and Cooling

The sun is a huge and largely untapped source of energy. The energy in sunlight shining on the United States in one day could power this country for a year. However, most of the sun's energy is reflected back into space or absorbed by the upper layers of the atmosphere.

Science and technology are working together to find new and better ways to use energy from the sun. Solar energy is being used for heating and cooling homes. Use of solar energy can conserve fossil fuels and reduce air pollution.

**Solar Heating** At the beginning of Chapter 3 you saw two houses heated by the sun's energy. In one house, solar energy was collected and stored in drums of water. In the other house, it was collected and stored in stone walls. The solar-heated house you see in Figure 22-1 absorbs heat from the sun by using collector panels. These panels have black energy-absorbing surfaces covered with glass or clear plastic. They are attached to pipes that circulate air or water throughout the house. The dark surfaces of the panels absorb solar energy and heat the air or water in the pipes. The heated materials transfer energy throughout the building.

Solar energy must be stored for use at times when it cannot be collected. Tanks of water and beds of large pebbles are two common methods of storage.

**Solar Cooling**  Energy is required to run air conditioners. Most air conditioners get this energy from electricity. The energy runs a refrigeration generator. The generator cools air by condensing and then evaporating a circulating liquid refrigerant.

Solar energy can supply the energy needed to run an air conditioning system. In 1975 an elementary school in Atlanta, Georgia installed a solar heating and cooling system for the entire building. This was the first such system in the world.

## Electricity from the Sun

The solar energy plant in Figure 22-2 uses a giant curved mirror to focus the sun's rays. The focused rays are used to heat water in a boiler. The energy produces steam. The steam, in turn, drives a turbine in a generator. The spinning turbine enables the generator to produce electricity.

**E**XPLORE
BY TRYING

**A HOMEMADE SOLAR COOKER**

**OBJECTIVE**
Use solar energy to cook marshmallows.

**MATERIALS**
bowl with rounded bottom, aluminum foil, sharpened pencil, marshmallow, towel

**PROCEDURE**
**1.** Line the inside of the bowl with foil, shiny side up. Put a marshmallow on the tip of the pencil.
**2.** Position the bowl in sunlight so that the foil gets the direct rays of the sun. Wrap the towel around the outside of the bowl to keep it in this position.
**3.** Carefully move your hand along the "optic axis" of the bowl. Find the hottest region of the solar cooker. Hold the marshmallow at this point.

**QUESTIONS**
**1.** What happened when you "cooked" the marshmallow?
**2.** What caused this effect?

*Figure 22-2. The town of Odeille, France, uses solar energy to produce electricity.*

**Solar Cells**   The building that you saw in the opening photograph is making use of electricity produced by a solar cell. A solar cell converts solar energy directly into electricity. *The direct conversion of sunlight into electricity is called the* **photovoltaic** (foh•toh•vohl•TAY•ik) *effect.*

A solar cell is two layers made largely from the element silicon. When the sun shines on the cell, electrons are released from the lower layer. These electrons are collected by one surface of the cell. The electrons can then travel through a path, or circuit, made of metal grids. This flow of electrons through a circuit is, as you know, an electric current.

By connecting many solar cells, you can increase the amount of current produced. Groups of solar cells have been used for communication and transportation. See Figure 22-3. Solar cells have also been used successfully in spacecraft.

**Solar Energy for the Future**   A major advantage of using solar energy is that it is clean. Solar energy produces little or no waste material. So it does not cause air pollution or waste disposal problems. Another advantage: energy from the sun is not going to run out for many years to come.

However, using solar energy does have some disadvantages. It can be collected only when the sun is

Solar cells are made largely from what element?

*Figure 22-3. Solar cells can be grouped together to supply larger amounts of electricity.*

shining. And some places do not get very much sunshine. The cost of installing solar heating and cooling systems is high. But once the systems are in operation, they save on fuel. Solar cells are also expensive at present. Scientists are searching for less expensive ways to produce solar cells.

## Wind Power

The wind is really a form of solar energy. It is produced by the uneven heating of the earth by the sun. About 2% of solar energy is changed into wind energy. Using wind energy to do work is not a new idea. Many centuries ago people began using wind to sail ships. And they started using wind-driven mills to grind grain.

The windmill you saw in the opening photograph can be used to do work. A windmill is a shaft with blades that turn in the wind. Wind energy does work when it turns the blades.

By 1900 the United States had a windmill industry. Windmills like the ones in Figure 22-4 were used on many farms to pump water or grind grain. Some were used to turn turbines that generated electricity. During the 1930's wind generators fell out of use. They were replaced with generators that used coal and water power to produce electricity.

Today scientists are designing large windmills like the one you saw in the opening photographs. The wind blows the propeller, or turbine, which runs an electric generator. The larger the propeller, and the faster it turns, the more electric energy it generates.

Wind energy is clean and, of course, free. But wind-driven generators are expensive. And they can produce electricity only when the wind blows. Some people also object to the noise and the appearance of these large machines.

The electric power from windmills is not great enough to supply our energy needs. It can save on fossil fuels. However, other sources are still needed to satisfy the demand for energy.

How is wind produced?

*Figure 22-4.* Windmills are being considered as alternative sources of energy.

**Figure 22-5.** Solar One uses mirrors to concentrate the rays from the sun.

● In the Mohave (moh•HAV•ee) Desert in California, a solar power plant is in operation. The plant, known as Solar One, is a 30-story tower surrounded by almost 2,000 flat mirrors. See Figure 22-5. Each mirror, which turns to face the sun throughout the day, reflects sunlight to the tower. Water circulating through pipes in the tower is heated to 515 °C and turned into steam. The steam then turns a turbine that generates electricity. Solar One has already met its goal of producing 10 million watts of electricity. Other, more efficient, solar power plants are being proposed for California, Arizona, and Texas.

**OBJECTIVES AND WORDS TO REVIEW**

1. (a) How do solar-heat buildings collect and store the sun's energy? (b) How do these buildings circulate energy?
2. Describe what happens to the silicon layers in a solar cell when the sun shines on it.
3. State two advantages and two disadvantages of using windmills to produce electricity.
4. Write a complete sentence for the term below. photovoltaic effect

# ENERGY FROM WATER

Rivers often start as small trickles of rain water or melting snow high in the mountains. Responding to the pull of gravity, the trickles flow downhill. They merge into larger and larger channels. High in the mountains, a river has a great store of potential energy. As it flows downhill, this potential energy changes into kinetic energy.

In this section you will find how the kinetic energy of flowing water can be tapped to produce electricity. You will also learn about the uses of a buried treasure in the hot water deep within the earth.

**OBJECTIVES**

**1.** Explain how moving water can produce electricity.

**2.** Describe two ways heat inside the earth is used to produce electricity.

**3.** List advantages and disadvantages of using hydrogen as a fuel.

## Hydroelectricity

A bladed wheel mounted over a river or stream can be used to harness the water's energy. During the 1800's such water wheels were used to run machines. See Figure 22-6. Today water turns the turbines of electric generators that produce electricity. *Electricity produced by flowing water is called* **hydroelectricity.**

Hydroelectricity has two main advantages. It produces very little pollution. And water in nature is never really used up. Liquid water does evaporate. But water vapor rises into the air, condenses into clouds, and returns to the earth as rain or snow.

However, hydroelectricity can sometimes cause a problem. In certain areas, dams have killed species of water animals and plants by interrupting the natural flow of water. This interruption can sometimes interfere with the reproductive cycles of these lifeforms. The problem can be prevented by careful study of river life before a dam is constructed. For example, many dams are now being built with "fish ladders." These structures provide a way for fish to swim around a dam. Thus, the dam does not interfere with the activities of the fish.

*Figure 22-6. Flowing water can be used to produce electricity.*

## Geothermal Energy

Figure 22-7 shows another way water can be used to produce electricity. You are looking at a geyser. A geyser shoots out jets of steam from water that boils naturally underground.

Underground water in a geyser is boiled by *geothermal energy.* **Geothermal energy** *is heat inside the earth.* Heat, remember, is energy transferred between materials that have different temperatures. Energy is transferred from rocks to water trapped below the surface. The water heats up and can change into steam. When steam forms, pressure builds up until it is released as a geyser.

Geothermal energy can be tapped by locating underground areas where steam or very hot water is trapped. The steam or hot water, once located, can be pumped out and used to turn turbines.

## A Fuel from the Ocean

The ocean may become another important source of electricity. Sea water can provide vast amounts of a fuel: hydrogen. Water, remember, is made of hydrogen and oxygen. *The process by which hydrogen is separated from the oxygen in water is* **electrolysis.**

Hydrogen can be used in place of fossil fuels to heat water and produce the steam for turning turbines. Unlike fossil fuels, hydrogen produces no pollution when it burns. Burning hydrogen produces ordinary water. However, hydrogen can burn explosively unless it is carefully controlled.

A problem with using hydrogen from the ocean as a fuel is that electrolysis requires energy. It takes electricity to separate hydrogen from water. If applied to a large amount of ocean water, electrolysis would require a great deal of electricity. As yet, no effective means of providing electricity for this process has been perfected. In many cases, it would take more electricity to get the hydrogen than the hydrogen could provide when it is burned. However, research is continuing.

*Figure 22-7. The energy contained in steam from a geyser can be used to produce electricity.*

What compound is formed when hydrogen burns?

*Figure 22-8. A tidal power plant.*

● The tides are still another source of electricity. The incoming and outgoing flow of water can be used to spin the blades of turbines. The spinning turbines then generate electricity.

An electric power plant on the Rance River in France is one place where tides are used to generate electric power. Another such power plant is located on the Annapolis River in Nova Scotia, Canada.

The use of tidal energy is limited to the coasts. There are not many suitable sites in the United States for tidal-powered electric generators. An ideal site would be a narrow inlet, where tides come in and go out along a rocky coast. See Figure 22-8.

## OBJECTIVES AND WORDS TO REVIEW

1. Explain how moving water can produce electricity.
2. Describe how geothermal energy can produce electricity.
3. State two advantages and one disadvantage of using hydrogen as a fuel.
4. Write one complete sentence for each term listed below.
   hydroelectricity        electrolysis        geothermal energy

## EXPLORE BY TRYING

### GEYSER POWER

**OBJECTIVE**
Show how steam can do work.

**MATERIALS**
teakettle, water, stove or hot plate, paper, scissors, metric ruler, pencil, pin

**PROCEDURE**
1. Boil a teakettle half full of water.
2. Cut a square of paper about 16 cm on an edge. Draw two lines so that they connect the opposite edge of the square.
3. Cut along each line to about 2 cm from the center.
4. Fold (*do not bend or crease*) the right tip of each triangle over so it overlaps the center of the square.
5. Push a pin all the way through the tips.
6. Push the pin into the wood at the top of a pencil *just far enough to hold the pin in.* You now have a pinwheel.
7. Hold your pinwheel over the steam from the teakettle. The blades must be horizontal to the top of the kettle.

**QUESTIONS**
1. What happened when the steam hit the pinwheel?
2. How is the pinwheel like a turbine?

# ENERGY FROM BIOMASS

You have seen that solar collector panels and solar cells trap the sun's energy. Green plants do much the same thing. They trap the sun's energy in a process called photosynthesis. In photosynthesis, plants make food from carbon dioxide and water in the presence of light. In this process, solar energy is changed into stored chemical energy in the food. This energy is passed on to animals when the plants are eaten.

Insuring energy for future generations is a vital responsibility. Perhaps in the future we may be able to release stored energy from plant and animal matter. Scientists are even trying to find ways to produce energy from waste products. In this section you will find out how scientists use *biomass* to produce energy. **Biomass** *includes plants, animal wastes, and all other organic matter that can be used as a source of energy.*

*Figure 22-9. How does a refuse-burning power plant remove the odors and polluting gases that it produces?*

## Energy from Solid Wastes

The amount of garbage produced in the United States is staggering. The average person produces more than 1,800 grams each day. This garbage is actually a treasure chest of energy. It contains much animal waste and other forms of biomass. It has been said that the solid wastes of large cities contain enough energy to light homes and businesses across the country for an entire year. The problem is how to get the energy from solid waste.

**Burning Garbage**   One way to release energy from solid wastes is to burn them. Before solid wastes can be burned, however, they must be processed and dried. In some countries, farmers have been processing such wastes for use as fuel for centuries. They simply dry solid animal wastes in sunlight.

Figure 22-9 is a photograph of a modern waste treatment plant. In it, solid wastes are processed so that they can be burned. Then the energy from the wastes is used to produce steam for an electric generator. The process releases waste gases that pollute the air. However, the plant helps dispose of the wastes by *scrubbing*. **Scrubbing** *is a way of cleaning waste smoke by using water.* Water is sprayed into the smoke, dissolving some of the polluting gases.

**From Garbage to Natural Gas**   Much solid waste material is dumped into landfills. Here bacteria take in and digest the waste. The bacteria then give off natural gas, which is made largely of methane.

Methane is a fuel used in homes and businesses around the world. Scientists are looking for ways to obtain more methane from landfills and dump sites. Doing so would also help solve a waste disposal problem.

The People's Republic of China has experienced an energy shortage for many years. People there have found a way to combat the shortage. They put organic wastes into a hole called a biopit. There, bacteria change the biomass into methane. The methane is collected and used as fuel.

What gas do bacteria release when they digest wastes?

## Energy from Alcohol

Have you ever seen campers cooking with solid alcohol? See Figure 22-10. Alcohol is a clean fuel that burns with a bright, hot flame. The source of alcohol is biomass.

**Ethanol**   Ethanol (ethyl alcohol) is an alcohol being tested for use in fuel for cars. It is produced by *fermentation* (fur•men•TAY•shuhn). **Fermentation** *is a process by which living yeast cells change sugar into alcohol and carbon dioxide.* The sugars in corn and other grains are used in the process. They give ethanol its common name, "grain alcohol."

*Ethanol is mixed with gasoline in a fuel called* **gasohol.** It has been used in gasoline engines to help conserve fossil fuel. However, the alcohol used must be very pure. Purifying the alcohol takes energy. As a result, gasohol is expensive.

**Methanol**   The car you see in Figure 22-11 uses methanol (methyl alcohol) as a fuel. Someday you may be asking for methanol at the gas pumps.

*Figure 22-10. Most of the substance in the can is ethanol. Why is ethanol a good fuel?*

## Farming an Energy Supply

Farming is becoming an important step in energy production. For example, if you visit Brazil, you may see its "fuel farms," fields of sugar cane with fermentation plants and storage tanks. Brazil has only a small oil supply. Cars in that country run on gasohol. The ethanol used in the gasohol comes from the fermentation of sugar cane on the fuel farms.

Water crops are becoming important as energy sources. For example, scientists are considering harvesting kelp for energy. Kelp is a fast-growing water

*Figure 22-11. The energy from methanol can power cars.*

*Figure 22-12.* How is the biomass from the kelp changed into methane?

plant. Kelp plants grow well in the ocean. Under good conditions, a giant kelp can grow 60 to 90 centimeters in one day. Kelp plants are sources of biomass. The action of bacteria on the remains of these plants yield methane gas. A research test farm with giant kelp is in operation off the coast of southern California. Scientists are trying to learn more about the effects of kelp farming on the environment. Figure 22-12 is a sketch of a test farm.

● The water hyacinth is another fast-growing water plant that is being studied as a source of biomass. See Figure 22-13. These plants are especially interesting to scientists because of their unique diet. Water hyacinths feed on raw sewage. As they feed, they clean up the water around them. So these plants are valuable on two accounts. They may be sources of fuel. And they are agents in the fight against pollution.

*Figure 22-13. Water hyacinths may be a source of biomass.*

## OBJECTIVES AND WORDS TO REVIEW

1. Explain two methods for getting useful energy from waste materials.
2. Ethanol and methanol are good fuels. Give an example of how each one is used.
3. List two fast-growing plants that may be used to produce methane.
4. Write one complete sentence for each term listed below.
   biomass        fermentation        scrubbing        gasohol

# WRITING A SCIENCE RESEARCH PAPER

## Preparation

Have you ever wanted to learn more about some topic? Writing a science research paper is one way. You can learn about anything from Andromeda to zirconium.

Scientists also write research papers. The papers give them the chance to explain their work to other scientists in their field. By so doing, ideas can be exchanged.

## Directions

When writing a science research paper, you should remember the following.

1. Select a fairly specific topic for your paper. If your topic is too broad, for example, outer space, you will find too much information. Your paper will be difficult to organize and to write. Pick one aspect of outer space, such as the history of the space shuttle or the life cycle of a star.

2. Once you have chosen a topic, go to the library to find informaton. Start with *The Reader's Guide to Periodical Literature.* It lists *magazine articles* by subject. To finds *books* on your topic, look in the card catalog. Your librarian may suggest other information sources.

3. Write down the author and title of each reference. For books, record the publisher and the date of publication. For magazine articles, include the name and date of the magazine, and its volume and issue number. Also indicate the page numbers where the reference is located.

4. As you read your references, decide what is important. In your own words, write down the information and where you found it. Keep your notes brief. Use phrases or short sentences. If you quote anything, copy the words exactly. Place quotation marks around them.

5. After you have read all your material and taken notes, study them. Pick out the main ideas and the subtopics. Use them to make a detailed outline. Once this is done, you are ready to write. Use your outline to set up headings. Use your notes to help you fill in the information under each heading. At the end of the paper, list the references you used.

Figure 1 summarizes the above steps.

*Figure 1.*

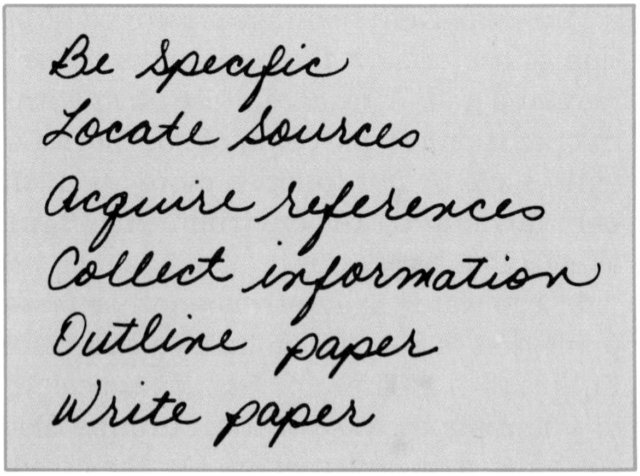

Be Specific
Locate Sources
Acquire references
Collect information
Outline paper
Write paper

## Practice

On a separate sheet of paper, take notes on any physical science article in a magazine. Be brief but thorough.

## Application

*Insulation* and *Alternate Energy Sources* are too broad to be good subjects for research papers. Using the information in Chapter 22, find three suitable subtopics from within each of these broad subjects. Write them on a separate sheet of paper. Choose one of these topics. Research and write a report about it.

## CONSERVING ENERGY
## BY INSULATION

### Objective
Compare the abilities of various insulators to retain heat.

### Background
Because of the high cost of fuels today, people are trying to conserve energy in their homes. Many homes have an insulating material in the walls. This material keeps heat in during the winter and out during the summer.

### Materials
water, hot plate or bunsen burner, empty juice can, empty soda can, fiberglass, cotton balls, newspaper, thermometer, pot holder

### Procedure
1. Heat a beaker of water to 80°C.
2. Put the juice can inside the soda can so that it is centered. Stuff the insulating material you are testing in the space between the juice can and the soda can. Pack the material tightly, almost to the top of the juice can.
3. (**CAUTION:** Hold the beaker with a pot holder.) Fill the juice can almost to the top with the hot water and put a thermometer in it. Record the temperature in a data table set up like Table 22-L. Record this first reading as 0 minutes.
4. Continue to record the temperature every 5 minutes for 20 minutes.
5. When all groups have completed the experiment, record the data obtained for the other materials (and for no material).
6. Plot each set of data in your table on a graph. Place temperature on the vertical axis and time on the horizontal axis. Put all four lines on the same graph. Label the lines *A, B, C,* and *D.*

### Questions
1. Why was data taken for a setup with no insulator?
2. Which of the materials tested is the best insulator? The worst? Explain.
3. **PROBLEM SOLVING** Which combination of materials makes the best insulator? Make a hypothesis based on your data. Then test your hypothesis.

| | **TABLE 22-L.** DATA TABLE | | | |
|---|---|---|---|---|
| **Time (min)** | **A. Fiberglass T (°C)** | **B. Cotton T (°C)** | **C. Newspaper T (°C)** | **D. No insulator T (°C)** |
| | | | | |

Do you look for ways to conserve energy at home? Perhaps you like drawing things, especially designs. The careers below involve interests like these. You might want to read about them.

### Environmental Designer

Environmental designers are architects with special training in energy conservation and environmental use. They try to design buildings that are attractive and that blend into the environment. They also try to prevent buildings from wasting energy. Many of their recent designs have included solar collectors for heating water and rooms.

Students in environmental design take five to six years of college. After graduating, they usually work in an architect's office for three years before taking licensing exams. The training is long, but the rewards of watching ideas turn into beautiful buildings make it all worthwhile.

For more information on a career as an environmental designer, write:

*The American Institute of Architects*
*1735 New York Avenue, NW*
*Washington, DC 20006*

### Heating and Air-Conditioning Technician

Heating and air-conditioning technicians help design, and service systems that control temperatures inside buildings. They may help engineers test experimental models at a manufacturing company. Or they may supervise sales, installation, and maintenance of heating and air-conditioning equipment for dealers.

One or two years of technical training at a junior or community college is very helpful in this career, especially for jobs in research and development or supervision. Courses in solar energy are also helpful for technicians who would like to work for solar energy companies.

More information on this career is available from:

*Air-Conditioning Contractors of America*
*1228 17th Street, NW*
*Washington, DC 20036*

# SUMMARY

1. Solar energy can be used to heat and cool buildings. It can be changed into electricity by solar cells. (22-1)

2. Windmills can produce electricity from the energy of wind. (22-1)

3. Water falling over a dam can generate electricity. (22-2)

4. Geysers and hot rocks are sources of geothermal energy, or heat within the earth. Geothermal energy can be used to generate electricity. (22-2)

5. Biomass, plant or animal matter, contains stored energy from photosynthesis. Energy can be obtained from solid waste biomass by burning or by the action of bacteria. (22-3)

6. The fuels produced from biomass include methane gas, methanol, and ethanol. Gasohol contains gasoline mixed with ethanol. (22-3)

# REVIEW

Number a sheet of paper from 1 to 25 and answer these questions.

**Building Science Vocabulary**  Write the letter of the term that best matches each definition.

| | |
|---|---|
| **a.** biomass | **g.** geothermal energy |
| **b.** electrolysis | **h.** hydroelectricity |
| **c.** ethanol | **i.** methanol |
| **d.** fermentation | **j.** photosynthesis |
| **e.** fossil fuel | **k.** photovoltaic effect |
| **f.** gasohol | **l.** turbine |

1. A mixture of gasoline and ethanol
2. The conversion of sunlight into electricity
3. Electricity produced by water falling or flowing from a higher level to a lower level

4. A process by which yeast changes sugar into alcohol and carbon dioxide

5. The breaking down of water into hydrogen and oxygen by electricity

6. A bladed wheel in an electric generator

7. Organic matter that can be used as a source of energy

8. Any fuel formed from dead plants and animals deep in the earth

9. Stored heat within the earth

10. A process by which green plants make food from water and carbon dioxide in the presence of light

**Finding Facts**  Select the letter of the answer that best completes each of the following.

11. Which of the following is *not* a fossil fuel?  (**a**) coal  (**b**) alcohol  (**c**) natural gas  (**d**) oil.

12. Solar cells are made from the element (**a**) silicon  (**b**) copper  (**c**) iron  (**d**) hydrogen.

13. A windmill is really a turbine that produces electricity by running a  (**a**) shaft  (**b**) generator  (**c**) propeller  (**d**) pump.

14. The energy stored in water comes from  (**a**) hydrogen  (**b**) electrolysis  (**c**) the wind  (**d**) the sun.

15. Hydroelectricity is most often associated with  (**a**) windmills  (**b**) nuclear power plants  (**c**) dams  (**d**) geysers.

16. Which of the following is a source of geothermal energy?  (**a**) hot rocks  (**b**) dams  (**c**) the wind  (**d**) biomass

17. A fuel gas obtained by the electrolysis of water is  (**a**) natural gas  (**b**) hydrogen  (**c**) oxygen  (**d**) steam.

18. Methane, a fuel gas, is produced from garbage by  (**a**) electrolysis  (**b**) photosynthesis  (**c**) the action of bacteria  (**d**) fermentation.

**19.** Which of the following is a high-power fuel used in racing cars? **(a)** ethanol **(b)** hydrogen **(c)** methane **(d)** methanol

**20.** A method in which water is used to remove wastes from smoke is **(a)** scrubbing **(b)** the photovoltaic effect **(c)** electrolysis **(d)** fermentation.

**Understanding Main Ideas** Complete the following.

**21.** Solar energy can be used to run air conditioners because the heat is used to run the _?_ generator.

**22.** Some dams can be harmful to the environment because a change in the natural flow of water can kill _?_ .

**23.** Before using kelp farms to produce biomass, scientists must learn more about the effect of kelp farms on the _?_ .

**24.** Some people object to using hydrogen as a fuel because hydrogen is _?_ .

**25.** Wood plants, animal wastes, and any other organic matter used for energy is called _?_ .

**Writing About Science** On a separate sheet of paper, answer the following as completely as possible.

**1.** Suppose you want to start a campfire. You have plenty of wood but no matches. How could you use a mirror to start the fire?

**2.** Why are hydroelectric power plants built at the bottom of a dam instead of at the top?

**3.** A British engineer was able to use a kite to help pull his yacht across the English Channel. How could this technique conserve fossil fuel?

**4.** What are some sources of biomass in your home?

**5.** (laboratory question) To help insulate houses, some storm windows contain two panes of glass with a region of air in between them. What is the insulator? Why does it work?

**Investigating Chapter Ideas** Try one of the following projects to further your study.

**1. Energy sources** Find a reference that lists the percentage of our energy supply provided by current energy sources. Find a chart that shows how these percentages may change over the next 30 years. Prepare a poster comparing these charts. How much will we have to increase alternative energy sources to keep up with our demand for energy? What will happen if nuclear power is not developed because of the dangers and construction problems involved? Can alternative energy sources make up the difference?

**2. Coal mining** Coal is mined in several areas of the United States by a variety of methods. Write a report on the various locations and ways coal is mined.

**3. Ocean thermal power plants** Read and report on the operating principles of an ocean thermal power plant.

**Reading About Science** Read some of the following books to explore topics that interest you.

Knight, C. 1976. **Harnessing the Sun.** New York: Morrow.

Lyttle, Richard B. 1982. **Shale Oil and Tar Sands: The Promises and Pitfalls.** New York: Watts.

Smith, Norman F. 1984. **Energy Isn't Easy.** New York: Coward.

MacDonald, Lucille. 1981. **Windmills: An Old-New Energy Source.** New York: Elsevier/Nelson.

# CHAPTER INVESTIGATIONS

## Objective
Investigate how scientists study nature.

## Background
Scientists carry out many activities in their search for answers about the world around them. They observe, question, record measurements, draw conclusions, and test their ideas. In this investigation, you will first take a closer look at these activities. Then you will carry out some of these activities as you investigate the way double-acting baking powder works.

## Materials (*needed for Part B only)
*double-acting baking
  powder
*250-mL beaker
*egg white
*stirring rod
*glass marking pencil
*metric ruler
*watch
*safety goggles
*Pyrex dish of hot
  tap water
*pot holders
*safety apron

## Procedure

### Part A    Identifying Scientific Activities
1. Look carefully at the activities being done by the people in Figure 1. On a separate sheet of paper, write down each activity being done.

### Part B    An Investigation with Baking Powder
2. Copy Table 1 onto a separate sheet of paper.
3. Place the baking powder into a beaker.
4. Pour the egg white into the beaker. Stir gently just enough to moisten the powder.
5. Immediately place a mark at the height of the mixture in the beaker. See Figure 2.
6. Measure and record the height in centimeters of the foam every minute for five minutes.
7. Use pot holders to transfer the dish of hot water to the laboratory table. **CAUTION:** Hot water can scald you. Handle all materials carefully. After 5 minutes place the beaker of foam in the dish. Wear goggles and apron.

8. Measure the height of the foam every minute for 5 minutes. Record your readings in your table.

*Figure 1.*

## Questions

### Part A

1. The following is a list of some activities that scientists do. Use words from this list to identify each of the scientific activities being done by the people in Figure 1. For example, the scientific activity "testing" is being done by the person labeled **A**. Note that a letter may be used more than once. And an activity may have more than one answer.

Scientific Activities: discussing results; following directions; making measurements; observing; recording information; researching a topic; testing

### Part B

2. Calculate how fast the foam rose in the beaker at room temperature. Use the formula in Figure 2.

3. Calculate how fast the foam rose in the beaker when it was placed in the hot water. Use the same formula.

4. Double-acting baking powder has two substances that combine with batter. One acts at room temperature. The other substance

*Figure 2.*

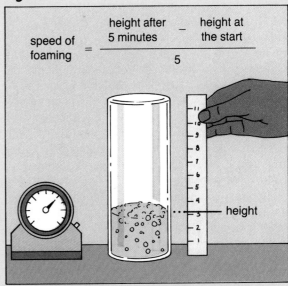

acts only at higher temperatures. Explain why double-acting baking powder contains these two substances.

5. Compare your results with others in the class. Explain any differences.

**TABLE 1.** BAKING POWDER READINGS

| Time (minutes) at Room Temperature | Height of Foam (cm) | Time (minutes) at Higher Temperature | Height of Foam (cm) |
| --- | --- | --- | --- |
| 1 | | 1 | |
| 2 | | 2 | |
| 3 | | 3 | |
| 4 | | 4 | |
| 5 | | 5 | |

# CHAPTER 2 INVESTIGATION

## Objective
Observe and identify chemical changes.

## Background
Physical and chemical changes are taking place all around you. In a physical change, substances keep their original identities. But in a chemical change, substances lose their original identities. They become one or more new substances with different properties. For example, an iron nail can combine with oxygen and change into rust. Rust is a substance with different properties from either original substance.

By observing what happens when substances are mixed, you can tell if a chemical change has taken place. For example, the change in color and texture of an iron nail are signs that a chemical change has occurred in the nail. In this investigation you will observe signs of chemical change. Then you will carry out some changes on your own. Based on your observations, you will then decide how to tell if a chemical change has taken place.

## Materials (*needed for Part B only)
*safety goggles
*steel wool
*3 test tubes
*test tube rack
*hydrochloric acid
*4 medicine droppers
*strip of colored cotton fabric
*chlorine bleach
*copper sulfate dissolved in water
*sodium hydroxide dissolved in water

*Figure 1.*

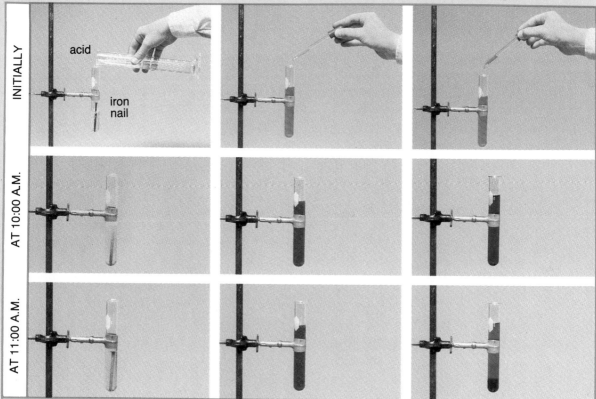

**TABLE 1.** DATA TABLE

| Reaction | Observations | |
|---|---|---|
| | 10:00 A.M. | 11:00 A.M. |
| Acid added to iron nail | | |
| Colorless liquid added to yellow liquid | | |
| Green liquid added to yellow liquid | | |

## Procedure

### Part A   Observing Chemical Changes
1. Copy Table 1 onto a separate sheet of paper.
2. Look carefully at each of the series of photos in Figure 1. Complete Table 1.

### Part B   Looking For Signs
CAUTION: Handle all chemicals with care. Report any spills to your teacher immediately. Always wear goggles when handling acids.
3. Place a loosely packed ball of steel wool about the size of a pea into a test tube.
4. Carefully half fill the test tube with acid. Observe for about 5 minutes. Write down any changes you see. After about an hour, record any further changes that you may see in the steel wool.
5. Place a small scrap of the cotton fabric in a second test tube.
6. Half fill the test tube with the chlorine bleach. Leave it alone for about 15 minutes. Record any observations you make.
7. Half fill a third test tube with the blue copper sulfate liquid.
8. Carefully add about 5 drops of sodium hydroxide to the third test tube. Record what you observe.

## Questions

### Part A
1. Based on your observations, list four possible signs of a chemical change.

### Part B
2. What happened when you added acid to the steel wool? Describe what happened to the steel wool as time passed.
3. What happened when the chlorine bleach was added to the cotton strip?
4. What happened when you added sodium hydroxide to the copper sulfate?
5. Based on your observations, which activities that you performed showed signs of a chemical change? Describe the signs.

# CHAPTER 3
# INVESTIGATION

## Objective
Make and test a hypothesis.

## Background
In addition to the natural chemicals in foods, other chemicals such as preservatives, flavors, and colors are often added to some foods. Chemicals such as these are called food additives. In this exercise you will study some artificial food coloring. Food coloring is a mixture of dyes. They can be separated by a process called paper chromatography. In this process, the dyes move at different rates through the fibers of paper.

A small amount of food coloring is placed on a strip of paper. When the food coloring is dry, a liquid is placed at the lower end of the strip. As it is absorbed by the strip, it rises through the fibers in the paper. See Figure 1. The rising liquid carries the different dyes in the food coloring up the paper. Different dissolved dyes travel through the paper at different rates. This difference in speed separates the parts of the mixture, leaving a record on the paper strip.

## Materials (*needed for Part B only)
*package of grape Kool-Aid™ (unsweetened), *water, *Whatman #1 chromatography paper, *1% sodium chloride (NaCl) solution, *large paper clip or wire, *600-mL beaker (or glass at least 12 cm high), *wood toothpick, *metric ruler, *small beaker, *balance, *stirring rod

## Procedure

### Part A   Identifying Food Dye Colors
1. Figure 1 is a chromatogram of three food colors: blue, green, and yellow. Which of the dyes are mixtures of colors? Each dye in a food color can be identified by the distance it travels up the paper compared with the distance the liquid travels. This is a ratio called the $R_f$. To find the $R_f$ of each colored dye, first measure the distance it traveled from the starting line (bottom pencil line). Measure this from the starting line to the center of the dye spot. Then measure the distance the liquid traveled from the starting line to the finishing line (top pencil line). The

**Figure 1.**

**Figure 2.**

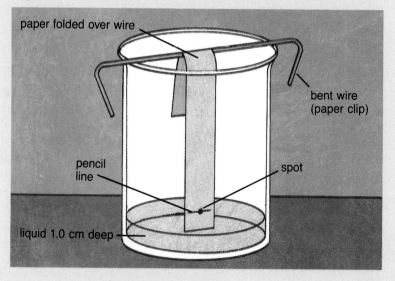

paper folded over wire

bent wire (paper clip)

pencil line

spot

liquid 1.0 cm deep

$R_f$ is the distance the dye traveled divided by the distance the liquid traveled. Copy Table 1 onto a separate sheet of paper and record your results.

2. Now use a metric ruler to measure the distance each colored dye in each food color traveled. Record these distances on a separate sheet of paper. Measure the distance the liquid traveled and record it.

3. Calculate the $R_f$ for each of the colored dyes in each food color. Record your results.

**TABLE 1.** DATA TABLE

| Food Color | Dyes Present | $R_f$ of Each Dye |
|---|---|---|
| Blue | | |
| Green | | |
| Yellow | | |

## Part B   Identifying the Colors in Grape Kool-Aid™

4. Your problem is to find out what colors give grape powder its purple color. State your hypothesis as an "If…then" sentence.

5. Now test your hypothesis with an experiment. Cut a strip of chromatography paper 15 cm long by 2 cm wide.

6. Draw a pencil line 1.5 cm from the bottom of the strip. Do not use ink.

7. Measure 5 g of grape powder and dissolve it in 10 mL of water in a small beaker. Stir it until no more dissolves.

8. Use a toothpick to place a small spot of the grape liquid on the paper strip. Spot it right on the starting line (pencil line). Allow a few minutes for the spot to dry. If the spot is very light after it dries, place another spot directly on top of the first spot. Allow it to dry.

9. Add 1% salt solution (sodium chloride) to the 600 mL beaker (or glass) until it is about 1 cm deep. Do not wet the sides of the beaker inside or outside. If you do, dry it before using.

10. Bend a large paper clip or wire into the shape you see in Figure 2. Place it across the beaker. Fold the top of the chromatography strip over the wire so that it is well supported. See Figure 2.

11. Place the wire with the paper strip on the beaker so that the bottom edge of the paper just dips into the liquid. The liquid will travel up the paper. Observe the process for 30 minutes.

12. After 30 minutes remove the paper from the beaker. Immediately make a pencil dot to mark the distance traveled by the liquid. Allow the strip to dry and then draw a pencil line where you marked the pencil dot. This is the finishing line for the liquid.

13. Calculate the $R_f$ values for each separate color as you did in Part A. Use Table 1 to determine which of the colored dyes is in grape drink.

## Questions

### Part A

1. What is the $R_f$ value of a dye if it traveled 3.5 cm from the starting line while the liquid traveled 10 cm?

2. List two factors that determine how far a dye will move up a chromatography strip.

### Part B

3. State the hypothesis you formed.

4. What two dye colors are in the grape powder?

5. **PROBLEM SOLVING** Suppose you are allergic to blue food dye. Grape powder drink makes you break out in a rash. Dark cherry drink is red, but maybe there is some blue mixed in it. How can you test your hypothesis?

## Objective

Use distance and time measurements to describe the motion of an accelerating object.

## Background

To describe the motion of an object accurately, you need distance and time data. Strobe photography is one method of obtaining this information. A strobe photograph allows measurements to be taken from a single picture. A strobe photograph takes many pictures of a moving object, all on the same film.

To make the strobe photographs in Figure 1, the camera shutter was kept open in a darkened room. A bright light flashed every tenth of a second. Each time the light flashed, a picture was taken of the moving object. In *Part A* you will study the motion of an accelerating object by making measurements on a strobe photograph. In *Part B* you will set up your own model of an accelerating object and find distance–time data.

## Materials (*needed for Part B only)

| | |
|---|---|
| *newspaper | *felt-tipped pen |
| *scissors | *book |
| *cellophane tape | *ping-pong ball |
| *2 meter sticks | *watch with second hand |
| | *graph paper |

## Procedure

### Part A   Measurements on a Strobe Photograph

1. Look at Figure 1. Measure the distance in centimeters from the dot on the object on the far left to the dot on the object in the second position from the left.

2. Measure the total distance traveled by the object from the starting point in 0.2 second, 0.3 second, etc.

3. Make a data table, showing the total distance traveled in one column and the travel time in another column.

*Figure 1.*

4. Make a graph of the motion of the object. Plot the total distance traveled on the vertical axis and the time of travel on the horizontal axis. Label your vertical axis from 0 to 90 cm and your horizontal axis from 0 to 0.5 s.

5. Calculate the average speed during the first 0.1 second for the motion in Figure 1.

*Figure 2.*

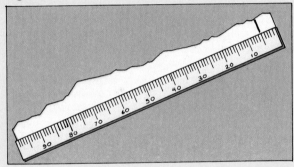

## Part B   A Model of Accelerated Motion

6. Cut a thin strip of newspaper about 1 m long by 1 cm wide. Tape it along the edge of a meter stick. Make a line at a position 5 cm from the edge of the meter stick. See Figure 2.

7. Set up the apparatus for this investigation as shown in Figure 3.

8. Place the ping-pong ball in the groove at the 5-cm line you marked on the newspaper.

9. Release the ball and begin timing. Every second say the word "now." Your partner should mark the position of the ball each time you say "now." Continue until the ball reaches the bottom of the ramp. (Try a few dry runs to practice the part that each of you will have in the investigation.)

10. Measure the distance from the 5-cm line to the next line.

11. Measure the total distance traveled by the ball from the starting point in 1.0 second, 2.0 seconds, etc.

12. Make a data table, showing the total distance traveled in one column and the travel time in another column.

13. Make a graph of the motion of the ball. Plot the total distance traveled on the vertical axis and the time of travel on the horizontal axis. Use appropriate divisions for your axes.

*Figure 3.*

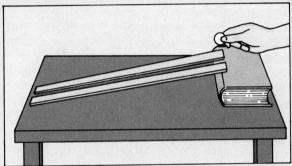

14. Calculate the average speed during the first 1.0 second for the motion of the ball.

## Questions

### Part A

1. Describe the speed of the object in Figure 1.

2. What is the average speed of the object during the first 0.1 second?

3. What is the average speed during the second 0.1-second interval (from 0.1 s to 0.2 s)?

4. What kind of motion is the object undergoing?

5. Describe the graph of the motion of the object.

### Part B

6. Describe the speed of the ball.

7. What is the average speed of the ball during the first second?

8. What is the average speed of the ball during the second 1.0-second interval (from 1.0 s to 2.0 s)?

9. What kind of motion is illustrated by the ball?

## Objective

Investigate how the force of friction can be changed.

## Background

A force of friction is exerted whenever the surfaces of two objects rub against each other. As Figure 1 shows, even the smoothest surfaces are very uneven when looked at on the microscopic level. And it is on the microscopic level where frictional forces occur. As the surfaces are rubbed together, the microscopic "peaks and valleys" tend to lock together. This locking causes the surfaces to resist being moved. This resistance results in friction.

Frictional forces can occur between any two states of matter. For example, they can occur between two solids, a solid and a gas, etc. In this investigation, you will study factors that change the amount of friction between the surfaces of two objects. First you will study the effect on friction of increasing mass. Then you will consider the use of water and oil as lubricants between two surfaces.

## Materials

| | |
|---|---|
| masking tape | watch with second hand |
| sheet of plastic | spring scale |
| jar lid | water |
| standard masses | vegetable oil |
| string | colored pencils |
| meter stick | graph paper |

## Procedure

1. Copy Table 1 onto a separate sheet of paper.
2. Tape a long sheet of plastic (about 1 meter) to a table. Place the jar lid on the plastic sheet and put a 100-gram mass in the jar lid. Attach the spring scale to the jar lid using some string. See Figure 2.
3. Slowly pull on the spring scale until the jar lid just begins to move. Record the force reading on the spring scale at which this occurs in Table 1. This force is called starting friction. It measures the friction between the jar lid and the plastic sheet.
4. Continue to pull on the spring balance so that the lid moves about 20 cm in 1 second. While the lid is moving, have a partner record the force reading on the spring scale. This force is called sliding friction. Sliding friction measures the friction between objects that are sliding over each other.

*Figure 1.*

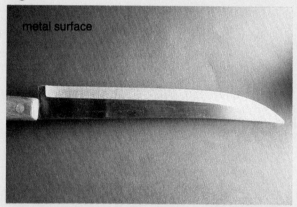
metal surface

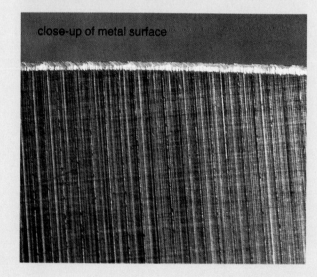
close-up of metal surface

**TABLE 1.**  DATA TABLE

| Cases | Mass | Starting Friction | Sliding Friction |
|---|---|---|---|
| 1.  Jar lid alone | 100<br>300<br>500 | | |
| 2.  Lid plus water | 100<br>300<br>500 | | |
| 3.  Lid plus vegetable oil | 100<br>300<br>500 | | |

5. Replace the 100-gram mass with 300 grams. Repeat steps 3 and 4. Then repeat with 500 grams. Your partner should record the results of each trial.

6. Place a few drops of water on the plastic and spread it around with the jar lid. Repeat steps 3 through 5.

7. Carefully wipe off all the water from the lid and the plastic so that both surfaces are completely dry. Then place a few drops of oil on the plastic and spread it with the jar lid. Repeat steps 3 through 5.

8. Plot a graph showing how the frictional force depends on the total mass pressing the jar lid on the plastic. Label the frictional force on the vertical axis and the mass on the horizontal axis. Do this for each case in Table 1. Plot the data from each case on the same graph. Use different colored pencils for each case.

## Questions

1. What happened to the force of friction between the surfaces involved as the mass in the jar lid increased?

2. For any particular case and mass, how does the starting friction and the sliding friction compare?

3. In which case was the sliding friction the greatest?

4. In which case was the starting friction the least?

5. The water and the oil are lubricants for this investigation. What effect does adding lubricants have on the friction between two surfaces? How could you explain this effect? (Hint: Refer to Figure 1 for a clue.) Do all lubricants seem to be equally effective?

*Figure 2.*

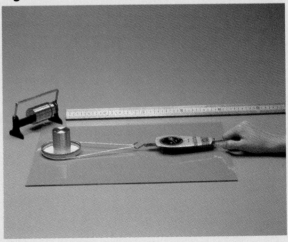

## Objective

Determine the work you do by driving a nail into wood.

## Background

Figure 1 shows a pile driver in action. A large mass is lifted and dropped on the cylindrical pile. Each time the mass hits the cylindrical pile, it exerts a force on the pile. The pile is driven deeper into the concrete.

In this investigation you will set up a model of a pile driver. You will do work by lifting an object a certain distance before you drop it on a nail.

**Figure 1.**

The work you do is equal to the weight of the object times the distance you lift it each time. You may be surprised at the total amount of work you have to do to drive the nail completely into a piece of wood.

## Materials

| | |
|---|---|
| wood (soft pine or balsa) | meter stick |
| | 1-kg mass |
| long iron nail | long weight hanger |
| hammer | 2-kg mass |

## Procedure

1. Copy Table 1 onto a separate sheet of paper.

2. Use a hammer to pound a nail a short distance into a block of wood. Make sure the nail is straight and positioned vertically. Measure the distance from the head of the nail to the wood. Record this distance in the table under "Trial 1, Distance Before Hitting."

3. Place a 1-kg mass (weight = 9.8 N) on a weight hanger. Then rest the weight hanger on the head of the nail as shown in Figure 2.

**Figure 2.**

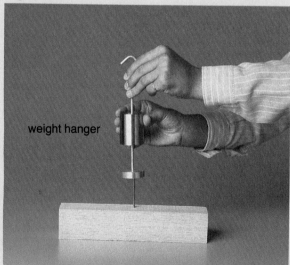

weight hanger

# POUNDING NAILS AND WORK

**TABLE 1.  WORK AND DISTANCE**

| Work Done by Lifting the Weight | Distance Nail Is Driven into Wood<br>$\left(\begin{array}{l}\text{Distance from nail head to wood}\\ \text{before hit} - \text{after hit}\end{array}\right)$ |
|---|---|
| Trial  weight × 0.10 m = _____ J | _____ − _____ = _____ |
| Trial  weight × 0.10 m = _____ J | _____ − _____ = _____ |
| Trial  weight × 0.10 m = _____ J | _____ − _____ = _____ |
| Total Work You Did _____ | Total Distance _____<br>Average distance = $\dfrac{\text{total}}{\text{\# trials}}$ = _____ |

Lift the mass a distance of 10 cm (0.10 m). Release the mass so that it pounds the nail.

4. Now measure again the distance from the head of the nail to the wood. Record it on the table under "Trial 1, Distance After Hitting." Then calculate the distance the nail was driven into the wood.

5. Calculate the work you did by lifting the 9.8-N weight. Record the work on the Table under "First Trial."

6. Repeat steps 2 to 5 until the nail has been driven completely into the wood. Determine the total work you did by adding the work done for all the trials. Find the average distance the nail was driven for each trial.

7. Repeat steps 1 to 6. However, replace the 1-kg mass with a 2-kg mass. As you start, be sure that you drive the nail with a hammer the same distance as in step 2.

## Questions

1. How many hits were required when you used the 1-kg mass? When you used the 2-kg mass? Explain the difference.

2. Was the total amount of work you did using the 1-kg mass different from the total you did using the 2-kg mass? Explain your answer.

3. What was the average distance the nail was driven into the wood during one hit for each mass? Explain any difference you may find.

4. Does the distance the nail was driven into the wood during a hit increase or decrease as the nail gets deeper into the wood? Explain your answer.

5. Suppose you lifted each mass 20 cm each time. How many hits do you think it would take for each mass to drive the nail into the wood? Explain your answer.

# CHAPTER 7
## INVESTIGATION

## Objective
Measure the efficiency of a simple machine.

## Background
Modern machines still use pulleys to make heavy construction work easier. Modern cranes use complex systems of pulleys to construct high-rise office buildings.

In this investigation you will make a few pulley systems and measure their efficiency. A pulley system allows you to move heavy objects with small forces. However, you have to do something extra when you are using the smaller force.

## Materials (*needed for Part B only)
*500-gram mass  *ring stand and clamp
*spring scale   *string
*two pulleys    *meter stick

## Procedure

### Part A  Different Pulley Systems
1. Study carefully the four pulley systems in Figure 1. To help guide your study, copy and complete Table 1.

### Part B  Setting Up Pulley Systems
2. Copy Table 2 onto a separate sheet of paper.
3. Hang a 500-gram mass on a spring scale and record its weight in newtons (N) in all the blanks under "Output Force" in Table 2.
4. Construct the pulley system in Figure 1A. Use the 500-gram mass as the load.
5. Slowly pull on the spring scale, moving it a distance of 20 cm (0.20 m). Read the force indicated on the scale as you move it. Record the force in Table 2 under "Input Force."
6. Measure the distance the load moved. Record the distance in Table 2 under "Output Distance."

*Figure 1.*

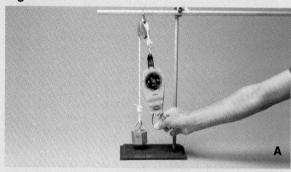

A

B

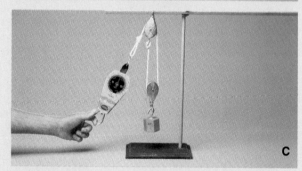

C

D

**TABLE 1.** CONTRASTING PULLEY SYSTEMS

|  | Number of Movable Pulleys | Number of Fixed Pulleys | Number of Strings That Support Load | Direction of Effort |
|---|---|---|---|---|
| Fig. 1A |  |  |  |  |
| Fig. 1B |  |  |  |  |
| Fig. 1C |  |  |  |  |
| Fig. 1D |  |  |  |  |

**TABLE 2.** INPUT AND OUTPUT DATA

|  | Input Force | Input Distance | Output Force | Output Distance | Work Input | Work Output | Efficiency |
|---|---|---|---|---|---|---|---|
| Fig. 1A |  | 0.2m |  |  |  |  |  |
| Fig. 1B |  | 0.2m |  |  |  |  |  |
| Fig. 1C |  | 0.2m |  |  |  |  |  |
| Fig. 1D |  | 0.2m |  |  |  |  |  |

7. Calculate the work output of the machine:

$$\text{Work Output} = \text{Weight of Load} \times \text{Distance Load Moved}$$

Record the work output in Table 2.

8. Calculate your work input:

$$\text{Work Input} = \frac{\text{Spring Scale Reading}}{} \times \frac{\text{Distance Spring Scale Moved}}{}$$

Record the work input in Table 2.

9. Repeat steps 4 through 8 for the pulley systems shown in Figures **B**, **C**, and **D**.

10. Calculate the efficiency of each pulley system:

$$\text{Efficiency} = \frac{\text{Work Output}}{\text{Work Input}} \times 100\%$$

Record each efficiency in Table 2.

## Questions

### Part A

1. Which system has the greatest number of strings that support the load?

2. Which systems change the direction of the force in order to lift the load?

### Part B

3. In which pulley system did you exert the least force to lift the load?

4. In which pulley system would you have to pull the string the greatest distance to lift the load 30 cm?

5. Which pulley system has the lowest efficiency?

6. Relate your answers to questions 3, 4, and 5 to your answer to question 1.

# CHAPTER 8 INVESTIGATION

## Objective

Observe the colors produced by some elements when heated in a flame.

## Background

According to the Bohr model, when atoms are heated, some electrons absorb energy. They move to higher orbits. These jumps to higher orbits, however, are only temporary. Soon the electrons give off the extra energy and return to their original, lower orbits. When they drop to lower orbits they emit energy in the form of light of various colors.

When you heat some elements in a flame you can see the colored light. If you view the flame with an instrument called a spectroscope you will discover that the colored light may be more than one color. (See page 419.) Many electrons in orbits of different energies are making jumps. Some elements can be identified by the colors they produce in a flame.

## Materials

bunsen burner, wood match sticks, cork or rubber stopper, marking pencil, 5 medicine droppers, saturated solutions of sodium chloride, calcium chloride, barium chloride, potassium chloride and copper sulfate (each in a separate beaker), five small watch glasses, spectroscope (optional)

### TABLE 1. DATA TABLE

| Solution | Flame Color | Element Present |
|----------|-------------|-----------------|
| 1 | | |
| 2 | | |
| 3 | | |
| 4 | | |
| 5 | | |

*Figure 1.*

calcium    sodium    lithium    barium    potassium

## Procedure

### Part A   Flame Colors

1. Figure 1 shows the colored flames produced by five different elements. On a separate sheet of paper, record the name of each element and the color of the flame produced.

2. Mark five small watch glasses 1, 2, 3, 4, and 5. From the beakers marked 1, 2, 3, 4, and 5 use medicine droppers to add a small amount of the solution to each watch glass having the corresponding number. Do not mix medicine droppers.

3. Light the bunsen burner. **CAUTION:** Ask your teacher to assist you.

4. Obtain five match sticks. Dip the unburned end of a match stick in the solution in watch glass 1. Dip the match stick several times or until the wood is very wet.

**Figure 2.**

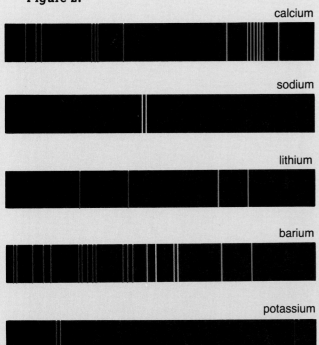

5. Hold the wet end of the match stick in the edge of the burner flame until you observe a color. You may have to dip the stick in solution again if it becomes dry. Observe the color of the flame. Match the color with Figure 1 and identify the element.

6. Copy Table 1 onto a separate sheet of paper. Record the results of step 5 in the Table.

7. Repeat steps 5 and 6 for the other four solutions.

### Part B   Observing Spectra

8. Figure 2 shows the colored bands of light (the spectra) produced by some common elements. On a separate sheet of paper, list the colors produced by each element.

9. (optional) If you have a student-type spectroscope, you may observe the spectra of some of the elements in the five solutions used in *Part A*. To do this work in pairs. One student holds the wet match stick in the flame. The other looks at the flame through the spectroscope.

## Questions

### Part A

1. Why do some of the spectra in Figure 2 have more than one colored line?

2. **Problem Solving** Sodium chloride and calcium chloride are commonly sprinkled on roads to melt the winter ice. Suppose someone gives you a bag of de-icing salt but the label does not tell you which compound it is. Based on this investigation explain how you would test the compound to find out what it is.

### Part B

3. Suppose you do a flame test on each of two different compounds. Each compound produces a green flame. You know that boron and barium each produce a green flame. How could you tell which is a boron compound and which is a barium compound?

## Objective

Study some properties and uses of three halogens.

## Background

Halogens are part of hundreds of compounds. Pure halogens are not found in the free, or uncombined, state in nature. They are always found as part of a compound. Fluorine is the most active halogen and is very poisonous. Figure 1 shows samples of pure chlorine, bromine, and iodine.

In *Part A* of this investigation you will look at some physical properties of pure chlorine, bromine, and iodine. In *Part B* you will use a special property of chlorine to test for its presence. When potassium iodide is added to a liquid containing chlorine, a chemical change takes place. The chlorine takes the place of the iodine in potassium iodide and iodine is set free. This is a chemical property of chlorine.

If starch is added to the mixture of chlorine and potassium iodide, another chemical change takes place. The iodine that is set free reacts with the starch. This causes the starch to turn blue. So when starch and potassium iodide are added to a liquid that contains chlorine, the starch turns blue. The more chlorine that is present, the darker will be the blue color.

## Materials (*needed for Part B only)

*two 500-mL beakers, *tap water, *balance, *chlorine bleach, *starch, *stirring rod, *potassium iodide, *graduated cylinder (50 mL or 100 mL), *medicine dropper, *small scrap of colored cotton cloth, *pool water (optional)

## Procedure

### Part A   Comparing Halogens

1. Study Figure 1. Note the phases (solid, liquid, gas) and color of each halogen. Copy Table 1 onto a separate sheet of paper and complete the table.

### Part B   Test for Chlorine

2. Let cold tap water run for several minutes. Then add about 225 mL of water into a beaker. Use a balance to measure out 0.2 g of potassium iodide (KI). Add it to the water and stir it.

*Figure 1.*

chlorine

bromine

iodine

3. Shake the bottle of starch mixture before using it. Add 10 mL of the starch mixture to the beaker in step 2. Stir it again. Observe and record any change you see.

4. To a second beaker add 225 mL of cold tap water. Use a medicine dropper to add 2 to 3 drops (not more) of chlorine bleach. **CAUTION:** Do not get bleach on yourself or your clothes. If you do, wash with water and tell your teacher. Stir the mixture. Add 0.2 g of potassium iodide and stir again. Then repeat step 3.

5. Clean the beaker used in step 2. Carefully use the medicine dropper to add 10 mL of chlorine bleach (a solution that contains a compound of chlorine). Then add 190 mL of water and stir it.

6. Soak a small scrap of colored cotton in the mixture of water and bleach for about 20 minutes. Record any changes you see.

7. (optional) If you have a sample of swimming pool water, you can test for chlorine by repeating steps 2 and 3. Use 225 mL of swimming pool water in place of tap water.

## Questions

### Part A

1. Which of the halogens in Figure 1 are present in more than one phase? What are the phases?

2. How many nonmetals in the Periodic Table are liquids?

### Part B

3. Did you observe a color change in step 2? If so, describe it.

4. Did you observe a color change when you tested tap water with potassium iodide and starch? The water containing chlorine bleach? Explain your answers.

5. List two chemical properties of chlorine and two of iodine observed in this experiment.

6. (optional) Did you observe a color change when you tested swimming pool water? If so, describe it.

7. **PROBLEM SOLVING** In an activity in which silver iodide was added to water containing halogen ions and starch, a deep blue color resulted. What might you conclude?

**TABLE 1.** DATA TABLE

| Halogen | Phases Present | Color of Each Phase |
|---------|----------------|---------------------|
| Chlorine | | |
| Bromine | | |
| Iodine | | |

# CHAPTER 10 INVESTIGATION

## Objective
Investigate a law of science by observing a chemical reaction.

## Background
The masses of the substances produced in a chemical reaction always equal the masses of the substances present before the reaction. This statement describes a law of science known as the Law of Conservation of Matter. This law, as well as all laws of nature, has been based on the observations of many people. However, laws are continually being tested. And, as more information is obtained, laws sometimes have to be changed. For example, it was once thought that matter could not be created or destroyed. However, as scientists learned about the nucleus, they learned that under certain conditions this law was not valid. Thus, the law was modified.

In this investigation you will test the Law of Conservation of Matter. You will observe what happens as two liquids are mixed. However, when liquids are mixed, it is sometimes hard to tell if a chemical reaction has occurred. To avoid this difficulty, you will use a property that some compounds possess when they are dissolved in water. When such water compounds are mixed, a solid is formed. This solid is evidence that a chemical reaction has taken place.

## Materials (*needed for Part B only)
| | |
|---|---|
| *10% solutions of | *2 100-mL beakers |
|    sodium carbonate | *graduated cylinder |
|    magnesium sulfate | *balance |
| *safety goggles | *safety apron |

## Procedure

### Part A  Testing A Law
1. Copy Table 1 onto a sheet of paper.

2. Figure 1A shows the reactants of a chemical reaction. They are sodium chromate ($Na_2CrO_4$) and zinc nitrate ($Zn(NO_3)_2$). Both compounds are dissolved in water. Record in Table 1 the names and formulas of the reactants. Record also the total mass of the system reactants + beakers (200 g).

3. Figure 1B shows the products of this reaction. They are sodium nitrate ($NaNO_3$) and zinc chromate ($ZnCrO_4$). Record in Table 1 the names and formulas of the products. Record also the total mass of the system products + beakers (200 g).

4. Note in your table any changes you see.

### Part B  Mixing Two Liquids Together
5. Add 10 mL sodium carbonate solution to a beaker. **CAUTION:** Wear goggles.

6. Add 10 mL magnesium sulfate solution to another beaker.

7. Place both beakers with their solutions on a balance. Record the total mass in Table 1.

**Figure 1.**

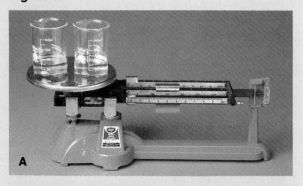

A

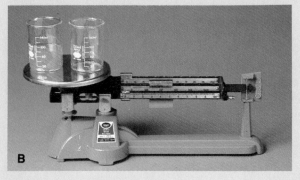

B

**TABLE 1.** DATA TABLE

| | | Reactants | ⟶ | Products | |
|---|---|---|---|---|---|
| **Part A** | Name | _____ + _____ | | _____ + _____ | |
| | Formula | _____ + _____ | | _____ + _____ | |
| | Total Mass | _____ | | _____ | |
| | Changes Observed | | | | |

| | | Reactions | ⟶ | Products | |
|---|---|---|---|---|---|
| **Part B** | Name | _____ + _____ | | _____ + _____ | |
| | Formula | _____ + _____ | | _____ + _____ | |
| | Total Mass | _____ | | _____ | |
| | Changes Observed | | | | |

8. Now pour the magnesium sulfate solution into the beaker of sodium carbonate. Record any changes you observe.

9. Place the empty beaker and the one containing the products of the reaction on the balance. Record the total mass.

## Questions

### Part A

1. How do you know that the mixing of the two solutions resulted in a chemical reaction?

2. Write a word equation for the reaction that occurred in Figure 1.

3. Using symbols for each substance, balance the equation for this reaction.

4. What kind of reaction is this?

5. What was the total mass of the system before the reaction? After the reaction?

6. How does this reaction show that matter is conserved?

### Part B

7. What evidence do you have that a chemical reaction occurred when you mixed the two liquids together?

8. In the investigation you performed, the two products formed were sodium sulfate ($Na_2SO_4$) and magnesium carbonate ($MgCO_3$). Write a word equation indicating the reactants and the products of the reaction.

9. Using symbols, write a balanced equation for this reaction.

10. What kind of chemical reaction took place?

11. What was the total mass of the system before the reaction (reactants plus beakers)? After the reaction (products plus beakers)?

12. Why did you not subtract the mass due to the beakers from your readings of the mass of the reactants and the products?

**Objective**
Grow and observe crystals of several solids.

**Background**
If you prepare a supersaturated solution of certain solids, you may watch crystals grow. Allow the solution to remain undisturbed several days. As the liquid evaporates, particles of the solute gradually "clump" together into crystal shapes. You can get faster results if you prepare only a small amount of solution and allow it to evaporate quickly. However, the crystals that result in this case are usually very small.

Crystals come in a variety of shapes and colors. The crystals of any substance have a

particular, identifiable shape. Figure 1 shows the six basic crystal shapes. Many crystals have identifiable colors as well. However, some crystals appear colorless unless viewed under polarizing film. Such film filters out light traveling in many paths, so that light emerging from the film travels in a single, uniform path. Light passing through the film and into a crystal may, in some cases, produce a color. The crystals of vitamin C in Figure 2 are shown in polarized light.

**Materials** (*needed for Part B only)
| | |
|---|---|
| *copper sulfate | *3 microscope slides |
| *balance | *wax marking pencil |
| *100-mL beaker | *stirring rod |
| *flat dish | *hand lens |
| *3 medicine droppers | *2 polarizing films |
| *10% solutions of | (optional) |
|   boric acid | *microscope |
|   vitamin C and MSG | (optional) |

*Figure 1.*

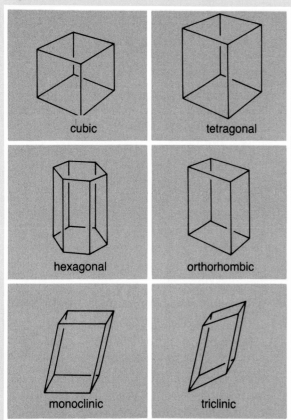

cubic     tetragonal

hexagonal     orthorhombic

monoclinic     triclinic

*Figure 2.*

## Procedure

### Part A   Observing Crystals

1. Figure 3 shows a variety of crystals that grow naturally in the earth's crust. On a separate sheet of paper, record the name and color of each crystal.

2. Now match each crystal with one of the basic shapes shown in Figure 1.

### Part B   Growing Crystals

3. Stir about 20 grams of powdered copper sulfate into 30 mL of hot tap water in a beaker. (**CAUTION:** Copper sulfate is poisonous. Wash your hands thoroughly after you work with it.) Allow the solution to cool for several days. Record your observations.

4. Using the dropper in the container of boric acid solution, add 3 drops of the solution to a microscope slide. Mark the slide *B*.

5. Using a stirring rod, spread the drops around to form a film about the area of a penny. Set the slide aside until the water evaporates.

6. Repeat steps 4 and 5 using two more slides and solutions of vitamin C and MSG. Mark the vitamin C slide *C* and the MSG slide *M*.

7. Use a hand lens to observe the crystals on each slide. Describe, or sketch, the crystals of boric acid, vitamin C, and MSG.

8. (optional) Place each of the three slides between two polarizing films and hold the "sandwich" up to the light. Slowly rotate the top film until you see colors. Then place this slide–film arrangement under a microscope. Your teacher will focus it for you. Describe what you see.

## Questions

### Part A

1. How would you recognize crystals of sodium chloride ( halite ) , sulfur, lead sulfide (galena), and calcium sulfate (gypsum)?

sulfur

gypsum

halite

galena

### Part B

2. What evidence do you have that the solution of copper sulfate you made in step 3 is supersaturated?

3. Describe the crystals of copper sulfate that grew in time.

4. Why could you not see particles of boric acid, vitamin C, and MSG in the solutions?

5. Describe the crystals of boric acid, vitamin C, and MSG.

6. (optional) What effect did polarized light have on each of the crystals on the slides?

## Objective
Measure pH with a wide range indicator.

## Background
You can measure pH with an acid–base indicator. Some indicators, such as litmus and phenolphthalein, only tell you whether the solution is acidic or basic. Others, like pH paper (see page 266), are sensitive over a wide range of pH values. To measure very exact pH values, scientists use a pH meter like the one in Figure 1.

The colored juices from some fruits and vegetables change color at various pH ranges. See Figure 2.

## Materials
plant juice (radish, red cabbage, blueberries, or turnips), two small beakers, stirring rod, graduated cylinder, test tube rack, four test tubes, marking pencil, dilute sodium hydroxide (NaOH), 10% solution white vinegar, 10% solution ammonia, club soda, safety goggles, safety apron

## Procedure

### Part A   Observing Changes in pH
1. Mark four test tubes from 1 to 4.
   #1 = vinegar, #2 = vinegar,
   #3 = ammonia, #4 = club soda

2. Add 5 mL of vinegar to tube #1. Leave the other tubes empty. **CAUTION:** Wear safety goggles and an apron. Always add acids to water.

3. Obtain 5 mL of the plant juice in a small beaker. Use a medicine dropper to add 10 drops of the juice indicator to tube #1. Stir the contents with a stirring rod and observe the color.

4. Copy Table 1 onto a separate sheet of paper.

5. Match the color with the pH scale in Figure 2 for your plant juice. Record the pH range in Table 1.

*Figure 1.*

**TABLE 1.   pH READINGS**

| Steps 4 to 8 Plant juice indicator used _____ | | | Steps 9 to 11 | | |
|---|---|---|---|---|---|
| Drops of NaOH added | Color of solution | pH range | Substance | Color of solution | pH range |
| 0 | | | Vinegar | | |
| 10 | | | Ammonia | | |
| 20 | | | Club soda | | |
| 30 | | | | | |
| 40 | | | | | |
| 50 | | | | | |
| 60 | | | | | |
| 70 | | | | | |

6. Add 5 mL of sodium hydroxide to a small beaker. Rinse the medicine dropper and use it to add 10 drops of sodium hydroxide to tube #1. **CAUTION:** Always add bases to water. Stir the contents with a stirring rod and observe the color.

7. Match the color with the pH scale in Figure 2. Record the pH range in Table 1.

8. Continue adding sodium hydroxide to tube #1, 10 drops at a time with stirring. Repeat step 7 until you have added a total of 70 drops.

### Part B   Measuring the pH of Some Home Chemicals

9. Rinse the graduated cylinder and use it to add 10 mL of vinegar to tube #2. Rinse the cylinder and add 10 mL of ammonia to tube #3. Rinse the cylinder and add 10 mL of club soda to tube #4.

10. Add 10 drops of juice indicator to tubes #2, 3, 4. Stir and rinse the stirring rod in between stirs.

11. Now match the color in tubes #2, 3, 4 with the pH scale and record the pH range of each in Table 1.

12. (optional) If you have a pH meter, you can check the pH values for vinegar, ammonia, and club soda. You will obtain an exact pH, such as 2.6. Ask your teacher for directions on using the meter.

### Questions

1. An environmental scientist reported that the rain water in an industrial area had a pH of 4.5. How do you think he measured this pH?

2. If you were to measure the pH of the rain water in question 1 with the plant juice you used in this investigation, what color would the solution be?

### Part B

3. What were the pH ranges for vinegar, ammonia, and club soda?

4. (optional) How did the pH values for the substances in question 3 compare with those measured using a pH meter?

*Figure 2.*

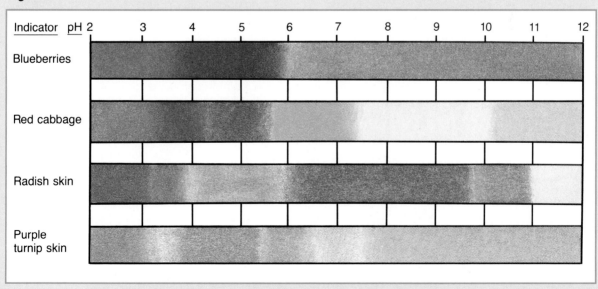

## Objective
Study some properties of plastics.

## Background
Technology has developed many different plastic materials with a variety of useful properties. Some plastics that may be familiar to you are the polyethylene used in sandwich bags, the polystyrene used in foam cups, and a special polyethylene fabric called TYVEK™. Figure 1 shows a house being wrapped in TYVEK™ before the final siding is put on. This special plastic stops drafts. However, it also lets the walls "breathe."

In this investigation you will find out why TYVEK™ is used to wrap the house. You will experiment with two plastic materials. You will compare their properties with those of regular paper. Your problem is to answer a question. Which plastic is best to use for the following

purposes: food storage bags, envelopes to mail videotapes, trash bags, protective suits to wear for cleaning up chemical spills.

## Materials (*needed for Part B only)
*computer disk sleeve (TYVEK™), *sandwich bag (polyethylene), *regular paper, *scissors, *ballpoint pen, *water, *three identical size drinking glasses, *graduated cylinder, *modeling clay

## Procedure

### Part A   Forming a Hypothesis
1. After reading the background information, you may want to go to the library and look up more information on polyethylene plastics. They are also called polymers.
2. Form your hypothesis, or educated guess, to solve the problem stated in the background information.

### Part B   Doing Tests
3. Use scissors to cut a 5-cm square of TYVEK™ polyethylene nonwoven fabric from a computer disk sleeve. Cut similar squares from regular paper and from a plastic sandwich bag.
4. Push a ballpoint pen through the three materials. **CAUTION:** Be careful not to push the point into your hand. Observe the difference in resistance to puncturing of each material. Copy Table 1 onto a separate sheet of paper and record your observations.
5. Now tear each material. Observe and record the differences in their strengths.
6. Soak the three materials (sandwich bag, TYVEK™, and regular paper) under water for 5 minutes. Remove the materials from the water and shake off excess water. Now test for puncture resistance and strength as you did in steps 4 and 5. Record your observations in Table 1.

*Figure 1.*

Adapted and reprinted with permission from CHEM MATTERS, April 1986, pp. 8–11. © 1986 American Chemical Society.

**Figure 2.**

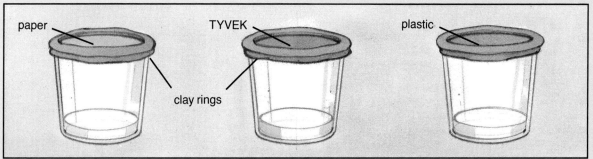

7. Place one of the drinking glasses upside down on a piece of TYVEK™ cut from a computer disk sleeve. Trace around it to make a circle. Cut out the circle with scissors. Do the same with the plastic sandwich bag and the paper.

8. Add 40 mL of water to each of the drinking glasses.

9. Form six rings of modeling clay and use them to seal the circle of TYVEK™ over one glass, the sandwich bag plastic over a second glass, and the paper over the third glass. See Figure 2.

10. Mark the water levels in each glass. Place them in a warm spot. Observe the water levels in each glass for several days. Record your observations in Table 1.

**Questions**

**Part A**

1. State your hypothesis.

**Part B**

2. Was there a control used in this experiment? If so what was it?

3. Based on your observations in step 10, did either plastic allow water vapor to pass through it?

4. Study your data table of the properties of the two plastics as compared with regular paper. What are your conclusions? The conclusions should be answers to the stated problem.

5. **PROBLEM SOLVING** Why is TYVEK™ used to wrap houses before the final siding is put on?

**TABLE 1.** DATA TABLE

| Material | Puncture Resistance | Strength | Strength After Soaking | Allows Water to Evaporate |
|---|---|---|---|---|
| TYVEK™ | | | | |
| Sandwich Bag | | | | |
| Paper | | | | |

## Objective
Relate the strength of the electric force between two objects to the distance between them.

## Background
Figure 1 shows a setup for measuring the amount of electric force between two objects. Charged metal sphere A is mounted on a balance. If equally charged sphere B is brought near the first, the spheres repel each other. As a result, sphere A moves down. Standard masses can be added to the balance to bring it into equilibrium again. The total weight of the standard masses needed to regain equilibrium equals the strength of the electric force between the spheres. At sea level, the weight in newtons of a standard mass can be found by multiplying the mass in grams by 0.0098.

## Materials

| | |
|---|---|
| 2 ping-pong balls painted with graphite | 2 ring stands and clamps |
| 2 plastic straws | meter stick |
| sharpened pencil | rubber rod |
| balance | piece of fur |
| cellophane tape | set of standard masses |
| | graph paper |

### Figure 1.

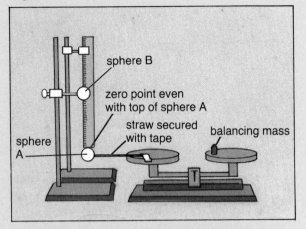

sphere B

zero point even with top of sphere A

straw secured with tape

balancing mass

sphere A

## Procedure
1. Copy Table 1 onto a separate sheet of paper.
2. Punch a hole in each ping-pong ball with the point of a pencil. Insert a plastic straw into each hole.
3. Position the balance in the middle of the rubber mat.
4. Attach sphere A to the balance. See Figure 1.
5. Place standard masses on the right-hand pan of the balance until the two pans are

**TABLE 1.** DISTANCE AND MASS DATA

| Trial | Distance Between the Two Spheres (cm) | Mass Needed for Equilibrium (g) | Electric Force (N) |
|-------|---------------------------------------|---------------------------------|--------------------|
| 1 | | | |
| 2 | | | |
| 3 | | | |
| 4 | | | |
| 5 | | | |
| 6 | | | |

balanced. Leave this total mass (the "balancing mass") on the pan throughout the investigation.

6. Stroke the rubber rod with the fur four times in the same direction. Touch sphere A with the rod. Now, holding onto the plastic straw, touch sphere B to sphere A. From here on, do not touch either sphere.

7. Use a clamp to fix the straw of sphere B to a ring stand. Raise the clamp on the ring stand until sphere B is near the top of the stand. Sphere B should be directly over sphere A.

8. Use another clamp to fix a meter stick to a second ring stand. The zero point on the meter stick should be even with the top of sphere A. Arrange the ring stands as shown in Figure 1.

9. Now slowly lower the clamp holding sphere B toward sphere A. Stop when you see the balance move. See Figure 2. Record the centimeter reading of the top of sphere B in Table 1. This is the distance between the two spheres.

10. Add masses to the right-hand pan until the top of sphere A once again is at the zero point of the meter stick. See Figure 3. Find the total mass you used. (Remember not to include the mass from step 5.) Record your data.

11. Calculate the force in newtons to which this mass corresponds. Record your results.

12. Lower the sphere by 5 cm and repeat steps 9–11. Repeat this procedure until the two spheres are 10 cm apart.

13. Make a graph showing how the electric force (vertical axis) is related to the distance between the two spheres (horizontal axis). Draw a smooth curve through your points.

**Figure 2.**

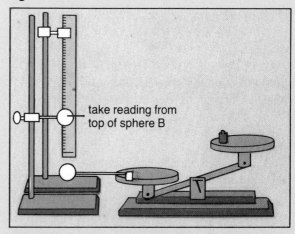

take reading from top of sphere B

**Figure 3.**

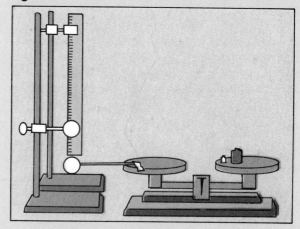

## Questions

1. Why did you not include the mass from step 5 in any measurements?

2. What was the electric force when the two spheres were 35 cm apart? 20 cm apart? 5 cm apart?

3. Describe how the electric force is related to the distance between two charged objects.

4. Suppose the two spheres were oppositely charged. How might you measure the force in that case?

## Objective
Study the operation of a transformer.

## Background
A coil of wire produces a voltage when it is moved through a magnetic field. This effect is called electromagnetic induction (EI). EI also occurs when the coil is not moving but the magnetic field is changing. A changing magnetic field is produced by sending a changing current through a coil of wire. Since a current creates a magnetic field, a changing current produces a changing magnetic field.

A transformer is a device made of two coils of wire wrapped around a piece of iron. It can be used to demonstrate EI. An alternating voltage in the first coil, the primary, creates a changing magnetic field. The changing magnetic field of the first coil then creates a voltage in the second coil, the secondary.

A transformer can increase or decrease the voltage. If voltage is increased, the transformer is a step-up transformer. If voltage is decreased, it is a step-down transformer. The kind of transformer (step-up or step-down) depends on the number of turns of wire in the secondary compared with the primary.

## Materials
graph paper

## Procedure
1. Copy Table 1 onto a separate sheet of paper.
2. The primary of the transformer in Figure 1 is connected to a voltage of 10 V. Study each of the photos. Record the number of turns of wire in the secondary coils in each photo.
3. Plot a graph of the Secondary Voltage (vertical axis) versus the Secondary Turns of Wire (horizontal axis).

4. Copy Table 2 and Table 3 onto a separate sheet of paper. Complete the tables by calculating the Voltage Ratio and the Turns Ratio.

*Figure 1.*

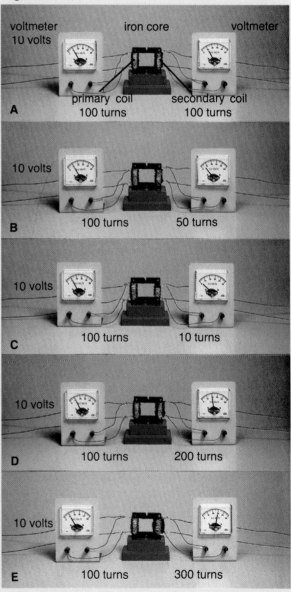

**TABLE 1.** DATA TABLE

| Transformer | Primary Voltage | Primary Turns of Wire | Secondary Voltage | Secondary Turns of Wire |
|---|---|---|---|---|
| A | 10 | 100 | 10 | |
| B | 10 | 100 | 5 | |
| C | 10 | 100 | 1 | |
| D | 10 | 100 | 20 | |
| E | 10 | 100 | 30 | |

## Questions

1. In which photo(s) is the transformer acting as a step-up transformer?
2. In which photo(s) is the transformer acting as a step-down transformer?
3. How many turns of wire in the secondary are needed to produce a voltage of 25 V?
4. How could you obtain an output voltage of 1000 V from the transformer used in the investigation?
5. Write a complete sentence stating the relationship between the voltages and turns of wire in a transformer. (Hint: Refer to step 2.)

**TABLE 2.** TURNS RATIO

| | Secondary Turns / Primary Turns = Turns Ratio | | |
|---|---|---|---|
| Fig. 1A | _____ | / 100 | = _____ |
| Fig. 1B | _____ | / 100 | = _____ |

**TABLE 3.** VOLTAGE RATIO

| | Secondary Voltage / Primary Voltage = Voltage Ratio | | |
|---|---|---|---|
| Fig. 1A | _____ | / 10 volts | = _____ |
| Fig. 1B | _____ | / 10 volts | = _____ |

## Objective
Study the frequency, wavelength, and speed of waves in a medium.

## Background
You can make many different waves in a long rope. Shorter waves are made when you shake one end of the rope up and down rapidly. Shake the end of the rope slowly and you make longer waves. In any medium, the wave's frequency (f), wavelength ($\lambda$), and speed (v) are related by the equation:

$$f\lambda = v$$

Figure 1 shows a system of rods connected together by a stiff metal band. When the metal band is twisted, wave energy is transferred from one rod to another. The rod system can be used to study the motion of transverse waves.

A rapid hand motion moves one end of the rods up and down, sending waves into the medium. If the hand turns fast, high-frequency waves are made. If the hand turns slowly, low-frequency waves are made.

## Materials
graph paper

## Procedure
1. Copy Table 1 onto a separate sheet of paper.

2. Study the photographs in Figure 2. Use a metric ruler to measure each wavelength (in centimeters). The best way to measure the wavelength is from crest to crest.

3. In Table 1 record the frequency (Hz) and wavelength (cm) for the wave in each photograph.

4. Find and record the speed of each wave.

5. Plot a graph of frequency (vertical axis) versus wavelength (horizontal axis).

*Figure 1.*

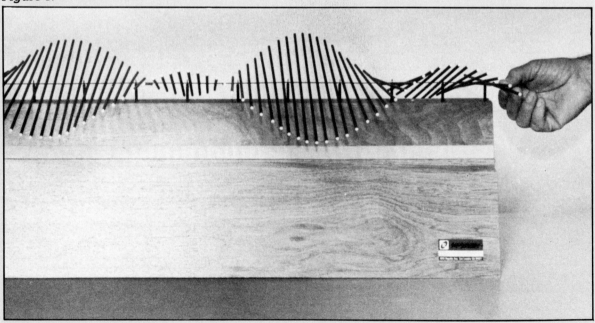

**Figure 2.**

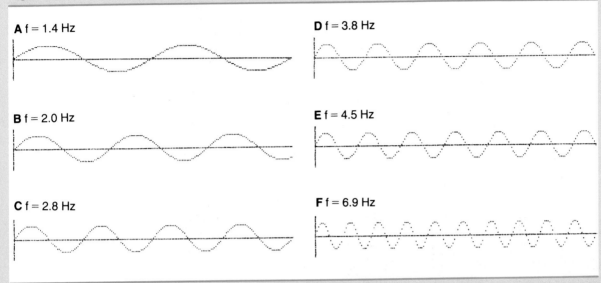

A f = 1.4 Hz

B f = 2.0 Hz

C f = 2.8 Hz

D f = 3.8 Hz

E f = 4.5 Hz

F f = 6.9 Hz

## Questions

1. Based on your graph, state the relationship between frequency and wavelength for waves in a medium.
2. Does the speed of the waves change when the frequency of the wave changes? State evidence to support your answer.
3. The frequency of a wave is 4 Hz and the wavelength is 3 cm. What is the speed of the wave?
4. If the frequency of the wave in question 3 was doubled, what would be the new wavelength and speed? If the frequency was halved, what would be the new wavelength and speed?

**TABLE 1.** DATA TABLE

| Photo | Frequency (Hz) | Wavelength (cm) | Speed of Wave (cm/s) |
|-------|----------------|-----------------|----------------------|
| A | 1.4 | | |
| B | 2.0 | | |
| C | 2.8 | | |
| D | 3.8 | | |
| E | 4.5 | | |
| F | 6.9 | | |

## Objective

Investigate how frequency affects the shape of a resultant wave.

## Background

Have you ever "seen" a sound? Electronic devices called oscilloscopes produce pictures of sounds. Look at the "sounds" in Figure 1. They show how complex simple sounds actually can be. Note how the amplitude of these sounds changes. Complex waves are the result of adding several simple waves. See Figure 2. In this investigation you will use a BASIC computer program to add waves. When you enter the program into a computer, you will be able to choose the frequencies of the waves you will add. Then you will be able to see the result when they are added.

## Materials

computer
graph paper

**Figure 2.** *"Visible" musical notes.*

**Figure 1.** *Adding waves together.*

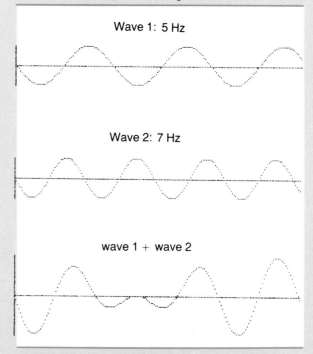

Wave 1: 5 Hz

Wave 2: 7 Hz

wave 1 + wave 2

## Procedure

1. Type the program into the computer *exactly* as shown in Table 1. Read Table 2 for an explanation of the program steps.
2. When you are ready to run the program, type in RUN and press the RETURN button.
3. When the computer asks for the frequency of the first wave, type 5 and press RETURN.
4. When the computer asks for the frequency of the second wave, type 7 and press RETURN.
5. After pressing RETURN, the computer will display the addition of the two waves. Sketch the waves that you see.
6. After you have sketched the waves, press RETURN to try runs with the frequencies shown in Table 3.
7. Turn the computer off when you have completed the investigation.

**TABLE 1.** COMPUTER PROGRAM

```
5   HOME : PRINT "MACMILLAN PHYSIC
    AL SCIENCE * WAVES": PRINT
10  PRINT "FREQUENCIES ** CHOOSE
    A FREQUENCY BETWEEN 1 AND 10
    HZ"
20  INPUT "FREQUENCY OF FIRST WAV
    E = ?";F1
30  INPUT "FREQUENCY OF SECOND WA
    VE = ?";F2
40  HGR : HCOLOR= 3
50  HPLOT 0,0 TO 0,30: HPLOT 0,50
    TO 0,80: HPLOT 0,90 TO 0,15
    0: HPLOT 0,15 TO 255,15: HPLOT
    0,65 TO 255,65: HPLOT 0,120 TO
    255,120
60  FOR I = 1 TO 255
70  W1 = 15 *  SIN (F1 * I / 50)
80  W2 = 15 *  SIN (F2 * I / 50)
90  HPLOT I,W1 + 15: HPLOT I,W2 +
    65: HPLOT I,W1 + W2 + 120
100 NEXT
110 VTAB 22: INPUT "PRESS <RETUR
    N> TO TRY AGAIN";A$
120 TEXT : GOTO 5
```

## Questions

1. What is the result when two waves of the same frequency are added?

2. Describe the result of adding two waves when one wave has twice the frequency of the second wave.

3. Describe the result of adding a wave with a frequency of 1 Hz to a wave with a frequency of 3 Hz.

4. Describe the result of adding a wave with a frequency of 2 Hz to a wave with a frequency of 6 Hz.

5. How could you use the computer to add three waves? Discuss with your teacher how to change the computer program to add three waves.

**TABLE 2.** EXPLANATION OF STEPS

Steps 5 and 10: These steps put introductory information on the TV screen.

Steps 20 and 30: These steps allow you to choose the frequency of the two waves.

Step 40: Tells the computer to get ready to plot graphs.

Step 50: Plots the axis for the graph of wave 1, wave 2, and the sum of the two waves.

Step 60: Tells the computer to calculate 255 parts for each wave.

Steps 70 and 80: Calculates each part of the two waves.

Step 90: Plots wave 1, wave 2, and the sum of the two waves.

Step 100: Part of step 60.

Step 110 and 120: Sends the program back to the beginning if you want another try.

**TABLE 3.** FREQUENCY FOR COMPUTER RUNS

| Run | Frequency 1 (in Hz) | Frequency 2 (in Hz) |
|---|---|---|
| 1 | 5 | 7 |
| 2 | any | same as frequency 1 |
| 3 | any | twice frequency 1 |
| 4 | 1 | 3 |
| 5 | 2 | 6 |
| 6 | any | any |

## Objective
Investigate the refraction of light.

## Background
A light ray bends when it travels from one medium into another. The bending—refraction—occurs at the boundary between the two media. Refraction depends on the two media and on the incident angle of the light ray.

A laser is ideal for studying properties of light. See Figure 1. A laser produces a narrow beam of intense light with a single wavelength. And since the beam of light is very narrow, it does not spread out very much. Laser light colliding with particles in the air scatters in all directions. The scattering allows you to see or photograph laser beams. If a laser beam passes from one medium to another, you can see clearly the refraction of light.

## Materials
graph paper       tracing paper

*Figure 1.*

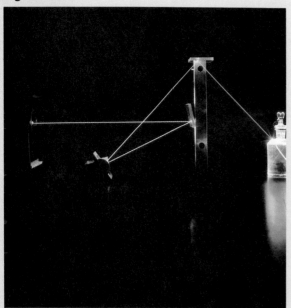

**TABLE 1.   DATA TABLE**

| Angle of Incidence | Angle of Refraction | |
| --- | --- | --- |
| | Air/Water | Air/Glass |
| 10 | | |
| 20 | | |
| 30 | | |
| 40 | | |
| 50 | | |
| 60 | | |

## Procedure
1. Copy Table 1 onto a separate piece of paper. Then, use tracing paper to draw the protractor shown in Figure 2. Figure 3 illustrates the refraction of laser light. The light beam travels from air into water (A) and from air into glass (B).
2. Use this protractor to estimate the refracted angle for each incident angle.

*Figure 2.*

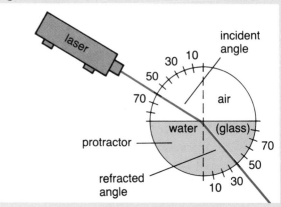

**3.** Record your data for this case in Table 1.

**4.** Graph your data. Plot the incident angle on the horizontal axis and the refracted angle on the vertical axis.

**5.** Repeat steps 2 through 4 for case B. However, graph the second set of data on the same set of axes as for case A.

**Questions**

**1.** If the incident angle is 45°, what is the refracted angle for the air-glass combination?

**2.** Which medium produces the greater amount of bending?

**3.** On the basis of your data, what do you think will be the angle of refraction if the incident angle is 0°?

*Figure 3.*    **A** FROM AIR INTO WATER

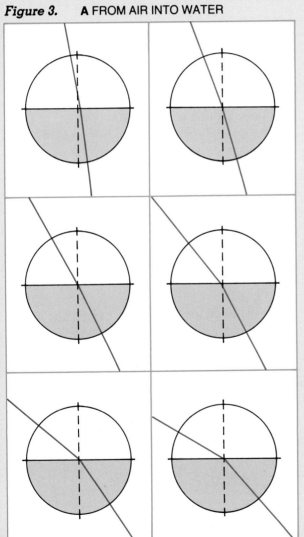

**B** FROM AIR INTO GLASS

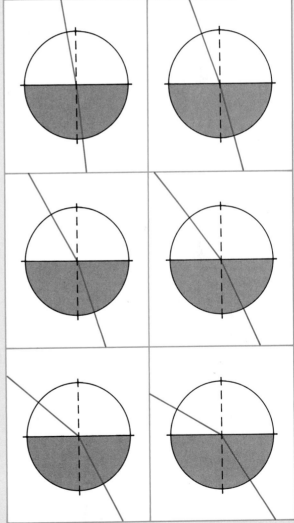

## Objective
Investigate energy changes in an atom.

## Background
An atom has both potential energy and kinetic energy. The potential energy is stored energy. It depends on the separation between the electron and proton, or the size of the electron's orbit. Larger electron orbits have more energy. The kinetic energy in the atom is the energy of the moving electron as it orbits the proton.

Imagine that an atom has a small amount of energy with its electron in a small orbit. If some energy were added to the atom, the size of the orbit would increase. The electron would jump to a larger orbit. However, an atom absorbs, or accepts, only certain amounts of energy. In this investigation you will determine which energies

a model atom will absorb. Your model atom is a computer model. If you choose a correct amount of energy, the electron will jump to a larger orbit.

In your model atom, the electron stays in the large, high-energy orbit for a short time. It then emits a photon, or bundle of electromagnetic energy. The electron drops down to the smallest energy orbit. In this investigation you will be able to calculate the frequency of the emitted photon.

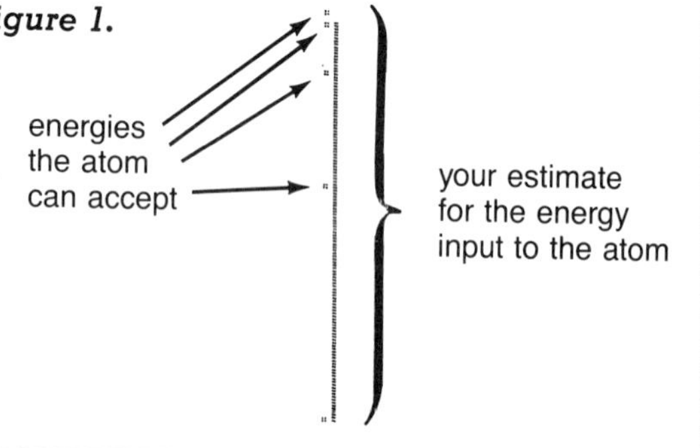

## Materials
computer, paper, pencil, calculator

## Procedure
1. Type the program into the computer exactly as shown in Table 1.
2. Copy Table 2 onto a sheet of paper.
3. When you are ready to run the program, type RUN and hit the RETURN key.
4. When the computer asks for the "ENERGY," type in a number between 10.0 and 14.9 and press RETURN. You are telling the computer what amount of energy you wish to add to the model atom. The vertical line that appears at the left of the screen represents your energy input. The dots near the vertical line show the energy levels the atom can absorb. See Figure 1.
5. If the atom did not absorb your energy input, repeat step 4 with another energy you think the atom can absorb.

Figure 1.

energies the atom can accept

your estimate for the energy input to the atom

Figure 2.

infrared region          visible region          ultraviolet region

$3.5 \times 10^{14}$ Hz   $4.6 \times 10^{14}$ Hz   $5.0 \times 10^{14}$ Hz   $5.2 \times 10^{14}$ Hz   $5.8 \times 10^{14}$ Hz   $6.4 \times 10^{14}$ Hz   $7.3 \times 10^{14}$ Hz   $8.8 \times 10^{14}$ Hz

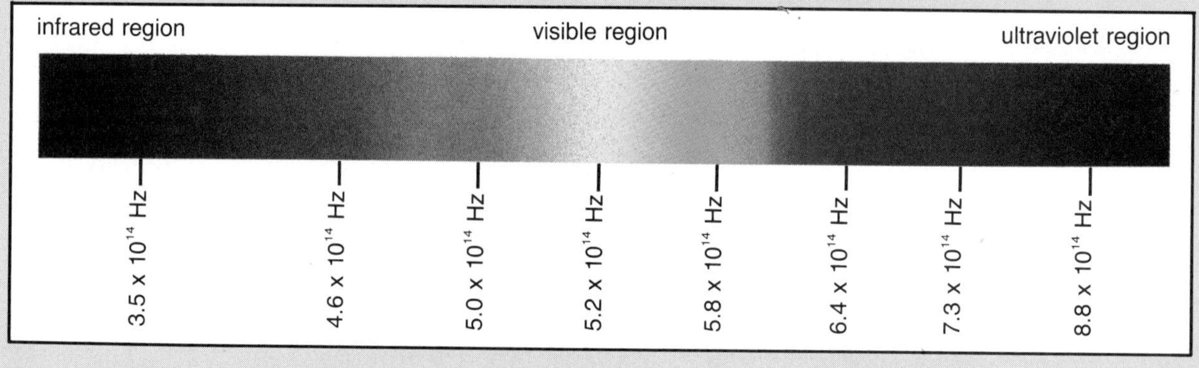

**6.** If the atom did absorb your energy input, write down the energy in your Table. Using the equation in Table 2, calculate the frequency of the emitted photon.

**7.** Repeat step 2 until you have found all four energies that your model atom can absorb. Calculate the frequencies of all the photons your atom can give off.

**TABLE 1.**

```
10   HGR2 : HCOLOR= 3
20   FOR I = 1 TO 20: HPLOT 150,70
     TO 100 *   RND (I),105 – 70 *
     RND (I): NEXT
30   TEXT
40   VTAB 24: NORMAL : INPUT
     "ENERGY =?";E
50 R = 5
60   GOSUB 160
70   POKE   – 16299,0
80   IF R > 6 THEN   GOSUB 250
90   FOR N = 2 TO 5
100 EN =   INT (10 * (14 – 14 /
     N ^ 2)) / 10
110  IF EN = E THEN R = 2.8 * N ^ 2
120  NEXT
130  GOSUB 160
140  IF R = 5 THEN   GOTO 350
150  GOTO 60
160  HGR : HCOLOR= 3: HPLOT 150,70
170  HPLOT 3,84: HPLOT 3,45: HPLOT
     3,26: HPLOT 3,18: HPLOT 3,16
180  HPLOT 5,84 TO 5,150 – 10 * E
190  VTAB 21
```

```
200  IF R > 6 THEN   PRINT "THE
     ENERGY HAS BEEN ABSORBED
     BY THE ATOM."
210  FOR I = 0 TO 10.6 STEP .31
220  HPLOT 150 + R * COS (I),70 –
     R *   SIN (I)
230  NEXT
240  RETURN
250  HGR : HCOLOR= 3
260  FOR J = 140 TO 110 STEP   – 2
270  CALL   – 198
280  HPLOT J,70 – 5 *   SIN (J / 2)
290  NEXT
300  HOME : VTAB 21
310  FLASH : PRINT "A PHOTON HAS
     BEEN EMITTED BY THE
     ATOM   WITH AN ENERGY OF ";E
320 R = 5
330  GOSUB 160
340  GOTO 40
350  VTAB 21: PRINT "THE ENERGY HAS
     NOT BEEN ABSORBED BY THE ATOM"
360  GOTO 40
```

**TABLE 2.**

| Energy Absorbed by Atom | Frequency of Photon Emitted by Atom $f = E \times 0.7 \times 10^{14}$ Hz |
|---|---|
| E = | f = |
| E = | f = |
| E = | f = |
| E = | f = |

## Questions

**1.** Why is the energy of the emitted photon equal to the energy you added to your atom?

**2.** What is the frequency of the photon that was emitted by the atom with the largest orbit?

**3.** Look at Figure 2. Which photons that were emitted by your model atom could be in the visible region of the spectrum?

**4.** **PROBLEM SOLVING** Imagine that the electron jumped from the highest energy orbit down to the next highest energy orbit. What is the energy of the photon that would be emitted?

### Objective

Investigate the conduction of heat using liquid crystals.

### Background

You learned that conduction is a transfer of energy by molecular collisions in a solid. The greater the difference in temperature, the faster the transfer occurs. If one end of a cold (0°C) metal sheet is placed on a hot object, the temperature of the different parts of the sheet increases. See Figure 1. Imagine a region of a certain temperature moving from the hot end through the rest of the sheet. The region or collection of all the points in the sheet having the same temperature is called an isotherm (IGH·soh·thurm). An isotherm of 22° moves from the hot end to the other end of the sheet.

The motion of isotherms can be detected by using a liquid crystal sheet. A liquid crystal is a material that changes the color of reflected light as its temperature changes. The liquid crystal shown in Figure 1 reflects orange light at 20°C,

**Time Photos**

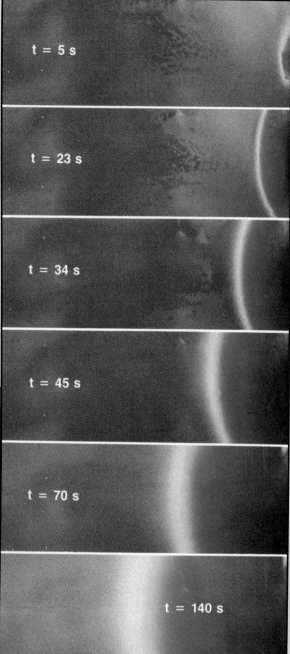

t = 5 s

t = 23 s

t = 34 s

t = 45 s

t = 70 s

t = 140 s

*Figure 1.*

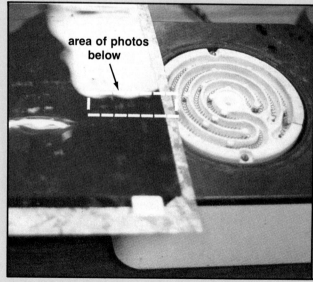

area of photos below

yellow light at 22°C, green light at 24°C, and blue light at 25°C. By measuring the positions of the colors, you can follow the motion of isotherms through the metal sheet.

## Materials
metric ruler, paper, pencil, graph paper

## Procedure
1. Copy Table 1 onto a separate sheet of paper.
2. A picture of the liquid crystal sheet was taken at the times shown in Figure 1. For each time, measure the distance from the hot end of the sheet to the 20° (orange) isotherm. Record the distances in Table 1.
3. Plot a graph of the movement of the 20° isotherm. Plot the distance on the vertical axis and the time on the horizontal axis. Connect the points with a smooth curved line.

**TABLE 1.**

| Distance to 20°C Isotherm (mm) | Time (s) |
|---|---|
|  |  |
|  |  |
|  |  |
|  |  |
|  |  |
|  |  |
|  |  |
|  |  |

*Figure 2.*

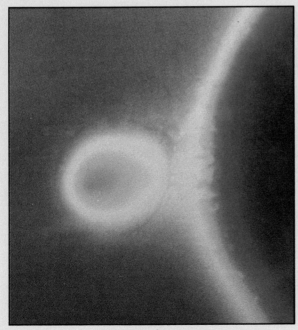

## Questions
1. Study your graph. Describe the movement of the 20° isotherm across the metal plate as it warmed up.
2. The slope of your curved-line graph shows how fast the 20° isotherm is moving across the metal plate. The speed of the isotherm is greatest when the graph has the greatest slope. When was the isotherm moving the fastest? When was the isotherm moving the slowest?
3. Why does the isotherm move faster in one part of the metal place and slower in another part?
4. Compare the first picture (t = 5 s) of the 20° (orange) isotherm to the last (t = 140 s) picture. Why is the orange color spread out over a larger region in the last picture?
5. **PROBLEM SOLVING** Study Figure 2. What do you think has been done to the metal plate?

## Objective
Investigate one way used to detect nuclear radiation.

## Background
In Chapter 21 you learned that nuclear radiation can be detected with an electroscope. This effect is possible because nuclear radiation can remove electrons from atoms in the air. The atoms then become positive ions.

An electroscope is only one device that can be used to detect nuclear radiation. Another device is a cloud chamber. See Figure 1. A cloud chamber is basically a glass container lined with a cloth strip soaked in alcohol. The alcohol evaporates from the strip and fills the chamber with vapor. The chamber is placed on a piece of dry ice. The air inside becomes very cold. The decreased temperature of the air causes the air to become supersaturated with alcohol.

*Figure 1.*

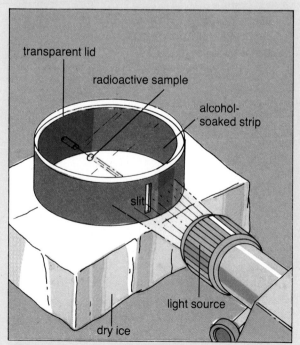

transparent lid

radioactive sample

alcohol-soaked strip

slit

light source

dry ice

When radiation passes through the cloud chamber, it collides with atoms of the air. Electrons and positive ions are produced. The alcohol vapor in the chamber condenses in the positive ions, forming clouds. A light is shined through the chamber to make the clouds, or tracks, more easily seen. Figure 2 shows tracks made by alpha particles and beta particles.

Scientists also use bubble chambers to study nuclear radiation. They fire alpha particles at nuclei in the bubble chamber. The tracks help scientists to study the results of the collisions. In some cases, nuclei of one element are changed into nuclei of different elements. Figure 3 shows bubble chamber tracks made when nuclei of certain elements are bombarded with alpha particles.

## Materials (*needed for Part B only)
*cloud chamber kit   *rubbing alcohol
  including:   *dry ice
  absorbent strip   *tongs
  cloud chamber   *projector
  radioactive sample

## Procedure

### Part A   Observing Particle Tracks
1. Study Figure 2 carefully. Observe the length and thickness of each track. Record what you see.

2. Look at Figure 3. Observe the length, thickness, and direction of possible alpha or beta particle tracks.

### Part B   Using A Cloud Chamber
3. Soak the absorbent strip with alcohol. Place the top on the cloud chamber and allow alcohol vapor to fill the chamber.

4. After a few minutes, place the chamber on a piece of dry ice. **CAUTION:** Always handle dry ice with laboratory tongs.

5. When the chamber has cooled, shine the projector light through it. Observe what happens.

6. Turn off the light. Now place the radioactive sample in the holder. Turn the light back on. Observe what happens in the lighted chamber.

7. Estimate the length of the tracks produced by the radiation. Compare the tracks with the ones you saw in Figure 2. Make a sketch of what you observed.

*Figure 2.*

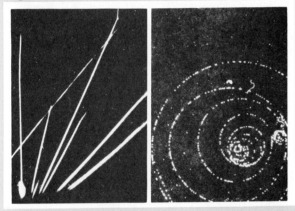

*Figure 3.*

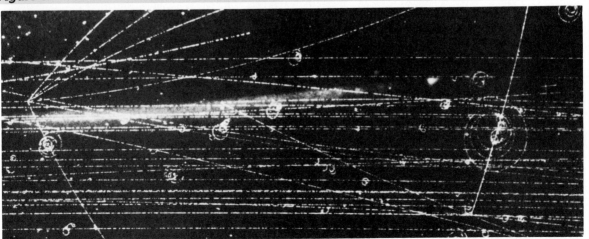

## Questions

### Part A

1. What differences do you observe in the tracks made by alpha particles and those made by beta particles in Figure 2?

2. Explain why alpha tracks are different from beta tracks.

3. How are the tracks made by the particles in Figure 3 alike?

4. How are the tracks made by the particles in Figure 3 different?

5. Considering the materials bombarded, why do you think the tracks that are shown in Figure 3 are different?

### Part B

6. What did you observe in step 5?

7. What did you observe in step 6 when you put the radioactive sample in the chamber?

8. What produced the tracks in the cloud chamber?

# CHAPTER 22
## INVESTIGATION

### Objective
Observe how insulation affects heat transfer.

### Background
Special kinds of cameras can take pictures with film sensitive to infrared radiation. Figure 1 shows prints, or thermograms, made from heat-sensitive film. With the help of the color scale, you can see that some parts of each picture are warmer than others. The warm areas—white, red, and orange—are places where the buildings in each picture are losing heat because of poor insulation. The cool areas—blue and purple—are not losing much heat. Thermograms help homeowners tell what parts of their homes need better insulation.

*Figure 1.*

warmer                              cooler

Proper insulation reduces heat loss and enables homeowners to save energy and money.

## Materials (*needed for Part B only)

*2 beakers (Pyrex or Kimax) 250 mL, 100 mL

*Styrofoam cup
*hot and cold water
*thermometer
*cloth pot holder

## Procedure

### Part A   Studying Thermograms

1. Study carefully the color scale and the thermograms. On a separate sheet of paper, list each color from warmest to coolest. Record the part of the buildings that you see in each color.

warmer                                    cooler

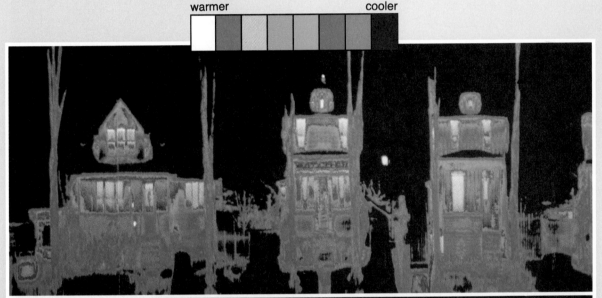

# CHAPTER 22
## INVESTIGATION

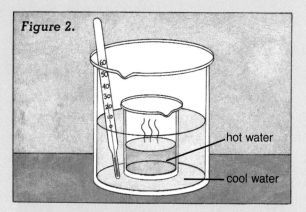

Figure 2.

hot water

cool water

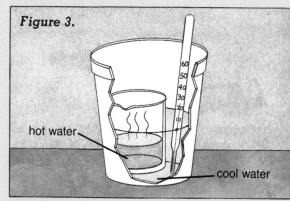

Figure 3.

hot water

cool water

## Part B   Testing Insulation Materials

2. Copy Table 1 onto a separate sheet of paper.
3. Fill a large beaker one third full of cool water (room temperature). Record its temperature.
4. Fill a small beaker with hot tap water. Record its temperature.
5. Place the small beaker of hot water in the beaker of cold water. See Figure 2.
   **CAUTION:** Hold the hot beaker with a cloth pot holder.
6. Record the temperature of the water in each container.
7. Record the temperature in each container every three minutes for 21 minutes. Allow a few seconds for the mercury to stop moving as you take each reading.
8. Repeat steps 3 through 7, this time placing the small beaker inside a Styrofoam drinking cup. See Figure 3. Do not cover the cup with a lid.

## Questions

### Part A

1. Were any of the buildings well insulated?
2. Were any of the buildings poorly insulated?
3. Which parts of the buildings did the thermograms show most needed insulation?

### Part B

4. What did you observe about the temperatures in the two beakers (steps 3–7) after 10 min?
5. What did you observe about the temperatures in the two beakers in step 8 after about 10 minutes?
6. What did you observe about the temperature changes in the two beakers (steps 3–7) between 10 and 21 minutes?
7. What effect did the Styrofoam cup have on the temperature changes observed in step 8?
8. How can you explain any effect the Styrofoam cup had on the results?

### TABLE 1.   TEMPERATURE READINGS

| Time (min) | Steps 3 to 7 | | | Step 8 (Steps 3 to 7 Repeated) | |
| | Temperature °C | | | Temperature °C | |
| | Cool Water (large beaker) | Hot Water (small beaker) | | Cool Water (Styrofoam cup) | Hot Water (small beaker) |
| --- | --- | --- | --- | --- | --- |

**546**  CHAPTER 22 • Investigation

# CONCEPT EXTENSIONS

## Tie-In to Chapter 9

Think of all the ways you group things together. You put together records that have similar singers or books that have similar themes. In Chapter 9, you saw that elements with similar properties are grouped together into families of the periodic table. Study the part of the periodic table shown in Figure 1. Look for a special similar property of members of each family: the arrangement of electrons.

## Directions

Find lithium, atomic number 3, at the start of period 2. The orange inner circle represents the nucleus with three protons (P) and four neutrons (N). The numbers in red are the numbers of electrons in each energy level. There are two electrons in the first level and one electron in the second level.

Now look at each element to the right of lithium in period 2. As you look from atom to atom, you find one more electron in the second level. When you reach neon, you find eight electrons in the second level. When you find eight electrons in the outermost energy level of an atom, you have reached the end of a period in the table. The following element begins the next period and has one more electron in the next higher energy level.

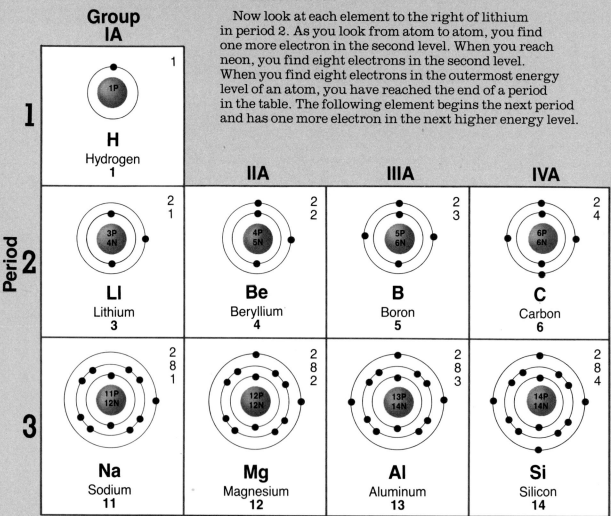

Figure 1.

# ELECTRON ARRANGEMENT IN ATOMS

**Practice**

1. How does the number of protons change as you look from atom to atom across a period? Sum up your findings in a general statement.

2. Study the arrangement of electrons in each member of Group IA. How are the arrangements similar? How are the arrangements of electrons similar in Group IIA, IIIA, IVA, VA, VIA, VIIA, and VIIIA?

3. The element following argon is potassium, atomic number 19. In which period and group is this element? How many electrons does an atom of this element have at each energy level?

4. If an atom has electrons in three energy levels, the third level holds up to eight electrons. However, if an atom has four or more energy levels, the third level can hold more than eight electrons, as many as 18. Draw an electron arrangement diagram for potassium, chromium, iron, and krypton. Find the electron count by looking at period four in the periodic table on page 182–183.

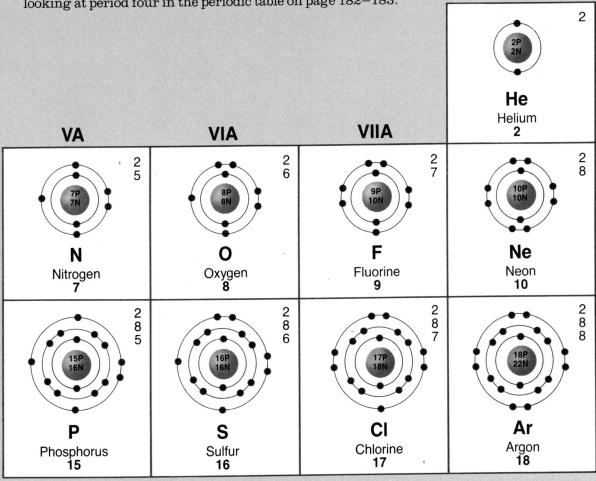

## Tie-In to Chapter 10

Usually, "+" means "to add," and "−" means "to subtract." When you learned about oxidation numbers, however, these signs seemed to have opposite meanings. For example, lithium has an oxidation number of 1+. This number indicates that lithium <u>loses</u> one electron when it forms an ionic bond. Fluorine has an oxidation number of 1−. This number indicates that fluorine *gains* one electron when it forms an ionic bond. How can "+" mean "to lose" and "−" mean "to gain?"

## Directions

**Lithium** Look at Figure 1**A**. Like all atoms, the lithium atom is neutral. It has the same number of electrons as protons. If you add the charges of these particles, the sum is zero. The overall charge is zero. Notice the addition in Figure 1**A**.

Atoms with one, two, or three electrons in the outermost level (valence shell), tend to lose these electrons when they form ionic bonds. When a lithium atom forms an ionic bond, it loses the one electron in its valence shell. See Figure 1**B**. The lithium atom becomes an ion. The ion has a charge of 1+ because it has three protons and only two electrons. Notice the addition in Figure 1**B**.

The charge of the lithium atom is the oxidation number of lithium. The lithium ion has a 1+ charge because the lithium atom "loses" a negatively charged particle, an electron.

*Figure 1.* A lithium atom LOSES an electron.

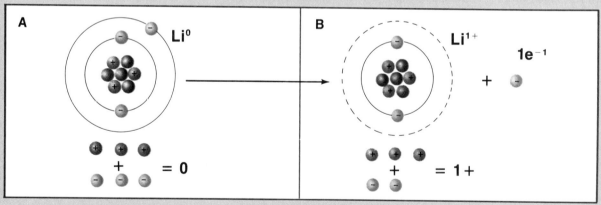

**Fluorine** Look at Figure 2**A**. The fluorine atom is neutral. It has nine protons and nine electrons. Notice that it has seven electrons in its valence shell. Atoms with five or more electrons in the valence shell tend to gain electrons when they form ionic bonds. They become stable when they gain enough electrons to have a total of eight electrons in the valence shell. When a fluorine atom forms an ionic bond, it gains one electron from another atom. See Figure 2**B**. The fluorine atom becomes an ion. The ion has a charge of 1− because it has one electron more than the number of protons.

The charge of the fluorine atom is the oxidation number of fluorine. The fluorine ion has a charge of 1 − because the fluorine atom "gains" a negatively charged particle, an electron.

**Figure 2.** The fluorine atom GAINS an electron.

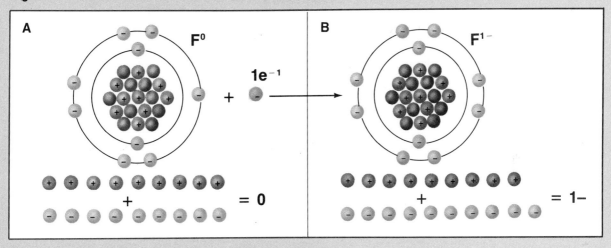

**Figure 3.** Does magnesium GAIN or LOSE electrons?

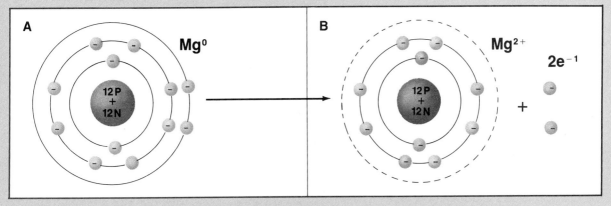

## Practice

1a. Add the red numbers in Figure 1**B.** How does the sum compare with the single red number in Figure 1**A**? Explain.

1b. Add the red numbers in Figure 2**A.** How do they compare with the single red number in Figure 2**B**? Explain.

2. Look at Figure 3. What is the oxidation number for magnesium? Be sure to indicate " + " or " − ." Explain your answer.

3. Look at Figure 1 on pages 548–549. Give the oxidation number for each of the following: beryllium, nitrogen, oxygen, chlorine.

4. Explain why all halogens have an oxidation number of 1 − .

### Tie-In to Chapter 10

Have you ever written messages in shorthand? With shorthand, you use symbols for letters and words to save space and time. You can use a simple shorthand method to show ionic and covalent bonds. This method uses electron-dots, dots that stand for electrons.

### Directions

Figure 1 shows how to use electron dots to represent atoms. Simply draw a dot for each electron in the outermost level (valence shell) of an atom. Notice that you need no more than eight dots to draw these atoms because they have no more than eight electrons in the valence shell. Dots for the first two electrons in the valence shell are drawn paired to the right of the symbol. (See beryllium.) The next three electrons are drawn as single dots. The last three electrons are drawn paired to the single electrons. (See oxygen to neon.)

*Figure 1.* The electron-dot diagram shows the electrons in the valence shell. The numbers in red refer to the positions of the electrons.

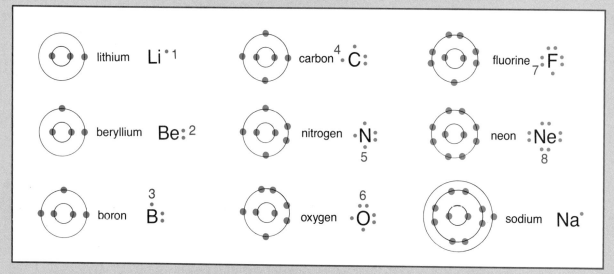

**Covalent Bonds** Figure 2 shows how to use electron-dot diagrams to represent covalent bonds. Figure 2**A** shows bonding that takes place in a water molecule. Each hydrogen atom shares its one electron with the six electrons of the oxygen atom. The oxygen atom shares one of its electrons with each hydrogen atom. The final molecule shows eight electrons surrounding the oxygen atom. A pair of shared electrons is shown between each hydrogen atom and the oxygen atom. To simplify the diagram of the molecule, replace each pair of shared electrons with a short line.

Look at Figure 2**B**. All electrons are the same. By using colors for electrons, however, you can show where each "dot" in the final molecule is from. The brown dots in the ammonia molecule are from the original hydrogen atoms.

# ELECTRON-DOT DIAGRAMS

**Figure 2.** Using electron dots to show **COVALENT BONDS**.

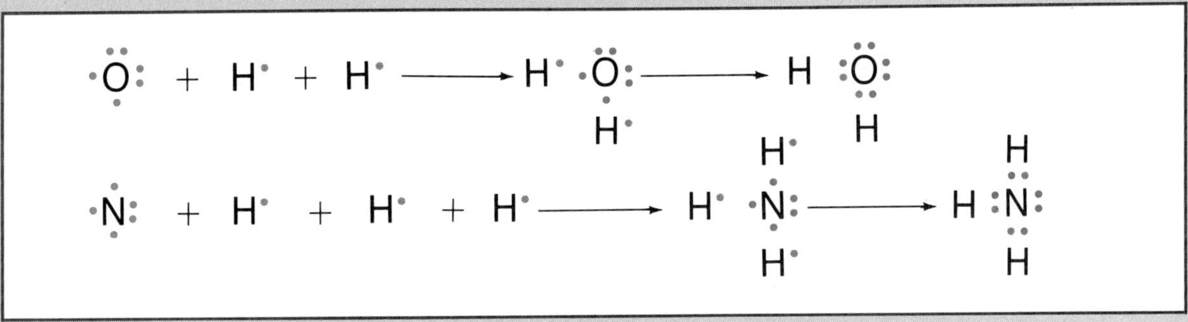

**Figure 3.** Using electron dots to show **IONIC BONDS**.

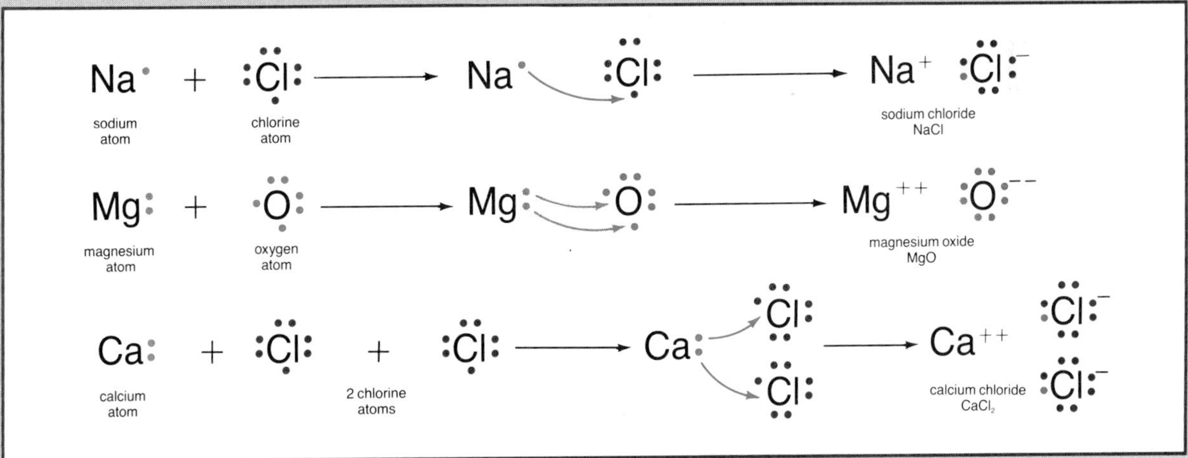

**Ionic Bonds** The dot diagrams in Figure 3 show ionic bonds. Look at the bonding in sodium chloride in Figure 3**A**. Before bonding, no charge signs are drawn. After bonding, the sodium ion has lost an electron and has becomes a positive ion. The chlorine atom has gained an electron and has become a negative ion.

## Practice
1. Draw electron-dot diagrams for: barium, cesium, aluminum, bromine, and argon. (Use the periodic table on pages 182-183.)
2. The electron-dot diagrams for lithium and sodium are the same. Explain why. Give another example of diagrams that are alike.
3. Explain how bonding takes place in magnesium oxide and calcium chloride.
4. Draw electron-dot diagrams to show covalent bonding in a molecule of hydrogen chloride (HCl).
5. Draw electron-dot diagrams to show an ionic bond in potassium chloride (KCl) and aluminum chloride ($AlCl_3$).

## Tie-In to Chapter 10

The chemical formula of a compound gives the relative number of atoms of each element present in the compound. For example, the formula $H_2SO_4$ tells you that there are two atoms of hydrogen and four atoms of oxygen for each atom of sulfur in that compound.

## Directions

You can write the formula of a compound if you know the charge that ions of its elements have. Table 1 lists the charges of common ions. Notice aluminum ions have a charge of 3+. This number is the oxidation number of aluminum. This number indicates that an aluminum atom loses 3 electrons when it forms bonds with other atoms. Notice copper has two ions. Copper atoms can lose one or two electrons when they form bonds. Thus, they form ions with a charge of 1+ or 2+. Find the polyatomic ions in the table. They form compounds as single-element ions do.

**TABLE 1.   COMMON IONS AND THEIR CHARGES**                    *indicates polyatomic ion

| Name | Symbol | Charge | Name | Symbol | Charge |
|------|--------|--------|------|--------|--------|
| aluminum | $Al^{+++}$ | 3+ | iron (III) | $Fe^{+++}$ | 3+ |
| ammonium | $*NH_4^+$ | 1+ | magnesium | $Mg^{++}$ | 2+ |
| barium | $Ba^{++}$ | 2+ | mercury (II) | $Hg^{++}$ | 2+ |
| calcium | $Ca^{++}$ | 2+ | potassium | $K^+$ | 1+ |
| copper (I) | $Cu^+$ | 1+ | silver | $Ag^+$ | 1+ |
| copper (II) | $Cu^{++}$ | 2+ | sodium | $Na^+$ | 1+ |
| iron (II) | $Fe^{++}$ | 2+ | zinc | $Zn^{++}$ | 2+ |
| bromide | $Br^-$ | 1− | nitrate | $*NO_3^-$ | 1− |
| chloride | $Cl^-$ | 1− | oxide | $O^{--}$ | 2− |
| fluoride | $F^-$ | 1− | phosphate | $*PO_4^{---}$ | 3− |
| hydroxide | $*OH^-$ | 1− | sulfate | $*SO_4^{--}$ | 2− |
| iodide | $I^-$ | 1− | sulfide | $S^{--}$ | 2− |

To write the chemical formula of a compound, you must be able to recognize positive and negative ions named in the compound. Refer to Table 1 to help you decide. Once you have made your decision, follow these steps:
1. Write down the symbol for each part of the compound, placing the positive ion first. Also, write down the charge on each ion.
2. Adjust the number of ions in the compound so that the *total* number of positive charges equals the *total* number of negative charges in the compound. Do this by placing as a subscript to the lower right of the ion the number that will balance the charges. With a polyatomic ion, place parentheses, ( ), around the ion before writing the subscripts.

# WRITING CHEMICAL FORMULAS

*Example*   Write the chemical formula for each of the following compounds: sodium fluoride, copper (II) chloride, potassium sulfide, calcium hydroxide, and aluminum oxide.

*Solution:*

### sodium fluoride

$$Na^+ \qquad F^-$$
$$+1 \qquad -1$$

Since the $+1$
balances the $-1$,
the formula is        NaF

Note: The $+$ and $-$ signs are not written in the final formula.

### copper (II) chloride

[ Note: The (II) means that copper has a $+2$ charge in this compound. ]

$$Cu^{++} \qquad Cl^-$$
$$+2 \qquad -1$$
$$+2$$

2 $Cl^-$ ions give a total charge of $2(-1) = -2$

The $+2$ balances the $-2$.
The formula is   $CuCl_2$

### potassium sulfide

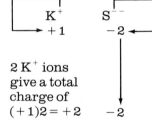

$$K^+ \qquad S^{--}$$
$$+1 \qquad -2$$

2 $K^+$ ions give a total charge of $(+1)2 = +2$

$-2$

The $+2$ balances the $-2$.
The formula is        $K_2S$

### calcium hydroxide

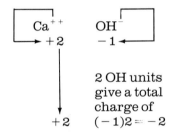

$$Ca^{++} \qquad OH^-$$
$$+2 \qquad -1$$

2 OH units give a total charge of $(-1)2 = -2$

$+2$

The $-2$ balances the $+2$.
The formula is        $Ca(OH)_2$

Note: The OH is put in parentheses before the subscript is written.

### aluminum oxide

$$Al^{+++} \qquad O^{--}$$
$$+3 \qquad -2$$

2 $Al^{+3}$ ions give a total charge of $(+3)2 = +6$

3 $O^{-2}$ ions give a total charge of $(-2)3 = -6$

$+6$ balances $-6$.
The formula is   $Al_2O_3$

The above discussion is based on ions and ionic compounds. A similar procedure can be used to write formulas for covalent compounds. The number of electrons shared is important in their formulas.

## Practice
1. Write chemical formulas for:
   silver chloride, zinc oxide, magnesium bromide, magnesium nitrate, aluminum sulfate, iron (III) oxide, copper (II) sulfate.
2. Classify each of the above compounds as <u>binary</u> or <u>ternary</u>.

## Tie-In to Chapter 10

You may have heard the expression "The whole is equal to the sum of the parts." For example, a house is equal to all the rooms put together. The same expression is true for molecules. If you had an infinitely small balance, you could determine the mass of a molecule. The mass of that molecule is equal to the sum of all the atoms that make up the molecule.

If you know the chemical formula of a molecule, you can determine the mass of the molecule from the masses of the atoms that make up the molecule.

## Directions
### Formula Mass of a Compound

The formula mass of a compound can be used to calculate how much of one element will react with a given amount of another element. The formula mass of a compound is the sum of the atomic masses of all the atoms in the formula. You can find the atomic mass of an element from the Periodic Table on pages 182–183. For example, the formula weight of sodium hydroxide can be found in the following way:

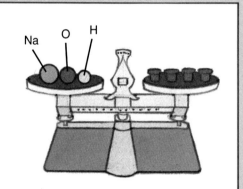

formula of sodium hydroxide: NaOH

| element | atomic mass | × | number of atoms in formula | = | total mass of element in compound |
|---------|-------------|---|----------------------------|---|-----------------------------------|
| Na | 23.0 | × | 1 | = | 23.0 |
| O | 16.0 | × | 1 | = | 16.0 |
| H | 1.0 | × | 1 | = | 1.0 |
| | | | | | 40.0 |

formula mass of NaOH is 40.0

As another example, find the formula mass of potassium sulfate

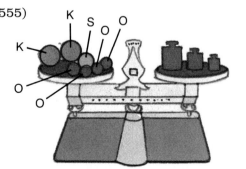

formula of potassium sulfate: $K_2SO_4$ (see pages 554, 555)

| element | atomic mass | × | number of atoms in formula | = | total mass of element in compound |
|---------|-------------|---|----------------------------|---|-----------------------------------|
| K | 39.1 | × | 2 | = | 78.2 |
| S | 32.1 | × | 1 | = | 32.1 |
| O | 16.0 | × | 4 | = | 64.0 |
| | | | | | 174.3 |

formula mass of $K_2SO_4$ is 174.3

## Percentage Composition of a Compound

If you know the formula mass of a compound, you can find the percentage composition of any element in that compound. To find the percentage composition (% comp) of an element in a compound, use the formula:

$$\begin{matrix}\text{\% comp} \\ \text{of element X}\end{matrix} = \frac{\text{total atomic mass of X in compound}}{\text{formula mass of compound}} \times 100\%$$

For example, the percentage composition of each element in the compound $K_2SO_4$ is:

$$\begin{aligned}\text{\% comp of K} &= \frac{\text{total atomic mass of K in compound}}{\text{formula mass of } K_2SO_4} \times 100\% \\ &= \frac{78.2}{174.3} \times 100\% \\ &= 0.449 \times 100\% \\ &= 44.9\%\end{aligned}$$

$$\begin{aligned}\text{\% comp of S} &= \frac{\text{total atomic mass of S in compound}}{\text{formula mass of } K_2SO_4} \times 100\% \\ &= \frac{32.1}{174.3} \times 100\% \\ &= 0.184 \times 100\% \\ &= 18.4\%\end{aligned}$$

$$\begin{aligned}\text{\% comp of O} &= \frac{\text{total atomic mass of O in compound}}{\text{formula mass of } K_2SO_4} \times 100\% \\ &= \frac{64.0}{174.3} \times 100\% \\ &= 0.367\% \times 100\% \\ &= 36.7\%\end{aligned}$$

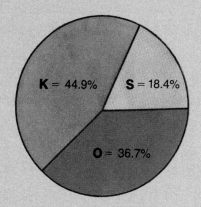

**Figure 1.** A circle graph illustrates that the whole (the complete circle or a molecule of $K_2SO_4$) equals the sum of its parts (the pieces of the circle or the parts of the molecule).

Therefore, % comp of K in $K_2SO_4$ is  44.9%
   % comp of S in $K_2SO_4$ is  18.4%
   % comp of O in $K_2SO_4$ is  36.7%
                              100.0%

Notice that the sum of all the percentages is 100%. See Figure 1.

## Practice

1. Find the formula mass of:
   HCl   $H_2O$   MgO
2. Find the percentage composition of NaOH.

### Tie-In to Chapter 14

In Chapter 14 you saw sample circuits. Setting up actual circuits in buildings is the job of an electrician. An electrician uses diagrams to map out the branches of circuits in different rooms. The illustrations you see here give you an idea of how detailed an electrician's diagrams must be.

### Directions

#### Part 1

An electrician uses symbols for each part of a circuit. See Chart 1. Now look at the circuit in Figure 1**A.** Compare with the diagram of the circuit in Figure 1**B.** Now compare the circuit and diagram in Figure 1 with those in Figure 2.

#### Part 2

Lamps and other loads can be connected in series and parallel circuits. If you want to use more than one dry cell in a circuit, you can connect the cells in series and in parallel as well. In Figure 3**A,** three dry cells are connected in series. In Figure 3**B,** they are connected in parallel. Study the electrician's diagram for each setup. Compare the way the wires are connected in each setup.

**Chart 1**

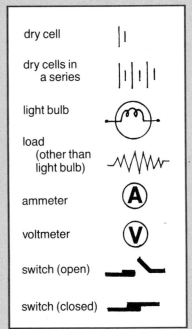

*Figure 1.*

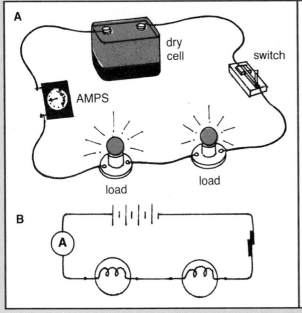

*Figure 2.*

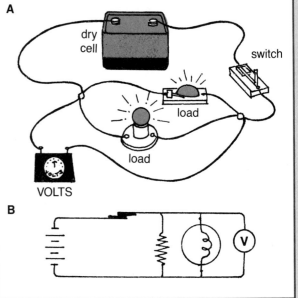

*Figure 3.*

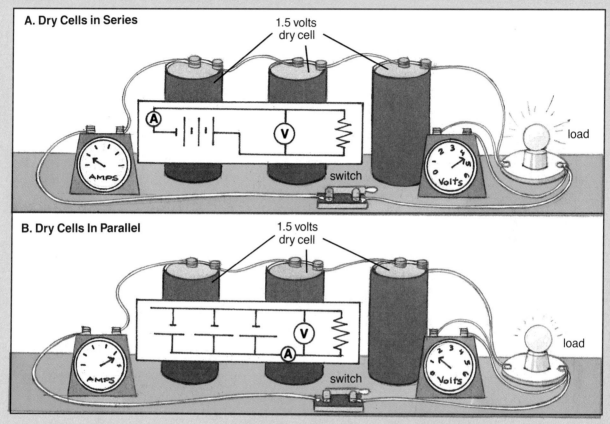

**A. Dry Cells in Series**

1.5 volts dry cell

AMPS

A

V

switch

load

2 3 4 5

Volts

**B. Dry Cells In Parallel**

1.5 volts dry cell

AMPS

V

A

switch

load

2 3 4 5

Volts

## Practice

### Part 1

1. Identify Figure 1 and Figure 2 as a series or a parallel circuit. Explain your answer. How does the electrician's diagram help you identify the parallel circuit?
2. From Figure 1 and 2, explain how an ammeter and a voltmeter are connected in a circuit.
3. Look at the complex circuit on page 321 of Chapter 14. Draw an electrician's diagram to represent this circuit.

### Part 2

4. When dry cells are connected in series, how are the wires arranged to connect one dry cell to another?
5. Why do you think an electrician might connect dry cells in series?
6. From Figure 3, how are wires used to connect dry cells in parallel?
7. Why might an electrician connect dry cells in a series? Explain.
8. Suppose you have four dry cells (1.5 volts per cell). How might you connect them in a circuit to have the greatest amounts of potential difference and current? Show an electrician's diagram of your circuit.

### Tie-In to Chapter 18

In Chapter 18 (page 392), you were asked to squint at a distant streetlamp one evening. If your eyes are nearly shut, you can see a pattern of bright and dim bands of light through your eyelashes. In 1801, the physicist Thomas Young studied this same observation. He used a setup similar to the modernized one in Figure 1. If the viewer's eye is replaced with a screen, the pattern of bands appears on the screen. Young offered a model to explain the pattern. His model suggests that light travels like waves on the surface of water.

### Directions

To understand Young's model, imagine two canoes roped together on a lake. See Figure 2**A**. A boat speeds by and produces waves. As the waves reach the canoes, they spread as they pass through the space between the canoes. The curving or spreading of waves is called diffraction.

*Figure 1.*

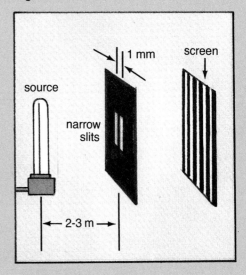

*Figure 2A.* The space between the canoes is like a slit in Young's model.

*Figure 2B.* Light waves spread through each of the two slits just as the water waves spread as they pass between the canoes.

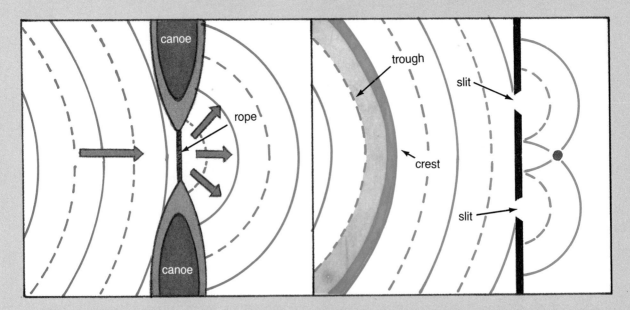

# DIFFRACTION AND INTERFERENCE

Compare Young's model in Figure 2**B** with Figure 2**A**. The light waves in **B** are drawn like water waves. Each solid line represents a crest. Each dashed line represents a trough. As the waves pass through the two slits, they curve around the edges of the slits, just as water waves curve around the raft. Notice that the crests meet at a point (marked with a heavy dot). At that point, the crests are interfering *constructively*. The amount of energy in one crest reinforces (or adds to) the amount in the other.

Now follow the shaded wave across Figures 3 and 4. The shaded wave helps you see how a series of waves reaches the screen and produces the pattern of bands. In Figure 4, dots are used to mark some of the points where crest meets crest and trough meets trough. These are points of constructive interference, where energy in one wave adds to the other. Circles mark some points where crest meets trough. These are points where the waves are interfering *destructively*. At these points, the combined energy of the waves is lower than at points where dots are drawn.

*Figure 3.*          *Figure 4.*

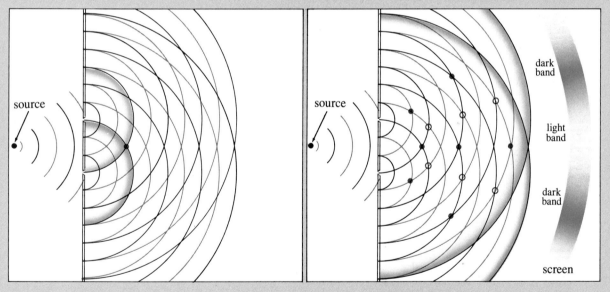

## Practice

1. Carefully trace Figure 4 onto tracing paper. On your copy, continue to mark: dots on *all* points where crest meets crest and where trough meets trough, circles on *all* points where crest meets trough.
2. Describe the patterns of dots (constructive interference) and of circles (destructive interference) that you drew. Using your completed diagram, offer an explanation for the pattern of bands that appear on the screen.

# CONCEPT EXTENSIONS

## Tie-In to Chapter 18

Have you ever read newsprint through a hand lens? A hand lens is a convex lens. If you put your eye near the lens and hold the lens to the print, you see magnified letters. However, if you move back from the print and move the lens back and forth, the image changes size and can even turn upside down. Why do you get different images with a convex lens?

## Directions

Look at the six diagrams shown here. You might pretend that the object you are looking at is newsprint. The image is the image of the print that you see. However, you might use a dim source of light as your object (such as a shaded lamp or a lighted aquarium). If the object is a source of light, it can project an image on a white index card (screen) if the image is real. (**CAUTION:** Never look through a lens at a bulb or other bright source of light.)

Stand in a dim room. Have a lighted aquarium at one end. Stand at the other end. Hold up a lens toward the aquarium. Hold an index card in front of the lens as in Figure 1. Move the card until you see a focused dot of light. You have just located the focus (F). The distance from the focus to the lens is the focal length. In all the diagrams, the focus is marked on both sides of the lens (F and F').

As you move the lens closer to the object (the aquarium), an inverted image eventually appears on the card. See Figure 2. As you keep moving the lens closer, the image changes. See Figures 3 and 4. However, if you move the lens until it is one focal length in front of the object, the image disappears. See Figure 5.

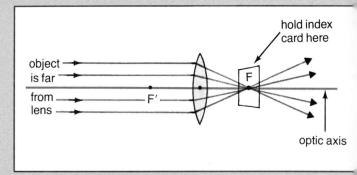

*Figure 1.* In this case, no image appears. You can see only a dot of light at the focus.

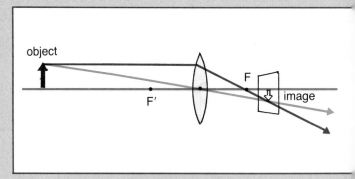

*Figure 2.* Keep moving the lens closer to the object until an image finally appears on the card.

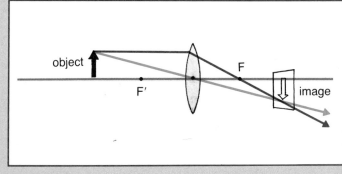

*Figure 3.* Move even closer than in Figure 2 and the image changes.

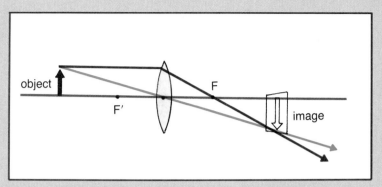

**Figure 4.** The image keeps changing as you approach one focal distance from the object.

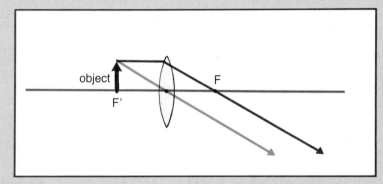

**Figure 5.** When the lens is one focal distance from the object, the image disappears.

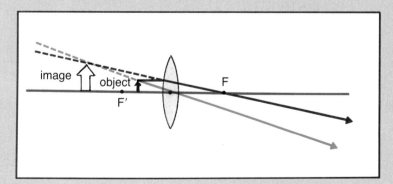

**Figure 6.** When the lens is closer than one focal distance from the object, an image appears when you look through the lens. (**CAUTION:** Never look at a lamp or other light source through a lens.)

**Practice**

1. How are the light rays that enter the lens different in Figure 1 from Figures 2-5? Explain why you do not see an image when light rays from a distant object enter a convex lens.

2. In Figures 2 to 6, two rays are drawn from the object through the lens. Explain what the red ray has in common in all the figures. Explain what the blue ray has in common.

3. Based on your answer to #2, explain why the image appears where it does in Figures 2, 3 and 4. How does the image change in each case?

4. Why is there no image in Figure 5, when the lens is one focal length away from the object?

5. Suppose you move the lens so close to the aquarium that it practically touches the glass side. Then you could look through the lens at the fishes and plants. (**CAUTION:** Never look at the aquarium lamp through a lens.) Describe the images you would see. Which figure from these pages best describes this situation?

6. If the object you are viewing is newsprint, the image does not appear on a screen. Where does the image appear?

7. Identify each image in Figures 2 to 6 as real or virtual. Explain your answers.

## Tie-In to Chapter 20

Suppose you left a cake of ice in the sun for several hours. When you return, the ice has disappeared. What happened to the ice? From what you learned in Chapter 20, you know the ice absorbed heat. As it absorbed heat, the molecules in the cake of ice gained kinetic energy. In the graphic shown here, you can get an idea of how an increase in kinetic energy can change a solid.

## Directions

A block of ice is made up of water molecules. The molecules are attracted to each other by forces that hold the molecules into a solid, a crystal. Even though they are held together, the molecules are moving slightly. They already have kinetic energy. Look at Figure 1. Part **A** represents the molecules in ice or the molecules of any solid. Follow the graph to Part **B** and Part **C**. Each part shows the same molecules, but with greater kinetic energy.

*Figure 1.*

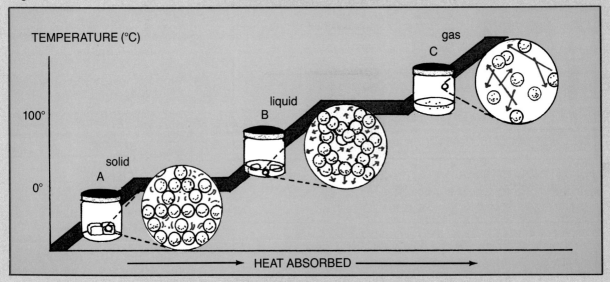

## Practice

1. What happens to the speed of the molecules from Part **A** to **B** to **C**?
2. What happens to the forces that hold the molecules together from Part **A** to **B** to **C**?
3. Figure 1 sums up the Kinetic Theory of Matter. According to this theory any substance can exist in three phases. However, in each phase, the molecules differ in the amount of kinetic energy they have. From Figure 1, describe the molecules in each phase.
4. Oxygen is a gas at room temperature. Yet oxygen is often stored for industry as a liquid. How can oxygen be changed from a gas to a liquid? How might liquid oxygen be changed to a solid?

# CONCEPT EXTENSIONS

## Tie-In to Chapter 20

In Chapter 20, you saw how one kind of cooling system, a refrigerator, works. Air conditioners are cooling systems also. Air conditioners work in different ways. Many use a vapor compression cycle. In this cycle, a substance called a refrigerant flows through a path inside the air-conditioning unit, changing from a liquid to a gas, from a gas to a liquid, and so on. As the liquid refrigerant evaporates, it absorbs heat from air in a room. A device compresses the gaseous refrigerant, raising its temperature higher than that of outside air. The refrigerant then transfers the heat it absorbed from the room to the outside air. Figure 1 shows how this cycle takes place.

## Directions

Look for the liquid refrigerant in Figure 1**B**. Notice that a blower pulls warm, moist air from the room across coils containing the refrigerant. Follow the path from where the refrigerant evaporates to where it is compressed in Figure 1**A**. In this part of the unit, air is pulled into the unit from the outside. The outside air flows over condensing coils containing the gaseous refrigerant. Here the refrigerant changes back to a liquid, and the cycle is repeated.

*Figure 1.* An air conditioner at work.

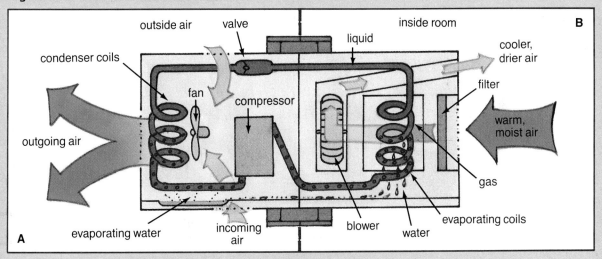

## Practice

1. Look at Figure 1**B**. What happens to air that enters the air conditioner from the room? How is this change related to the change of the refrigerant from liquid to gas?
2. Why are droplets of water dripping from the evaporating coils? What eventually happens to these droplets?
3. Look at Figure 1**A**. A fan pulls outside air into the unit. How does this air change as it passes over the condensing coils? How is this change related to the change of the refrigerant to a liquid?

# CONCEPT EXTENSIONS

## Tie-In to Chapter 20

If you squeeze a balloon, its volume changes. If you place a balloon in a freezer or in bright sunlight, the volume changes. These examples illustrate Boyle's Law and Charles' Law. In each case, the volume of air inside the balloon changes because the air molecules can spread out or be compressed.

## Directions

The diagrams on these pages can help you understand and apply the two gas laws.

## BOYLE'S LAW

At a constant temperature, the volume of a definite amount of gas decreases as the pressure it exerts increases. See Figure 1. A formula you can use is:

P(initial) × V(initial) = P(final) × V(final)

**Example:** Suppose the pressure of 30 mL of hydrogen gas changes from 740 mm of mercury (mm of mercury is a common way of expressing pressure of a gas) to 360 mm of mercury. What new volume will the gas occupy? (See Figure 2.)

**Solution:**

P(initial) = 740 mm mercury
V(initial) = 30 mL
P(final) = 360 mm mercury
V(final) = ?

P(initial) × V(initial) = P(final) × V(final)
V(final) × 360 = 30 × 740
V(final) × 360 = 22,200
$$= \frac{22,200}{360}$$
V(final) = 61.7 mL

## CHARLES' LAW

At a constant pressure, the volume of a definite amount of gas increases as its temperature increases. See Figure 3. The temperature of the gas must be expressed in kelvins (K). To change from degrees Celsius (°C) to kelvins, add 273. So, 10°C = 10 + 273 = 283 K. A formula you can use when applying Charles' Law is:

$$\frac{V(initial)}{V(final)} = \frac{T(initial)}{T(final)}$$

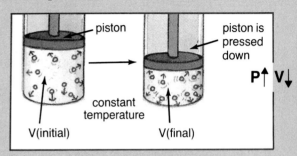

**Figure 1.** As the piston moves down, the volume of the gas decreases. The pressure increases.

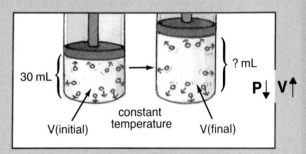

**Figure 2.** The piston moves up. The volume increases. The molecules exert less pressure on the container.

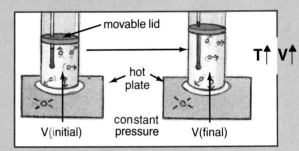

**Figure 3.** Suppose a plastic lid is placed over a volume of gas in a beaker. As the temperature of the gas increases, the volume also increases.

# BOYLE'S LAW AND CHARLES' LAW

**Example:** A gas occupies a volume of 250 mL at 27°C. What volume will it occupy when its temperature is raised to 177°C?

**Solution:**

V(initial) = 250 mL
T(initial) = 27°C = 27 + 273 = 300 K
T(final) = 177°C = 177 + 273 = 450 K
V(final) = ?

$$\frac{V(initial)}{V(final)} = \frac{T(initial)}{T(final)}$$

$$\frac{250}{V(final)} = \frac{300}{450}$$

Cross multiply: V(final) × 300 = 250 × 450
V(final) × 300 = 112,500

$$V(final) = \frac{112,500}{300}$$

V(final) = 375 mL

## COMBINING THE LAWS

In most situations, a change in one of the three properties (temperature, pressure, volume) causes a change in both of the other properties. A formula that gives the relationship among all these properties is:

$$\frac{P(initial) \times V(initial)}{T(initial)} = \frac{P(final) \times V(final)}{T(final)}$$

Remember, the temperature must always be expressed in kelvins.

**Example:** In a laboratory experiment, 50 mL of a gas at 25°C and 752 mm of mercury was expanded to three times its original volume. If at the same time the pressure was reduced to 376 mm of mercury, what was the final temperature of the gas?

**Solution:**

P(initial) = 752 mm mercury
V(initial) = 50 mL
T(initial) = 25°C = 25 + 273 = 298 K
P(final) = 376 mm mercury
V(final) = 150 mL (= 3 × orig vol)
T(final) = ?

$$\frac{P(initial) \times V(initial)}{T(initial)} = \frac{P(final) \times V(final)}{T(final)}$$

$$\frac{(752) \times (50)}{298} = \frac{(376) \times (150)}{T(final)}$$

Cross multiply: T(final) × 752 × 50 = 298 × 376 × 150

$$T(final) = \frac{298 \times 376 \times 150}{752 \times 50}$$

T(final) = 447 K = 447 − 273 = 174°C

## Practice

1. Suppose a gas is kept in a container at a pressure of 370 mm of mercury. The volume of the gas is 80 mL. The pressure is then changed to 740 mm and the temperature remains constant. What is the new volume? (Show all work.)
2. A gas is stored in a container at 127°C. The volume of the gas is 80 mL. The temperature drops to 27°C although the pressure does not change. What is the new volume?
3. Suppose 80 mL of gas is stored at a pressure of 370 mm of mercury at a temperature of 127°C. The pressure changes to 740 mm and the temperature changes to 27°C. What is the new volume?

**FOR USE WITH CHAPTER 21**

## Tie-In to Chapter 21

When an isotope of an element loses an alpha or beta particle, it becomes an isotope of another element. You can set up an equation to show this kind of change.

## Directions

An isotope of radium decays by losing an alpha particle (alpha decay). The isotope of radium changes into an isotope of radon in the process. To show this change, set up an equation as in Figure 1. The figure shows one reactant, radium. There are two products of the reaction: the isotope of radon plus the alpha particle that was given off. Notice that the reaction is balanced. The sum of atomic numbers on each side of the equation is the same. The sum of the atomic masses on each side of the equation is the same.

*Figure 1.*

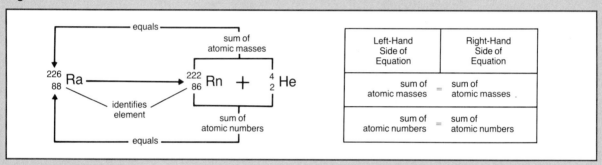

Once you know how to set up an equation. You can use the skill of balancing the equation to identify the decay product.

**Example:** $^{222}_{86}$Rn decays by emitting an alpha particle, $^{4}_{2}$He. What is the product?

$$^{222}_{86}\text{Rn} \longrightarrow \,^{4}_{2}\text{He} + \,^{m}_{z}\text{x}$$

Step 1: Sum of Atomic Masses

$$\begin{array}{r} 222 = \quad 4 + m \\ \underline{-4 \qquad -4} \\ 218 = \qquad m \end{array}$$

Step 2: Sum of Atomic Numbers

$$\begin{array}{r} 86 = \quad 2 + Z \\ \underline{-2 \quad -2} \\ 84 = \qquad Z \end{array}$$

Step 3: Identity of Product

Atomic Number = 84.   Element is Po.   Product is $^{218}_{84}$Po.

## Practice

Find the decay product in each of the following:

$$^{214}_{84}\text{Po} \longrightarrow \,^{4}_{2}\text{He} + \,^{m}_{z}\text{X} \text{ (alpha decay)}$$

$$^{214}_{82}\text{Pb} \longrightarrow \,^{0}_{-1}\text{e} + \,^{m}_{z}\text{X} \text{ (beta decay)}$$

# THE METRIC SYSTEM

The metric system of measurement is used throughout the world. Common measurements made in **Macmillan Physical Science** are of length, mass, time, and temperature. The metric unit for these measurements is shown in Table 1.

**TABLE 1. USEFUL BASE METRIC UNITS**

| Measurement | Base Unit | Symbol |
|---|---|---|
| Length | meter | m |
| Mass | kilogram | kg |
| Time | second | s |
| Temperature | Kelvin or degree Celsius | K °C K = °C + 273 |

Other units are derived from these base units. Table 2 presents a few examples.

**TABLE 2. USEFUL DERIVED METRIC UNITS**

| Measurement | Derived Unit | Symbol | How Derived |
|---|---|---|---|
| Volume | cubic meter | $m^3$ | length x length x length $= m \times m \times m = m^3$ |
| Density | kilogram per cubic meter | $kg/m^3$ | mass ÷ volume $= kg/m^3$ |
| Force | newton | N | mass x acceleration $= kg \times \dfrac{m}{s^2} = N$ |

To convert from the English system of measurement to the metric system, use Table 3.

**TABLE 3. ENGLISH-METRIC CONVERSION FACTORS**

| To Convert From | To | Multiply By |
|---|---|---|
| Inches | centimeters | 2.54 |
| Pounds of force | newtons | 4.45 |
| Horsepower | watts | 746 |

For example, to convert 7 inches to centimeters: 7 x 2.54 = 17.8, rounded off to nearest tenth.

# LABORATORY
## TECHNIQUES

To complete laboratory activities safely and successfully, you must develop proper laboratory techniques. The correct way to use laboratory instruments is described in this appendix.

## READING A GRADUATED CYLINDER

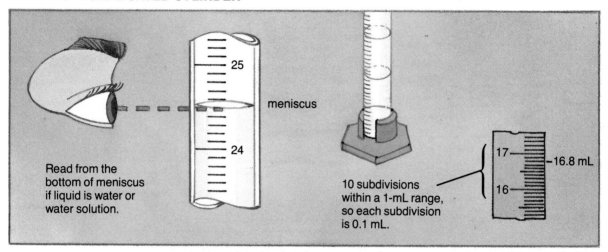

Read from the bottom of meniscus if liquid is water or water solution.

meniscus

10 subdivisions within a 1-mL range, so each subdivision is 0.1 mL.

16.8 mL

## USING A METRIC RULER OR METER STICK

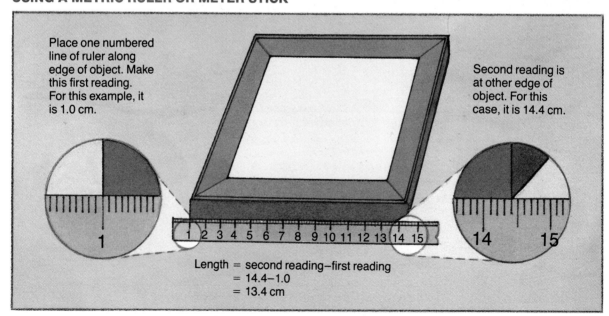

Place one numbered line of ruler along edge of object. Make this first reading. For this example, it is 1.0 cm.

Second reading is at other edge of object. For this case, it is 14.4 cm.

Length = second reading−first reading
     = 14.4−1.0
     = 13.4 cm

## HANDLING ACIDS AND BASES SAFELY

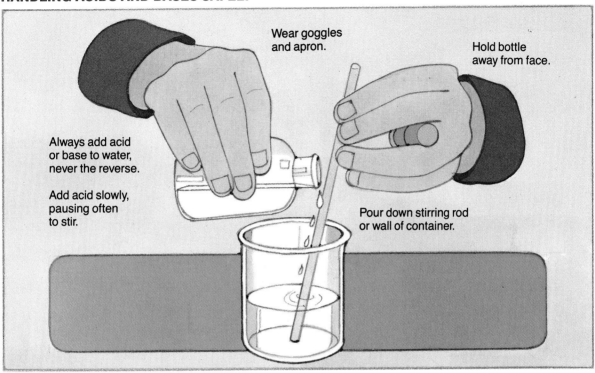

Wear goggles and apron.

Hold bottle away from face.

Always add acid or base to water, never the reverse.

Add acid slowly, pausing often to stir.

Pour down stirring rod or wall of container.

## INVESTIGATING AN ODOR SAFELY

wafting motion

## MAKING A FILTER

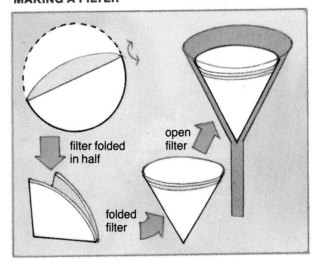

filter folded in half

folded filter

open filter

# LABORATORY TECHNIQUES

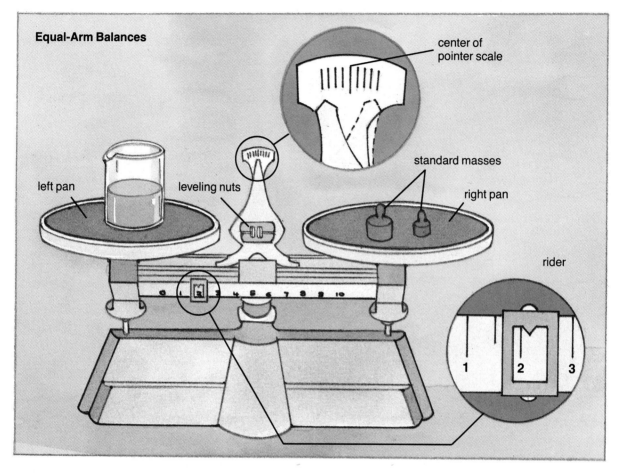

**Equal-Arm Balances**

center of pointer scale

standard masses

left pan

leveling nuts

right pan

rider

1. To protect the pans from corrosive substances and wear, place a clean piece of filter paper on each pan of the balance.
2. Remove all masses from both pans. Move rider all the way to the left. Check to see if pans are level. Do this by lightly touching one of the pans. If the pointer swings the same amount to both sides of the center of the pointer scale, the balance is leveled. If not, adjust the leveling nuts until the amount of swing is equal.
3. Place the object whose mass you want to find on the left pan.
4. Place standard masses on the right pan until the pointer moves equally on both sides of the center of the scale.
5. Use the rider to help balance the unknown mass. The rider gives readings between 0 and 1 gram.
6. The unknown mass is the sum of the standard masses and the rider reading.

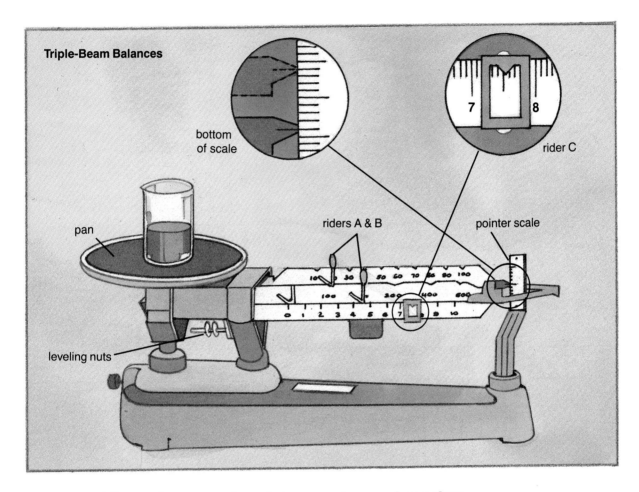

**Triple-Beam Balances**

bottom of scale

rider C

pan

riders A & B

pointer scale

leveling nuts

1. To protect the pan from corrosive substances and wear, place a clean piece of filter paper on the pan.
2. Make sure all riders are all the way to the left. If pointer swings equally on both sides of the center of the pointer scale, the balance is level. If not, adjust leveling nuts until the amount of swing is equal.
3. Place the unknown mass on the pan.
4. Move rider A up one notch at a time until the pointer remains at bottom of scale. Move the rider to the notch just before this one. Readings on rider A range from 0 to 500 g.
5. Repeat step 4 with rider B. Readings on rider B range from 0 to 100 g.
6. Move rider C to the right until the pointer swings equally on both sides of center of pointer scale. Readings on rider C range from 0 to 10 g.
7. Read the unknown mass by adding up the mass readings of the three riders. The reading on the scale shown here is 227.5 g.

# LABORATORY TECHNIQUES

## USING A BUNSEN BURNER SAFELY

Wear goggles and safety apron.

Light with air off and gas low. Bring lighted match up side of barrel.

Do not look directly into barrel when lighting.

If flame is yellow, turn the air adjustment knob to allow more air to enter.

Decrease amount of air entering if there is space between barrel top and flame.

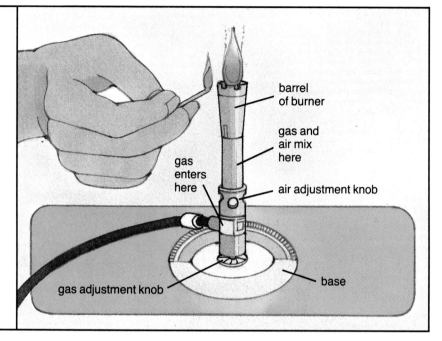

barrel of burner

gas and air mix here

gas enters here

air adjustment knob

gas adjustment knob

base

## HEATING A LIQUID IN A TEST TUBE SAFELY

Use goggles and safety apron.

Use test tube holder.

Do not use an open flame to heat flammable materials.

Keep mouth of test tube pointed away from yourself and others.

Shake test tube gently and heat just below surface of liquid.

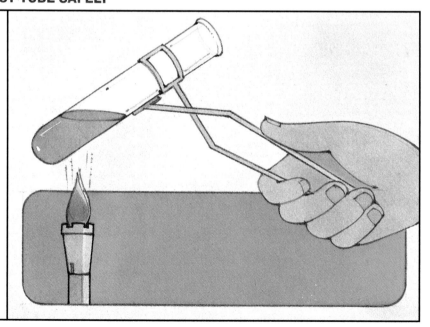

## IMPORTANT SAFETY RULES

Wear goggles and apron. Tie back long hair.

Stir mixtures with stirring rods. Never use a thermometer to stir mixtures.

Cap all bottles and jars of chemicals when you are finished using them.

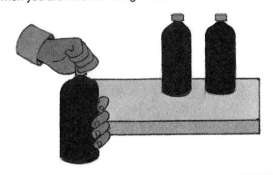

Never touch a solution jar that is wet on the outside. The liquid may be an acid or base or other material that can burn your skin.

Never touch broken glassware.

Never use a dirty spatula or spoon to remove a chemical from a jar.

# IMPORTANT ELEMENTS

| Element | Symbol | Atomic Number | Atomic Mass | Property, Use, or Interesting Fact |
|---|---|---|---|---|
| aluminum | Al | 13 | 27.0 | most abundant metal in earth's crust |
| antimony | Sb | 51 | 121.8 | used in making semiconductors |
| argon | Ar | 18 | 39.9 | gas used in light bulbs and lasers |
| arsenic | As | 33 | 74.9 | is a poison, has garlicky odor |
| barium | Ba | 56 | 137.3 | used in making paints and glass |
| beryllium | Be | 4 | 9.0 | has one of highest boiling points of all metals |
| bismuth | Bi | 83 | 209.0 | pink-colored metal |
| boron | B | 5 | 10.8 | used in semiconductors and control rods |
| bromine | Br | 35 | 79.9 | only liquid nonmetal |
| cadmium | Cd | 48 | 112.4 | metal that can be cut with a knife |
| calcium | Ca | 20 | 40.1 | essential part of bones and teeth |
| carbon | C | 6 | 12.0 | more than a million carbon compounds known to exist |
| chlorine | Cl | 17 | 35.5 | combines with nearly all elements |
| chromium | Cr | 24 | 52.0 | all its compounds have beautiful colors |
| cobalt | Co | 27 | 58.9 | used in radiotherapy |
| copper | Cu | 29 | 63.5 | known for more than 5000 years |
| fluorine | F | 9 | 19.0 | most reactive element |
| gallium | Ga | 31 | 69.7 | metal that melts in your hand |
| germanium | Ge | 32 | 72.6 | important semiconductor |
| gold | Au | 79 | 197.0 | gold crystals often found in veins of quartz |
| helium | He | 2 | 4.0 | first discovered in the sun |
| hydrogen | H | 1 | 1.0 | most abundant element in universe |
| iodine | I | 53 | 126.9 | changes directly from solid to gas |
| iridium | Ir | 77 | 192.2 | was used in making standard meter bar in Paris |
| iron | Fe | 26 | 55.8 | fourth most abundant element |
| krypton | Kr | 36 | 83.8 | now used to define the meter |
| lead | Pb | 82 | 207.2 | Scientists are investigating possibility that poisoning from lead pots may have contributed to fall of Roman empire. |
| lithium | Li | 3 | 6.9 | lightest metal |
| magnesium | Mg | 12 | 24.3 | eighth most abundant element in earth's crust |
| manganese | Mn | 25 | 54.9 | clumps found on floor of ocean |

| Element | Symbol | Atomic Number | Atomic Mass | Property, Use, or Interesting Fact |
|---------|--------|---------------|-------------|-------------------------------------|
| mercury | Hg | 80 | 200.6 | only metal liquid at room temperature |
| neon | Ne | 10 | 20.2 | very inert gas used in advertizing |
| nickel | Ni | 28 | 58.7 | found in most meteorites |
| nitrogen | N | 7 | 14.0 | 78% of air by volume |
| osmium | Os | 76 | 190.2 | may be the heaviest known element |
| oxygen | O | 8 | 16.0 | third most abundant element in the sun |
| phosphorus | P | 15 | 31.0 | used in making safety matches and water softener |
| platinum | Pt | 78 | 195.1 | mined by American Indians before the time of Columbus |
| potassium | K | 19 | 39.1 | symbol comes from *kalium,* the Latin word for the element |
| radium | Ra | 88 | 226 | discovered by the Curies |
| radon | Rn | 86 | 222 | heaviest known gas |
| rubidium | Rb | 37 | 85.5 | metal used to generate electricity |
| selenium | Se | 34 | 79.0 | metal essential to life |
| silicon | Si | 14 | 28.1 | second most abundant element in earth's crust |
| silver | Ag | 47 | 107.9 | used as early as 3000 B.C. |
| sodium | Na | 11 | 23.0 | sixth most abundant element on earth |
| sulfur | S | 16 | 32.1 | used to treat rubber to make it hard |
| technetium | Tc | 43 | 98.9 | first element made artificially |
| tellurium | Te | 52 | 127.6 | used in making semiconductors |
| thallium | Tl | 81 | 204.4 | named after the beautiful green flame it gives off when heated |
| thorium | Th | 90 | 232.0 | more energy available from thorium than from uranium and fossil fuels combined |
| tin | Sn | 50 | 118.7 | When a tin bar is bent, a "tin cry" is heard due to breaking of crystals. |
| titanium | Ti | 22 | 47.9 | ninth most abundant element in earth's crust |
| tungsten | W | 74 | 183.9 | once known as wolfram |
| uranium | U | 92 | 238 | thought to be cause of much of internal heat of earth |
| xenon | Xe | 54 | 131.3 | found in atmosphere of Mars |
| zinc | Zn | 30 | 65.4 | used in making brass and solder |

# GLOSSARY

The glossary defines the important science terms in *Macmillan Physical Science.* Phonetic spellings are given for those words having unfamiliar pronunciations. The phonetic spellings are broken into syllables and respelled according to the key below. The emphasized syllable is given in capital letters.

## PRONUNCIATION KEY

| Phonetic Symbol | | |
|---|---|---|
| a | **a** | **a** as in **at, bad** |
| ay | **ā** | **a** as in **ape, ai** as in **pain, ay** as in **day** |
| ah | **ä** | **a** as in **father, car, o** as in **odd** and **hot** |
| e | **e** | **e** as in **end, pet** |
| ee | **ē** | **e** as in **me, ee** as in **feet, ea** as in **meat, ie** as in **piece, y** as in **finally** |
| i | **i** | **i** as in **it, pig** |
| igh | **ī** | **i** as in **ice, fine, ie** as in **lie, y** as in **my** |
| oh | **ō** | **o** as in **old, oa** as in **oat, ow** as in **low, oe** as in **toe** |
| aw | **ô** | **o** as in **coffee, fork, au** as in **author, aw** as in **law, a** as in **all** |
| oo | **oo** | **oo** as in **wood, u** as in **put** |
| ew | **oo** | **oo** as in **fool, ue** as in **true, ew** as in **crew** |
| oy | **oi** | **oi** as in **oil, oy** as in **boy** |
| ow | **ou** | **ou** as in **out, ow** as in **cow** |
| u | **u** | **u** as in **up, mud, o** as in **oven, love** |
| ur | **ur** | **ur** as in **turn, er** as in **term, ir** as in **bird, or** as in **word** |
| yew | **yoo** | **u** as in **use, ue** as in **cue, ew** as in **few, eu** as in **feud** |
| uh | **ə** | **a** as in **ago, e** as in **taken, i** as in **pencil, o** as in **lemon, u** as in **helpful** |
| b | **b** | **b** as in **bat, above, job** |
| ch | **ch** | **ch** as in **chin, such, tch** as in **hatch** |
| d | **d** | **d** as in **dear, soda, bad** |
| f | **f** | **f** as in **five, defend, leaf, ff** as in **off** |
| g | **g** | **g** as in **game, ago, fog** |
| h | **h** | **h** as in **hit, ahead** |
| | **hw** | **wh** as in **white, which** |
| j | **j** | **j** as in **joke, enjoy, g** as in **gem, dge** as in **edge** |
| k | **k** | **k** as in **kit, baking, seek, ck** as in **tack, c** as in **cat** |
| l | **l** | **l** as in **lid, sailor, feel, ll** as in **ball, allow** |
| m | **m** | **m** as in **man, family, dream** |
| n | **n** | **n** as in **not, final, on** |
| ng | **ng** | **ng** as in **singer, long, n** as in **sink** |
| p | **p** | **p** as in **pail, repair, soap** |
| r | **r** | **r** as in **ride, parent, four** |
| s | **s** | **s** as in **sat, aside, cats, e** as in **cent, ss** as in **pass** |
| sh | **sh** | **sh** as in **shoe, wishing, fish** |
| t | **t** | **t** as in **tag, pretend, hat** |
| th | **th** | **th** as in **thin, ether, both** |
| th | **th** | **th** as in **this, mother, smooth** |
| v | **v** | **v** as in **very, favor, salve** |
| w | **w** | **w** as in **wet, reward** |
| y | **y** | **y** as in **yes** |
| z | **z** | **z** as in **zoo, gazing, zz** as in **jazz, s** as in **rose, dogs** |
| zh | **zh** | **s** as in **treasure, z** as in **azure, ge** as in **garage** |

# A

**absorption spectrum**  The radiation pattern absorbed by a single atom.

**acceleration** (ak•sel•uh•RAY•shuhn)  A change of velocity per unit of time.

**acid**  A substance that, when added to water, increases the concentration of hydronium ions.

**aeration** (ayr•AY•shuhn)  Spraying water into the air.

**air resistance**  A force that opposes the motion of objects in air.

**alcohols**  Organic compounds that contain a hydroxyl group of atoms (—OH).

**alloy**  A mixture of two or more elements having the properties of a metal.

**alpha particle** (AL•fuh)  A positively charged particle consisting of two protons and two neutrons.

**alternating current**  A current that reverses its direction of flow.

**ammeter** (AM•mee•tur)  An instrument that measures current.

**ampere** (AM•payr)  A unit in which current is measured.

**amplifier**  A device that converts a small input current into a large output current.

**amplitude** (AM•pluh•tewd)  The distance from the crest of a wave to the normal position of the medium.

**applied research**  The investigation of ways of using scientific knowledge to benefit human beings.

**Archimedes' Principle**  An object placed in any fluid is acted upon by an upward force equal to the weight of the fluid displaced by the object.

**armature** (AHR•muh•chur)  The rotating electromagnet in a motor.

**aromatic hydrocarbon** (ar•uh•MAT•ik)  A hydrocarbon that has molecules built from a ring of six carbon atoms joined by single and double bonds.

**atom**  The smallest particle of an element that has the properties of the element.

**atomic mass**  The average of the masses of the atoms of an element.

**atomic mass unit**  The standard for measuring the mass of an atom. Abbreviation amu.

**atomic number**  The number of protons in the nucleus of an atom.

# B

**base**  A compound that increases the concentration of hydroxyl ions in water.

**basic research**  A careful study in some field of knowledge.

**beat**  One of a series of loud and soft sounds.

**beta particle** (BAY•tuh)  An electron.

**binary compound**  A compound made of two elements.

**biomass**  Plants, animal wastes, and all other organic matter that can be used as a source of energy.

**boiling point**  The temperature at which a liquid begins to change into a gas.

**Boyle's Law**  If the temperature remains constant, a decrease in the volume of a gas causes an increase in its pressure.

**Brownian motion**  The random motion of colloid particles suspended in a fluid.

**buoyant force** (BOY•uhnt)  An upward force applied by water and other fluids on objects immersed in them.

# C

**carbohydrate** (kahr•boh•HIGH•drayt)  An organic compound that contains carbon, hydrogen, and oxygen, with two atoms of hydrogen for every atom of oxygen.

**catalyst** (KAT•uh•list)  A substance that speeds up a chemical reaction.

**cathode ray tube**  An electronic component that produces a stream of electrons. Abbreviation CRT.

**centripetal force** (sen•TRIP•uh•tuhl)  The inward force that keeps an object moving in a circle.

**chain reaction**  A reaction in which some of the products of the reaction cause the reactions to keep going.

**charge**  A model that explains how some particles attract each other and others push apart, or repel, each other.

**Charles' Law**  At a constant pressure, an increase in temperature causes an increase in the volume of a gas.

**chemical bond**  A force of attraction that holds atoms together.

**chemical change**  Any change of a substance into one or more other substances.

**chemical equation**  An arrangement of numbers and symbols that describes a chemical reaction.

**chemical formula**  A shorthand way of showing the composition of substances by using symbols and subscripts.

**chemical property**  A property that can be observed only by changing the identity of a substance.

**chemistry**  The study of what substances are made of and the changes that occur in their make-up.

**circuit breaker**  A safety device that switches off when too much current goes through it.

**cloud chamber**  A container in which radioactive particles are detected by leaving a trail.

**colloid** (KAHL•oyd)  Undissolved particles or droplets that stay mixed in another substance.

**combustion** (kuhm•BUS•chuhn)  Rapid oxidation with the release of heat and light.

**commutator** (KOM•yew•tay•tur)  A split ring in a motor where wires from the circuit touch the armature.

**composition reaction**  The combining of two substances to form a compound.

**compound** (KAHM•pownd)  A substance made up of two or more elements that have been chemically combined.

**compression**  A region where particles of a medium are close together.

**concave lens**  A lens that is thinner at the center than at the edges.

**concentrated solution** (KAHN•sen•tray•tid)  A solution having a relatively large amount of solute compared with the amount of solvent.

**concentration** (kahn•sen•TRAY•shuhn)  The number of particles present in a given space.

**conclusion**  A judgment based on the data gathered in an experiment.

**condensation** (kahn•den•SAY•shuhn)  The change in phase from gas to liquid.

**conduction**  The transfer of energy from molecule to molecule by collisions.

**conductor**  A material that allows electricity to flow through it easily.

**Conservation of Energy (Law of)**  Total energy of an object or group of objects remains the same. When applied to heat, the heat lost by any material in an insulated system is equal to heat gained by another material in the system.

**Conservation of Mass (Law of)**  Mass does not change in a chemical reaction.

**Conservation of Momentum (Law of)**  The total momentum of any group of objects remains the same unless outside forces act on the group.

**control**  An extra setup in which all the conditions are the same except for the variable being tested.

**convection** (kuhn•VEK•shuhn)  The transfer of energy by the flow of a liquid or a gas.

**convection current**  The flow within a fluid due to changes in density.

**convex lens**  A lens that is thicker in the middle than at the edges.

**corrosion** (kuh•ROH•zhuhn)  The gradual eating away of a metal in which the metal element is changed into a metallic compound.

**covalent bond** (koh•VAY•luhnt)  A bond formed when two atoms share electrons.

**crest**  The high point of a wave.

**crystal** (KRIS•tuhl)  A solid with a geometric shape having flat surfaces at definite angles to each other.

**cubic centimeter**  A standard unit of volume. Abbreviation $cm^3$.

**current**  The number of electrons that flow past a point in a circuit each second.

# D

**data**  Measurements and information that a scientist gets from an experiment.

**deceleration** (dee•sel•uh•RAY•shuhn)  The kind of acceleration in which speed decreases.

**decibel** (DES•i•buhl)  A unit in which the volume of a sound is measured. Abbreviation dB.

**decomposition reaction**  The breaking down of a compound into two or more simpler substances.

**degree Celsius**  Unit of temperature in the metric system. Abbreviation °C.

**density** (DEN•suh•tee)  The mass of a substance contained per unit of volume.

**diatomic molecule** (digh·uh·TAHM·ik) A molecule that contains two of the same kind of atom joined by a covalent bond.

**diffraction** The bending of waves around the edges of an object.

**digestion** The breaking down of proteins, fats, and carbohydrates into smaller molecules.

**dilute solution** (digh·LEWT) A solution with only a small amount of solute compared with the amount of solvent.

**direct current** A current that flows in one direction.

**distance** The length between any two points in the path of an object.

**distance-time graph** A graph showing the relationships between distance and time.

**distillation** (dis·tuh·LAY·shuhn) A process that evaporates a liquid by heating and changes the gas back to a liquid by cooling.

**Doppler effect** (DAHP·lur) The change in the frequency of waves from a moving source.

**double replacement reaction** The replacement of parts of two compounds with each other.

**ductile** (DUHK·tuhl) Capable of being drawn into wires.

# E

**echo** A sound produced by reflected sound waves.

**efficiency** A measure of the useful work a machine can do.

**effort** An applied force.

**elastic force** (i·LAS·tik) A force produced by any bent or stretched object that returns to its original shape.

**electric circuit** A path along which electrons can flow.

**electric field** The region around a charged object where electric forces on other charged objects can be observed.

**electric force** A force that attracts or repels charged objects.

**electrolysis** The process by which hydrogen is separated from the oxygen in water.

**electrolyte** (i·LEK·truh·light) A substance that conducts electricity in water solutions.

**electromagnet** (i·lek·troh·MAG·nit) A coil of wire that acts like a magnet when an electric current passes through it.

**electromagnetic induction** (in·DUHK·shuhn) Producing a current by moving a coil of wire across a magnetic field.

**electromagnetic wave** A transverse wave that can travel through a vacuum.

**electron** (i·LEK·trahn) A negatively charged atomic particle.

**electronics** The study of the motion of electrons for use in devices in home and industry.

**electroscope** (i·LEK·truh·skohp) A device used to study static electricity.

**element** (EL·uh·muhnt) A substance that cannot be broken down into other substances.

**emission spectrum** The wavelength pattern given off by a single atom.

**emulsifier** (ee·MUL·si·figh·ur) A substance that keeps the parts of an emulsion mixed together.

**emulsion** (ee·MUL·shuhn) A suspension of two liquids that usually do not mix.

**endothermic reaction** (en·duh·THUR·mik) A reaction that absorbs heat as it progresses.

**energy** (EN·uhr·jee) The ability to cause changes in matter.

**enzyme** (EN·zighm) A catalyst that helps speed up a chemical reaction in living things.

**ester** An organic compound formed by the reaction of an organic acid with an alcohol.

**evaporation** (i·va·poh·RAY·shuhn) The change in phase from liquid to gas.

**excited electrons** Electrons that have absorbed energy and moved farther from the nucleus.

**exothermic reaction** (ek·soh·THUR·mik) A reaction that releases heat.

**experiment** A scientific test designed to give information under carefully controlled conditions.

# F

**fermentation** (fur·men·TAY·shuhn) A process by which living yeast cells change sugar into alcohol and carbon dioxide.

**filter** A material that transmits certain colors of light and absorbs others.

**First Law of Motion, Newton's**   An object at rest remains at rest unless acted on by an unbalanced force. An object in motion continues to move at a constant speed and in a straight line unless acted on by an unbalanced force.

**fluorescent material** (floor•ES•uhnt)   A material that absorbs ultraviolet rays and changes some of the energy into visible light.

**focal length**   The distance between a mirror or lens and its focus.

**focus** (FOH•kuhs)   The point through which all rays striking a mirror or lens parallel to the optic axis are reflected.

**force**   Any cause of a change in motion.

**formula**   A shorthand way of showing what elements make up a compound.

**fossil fuel**   A fuel that forms in the earth from the decay of dead plants and animals.

**free electrons**   Electrons in a metal that are not tightly held by the atoms.

**frequency** (FREE•kwuhn•see)   The number of waves produced each second.

**friction** (FRIK•shuhn)   A force that opposes the motion of one surface past another.

**fulcrum** (FUL•kruhm)   The pivot point of a lever.

**fundamental frequency**   The lowest frequency of a string, produced when the string vibrates as a whole.

**fuse**   A safety device in a circuit that melts before the wires in the circuit become too hot.

## G

**gamma ray**   One of the rays having the shortest wavelengths of all electromagnetic waves.

**gas**   A phase of matter that has no definite shape or volume.

**gasohol**   A fuel containing ethanol mixed with gasoline.

**gear**   A wheel with teeth cut into the rim.

**Geiger counter**   An instrument that detects radioactivity by an electric current.

**generator**   A device that uses energy of motion to produce electricity.

**geothermal energy**   Heat inside the earth.

**gram**   A unit of mass in the metric system.

**gravitational potential energy**   The potential energy an object has due to its position above the earth's surface. Abbreviation GPE.

**gravity** (GRAV•uh•tee)   A force of attraction between two objects.

**grounding**   The removal of static electricity by conduction to the earth.

**groups**   The columns of the Periodic Table of the Elements.

## H

**half-life**   The time it takes for one half of the starting amount of an element to decay.

**hard water**   Water containing dissolved metal ions that keep the water from lathering when soap is added.

**heat**   The energy transferred between materials (or parts of a material) that have different temperatures.

**heat engine**   An engine that uses energy from burning fuel to make something move.

**heat of fusion**   The energy needed to change one gram of a material from a solid into a liquid.

**heat of vaporization** (vay•pur•i•ZAY•shuhn)   The energy needed to change one gram of a material from a liquid into a gas.

**hertz** (HURTZ)   A unit of frequency equal to one wave per second. Abbreviation Hz.

**horsepower**   A unit of power in the British system of measurement.

**hydrocarbon** (high•droh•KAHR•buhn)   An organic compound that contains only hydrogen atoms and carbon atoms.

**hydroelectricity**   Electricity produced by flowing water.

**hydronium ion** (high•DROH•nee•uhm)   An ion group made of a water molecule and a hydrogen ion.

**hydroxyl ion** (high•DRAHK•suhl)   An ion group made of an oxygen atom joined to a hydrogen atom.

**hypothesis** (high•PAHTH•uh•sis)   An educated guess about the answer to a problem or question.

# I

**inclined plane** (in·KLIGHND)  A straight, slanted surface.

**index of refraction**  A measure of the amount of refraction that occurs as light passes into a substance.

**indicator** (IN·duh·kay·tur)  A substance that changes color in the presence of an acid or a base.

**induced current**  The current produced by electro-magnetic induction.

**inert** (in·URT)  Inactive.

**inertia** (in·ur·shuh)  The tendency of any object to oppose a change in motion.

**infrared ray** (IN·fruh·red)  One of the electro-magnetic waves with wavelengths between those of visible light and radio waves.

**infrasonic wave** (in·fruh·SAHN·ik)  A sound wave with a frequency below 20 Hz.

**insoluble** (in·SAHL·yew·buhl)  Cannot be dis-solved.

**insulator** (IN·suh·lay·tur)  A material that hinders the flow of electricity through it.

**integrated circuits** (IN·tuh·gray·tuhd)  Circuits that combine hundreds of electronic components on a single chip.

**interference** (in·tur·FEER·uhns)  The interaction of two or more waves when they meet.

**ion** (IGH·ahn)  An atom that has unequal numbers of electrons and protons.

**ionic bond**  A bond formed by the transfer of elec-trons.

**isomers** (IGH·soh·murz)  Compounds that share the same chemical formula but have different structural formulas.

**isotope** (IGH·suh·tohp)  Atoms of an element hav-ing the same number of protons in the nucleus, but different masses.

# J

**joule** (JEWL)  The amount of work done when a force of one newton is exerted over a distance of one meter. Abbreviation J.

# K

**kinetic energy** (ki·NET·ik)  The energy of motion. Abbreviation KE.

**laser**  A device that amplifies light.

**lever**  A simple machine made of a rigid bar that is free to pivot.

**liquid**  A phase of matter that has a definite vol-ume but no definite shape.

**liter**  A unit of volume in the metric system. Abbre-viation L.

**load**  A device that uses energy.

**longitudinal wave** (lawn·juh·TEW·di·nuhl)  The kind of wave that moves along the same direction as the moving particles of the medium.

**luster**  Shininess.

# M

**magnetic domain** (doh·MAYN)  A region where atomic magnetic fields line up in one direction.

**magnetic field**  The space around a magnet in which its force affects objects.

**malleable** (MAL·ee·uh·buhl)  Capable of being hammered or shaped without breaking.

**mass**  The amount of material an object contains.

**mass number**  The sum of the protons and neu-trons of an atom.

**matter**  Anything that has mass and volume.

**mechanical advantage**  The number of times a simple machine multiplies effort. Abbreviation MA.

**medium** (pl. media)  The material through which a wave travels.

**melting point**  The temperature at which a solid becomes a liquid.

**metallic bond**  The sharing of many freely mov-ing electrons among the atoms of a solid metal.

**metalloids** (MET·uhl·oydz)  Elements that have properties in between metals and nonmetals.

**meter**  A unit of length in the metric system. Abbreviation m.

**mixture**  Any combination of two or more substances in which the substances keep their own properties.

**model**  A description that uses familiar ideas to explain unfamiliar ones.

**molecule** (MAHL·i·kyewl)  The smallest particle of a substance that can exist independently.

**momentum** (moh·MEN·tuhm)  The mass times the velocity of an object.

**motion**  A change in position relative to fixed objects.

**muscular force** (MUS·kyuh·lur)  A force that comes from the expanding and contracting of muscle tissue.

# N

**neutralization** (new·truh·luh·ZAY·shuhn)  A chemical reaction in which hydronium ions combine with hydroxyl ions and form water.

**neutral solution**  Having the properties of neither an acid nor a base.

**neutron** (NEW·trahn)  A particle in the nucleus that has no charge.

**newton**  A unit for measuring force. Abbreviation N.

**nuclear fission** (FISH·uhn)  The splitting of a nucleus with a large mass into two nuclei with smaller masses.

**nuclear fusion**  The joining of several nuclei with smaller masses into one nucleus with a larger mass.

**nuclear reactor**  A device that produces energy from radioactive fuels through controlled chain reactions.

**nucleus** (NEW·klee·uhs)  The dense, central part of an atom.

# O

**ohm**  A unit of electric resistance.

**Ohm's Law**  The current is equal to the potential difference divided by the resistance.

**opaque material** (oh·PAYK)  A material that can absorb light without transmitting it.

**optic axis**  A line drawn through the center of a mirror.

**optics**  The study of the production of images by the reflection and refraction of light.

**organic acids**  Organic compounds that contain a –COOH group of atoms.

**organic chemistry**  The study of the compounds of carbon.

**output force**  The force produced by a machine.

**overtone**  Sound waves with frequencies higher than the fundamental, produced by a string or air column vibrating in parts.

**oxidation** (ahk·si·DAY·shuhn)  The chemical combination of oxygen with another substance.

**oxidation number**  The number of electrons an atom loses, gains, or shares in bonding.

**oxides**  Compounds of oxygen and another element.

# P

**parallel circuit**  A circuit that provides more than one path for electrons to move along.

**pascal** (pas·KAL)  A unit of pressure. Abbreviation Pa.

**periodic property**  A property repeated within a regular interval.

**periods**  The rows across the Periodic Table of the Elements.

**petroleum** (puh·TROH·lee·uhm)  A liquid mixture of hydrocarbons obtained from below the earth's surface.

**pH**  A measure of the concentration of hydronium ions in a solution.

**phenolphthalein** (fee·nohl·THAY·leen)  An indicator.

**photon** (FOH·tahn)  A tiny packet or bundle of energy with a particular wavelength.

**photovoltaic effect** (foh·toh·vohl·TAY·ik)  The direct conversion of sunlight into electricity.

**physical change**  A change that does not produce a new substance.

**physical property** A property that can be observed without changing the identity of a substance.

**physics.** The study of matter and energy and how they are related.

**pitch** The highness or lowness of a sound.

**plasma** A gaslike phase consisting of ions and free electrons.

**plastic** A material that can be molded while soft, and then hardened by heat, cooling, or exposing to air.

**polarized wave** (POH•lur•ighzd) A wave that vibrates along a single plane.

**polar molecules** (POH•lur) Molecules that have ends with partial negative and partial positive charges.

**pollution** The presence of unwanted or harmful substances in the environment.

**pollutants** (puh•LEWT•uhnts) Impurities in air and water that may be harmful to life.

**polyatomic ion** An ion that is made up of more than one atom acting as a single unit.

**polymer** (PAHL•i•mur) An organic compound that has molecules made of long chains of smaller molecules.

**potential difference** The work needed to move a charge from one point to another.

**potential energy** (puh•TEN•shuhl) Stored energy. Abbreviation PE.

**power** A measure of how fast work is done.

**precipitate** (pri•SIP•uh•tayt) An insoluble solid that separates out of a solution.

**pressure** The force exerted on each unit of area of a surface.

**primary colors** Red, green, and blue.

**primary pigments** Magenta, yellow, and cyan.

**prism** (PRIZ•uhm) A clear piece of glass or plastic shaped like a wedge.

**projectile** (pruh•JEK•tuhl) Any object that is thrown or shot and travels in a curved path.

**protein** (PROH•teen) An organic compound used in building and repairing cells.

**proton** A positively charged particle in the nucleus of an atom.

**pulley** A grooved wheel that turns by the action of a rope in the groove.

# Q

**quality** The difference between sounds of the same pitch and volume.

# R

**radiation** The transfer of energy by electromagnetic waves.

**radioactive decay** The change of one element into another element by the release of radiation.

**radioactivity** (ray•dee•oh•ak•TIV•uh•tee) Breakdown of atomic nuclei by release of particles or electromagnetic radiation.

**radio wave** One of the waves that have the longest wavelengths in the electromagnetic spectrum.

**rarefaction** (rayr•uh•FAK•shuhn) A region where the particles of a medium are spread apart.

**ray** A straight line that starts at a point and keeps going in one direction.

**real image** An image formed when light actually passes through the point where the image appears.

**rectifier** A device that changes alternating current into direct current.

**reflection** (ri•FLEK•shuhn) The bouncing of a wave off a surface.

**refraction** (ri•FRAK•shuhn) The change in direction of a wave as it moves into a different medium.

**relative mass** The mass of an atom expressed in terms of the mass of the standard atom.

**resistance** The ability of a material to resist, or oppose, the flow of electrons through it.

**resonance** (REZ•uh•nuhns) A large-amplitude vibration that is produced at a certain frequency.

**respiration** The release of energy from digested carbohydrates.

**resultant** (ri•ZUL•tuhnt) A single force that has the combined effect of all the forces acting on an object.

**retina** A layer of light-sensitive cells in the rear of the eye.

# S

**salt**   A compound formed by the positive ions of a base and the negative ions of an acid.

**saturated hydrocarbon**   A hydrocarbon in which each carbon atom is joined by single bonds to four other atoms.

**saturated solution** (SACH•uh•ray•tuhd)   A solution in which at any given temperature no more solute may be dissolved.

**science**   The search for knowledge about how things behave as they do.

**scientific law**   A statement that describes how something behaves.

**scrubbing**   A way of cleaning waste smoke by using water.

**Second Law of Motion, Newton's**   An unbalanced force that is acting on an object will produce an acceleration.

**semiconductor**   A material that has a resistance between that of an insulator and a conductor.

**series circuit**   A circuit that provides only one path for electrons to move along.

**shock wave**   A region of compressed air molecules produced when a source is traveling faster than sound.

**simple machine**   A device that helps you do work.

**single replacement reaction**   The replacement of one element in a compound by a free element.

**slope**   The steepness of a line.

**soap**   A metallic salt of a fatty acid.

**solid**   The phase of matter that has a definite shape and volume.

**solubility** (SAHL•yew•bil•uh•tee)   The amount of solute that can be dissolved in a given amount of solvent at a given temperature.

**soluble** (SAHL•yuh•buhl)   Capable of being dissolved.

**solute** (SAHL•yewt)   The substance that becomes dissolved.

**solution** (suh•LEW•shuhn)   A mixture of one substance dissolved in another so that the properties are the same throughout.

**solvent** (SAHL•vent)   The part of a solution that dissolves a substance.

**specific heat**   The energy needed to change the temperature of one gram of a material by one Celsius degree. Abbreviation $c_p$.

**spectrum** (pl. spectra) (SPEK•truhm)   A band of colors produced when wavelengths of white light are separated.

**speed**   The distance traveled each second.

**speed, average**   The total distance traveled divided by the total time passed.

**stable electron arrangement**   All the electrons of an atom in the lowest possible energy levels.

**standard**   A fixed quantity to which all measurements are compared.

**standing wave**   A wave that results from the meeting of two waves with the same frequency and amplitude traveling in opposite directions.

**static electricity**   A charge that is not moving.

**structural formula**   A formula showing the number and arrangement of atoms in a molecule.

**substituted hydrocarbon**   A compound made by replacing some of the hydrogen atoms of a hydrocarbon with other atoms.

**supersaturated solution**   A solution that contains more solute than it normally has at a given temperature.

**supersonic speed**   A speed greater than the speed of sound.

**suspension** (suh•SPEN•shuhn)   A mixture made of parts that separate upon standing.

**switch**   A device that opens or closes a circuit.

**symbol**   One or two letters that stand for an element.

# T

**technician** (tek•NISH•uhn)   A skilled laboratory worker who carries out much of the actual work of a test.

**technology**   The use of scientific knowledge to serve human needs.

**temperature**   A measure of the average kinetic energy of the molecules in a material.

**terminal speed**   The constant speed a falling object reaches when air resistance balances gravity.

**ternary compound**  A compound made of three elements.

**theory**  An explanation for the way something behaves.

**Third Law of Motion, Newton's**  For every action there is an equal and opposite reaction.

**tincture** (TING•chur)  Solutions in which alcohol is the solvent.

**transformer**  A device that changes voltage.

**transistor**  A small device that controls current flow.

**transparent material** (tranz•PAR•uhnt)  A material that can be seen through.

**transverse wave** (tranz•VURS)  A wave that moves at right angles to the moving particles of the medium.

**trough** (TRAWF)  The low point of a wave.

**turbine**  A rotating wheel with blades.

# U

**ultrasonic wave** (uhl•truh•SAHN•ik)  A sound wave with a frequency above 20,000 Hz.

**ultraviolet ray**  An electromagnetic wave with a wavelength just shorter than that of visible light.

**unsaturated hydrocarbon**  A hydrocarbon in which each carbon atom is bonded to only two or three atoms.

**unsaturated solution**  A solution in which more solute can be dissolved.

# V

**vacuum**  A region from which all matter has been removed.

**valence electron** (VAY•luhns)  An electron that takes part in a chemical bond.

**variable** (VAR•ee•uh•buhl)  Any condition that can be changed.

**velocity** (vuh•LAHS•uh•tee)  The speed in a particular direction of a moving object.

**virtual image**  An image that only seems to be where it is.

**volt**  A unit used to measure potential difference. Abbreviation V.

**voltmeter** (VOHLT•mee•tur)  An instrument that measures the amount of work done as electrons move between two points.

**volume** (VOL•yewm)  1. The amount of space an objects takes up. 2. The loudness of a sound.

# W

**watt**  An amount of power equal to one joule per second. Abbreviation W.

**wave**  A disturbance that travels through matter or space.

**wavelength**  The distance from one crest to the next crest.

**weight**  A measure of the pull of gravity on an object.

**wheel and axle**  A simple machine consisting of a handle or axle attached to the center of a wheel.

**work**  The amount of force exerted on an object times the distance the object moves in the direction of the force.

**work input**  The amount of work you put into a machine when you use it.

**work output**  The amount of work you obtain from a machine when you use it.

# X

**X ray**  One of the electromagnetic waves with wavelengths just shorter than those of ultraviolet rays.

# INDEX

NOTE: Page numbers in *italics* refer to definitions, and page numbers in **boldface** refer to illustrations.

## A

Absorption spectrum, *420,* **421**
Acceleration, *75,* 76
　amount of force and, 90
　free fall, 101–2
　mass and, 91, 98
　Second Law of Motion and, 92
Acetylene, 284
Acid rain, 256, **256**
Acids, 254–59, *257,* 263 (table)
　chemists' definition of, 256, *257*
　effect on litmus, **254**
　industrial, 258–59
　measuring strength of, 264–65
　organic, *286,* **286**
　properties of, 254–56
　reactions between bases and, 266–68
　strong and weak, 257–58, 258 (table)
Aeration, *242*
Airplanes, 5–6
Air resistance, *102*
Alcohols, 286, *286,* **286**
　energy from, 494
Alkali metals, 184 (chart), 184–85
Alkaline earth metals, 185 (chart), 185
Alloys, 187, *187,* 187 (table), 234–35
Alpha particles, 159, 178, *460*
Alternating current, *336*
Aluminum sulfate, 269–70
Aluminum 22, 470
Amino acids, 291, **291**
Ammeter, *316,* 317
Ammonium hydroxide (ammonia water), 261, 263
Amperes, *316*
Amplifiers, *342*
Amplitude of a wave, *362,* 373, 381
AM radio waves, 413–14
Animal substances, effect of bases on, **260,** 260–61

Applied research, *14*
Archimedes' Principle, *105*
Armature, *333,* 333–34
Aromatic hydrocarbons, *284,* 284–85
Atomic energy, 16–17
Atomic mass, *167,* 167 (table)
Atomic mass unit (amu), *166,* 166–67, 167 (table)
Atomic number of elements, *165,* 167 (table), 177
Atomic weight, arrangement of elements by, 176–77
Atomists, 156
Atoms, *31–32*
　ancient Greeks and, 156, 157
　atomic number of, *165,* 167 (table)
　Bohr's model of, 162–163, 162–63 (chart), 168, **168**
　chemical bonds between, 202–11, *203*
　Dalton's theory of, 157–58
　electrons in, 162–164, 168, **168**
　ions of, *208*
　models of, *36,* **38,** 39
　nucleus of, 165
　particles of, 36–39
　parts of, **168**
　relative mass of, *166*
　resistance and kinds of, 317
　Rutherford's model of, 159, 160–61 (chart), 162
　Thomson's model of, 159, 160–61 (chart)
　wavelengths from, **419,** 419–21, **421**
　wave model of, 163, 163–64
Average speed, *74,* 74–75

## B

Balanced equations, 214
Balanced forces, 80
Bases, 260–63, *262,* 263 (table)
　chemists' definition of, 261–62, *262*
　measuring strength of, 264–65
　properties of, 260–61, **260, 261**
　reactions between acids and, 266–68
　uses of, 263
Basic research, *13,* 13–14
Beats, *377*

Beautician, 300, **300**
Becquerel, Henri, 458
Benzene, 284, **284**
Beta particles, *460,* 460–61
Binary compound, *209,* 209
Binary number system, 343
Biomass, *492*
　energy from, 492–95
Bitter taste of bases, 260
Bohr, Niels, 162–63 (chart), 163, 168, **168,** 419
Boiling point, *209*
Bonds. *See* Chemical bonds
Books and journals, 53
Boron, 194
Boyle's Law, 450
　calculations with, 566–67
Brownian motion, *246,* **246**
Bubble chambers, 463, **463**
Buoyant force, *103,* 103–4

## C

Cameras, 397
Carbohydrates, *289,* 289–90
Carbon, 278–79
　atoms of, 279
Carbon-12, 166–67, 465, 466
Carbon-14, 465
Carbon compounds, 280–82. *See also* Organic compounds models of, **281,** 281–82
Carbon dioxide, 280, 280 (chart)
Carbon monoxide, 280, 280 (chart)
Careers, 64, 150, 226, 300, 348, 430
Catalysts, 221, *222*
Cathode ray tube (CRT), *341,* **341**
Cellulose, 296–97
Cement mason, 226, **226**
Centripetal force, *83*
Ceramic engineer, 226, **226**
Chadwick, James, 166
Chain reactions, *472*
Change of phase, heat transfer and, 444–46, **445**
Charge, *36,* **37,** *306,* 310
Charles' Law, 450
　calculations with, 566–67

## TABLE 9-1. THE PERIODIC TABLE OF THE ELEMENTS

**Group**

**ELEMENT KEY**

- 2 electrons (1st level)
- 4 electrons (2nd level)

Center: 6p 6n

Atomic Number → (2, 4) 6

Electron Arrangement

Symbol of Element → C

Average Atomic Mass → 12.0

Element Name → carbon

**COLOR KEY**
Yellow: metals
Blue: nonmetals
Green: metalloids

**Period**

| IA | IIA | | | | | | | |
|---|---|---|---|---|---|---|---|---|
| 1<br>**H**<br>1.0<br>hydrogen | | | | | | | | |
| 2,1 3<br>**Li**<br>6.9<br>lithium | 2,2 4<br>**Be**<br>9.0<br>beryllium | | | | | | | |
| 2,8,1 11<br>**Na**<br>23.0<br>sodium | 2,8,2 12<br>**Mg**<br>24.3<br>magnesium | | | | | | | |
| 2,8,8,1 19<br>**K**<br>39.1<br>potassium | 2,8,8,2 20<br>**Ca**<br>40.1<br>calcium | 2,8,9,2 21<br>**Sc**<br>45.0<br>scandium | 2,8,10,2 22<br>**Ti**<br>47.9<br>titanium | 2,8,11,2 23<br>**V**<br>50.9<br>vanadium | 2,8,13,1 24<br>**Cr**<br>52.0<br>chromium | 2,8,13,2 25<br>**Mn**<br>54.9<br>manganese | 2,8,14,2 26<br>**Fe**<br>55.8<br>iron | 2,8,15,2 27<br>**Co**<br>58.9<br>cobalt |
| 2,8,18,8,1 37<br>**Rb**<br>85.5<br>rubidium | 2,8,18,8,2 38<br>**Sr**<br>87.6<br>strontium | 2,8,18,9,2 39<br>**Y**<br>88.9<br>yttrium | 2,8,18,10,2 40<br>**Zr**<br>91.2<br>zirconium | 2,8,18,12,1 41<br>**Nb**<br>92.9<br>niobium | 2,8,18,13,1 42<br>**Mo**<br>95.9<br>molybdenum | 2,8,18,13,2 43<br>**Tc**<br>98.9<br>technetium | 2,8,18,15,1 44<br>**Ru**<br>101.1<br>ruthenium | 2,8,18,16,1 45<br>**Rh**<br>102.9<br>rhodium |
| 2,8,18,18,8,1 55<br>**Cs**<br>132.9<br>cesium | 2,8,18,18,8,2 56<br>**Ba**<br>137.3<br>barium | 57–71*<br>see below | 2,8,18,32,10,2 72<br>**Hf**<br>178.5<br>hafnium | 2,8,18,32,11,2 73<br>**Ta**<br>180.9<br>tantalum | 2,8,18,32,12,2 74<br>**W**<br>183.9<br>tungsten | 2,8,18,32,13,2 75<br>**Re**<br>186.2<br>rhenium | 2,8,18,32,14,2 76<br>**Os**<br>190.2<br>osmium | 2,8,18,32,15,2 77<br>**Ir**<br>192.2<br>iridium |
| 2,8,18,32,18,8,1 87<br>**Fr**<br>223<br>francium | 2,8,18,32,18,8,2 88<br>**Ra**<br>226<br>radium | 89–103**<br>see below | 2,8,18,32,32,10,2 104<br>261 | 2,8,18,32,32,11,2 105<br>260 | 2,8,18,32,32,12,2 106<br>263 | 2,8,18,32,32,13,2 107<br>261 | 108<br>265 | 2,8,18,32,32,15,2 109<br>267 |

**\* Lanthanoid Series**

| | | | | | | |
|---|---|---|---|---|---|---|
| 2,8,18,18,9,2 57<br>**La**<br>138.9<br>lanthanum | 2,8,18,20,8,2 58<br>**Ce**<br>140.1<br>cerium | 2,8,18,21,8,2 59<br>**3Pr**<br>140.9<br>praseodymium | 2,8,18,22,8,2 60<br>**Nd**<br>144.2<br>neodymium | 2,8,18,23,8,2 61<br>**Pm**<br>145<br>promethium | 2,8,18,24,8,2 62<br>**Sm**<br>150.4<br>samarium | 2,8,18,25,8,2 63<br>**Eu**<br>152.0<br>europium |

**\*\* Actinoid Series**

| | | | | | | |
|---|---|---|---|---|---|---|
| 2,8,18,18,9,2 89<br>**Ac**<br>227.0<br>actinium | 2,8,18,32,18,10,2 90<br>**Th**<br>232.0<br>thorium | 2,8,18,32,20,9,2 91<br>**Pa**<br>231.0<br>protactinium | 2,8,18,32,21,9,2 92<br>**U**<br>238.0<br>uranium | 2,8,18,32,22,9,2 93<br>**Np**<br>237.0<br>neptunium | 2,8,18,32,24,8,2 94<br>**Pu**<br>244<br>plutonium | 2,8,18,32,25,8,2 95<br>**Am**<br>243<br>americium |